THE CANADIAN YEARBOOK OF INTERNATIONAL LAW

2003

ANNUAIRE CANADIEN DE DROIT INTERNATIONAL

The Canadian Yearbook of International Law

VOLUME XLI   2003   TOME XLI

Annuaire canadien de Droit international

Published under the auspices of
THE CANADIAN BRANCH, INTERNATIONAL LAW ASSOCIATION
AND
THE CANADIAN COUNCIL ON INTERNATIONAL LAW

Publié sous les auspices de
LA SECTION CANADIENNE DE L'ASSOCIATION DE DROIT INTERNATIONAL
ET
LE CONSEIL CANADIEN DE DROIT INTERNATIONAL

UBC Press
VANCOUVER / TORONTO

Printed in Canada on acid-free paper ∞

ISBN 0-7748-1124-2
ISSN 0069-0058

Library and Archives Canada Cataloguing in Publication

The National Library of Canada has catalogued this publication as follows:

The Canadian yearbook of international law — Annuaire canadien de droit international

    Annual.
    Text in English and French.
    "Published under the auspices of the Canadian Branch, International Law Association and the Canadian Council on International Law."
    ISSN 0069-0058

    1. International Law — Periodicals.
I. International Law Association. Canadian Branch.
II. Title: Annuaire canadien de droit international.
JC 21.C3   341'.05   C75-34558-6E

Catalogage avant publication de la Bibliothèque et Archives Canada

Annuaire canadien de droit international — The Canadian yearbook of international law

    Annuel.
    Textes en anglais et en français.
    "Publié sous les auspices de la Branche canadienne de l'Association de droit international et le Conseil canadien de droit international."
    ISSN 0069-0058

    1. Droit international — Périodiques.
I. Association de droit international. Section canadienne.
II. Conseil canadien de droit international.
III. Titre: The Canadian yearbook of international law.
JC 21.C3   341'.05   C75-34558-6E

UBC Press
University of British Columbia
2029 West Mall
Vancouver, BC V6T 1Z2
(604) 822-3259
www.ubcpress.ca

The Board of Editors, the Canadian Branch of the International Law Association, the Canadian Council on International Law, and the University of British Columbia are not in any way responsible for the views expressed by the contributors, whether the contributions are signed or unsigned.

Les opinions émises dans le présent *Annuaire* par nos collaborateurs, qu'il s'agisse d'articles signés, ne sauraient en aucune façon engager la responsibilité du Comité de rédaction, de la Section canadienne du Conseil canadien de droit international ou de l'Université de Colombie Britannique.

Communications to the *Yearbook* should be addressed to:

Les communications destinées à l'*Annuaire* doivent être adressées à:

THE EDITOR, THE CANADIAN YEARBOOK OF INTERNATIONAL LAW
FACULTY OF LAW, COMMON LAW SECTION
UNIVERSITY OF OTTAWA
57 LOUIS PASTEUR
OTTAWA, ONTARIO K1N 6N5 CANADA

Contents / Matière

Book Reviews / Recensions de Livres

THE CANADIAN YEARBOOK OF
INTERNATIONAL LAW

2003

ANNUAIRE CANADIEN
DE DROIT INTERNATIONAL

International Law at the University of British Columbia, 1945-2000

R. ST. J. MACDONALD

INTRODUCTION

Recent prominence given to the study and teaching of international law in Canada represents something of a departure for a discipline often seen as being at the margins of the legal academy. Historically, the place of international legal subjects within the law school curriculum has ebbed and flowed with changing academic cultures. For the most part, however, international law has been seen as a marginal or isolated area of legal study. An exception has been the Faculty of Law at the University of British Columbia (UBC) where public international law was for many years a required course. The early period in the history of the UBC law school reveals an unusual commitment to the study of international law. The effect of this commitment was to position UBC as one of Canada's strongest international law faculties.

In the article that follows, I will trace the history of the teaching of international law at UBC from the time of the establishment of the law school in 1945 to the year 2000. I will offer an historical survey of the international law curriculum in order, first, to document the institutional and individual forces that shaped the development

R. St. J. Macdonald, LL.D. Honorary President, Canadian Council on International Law, formerly Judge at the European Court of Human Rights, Strasbourg 1980–98. The author wishes to recognize with pleasure and gratitude the outstanding assistance of Doris E. Buss (B.A. Carleton, LL.B. Dalhousie, LL.M. University of British Columbia [hereinafter UBC]) of the Department of Law, Carleton University, in the preparation of this article. Joost Blom, Charles Bourne, Gordon Jahnke, and Ikechi Mgbéoji kindly read the first draft and made useful comments. Maurice Copithorne was generosity itself in sharing information and helping to improve the text.

of the teaching of the subject at UBC, and, second, to provide a context within which to better understand the changing nature of international law teaching and scholarship in relation to other courses, seminars, and faculty offerings in the general domain of international and comparative law.

The discussion is divided into four periods: 1945-50, 1951-69, 1970-86, and 1986-2000. These periods correspond to significant changes in the law school curriculum at UBC, either through the addition or departure of members of faculty or through substantive changes to the overall curriculum. For each of these periods, I will provide an overview of the faculty's operation and a discussion of the place of international law in the curriculum. In conclusion, I will offer a few comments on the present status of international law at UBC and the challenges the faculty faces in responding to a rapidly changing international legal order.

Early Days, 1945-50

The Faculty of Law at UBC emerged almost overnight in the heady days following the end of the Second World War. The prospect of thousands of veterans returning from overseas convinced the provincial government and the Law Society of British Columbia that the time had finally arrived for the establishment of a university law school in the province. Earlier efforts to establish a law school at UBC had been thwarted by external events: fiscal crises at the Law Society of British Columbia in the 1920s, the depression of the 1930s, and the outbreak of the Second World War in 1939. Finally, in July 1945, after much effort by the Law Society of British Columbia, Senator Wallace Farris, and the newly appointed president of UBC, N.A.M. MacKenzie, the government of British Columbia agreed to provide $10,000 to assist with the establishment of a law school. Over the next three months, George F. Curtis of Dalhousie University was hired as dean, and the new school prepared to start teaching classes as early as October.[1]

---

[1] See W. Wesley Pue, *Law School: The Story of Legal Education in British Columbia* (Vancouver: University of British Columbia, Faculty of Law, 1995) at 137, 139-44; P.B. Waite, *Lord of Point Grey: Larry MacKenzie of UBC* (Vancouver: UBC Press, 1987) at 124, 125. These two books are essential reading for anyone interested in the subject matter of this article. The story of how the Faculty of Law came into being has been told by Dean Curtis, in his inimitable off-the-cuff style, in *The Gryphon* (UBC Law Magazine) (Fall 1995) at 6. See also the address by Prime Minister Louis St. Laurent at the formal opening ceremonies of the Faculty of Law building on September 4, 1952, in (September-October 1952) 10 The Advocate 170; and the

In its first year of operation, the Faculty of Law comprised eighty-six students, the majority of whom were veterans, two full-time faculty members, Dean Curtis and Professor Frederick Read, and two books: *McLaren on Bills and Notes* and *Salmond on Torts*.[2] In its second year, the faculty numbered 240 students with two additional full-time members of faculty, George McAllister and Gilbert Kennedy. By 1949, student enrolment had jumped to 400 students.[3] During these early years, the law school was housed in army huts that had been made available by the government of Canada — a new law building was constructed in 1951.[4] Throughout this period, when the faculty was struggling to accommodate the influx of returning soldiers, classes were taught as large lectures.[5] In 1948, the university agreed to the hiring of two additional professors, M.M. MacIntyre and John Westlake as well as a lecturer, A.W.R. Carrothers. The faculty thus numbered six to seven full-time professors, which was an unusually high number for that time and the subject of friendly rivalry at Toronto, McGill, and Dalhousie.

LAW SCHOOL CURRICULUM AND INTERNATIONAL LAW

In a bold and innovative move, Dean George Curtis added international law to the second year curriculum as a required course.[6] At this time, Toronto, McGill, and Dalhousie were the only Canadian law schools to have made international law a required subject, and at Dalhousie the course, regrettably, lost this status upon the

---

useful article by W. Wesley Pue, "An Ancient, Honourable and Learned Profession" (1995) 53 The Advocate 345. On the geographical and economic background, see Geoffrey Molyneux, *British Columbia: An Illustrated History* (Vancouver: Polestar Press, 1992); Kevin Griffin, *Vancouver's Many Faces: Passport to the Cultures of a City* (Vancouver and Toronto: Whitecap Books, 1993); and Terry Rekstan, *Illustrated History of British Columbia* (Vancouver: Douglas and McIntyre, 2001).

[2] Interview with Dr. George Curtis by Dean F. Murray Fraser (*British Columbia Legal History Collection Project*, Aural History Program, Faculty of Law, University of Victoria, transcript, February 1980) at 61 [hereinafter Curtis Interview 1980].

[3] Robin S. Harris, *A History of Higher Education in Canada 1663-1960* (Toronto and Buffalo: University of Toronto Press, 1970) at 53.

[4] Pue, *supra* note 1 at 185, 252.

[5] The size of the classes increased dramatically after 1945. In 1946, class size was 150, but, by 1947, it was 250. Faculty-to-student ratio was as high as 100:1. Pue, *supra* note 1 at 169, 185-6.

[6] *University of British Columbia Calendar, 1946-1947* (Vancouver: University of British Columbia, 1946) at 321 [hereinafter *UBC Calendar,* followed by the year and page number].

outbreak of the Second World War in 1939. When asked why international law had been added to the curriculum, Curtis replied that international law was what the "Second World War [had] been fought about and it seemed to me that [it] should find a place amongst the subjects."[7]

It is instructive to recall that in 1945, and indeed throughout the period surrounding the launching of the new law school, professionals in Vancouver saw the study and practice of law as something more than domestic legal practice. It involved larger issues of international peace and security, global cooperation, and the protection of human rights. In his address at the opening of the new school, the Honourable Wendell Farris, chief justice of the Supreme Court of British Columbia, emphasized that the world was facing a "new era" in which lawyers would "play a more prominent part in world affairs than at any time in history."[8] The end of the war had brought about the "new rule of International Law" and with it a role for lawyers as public servants:

It is the duty of lawyers to give leadership ... to maintain the freedom which is our heritage and which has been maintained for us by the gallant sacrifice of such young men and women who largely compose the members of the student body of the Law School.

We must work together as one body, realizing the great privileges we have and the responsibility which comes with privilege. Never in the history of the world has the opportunity been as great as at present to give leadership at this time, but it is our privilege to do so. We must stand together and while maintaining the individuality of the great traditions of our profession, march with the rest of decent society for the betterment of mankind.[9]

This sentiment was fully shared by the founding dean, who emphasized the role of lawyers in public service: "Lawyers have always been leaders in the national life of the country. I thought it proper that the lawyers graduating from UBC should have as part of their requirement an understanding of the basic principles and doctrines of international law."[10]

---

[7] Curtis Interview 1980, *supra* note 2 at 87.

[8] Pue, *supra* note 1 at 155.

[9] *Ibid.* at 156.

[10] Interview with Dean Curtis by Doris Buss (UBC Faculty of Law, May 1996) [hereinafter Curtis Interview 1996]. On Curtis, see Elisabeth Lumley, ed., *Canadian Who's Who 2002*, vol. 37 (Toronto: University of Toronto Press, 2002) at 304; R.H. Tupper, "Dean George Curtis, A Tribute by R.H. Tupper, Q.C." (1971) 29 The Advocate 154; Anthony J.F. Sheppard, "The Ceremonial Opening

Curtis's interest in, and dedication to, international law was a product of his legal education in Saskatchewan, his post-graduate education at Oxford, where he had been a brilliant student of the great international law scholar James Brierly, and the cultural traditions of Dalhousie Law School, where he had been an outstanding professor for many years and had taught the international law course in the early days of the Second World War.[11] As a result of his interest in international law, Curtis had been asked by J. McGregor Stewart of Halifax to stand in for him at the Ottawa meeting of the Special Committee of the Canadian Bar Association (CBA) on the Statute of the International Court of Justice. Curtis's involvement with this committee was important in two respects. First, it reinforced his convictions about the need for international lawyers in the post-war world, and, second, it led to a professional relationship with Chief Justice Wendell Farris, chair of the CBA Committee,

---

of the George F. Curtis Building, Faculty of Law, University of British Columbia" (December-January 1977) 35(1) The Advocate 31; Thomas H. Shorthouse, compiler, *A Scrapbook of Reminiscences by George F. Curtis*, UBC Law Library (call no. KB 15 C 876 A1 1998); Christina Parkin, George Curtis, and the UBC Law School, *A Crucial Phase in the History of Canadian Legal Education*, UBC Law Library (call no. KB 15 CB76 P37, 1988). See also the unsigned note on Curtis's ninetieth birthday party in *The Gryphon* (Winter 1997) at 9.

In the opinion of Chief Justice Bora Laskin, "George Curtis has played a major role in legal education in this country, especially in interpreting its university and theoretical orientation to a legal profession which, caught up in busy practice, sometimes forgets how necessary it is to have free albeit disciplined inquiry into the foundations of our legal order and into the adequacy of its controlling principles. This is an occasion when it is permissible to salute all of those who have dedicated themselves to one of the noblest of endeavours, the teaching of our youth to understand and appreciate the democratic values which underpin our legal system and to prepare them to preserve and advance those values, and to adapt them to the needs of an ever changing society" (Sheppard at 34). In the opinion of John Willis, Curtis's "true métier was oral communication both inside and outside the School." John Willis, *A History of Dalhousie Law School* (Toronto: University of Toronto Press, 1979) at 122, 130, and 136.

[11] Pue explains that Curtis's approach to the UBC curriculum was a reflection of a particular "cultural" approach to the study of law that drew from the traditions of legal education in the prairies and at Dalhousie Law School in Halifax, where the influence of Richard Chapman Weldon was pervasive. Weldon, who had made international law a compulsory course from the start of his school in 1883, emphasized the idea of "legal education for the public good." Curtis combined this cultural tradition with a pragmatic recognition of the changing nature of Canadian society. "The objective was to fully take on board the post-New Deal welfare state. Courses and course content were added to the traditional 'cultural' curriculum in order to meet this new social reality." Pue, *supra* note 1 at 171.

who subsequently became Curtis's ally in developing the curriculum at UBC.[12]

Curtis's constructive role in promoting international law and legal scholarship at UBC — indeed in Canada as a whole — cannot be overstated. While he did not publish in the area, he was a tireless promoter of international legal education and scholarship in other ways. During his long tenure as dean of law at UBC, where he was the last of the Rolls Royce deans — good for a life-time — he provided decanal direction and encouragement for international legal studies, built up staff in the international law area, actively sought out and encouraged students to pursue graduate studies in international law, assembled an international law research library, and encouraged important initiatives, such as the creation of the *Canadian Yearbook of International Law*, which was housed at UBC from 1961 to 1993 and is still published by UBC Press.[13]

PUBLIC INTERNATIONAL LAW COURSE

Interestingly, international law had been taught at UBC, as part of the political science program, prior to 1946. The subject first appeared in the UBC calendar in 1942-43, with the following, fairly comprehensive, description: "The nature, sources, and sanctions of international law; the notion of nationhood, with particular reference to the status of the British Dominions; jurisdiction, nationality, normal relations between states; settlement of international disputes; war; organization of peace after the present conflict." Taught for three hours a week, the course was based on Manley O. Hudson's *Cases on International Law* and A. Berriedale Keith's, *The*

---

[12] Curtis Interview 1996, *supra* note 10. On the fascinating account of the statement of principles and joint action by the Canadian Bar Association and the American Bar Association on planning a post-world war court, see George Curtis, "Dalhousie and the World Court, 1945 — a Recollection" (Fall 1987) 3(1) Hearsay 18. This story ought to be more widely known. Curtis played a role. On J. McGregor Stewart, see Barry Cahill, *The Thousandth Man: A Biography of James McGregor Stewart* (Toronto: University of Toronto Press for the Osgood Society for Canadian Legal History, 2000).

[13] Curtis served as dean for twenty-six years, the longest deanship ever held in Canada. On the *Canadian Yearbook of International Law*, see R. St. J. Macdonald, "Charles B. Bourne: Scholar, Teacher and Editor: Innovator in the Development of the International Law of Water Resources" (1996) 24 Can. Y.B. Int'l L. 3 at 34 ff.; Curtis to R. St. J. Macdonald (May 31, 1972); Curtis Interview 1996, *supra* note 10. For MacKenzie's succinct and still-useful statement on the background, see his foreword in (1963) 1 Can. Y.B. Int'l L. 7.

Dominions as Sovereign States.[14] In 1946, when the subject, which was now part of the curriculum of the Faculty of Law, was available to political science as well as law students, the course was dropped from the political science curriculum.

With a large student body and a small faculty, Curtis looked around for part-time instructors to assist with the teaching. In the case of public international law, he turned to no less than N.A.M. MacKenzie, the formidable president of the university. MacKenzie, a prominent professor of international law of fourteen years standing at the University of Toronto, was a fully trained scholar of the subject. A graduate of Dalhousie, Harvard, and Cambridge, he had served as an informal member of Canada's delegation to the League of Nations and as the assistant English language legal advisor at the International Labour Office in Geneva before joining the faculty of law in Toronto.[15] As Diana M. Priestly, a student at the UBC law school in the early years and later its first full-time law librarian, recalls, the active participation of the dean of law and the president of the university meant the law school obviously had "great strengths in Public International Law and I found that just fascinating."[16]

While MacKenzie was able to draw on his reservoir of learning, his experience in Geneva, his vast professional network, and his natural gifts as a lecturer to enhance the presentation of his classes, his very demanding schedule, as president of one of Canada's most important universities, prevented him from giving the course the

---

[14] *UBC Calendar 1942-43, supra* note 6 at 142. Hudson's casebook, widely used in the United States, was a "natural" for UBC since MacKenzie knew Hudson at Harvard and elsewhere. Hudson's first edition appeared in 1929, the third edition in 1951. For his evaluation of other collections in the field, see Manley O. Hudson, "Twelve Casebooks on International Law" (1938) 32 Am. J. Int'l L. 447 and for a discussion of earlier casebooks and treatises on international law in the United States, see Benjamin Akzin, "On the Teaching of International Law" (1934) 20 Iowa L. Rev. 774. See my brief comment on Canadian casebooks, in note 114.

[15] Waite, *supra* note 1.

[16] Interview with Diana M. Priestly by Balfour J. Halevy and Maryla Waters (British Columbia Legal History Collection Project, Aural History Program, Faculty of Law, University of Victoria, transcript, September-October 1988) at 15 [hereinafter Priestly Interview]. For information on Diana Priestly, see Margaret A. Banks, "The Canadian Association of Law Libraries: A History," Canadian Association of Law Libraries Newsletter / Bulletin Special Issue 1988, reprinted in Joan N. Fraser, ed., *Law Libraries in Canada: Essays in Honour of Diana M. Priestly* (Toronto: Carswell, 1988) at 191.

attention it required. Former students agree that his lectures were stimulating because of the man MacKenzie was, but that details of the subject were sadly neglected as a result of his anecdotal style of teaching. He simply could not and did not prepare. Neil M. Fleishman of the Class of 1948 recalls:

> [W]hat we did learn about International Law was how joyful it was for Dr. MacKenzie to have travelled down the Danube with Dr. Lauterpacht and his attractive daughter. When exam time came close, some of us approached Dr. MacKenzie and asked him just how we were to answer the questions on International Law. Dr. MacKenzie's reply was a magnificent piece of advice: "If you students carefully and assiduously read Time Magazine, you will have no trouble passing International Law." We looked up to Dr. MacKenzie because we knew he had the Military Medal and two Bars in the Great War. Well, we all passed international law.[17]

Diane Priestly recalls the following about MacKenzie's course:

> I liked international law ... but the class as a whole felt very aggrieved because Dr. MacKenzie [later President MacKenzie] assigned essays and we thought that as law students we were above essay writing and so what happened in the school was you inherited, because they were always the same topics given out for essays, you inherited your essay topics along with your books. The person who sold you their books gave you their two essays ... and you just wrote them out in your own handwriting and handed them in ... [One year a person hired to do the marking for Dr. MacKenzie discovered that] ... there were quite a lot of exactly similar essays, and [he] thought that something wrong was going on and reported this. Well! There was a tremendous faculty meeting I gather about it. [A faculty member] thought we should be expelled. Dr. Mac[Intyre] was in the school by this time and he volunteered to come in and speak sternly ... about this.[18]

For Dean Curtis, the problem of the quality of the instruction in international law was obvious.[19] Once it became apparent that MacKenzie's schedule would not permit him to spend time on the subject, Curtis himself stepped in to assist.[20] However, as founding

---

[17] Neil M. Fleishman, "The Fabulous Forties — Class of '48" UBC Law Faculty Newsletter (Autumn 1991) at 10. MacKenzie was twice decorated for bravery. There is now a substantial literature on Lauterpacht, including important essays by Sir Gerald Fitzmaurice, Stephen M. Schwebel, Martii Koskenniemi, Donald Greig, Michael Reisman, and Benedict Kingsbury.

[18] Interview with Diana Priestly by Jim MacIntyre (University of British Columbia Law School, Vancouver, September 23, 1994) as quoted in Pue, *supra* note 1 at 202.

[19] Curtis Interview 1996, *supra* note 10.

[20] *UBC Calendar 1948-49*, *supra* note 6 at 403.

dean of a dynamic faculty in an expanding university, Curtis was also busy, and he soon hired Michael Goldie to assist MacKenzie. Michael Goldie, a brilliant student just back from Harvard, was fortunately able to fill in as a highly competent part-time lecturer.[21] In 1946, the first year the course was taught, MacKenzie relied on Oppenheim's *International Law*, Brierly's *The Law of Nations*, and MacKenzie and Laing's *Canada and the Law of Nations*. The latter was the first hard-covered casebook on international law produced by Canadians. In 1947, the materials were supplemented with Shuman's *International Politics*, which was soon afterwards replaced by Nussbaum's *Concise History of the Law of Nations*. These materials, which were one-third British, one-third American, and one-third Canadian, represented a solidly balanced and professionally respectable basis for an introductory course on international law at the time. They remained the recommended materials until the course was revised by Charles B. Bourne.

George Curtis was not the first dean of law to make public international law mandatory in a Canadian law school. This honour belongs to Maximilien Bibaud at the College St. Marie in Montreal in 1851 and, in English Canada, to Richard Chapman Weldon at Dalhousie University in Halifax in 1883.[22] Yet in the promising period following the end of the Second World War, Curtis was the first dean of law to publicly and continually proclaim the importance of the subject. A man of good judgment, he was widely respected and greatly liked.

As for MacKenzie, we need to remember that he was a popular and widely admired public figure in Canada. Everybody knew him and he knew everybody. He was in his time a founding member of the Canadian Institute of International Affairs, president of the University of New Brunswick, a member of the Massey Commission, a charter member of the Canada Council, an active member of innumerable organizations and associations, a senator, and well connected politically. In the words of his biographer, "Larry was unique in being a university president who moved effortlessly among three worlds, university, politics, and business, and he was a

---

[21] *Ibid.* On Goldie, see my article on Charles Bourne, *supra* note 13 at 16. See also the unsigned note, "New Judges: The Honourable Mr. Justice D.M.M. Goldie" (November 1991) 49(6) The Advocate 931.

[22] On Bibaud, see R. St. J. Macdonald, "Maximilien Bibaud 1823-1887: The Pioneer Teacher of International Law in Canada" (1988) 11 Dalhousie L. J. 721. On Weldon, see Della Stanley, "Richard Chapman Weldon 1849-1925 Fact, Fiction and Enigma" (1989) 12 Dalhousie L. J. 539.

near-genius at explaining the one to the other."[23] And he was on a first-name basis with virtually all the heavyweight international lawyers of the Anglo-American world of his day, Brierly, Hudson, Jenks, Jessup, Lauterpacht, and McNair.

MacKenzie and Curtis did not publish anything of consequence on or about international law during their days at UBC. They were not productive scholars of the subject, but this fact did not really matter. They contributed in other ways. Both were evangelists for the university and for the subject they regarded as fundamental. They travelled extensively in Canada and abroad announcing to all and sundry that international law was important, that those at UBC needed to recognize this fact and do something about it, and that the government of Canada needed to take it seriously. Their reputations were such that professionals in legal, educational, and governmental circles agreed that if these two men said so then it must be so. In short, they established a culture of international law at UBC.[24]

---

[23] Waite, *supra* note 1 at 218. "There wasn't a university president in Canada who could touch him in public relations" (at 178). According to Curtis, "Larry MacKenzie — He was enormously human ... he was 'a bit of a giant, you know'," in *UBC Reports*, February 6, 1986 at 3. According to Gordon Shrum, "MacKenzie was quite a gambler — it was one of the many things I liked about him," in Clive Cocking, ed., *Gordon Shrum, An Autobiography* (Vancouver: UBC Press, 1986) at 64. Gordon Shrum (at 145) thought: "The trouble with Canadians is that they don't know what their potential is; nobody has ever given them encouragement to develop their potential." That was not true of MacKenzie. For brief comments at the time of MacKenzie's death, see *The Ubyssey* (January 28, 1986) at 1 and Bruce McLean, "Goodbye, Old Friend," *The Province* (January 30, 1986) at 14.

[24] N.A.M. MacKenzie is sometimes referred to as "the father of international law" in Canada. The accuracy of this remark would depend on an evaluation of MacKenzie's work in the domain of international law specifically, in the context of the work of those in the field who preceded him, from Bibaud in the nineteenth century, to those who followed, especially Percy E. Corbett, John E. Read, and John P. Humphrey. If MacKenzie's intellectual contributions were less impressive than those of Corbett, Read, and Humphrey, his talents as proselytizer, communicator, and administrator were superior. MacKenzie taught at universities in three provinces, struggled for better research and resources (see (1932) 10 Can. Bar Rev. 519), produced the first hard-back casebook on international law in Canada, supported the creation of a yearbook, anticipated the establishment of what became the Canadian Council on International Law, spoke publicly and nationally about the importance of the subject, and recognized the need for good professional relations with government officials in Ottawa. A study of his legal life brings into consideration the part to be played by individual members of the international law community in Canada. Hopefully, the new generation of international lawyers in Canada will re-examine MacKenzie's

INTERNATIONAL LAW COMES OF AGE AT UBC, 1951-69

The 1950s was a period of relative calm at the UBC law school. In 1951, the desperately needed new law building was completed, and most of the veterans had graduated and moved on, thus causing the population of the law school to drop. By the mid-1950s, the student population was around 200, increasing by about five to ten students per year.

BUILDING THE INTERNATIONAL LAW TRADITION: THE 1950S

The difficulty of finding someone to teach international law was resolved with the fortuitous appointment of Charles Beresford Bourne in 1951. A Barbadian, he had received a Bachelor of Arts with great distinction from the old Honours Law Course at the University of Toronto and an LL.B., later redesignated as an LL.M., with a "starred" first from Cambridge University in England. He came to UBC from the College of Law at the University of Saskatchewan, where for three years he had, in the tradition of the times, taught across the board, which meant teaching as many as four subjects every term. His assignment at UBC was to assist MacKenzie with public international law, teaching classes whenever MacKenzie was unavailable.[25]

With MacKenzie away most of the time, able to give only about six lectures a year, Bourne taught the bulk of the course. As the principal instructor, he was able to change its nature from one based on anecdotal accounts of MacKenzie's career to one emphasizing case law: "I taught it as a law course using case materials whenever I could. I do not know that the students ever became convinced that there was such a thing as international law but at least they were exposed to it and used the materials that they would need in looking at a legal system."[26] Although Larry MacKenzie ceased teaching public international law, he never abandoned his interest and commitment to the subject. He referred to it throughout his

---

professional career. For a list of his publications, see Christian L. Wiktor, *Canadian Bibliography of International Law* (Toronto: University of Toronto Press, 1984) at 723. In the context of this article, we need to remember that MacKenzie's principal work in international law took place in Toronto, not Vancouver. For his Toronto experience, see Waite, *supra* note 1; and Martin L. Friedland, *The University of Toronto: A History* (Toronto: University of Toronto Press, 2002).

[25] Macdonald, *supra* note 13.

[26] Interview with Professor Charles Bourne by Kathleen Fisher (Vancouver, December 12, 1992) at 3-4 [hereinafter Bourne Interview].

public addresses, remained the formal instructor in the course, and insisted that he be listed in the university calendar as "Honorary Professor of Public International Law."[27]

When Charles Bourne started teaching public international law, he added two new texts to the list of recommended materials: L.B. Sohn's pioneering *Cases and Materials on World Law* and J.G. Starke's *Law of Nations.* These materials remained standard throughout the 1950s and most of the 1960s. In addition, Bourne drew extensively on current world events and their implications for the application and development of the subject. A review of essay topics assigned to the political science students enrolled in the public international law course shows that students were addressing issues such as: "legal problems in the regulation of sea fisheries" (November 1957); "legal problems in the use of space" and "the issues in the Icelandic fishery dispute" (November 1959); "the legality of the US 'quarantine' of Cuba" (1962-63); "the Eichmann trial and international law" (1962-63); and "Canada's claim to twelve miles from straight baselines drawn between headland points on the coast of Canada" (1960-61). From his earliest days as an internationalist, Bourne was, as he remained throughout his career, informed, wide-ranging, and relevant.[28]

The 1950s was a period of growth for international law at UBC. During this period, Bourne began what was to become his universally admired work on the international law of rivers. He was active with the International Law Association's (ILA) Committee on International Water Resources Law and with the Vancouver Branch of the Canadian Institute of International Affairs. Although his teaching responsibilities were divided between public international

---

[27] *UBC Calendar 1965-66, supra* note 6 at 7.

[28] It is instructive to note other topics assigned by Bourne: "The disposition of claims to Formosa, Quemoy and Matsu in accordance with International Law" (1958-59); "An International Bill of Rights" (1958-59); "The Legality of Establishing Danger Zones on the High Seas for Testing Nuclear Devices" (1962-63); "The Influence of the Concept of "Natural Law" on the Development of International Law" (1953-54); "The Economic and Social Council of the UN: Its Contribution to the Achievement of the Purposes of the UN," "The Voting Provisions of the UN Charter," and "The Proposal for an International Criminal Court of Justice" (1955-56), "The Secretariat of the UN" (1961-62), "The Exercise of Police Powers in the International Community" (1960-61); "The Extra-Territorial Application of United States' Laws, with Particular Reference to Their Application to Canada" (1959-60), all contained in Manuscripts of Charles B. Bourne, box 21, file 9, Special Collections and University Archives Division, University of British Columbia Library.

law, administrative law, and constitutional law, his scholarship and research began to move towards international law. In 1961, he became president of the Canadian branch of the ILA. At the same time, he became the founding editor-in-chief of the *Canadian Yearbook of International Law*, a position that he held for the remarkable period of thirty-one unbroken years during which he supervised the production of thirty volumes. The yearbook was made possible by Bourne's availability and enthusiasm, the support of MacKenzie and Curtis, and a grant from the Koerner Foundation, which was a local charitable trust for the support of higher education.[29] The yearbook was housed at UBC until 1993 when it moved under the editorship of D.M. McRae to the University of Ottawa.

During this same period, Curtis himself was not inactive in the domain of international law. During the 1950s, he drafted Canadian proposals for the first UN Conference on the Law of the Sea in 1958, where he played a key role within the Canadian delegation.

EXPANDING THE INTERNATIONAL LAW CURRICULUM

1964 Curriculum Review

Until 1960, the curriculum at the law school was prescribed.[30] In 1960-61, when seminars became available, a measure of choice was introduced into the third-year program.[31] In addition to the required courses, students were required to choose a seminar, and by 1961-62 seminars were being offered in Legal Theory and Legislation; Public Law (taught by Bourne); Commercial Transactions; Comparative Law; Trade Regulation; Problems in the Common Law; Acquisition; and Control of Land by the State; and, in international law, in Current Problems in International Law (taught by John M. Flackett) and International Economic Law (taught by L. Gordon Jahnke).[32]

---

[29] See the references in Waite, *supra* note 1 at 34-36. For an amusing episode involving MacKenzie and Koerner, see P.B. Waite, "A Tale of Three Presidents: UBC, Western, and Dalhousie 1945-1967" (forthcoming).

[30] In third year, students could choose between either Legislation or Taxation and either Municipal Law or Shipping: *UBC Calendar 1958-59, supra* note 6 at 256-57.

[31] *Report of the Curriculum Committee to the Faculty of Law, UBC*, February 1964 at 3, on file at the UBC Faculty of Law [hereinafter *Curriculum Report* 1964].

[32] *UBC Calendar 1961-62, supra* note 6 at 284. Charles Bourne to R. St. J. Macdonald Outlining Courses and Instructors in International Law from 1945-66 (undated).

This expansion of course offerings required additional faculty. John Flackett and Gordon Jahnke, both of whom became more heavily involved in the teaching of international law, were hired in the early 1960s. Flackett had been educated at the University of Birmingham, and Jahnke held an LL.B. from Saskatchewan and an LL.M. in international law from the University of London. Jahnke remained for twenty years as an important member of the full-time staff, teaching international economic law and public international law and co-editing the first casebook on the subject with Bourne, but he and Flackett did finally depart.[33] For a time, public international law was taught by Anthony Hooper of Cambridge, who is now Sir Anthony Hooper in the United Kingdom.[34] In 1968, Peter T. Burns joined the faculty and assisted Bourne and Jahnke in teaching the basic course.[35]

The pressure on the faculty to increase the number of courses and the variety of course arrangements continued throughout the 1960s, and, in 1964, the faculty undertook a review of course offerings, required courses, and seminars.[36] As a result of this review, some courses in second and third year were made optional, but, significantly, public international law was retained as a required two-hour course. The committee justified this important decision in a statement of the utmost significance for the purposes of this survey. The committee said that international law

is the most important and exciting legal development of the twentieth century ... The adaptation of peaceful procedures for settling disputes in the international arena; of the rules of commercial law to international law; of constitutional law to supr-national [sic] organizations; and of property law to the resources of the oceans and space — all these face the law with a test and opportunity of unparalleled magnitude. Every law student of today, whether he [sic] is going to be an international lawyer or a conveyancer in Vancouver, should be made award [sic] of this development and the creative opportunities it offers.[37]

[33] *UBC Calendar 1964-65 supra* note 6 at 13, 19.

[34] *UBC Calendar 1967-68, supra* note 6 at 7.

[35] "Timetables and Teaching Assignments, 1968," Faculty of Law Records, box 6, file 23, Special Collections and University Archives Division, University of British Columbia Library. Peter Burns served as dean of the law school from 1982-91, and he was a member of the United Nations Committee against Torture and Cruel, Inhuman or Degrading Treatment or Punishment 1987-2003. He continues to serve as president of the International Society for Criminal Law Reform and Criminal Justice Policy: *UBC Calendar 1998-2000, supra* note 6 at 10.

[36] *Curriculum Report* 1964, *supra* note 31.

[37] *Ibid.* at 23.

Interestingly, the Curriculum Committee recommended that public international law should not be taught as a traditional law course "dealing with a number of rules." It was preferable, said the committee, to concentrate on the "current evolution of international law" than with all of its traditional aspects, many of which are "irrelevant today." The committee rightly thought it more relevant to consider "international organizations and the claims of states to areas of the sea and space than it is to study the independence of states and diplomatic immunities."[38]

International Law Courses

Public International Law Course

As a result of the curriculum review in 1964, the Public International Law course was renamed "International Law" and described in the calendar as follows: "History, sources and evidence of international law and its relation to municipal law. International personality, state jurisdiction, treaties and international organizations."[39] This (very traditional) course was taught by Bourne and Jahnke and was offered in each term. Recommended materials included Oppenheim's *International Law;* Brierly's *The Law of Nations;* MacKenzie and Laing's *Canada and the Law of Nations;* Nussbaum's *Concise History of the Law of Nations;* and Sohn's *Cases and Materials on United Nations Law.*[40] These materials were virtually identical to those on the original list of 1946.

In 1967, Bourne and Jahnke published a mimeographed collection of their own materials.[41] The topics covered included sources and evidences of international law; relations between international and municipal law; the persons of international law; the continuing personality of states; the recognition of states and governments; the jurisdiction of states; state responsibility for injuries to aliens; nationalization and expropriation; and international agreements. The materials in this volume, which was one of the first of its kind in Canada, comprised mostly primary sources: Canadian, American, British, and international case law, treaties and conventions,

---

[38] *Ibid.*

[39] *UBC Calendar 1965-66, supra* note 6 at 14.

[40] *Ibid.*

[41] C.B. Bourne and L.G. Jahnke, *Cases and Materials on Public International Law* (Vancouver: University of British Columbia, Faculty of Law, 1967, updated 1969, 1972, 1974).

international law documents, and basic UN instruments, such as the Charter of the United Nations. The primary sources were supplemented by academic writings by, for example, Manfred Lachs's *The International Law of Outer Space* and R. St. J. Macdonald's "Public International Law Problems Arising in Canadian Courts."[42]

In the late 1960s, students and faculty at UBC were continuing to agitate, as were their counterparts elsewhere, for an overall reform of the curriculum. Surveys were undertaken, and these surveys provide a glimpse of what the students of the time thought about international law. For example, in a 1968 survey of second-year students, the respondents said that the course could be shortened to a half year; that there was "too much emphasis" on international law in the law school; that the subject was "useless;" and that the course should be elective rather than required.[43] In a second student survey, conducted under the auspices of the Law Students' Association during the year 1967-68, most respondents taking international law from Bourne returned generally favourable comments.[44] In their opinion, Bourne was well-organized, prepared good materials, and conveyed a sense of interest in the subject. His approach to the course was described as "solid, predictable, well-organized," but with little scope for class participation. A few felt that Bourne was "at times overly dogmatic in his pursuit of the general principles in international law."

International Law Seminars

On his return from sabbatical leave at Harvard Law School in 1964, Charles Bourne took over the seminar on international law problems, the aim of which was to examine some of the issues touched on in the basic course.[45] It was described in the course calendar as "[a] research seminar in which selected problems of international law and government of current interest and importance will be investigated; examples are the financing of the United Nations, offshore fishing limits, the Cyprus situation, peaceful

---

[42] Manfred Lachs, *The International Law of Outer Space* (Leiden: Sifothoff, 1972); and R. St. J. Macdonald, "Public International Law Problems Arising in Canadian Courts" (1955-56) 11 U. Toronto L.J. 224.

[43] "1968 Survey of Second-Year Students," Faculty of Law Records, box 6, file 12, Special Collections and University Archives Division, University of British Columbia Library.

[44] *Ibid.*

[45] Bourne Interview, *supra* note 26 at 2.

coexistence, etc."[46] A review of Bourne's course notes indicates that he covered a different problem each week, usually drawing on current world events. In 1968, for example, the class considered "[t]he Withdrawal of UNEF [United Nations Emergency Force] from Sinai, May 1967."[47] Two of Bourne's favourite topics throughout the 1960s were "the trial of Eichmann" and "intervention in Vietnam."[48] He relied mostly on primary sources: American, English, and international case law, reports of United Nations and domestic government bodies, and treaties. In addition, he prescribed readings from the standard international law texts, such as Oppenheim's *International Law* (8th edition), O'Connell's *International Law,* Brierly's *The Law of Nations* (6th edition), and McNair's *The Law of Treaties.*

In addition to Bourne's seminar, Jahnke offered a seminar on international law and transactions, which was described in the course calendar as "[p]rinciples of international law in the context of economic transactions. The first part will be concerned with public transactions, particularly public economic institutions and treaties with economic significance. The latter part will be devoted to an examination of the effects of these institutions, treaties and principles upon private international transactions."[49] In the academic year 1968-69, Jahnke refocused this seminar to look at specific international and domestic activities affecting international

---

[46] *UBC Calendar 1965-66, supra* note 6 at 18.

[47] Students were asked to read Meg Greenfield, "A Story of Forty-Eight Hours," *The Reporter,* June 15, 1967; D.W. Bowett, *United Nations Forces: A Legal Study of United Nations Practice* (London: Stevens, 1964); and Dag Hammarskjold, *Aide Memoire* (1956).

[48] For the seminar on the *Eichmann* trial (which Bourne listed as abduction, jurisdiction, and retroactivity), students were asked to read Pierre Achille Papadatos, *The Eichmann Trial* (London: Stevens, 1964) at chapter 2; *Frisbie* v. *Colins,* (1951) 342 U.S. 519; *Ex. P. Elliot,* [1949] 1 All E.R. 373; and the *Lotus* case. On intervention in Vietnam, he assigned the Agreement Relating to the Situation in Viet Nam, reprinted in "Vietnam and International Law" (1966) 60 Am. J. Int'l L. 137-50, 629-49; "The Legality of United States Participation in the Defense of Viet Nam," a legal memorandum prepared by Leonard C. Meeker, Legal Adviser of the Department of State, submitted to the Senate Committee on Foreign Relations on March 8, 1966, reprinted in (1966) 60 Am. J. Int'l L. 565-885. Other topics assigned by Bourne included the position of English courts with respect to the Act of State Doctrine and the violation of international law; the recognition of states and governments: international law and Canadian practice (post-1945); doctrine of *rebus sic stantibus;* private broadcasting from international waters, state succession and the problem of treaty applicability in international law, and the extra-territorial effects of the United States maritime commission.

[49] *UBC Calendar 1965-66, supra* note 6 at 18.

trade. In the first part of the seminar, students considered "one or more typical bilateral international commercial agreements" as well as the General Agreements on Tariffs and Trade. "Against this background," students then looked at international trade barriers, "problems relating to the trade contract, export procedures and the financing of exports from Canada."[50] Statistics on student enrolment for 1968-70 show that Jahnke's seminar on international law and economic transactions attracted seven students in 1968-69 and nine students in 1969-70. The seminar on international law problems had eight students enrolled in 1968-69, which is the only date for which statistics are available. Bourne estimates that his seminar generally attracted between ten and fourteen students.[51]

Institutional Support

In retrospect, we can see that the years 1950-69 marked the growth and development of UBC's strength in international legal scholarship. As I have already indicated, the basis of this development was the university's general commitment to international law as an important part of legal education, the universalist perspective of the early student body, the institutional support given to the subject through the hiring of outstanding faculty, the acquisition of international legal literature, and, of great importance, the insistence that the course should be compulsory. An example of institutional commitment was the establishment in 1960-61 of the Norman MacKenzie Prize in Public International Law, a prize "in honour of Dr. Norman MacKenzie" offered annually to the student in law obtaining the highest standing in public international law.[52] In 1965-66, the prize was worth $125 and by 1982-83 it was worth $600. It was described as "established by Walter H. Gage, for the best student in Public International Law."[53]

GROWING PAINS: 1970-86

The period 1970-83 was a period of both strength and weakness for international law at UBC. In 1971, George Curtis completed

---

[50] "Course Options and Seminars," Faculty of Law Records, box 6, file 8, Special Collections and University Archives Division, University of British Columbia Library.

[51] Bourne Interview, *supra* note 26 at 2.

[52] *UBC Calendar 1962-63, supra* note 6 at 468.

[53] *UBC Calendar 1982-83, supra* note 6 at 40.

his long tenure as dean and was succeeded by Albert McClean. In 1972, Donald M. McRae, a young New Zealand scholar, joined the faculty from the University of Western Ontario, reinforcing the expertise of MacKenzie, Curtis, and Bourne.[54] As a direct result of the fruitful partnership between Bourne and McRae, the Faculty of Law not only retained, but also greatly increased, its strength in international law, at least for the short term. However, the failure to develop junior professors in international law took its toll when Bourne and McRae left in the 1980s. Bourne, who had been moving slowly away from full-time involvement in the faculty in the late 1970s,[55] retired in 1986. McRae who, from 1983 to 1986 had spent three years with the Department of External Affairs in Ottawa, was appointed dean of the Common Law Section of the Faculty of Law at the University of Ottawa in 1987 and moved away to the nation's capital. Maurice Copithorne, a retired former legal adviser to the Department of External Affairs, arrived in 1986 to take up a visiting chair and, on McRae's departure, took over the teaching of the basic course as well as an advanced seminar. Enrolment grew steadily over the following years, and a new faculty member, Karen Mickelson, began teaching a second section of the introductory course in 1990-91.

1969 CURRICULUM REVIEW

In the latter half of the 1960s, student enrolment at the law school increased dramatically. By 1970-71, there were 620 students and enrolment was capped at 700.[56] This increase in numbers, combined with an activist student body, put pressure on faculty to review what and how it was teaching. The Curriculum Committee responded to these pressures from faculty as well as from students by undertaking a survey of the curriculum. As a result of this

---

54 McRae obtained an LL.B. and LL.M. (first-class honours) from the University of Otago and a Diploma in International Law from Cambridge. He attended Columbia University in 1969-70, taught at University of Western Ontario in 1970-72 and served as associate dean of law at UBC in 1980-82.

55 Bourne was increasingly away from the Faculty of Law during the 1970s. In 1970-71, he was the academic-in-residence at External Affairs. In 1975, he began working part-time for the incoming president of UBC, Douglas Kenny, eventually taking on a full-time position as special advisor to the president. However, he continued to teach the basic course on international law throughout his years at UBC. See my paper on Bourne, *supra* note 13 at 26-29.

56 A.J. McClean, "The Faculty of Law, University of British Columbia, 1970-1981" (1984) 8 Dalhousie L.J. 185.

survey, the committee prepared a report in which a central theme
was the compulsory status of several courses, including international
law.[57] While some teachers felt that international law should remain
compulsory, Charles Bourne offered what might have been a conciliatory gesture, suggesting that the curriculum could be restructured
to allow a student to choose between International Law, International Organizations, and International Business Transactions.
The committee concluded that decisions concerning the status of
courses such as International Law, Jurisprudence, and Legal Institutions II involved "over-riding questions of faculty policy," which
required greater in-depth consideration of the whole curriculum.

In 1969, the faculty conducted its second major review of the
curriculum as a result of which the teaching of international law
was fundamentally changed. The purpose of the 1969 review was to
"structure UBC Faculty of Law's curriculum to reflect its position
as a top school in Canada and North America."[58] As a result of the
recommendations of the review committee, the curriculum in second and third year was made largely optional, with only Evidence
being a required course. In addition, second-year students were
required to choose at least one course from each of two groupings:
Legal Philosophy and Public International Law.[59] The committee offered the following three reasons for its decision to "open up"
the curriculum: (1) changes in legal education in Ontario; (2) its
desire to give students an opportunity to take a wider variety of
courses and to specialize in different areas; and (3) its perception
that the curriculum was dominated by private law and, in particular, by commercial law courses.[60]

The international law grouping recommended by the Curriculum Committee comprised Public International Law, International
Business Transactions, International Organizations, Conflict of
Laws, and Comparative Law. Although the report recognized that
this grouping was not without controversy, it emphasized, in favour
of the suggested grouping, the need to: (1) give students an understanding of the international legal order and the increasing relationships between Canadian and other legal systems; (2) retain

---

[57] D.J. MacDougall, "Summary of the Curriculum Committee Survey 1968-1969"
(Curriculum Committee, February 1969).

[58] *Report of the Curriculum Committee to the Faculty of Law, UBC,* November 1969, on
file at the UBC Faculty of Law [hereinafter *Curriculum Report* 1969].

[59] *Ibid.* and *UBC Calendar 1970-71, supra* note 6 at 11.

[60] *Curriculum Report* 1969, *supra* note 58.

some required courses in order to maintain a balance in an increasingly specialized curriculum; and (3) provide special protection for the study of international law. Of great interest for the present discussion was the committee's statement that UBC has "always maintained a pre-eminent position within Canada insofar as the study of International Law is concerned."[61] Against the suggested grouping were statements that there was "no basis for elevating these courses over others" and that the courses in the "proposed group (including Conflicts and Comparative Law)" were not necessarily related.[62]

In addition to making most of the courses in second and third years optional, the Curriculum Committee recommended the development of new courses, in particular, seminar courses. In fact, the changes brought about by this 1969 review resulted in a 40 per cent increase in the number of courses and a doubling of the number of seminars.[63] As with the courses, seminars were divided into subject groupings — International Legal Studies being one subject area. Two seminars, International Legal Problems and Problems in Conflict of Laws, made up the International Legal Studies grouping.[64] The International Law Problems seminar was a research seminar on "selected problems of international law and organizations." The Conflict of Laws seminar, which examined the "methods and objectives in conflict of laws," focused primarily on conflict issues arising out of domestic, particularly British Columbia, law.

INTERNATIONAL LAW COURSES 1970-81

In addition to making the basic course on international law optional, the curriculum review of 1969 brought in changes to other courses on the subject. Importantly, having regard for its neglect in Canada, a new course entitled International Organizations was created to cover in detail some of the material that had been touched on in the basic course. It was described in the calendar as "[a] study of current international organizations including the United Nations, international economic and social organizations and the institutional aspects of the European Communities. Particular attention is

---

[61] *Ibid.* at 30.

[62] *Ibid.*

[63] *Report of the Senate Curriculum Committee,* February 1970, Faculty of Law Records, box 6, file 8 at 4, Special Collections and University Archives Division, University of British Columbia Library [hereinafter *Senate Report* 1970].

[64] *Curriculum Report* 1969, *supra* note 58 at 41.

paid to the law-creating role and processes of these organizations."[65] Both International Law and International Law and Economic Transactions underwent a name change to Public International Law and International Business Transactions respectively. International Taxation, which was added as a new seminar, offered a comparative analysis of national tax systems considered in "their relation with international tax conventions in the fields of commercial, personal, and estate taxes."[66]

In 1970-71, Bourne taught Public International Law, which was offered in the first term only, and International Organizations, which was offered in the second term.[67] During the academic year of 1971-72, while Bourne was serving as the first academic-in-residence at the Department of External Affairs in Ottawa, Public International Law and International Organizations were taught by P. Vaver.[68] In 1972, D.M. McRae joined the faculty and taught Public International Law with Bourne, while Joost Blom took over the seminar on International Organizations.[69] Bourne resumed teaching the International Law seminar and Jahnke taught International Business Transactions.

By 1973, Jahnke had moved out of the field of international law, and teaching resources for the international courses were stretched. Fortunately, McRae took over the International Organizations course, which he taught for the rest of his time at UBC, and he joined Blom in teaching Conflicts. Bourne continued to teach Public International Law. In 1974-75, Public International Law was taught by Bourne and Martin Thomas.[70] During this period, Bourne was working with Mark Zacher of the Institute of

---

[65] *UBC Calendar 1970-71, supra* note 6 at 13; and *Senate Report* 1970, *supra* note 63.

[66] *UBC Calendar 1970-71, supra* note 6 at 16.

[67] "Teaching Assignments 1970-71," Faculty of Law Records, box 6, file 8, Special Collections and University Archives Division, University of British Columbia Library.

[68] "Teaching Assignments and Timetable 1971-72," Faculty of Law Records, box 6, file 10, Special Collections and University Archives Division, University of British Columbia Library.

[69] Joost Blom obtained a B.A. (1967) and an LL.B. (1970) from UBC, a B.C.L. from Oxford in 1972 and an LL.M. from Harvard in 1996. He joined the faculty in 1972, was called to the Bar of British Columbia in 1978, appointed Queen's Counsel in 1985, and made dean of the faculty in 1997. *UBC Calendar 1998-2000, supra* note 6 at 9.

[70] "Teaching Assignments 1974-75," Faculty of Law Records, box 10, file 23, Special Collections and University Archives Division, University of British Columbia Library.

International Relations at UBC on a new course, relevant and timely, on the regulation of the oceans. Offered on a multidisciplinary basis, this course covered the general perspectives on the development of the law of the sea, the regulation of international fisheries, the control of marine pollution, and the international regulation of the seabed.[71]

When, in 1975, Bourne began working half-time in the office of the president of the university, teaching resources for international law were stretched once again. Bourne taught Public International Law and International Law Problems with Martin Thomas, and McRae continued with International Organizations and Public International Law.[72] However, as Bourne became more involved at the president's office, his teaching load dropped to just Public International Law — a development that was not without controversy. In 1976, he was originally scheduled to teach both Public International Law and Administrative Law but felt his responsibilities at the president's office would not allow him to satisfactorily handle two major courses. The matter was resolved in his favour.[73]

During the period 1970-74, enrolment in Public International Law fluctuated between a low of twenty-six students in 1972-73 to a high of fifty-four in 1973-74. International Organizations attracted thirty-six students in 1970-71, which was the first year it was offered, with a low of twelve students in 1972-73. The seminars on International Law Problems and International Business Transactions did not have consistent enrolment during this period, probably because neither seminar was offered consistently each year.[74]

---

[71] Correspondence between Mark Zacher and Charles Bourne, Manuscripts of Charles B. Bourne, box 1, file 3, Special Collections and University Archives Division, University of British Columbia Library. This course was structured to accommodate a series of guest lecturers who lectured on: trends in fish populations, economic dimensions of fisheries problems, economic dimensions of marine pollution, present knowledge of seabed minerals and the nature of exploitative technologies, the effects of marine pollutants, national policies towards seabed mining, the international regulation of fisheries, and the development of Canadian policy.

[72] "Teaching Assignments 1975/76," Faculty of Law Records, box 10, file 22, Special Collections and University Archives Division, University of British Columbia Library.

[73] Exchange of Correspondence between Dean Lysyk and Charles Bourne, Faculty of Law Records, box 10, file 19, Special Collections and University Archives Division, University of British Columbia Library.

[74] Charles Bourne to R. St. J. Macdonald (January 24, 1974). International Law Problems was not offered in 1970-71 or 1971-72. International Business Transactions was not offered in 1972-73.

International Law Problems had nine students in 1972-73 and ten students in 1973-74. International Business Transactions fluctuated between nine students in 1970-71 and three students in 1973-74.

The faculty conducted its third major review of the curriculum in 1978-79 — a review that resulted in a restructuring of the place of seminars in the curriculum. Under the new approach, which is still partly in place today, seminars were structured around specific topics within a larger subject grouping. For example, topics in international law would include seminars in a variety of areas related to international law and would vary from year to year, depending on student and faculty interest. Following this third review, McRae wisely reorganized the seminar on International Law Problems, which he had taken over from Bourne, so that it could run in two sections, one as a seminar on law of the sea for students who had not taken Public International Law and the other as a more advanced seminar for students who had completed the basic course.[75] The course on International Business Transactions, which had been resurrected by Robert Paterson, a new addition to the faculty,[76] was designed to "provide a widely based examination of various legal problems associated with business conducted internationally from the local exporter to the multinational corporation. Thus such schemes as exporter's risk insurance will be looked at as well as international approaches to regulation of multinational companies."[77]

The third curriculum review also resulted in the creation of a new course, entitled Law of the Sea. First offered by D.M. McRae in 1979-80, it attracted twenty-three students. The introduction of this course was justified on the ground that it was obviously important and of particular interest at UBC. The Institute of International Relations at the university had been conducting research on Canada and the international management of oceans and there

---

[75] "Clinical and Seminar Descriptions — 1978-79," Faculty of Law Records, box 10, file 19, Special Collections and University Archives Division, University of British Columbia Library.

[76] Robert Paterson received his legal education in New Zealand and at Stanford. He chaired the BC Task Force on International Commercial Arbitration, anchored the collection *Canadian Regulation of International Trade and Investment* (Toronto: Carswell, 1986), which is now entitled *International Trade and Investment Law in Canada* (Toronto: Carswell, 2nd. ed. 1994), and co-edited a text for United Nations Commission on International Trade Law.

[77] "Clinical and Seminar Descriptions — 1978-79," *supra* note 75. The course was first offered in 1977-78.

existed a cooperative spirit among several disciplines at the university, including law. Topics covered in the new course included the history of the international law of the sea, coastal state jurisdiction, the high seas, the extension of coastal state jurisdiction, the continental shelf, maritime boundaries, the deep-sea bed, and the international regulation of the oceans.[78]

In his course on International Organizations, which was one of the very few courses on this highly important subject in any Canadian law school, McRae examined the history, structure, and functions of international organizations; membership, voting, and financing; the powers of the organs; the judicial review of the actions of international organizations; the amendment of constitutions; the law on employees of international organizations; the international and national legal status of organizations; succession; and the legal effect of decisions of international organizations at both the domestic and international levels.[79] In view of the

---

[78] "Curriculum Proposals: Second and Third Years: Rationale and Overview," December 30, 1980, Faculty of Law Records, box 13, file 3(2), Special Collections and University Archives Division, University of British Columbia Library. McRae's materials included the Hague Codification Conferences, the ILC Draft Articles on the Law of the Sea, the 1958 Conventions on the High Seas and Continental Shelf, international cases and arbitral decisions, and domestic legislation and bilateral agreements. Students were required to read excerpts from Jessup, *The Law of Territorial Waters and Maritime Jurisdiction* (1927); H.A. Smith, *The Law and Custom of the Sea* (1959), Myres McDougal and William Burke, *The Public Order of the Oceans* (1962); C.J. Colombos, *International Law of the Sea*, 6th ed. rev. (1967); O'Connell, *International Law*, 2 vols (2nd ed. 1970); B. Johnson and M.W. Zacher, *Canadian Foreign Policy and the Law of the Sea* (1977). See D.M. McRae, *Law of the Sea: Course Outline and Reading List* (Vancouver: University of British Columbia, 1979-80). McRae's additional readings included D.W. Bowett, *The Law of the Sea* (1967); E.D. Brown, *The Legal Regime of Hydrospace* (1971); J. Dupuy, *The Law of the Sea* (1974); Waldock, "The Anglo-Norwegian Fisheries Case" (1951) 28 Br. Y.B. Int'l L. 114; Donat Pharand, *The Law of the Sea of the Arctic*; Shigeru Oda, "The Concept of Continuous Zone" (1962) 11 I.C.L.Q. 131.

[79] McRae compiled his own materials for International Organization. The course outline (1979) directed students to the United Nations Charter, the Treaty Establishing the European Community, case law, and other treaties. Students were required to read D.W. Bowett, *Law of International Institutions* (3rd ed., 1975). Listed references included H.F. van Panhuys, Brinkhorst and Maas, *International Organization and Integration* (1968); Sweet and Maxwells, *European Community Treaties* (1972); Goodrich, Hambro, and Simons, *The Charter of the United Nations* (3rd ed. rev. 1969); Lasok and Bridge, *An Introduction to the Law and Institutions of the European Communities* (1973); Schermers, *International Institutional Law* 3 vols., (1977). See D.M. McRae, *Cases and Materials on International Organization* (Vancouver: UBC, 1979).

unfortunate, and indeed inexplicable, neglect of this topic in most Canadian law schools, it is relevant to emphasize that UBC was one of the first major law schools in Canada to recognize the central and increasing role of international organizations in the development of the international legal system.

During the period from 1975 to 1980-81, enrolment in Public International Law declined from seventy-two students in 1975-76 to an average of thirty-five to fifty students thereafter.[80] International Organizations fluctuated from twelve students in 1975-76 to twenty-five students in 1976-77 and 1979-80. Paterson's International Business Transaction course was generally popular — it attracted twenty-three students when it was first offered in 1977-78, nineteen students the next year, and nine students in 1979-80.

INTERNATIONAL LAW COURSES 1982-86

With McRae on leave at the Department of External Affairs from 1983 to 1986 and Bourne at the president's office, international law lost ground in the law school. Although Bourne was still offering the basic course, and other faculty members were adding interesting new courses to the curriculum, the faculty was without a senior, full-time international law scholar to provide long-term leadership, as Bourne had done so admirably throughout the previous three decades. In addition, the faculty, along with the rest of the university, was experiencing financial difficulties since university funding had been reduced during this period, and it had become difficult to hire much-needed teaching staff.

Due to these circumstances, the faculty had been relying on temporary and visiting lecturers. In 1983, International Organizations and Law of the Sea were offered as a single course. In 1984-85, Michael Vechsler, a research associate with the Max Bell Foundation, and Herbert Adelman, a visiting professor, assisted with the teaching of International Law.[81] In 1986, the faculty was extraordinarily fortunate to attract Maurice D. Copithorne and Chris Thomas. The latter had been scheduled to teach International

---

[80] "Trends in Enrolment from 1976-1980," Faculty of Law Records, box 13, file 4, Special Collections and University Archives Division, University of British Columbia Library; and Charles Bourne to R. St. J. Macdonald (November 28, 1979).

[81] D.M. McRae to R. St. J. Macdonald (August 13, 1984); and Tom J. Shorthouse to R. St. J. Macdonald (July 27, 1984).

Trade Law in 1986-87 but was seconded to the office of the Honourable Pat Carney as senior policy advisor and did not in fact teach. Maurice Copithorne, one of Canada's most senior and distinguished international lawyers, who was a former legal advisor to the Department of External Affairs and a member of the Canadian Delegation to the Sixth Committee of the General Assembly, was appointed to the Douglas McK. Brown Chair in 1987-88. Fortunately for the law school, he remained on faculty to anchor the international law program while practising law with Ladner Downs in Vancouver.[82] Karin Mickelson joined him in 1990-91.

While the core subjects of international law were understaffed during the 1982-86 period, the faculty nevertheless developed innovative courses in related disciplines, such as foreign direct investment, international commercial arbitration, Japanese law, and the law of international human rights. These courses will be discussed presently. In 1984-85, a projected course on International Commercial Arbitration, which was expected to be taught by Herbert Adelman, attracted few students and was therefore combined with International Business Transactions.[83] In addition, Paterson started a new seminar on Foreign Direct Investment. Also in 1984, the Curriculum Committee added a new seminar on international economic law, which was devoted to the international and national regulation of trade in goods and services and to foreign investment.[84]

One of the most innovative changes in the curriculum during the 1980s was the establishment of a program in Japanese legal studies. As early as 1969, the Faculty of Law had considered the desirability of developing courses in Asian legal studies to reflect Vancouver's position on the Pacific Rim, but it was only in 1980 that the program started up with a grant from the Law Foundation of British

[82] Copithorne joined the faculty after thirty years distinguished service as a foreign service officer in the Department of External Affairs. See (Summer 1987) 5 UBC Law Faculty Newsletter at 2; Elizabeth Lumley, ed., *Canadian Who's Who,* vol. 38 (Toronto: University of Toronto Press, 2003) at 283. From 1995 to 2002, he served as UN special representative on the human rights situation in Iran.

[83] Herbert E. Adelman to R. St. J. Macdonald (August 28, 1984). The combined course focused on international trade but contained a segment on international commercial arbitration.

[84] *Report of the Curriculum Committee to the Faculty of Law, UBC,* 1984-85, on file with the UBC Faculty of Law; *UBC Calendar 1985-86, supra* note 6 at 34. At the same time, the Curriculum Committee deleted International Taxation, which had not been offered for the previous five years.

Columbia.[85] Courses were offered in comparative and Japanese law. The program was supported by faculty research and a growing library collection of Japanese legal materials. In 1986-87, the school received a grant of $98,000 from the British Columbia government to expand the Asian Law Programme to include legal studies relating to China, Japan, and Korea.[86] The directors of the Clinic and Japan programs were specialists with language skills.

It is not surprising that staff and students soon recognized the need for courses and seminars on international trade and on Japanese law. In a message commemorating the law school's fortieth anniversary, Dean Burns noted that "[t]he horizons of legal education, however, continue to widen in spite of financial stringency. Japanese and Chinese Legal Studies, a growing emphasis on International Trade Law and International Commercial Dispute Resolution ... all present opportunities for growth for our Law School."[87]

Malcolm Smith, the first director of the Japanese Law Programme until Stephan Salzberg joined the faculty in 1988, began teaching the basic course in Japanese law in 1983, when it was offered to second- or third-year students in the fall term.[88] This course attracted between twenty and forty students and covered the sources of Japanese law, the role of law in Japanese society, the reception of

[85] In 1969, the Curriculum Committee recommended that "it may be necessary in the near future for this law school to consider introducing an Asian Law programme." *Senate Report* 1970, *supra* note 63 at 3. In his 1978-79 report to the president of UBC, Dean Lysyk noted that the faculty was considering adding Japanese Law to the curriculum: "The growing economic importance of the relationship between Canada and Japan has created a need for understanding in Canada of Japanese law and institutions. UBC is the logical place for a programme in Japanese law having regard to British Columbia's geographical location on the Pacific Rim and to the fact that Asian Studies is already an area of concentration and distinction at the University of British Columbia." Faculty of Law Records, box 11, file 6, Special Collections and University Archives Division, University of British Columbia Library.

[86] *UBC Calendar 1986-87, supra* note 6 at 16-17; and (summer 1987) 5 UBC Law Faculty Newsletter 1 at 5. The newsletter noted that the expanded Asian Legal Studies Programme was meant to interlock with the Faculty of Law's emphasis on international law, international trade law, and the resolution of international commercial disputes.

[87] Dean Burns, "Message" (summer 1986) 4 UBC Law Faculty Newsletter 1 at 2.

[88] See *UBC Calendar 1985-86, supra* note 6 at 16-17 and *UBC Calendar 1988-89, supra* note 6 at 17. Malcolm Smith, LL.B., LL.M. (Melbourne), LL.M., S.J.D. (Harvard) came to UBC from the Faculty of Law at Morash University as an Ohira Programme visiting professor. Stephan Salzberg received an M.A. from UBC and a J.D. from Washington University.

Western legal systems, the structure of the codes, contract law, the courts, the constitution and the legislature, the administrative process, and the lawyer's role in Japan.[89] In the following year, the Max Bell Foundation funded a continuing flow of exchanges with Japanese universities. For its part, the Chinese program developed in parallel ways.

STUDENT INTEREST AND EXTERNAL SUPPORT
FOR INTERNATIONAL LAW

During the period 1970-86, student interest in international law fluctuated. When the subject was made optional in 1970, enrolment declined and the subject reached a low in student interest. In the mid-1970s, student interest reawakened and led to the establishment of an international law club. With the assistance of Charles Bourne, the club brought in speakers, including Maurice Copithorne, but in the late 1970s, student interest dropped off once again. When asked about this decline, Bourne referred to "a sense of disappointment that we have not been able to build more quickly on the foundations [of international law scholarship in Canadian universities] laid in the preceding two decades."[90]

The absence of concentrated leadership in the teaching of international law at UBC during the early 1980s contributed in no small measure to declining student interest in the subject and in related courses. Nevertheless, there remained a core of interested students who found encouragement at UBC. Their presence was partly due to an infrastructure of support for scholarship. The Law Foundation of British Columbia supported international legal scholarship by funding students to participate in the Jessup moots and to attend meetings of the Canadian Council on International Law in Ottawa.[91]

---

[89] Joost Blom, "The Faculty of Law, University of British Columbia 1981-1990" (1991) 14 Dalhousie L. J. 195; Malcolm Smith, "Japanese Law: Reading Guide and Class Schedule," mimeograph (1983). The basic materials were A. Morishma, *Cases and Materials* (mimeographed), and H. Tanaka, *The Japanese Legal System* (1976).

[90] Charles B. Bourne to R. St. J. Macdonald (November 28, 1979).

[91] For example, in 1975-76, the Law Foundation of British Columbia provided $1000 for expenses involved with the Jessup moot competition and $408 for attendance at the Canadian Council on International Law. In 1977, the Law Foundation of British Columbia gave the fledging student international law association $278.25, see "Dean's Reports," Faculty of Law Records, box 7, file 26, Special Collections and University Archives Division, University of British Columbia Library.

Importantly, the Faculty of Law's dynamic graduate program, which was expanded in the 1980s, attracted students interested in international law research. The Law Foundation of British Columbia, once again, played an important role by providing funding for graduate studies at UBC.[92]

CHARLES BOURNE'S RETIREMENT AND THE END OF AN ERA

In 1986, Charles Bourne formally retired as a professor of law at the University of British Columbia, where he was made professor emeritus. Although he remained an active presence, his retirement signalled the end of an era for the teaching of international law at UBC as well as the start of a new one. With his retirement in 1986 and McRae's departure in 1987, the law school faced a huge problem. It responded over the next ten years by developing a broad, multidisciplinary approach to international law that involved innovation in the areas of international trade, international environmental law, and comparative law.

INTERNATIONAL LAW TEACHING: 1986-2000

UBC is the second largest law school in Canada. It admits 190 students to first year for a total of approximately 590 undergraduates. There are forty-three full-time members of faculty.[93] The availability of seminars, which were made possible by changes to the curriculum, have led to a move away from traditional case-based methods of instruction to a broader range of teaching approaches.[94] In addition to standard lecture courses, many upper-year subjects were offered as small-group seminars. Classes were also organized as workshops, problem-oriented seminars, and, in the case of one

---

[92] For example, in 1977, the Law Foundation of British Columbia doubled its grant for graduate scholarships from $15,000 to $30,000 (*ibid.*) The Law Foundation continued to play an instrumental role in financing UBC graduate students.

[93] *UBC Calendar 1998-2000, supra* note 6 at 8, 58.

[94] First-year courses are mandatory. In second and third year, students are free to design their own curriculum but must take evidence, constitutional law (or Canadian Charter of Rights and Freedoms and Canadian Federalism), Moot Court, and they must write an independent research paper that is generally done as part of a seminar requirement. Second- and third-year students select their curriculum from approximately 100 seminars and courses offered in a given year. Seminars are offered as smaller classes, usually less than twenty-five students and are generally graded on the basis of a paper. *UBC Calendar 1998, supra* note 6 at 24.

section of Evidence, an Internet-based course. No longer tied to the traditional "core" courses, the school expanded its offerings to include courses on legal theory (Philosophy of Law and Feminist Legal Studies, for example), law and social policy (Issues of Equality and Social Policy and Aboriginal and Treaty Rights, for example) as well as topic-specific courses, such as First Nations Self-Government, Municipal Law, Fisheries Law, Intellectual Property, and so on.[95]

During the years 1986-2000, international law offerings were increased, though not as extensively perhaps as courses in other areas. A review of the course descriptions over the five-year period 1995-2000 shows an impressive array of courses on international law and related fields, such as environmental law, comparative law, and private international law subjects, such as trade, investment, copyright, and taxation. Strangely missing from the list are courses of a critical or theoretical orientation exploring the changing nature of the "international" in an increasingly globalized world order.[96] Many of the courses touch on, or are a result of, an expanding international order in which economic, social, cultural, and political relations are identified and briefly considered, but few investigate how and why these developments have occurred and the implications they might have for the role and scope of law.

This is not to suggest that international law teaching and research is weak at UBC. Quite the opposite. There exists at UBC a broad-based research and teaching interest in international law and related subjects. The result is a dynamic, if fragmented, scholarly community of professors, adjunct teachers, graduate students, researchers, special students, and undergraduate students committed to, and interested in, exploring most, if not all, aspects of international law. And it would seem, at least to an outsider, that this community is more than a product of the existence of individual courses. It results from the confluence of three factors: an active forward-looking international law faculty with a strong commitment to research, a number of international law-related programs and projects in other parts of the university affiliated with the Faculty of Law, and a variety of course offerings.

---

[95] *Course Descriptions, Fall 1999/Spring 2000* (Vancouver: Faculty of Law, University of British Columbia, 7 June 1999) [hereinafter *1999 Course Descriptions*].

[96] A notable exception is Ruth Buchanan's seminar "The Regulatory Impact of Globalization," *infra* note 122.

NEW FACULTY MEMBERS

Following the departure of Bourne and McRae, the law school slowly began the process of building a full-time international law faculty that could grow within the institution. Four full-time appointments were made: Ian Townsend Gault in 1989, Ivan Head and Karin Mickelson in 1991, and Jutta Brunnée in 1995. Fortunately for all concerned, Maurice Copithorne, whose basic course I will refer to later in this article, continued his influential involvement on a part-time basis.

Both Townsend Gault and Head brought with them established research interests and projects that provided important additions to the culture of international law at UBC. Townsend Gault, who arrived from Dalhousie University law school in Halifax, brought several projects involving the South China Sea as well as professional expertise in marine resource law and the law of the sea.[97] Ivan Head, who was an influential mandarin in Ottawa, brought vast international experience, influence at high levels of government, and prestige throughout the global community. An international lawyer by training as well as a distinguished former president of the International Development Research Centre in Ottawa and Prime Minister Pierre Trudeau's principal foreign affairs advisor, Ivan Head was asked to join UBC to develop an interdisciplinary focus on South-North issues. He taught a course jointly in the Department of Political Science and at the law school and served as chair of the program in South-North studies.[98] Although not engaged in the teaching of international law at UBC, he was notably active in the supervision of graduate students. When he retired, he left a lasting legacy as a result of his work to establish the Liu Centre for the study of global issues, including a particularly distinguished international panel of advisors. The mandate of this centre, which was a self-governing unit within the Faculty of Graduate Studies, is to explore international and domestic implications of globalization.

[97] For biographical information, see Canadian Association of Law Teachers, *Directory of Law Teachers, 1993-1994* (Scarborough, ON: Carswell, 1993-94) at 149.

[98] On Ivan Head, see foreword, preface, and first chapter of Obiora Chinedu Okafor and Obijiofor Aginam, *Humanizing Our Global Order: Essays in Honour of Ivan Head* (Toronto: University of Toronto Press, 2003) at vii-x2. For information on the Liu Centre, see UBC website at <http://www.liucentre.ubc.ca/>. During the Trudeau era, no major foreign or defence policy decision or initiative was taken, conference attended, or speech delivered by the prime minister without Head's involvement. See Ivan L. Head and Pierre Elliott Trudeau, *The Canadian Way: Shaping Canada's Foreign Policy 1968-1984* (Toronto: McClelland and Stewart, 1995) at 8.

Karin Mickelson, who was also appointed in 1991, assumed responsibility for one section of the basic course and a seminar on international environmental law. Her research interests included Third World approaches to international law, especially environmental law. She also worked in South-North relations, publishing and speaking on the problems involved, including the role of international law.[99]

Jutta Brunnée, a McGill professor appointed in 1995, brought widely recognized expertise in international environmental law. The holder of a doctorate in law from Johannes Gutenberg University in Germany and an LL.M. from Dalhousie University in Canada, she had previously taught at the University of Western Ontario and at McGill. The author of a highly regarded textbook on acid rain and ozone layer depletion as well as numerous journal articles, she came to UBC as an established scholar and highly competent teacher. In 1998-99, she took a year's leave from UBC to serve as scholar-in-residence in the Legal Bureau of the Department of Foreign Affairs in Ottawa — the first time this position had been filled since McRae held it in the early 1980s. She was thus the third faculty member from UBC to hold this sought-after position. Unfortunately for UBC, Brunée was lured away to the University of Toronto in 2000.[100]

Ruth Buchanan, who was hired in 1997, does not teach within the core international law curriculum, but her research on globalization and economic restructuring involves innovative analyses of the changing international order. As with Mickelson and Brunnée, her scholarly approach and commitment to research are important elements in the maintenance of an international law community within the law school.[101]

---

[99] A graduate of Duke University and UBC Law School, Karin Mickelson holds an LL.M. from Columbia University in New York. *UBC Calendar 1998, supra* note 6 at 15.

[100] Currently Professor of Law and Metcalf Chair in Environmental Law at the University of Toronto, Brunnée was the editor-in-chief of the *Yearbook of International Environmental Law* from 1995 to 2000 and co-chair of the American Society of International Law Interest Group on International Environmental Law. For further information, see the University of British Columbia, Faculty of Law website at <http//www.law.ubc.ca/faculty/brunnee /index.htm>.

[101] Ruth Buchanan received an B.A. from Princeton, an LL.B. from the University of Victoria, and an LL.M. from Wisconsin. She is completing a Ph.D. at the University of Wisconsin on globalization, economic restructuring, and women's work. *UBC Calendar 1998, supra* note 6 at 10.

The addition of Townsend Gault, Head, Mickelson, Brunnée, Buchanan, and the continuing association of Maurice Copithorne with the Faculty of Law, broadened the range of available offerings to include courses in marine resources, European Community law, the international law of South-North relations, international environmental law, and globalization. These new courses, together with other courses taught by Douglas Sanders on international human rights and Aboriginal law and courses offered by the trade lawyers, such as Robert Paterson and Pitman Potter, represent the core of the teaching and supervision in international law at UBC.[102]

PROGRAMS AND PROJECTS AT THE FACULTY OF LAW

Asian Legal Studies. Reflecting its location on the Pacific rim, the law school supplemented its core courses on international law with courses on Asian legal systems. In 1987, the Japanese Legal Studies program became part of a larger North Asian Legal Studies program, offering courses, research, and exchange opportunities with Asian countries. This new program, which is now the Centre for Asian Legal Studies, was designed to reflect the growing trade, as well as financial, social, and cultural links, with Japan, China, Hong Kong, and Korea.[103] Recognizing the evolving legal relationships involved in the growth of trade and contact with the Pacific Rim, the Asian Legal Studies program encourages the exploration of different legal issues and systems from a position of knowledge and understanding. It also underscores the growing interest and expertise at the faculty in international trade and investment law.[104] Complementing the Asian Legal Studies programs, the school offered courses in International Business Transactions and International Economic Law as well as opportunities for directed research and graduate study in these areas.

The Centre for Asian Legal Studies was strengthened in 1991 when Pitman Potter joined the faculty as director of Chinese Legal Studies. In addition to holding J.D. and Ph.D. degrees from the University of Washington, Potter had practised law in Beijing and

---

[102] Maurice Copithorne has been a pillar of strength in the Faculty of Law. He taught a section of the basic course for twelve years and continues to conduct an upper-year seminar on international law and politics.

[103] *UBC Calendar 1987-88, supra* note 6 at 16-17; and *UBC Calendar 1991-92, supra* note 6 at 17.

[104] *UBC Calendar 1998, supra* note 6 at 52.

San Francisco. His strong scholarly background and commitment to research provided additional strength to the graduate studies program, which he headed until 1996. Under his guidance, the China Law program strengthened its course offerings in comparative law and Chinese legal systems in particular. Drawing on his practical experience and academic training, Potter introduced an additional seminar on trade and investment with the People's Republic of China and broadened possibilities for directed research and graduate study in Chinese law and international trade law.

International Criminal Law. In 1991, the Faculty of Law expanded its course offerings as a result of the establishment of the International Centre for Criminal Law Reform and Criminal Justice Policy. This centre, which is an autonomous non-academic research and international assistance facilitator, is a joint venture between the UBC Faculty of Law, Simon Fraser University School of Criminology, and the Society for Reform of Criminal Law — the latter being an international non-governmental association of judges, legislators, lawyers, academics, government officials, and public interest advocates who work to improve criminal law and the administration of criminal justice domestically and internationally. The centre is part of the United Nations' worldwide network of crime prevention and criminal justice institutions. Its primary task is to "improve the quality of justice through reform of criminal law, policy and practice."[105] For its part, the law school began offering a course on comparative sentencing structures and a course on the proceeds of crime legislation.

South China Sea Projects. Not reflected in the course calendar but relevant to the teaching of international law at UBC are several projects, supervised by Townsend Gault, that are related to the South China Sea. For some years after 1989, Townsend Gault managed to encourage scientific and environmental cooperation between neighbouring countries in the South China Sea area. Funded by the Canadian International Development Agency, the project developed and pursued initiatives to encourage peace in the South China Sea through cooperation on issues such as marine environment and scientific research, navigational safety, fisheries, and security. Townsend Gault's group managed a series of meetings between South Asian governments in which participants examined questions of resource management, shipping, navigation, and

---

[105] The centre's website is at <http://www.icclr.law.ubc.ca/html>.

environment. Although these issues were, and are still, tangential to
the larger issues of jurisdiction in the South China Sea, the group
was able to work around the impasse of this intractable question.
In addition, a series of technical working groups on, for example, marine scientific research (Manila) and resource assessment
(Jakarta) were organized in 1993. The workshop structure of the
meetings and their informal settings facilitated the establishment
of an environment of cooperation, which played down contested
sovereignty and jurisdictional disputes.[106]

Graduate Program. The Faculty of Law received permission to offer a
graduate degree in 1961, and the first LL.M. students were admitted in 1965. As stated by McLean: "When the program was first
established it was decided that it would emphasize three areas of
law: international law, labour law and natural resources. That
degree of specialization never materialized, and the Faculty [was]
prepared to accept students in any area of study, provided it [had]
the personnel and other necessary resources. For many years there
were not more than two or three students per year who took the
degree."[107]

The graduate program was modest throughout the 1960s and
1970s, as it was in virtually every common law school in Canada.
Interest slowly increased in the 1980s as student priorities changed
and more funding became available. In 1989, the Graduate Committee proposed an expansion of the program from twelve to twenty-
four students each year as well as two additional faculty positions to
oversee the program.[108] The committee's aim in recommending an
expansion of the program was to attract a "critical mass" of gradu-
ates who would support graduate courses in the faculty's key areas
of interest: human rights, resources, the environment and international law, law and society, the regulation of international trade
law, and research methodology. As a result of the committee's proposal, a director of the graduate program was appointed, and, in
1993, UBC began offering a Ph.D. in law, admitting two students

---

[106] See Ian Townsend Gault's "Testing the Waters: Making Progress in the South
China Sea" (Spring 1994) 17 Harvard Int'l Rev. 16; William G. Stormont,
"Managing Potential Conflicts in the South China Sea" (1994) 18(4) Marine
Policy 353.

[107] McClean, *supra* note 56 at 197; and *The Master of Law (LL.M.) Programme* (Vancouver: Faculty of Law, University of British Columbia, January 1984).

[108] Graduate Committee, "Memorandum Re: Five Year Plan for the Graduate Programme in Law," UBC Faculty of Law, November 20, 1989.

in its first year.[109] A steady flow of candidates was admitted in the following years, and in 1999-2000, four new candidates were admitted for a total of fourteen students in the Ph.D. program. At the LL.M. level, the faculty was admitting approximately twenty students each year.[110]

International law and related subjects, such as Chinese Legal Studies and International Criminal Law, attract a significant number of graduate students; approximately 30-35 per cent of the Master's students pursue research on international law-related subjects. It is thus apparent that the graduate program has served, and continues to serve, as an important stimulus to teaching and research in international law at UBC.

INTERNATIONAL LAW COURSES

Starting in 1990, the school moved away from the traditional distinction between "public" and "private" international law to a more problem-based, integrated approach to international law in general. This change was reflected in the development of topic specific courses, such as environmental law and South-North relations, combining a theoretical and interdisciplinary component with an analysis of the operation of international law. One of the principal strengths of the teaching of international law at UBC is that it offered students opportunities to explore "applied" international law, whether through ongoing international law projects, such as the South China Sea project, or through specialized courses on the environment and peacekeeping.

In order to indicate the multi-dimensional approach to the teaching of international law at UBC, I will briefly refer not only to the faculty's core international law courses but also to a few of the many comparative and topic specific courses and projects that touch on, and form an important part of, the overall international law

---

[109] Ph.D. students are required to complete a two-part Ph.D. seminar, comprehensive examination, doctoral thesis, and an oral examination. LL.M. students must take the graduate seminar, which is a full-year course designed to illustrate different perspectives from which law can be approached. Students must also complete a thesis and twelve credits of course work. *UBC Calendar 1998, supra* note 6.

[110] For example, twenty-one students were admitted in 1993-94, twenty-five in 1995-96, and twenty-one in 1999-2000. No new money was involved in the expansion of the law school's graduate program. The expansion, which was part of the university's over-all emphasis on the importance of graduate work, was achieved by reducing the intake of the first-year class by 25 per cent.

program.[111] I have divided this discussion into two sections: core international law courses and courses with an international law component. While there may be reasons for saying that the latter involve the study of international law, there is a need to distinguish them. The discipline of international law is generally defined as the study of principles and rules governing relations between states. However, the dramatic enlargement of the international sphere of activities, primarily as a result of capital mobility, trade liberalization, technological innovation, the exportation of culture, and regionalization, has resulted in the internationalization of subjects normally thought of as being exclusively domestic. Taxation, cultural property, dispute resolution, and competition law, to mention only a few examples, have important international aspects. While these and other subjects involve the study of international law in a broad sense, their focus is not so much on this subject as such as it is on the internationalization of aspects of domestic law.

Core International Law Courses

Perspectives on Law: This mandatory first-year course was designed to give students an appreciation of the underlying social forces and values that shape the law and an understanding that those forces can be analyzed from a variety of perspectives. Over the academic year, students were to complete three six-week units chosen from a series of options that included Feminist Perspectives on Law, Law and First Nations, the Western Idea of Law, and International Law, which was offered for the first time in 1994-95. Taught by Townsend Gault, the international law component, entitled International Law Perspectives, although optional, was popular. In 1999, it was attended by almost half of the first-year class. Townsend Gault taught this mini-course as an introduction to the international dimension of law, addressing issues such as sustainable development, environmental protection, human rights, and the impact of international law-making treaties on domestic law. Students were assessed on a short paper on an international law issue.

International Law: This three-credit, introductory course was offered in two sections — in the fall term by Maurice Copithorne and in the spring term by Karin Mickelson. The course offered a

---

[111] All international law courses and seminars at the Faculty of Law are optional. The first-year perspectives course is mandatory and includes a segment on international law.

survey of the basic principles of public international law and the international law-making process. Its object was to provide an appreciation of the major characteristics of international law and a basic knowledge of its sources and skills. The focus of the two sections differed. Mickelson focused on doctrinal and procedural aspects of international law, while Maurice Copithorne, bearing in mind that 50 per cent of the class were international relations students, emphasized the interaction of law and politics. Copithorne used Peter Malanczuk's *Akehurst's Modern Introduction to International Law*,[112] supplemented by several hundred pages of contemporary material, while Mickelson used Hugh Kindred et al.'s *International Law: Chiefly as Interpreted and Applied in Canada*.[113] Students in both sections were evaluated on a 100 per cent final exam.[114]

International Human Rights: In 1994, this seminar focused on the legal and political status of indigenous peoples in various parts of the world and their inclusion in contemporary human rights concerns at the United Nations and before inter-governmental organizations. In 1995, the focus shifted to an examination of the international protection of human rights with reference to the European human rights system, the Canadian Charter of Rights and Freedoms, and the individual complaints procedure under the International Covenant on Civil and Political Rights. Throughout the 1990s, this seminar was supplemented by additional classes taught by visiting scholars and adjunct teachers.[115]

---

[112] Peter Malanczuk, *Akehurst's Modern Introduction to International Law,* 7th revised edition (London and New York: Routledge, 1997).

[113] Hugh Kindred et al., *International Law: Chiefly as Interpreted and Applied in Canada* (Toronto: Emond Montgomery, 2000).

[114] *1999 Course Descriptions, supra* note 95. It is regrettable that there are so few discussions of the teaching materials on international law used in Canada. We need a good narrative account and constructive analysis of the international law casebooks in Canada from the time of Henry F. Munro (1921) to MacKenzie and Laing, Bourne and Jahnke, Castel, Williams and de Mestral, Kindred, and the collections put together at Université de Montreal by Daniel Turp in 1986 and at the University of Toronto in the 1980s by W.C. Graham, who is now Canada's foreign minister. Why are there so few reviews of Kindred? And why, oh why, has there been no continuation of the discussion initiated by Claydon and McRae as long ago as 1985? See John E. Claydon and D.M. McRae, "International Legal Scholarship in Canada" (1986) 23 Osgoode Hall L. J. 477.

[115] For example, Adjunct Professor Marcia Kran, taught a seminar on the international law of human rights.

International Law Problems: Over the years, Copithorne's seminar for second- and third-year students as well as international relations students and graduate students in law and in political science varied its focus depending on the issues of the day. In 1997, it considered whether there was a consensus for a new activism on the part of the United Nations in the fields of preventive diplomacy, peacemaking, peacekeeping, and post-conflict peace. The 1999 course considered the role and influence of ethics and morality on the evaluation of international legal norms and their implementation. Building on his previous analysis of Somalia and Kosovo, Copithorne also examined the *Pinochet* case in the United Kingdom. Evaluation was based on class participation and a major term paper. The recommended text was Joel H. Rosenthal's *Ethics and International Affairs: A Reader.*[116]

International Environmental Law: This four-credit seminar, which is normally taught by Karin Mickelson, was co-taught with Jutta Brunnée until her departure in 2000. It provided a general overview of international environmental law with a consideration of cross-cutting issues, such as approaches to compliance and enforcement, the interface of environment and trade, and South-North dimensions to international environmental regulation. Selected issues, such as acid rain, the degradation of freshwater resources, stratospheric ozone depletion, and forest decline were examined in the context of regime building and normative development.[117]

International Trade Law: This course presents an overview of the major international treaties affecting Canadian foreign trade, such as the Marrakesh Agreement Establishing the World Trade Organization and the North American Free Trade Agreement. Canada's international trade and investment laws are examined together with a number of recent trade disputes and the means of resolving them.

Natural Resources Law: International Law and Resources. This four-credit seminar considers specific topics designed to develop students' skills in legal analysis and evaluation, legal research, and written and oral expression. It explores the sources and application of international law, problems in international water law, problems in

---

[116] *1999 Course Descriptions, supra* note 95. Joel H. Rosenthal, ed., *Ethics and International Affairs: A Reader* (Washington, DC: Georgetown University Press, 1995). The reading list for this seminar, open to non law students and including masters and doctoral students from law and other faculties, is impressive.

[117] *Ibid.*

economic well-being, and problems in socio-political justice. The recommended text is the splendid collection by Burns Weston, *International Law and World Order*.[118]

International Criminal Law. This graduate-level seminar, which was taught by Peter Burns, covered sovereignty and jurisdiction, immunity from criminal jurisdiction, war crimes, piracy and terrorism, the international control of narcotics and money laundering, and the role of the United Nations in developing a modern international criminal law regime. Burns relied on Cherif Bassioune's *International Criminal Law*, Gerhard O.W. Mueller and Edward M. Wise's *International Criminal Law*, and Sharon A. Williams and Jean Gabriel Castel's *Canadian Criminal Law: International and Transnational Aspects*.[119] These texts were supplemented by information compiled specifically for the course. Evaluation was based on participation in the seminar (30 per cent) and a research paper of at least 7,500 words.

International Law-Related Courses

In addition to the core courses, the Faculty of Law offered a number of courses that I have classified as international law related. This category includes topic-specific courses with obvious international dimensions, courses with a comparative law focus, and courses that are primarily about domestic law in which the international aspect influences domestic application.

Marine Resources Law. This four-credit seminar, taught by Townsend Gault, explored the way countries and regions undertook legal development for the exploration and development of ocean resources. Covering the basic rules of the law of the sea, the seminar sought to explain the nature and extent of states rights and responsibilities respecting resource development in marine areas. By focusing on particular regions, the South China Sea, southeast Asia, the South Pacific, and the Indian Ocean, for example, Townsend Gault was

---

[118] Burns H. Weston, *International Law and World Order* (Livingston-on-Hudson, NY: Transnational Publishers, 1994).

[119] Cherif Bassiouni, ed., *International Criminal* Law, 3 vols. (Dobbs Ferry, NY: Transnational Publishers, 1986); Gerhard O.W. Mueller and Edward M. Wise, eds., *International Criminal Law* (South Hackensack, NJ: Fred B. Rothman and Company, 1965); and Sharon A. Williams and Jean Gabriel Castel, *Canadian Criminal Law: International and Transnational Aspects* (Toronto: Butterworths, 1981).

able to relate the course to his research projects in those areas. Students were involved in his work in these regions. In addition, Richard Paisley taught various courses and seminars on international fisheries and other aspects of the law of the sea and on international environmental problems.

International Dispute Resolution. The Faculty of Law offered two separate seminars on dispute resolution in international contexts. The first, Robert Paterson's four-credit course on Dispute Resolution in International Trade and Investment, which was offered in the fall term, examined dispute resolution and arbitration in the context of international business disputes. The second seminar, entitled International Commercial Disputes, which was a three-credit seminar taught by a practitioner, Henry Alvarez, dealt with "alternative dispute resolution, the nature and evolution of international commercial arbitration, the arbitration agreement, applicable procedural law, the organization of arbitrations, the law applicable to the merits of the dispute, recognition and enforcement of arbitral awards, and arbitrations involving state parties."[120]

Cultural Property and the Law. Paterson's seminar on cultural property examined the legal, cultural, economic, and ethical issues surrounding international trade in cultural property (art, artifacts, and archaeological remains). These issues were addressed in light of relevant treaty obligations and the rights of indigenous peoples as well as private individuals and sovereign states. Approximately two-thirds of the course was devoted to examining international laws pertaining to cultural property, while the remaining one-third of the course concentrated on domestic issues. Guest lectures were given by collectors, dealers, anthropologists, museum officials, and law enforcement officials.[121]

Regulatory Impact of Globalization. This important bi-university, multimedia course, which was collaboratively taught by Ruth Buchanan at UBC and Sundhya Pahuja at Melbourne University in Australia, examined the regulatory impact of globalization on labour and employment standards, financial markets, social welfare, immigration, intellectual property, and trade. It brought to bear (on a web-based

---

[120] This course was taught as a series of introductory lectures followed by a discussion of student research. Professor Alvarez compiled his own materials.

[121] Students were graded on the results of a major term paper. See Robert K. Paterson, "Cases and Materials: Cultural Property and Law 330" (Vancouver: UBC Faculty of Law, 1994).

format) a theoretical interest in the relocation of governance in the context of globalization and the intersection between global integration and local identification.[122]

In addition to the foregoing, the faculty offered a number of courses with a comparative law orientation. Most prominent among these were courses in the Asian Legal Studies program, including, for example, courses on the introduction to Asian legal systems,[123] and more advanced seminars such as Trade and Investment in the People's Republic of China. Other courses with a comparative flavour were European Union Law and International and Comparative Law of Copyright and Related Rights.[124] Finally, the faculty, as expected, continued to offer the usual domestic law courses that now contain an increasing number of international elements:

[122] Students were asked to consider the changing role of law (domestic and international) in the global economy. A web-based format was used to facilitate discussions and collaboration between the two classrooms. The website had links to the websites of a number of international economic institutions, including the World Trade Organization, International Labour Organization, and the World Bank, with which students became familiar. The course was organized through a series of modules on the website that combined a range of theoretical approaches with case studies in key areas where global flows are at their most turbulent. The topics included international economic institutions, trade and environment conflicts, labour regulation, North/South conflicts in the area of intellectual property, immigration, and the role of non-governmental organizations in global governance. For background, see David M. Trubek, Yves Dezalay, Ruth Buchanan, John R. Davis, "Global Restructuring and the Law: Studies of the Internationalization of Legal Fields and the Creation of Transnational Arenas" (1994) 44 Case Western Reserve L. Rev. 407-498.

[123] This three-credit course was team-taught by Potter (People's Republic of China), Salzberg (Japan), and Townsend Gault (Southeast Asia — Indonesia, Malaysia, and Vietnam). Visiting Asian scholars taught segments of the course, depending on their availability. The course emphasized comparative law theory as well as aspects of the legal systems of each country and a few of their common legal problems. Most of the assigned material comprised articles and commentaries published in North America, supplemented by domestic laws in translation and articles and commentaries by Asian scholars. Students were assessed by way of a 100 per cent final examination. *Introduction to Asian Legal Systems: Topics in Comparative Law* (Vancouver: Faculty of Law, UBC, 1993).

[124] This three-credit seminar examined copyright and related rights in an international and comparative law context. The course was divided into three parts: (1) national legislation; (2) international conventions and treaties, including, for example, the Berne Convention for the Protection of Literary and Artistic Works and the World Trade Organization's Trade-Related Agreement on Intellectual Property Rights; and (3) special topics, such as European Community directives on competition law.

Immigration and Refugee Law, Conflict of Laws, International Taxation, and, as a graduate seminar, Proceeds of Crime and Money Laundering.

CONCLUDING REMARKS

The history of the teaching of international law at UBC is unique in the Canadian experience. Strong support from the then-president of the university and the dean of the law school, together with their insistence that international law occupy a required place in the curriculum, established a culture of international law at the law school. Their policies were actively reinforced by the presence of several outstanding professors, Bourne, McRae, Copithorne, and Brunnée, all highly respected names in Canada's international law community, supported by an able student body and a stimulating graduate program. There are now a large number of optional courses related to international law and a corresponding rise in student interest. In the academic year, 1999-2000, student interest in international law continued to increase, with almost half of the first-year class electing to take the international law component of the mandatory perspectives course. In addition, student interest in the basic course increased to the point of necessitating regular waiting lists.

The increase in student interest can be attributed to a number of factors. First, it is now widely recognized that for those interested in practising law it is no longer possible to ignore its international dimensions. Second, student interest in general is increasingly driven by a broader agenda. No longer simply interested in a career in private practice, some students want to explore law-related careers in public interest advocacy, human rights, international aid, and so on. Third, students are increasingly multilingual and internationally mobile. Many expect to live and work in various countries, and, in their view, a grounding in international and comparative law is rightly seen as being necessary. Finally, international law is attractive for some students simply because it is the subject least like law. A diverse student body means that the traditional core curriculum of forty-five years ago is less appealing than it once was.

The growth in student interest, coupled with an expanding political and legal international space, has research and pedagogical implications. The study of international law over the last fifteen years has been complicated by increasingly sophisticated and diverse theoretical contributions. This so-called "new stream" of scholarship has brought to bear on the study of international law the gaze of critical, feminist, and Third World theorists.[125] The result is a multi-layered, nuanced critique of the subject that challenges both teachers and researchers to explore the complex ways in which international law operates.[126] This development means that for those teaching the subject it is important to situate international law in a social, political, and economic context. Traditional case-based approaches are seen today as isolating international law in an artificially narrow disciplinary conception that does not recognize the ways in which it intersects with, and informs, other social, economic, cultural, and political disciplines and institutions.

Has the UBC Faculty of Law responded to the growing importance of international law and the challenges of a changing international law discipline? The answer is resoundingly affirmative. The concentration of able scholars working in international law-related areas, such as Asian legal studies, international criminal law, environmental law, trade law, and human rights, evidences a dynamic scholarly community strengthened by the presence of relatively large numbers of graduate and research students. This concentrated research interest is perhaps more a product of an historic institutional commitment to the teaching of international law than it is to a focused academic plan. Moreover, the seemingly ad hoc nature of recruiting and retaining teachers of international law and of international legal study at UBC has implications for the future. Uncertainty in university funding means there is no guarantee that the "community" of interested faculty members and graduate

---

[125] On "new stream" scholarship, see Nigel Purvis, "Critical Legal Studies in Public International Law" (1991) 32 Harv. Int. L.J. 81; David Kennedy, "A New Stream of International Law Scholarship" (1988) 7 Wis. Int'l L. J. 1. On the "crits," see, for example, Martti Koskenniemi, *From Apology to Utopia: The Structure of International Legal Argument* (Helsinki: Finnish Lawyers' Publishing Company, 1989), and Deborah Z. Cass, "Navigating the Newstream: Recent Critical Scholarship in International Law" (1996) 65 *Nordic Journal of International Law* 341. On the feminists, see, for example, Hilary Charlesworth, Christine Chinkin, and Shelley Wright, "Feminist Approaches to International Law" (1991) 85 Am. J. Int'l .L. 613; and on the Third World, see, for example, Karin Mickelson, "Rhetoric and Rage: Third World Voices in International Legal Discourse" (1998) 16 Wisc. Int'l L. J. 353.

[126] For discussion of the changing nature of international law methodology, see Steven R. Ratner and Anne-Marie Slaughter, "Symposium on Method in International Law" (1999) 93 Am. J. Int'l L. 291. See also draft of *I.L.A. Committee on the Teaching of International Law*, Hilary Charlesworth, chair, John King Gamble, rapporteur, March 24, 2000, with bibliography of articles in English published since 1980, and report of September 7, 1999. Biennal Conference of the ILA (New Delhi, April 2-7, 2002 (with syllabi)).

students will always be there. A more concrete institutional commitment to the subject, including the attraction of senior scholars, may be necessary.[127]

If the foregoing account of the teaching of international law at UBC has been laudatory, I can only say that it was intended to be. Even a brief review of the relevant events of the last fifty years makes it crystal clear that, in the words of the 1969 report of the Curriculum Committee, the faculty has indeed "maintained a pre-eminent position within Canada insofar as the teaching of international law is concerned." Praiseworthy and encouraging as these achievements have undoubtedly been, there nevertheless remains a matter of fundamental importance that I have not been able to deal with in this article — the wisdom of the decision of the UBC law faculty to abandon the great tradition of its founders in regard to the need for a mandatory basic course.

In my opinion, diversification and increases in the number of international law-related courses, including segments of a first-year perspectives course, are not adequate substitutes for a mandatory introductory course taught (probably) in the first term of the second year. I believe that no student should graduate from any Canadian law school or be called to the Bar in any part of Canada without having had a solid general course in international law. In espousing this belief, I am aligning myself with the recommendations of the Institut de droit international, the opinion of the Legal Counsel of the United Nations, and the observations of the president of the International Court of Justice.[128] In a letter, dated July 15, 1993, the distinguished Cambridge law scholar, Sir Robert Jennings, then president of the International Court of Justice, wrote to the writer as follows:

---

[127] For recent discussion of faculty thinking, see Dean Joost Blom, "Looking Ahead in Canadian Law School Education" (1999) 33 UBC Law Review 7.

[128] *Annuaire de l'Institut de droit international*, vol. 67 (Session de Strasbourg, 1997) at 123-219; Hans Corell, "An Appeal to Deans of Law Schools Worldwide," August 2000, available at <www.un.org/law/counsel/info.htm> at 2. See also the vigorous acceptance speech by Shabtai Rosenne when he received the Hague Prize for International Law, June 18, 2004 (Leiden: Martinus Nijhoff, 2004), 6-20. International law "must become a compulsory subject for membership in every national Bar ... My suggestion is motivated exclusively by ... practical considerations, relating, above all, to ... what the average man or woman is entitled to expect when approaching a duly qualified attorney for legal advice" (18-19).

[T]he chief need is more elementary and comprehensive courses in public international law in general. The ideal situation is the one that, I am glad to say, still obtains in the University of Cambridge: that *every* law student taking his or her normal course in law will have to learn the elements of public international law in precisely the same way as they are required to become acquainted with the elements of the law of contracts. The aim is that more practising lawyers, and Judges, should have a basic knowledge of international law. For then they will be prepared to see it applied as a routine matter in domestic as well as international tribunals. But if the system is entirely strange to them, they will resist the relevance of international law. Maitland's aphorism is still true: "taught law is tough law."

Moreover, I would say that there ought to be such a general course in the elements of the system in any Faculty that purports to teach any *aspect* of international law. In many universities there are courses in trendy aspects of international law — such as, the environment or human rights; though what those subjects will be in 5 years time one can only guess, for trends by definition change rapidly. But nobody should be *allowed* to do such subjects unless they also take a course in general public international law. Otherwise one breeds utterly useless persons such as one with a "specialists" knowledge of, say human rights, though lacking any proper training in the law of treaties.

I realize that in asking for something that would have been an obvious requirement not needing a mention, say 50 years ago, I am now asking for something almost impossible of achievement. For faculties get funds for teaching what makes headlines in newspapers. But *unless* more *lawyers* are trained in the elements of the subject *as a whole system,* the outlook for international law is bleak.[129]

Sommaire

Droit international à l'University of British Columbia de 1945 à 2000

Depuis la fondation de la Faculté de droit à l'University of British Columbia en 1945, le droit international y occupe une place de choix. L'auteur trace l'historique de l'enseignement du droit international à cette faculté, depuis ses débuts en tant que cours obligatoire jusqu'en 2000, en soulignant les personnalités qui ont collaboré à cet enseignement ainsi que les questions qui ont influencé l'évolution de cet l'enseignement au fil des années.

---

[129] Letter from Sir Robert Jennings to R. St. J. Macdonald (July 15, 1993) at 1, 2. In my own view, the reasons for making public international law a required subject in the law school curriculum are similar to the reasons for making constitutional law a mandatory law school subject: maintenance and development of the democratic international constitutional system requires, first, understanding and, second, support from lawyers in particular. Legal supranationalism is an inextricably linked complementary feature of national constitutional traditions.

Summary

International Law at the University of British Columbia, 1945-2000

Since the founding of the UBC law school in 1945 international law has had a prominent place. The author traces the teaching of international law from the days when it was a compulsory course to 2000 and discusses the personalities who have taught the subject and the issues that have affected the teaching of international law over those years.

Les juridictions traditionnelles et la justice pénale internationale

PACIFIQUE MANIRAKIZA

[L]a justice est trop importante pour la laisser aux seuls juristes.

— C. de Bueule[1]

Les années 90 ont été caractérisées par une prise de conscience par la communauté internationale de l'extrême gravité de la criminalité internationale et de l'ampleur de l'impunité qui en résulte. Ainsi, une lutte acharnée contre ce fléau est actuellement en cours. Des juridictions pénales internationales[2] ou mixtes[3] ont

---

Pacifique Manirakiza est professeur à la Faculté de droit, Université d'Ottawa.

[1] C. de Bueule, "La justice internationale peut-elle contribuer à la construction de la Paix dans la région des Grands Lacs?" Journée européenne-Rwanda organisée sous le thème *La Justice internationale face à la crise rwandaise*, Lille, le 16 février 2002.

[2] Il s'agit du Tribunal international pour juger les personnes présumées responsables de violations graves du droit international humanitaire commises sur le territoire de l'ex-Yougoslavie depuis 1991, en sigle TPIY, créé le 25 mai 1993 par le Conseil de Sécurité des Nations Unies, agissant en vertu du Chapitre VII de la Charte des Nations Unies, voir Doc. NU S/RES/827 (1993); du Tribunal pénal international chargé de juger les personnes présumées responsables d'actes de génocide ou d'autres violations graves du droit international humanitaire commis sur le territoire du Rwanda et les citoyens rwandais présumés responsables de tels actes ou violations commis sur le territoire d'États voisins entre le 1er janvier et le 31 décembre 1994, en sigle TPIR, créé le 8 novembre 1994 par le même Conseil de sécurité, voir Doc. NU S/RES/955 (1994); de la Cour pénale internationale (C.P.I.) dont le Statut a été adopté le 17 juillet 1998 par la Conférence diplomatique de plénipotentiaires des Nations Unies sur la création d'une Cour criminelle internationale tenue à Rome, Italie, voir Doc. NU A/CONF. 183/9.

[3] Il s'agit par exemple, pour la Sierra Leone, du Tribunal spécial pour la Sierra Leone créé par suite de l'Accord entre l'Organisation des Nations Unies et le Gouvernement sierra-léonais sur la création d'un Tribunal spécial pour la Sierra Leone; voir *Rapport de la mission de planification en vue de la création d'un Tribunal spécial pour la Sierra Leone*, DOC. ONU S/2002/246, 8 mars 2002. Pour le Timor Oriental, voir la *Regulation No. 2000/15 on the establishment of panels with exclusive jurisdiction over serious criminal offences*, UNTAET/REG/2000/15, 6 juin 2000.

été mises en place dans le but de poursuivre, de juger et, le cas
échéant de condamner les personnes responsables des violations
graves du droit international humanitaire et du droit international
des droits de l'homme constitutives d'infractions internationales.
Parallèlement à ces efforts internationaux, des initiatives étatiques
en vue de réprimer les crimes internationaux les plus graves sont en
cours dans quelques pays agissant individuellement sur base de la
compétence territoriale,[4] personnelle[5] ou universelle.[6]

Force nous est cependant de faire constater qu'en dépit de ces
efforts déployés au niveau tant national qu'international, il n'est
pas facile de venir à bout de l'impunité du crime international
au regard de son ampleur. On doit par ailleurs noter que les tribunaux internationaux ou mixtes sont dotés d'une compétence
limitée quant au temps, à l'espace, aux crimes et aux personnes
à poursuivre.[7] En plus de la compétence limitée des institutions
judiciaires internationales ou mixtes, les quelques États agissant
individuellement ne sont pas généralement pourvus d'assez de
moyens et de ressources humains, logistiques et financiers qui leur
permettraient de combattre efficacement la criminalité internationale.[8] De même, l'efficacité des structures judiciaires dont ils

---

[4] Le Rwanda est par exemple en plein processus de répression des crimes qui ont
été commis sur son territoire entre le 1er octobre 1990 et le 31 décembre 1994.

[5] La Belgique réclame M. Ntuyahaga, ancien major dans l'armée rwandaise et
actuellement en détention en Tanzanie aux fins de répondre des accusations relatives à l'assassinat des 10 casques bleus du contingent militaire belge opérant
dans le cadre de la MINUAR au Rwanda en 1994.

[6] Certains pays ont engagé des poursuites contre des suspects criminels internationaux présents sur leurs territoires. C'est le cas de la Belgique; voir notamment
l'affaire *Ministère public* c. *Ntezimana et al.*, Cour d'assises, Bruxelles, juin 2001; de
la France, voir notamment l'affaire *Dupaquier et autres* c. *Munyeshyaka*, Chambre
d'accusation de la Cour d'appel, Nîmes, 20 mars 1996, n° 96-0160; de la Suisse,
voir notamment l'affaire *Niyonteze*, en ligne: http://www.diplomatiejudiciaire.
com/Niyonteze.htm, dernière visite en date du 15 octobre 2002; etc.

[7] Ainsi, le TPIR est compétent pour les crimes commis au Rwanda entre le 1er
janvier et le 31 décembre 1994, la CPI est compétente pour les crimes commis à
partir du 1er juillet 2002, date d'entrée en vigueur du statut qui l'institue, etc.

[8] Au Rwanda par exemple, avec la guerre de 1994, beaucoup de magistrats ont été
soit tués soit contraints à l'exil. À la fin d'octobre 1995, le Ministère de la justice
comptait en son sein 387 juges, 110 greffiers, 20 officiers du ministère public et
312 inspecteurs de police judiciaire; mais ces chiffres demeurent largement en
deçà des besoins en personnel judiciaire. Ceux-ci sont estimés par l'Opération
droits de l'homme au Rwanda — et seulement pour le "démarrage" — à 664 magistrats, 330 greffiers, 163 officiers du ministère public et 312 inspecteurs de
police judiciaire. Voir *Rapport sur la situation des droits de l'homme au Rwanda soumis*

sont dotés est parfois compromise par le volume des affaires à traiter.[9] Ainsi, certains États ont adopté de nouveaux mécanismes quasi juridictionnels ou juridictionnels afin de renforcer la capacité institutionnelle actuellement déployée dans la répression des crimes internationaux. Il s'agit en l'occurrence des commissions dites de vérité et de réconciliation[10] et des juridictions traditionnelles ou communautaires.[11]

Dans cet article, nous nous proposons d'analyser l'opportunité de l'intervention des juridictions traditionnelles ou communautaires dans la répression des crimes internationaux.[12] Notre postulat est que dans les États où des violences massives ont eu lieu

---

par M. René Degni-Ségui, Rapporteur spécial de la Commission des droits de l'homme, en application du paragraphe 20 de la résolution S-3/1 du 25 mai 1994, Doc. NU E/CN.4/1996/68, 29 janvier 1996 au par. 49. Pourtant, on devrait juger, au début du processus, plus de 200 000 détenus inculpés de génocide et/ou de crimes contre l'humanité et satisfaire le besoin de justice d'autant de victimes, y compris la communauté internationale.

[9] Neuf ans après la tragédie rwandaise de 1994, plus de 103 000 personnes sont encore détenues et accusées de génocide et de crimes contre l'humanité. Voir Amnesty International, *Gacaca: une question de justice*, Doc. AFR 47/004/02, Londres, novembre 2002 à la p.1.

[10] C'est le cas en Afrique du Sud de la *Truth and Reconciliation Commission* mise en place après la chute du régime d'apartheid.

[11] C'est le cas du Rwanda qui a reconnu la compétence aux tribunaux traditionnels dits *Gacaca* de réprimer les crimes de génocide et les crimes contre l'humanité; voir à cet effet la *Loi organique n° 40/2000 du 26/01/2001 portant création des "juridictions Gacaca" et organisation des poursuites des infractions constitutives du crime de génocide ou de crimes contre l'humanité, commises entre le 1er octobre 1990 et le 31 décembre 1994*, dans J.O.R.R., n° 6 du 15 mars 2001 (ci-après "Loi 40/2000"). Elle a été amendée par la *Loi organique n° 33/2001 du 22/06/2001 modifiant et complétant la loi organique n° 40/2000 du 26/01/2001 portant création des "juridictions Gacaca" et organisation des poursuites des infractions constitutives du crime de génocide ou de crimes contre l'humanité, commises entre le 1er octobre 1990 et le 31 décembre 1994*. Voir J.O.R.R. n° 14 du 15 juillet 2001 à la p. 15 et s.

[12] On dénombre à peu près 25 catégories de crimes internationaux; pour une énumération de ces crimes; voir M.C. Bassiouni, "The sources and content of international criminal law: a theoretical framework" dans M.C. Bassiouni, *International criminal law: Crimes*, vol. 2, 2e éd., 1999 à la p. 48; voir également M.C. Bassiouni, "The Nuremberg legacy" dans M.C. Bassiouni, *International criminal law: Enforcement*, vol. 3, 2e éd., New York, Transnational Publishers, 1999 aux pp. 209-230 (ci-après *Enforcement*). Aux fins de cet article, nous entendons, par crimes internationaux, le crime de génocide, les crimes contre l'humanité et les crimes de guerre, infractions considérées comme les plus graves en ce sens qu'elles "*défient l'imagination et heurtent profondément la conscience humaine*" (Statut de la CPI, *supra* note 2, préambule au par. 2).

impliquant la participation de la population, il est important que celle-ci ainsi que les institutions populaires existantes soient impliquées dans le règlement de la crise afin de mieux définir de nouvelles bases de cohabitation sociale. Cette implication peut prendre plusieurs formes mais nous nous en tiendrons à l'aspect judiciaire. Ce qui revient en réalité à nous demander, dans ces quelques lignes, si la population et les institutions judiciaires traditionnelles ou communautaires, là où elles existent, peuvent intervenir dans le jugement des personnes présumées responsables des crimes internationaux.

De prime abord, après des notions préliminaires sur ces institutions (§1) et une analyse des bases juridiques internationales de leur action répressive (§2), nous soutenons que les juridictions traditionnelles et communautaires accusent une incapacité notoire à participer à la lutte contre l'impunité du crime international en raison de leur structure, de leur composition et de leur compétence matérielle habituelle et du droit normalement applicable aux crimes internationaux (§3). Cependant, dans le but de ressouder le tissu social et d'alléger la charge judiciaire des tribunaux ordinaires, il est important de voir comment on pourrait, dans une moindre mesure et dans une perspective dissuasive et préventive, associer ces juridictions dans tout le processus de redressement judiciaire de la société (§4). De même, la participation de la population dans l'administration nationale de la justice pénale internationale devrait être clarifiée dans cet article (§5).

I   NOTIONS GÉNÉRALES SUR LES INSTITUTIONS JUDICIAIRES TRADITIONNELLES OU COMMUNAUTAIRES

A   LES INSTITUTIONS JUDICIAIRES TRADITIONNELLES

Dans beaucoup de pays, surtout ceux de tradition orale, il existe une coexistence de deux systèmes judiciaires:

- un système dit moderne calqué sur le modèle judiciaire occidental et qui est composé de cours et tribunaux qui appliquent essentiellement le droit écrit;
- un système de droit coutumier sous-tendu par des instances judiciaires qui font exclusivement recours aux coutumes locales pour régler des différends qui surgissent au sein de la communauté.

Ce dernier système nous intéresse aux fins de cet article. Il est articulé sur des juridictions traditionnelles qui sont encore appelées juridictions coutumières en ce sens qu'elles appliquent du droit coutumier. Ces institutions judiciaires ont pour principale mission de maintenir l'ordre au sein de la communauté par le biais de la résolution, par voie de conciliation, des différends qui opposent ses membres. Les juges qui y siègent sont généralement des chefs tribaux, familiaux ou simplement des sages qui incarnent le système.[13] Ils sont assistés par des notables-conseillers promus suivant des rites traditionnels d'initiation à la sagesse.[14] Au Pakistan, "les anciens des tribus ou les personnes particulièrement instruites comme les instituteurs ou autres notables locaux peuvent jouer le rôle de *musheer,* conseiller ou avocat auprès de la *jirga.* Cet avis donné par un tiers est généralement accepté et on considère comme un grand honneur d'être appelé à jouer ce rôle."[15]

Dans plusieurs pays d'Afrique, la population participe également dans toute instance judiciaire avec le droit, pour les personnes adultes, d'interroger les parties et/ou les témoins et, le cas échéant, de donner leurs points de vue sur les questions litigieuses. Au Pakistan, les *Sardars* sont les seuls véritables juges bien qu'ils peuvent recevoir des avis d'autres personnes éclairées.[16] Dans tous les cas, il importe de souligner cependant que ces instances judiciaires sont fortement marquées par le système patriarcal et sont partant discriminatoires envers les femmes qui ne peuvent pas participer de manière active ou passive dans la tenue et le déroulement des procès. Elles ne peuvent donc pas siéger; en Afrique, elles peuvent assister mais elles n'ont pas le droit de poser des questions contrairement à leurs congénères masculins. Au Pakistan, seuls les hommes peuvent participer aux *jirgas;* les femmes ne peuvent pas comparaître devant les tribunaux tribaux, que se soit

---

[13] Au Pakistan, les juridictions traditionnelles connues sous l'appellation de *jirga* sont pilotées par des chefs tribaux appelés *Sardar;* voir Amnesty International, *Pakistan — Le système de justice tribale,* ASA 33/024/02, Londres, octobre 2002. Au Rwanda, les juridictions coutumières *Gacaca* sont coordonnées par des sages appelées *Inyangamugayo;* voir notamment Charles Ntampaka, "*Le gacaca: une juridiction pénale populaire.*"Voir en ligne: http://droit.Francophonie.org/acct/rfj/actu/11Lepin.htm, dernière visite: le 12 septembre 2002; Felip Reyntjens, "Le gacaca ou la justice du gazon au Rwanda" (1990) 40 Revue politique Africaine 31, Le droit et ses pratiques; Loi organique n° 40/2000, *supra* note 11.

[14] On peut signaler par exemple la cérémonie d'initiation dite *Ukwatirwa* en vigueur au Burundi au cours de laquelle une assemblée de sages reconnaît et confère publiquement la qualité de personne intègre (UMUSHINGANTAHE) aux candidats après quoi ils peuvent siéger et prendre part aux séances de délibérations à l'issue des audiences publiques.

[15] Amnesty International, *supra* note 13 à la p. 13.

[16] *Ibid.* et texte correspondant.

comme accusées, plaignantes ou témoins; elles ne peuvent même
pas observer en simples spectateurs.[17]

B   LES JURIDICTIONS COMMUNAUTAIRES

En plus des institutions judiciaires traditionnelles, la justice
ordinaire cohabite avec des juridictions communautaires. Celles-
ci remontent généralement à un courant qui a pris naissance en
Europe dans les années 80 et qui visait l'implication de la communauté dans l'administration de la justice pénale. Il était question
de mettre en place un système informel et extrajudiciaire capable
de désengorger les tribunaux ordinaires,[18] d'administrer la justice
pénale pour infractions mineures suivant une procédure sommaire
et simplifiée mais aussi de trouver et de prononcer des sanctions alternatives à la prison.[19] Cette participation communautaire
présente des avantages évidents notamment la réduction des coûts
judiciaires et la responsabilisation de la communauté dans le traitement des problèmes en rapport avec la criminalité et son contrôle.[20]

Contrairement aux juridictions traditionnelles dont les juges
sont des chefs traditionnels ou tribaux dont l'autorité incontestée
relève de leur place primordiale dans la société ou au sein de leurs
tribus, les juges des juridictions communautaires sont des personnes élues dans les villages ou villes dans lesquels ils vivent. Ceci
est le cas des *Resistance Committee Courts* ougandais.[21] D'abord mis en
place d'une manière informelle à travers tout le pays depuis la
prise du pouvoir par le Président Yoweri Museveni en 1986, ces tribunaux populaires trouvent aujourd'hui une assise légale en droit

---

[17]   Amnesty International, *supra* note 13 à la p. 14.

[18]   H.J. Albrecht, *Settlements out of court: a comparative study of European criminal justice
systems*, South African Law Commission, Project 73, 2001 à la p. 7. Dans ce rapport, le Prof. Albrecht écrit: "Among the crime phenomena that are placing
criminal justice systems under new strains, mass crime and mass delinquency
rank high ... Mass crimes and complex crimes have caused capacity and over-
load problems and have contributed to a significant trend towards simplification
and streamlining of basic criminal law and criminal procedure."

[19]   Sur la notion de sanctions alternatives à la prison, voir les rapports de l'ONG
Penal Reform International, en ligne <http://www.penalreform.org/francais/
frset_bib_fr.htm>.

[20]   Albrecht, *supra* note 18 à la p. 23.

[21]   South African Law Commission, *The harmonisation of the common law and indigenous law: Traditional courts and the judicial function of traditional leaders*, Projet 90,
mai 1999 à la p. 17, par. 5.3.

ougandais.[22] Il en est de même pour les *Comrade courts* créées dans les États de l'ancien bloc socialiste.[23] Dans ce dernier cas, le fondement idéologique de l'implication communautaire découle du principe à la base même du socialisme, à savoir la participation de la population dans la gestion de ses affaires par des comités révolutionnaires qu'elle met en place, ainsi que de l'idéologie marxiste qui consiste dans la disparition de l'État au profit de la dictature du prolétariat.

Tout comme les juridictions traditionnelles, les instances communautaires poursuivent le maintien et le rétablissement de l'ordre social par la conciliation ainsi que la réconciliation des membres de la communauté. En Ouganda par exemple, les *Resistance Committee Courts* sont "charged with keeping the peace, supplementing police, and resolving disputes."[24] Ainsi, en dépit de quelques différences au niveau de la mise en place de ces juridictions et de leurs juges, les deux ordres juridictionnels jouissent de la même compétence et suivent des règles de procédure et un régime de sanctions identiques.

C COMPÉTENCE, PROCÉDURE ET RÉGIME DES SANCTIONS

Les juridictions traditionnelles ou communautaires sont généralement dotées d'une compétence et appliquent une procédure et des sanctions spécialement conçues pour leur permettre d'atteindre leur objectif de maintien de l'ordre et de la paix communautaires. S'agissant de leur compétence, certaines juridictions n'ont qu'une compétence en matière civile et tranchent des litiges civils par voie de conciliation.[25] D'autres cumulent les compétences civile et pénale.[26] Il convient de noter cependant que, dans ce dernier cas, la compétence pénale est plus ou moins étendue suivant les pays. Dans certains cas, ces fora judiciaires ne connaissent pas des infractions qui portent atteinte, d'une manière particulièrement grave, à

---

[22] Voir le *Resistance Committees (Judicial Powers) Statute, No. 1 of 1988* qui porte sur l'organisation et la compétence de ces institutions judiciaires.

[23] Albrecht, *supra* note 18 à la p. 24.

[24] O. Onyango *et al.,* "Popular Justice and Resistance Committee Courts in Uganda" mimeo, Kampala, 1994, cité par South African Commission, *supra* note 21 à la p. 17, par. 5.3.

[25] C'en est le cas avec les *Traditional Leaders' Courts* du Zimbabwe et les *Resistance Committee Courts* de l'Ouganda.

[26] Les *jirgas* tranchent les questions de terres et de l'eau et sont compétentes pour les homicides et autres atteintes à l'intégrité physique ou morale des personnes.

l'ordre public d'un État donné. Elles répriment uniquement les infractions mineures. Ainsi, au Timor oriental, "[L]es systèmes de justice traditionnels jouent un rôle important pour ce qui est de prévenir les crimes mineurs dans les districts ou de régler les affaires correspondantes grâce à l'établissement d'un comité de l'ordre public composé du chef du village, d'un prêtre, de représentants d'organisations locales et d'un policier civil."[27] De même, s'agissant des juridictions communautaires, le Prof. Hans J. Albrecht écrit que "small-scale crime and lesser conflicts not seen to be a threat to the social and political fabric were relegated to extra-judicial settlement of disputes and small scale sanctions."[28] Par contre, la compétence des *jirgas* pakistanaises est très étendue. C'est ainsi qu'elles connaissent des crimes graves comme les viols collectifs, les meurtres et les crimes "d'honneur."[29]

Dans tous les cas, contrairement au système dit moderne qui connaît des magistrats professionnels, les institutions judiciaires traditionnelles et communautaires fonctionnent avec des juges-citoyens qui incarnent le système. Elles rendent une justice de proximité dans un souci permanent de protéger et de promouvoir les intérêts de la société.[30]

En ce qui est du droit et de la procédure applicables, les jugements sont généralement rendus selon la coutume et en équité.[31] Le droit applicable, tout au moins devant les juridictions traditionnelles, est connu de tous car il émane des comportements, des attitudes, des modes de vie ou des traditions ayant acquis force de coutumes dans une communauté donnée. C'est ainsi que tout le

---

[27] *Rapport du Secrétaire général sur l'Administration transitoire des Nations Unies au Timor oriental* (pour la période du 27 juillet 2000 au 16 janvier 2001), Doc. NU S/2001/42, 16 janvier 2001, par. 27.

[28] Albrecht, *supra* note 18 à la p. 24.

[29] Dans la société pakistanaise traditionnelle, l'inconduite sexuelle d'une femme ou toute agression sexuelle contre une femme portent atteinte à l'honneur de sa famille, en particulier les hommes. Elles constituent ainsi un crime "d'honneur" qui doit être sévèrement réprimé; voir Amnesty International, *supra* note 13 aux pp. 8-9.

[30] Contrairement à la justice pénale occidentale qui met en avant les droits individuels et favorise la détermination du gagnant et du perdant, les juridictions traditionnelles favorisent la réconciliation et privilégient les intérêts du groupe et la conciliation au conflit. On vise donc l'harmonie sociale tout en réglant les différends qui opposent des membres d'une communauté donnée.

[31] South African Law Commission, *supra* note 21 à la p. vii, par. 2: "These community courts should apply the general sense of justice and common sense."

processus est entièrement piloté par les gens d'un certain âge qui sont censés connaître le droit coutumier.[32]

Quant aux règles qui gouvernent la procédure devant les juridictions traditionnelles et communautaires, elles ne sont pas fixes et inamovibles; elles se plient aux exigences impérieuses du maintien de l'harmonie et de la paix sociales. La procédure est donc simple, informelle et très flexible. L'absence d'arcanes procéduraux facilite la recherche rapide d'une solution car tout le monde, y compris les accusés, comprend la procédure qu'on peut ainsi manier aisément. Celle-ci est en outre inquisitoriale; ce qui permet aux juges-citoyens et à l'assistance (sous-entendu les adultes masculins) de participer activement dans la recherche de la vérité judiciaire par le biais de l'interrogatoire et du contre-interrogatoire des témoins et des parties. On peut néanmoins déplorer, pour le cas du Pakistan, certains procédés utilisés pour avoir une preuve de culpabilité. Il s'agit notamment de la tradition de faire marcher les gens dans le feu ou sur des charbons ardents étant donné que la plupart admettent que seuls les pieds des coupables seront brûlés mais que l'innocence protège de tout mal.[33]

Il n'existe pas de rapport sur le déroulement des audiences ou la motivation du jugement. La partie perdante peut, lorsque cela est possible, interjeter appel devant les tribunaux ordinaires qui sont obligés, en l'absence de procès-verbal d'audience et de motivations écrites du jugement rendu, d'examiner *de novo* l'affaire dans son fonds.

En outre, le système judiciaire traditionnel ne connaît pas la représentation légale. En Afrique du sud par exemple, le *National Development and Restoration of Traditional Customs Forum,* une organisation des chefs traditionnels estime que "no legal representation is necessary as the procedure is so uncomplicated that anyone can prosecute and defend a case."[34] Cette 'lacune' est inhérente à la nature juridique des juridictions coutumières. En effet, il est généralement reconnu que ces institutions consistent ou agissent beaucoup plus en un forum d'arbitrage de différends qu'en véritables

---

[32] *Ibid.* à la p. 29, par. 6.3.1: "As far as customary law is concerned, every adult member of the ethnic group is supposed to know it, and since the chiefs are supposed to be the custodians of the law of their community they are presumed to know the customary law. Even the parties are expected to know the law, the only question being the application of the law to the facts."

[33] Amnesty International, *supra* note 13 à la p. 13.

[34] South African Law Commission, *supra* note 21 à la p. 10.

cours de justice. C'est ainsi que même dans quelques pays où on leur reconnaît une compétence pénale, leur juridiction est orientée vers le rétablissement de l'harmonie sociale en poursuivant, autant que faire se peut, la remise des choses dans leur parfait état.[35] De même, la représentation légale n'est pas de mise pour une raison tirée du pragmatisme financier pouvant être préjudiciable aux accusés. En effet, les "litigants in these courts are normally the very poor who cannot afford lawyers' fees which means that in civil cases, a poor litigant confronting or confronted by a wealthy opponent is likely to be prejudiced."[36] Cette situation pousse certains pakistanais à préférer la juridiction de la *jirga* au système de justice pénale officiel: "Dans les tribunaux réguliers nous devons payer le wakeel [avocat], les policiers, les chaprassis [gardes], les greffiers et les autres. Ensuite les affaires traînent pendant des années et nous sommes écrasés financièrement par cet état de fait. C'est pourquoi je me suis adressé à Sardar sahib qui annoncera sa décision sur mon affaire dans la journée et cela également sans payer."[37]

En ce qui concerne le régime des sanctions, les juridictions traditionnelles et communautaires condamnent les fautifs à la restitution ou au paiement des dommages intérêts compensatoires:

Chiefs' courts are permitted to award compensation and restitution. The purpose of customary proceedings is to bring about reconciliation of the parties and restore harmony in the community, rather than retribution or the award of deterrent damages as at common law. Where no actual damage or injury is suffered then an apology suffices. These remedies should be retained as appropriate and should be encouraged even in other courts.[38]

Ce genre de sanctions doit être encouragé étant donné qu'elles sont "conceived not as a mere alternative to traditional criminal sanctions, but as being essentially a procedural alternative to the traditional concept of criminal procedure based on confrontation and conflict."[39] Il importe de faire remarquer que ces sanctions

---

[35] *Ibid.*, à la p. vii, par. 2: "These community ... should aim at reconciling the disputants and establishing harmony in the community."

[36] South African Law Commission, *supra* note 21 au par. 7.5.2.

[37] Propos d'un plaignant devant une *jirga* rapportés par Amnesty International, *supra* note 13 à la p. 26.

[38] South African Law Commission, *supra* note 21 au par. 6.4.5.

[39] Albrecht, *supra* note 18 à la p. 26.

sont compatibles avec la nouvelle perspective de la protection de la victime d'un crime mais aussi de sa réconciliation avec l'auteur dudit crime.[40]

Cependant, dans les pays comme le Pakistan, en plus de la compensation en nature, la réparation est parfois matrimoniale. Celle-ci concerne généralement les crimes d'honneur où le dédommagement prend souvent la forme d'une femme donnée en compensation du tort afin de mettre fin au conflit en rapprochant les familles ennemies par le lien de mariage.[41] Au même pays, certains châtiments sont dégradants et inhumains; il s'agit notamment du viol punitif souvent prononcé même à l'encontre des femmes qui n'ont aucune responsabilité dans une affaire, de la sanction consistant à faire marcher le supplicié sur des tisons ardents,[42] etc.

Dès lors et au regard de ce qui précède, peut-on concevoir la participation des juridictions traditionnelles et communautaires dans la répression des crimes internationaux comme cela est en train d'être tenté au Rwanda?[43] Avant de répondre à cette question, nous tenterons de trouver un fondement juridique à cette mission.

[40] L'administration de la justice pénale met traditionnellement un accent sur les droits des accusés, en l'occurrence le droit à un procès équitable, et la protection de la société en général. Jusqu'à une certaine époque, les victimes ne sont pas, en tant que telles, prises en considération par les tribunaux répressifs. C'est dans ce cadre que les victimes ne peuvent pas intervenir devant les juridictions internationales *ad hoc* sauf à titre de témoins à charge. Néanmoins, elles jouissent désormais d'une protection internationale aux termes de la *Déclaration des principes fondamentaux de justice relatifs aux victimes de la criminalité et aux victimes d'abus de pouvoir;* voir Doc. NU A/Rés/40/34 adoptée par l'Assemblée générale en 1985; voir également les art. 75 et 79 du Statut de la CPI, *supra* note 2; voir aussi *Ensemble de principes et de directives fondamentaux concernant le droit à des victimes de violations flagrantes des droits de l'homme et du droit humanitaire établi par* M. *Theo van Boven en application de la décision 1995/171 de la Sous-commission (des Nations Unies) de la lutte contre les mesures discriminatoires et de la protection des minorités,* Doc. NU E/CN.4/Sub.2/1996/17, p. 4, §7. Ces principes ont été dégagés sur base d'une étude menée par M. Theo van Boven (Rapporteur spécial de la Sous-commission), *Étude concernant le droit à la restitution, compensation et réhabilitation des victimes des violations graves des droits de l'homme et des libertés fondamentales,* Doc. NU, E/CN.4/sub.2/1996/17.

[41] Amnesty International, *supra* note 13 à la p. 15.

[42] *Ibid.* à la p. 35.

[43] Voir *supra* note 11.

II FONDEMENT JURIDIQUE DE LA PARTICIPATION DES INSTITUTIONS JUDICIAIRES TRADITIONNELLES ET COMMUNAUTAIRES DANS LA RÉPRESSION DES CRIMES INTERNATIONAUX

Avant de discuter de l'éventuel rôle judiciaire que les juridictions traditionnelles et communautaires peuvent jouer dans ce domaine précis de l'administration de la justice pénale internationale, il importe de savoir si le droit international peut, dans une certaine mesure, servir de base juridique à l'intervention de ces institutions dans la répression des crimes internationaux. D'entrée de jeu, il sied de noter que les État sont habilités, voire même obligés, en vertu du droit international conventionnel, à traduire en justice devant leurs juridictions, les personnes suspectées d'avoir commis les crimes internationaux les plus graves. Ainsi, en matière de crimes de guerre, les Conventions de Genève stipulent:

> Les Hautes Parties contractantes s'engagent à prendre toute mesure législative nécessaire pour fixer les sanctions pénales adéquates à appliquer aux personnes ayant commis, ou donné l'ordre de commettre, l'une ou l'autre des infractions graves à la présente Convention définies à l'article suivant.
> Chaque Partie contractante aura l'obligation de rechercher les personnes prévenues d'avoir commis, ou d'avoir ordonné de commettre, l'une ou l'autre de ces infractions graves, et elle devra les déférer à ses propres tribunaux, quelle que soit leur nationalité. Elle pourra aussi, si elle le préfère, et selon les conditions prévues par sa propre législation, les remettre pour jugement à une autre Partie contractante intéressée à la poursuite, pour autant que cette Partie contractante ait retenu contre lesdites personnes des charges suffisantes.[44]

En matière de génocide, l'art. V de la Convention sur le génocide prescrit que les personnes accusées de génocide ou de l'un quelconque des autres actes énumérés à l'article III seront traduites

---

[44] Voir *Convention de Genève pour l'amélioration du sort des blessés et des malades dans les forces armées en campagne*, RTNU, 1950, n° 970 à la p. 32, art. 49 (ci-après Convention de Genève I); *Convention de Genève pour l'amélioration du sort des blessés, des malades et des naufragés des forces armées sur mer*, RTNU, 1950, vol. 971 à la p. 86, art. 50 (ci-après Convention de Genève II); *Convention de Genève relative au traitement des prisonniers de guerre*, RTNU, 1950, n° 972 à la p. 136, art. 129 (ci-après Convention de Genève III); *Convention de Genève relative à la protection des personnes civiles en temps de guerre*, RTNU, 1950, n° 973 à la p. 288, art. 146 (ci-après Convention de Genève IV); *Protocole additionnel aux Conventions de Genève du 12 août 1949 relatif à la protection des victimes des conflits armés internationaux*, RTNU, 1979, n° 17512 à la p. 271, art. 85 (ci-après Protocole I). Ces textes peuvent être consultés en ligne sur le site du CICR: http://www.icrc.org/ihl.

devant les tribunaux compétents de l'État sur le territoire duquel l'acte a été commis. De même, dans les *Principes de coopération internationale en ce qui concerne le dépistage, l'arrestation, l'extradition et le châtiment des individus coupables de crimes de guerre et de crimes contre l'humanité*,[45] il est stipulé: "Les individus contre lesquels il existe des preuves établissant qu'ils ont commis des crimes de guerre et des crimes contre l'humanité doivent être traduits en justice et, s'ils sont reconnus coupables, châtiés, en règle générale, dans les pays où ils ont commis ces crimes."[46]

Bien que ce texte ne soit pas, de par sa nature elle-même, un instrument juridique contraignant vis-à-vis des États, la jurisprudence belge[47] et française[48] estime que cette résolution emporte une force obligatoire. Les tribunaux belges et français se fondent à cet effet sur la formulation normative ("doivent") de l'art. 1er de cette résolution 3074 (XXVIII) qui consacre une pratique où les États montrent qu'ils ont le sentiment de se conformer à ce qui équivaut à une règle juridique.[49] Ce faisant, cette jurisprudence confirme une évolution positive du droit qui confère un caractère coutumier à cette résolution avec pour effet qu'elle s'impose désormais à tous les États, en dépit néanmoins du fait que normalement une résolution soit en principe dénuée de force obligatoire.[50]

---

[45] *Principes de coopération internationale en ce qui concerne le dépistage, l'arrestation et le châtiment des individus coupables de crimes de guerre et de crimes contre l'humanité*, 3 décembre 1973, Doc. NU, A/RES 3074 (XXVIII).

[46] *Ibid.*, Doc. NU, A/RES 3074 (XXVIII), principe 5.

[47] Le juge d'instruction belge Vandermeersch considère "... qu'il existe une règle coutumière du droit des gens, voire du *jus cogens*, reconnaissant la compétence universelle et autorisant les autorités étatiques nationales à poursuivre et à traduire en justice, en toutes circonstances, les personnes soupçonnées de crimes contre l'humanité." Voir Tribunal de première instance (Bruxelles), juge d'instruction, Ordonnance n° 216/98, (1999) 2 Rev. dr. pén. et crim. 286 à la p. 288.

[48] Voir Affaire *Javor et autres*, résumée dans M. Sassoli et A.A. Bouvier, *How does law protect in war? Cases, documents and teaching materials on contemporary practice in international humanitarian law*, Genève, CICR, 1999 à la p. 1252 et s. Dans cette affaire, le juge d'instruction Getti soutient que "... contrairement à ce qui est soutenu par le ministère public, les principes de coopération internationale concernant le dépistage et le châtiment, notamment, des individus coupables de crimes de guerre, ont bien la force obligatoire et l'effet direct d'un texte conventionnel."

[49] Ordonnance n° 216/98, *supra* note 47 à la p. 288.

[50] Il faut noter par ailleurs que cette jurisprudence relative à la force obligatoire de cette résolution peut trouver un fondement solide dans l'avis de la CIJ sur la

En outre, le Statut de Rome instituant la Cour pénale internationale (CPI) accorde une priorité juridictionnelle aux États dans
la répression des crimes qu'il prohibe. C'est le sens qu'il convient
de donner au principe fondamental de la complémentarité de la
CPI par rapport aux juridictions étatiques.[51]

À travers ces quelques instruments internationaux, on se rend
aisément compte que les juridictions étatiques ont un fondement
juridique solide en droit international pour réprimer les crimes
internationaux, que ceux-ci aient été commis sur le territoire étatique[52] ou à l'étranger.[53] En outre, on constate que le droit international n'opère pas de distinction quant aux ordres juridictionnels
en vigueur dans un État donné, c'est-à-dire qu'il ne recommande
pas les tribunaux classiques au détriment des tribunaux traditionnels ou communautaires — là où ils existent — ou vice-versa. Ce qui

---

Licéité de la menace ou de l'emploi d'armes nucléaires. Dans cet avis, la CIJ a estimé
que "les résolutions de l'Assemblée générale, même si elles n'ont pas force
obligatoire, peuvent parfois avoir une valeur normative. Elles peuvent, dans certaines circonstances, fournir des éléments de preuve importants pour établir
l'existence d'une règle ou l'émergence d'une *opinio juris.* Pour savoir si cela est
vrai d'une résolution donnée de l'Assemblée générale, il faut en examiner le
contenu ainsi que les conditions d'adoption; il faut en outre vérifier s'il existe
une *opinio juris* quant à son caractère normatif," Affaire de la *Licéité de la menace
ou de l'emploi d'armes nucléaires,* CIJ, Avis consultatif, 8 juillet 1996 au par. 70.

[51] Statut de la CPI, *supra* note 2, art. 1er.

[52] Elles le feraient en vertu de la compétence territoriale car, comme le dit C. Beccaria, un des fervents défenseurs du principe de la territorialité, "le lieu du
châtiment ne peut être que le lieu du délit, attendu que c'est là et non ailleurs
qu'existe l'obligation de sévir contre un particulier pour défendre le bien public." Voir C. Beccaria, *Des délits et des peines,* Genève, Droz 1965, c. XXIX à la
p. 55. (Paru en 1766 en italien sous le titre *Dei delitti e delle pene,* cet ouvrage a été
traduit en français par Maurice Chevalier en 1965).

[53] Elles agiraient en vertu des principes de la personnalité ou de l'universalité
selon que l'auteur ou la victime du crime est un national de l'État poursuivant
ou non. Sur ces principes de compétence juridictionnelle, voir notamment
M. Henzelin, *Le principe de l'universalité en droit pénal international. Droit et obligation
pour les États de poursuivre et juger selon le principe de l'universalité,* Genève, Helbing
& Lichtenhahn, Faculté de droit de Genève, 2000 à la p.123; voir également
United States c. *Yunis,* District Court, DC, 12 février 1988, dans ILR, 1990, vol. 82
aux pp. 347-50 et 353. Signalons à toutes fins utiles que l'exercice de la compétence universelle est désormais soumis à l'arrêt *Yerodia* qui reconnaît l'immunité
juridictionnelle des Ministres des Affaires étrangères pour les crimes commis
pendant l'exercice de leurs fonctions; voir *Affaire du Mandat d'arrêt international*
(*République démocratique du Congo* c. *Belgique*), CIJ, arrêt du 12 février 2002; voir
en ligne: <http://www.icj-cij.org/cijwww/cdocket/cCOBE/cCOBEframe.htm>,
dernière visite: 15 octobre 2003.

est requis est une action étatique de telle sorte que les criminels de droit international présents sur son territoire ne jouissent pas d'une quelconque impunité. En conséquence, nous estimons que l'implication des juridictions communautaires et traditionnelles dans la répression des crimes internationaux trouve des assises juridiques en droit international. Néanmoins, si théoriquement ces institutions sont légalement fondées à participer à l'action répressive, nous doutons sérieusement de leur capacité potentielle, à moins d'un amendement substantiel de leurs bases légales nationales, de rendre une justice humanitaire qui serait reconnue comme telle par la communauté internationale au nom et pour le compte de laquelle la justice est rendue.[54]

III   ABSENCE DE CAPACITÉ OPÉRATIONNELLE DANS LE CHEF DES INSTITUTIONS JUDICIAIRES TRADITIONNELLES OU COMMUNAUTAIRES POUR ASSURER UNE RÉPRESSION ADÉQUATE DES CRIMES INTERNATIONAUX

Nous venons de voir que l'intervention des juridictions tradition-nelles et communautaires a de fortes assises en droit international, tout au moins théoriquement. Cependant, au regard de la brève analyse faite ci-dessus sur la notion même des juridictions coutu-mières et communautaires, de leur compétence inhérente et du droit applicable devant elles, on peut se demander si ces instances sont juridiquement et logistiquement outillées pour assurer une répression des crimes internationaux. De façon préliminaire et au regard de cette analyse, nous postulons d'emblée que les juges-citoyens des instances traditionnelles ne sont pas capables de réprimer et de juger les personnes responsables des crimes de droit international en raison de la nature de ces derniers (A), de la com-plexité du droit applicable (B), de la qualité des juges (C) et du

---

[54] Le *Committee on International Human Rights Law and Practice* de l'*International Law Association* soutient par exemple, dans son rapport de 2000, que "domestic courts and prosecutors bringing the perpetrators to justice are not acting on behalf of their own domestic legal system but on behalf of the international legal order." Voir International Law Association, Conférence annuelle, Londres, 2000. Voir également l'arrêt *Demjanjuk*: "The underlying assumption is that the crimes are offenses against the law of nations or against humanity and the pros-ecuting nation is acting for all nations. This being so, Israel or any other nation regardless of its status in 1942 or 1943, may undertake to vindicate the interest of all nations by seeking to punish the perpetrators of such crime," *Demjanjuk* c. *Petrovsky*, 776F. 2D 571, US Court of Appeal, 6th circuit, 31 Octobre 1985, publié dans A.J.I.L., vol. 80, 1986 aux pp. 656-58.

non-respect de certaines normes juridiques internationales relatives à un procès équitable (D).

Les juridictions locales, là où elles existent, ont généralement une compétence civile et gracieuse qui consiste dans la conciliation des parties.[55] Dans beaucoup de pays, il ne leur est pas reconnu une compétence pénale, sauf pour les infractions mineures. En Afrique du sud par exemple,

[C]hiefs' and headmen's courts have criminal jurisdiction over statutory offences, offences under the common law or customary law offences except those specified under the third Schedule of the Black Administration Act. The excluded offences are mainly the more serious offences such as treason, sedition, murder, culpable homicide, rape, arson, robbery. However, the list includes less serious offences but whose elements may be difficult to prove such as indecent assault, receiving stolen property knowing it to have been stolen and breaking and entering any premises with intent to commit a crime.[56]

Or, les crimes dont il est question dans cet article ne sont pas des infractions mineures mais sont plutôt les crimes des crimes.[57] Par conséquent, ces infractions ne rentrent pas dans le cadre de la compétence naturelle et traditionnelle des institutions judiciaires locales telle qu'exposée.[58] Ce sont au demeurant des infractions dont la qualification n'est pas très aisée même pour les professionnels du droit général en ce sens qu'elle fait appel à des connaissances et à une expérience juridiques poussées et spécialisées qui font évidemment défaut chez les juges traditionnels.[59] Il serait donc très hasardeux d'étendre la compétence *ratione materiae* des juges coutumiers sans aucune formation juridique pour embrasser les crimes de droit international.

---

[55] Ci-dessus, aux pp. 57-58.

[56] South African Law Commission, *supra* note 21 au par. 6.5.1.

[57] S'agissant du génocide, voir à cet effet les affaires *Procureur c. Kambanda* (1998), Affaire ICTR-97-23-S (TPIR, Chambre de première instance I), Sentence, par. 10-16; *Procureur c. Akayesu* (1998), Affaire ICTR-96-4-T (TPIR, Chambre de première instance I), Sentence, par. 11.

[58] Voir ci-dessus, aux pp. 57-58.

[59] Par exemple, la qualification de l'infraction de génocide n'est pas un exercice facile en ce sens qu'elle exige la détermination du *dolus specialis* juridiquement requis pour conclure à son existence. Voir jugement *Kambanda, supra* note 57 au par. 16; aussi *Procureur c. Akayesu* (1998), affaire ICTR-96-4-T, (TPIR, Chambre de première instance I), jugement, par. 498.

B   LA COMPLEXITÉ DU DROIT APPLICABLE

Le droit applicable aux crimes de droit international est, même devant les tribunaux internes, sans nul doute inspiré du droit pénal international, branche dont originairement relèvent les crimes en question. Or, de manière générale, les instances judiciaires traditionnelles ou communautaires appliquent, là où elles fonctionnent toujours, des lois non écrites qui s'imposent dans les rapports sociaux au titre des coutumes. Le rapport de la *South African Law Commission* conforte cette position: "[T]raditional courts apply customary law. Chiefs' and headmen's courts have no jurisdiction to hear cases arising out of common law. This should continue to be the case since *judicial officers not trained in the common law would cause a travesty of justice if they attempted to apply it.*"[60] En nous appuyant sur cet exemple sud-africain, nous soutenons que les institutions judiciaires traditionnelles ou communautaires ne peuvent pas administrer une justice pénale internationale en raison des connaissances juridiques limitées des juges-citoyens. En effet, si ceux-ci maîtrisent les coutumes locales, force nous est malheureusement de faire constater que les crimes internationaux ne peuvent pas être jugés sur cette base juridique coutumière. La coutume qui peut éventuellement être de mise est d'une autre nature: il s'agit de la coutume internationale. Or, nous pouvons prendre le risque d'affirmer que cette source du droit reste fondamentalement inconnue dans les communautés locales traditionnelles. Ainsi, les juges-citoyens ne peuvent pas passer le test de la compétence qui est une exigence légale chez toute personne appelée à rendre justice.[61]

C   LA DOUBLE QUALITÉ DES JUGES

Dans les procédures judiciaires traditionnelles, les juges interviennent à la fois comme juge et partie au procès. Ils accusent et

---

[60] South African Law Commission, *supra* note 21 à la p. 29, par. 6.3.1 (notre emphase).

[61] "[L]es personnes sélectionnées pour remplir les fonctions de magistrat doivent être intègres et compétentes et justifier d'une formation et de qualifications juridiques suffisantes." Voir *Principes fondamentaux relatifs à l'indépendance de la magistrature*, adoptés par le septième Congrès des Nations Unies pour la prévention du crime et le traitement des délinquants qui s'est tenu à Milan du 26 août au 6 septembre 1985 et confirmés par l'Assemblée générale dans ses résolutions 40/32 du 29 novembre 1985 et 40/146 du 13 décembre 1985, principe 10. Il faut noter que ces principes ont été établis pour les juges de carrière, "mais ils s'appliquent aussi, le cas échéant, aux juges non professionnels." Voir *ibid.*, préambule au par. 10.

jugent les parties. Sous cet angle, leur intervention au titre de juge et procureur porte en elle-même les germes d'injustice surtout dans une situation où sévissent toujours des tensions politiques et/ou ethniques comme au Rwanda et où les gens qui jugent représentent en grande majorité ou même en apparence une ethnie et/ou une tendance politique rivale des autres.[62] En effet, le risque est grand d'assister à une justice inéquitable et populaire synonyme de vengeance. Ainsi, cette situation juridique est inacceptable sur le plan international car elle consacre une atteinte au principe sacro-saint de la séparation des pouvoirs et à celui du droit d'un accusé à un procès juste et équitable.

D   LE NON-RESPECT DE CERTAINES NORMES JURIDIQUES
       INTERNATIONALES RELATIVES À UN PROCÈS ÉQUITABLE

Dans la plupart des cas, les procédures pénales devant les juridictions traditionnelles et communautaires se déroulent au mépris des garanties juridiques internationalement reconnues. Tantôt les justiciables sont à la merci des juges qui accusent et jugent en même temps sans aucune assistance légale, tantôt ces derniers recourent à des procédures et à des sanctions qui constituent des violations graves des droits fondamentaux de la personne.

*1   L'absence de représentation légale devant les juridictions
       traditionnelles et communautaires*

L'octroi aux juridictions traditionnelles d'une compétence pour juger les crimes internationaux est manifestement incompatible avec l'absence de représentation légale qui caractérise les systèmes judiciaires traditionnels et communautaires.[63] Cette lacune pose des questions importantes d'ordre constitutionnel dans la mesure où les constitutions de la plupart des pays reconnaissent le droit à un avocat dans toute procédure judiciaire. En outre, cette omission heurte profondément une protection fondamentale de la personne humaine à savoir le droit à un avocat considéré comme un élément

---

[62] Au Rwanda par exemple, l'appareil judiciaire est dominé par les Tutsi et le Front patriotique rwandais (FPR) vainqueur de la guerre de 1994. Il est vu et en fait agit comme un organe étatique destiné à juger uniquement les Hutu et à protéger les intérêts des Tutsi au détriment de ceux des autres groupes ethniques. Ce que le Prof. Cousineau appelle la "tutsification" du système judiciaire; voir M. Cousineau, "L'établissement de l'État de droit au Rwanda: un but irréalisable" (1996-1997) R.D. Ottawa 83.

[63] Voir ci-dessus, aux pp. 59-60.

important du droit à un procès équitable.[64] La communauté internationale pour le compte de laquelle la justice est rendue tolérerait difficilement une entorse juridique d'une telle gravité. Ainsi, le droit à un avocat s'impose en droit pénal international[65] où les suspects font face à des accusations graves qui, une fois juridiquement prouvées et judiciairement établies, emportent pour les accusés une sanction pénale conséquente qui tient compte de la gravité des crimes. Dans cette hypothèse, il serait impensable d'envisager des poursuites devant une institution qui ne reconnaît pas aux accusés le droit à une assistance juridique alors qu'ils courent le risque de sanction pénale grave comme l'emprisonnement à vie voire même la peine de mort dans les pays non abolitionnistes. La seule intégrité morale ou la sagesse des juges ne suffit pas pour garantir un procès juste et équitable étant donné la complexité des crimes internationaux quant à leur nature et au droit applicable.

2   *Des sanctions et des moyens de preuve inadmissibles au regard du droit pénal international*

Dans certains pays, les sanctions pénales susceptibles d'être prononcées par les tribunaux traditionnels sont très critiquables sous l'angle du droit international. C'est le cas du dédommagement matrimonial qui implique la remise d'une femme ou d'une fille en mariage en guise de compensation d'un tort subi et ce, en l'absence de tout consentement de ces dernières. C'est également le cas des châtiments consistant en viols collectifs et punitifs ou en atteintes à l'intégrité physique des individus.[66] De même, le recours à la torture pour réunir la preuve de culpabilité est contraire aux

---

[64] Sur l'importance de l'avocat dans une procédure judiciaire, voir Hon. J. Lachapelle et W.A. Schabas, *Pour un système de justice au Rwanda*, Rapport révisé d'une mission exploratoire effectuée au Rwanda du 27 novembre au 6 décembre 1994, Montréal, Centre international des droits de la personne et du développement démocratique, 1994 à la p. 16.

[65] Il faut noter que le droit pénal international reconnaît cette garantie judiciaire pour toute personne accusée de crimes internationaux: "En toutes circonstances, les inculpés bénéficieront de garanties de procédure et de libre défense qui ne seront pas inférieures à celles prévues par les articles 105 et suivants de la Convention de Genève relative au traitement des prisonniers de guerre du 12 août 1949." Voir Convention de Genève I, art. 49, par. 4; Convention de Genève II, art. 50, par. 4; Convention de Genève III, art. 129, par. 4; Convention de Genève IV, art. 146, par. 4.

[66] Ci-dessus, aux pp. 58-59.

droits de la personne.[67] Toutes ces lacunes n'autorisent donc que l'on puisse tolérer l'implication des fora judiciaires traditionnels dans l'administration d'une justice rendue au nom de l'humanité.

En bref, pour toutes ces raisons exposées ci-dessus, permettre des poursuites pénales pour crimes internationaux devant des juridictions traditionnelles manifestement incapables de s'acquitter de cette lourde responsabilité équivaudrait à tolérer des parodies judiciaires ainsi qu'une banalisation des crimes inacceptable aux yeux de la communauté internationale. Il serait ainsi difficile d'invoquer l'argument tiré du principe de la priorité juridictionnelle des tribunaux étatiques si la Cour pénale internationale décide par exemple de poursuivre et de juger un suspect criminel international en vertu du principe de la complémentarité.

Dès lors, devons-nous conclure à l'exclusion totale des instances judiciaires traditionnelles ou de la population dans tout processus de répression nationale des crimes internationaux? En dépit de nos inquiétudes exprimées ci-dessus, nous pensons que les juridictions traditionnelles et communautaires peuvent, dans une certaine mesure, se voir attribuer une compétence judiciaire limitée tandis que la population peut jouer un rôle quasi judiciaire dans le processus. Une telle implication active se justifie notamment par l'ampleur de la criminalité internationale mais aussi par une préoccupation grandissante sur le sort et la place des victimes dans un procès pénal[68] ainsi que l'objectif de dissuasion et de réconciliation nationale poursuivi par la justice pénale internationale, que celle-ci soit rendue devant les juridictions internationales ou nationales.

IV   COMPÉTENCES JUDICIAIRES DES INSTITUTIONS
      TRADITIONNELLES ET COMMUNAUTAIRES EN MATIÈRE
      DE CRIMES INTERNATIONAUX

Il a été démontré que les juridictions traditionnelles et communautaires assument un rôle judiciaire important afin de maintenir l'ordre et promouvoir la réconciliation au sein d'une communauté.[69] Face à une criminalité internationale de grande ampleur et qui souvent dépasse les capacités du système judiciaire classique, il y a lieu de se demander si on ne pourrait pas capitaliser sur l'expérience de ces institutions de façon à les impliquer, d'une manière

---

[67] Ci-dessus, à la p. 59.

[68] Voir *supra* note 40.

[69] Ci-dessus, à la p. 57.

ou d'une autre, dans la lutte contre l'impunité qui risque de se généraliser. Notre conclusion préliminaire est qu'il est toujours possible, voire même souhaitable, de tirer avantage de cette expérience des juges-citoyens, notamment en leur reconnaissant explicitement la compétence de juger les infractions mineures commises à l'occasion de la perpétration des crimes internationaux, en l'occurrence celles contre les propriétés (A) ou en les impliquant dans un système de jury (B).

A   RÉPRESSION DES INFRACTIONS MINEURES COMMISES À
    L'OCCASION DE LA PERPÉTRATION DES CRIMES
    INTERNATIONAUX

Si nous nous avons été très critique vis-à-vis de l'implication des institutions traditionnelles et communautaires dans la répression des crimes internationaux principalement en raison de la complexité du droit applicable et de la nature exceptionnelle des crimes, notre position reste vulnérable pour ce qui est des infractions mineures, en l'occurrence celles exclusivement dirigées contre les propriétés. En effet, même si ces infractions sont commises à l'occasion de la perpétration des crimes internationaux comme le génocide, elles sont par nature très proches des délits relevant de la compétence inhérente des institutions judiciaires traditionnelles et communautaires.[70] À ce titre, nous ne voyons pas d'inconvénient à ce que les mêmes juridictions puissent connaître de ces infractions dans le but de prononcer des peines relatives à l'indemnisation des victimes.[71] De cette façon, la charge judiciaire des tribunaux spécialisés serait considérablement allégée étant donné que ces infractions sont parfois les plus nombreuses, ce qui leur permettrait d'assurer la célérité de la justice dans les autres affaires beaucoup plus graves impliquant notamment des crimes de sang.[72] De même,

---

[70] Ci-dessus, aux pp. 57-58.

[71] Les tribunaux ordinaires internes prononcent, à l'encontre des personnes reconnues responsables de ces infractions, des peines pécuniaires, sous forme d'amendes ou d'indemnités de compensation pour les victimes. Donc, même au niveau de la peine, il n'y a pas de grande différence entre les deux systèmes pénaux.

[72] La South African Law Commission soutient que "if magistrates' courts are not to be overwhelmed, that at least some minor offences continue to be within the jurisdiction of the traditional leaders' courts while the more serious are excluded from such courts and left to be administered by magistrates' courts or higher," Voir South African Law Commission, *supra* note 21 au par. 6.6.3.

la compensation par voie de restitution de biens ou de réparation par équivalent est facile et rapide au sein d'une même communauté de vie, ce qui favorise l'harmonie sociale et la réconciliation nationale, autres objectifs importants que poursuit la justice pénale pour crimes internationaux.

Un autre atout important de cette solution est d'ordre institutionnel: si on reconnaît aux juges populaires une compétence pour les infractions mineures comme celles contre les biens, le système judiciaire traditionnel reste intact et n'est en aucune manière dénaturé comme cela résulterait de l'implication totale des tribunaux traditionnels dans la répression des infractions internationales. En effet, sous peine de déséquilibre social important, il faudrait éviter, autant que faire se peut, toute dénaturation d'un système judiciaire qui s'est construit au fur des ans, non sans quelques casses parfois, et qui se transmet de génération en génération. Ainsi, toute volonté politique visant la 'modernisation' et le 'développement' brusques des institutions coutumières, notamment en leur octroyant des tâches qui dépassent de loin leurs capacités et leurs compétences intellectuelles, matérielles et logistiques comme c'est le cas au Rwanda, produirait des effets pervers tant en défaveur des citoyens que de tout le système. À notre sens, permettre aux juridictions coutumières de poursuivre et de juger les personnes présumées responsables de crimes internationaux serait, d'une part, contribuer à créer une grande insécurité juridique inacceptable chez de paisibles citoyens en ce sens qu'elles ne constituent pas un forum judiciaire naturel qui peut offrir des garanties d'un procès équitable pour des accusations d'une telle gravité. D'autre part, les doter d'une telle compétence exorbitante dont elles ne sont pratiquement pas outillées à exercer serait augmenter considérablement le risque de dépréciation des institutions coutumières réputées avant-gardistes de l'harmonie sociale, sous peine de précipiter leur dissolution.

Par ailleurs, il est impérieux de bannir certaines procédures ou certains châtiments dégradants et inhumains incompatibles avec les normes internationales relatives à un procès équitable. De même, il faudrait revoir la composition sexiste des sièges des juridictions traditionnelles pour donner une place active et significative aux femmes. Il est en effet insoutenable de prétendre que la droiture, le sens de l'équité ainsi que la connaissance des coutumes soit l'apanage des seuls hommes. Nous pouvons relever et saluer l'exemple du Rwanda où le système judiciaire traditionnel *Gacaca* rénové comporte des femmes juges en son sein. À notre avis, il n'en devrait pas être autrement étant donné la situation et le rôle actuels des femmes dans la société rwandaise d'aujourd'hui. En effet, ces dernières sont largement majoritaires sur les collines, étant donné que la plupart des hommes sont morts ou sont emprisonnés pour crimes en rapport avec la tragédie de 1994, ce qui fait d'elles de véritables chefs de familles dans la plupart des ménages. Cette situation en fait également des témoins privilégiés. En outre, l'ampleur des crimes, en l'occurrence ceux à caractère sexuel[73] ou ceux commis par des enfants mineurs, milite en faveur de la participation des femmes dans le processus.

Enfin, il est fondamental que les juridictions soient assistées, dans l'accomplissement de leurs nouvelles attributions, par un corps de gens dotés d'une formation juridique en droit coutumier et en droit de preuve et de la procédure. Nous estimons que la proposition que la South African Law Commission fait pour les tribunaux coutumiers sud-africains[74] vaut également, *mutatis mutandis,* pour toutes les autres situations similaires. Ces assistants tiendraient notamment le registre des décisions prises dont ils auraient dressé des rapports synthétiques d'audiences.

B   PARTICIPATION DANS UN SYSTÈME DE JURY

En plus de la compétence en matière d'infractions mineures, les juges-citoyens peuvent être impliqués dans l'administration de la justice internationale comme membres d'un jury. En effet, le système de jury en vigueur dans plusieurs États[75] permet d'associer, dans un procès pénal pour des crimes d'une certaine gravité, des juges professionnels et des personnes reconnues pour leur intégrité, leur moralité, leur droiture et leur probité. Le rôle des juges professionnels est d'éclairer le jury sur les prescriptions légales

[73] Voir à cet effet Human Rights Watch, *Shattered lives: Sexual Violence during the Rwandan Genocide and its Aftermath,* Washington, DC, 1996.

[74] "[T]rained para-legals should be appointed by the Ministry of Justice to assist traditional courts as clerks of court. This would help the courts to assess and avoid decisions that might be in violation of the Constitution or the law or that are beyond the jurisdiction of the court." Voir South African Law Commission, *supra* note 21 au par. 5.7.

[75] Au Canada, en vertu de l'art. 471 du Code criminel, le procès devant un jury est un principe obligatoire en matière criminelle, à moins que le procureur et l'accusé consentent à la renonciation de ce droit pour certaines catégories d'infractions, notamment celles prévues à l'art. 469. Voici son prescrit: *"Sauf disposition expressément contraire de la loi, tout prévenu inculpé d'un acte criminel doit être jugé par un tribunal composé d'un juge et d'un jury."*

pertinentes, leur contenu ainsi que la fixation de la peine en cas de condamnation. Les 'juges de circonstance' sont, quant à eux, compétents pour se prononcer sur la culpabilité ou l'innocence des accusés. Étant donné que les juges-citoyens des juridictions traditionnelles sont déjà familiarisés à la profession d'administrer et de rendre la justice, leur nomination comme membres de jury dans des affaires relatives aux poursuites pour crimes internationaux serait souhaitable.

Au Rwanda par exemple, au lieu de laisser le processus entre les mains des juges-citoyens opérant dans le cadre des juridictions *Gacaca,* il est recommandable de mettre en place un système de jury dans le jugement des personnes responsables des crimes internationaux.[76] À notre sens, c'est à travers l'institution d'un tel système qu'il faudrait encore mettre à contribution l'expérience des anciens juges des chambres spécialisées qui avaient déjà acquis une expérience dans le traitement des dossiers de génocide. Ainsi, ceux-là agiraient comme des magistrats professionnels à côté des juges-citoyens ayant la charge de déterminer la culpabilité ou l'innocence de l'accusé.

Par conséquent, avec l'assistance et sous la supervision éclairée d'un ou des magistrats professionnels, les juges-citoyens peuvent ainsi participer directement à l'administration interne de la justice pénale internationale. La population peut également intervenir mais cette intervention est d'une autre nature: elle est quasi judiciaire.

V INTERVENTION QUASI JUDICIAIRE DE LA POPULATION

Un regard rétrospectif sur la plupart des conflits armés et autres violences massives de ces dernières années révèle une implication directe et active de la population dans la perpétration des génocides, des crimes contre l'humanité et des crimes de guerre (ex.: Rwanda, Burundi, etc.). À l'inverse, la commission de ces crimes fait également de la population civile la première victime, tout au moins sur le plan du nombre.[77] Aujourd'hui, rien ne semble clairement indiquer un quelconque changement de cibles et d'acteurs

---

[76] Le Prof. C. Ntampaka est également de cet avis; voir Ntampaka, *supra* note 13.

[77] Selon Bassiouni, "Since World War II alone, it is estimated that more than 250 conflicts of non-international character, internal conflicts and tyrannical regime victimization have occured. These post-World War II situations have resulted in an estimated 86 million casualties." Voir M.C. Bassiouni, "The need for international accountability" dans *Enforcement, supra* note 12 à la p. 4.

pour les conflits de demain. Outre l'implication de la population en tant qu'auteur ou victime des crimes internationaux, il est à signaler que ces derniers sont généralement commis sous ses yeux. Dès lors, la population peut être appelée à jouer un rôle de premier plan dans la recherche de la vérité historique (A) et dans la manifestation de la vérité judiciaire (B).

A RECHERCHE DE LA VÉRITÉ HISTORIQUE

Tout comme les institutions traditionnelles et communautaires, la population en tant que telle n'est pas juridiquement outillée pour administrer la justice dans des affaires complexes de génocide, de crimes contre l'humanité et de crimes de guerre. Sa contribution reste cependant indispensable dans la révélation de ce qui s'est passé afin de connaître la vérité sur certains faits autour desquels on entretient souvent des mystères. Ainsi, la population peut intervenir dans le cadre des Commissions Vérité et Réconciliation (CVR) qui sont souvent complémentaires au processus de responsabilisation judiciaire qui aboutit généralement à des condamnations pénales.[78] La connaissance de la vérité peut servir à des fins pédagogiques afin de prévenir une récurrence d'autres événements malheureux. Ceci a été fait en Afrique du Sud avec la fameuse *Truth and Reconciliation Commission* ainsi que dans certains pays d'Amérique du Sud comme l'Argentine et le Chili. Le principal objectif de ces commissions "is to reveal the facts of human rights violations under the previous regime. They explicitly do not have the objective of adjudication, but of reconciliation after the facts have been revealed."[79] De telles institutions ont donc pour mission

---

[78] Monseigneur Desmond Tutu, président de la *Truth and Reconciliation Commission* en Afrique du Sud soutient le caractère complémentaire de cette institution quand il dit que "it is just a small part of a process in which the whole nation must be engaged," propos cités par P. R. Baehr, 'How to deal with the past,' in C. Joyner et M.C. Bassiouni (eds.), *Reining in impunity for international crimes and serious violations of fundamental human rights: proceedings of the Siracusa conference,* Toulouse, Ères, 17-21 Septembre 1998, à la p. 424. Le Secrétaire général des Nations unies soutient aussi que "[L]a vérité et la réconciliation ne sauraient toutefois se substituer à la mise en cause devant la justice des responsabilités individuelles," voir *Rapport du Secrétaire général au Conseil de sécurité sur la protection des civils dans les conflits armés,* DOC. ONU S/2001/331, 30 mars 2001 au par. 13. Pour une analyse de certains mécanismes complémentaires aux poursuites pénales, voir notamment L. Olson, "Mechanisms complementing prosecution," 84 (2002) 845 RICR à la p. 173.

[79] Baehr, *supra* note 78 à la p. 424.

d'enregistrer les actes regrettables du passé afin d'éviter qu'ils ne se reproduisent. Ce genre de forum est important en ce sens qu'il permet aux victimes de rencontrer indirectement leurs bourreaux et d'accorder pardon à ceux qui reconnaissent leurs forfaits et le demandent explicitement.

On doit par ailleurs signaler qu'à côté de la réconciliation qu'une CVR est capable de faciliter, l'autre objectif important d'une telle commission est la reconnaissance officielle d'un passé douloureux que l'on voudrait conjurer et dont on voudrait prévenir la réédition.[80] De même, en plus de la constitution des archives de l'histoire, une CVR peut recueillir des éléments susceptibles d'être utilisés dans l'administration de la preuve devant une instance judiciaire.[81]

À notre sens, chaque État ayant connu des violences massives de l'ampleur d'un génocide, de crimes de guerre ou de crimes contre l'humanité devrait, parallèlement à un processus de répression, mettre en place une Commission Vérité et Réconciliation.[82] Celle-ci trouve un fondement juridique dans le droit inaliénable à la vérité reconnu aux peuples[83] et aux victimes[84] ainsi que dans leur devoir de mémoire.[85] En outre, les objectifs de prévention et de réconciliation sont nobles et le forum s'y prête bien. Monseigneur Tutu , Président de la Truth and Reconciliation Commission est à cet égard éloquent:

[T]here are some people who have tried to be very facile and let bygones be bygones: they want us to have a national amnesia. And you have to keep saying to those people that to pretend that nothing happened, not to acknowledge that something horrendous did happen to them, is to

---

[80] M. Baehr soutient que "the first and foremost task of the commission is to present the true facts, or rather to recognize those facts. After all, often the true facts are already well-known among the people involved, but they ask for an official recognition." Voir Baehr, *supra* note 78 à la p. 425.

[81] J.P. Biramvu, *Justice et lutte contre l'impunité au Rwanda: la poursuite des crimes de génocide et des crimes contre l'impunité*, en ligne: http://droit.Francophonie.org/acct/rfj/actu/08Biramv.htm, dernière visite: le 12 septembre 2003.

[82] Il nous faut néanmoins préciser que le pardon auquel aboutit généralement ce processus ne peut pas être accordé aux gens qui donnent leurs témoignages de la vérité factuelle mais dont les comportements ont été caractérisés par une gravité d'une grande ampleur qui les rangeraient dans la catégorie juridique de crimes internationaux sous examen dans cet article. En effet, comme le dit le Prof. H. Ascensio, la réconciliation pour ces crimes doit passer par des procès car "s'il n'y a pas de procès, il y a un passé qui ne passe pas." Voir l'intervention du Prof. Ascensio au colloque organisé à Limoges les 22-23 novembre 2001 et rapportée dans S. Gaboriau et H. Pauliat, *La justice pénale internationale*, Limoges, PULIM, 2002 à la p. 53.

victimise the victims yet again. But even more important, experience worldwide shows that if you do not deal with a dark past such as ours, effectively look the beast in the eye, that beast is not going to lie quietly. It is going, as sure as anything, to come back and haunt you horrendously. We are saying we need to deal with this past as quickly as possible—acknowledge that we have a disgraceful past—then close the door on it and concentrate on the present and the future. This is the purpose of the Commission it is just a small part of a process in which the whole nation must be engaged.[86]

B   MANIFESTATION DE LA VÉRITÉ JUDICIAIRE

À part la relation des faits à sa connaissance devant des Commissions Vérité et Réconciliation, la population peut intervenir directement devant les cours et tribunaux, au titre de témoins à charge ou à décharge. Cela est déjà une pratique courante dans tous les États en vertu du droit commun. En matière de poursuites internes des crimes de droit international, les témoignages gardent une place primordiale dans la découverte de la vérité judiciaire. Contrairement à l'Allemagne nazie où l'accusation a pu mettre la main sur une documentation impressionnante sur la planification et les moyens d'exécution des crimes odieux,[87] facilitant ainsi l'administration

[83] "Chaque peuple a le droit inaliénable de connaître la vérité sur les événements passés, ainsi que sur les circonstances et les raisons qui ont conduit, par la violation massive ou systématique des droits de l'homme, à la perpétration de crimes aberrants. L'exercice plein et effectif du droit à la vérité est essentiel pour éviter qu'à l'avenir les violations ne se reproduisent." Voir *Ensemble de principes pour la protection et la promotion des droits de l'homme par la lutte contre l'impunité*, annexé au *Rapport final révisé établi par M.L. Joinet, en application de la décision 1996/119 de la Sous-Commission*, adopté par la Commission des droits de l'homme (Sous-commission de la lutte contre les mesures discriminatoires et de la protection des minorités), Doc. NU E/CN.4/Sub.2/1997/20/Rev.1 du 2 octobre 1997, principe 1.

[84] *Ibid.* principe 3: "Indépendamment de toute action en justice, les victimes, ainsi que leurs familles et leurs proches, ont le droit imprescriptible de connaître la vérité sur les circonstances dans lesquelles ont été commises les violations et, en cas de décès ou de disparition, sur le sort qui a été réservé à la victime."

[85] *Ibid.* principe 2: "La connaissance par un peuple de l'histoire de son oppression appartient à son patrimoine et, comme telle, doit être préservée par des mesures appropriées au nom du devoir de mémoire qui incombe à l'État. Ces mesures ont pour but de préserver de l'oubli la mémoire collective, notamment pour se prémunir contre le développement de thèses révisionnistes et négationnistes."

[86] Baehr, *supra* note 78 aux pp. 423-24.

[87] Le gouvernement du 3ᵉ Reich tenait régulièrement les procès-verbaux des réunions où se planifiaient les crimes. Ces documents ont constitué une mine d'informations et de preuves à l'accusation.

de la preuve, il n'en va pas de même pour d'autres pays. Au Rwanda par exemple, on n'est pas encore parvenu, même au TPIR, à avoir des documents qui révéleraient l'existence d'un plan de génocide et de crimes contre l'humanité. Les bribes de renseignements à ce sujet proviennent essentiellement des très controversés aveux de culpabilité de M. Kambanda,[88] premier ministre d'alors, ainsi que du témoignage d'un agent Interahamwe livré au Général canadien Roméo Dallaire, Commandant en chef de la MINUAR. Dans ces circonstances, la preuve de culpabilité des accusés devient relativement difficile. Ainsi, les poursuites qui se sont déroulées devant le TPIR ou les chambres spécialisées dépendent énormément, pour ce qui est de l'administration de la preuve, des témoignages verbaux des personnes sous les yeux desquelles les crimes ont été commis ou celles qui en détiennent des informations par ouï-dire.[89]

Ainsi, dans tout processus interne de répression des crimes internationaux, la population devrait garder son statut habituel de témoin potentiel, à charge ou à décharge, qui découle de la procédure coutumière. En effet, comme elle assiste impuissamment à la perpétration des crimes, elle a un rôle judiciaire important dans l'administration des moyens de preuve. Cela constitue actuellement une réalité sur le plan des procédures internationales[90] ou nationales.[91]

---

[88] *Kambanda* c. *Procureur* (2000), Affaire n° ICTR-97-23-A (TPIR, Chambre d'appel), par. 10(3). L'accusé a invoqué comme motif d'appel que la Chambre de première instance "a accepté la validité de l'Accord de plaidoyer sans s'être assurée que l'aveu de culpabilité était volontaire, a été fait en toute connaissance de cause, était sans équivoque et reposait sur des faits propres à établir le crime et la participation de l'Appelant à sa commission compte tenu soit d'indices indépendants, soit de l'absence de tout désaccord fondamental entre les parties sur les faits de la cause."

[89] Voir notamment Ligue rwandaise pour la promotion et la défense des droits de l'homme (LIPRODHOR), *Problématique de la preuve dans les procès de génocide: l'institution imminente des juridictions Gacaca constitue-elle une panacée?*, Kigali, Centre de Documentation et d'Information sur les Procès de Génocide (CDIPG), juin 2000 à la p. 50.

[90] Les TPI *ad hoc* ont essentiellement recours aux témoignages des personnes privées, victimes ou pas, pour reconstituer la base factuelle de la vérité. Le procureur entend par exemple, à lui seul, appeler à la barre plus de 228 témoins et produire 500 documents dans l'affaire *Procureur* c. *Milosevic et autres*, affaire IT-99-37, TPIY, Conférence de mise en l'État (relativement à l'acte d'accusation du Kosovo), 30 Octobre 2001 et 250 témoins dans le dossier dit des militaires devant le TPIR (*Procureur* c. *Bagosora et autres*, affaire ICTR-98-41-T, TPIR, Chambre de première instance III).

[91] Devant les Chambres spécialisées, la LIPRODHOR affirme que 95 % de la preuve est obtenue par le biais de témoignages, voir LIPRODHOR, *supra* note 89.

VI CONCLUSION GÉNÉRALE

La justice pénale internationale, qu'elle soit rendue devant des juridictions internationales ou nationales, poursuit principalement deux objectifs majeurs: la dissuasion et la réconciliation nationale.[92] Or, la réalisation de ces deux objectifs ne peut pas être l'apanage des seuls spécialistes du droit intervenant dans le cadre des structures judiciaires ordinaires ou spécialisées. Les institutions judiciaires locales jouissant d'une renommée dans le maintien de l'harmonie sociale ont certainement un rôle complémentaire important à jouer dans tout le processus de dissuasion judiciaire et de réconciliation nationale. Elles peuvent intervenir pour juger les responsables des infractions mineures, en l'occurrence celles contre les propriétés mobilières ou immobilières, commises à l'occasion de la perpétration des crimes les plus effroyables qui portent atteinte à la conscience de toute l'humanité. À cet égard, elles suivraient une procédure simple orientée vers la restauration de la concorde sociale et fondée sur un système de sanctions qui visent le renforcement des rapports sociaux et la réconciliation nationale. Les juges-citoyens peuvent également intervenir dans le cadre d'un système de jury piloté par un ou des juges professionnels. Par contre, nous estimons que les juridictions traditionnelles et communautaires ne sont ni techniquement ni logistiquement outillées pour participer pleinement à l'œuvre répressive des crimes internationaux. Une telle incapacité découle de leur nature intrinsèque, de la gravité extrême des crimes internationaux dont il est question mais aussi de la nature particulièrement complexe du droit applicable.

S'agissant de la population en général, il est important de la faire participer dans le processus de redressement judiciaire d'une société déchirée, étant donné que les crimes se commettent souvent sous ses yeux par ses membres et contre ses membres. Son intervention devant une CVR permettrait de reconstituer la réalité historique d'un passé douloureux afin de bien baliser l'avenir. De même, par ses témoignages, la population joue et continuera à

---

[92] Voir la Résolution 955 (1994), *supra* note 2 qui énonce, au par. 7 de son préambule: "Convaincu que, dans les circonstances particulières qui règnent au Rwanda, des poursuites contre les personnes présumées responsables d'actes de génocide ou d'autres violations graves du droit international humanitaire permettraient d'atteindre cet objectif et contribueraient au processus de réconciliation nationale ainsi qu'au rétablissement et au maintien de la paix;" voir également M. de Bueule pour qui "la justice n'est pas un but en elle-même, mais un instrument de régulation de l'ordre dans la société;" voir de Bueule, *supra* note 1.

jouer un rôle important dans l'administration de la justice en cas de crimes internationaux. Il est évident que les témoignages influent beaucoup sur la découverte et la manifestation de la vérité judiciaire. À cet effet, il revient donc au procureur, à la défense et au juge qui interviennent dans un procès interne pour crimes internationaux de faire preuve de perspicacité pour juger de leur pertinence. Cette implication populaire a un grand effet pédagogique quant à l'importance et à la valeur des lois, en l'occurrence celles relatives à la dignité, à la liberté et à l'intégrité personnelles. Ce qui contribuerait à la promotion d'une culture du respect des lois et des droits de l'homme prélude à l'instauration de l'État de droit dans un pays donné.

Summary

Traditional Courts and International Criminal Justice

The extent of international crime and the resulting impunity forces the international community to develop new strategies in order to overcome this phenomenon. Although international criminal courts are often presented as a cure-all, we must acknowledge that state courts do intervene in order to assist the latter in the struggle against impunity. This article aims to examine the opportunities for intervention by traditional and community state courts in the administration of international criminal justice. Having established that there are grounds for state court intervention in international law, the author concludes that traditional courts are not equipped, legally or logistically, to control the most severe international crimes. However, in states where massive violence has occurred, in which the population was involved, the author believes that the latter as well as existing popular institutions can take part in the judicial resolution of the crisis in order to ensure greater efficiency in defining new neighbourhood principles. The judicial implication of traditional institutions is possible at two levels: the repression of minor offences, such as property offences occurring at the time of commission of heinous crimes that, on the one hand, offend the conscience of humanity as a whole, and on the other, require the involvement of citizen-judges as juries in the context of proceedings for international crimes as such. The population, per se, can be called upon to play a lead role in the search for historical truth and the demonstration of judicial truth.

Sommaire

Les juridictions traditionnelles et la justice pénale internationale

L'ampleur de la criminalité internationale et de l'impunité qui en résulte exige que la communauté internationale développe de nouvelles stratégies afin de venir à bout de ce phénomène. Bien que les juridictions pénales internationales soient souvent présentées comme une panacée, force est de constater que les juridictions étatiques interviennent pour leur prêter main forte dans la lutte contre l'impunité. Cet article se propose d'analyser l'opportunité de l'intervention des juridictions étatiques traditionnelles ou communautaires dans l'administration de la justice pénale internationale. Après avoir établi que leur intervention trouve des assises en droit international, l'auteur conclut que les juridictions traditionnelles ne sont pas juridiquement ni logistiquement outillées pour réprimer les crimes internationaux les plus graves. Néanmoins, dans les États où des violences massives ont eu lieu impliquant la participation de la population, l'auteur estime que celle-ci ainsi que les institutions populaires existantes peuvent être associées dans le règlement judiciaire de la crise afin de mieux définir de nouvelles bases de cohabitation sociale. L'implication judiciaire des institutions traditionnelles est envisageable à deux niveaux: la répression des infractions mineures, en l'occurrence celles contre les propriétés, qui sont commises à l'occasion de la perpétration des crimes odieux qui offensent la conscience de toute l'humanité d'une part, et, d'autre part, l'implication des juges-citoyens comme jurés dans le cadre des procès pour crimes internationaux proprement dits. La population quant à elle peut être appelée à jouer un rôle de premier plan dans la recherche de la vérité historique et dans la manifestation de la vérité judiciaire.

Overlaps and Conflicts of Jurisdiction between the World Trade Organization and Regional Trade Agreements

KYUNG KWAK AND GABRIELLE MARCEAU

Introduction

The relationship between the dispute settlement mechanism of the World Trade Organization (WTO) and that of regional trade agreements (RTAs) demonstrates the difficulties surrounding the issues of overlaps/conflicts of jurisdiction and of hierarchy of norms in international law.[1] Jurisdiction is often defined in terms of either legislative or judicial jurisdiction — that is, the authority to legislate or to adjudicate on a matter. Jurisdiction may be analyzed from horizontal points of view (the allocation of jurisdiction among states or among international organizations) and from a

Gabrielle Marceau, Ph.D., is counsellor in the Legal Affairs Division of the Secretariat to the World Trade Organization [hereinafter WTO] and Kyung Kwak is an associate of a law firm, Ashurst, in Brussels. The views expressed in this article are strictly personal to the authors and do not engage the WTO Secretariat or its members. We are grateful to John Kingery, Maria Pellini, Carmen Pont-Vieira, and Yves Renouf for their useful comments on earlier drafts. Mistakes are only our own.

[1] On the issue of jurisdiction generally and the relationship between the jurisdiction of the World Trade Organization [hereinafter WTO] and that of other treaties and institutions, see Joel Trachtman, "Institutional Linkages: Transcending 'Trade and ...'" (2002) 96(1) A.J.I.L 77. On the issue of universal jurisdiction, see the recent judgment of the International Court of Justice [hereinafter ICJ] in *Case Concerning the Arrest Warrant of 11 April 2000 (Democratic Republic of Congo v. Belgium)*, February 14, 2002. The full text of the judgment (including separate and dissenting opinions) is available at <www.icj-cji.org>.

vertical point of view (the allocation of jurisdiction between states and international organizations).[2]

This article addresses the issue of horizontal allocation of judicial jurisdiction between RTAs and the WTO, as expressed in the dispute settlement provisions of each treaty. The choice of a dispute settlement forum is often an expression of the importance that states give to the system of norms that may be enforced by the related dispute settlement mechanism. For instance, if the same states — which are parties to two treaties A and B that contain similar obligations — provide that priority or exclusivity is given to the dispute settlement mechanism of A over that of B, it may be that the states are expressing their choice to favour the enforcement of treaty A over treaty B.

In the case of RTAs, the situation is further complicated because the General Agreement on Tariffs and Trade (GATT)[3] authorizes WTO members to form regional trade agreements. The WTO jurisprudence has made it clear that members have a "right" to form preferential trade agreements. This right is however conditional. In the context of an RTA, Article XXIV may justify a measure that is inconsistent with certain other GATT provisions. However, in a case involving the formation of a customs union, this RTA "defence" is available only when two conditions are fulfilled. First, the party claiming the benefit of this defence must demonstrate that the measure at issue is introduced upon the formation of a customs union that fully meets the requirements of sub-paragraphs 8(a) and 5(a) of Article XXIV. Second, this party must demonstrate that the formation of the customs union would be prevented if it were not allowed to introduce the measure at issue. Again, *both* of these conditions must be met to have the benefit of the defence under Article XXIV of GATT.[4]

---

[2] This categorization is suggested by Joel P. Trachtman who argues that the linkage problem between "[t]rade and ... is a problem of allocation of jurisdiction; he suggests that there are three basic, and related, types of allocation of jurisdiction: (i) horizontal allocation of jurisdiction among States, (ii) vertical allocation of jurisdiction between states and international organizations and (iii) horizontal allocation of jurisdiction among international organisation." Trachtman, *supra* note 1 at 79.

[3] General Agreement on Tariffs and Trade, October 30, 1947, 61 Stat. A-11, TIAS 1700, 55 U.N.T.S. 194 [hereinafter GATT].

[4] *Turkey — Restrictions on Imports of Textile and Clothing Products*, Appellate Body Report, October 22, 1999, Doc. WT/DS34, para. 58. Presently, Article XXIV and WTO jurisprudence clearly establish that it is for the parties to the regional trade

Many RTAs include (substantive) rights and obligations that are parallel to those of the Marrakesh Agreement Establishing the World Trade Organization (WTO Agreement).[5] Generally, these RTAs may provide for their own dispute settlement mechanism, which makes it possible for the states to resort to different but parallel dispute settlement mechanisms for parallel or even similar obligations. This situation is not unique as states are often bound by multiple treaties, and the dispute settlement systems of these treaties operate in a parallel manner.[6] At the same time, the WTO dispute settlement system claims to be compulsory and exclusive. Article 23 of the Understanding on Rules and Procedures Governing the Settlement of Disputes (DSU)[7] mandates exclusive jurisdiction in favour of the DSU for WTO violations. By simply alleging that a measure affects or impairs its trade benefits, a WTO member is entitled to trigger the quasi-automatic, rapid, and powerful WTO dispute settlement mechanism, excluding thereby the competence of any other mechanism to examine WTO law violations. The challenging member does not need to prove any specific economic or legal interest nor provide any evidence of the trade impact of the challenged measure in order to initiate the DSU mechanism.[8] The

---

agreement [hereinafter RTA] to prove that the concerned free trade area or customs union is compatible with Article XXIV of GATT (and/or Article IV of the General Agreement on Trade in Services [hereinafter GATS] in World Trade Organization, Results of the Uruguay Round Multilateral Trade Negotiations: The Legal Texts, 325, text is also available at <http://www.wto.org/english/docs_e/legal_e/legal_e.htm#services>.) This test has, however, been severely criticized for being unrealistic.

5   Marrakesh Agreement Establishing the World Trade Organization, in World Trade Organisation, Results of the Uruguay Round Multilateral Trade Negotiations: The Legal Texts, 33, text is also available at <http://www.wto.org/english/docs_e/legal_e/14-ag.pdf> [hereinafter WTO Agreement].

6   The arbitral tribunal of the International Centre for the Settlement of Investment Disputes/International Tribunal for the Law of the Sea stated that "[t]here is frequently a parallelism of treaties, both in their substantive content and in their provisions for settlement of disputes arising thereunder." *Southern Bluefin Tuna* (*New Zealand v. Japan; Australia v. Japan*), Provisional Measures Order of 27 August 1999 (International Tribunal for the Law of the Sea), Award on Jurisdiction and Admissibility of 4 August 2000, p. 91 [hereinafter *Southern Bluefin Tuna* case].

7   Understanding on Rules and Procedures Governing the Settlement of Disputes, 1994, Annex 2 to the WTO Agreement, *supra* note 5 [hereinafter DSU].

8   The WTO jurisprudence has confirmed that any WTO member that is a "potential exporter" has the sufficient legal interest to initiate a WTO panel process (*European Communities — Regime for the Importation, Sale and Distribution of Bananas,*

WTO will thus often "attract" jurisdiction over disputes with (potential) trade effects even if such disputes could also be handled in fora other than that of the WTO.

OVERLAPS OF JURISDICTION BETWEEN RTAS AND THE WTO

Overlaps of jurisdiction in dispute settlement can be defined as situations where the same dispute or related aspects of the same dispute could be brought to two distinct institutions or two different dispute settlement systems. Under certain circumstances, this occurrence may lead to difficulties relating to "forum-shopping," whereby disputing entities would have a choice between two adjudicating bodies or between two different jurisdictions for the same facts. When the dispute settlement mechanisms of two agreements are triggered in parallel or in sequence, there are problems on two levels: first, the two tribunals may claim final jurisdiction (supremacy) over the matter and, second, they may reach different, or even opposite, results.[9]

Various types of overlaps of jurisdiction may occur. For the purpose of the present discussion, an overlap of jurisdiction occurs: (1) when two fora claim to have exclusive jurisdiction over the matter; (2) when one forum claims to have exclusive jurisdiction and the other one offers jurisdiction, on a permissive basis, for dealing with the same matter or a related one; or (3) when the dispute settlement mechanisms of two different fora are available (on a non-mandatory basis) to examine the same or similar matters. Conflicts are possible in any of these three situations. All of the

---

Appellate Body Report, April 9, 1999, WTO Doc. WT/DS27/ARB at para. 136); and in WTO disputes, there is no need to prove any trade effect for a measure to be declared WTO inconsistent (DSU, *supra* note 7 at Article 3.8). This is to say, in the context of a dispute between two WTO members, involving situations covered by both the RTA and the WTO Agreement, any member that considers that any of its WTO benefits have been nullified or impaired has an absolute right to trigger the WTO dispute settlement mechanism and request consultations and the establishment of a panel (*United States — Measures Affecting Imports of Woven Wool Shirts and Blouses from India*, Appellate Body Report, Doc. WT/DS33, para. 13). Arguably, a single WTO member cannot even agree to take its WTO dispute in another forum.

[9] The issue of forum shopping is not new. In the old GATT days, parties to the Tokyo Round codes had the choice between the general GATT dispute settlement mechanism and that of the codes (Agreement on Implementation of Article VI of the General Agreement on Trade and Tariffs (1979), Article 15, text is available at <http://www.wto.org/english/docs_e/legal_e/tokyo_adp_e.doc>).

[handwritten marginalia: But what if 2 WTO members agree to go elsewhere]

[handwritten marginalia at bottom: i.e. is Art 23 only re unilateralism? — N: What about Dunkel Draft?]

RTAs examined in Table 1 at the end of this article have dispute settlement mechanisms with jurisdiction that may potentially overlap with that of the WTO Agreement.

Table 1 examines different dispute settlement mechanisms of RTAs and attempts to describe systematically the dispute settlement mechanisms provided in the RTAs according to two different categories —the characteristics of the dispute settlement system and the region. Furthermore, the table identifies several elements in RTAs, including: (1) the compulsory or non-compulsory nature of the RTA jurisdiction; (2) the reference to the GATT/ WTO dispute settlement mechanism; (3) the exclusive or priority forum prescription clause; (4) the choice of forum clause; (5) the binding nature of dispute settlement conclusions; and (6) the remedy provided by the agreement, including the explicit right to take countermeasures in trade matters with or without the permission of RTA dispute settlement bodies.

EXAMPLES OF OVERLAPS OF JURISDICTION BETWEEN THE WTO'S AND RTAS' DISPUTE SETTLEMENT MECHANISMS

Canada-United States Free Trade Agreement / North American Free Trade Agreement (NAFTA) and the GATT/WTO Dispute Settlement Mechanisms

NAFTA[10] provides that a forum can be chosen at the discretion of a complaining party and gives preference to the NAFTA forum when the action involves environmental, sanitary and phytosanitary (SPS) measures, or standards-related measures.[11] At the time of the conclusion of NAFTA, these provisions were more advanced than those of GATT. It further provides that, if the complaining party has already initiated GATT procedures on the matter, the complaining party shall withdraw from these proceedings and may initiate dispute settlement mechanism under NAFTA.[12]

---

[10] North American Free Trade Agreement, December 17, 1992; Model Rules of Procedure for Chapter Twenty of the North American Free Trade Agreement; Code of Conduct for Dispute Settlement Procedures under Chapters 19 & 20 of the North American Free Trade Agreement [hereinafter NAFTA], text is available at <http://www.sice.oas.org/cp_disp/English/dsm_II.asp>.

[11] NAFTA, *supra* note 10 at Article 2005(3).

[12] NAFTA, *supra* note 10 at Article 2005(7), concludes that for purposes of Article 2005, dispute settlement proceedings under the GATT are deemed to be initiated by a party's request for a panel, such as under Article XXIII:2 of GATT 1947. Indeed, the explicit references to "GATT" and to the "General Agreement

However, in light of Article 23 of the DSU, which provides that a violation of the WTO Agreement can be addressed only according to the WTO/DSU mechanisms, would the invocation of this NAFTA provision be sufficient to halt the WTO adjudicating body? How can Article 23 and the quasi-automatic process of the DSU be reconciled with the preference and, in some circumstances, the exclusive priority given to the NAFTA dispute settlement mechanism for obligations that are similar in NAFTA and in the WTO for the same facts? For instance, Article 301 of NAFTA explicitly refers to Article III of GATT. In a hypothetical case where a NAFTA state's domestic regulation violates Article III of GATT and Article 301 of NAFTA, the defending party may prefer to have the matter submitted to a NAFTA panel — it may have a valid defence under NAFTA — but the complaining party may prefer to have the matter addressed in the WTO. The situation may also be reversed if the defending party sees some procedural or political advantage in having its case debated in the WTO.[13]

In light of the quasi-automaticity of the mechanism, once a dispute is initiated under the DSU, it is unlikely that a WTO panel would give much consideration to the defendant's request to halt the procedures just because similar or related procedures are being pursued under a regional arrangement. To take the NAFTA/WTO example again, a WTO panel would not examine any allegation of a NAFTA violation, rather it would be asked to examine an alleged WTO violation, which would be similar to a NAFTA violation. Could it be said that the NAFTA and the WTO provisions are dealing with the same subject matter (which could be defined as the measure plus the type of obligation imposed by the law)? Strictly speaking, the matter is different, although the content of the obligations is similar. For instance, the Free Trade Agreement between

on Tariffs and Trade 1947" raise the question whether the same rules would continue to apply to the new DSU of the WTO. However, since the first paragraph of Article 2005 refers to "any successor agreement (GATT)" and the recent NAFTA panel described GATT as "an evolving system of law" that includes the results of the Uruguay Round, the provisions of Article 2005 of NAFTA would be applicable to the dispute settlement rules of the WTO. Arbitral Panel Established Pursuant to Article 2008 of the North American Free Trade Agreement, *In the Matter of Tariffs Applied by Canada to Certain US — Origin Agricultural Products*, Final Report (December 2, 1996).

13 *Canada — Certain Measures Concerning Periodicals,* July 30, 1997, Doc. WT/DS31/AB/R is a good example of potential overlap. The United States initiated its dispute against Canada under the DSU of the WTO rather than that of the NAFTA.

the EU and Mexico[14] states that arbitration proceedings established under this agreement will not consider issues relating to parties' rights and obligations under the WTO Agreement. Would the insertion of this type of provision mitigate the problem of conflicts of jurisdiction or would it aggravate the situation?

If there is an allegation of WTO violation, it would be difficult for a WTO panel to refuse to hear a WTO member complaining about a measure claimed to be inconsistent with the WTO Agreement on the ground that the complaining or defending member is alleged to have a more specific or more appropriate defence or remedy in another forum concerning the same legal facts. Before a WTO panel, should the NAFTA parties have explicitly waived their rights to initiate dispute settlement proceedings under the WTO, the situation would be the same. However, in such a case, in initiating a parallel WTO dispute, a NAFTA party may be found to be violating its obligation under NAFTA — that is, not to take a dispute outside of NAFTA. In these circumstances, the NAFTA party opposed to the parallel WTO panel (the "opposing NAFTA party") could claim that the WTO panel initiated by the other NAFTA party is impairing some of its benefits under NAFTA. The opposing NAFTA party would arguably win this claim before the NAFTA panel. Theoretically, that opposing NAFTA party would then be entitled to some retaliation — the value of which could probably correspond to (part of) the benefits that the other NAFTA party could gain in initiating its WTO panel.

In other words, even if it may not be practical or useful for a NAFTA party to duplicate in the WTO a dispute that should be handled in NAFTA, there does not seem to be any legal impediment against such a possibility, since, legally speaking, the NAFTA and WTO panels would be considering different "matters" under different "applicable law," providing for different remedies and offering a different implementation and retaliation mechanisms.

---

[14] Free Trade Agreement between the EU and Mexico, Decision no. 2/2000 of the EC/Mexico Joint Council of 23 March 2000 (covering trade in goods, government procurement, cooperation for competition, consultation on intellectual property rights, dispute settlement), Article 41, entered into force on July 1, 2000, text is available at <http://europa.eu.int/comm/trade/bilateral/mexico/fta.htm >.

Other Free Trade Agreements with a "Forum Election Clause"
and an "Exclusivity Forum Clause"

Some recent free trade agreements contain even further detailed
and articulate provisions on the overlap with the WTO dispute settlement system. The Free Trade Agreement between the European
Free Trade Association States and Singapore[15] explicitly provides
that disputes on the same matter arising under both this agreement
and the WTO Agreement, or under any agreement negotiated
thereunder, to which the parties are party, may be settled in either
forum at the discretion of the complaining party but that the forum
thus selected shall be used to the exclusion of the other.[16]

The Free Trade Agreement between Canada and Costa Rica contains a general provision on the compulsory nature of the dispute
settlement system provided for in the same agreement.[17] The agreement also provides that "[s]ubject to paragraph 2, Article VI.4
(Dispute Settlement in Emergency Action Matters), Article VII.1.5
(Antidumping Measures), Article IX.5.1.2 (Sanitary and Phytosanitary Measures) and Article XI.6.3 (Consultations), disputes regarding any matter arising under both this Agreement and the WTO
Agreement, any agreement negotiated there under, or any successor agreement, may be settled in either forum at the discretion of
the complaining Party."[18] It also adds that once dispute settlement
procedures have been initiated under Article XIII.8 or dispute settlement proceedings have been initiated under the WTO Agreement, the forum selected shall be used to the exclusion of the other
unless a party makes a request pursuant to paragraph 2.[19]

These free trade agreements prohibit their members from initiating a second dispute on the same or related matters once the dispute
settlement process of these free trade agreements or of the WTO has
been initiated. It is doubtful whether this type of provision would

---

[15] Free Trade Agreement between the European Free Trade Association States
and Singapore, signed on June 26, 2002, entered into force on January 1,
2003, text is available at <http://secretariat.efta.int/Web/ExternalRelations/
PartnerCountries/Singapore/SG/SG_FTA.pdf>.

[16] *Ibid.* at Article 56(2).

[17] Free Trade Agreement between the Government of Canada and the Government
of the Republic of Costa Rica, Article XIII:6, entered into force on November 1,
2002, text is available at <http://www.dfaitmaeci.gc.ca/tna-nac/Costa_Rica_toc-
en.asp>.

[18] *Ibid.*

[19] *Ibid.*

suffice to allow a WTO panel to refuse to hear the matter in situations where the dispute settlement process of the free trade agreement has been triggered. It may be difficult at the early stage of a WTO panel to assess whether the matter is indeed exactly the same as the one raised in the free trade area forum. The WTO panel may simply continue its investigation to find out whether the measure is inconsistent with the WTO provisions while assessing whether the obligations are the same under both treaties. However, the WTO member party to the free trade agreement who initiates a WTO dispute process in parallel or subsequently to that of the free trade agreement could very well be in violation of that free trade agreement and lose, in application of the free trade agreement, all the benefits that it would/could otherwise have obtained from the WTO dispute settlement system.

MERCOSUR/WTO Dispute Settlement Mechanisms

The Southern Common Market (MERCOSUR)[20] provides that "[t]he controversies which arise between the State Parties regarding the interpretation, application or non-compliance of the dispositions contained in the Treaty of Asuncion, of the agreements celebrated within its framework, as well as any decisions of the Common Market Council and the resolutions of the Common Market Group, will be submitted to the procedure for resolution established in the present Protocol (of Brazilia): 'the state parties declare that they recognize as obligatory, *ipso facto* and without need of a special agreement, the jurisdiction of the Arbitral Tribunal which in each case is established in order to hear and resolve all controversies which are referred to in the present Protocol.'"[21] The Protocol of Olivos[22] now provides that the forum chosen by the complaining party should be the forum of the dispute and adds

---

[20] The Southern Common Market [hereinafter MERCOSUR] was created by the 1991 Treaty of Asunción, approved by Act 23981/91 (Argentina, Official Bulletin, September 12, 1991), text is available at <www.mercosul.org.uy/pagina1esp.htm>.

[21] Protocol of Brasilia, Council Decision MERCOSUR/CMD/DEC NO. 01/91; Protocol of Brasilia for Dispute Settlement, Article 1, signed on December 17, 1991, text is available at <http://www.mercosul.gov.br/textos/default.asp?Key=231>.

[22] Protocol of Olivos for the Settlement of Disputes in MERCOSUR, Article 1, signed on February 18, 2002, text is available at <http://www.mercosul.gov.br/textos/default.asp?Key=232>.

that once a forum has been selected it shall deal with the dispute at the exclusion of other fora.

In 2000, Argentina decided to impose safeguard quotas on entries of certain cotton products from Brazil, China, and Pakistan. Brazil asked an arbitral panel to rule on the trade dispute. The three arbitrators concluded that Argentina's safeguard measure was incompatible with the MERCOSUR agreement. Argentina did not remove its quotas immediately, thus Brazil asked the WTO Textiles Monitoring Body (TMB) to review the legality of the Argentina quotas.[23] Although the WTO rules on textiles allow members to take some safeguard actions, the TMB concluded that Argentina's safeguard measures were incompatible with the WTO Agreement. Since Argentina continued to refuse to comply, Brazil was forced to take the dispute to the dispute settlement body (DSB) and could have requested the establishment of a panel. In the end, the parties settled amicably.

In 2002, Brazil initiated a WTO dispute complaint relating to the imposition of anti-dumping measures against the importation of poultry from Argentina.[24] Before the WTO panel, Argentina argued that Brazil had failed to act in good faith by first challenging Argentina's anti-dumping measure before a MERCOSUR ad hoc tribunal and then, having lost that case, initiating WTO dispute settlement proceedings against the same measure. Argentina raised a preliminary issue concerning the fact that, prior to bringing WTO dispute settlement proceedings against Argentina's anti-dumping measure, Brazil had challenged that measure before a MERCOSUR ad hoc arbitral tribunal.[25] According to Argentina, a member is not acting in good faith if it first has recourse to the mechanism of the integration process to settle its dispute with another WTO member and, then, dissatisfied with the outcome, files the same complaint within a different framework, making matters worse by omitting any reference to the previous procedure and its outcome.[26] Argentina considered that "Brazil's conduct in

---

[23] The legal issues in the WTO were slightly different from those before the MERCOSUR arbitrators and could have led to very complicated questions relating to the WTO compatibility of the MERCOSUR customs union and whether countries in a customs union can impose safeguard measures against imports from another member.

[24] See *Argentina — Definitive Anti-Dumping Duties on Poultry from Brazil*, Panel Report, May 22, 2003, Doc. WT/DS241/R.

[25] *Ibid.* at para. 7.17.

[26] *Ibid.* at para. 7.19.

bringing the dispute successively before different fora, first MER-
COSUR and then the WTO, constitutes a legal approach that is
contrary to the principle of good faith which, in the case at issue,
warrants invocation of the principle of estoppel."[27] Argentina requested that, in light of the prior MERCOSUR proceedings, the
panel refrain from ruling on the claims raised by Brazil in the
present WTO dispute settlement proceedings. In the alternative,
Argentina submitted that the panel should be bound by the ruling
of the MERCOSUR tribunal. In the alternative, Argentina submitted that "in view of the relevant rule of international law applicable
in the relations between parties pursuant to Article 31.3(c) of the
Vienna Convention the Panel cannot disregard, in its consideration
and substantiation of the present case brought by Brazil, the precedents set by the proceedings in the framework of Mercosur."[28]

According to Brazil, the simple fact that it had brought a similar
dispute to the MERCOSUR tribunal did not represent that Brazil
had consented not to bring the current dispute before the WTO,
especially when the dispute before this panel was based on a different legal basis than the dispute brought before the MERCOSUR
tribunal. Brazil asserted that the MERCOSUR Protocol of Olivos
on Dispute Settlement, signed on 18 February 2002, could not be
raised here as an implicit or express consent by Brazil to refrain
from bringing the present case to the WTO dispute settlement,
again because the object of the earlier MERCOSUR proceedings
was different from that of the present WTO proceedings. Furthermore, the Protocol of Olivos did not apply to disputes that had
already been concluded under the Protocol of Brasilia.[29]

It is worthwhile to note the United States's argument as a third
party. The United States submitted that the MERCOSUR dispute
settlement rules are not within the panel's terms of reference:

Article 7.1 of the *DSU* makes quite clear that a Panel's role in a dispute is
to make findings in light of the relevant provisions of the "covered agreements" at issue. The Protocol of Brasilia is not a covered agreement, and
Argentina has not claimed that Brazil's actions with respect to the Protocol
breach any provision of a covered agreement. Rather, Argentina's claim
appears to be that Brazil's actions could be considered to be inconsistent
with the terms of the Protocol. A claim of a breach of the Protocol is not
within this Panel's terms of reference, and there are no grounds for the

[27] *Ibid.* at para. 7.18

[28] *Ibid.*

[29] *Ibid.* at para. 7.22.

Panel to consider this matter. Argentina may, however, be able to pursue that claim under the MERCOSUR dispute settlement system.[30]

The panel decided to limit itself to the arguments raised by Argentina — allegations of bad faith on the part of Brazil and the invocation of estoppels that would prohibit Brazil from challenging Argentina's actions before the WTO — and to reject them as inherently inconsistent. The panel concluded that "two conditions must be satisfied before a Member may be found to have failed to act in good faith. First, the Member must have violated a substantive provision of the WTO agreements. Second, there must be something 'more than mere violation.' With regard to the first condition, Argentina has not alleged that Brazil violated any substantive provision of the WTO agreements in bringing the present case. Thus, even without examining the second condition, there is no basis for us to find that Brazil violated the principle of good faith in bringing the present proceedings before the WTO."[31] The panel then discussed the international law criteria for estoppel and concluded that there was nothing on the record to suggest that Argentina actively relied in good faith on any statement made by Brazil, either to the advantage of Brazil or to the disadvantage of Argentina. There was nothing on the record to suggest that Argentina would have acted any differently had Brazil not made the alleged statement that it would not bring the present WTO dispute settlement proceedings.

The panel also rejected Argentina's argument based on Article 3.2 of the DSU and Article 31.3(c) of the Vienna Convention on the Law of Treaties.[32] The panel recalled that Article 3.2 of the DSU is concerned with international rules of treaty interpretation:

Article 3.2 of the DSU is concerned with treaty *interpretation*. Article 31.3(c) of the *Vienna Convention* is similarly concerned with treaty *interpretation*. However, the Panel noted that Argentina has not sought to rely on any law providing that, in respect of relations between Argentina and Brazil, the WTO agreements should be *interpreted* in a particular way. In particular, Argentina has not relied on any statement or finding in the MERCOSUR Tribunal ruling to suggest that we should interpret specific provisions of the WTO agreements in a particular way. Rather than concerning itself with the interpretation of the WTO agreements, Argentina

[30] *Ibid.* at para. 7.30.

[31] *Ibid.* at para. 7.36.

[32] Vienna Convention on the Law of Treaties, May 23, 1969, Can. T.S. 1980 No. 37 (entered into force January 27, 1980) [hereinafter Vienna Convention].

actually argues that the earlier MERCOSUR Tribunal ruling requires us to *rule* in a particular way. In other words, Argentina would have us *apply* the relevant WTO provisions in a particular way, rather than *interpret* them in a particular way. However, there is no basis in Article 3.2 of the *DSU*, or any other provision, to suggest that we are bound to rule in a particular way, or apply the relevant WTO provisions in a particular way. However, there is no basis in Article 3.2 of the *DSU*, or any other provision, to suggest that we are bound to rule in a particular way, or apply the relevant WTO provisions in a particular way.[33]

This report was not appealed to the Appellate Body.[34] It is clear that WTO adjudicating bodies do not have the authority to enforce provisions of a RTA as such.[35] In a case such as this one, however, the WTO adjudicating bodies would seem to be assessing the concerned states' situation in light of their WTO obligations and not in light of their MERCOSUR obligations. Yet, contrary findings based on similar rules from the MERCOSUR and WTO institutions would have unfortunate consequences for the trust that the states are to place in their international institutions.

How Can States and WTO Panels Deal with Overlaps of Jurisdiction between Dispute Settlement Mechanisms of RTAs and the WTO?

SOLUTIONS SUGGESTED BY INTERNATIONAL LAW

Overlaps and conflicts of jurisdictions are now of relevance in international law generally because of the multiplication of international jurisdictions. In recent years, treaties and organs of jurisdiction have increased drastically in number. An obvious example is the multiplicity of treaties, organs, and jurisdictions that are involved in human rights issues.[36] The accepted practice seems to be that states may adhere to different but parallel dispute settlement

---

[33] *Argentina — Definitive Anti-Dumping Duties on Poultry from Brazil*, *supra* note 24 at para. 7.41.

[34] It is interesting to note that the new Protocol of Olivos on Dispute Settlement, *supra* note 22, now contains an exclusive forum clause: "Once a dispute settlement procedure pursuant to the preceding paragraph has begun, none of the parties may request the use of the mechanisms established in the other fora, as defined by article 14 of this Protocol." At the time of this dispute, it was not yet in force.

[35] *United States — Margin of Preferences*, BISD II/11, Decision of August 9, 1949.

[36] See Emmanuel Roucounas, *Engagements parallèles et contradictoires*, Cours de la Haye (1987), 197.

mechanisms for parallel or even similar obligations. The arbitral tribunal of the International Centre for the Settlement of Investment Disputes/International Tribunal for the Law of the Sea in the recent *Southern Bluefin Tuna (New Zealand v. Japan; Australia v. Japan)* case stated:

But the Tribunal recognizes as well that there is a commonplace of international law and State practice for more than one treaty to bear upon a particular dispute. There is no reason why a given act of a State may not violate its obligations under more than one treaty. *There is frequently a parallelism of treaties, both in their substantive content and in their provisions for settlement of disputes arising thereunder* ... the conclusion of an implementing convention does not necessarily vacate the obligations imposed by the framework convention upon the parties to the implementing convention.[37]

A call for increased coherence was also made by a former president of the International Court of Justice (ICJ), Stephen Schwebel,[38] and again by Gilbert Guillaume,[39] against the dangers of forum shopping and the development of fragmented and contradictory international law. Roselyn Higgins believes, however, that there may not be any need for such an international structure and that coherence may be best ensured through awareness and exchanges between jurisdictions:

With the greatest respect to the past two Presidents of the International Court, I do not share their view that the model of Article 234 (the renumbered Article 177) of the Rome Treaty provides an answer. It is simply cumbersome and unrealistic to suppose that other tribunals would wish to refer points of general international law to the International Court of Justice. Indeed, the very reason for their establishment as separate judicial instances militates against a notion of intra-judicial reference.

---

[37] *Southern Bluefin Tuna* case, *supra* note 6 at 91 [emphasis added].

[38] "[I]n order to minimize such possibility as may occur of significant conflicting interpretations of international law, there might be virtue in enabling other international tribunals to request advisory opinions of the International Court of Justice on issues of international law that arise in cases before those tribunals that are of importance to the unity of international law ... There is room for the argument that even international tribunals that are not United Nations organs, such as the International Tribunal for the Law of the Sea, or the International Criminal Court when established, might, if they so decide, request the General Assembly — perhaps through the medium of a special committee established for the purpose — to request advisory opinions of the Court." Stephen M. Schwebel, President of the ICJ, Address to the Plenary Session of the General Assembly of the United Nations, October 26, 1999, text is available at <http://www.icj-cij.org/>.

[39] See, for instance, the note by Gilbert Guillaume, "La mondialisation et la Cour internationale de justice" (2000) 2(4) Forum (ILA) at 242.

The better way forward, in my view, is for us all to keep ourselves well informed. Thus the European Court of Justice will want to keep abreast of the case law of the International Court, particularly when it deals with treaty law or matters of customary international law; and the International Court will want to make sure it fully understands the circumstances in which these issues arise for its sister court in Luxembourg. Many ways of achieving this can be suggested; and events such as this lecture may perhaps be seen as counting among them.[40]

In the absence of provisions such as a choice of forum clause and an exclusive forum clause, it is possible that the dispute settlement forum of an RTA and that of the WTO may be seized, at the same time or sequentially, of very similar matters, to the extent that obligations under the RTA and the WTO are similar and applicable. In the absence of any other specific treaty prescription, the rules and principles of treaty interpretation and of conflicts applicable to the substantive provisions of treaties would also be applicable to the issue of the overlap or conflict of their respective dispute settlement mechanisms. The issue is whether these rules of conflict *(lex posterior* and *lex specialis)* are such as to be able to invalidate the WTO dispute settlement process or nullify its access. It is doubtful.

As long as a treaty provides for a dispute settlement mechanism in its text, parties to the treaty may invoke that mechanism to settle a dispute concerning the interpretation or application of the treaty. In the absence of any clear prescription, such a cumulative application of various dispute settlement mechanisms under different treaties seems possible. In initiating a WTO dispute, the RTA member may, however, nullify the benefits of another RTA member and may be subject to RTA dispute settlement procedures and eventually retaliation in the RTA context. The WTO recognizes the legitimacy of RTAs (with conditions). It may be argued that RTAs' dispute settlement mechanisms are used to enforce the disciplines of RTAs (which themselves must be compatible with Article XXIV and with the GATT/WTO) and are therefore "necessary" to allow members to enforce RTA rules (and the related countermeasures).

Treaty Clauses Addressing Dispute Settlement Mechanisms of Other Treaties

Article 23 of the DSU is a specific treaty clause[41] that seems to prevent other jurisdictions from adjudicating WTO law violations.

---

[40] Roselyn Higgins, "The ICJ, The ECJ, and the Integrity of International Law" (2003) 52 I.C.L.Q. 1-20 at 20.

[41] Vienna Convention, *supra* note 32 at Article 30.2.

However, Article 23 cannot prohibit tribunals established by other treaties from exercising jurisdiction over the claims arising from their treaty provisions that run parallel to, or overlap with, the WTO provisions. Hence, there is a need for WTO members to further address the issue of overlapping WTO/RTA dispute settlement jurisdictions. Table 1 at the end of this article identifies a number of aspects relevant to RTA jurisdiction. A large number of RTAs provide for compulsory jurisdiction mandating the parties to refer their disputes to an institution established by the constituting treaty. Some RTAs provide for forum shopping or a forum choice clause, allowing for the settlement of disputes either in the RTA forum or in the GATT forum at the discretion of the complaining party. Other RTAs contain exclusive forum clauses, in addition to the choice of forum clause, providing that, once a matter has been brought before either forum, the procedure initiated shall be used to the exclusion of any other, as is the case with NAFTA and the free trade agreements between the United States and Singapore,[42] Japan and Singapore,[43] or Singapore and Australia.[44] The purpose of this rule was not to recognize the existence of *res judicata* as such (since the applicable law was strictly different — the law of the free trade agreement in one forum, GATT law in the other) but rather to introduce certainty and avoid multiple dispute settlement proceedings. In fact, NAFTA goes further than the Canada-United States Free Trade Agreement,[45] which preceded NAFTA and, in the area of sanitary and phytosanitary measures (SPS) and environment and other standard disputes, obliges a NAFTA state to

[42] United States — Singapore Free Trade Agreement, signed on May 6, 2003, text is available at <http://www.ustr.gov/new/fta/Singapore/final.htm>.

[43] Agreement between Japan and the Republic of Singapore for a New-Age Economic Partnership, signed on January 13, 2002 and entered into force on November 30, 2002, text is available at <http://www.mti.gov.sg/public/FTA/frm_FTA_Default.asp?sid=28>.

[44] Singapore — Australia Free Trade Agreement, signed on February 17, 2003 and entered into force on July 28, 2003, text is available at <http://www.austlii.edu.au/au/other/dfat/treaties/2003/16.html>. Article 1801 of the Canada-United States Free Trade Agreement, *infra* note 45, envisaged that disputes arising under both this agreement and GATT (including the Tokyo Round codes) could be settled in either forum at the discretion of the complaining party but that once a matter has been brought before either forum, the procedure initiated shall be used to the exclusion of any other.

[45] Canada — United States Free Trade Agreement, signed on January 2, 1989, text is available at <http://wehner.tamu.edu/mgmt.www/nafta/fta/complete.pdf>.

withdraw from a GATT dispute if the other NAFTA state prefers the NAFTA jurisdiction.[46] The Free Trade Agreement between Chile and Mexico[47] and the Free Trade Agreement between Canada and Chile[48] have similar provisions.[49]

There is no clear rule in regard to the relationship between the WTO jurisdiction and other jurisdictions. Article XXIV of GATT does not make any reference to the dispute settlement mechanisms of RTAs. In order to govern the legal relationships between RTAs' dispute settlement mechanisms and those of the WTO, a set of principles can be devised. If both processes were triggered at the same time, it is quite probable that the WTO panel process would proceed much faster than the RTA process. What arguments may be raised before a WTO adjudication body with respect to the RTA dispute settlement mechanism? Are there rules of general international law that may be useful? Principles and rules that have

[46] Article 2005 of NAFTA, *supra* note 10, provides that after consultation "the dispute normally shall be settled under this Agreement." Paragraphs 3 and 4 of Article 2005 go further and prescribe the exclusive application of NAFTA to the detriment of GATT: When the responding party claims that its action is subject to Article 104 of the Environmental and Conservation Agreements (inconsistency with certain environmental and conservation agreements), sanitary and phytosanitary measures, or standards-related measures adopted or maintained by a party to protect its human, animal or plant life or health, or its environment, and that raises factual or scientific issues on these aspects, "the complaining Party may, in respect of that matter, thereafter have recourse to dispute settlement procedures solely under [NAFTA]." According to paragraph 5 of Article 2005, if the complaining party has already initiated GATT procedures on the matter, "the complaining Party shall promptly withdraw from participation in those proceedings and may initiate dispute settlement procedures under Article 2007." See the Agreement between the Government of Canada and the Government of the United States of America Concerning the Transboundary Movement of Hazardous Waste, signed on October 28, 1986; and the Agreement between the United States of America and the United Mexican States on Cooperation for the Protection and Improvement of the Environment in the Border Area, signed on August 14, 1983.

[47] Free Trade Agreement between the Government of the Republic of Chile and the Government of the United Mexican States, signed on April 17, 1998 and entered into force on August 1, 1999, text is available at <http:www.sice-oas.org>.

[48] Free Trade Agreement between the Government of Canada and the Government of the Republic of Chile, signed on December 5, 1996, text is available at <http://www.dfait-maeci.gc.ca/tna-nac/cda-chile/menu-en.asp>.

[49] Article N-05 of the Free- Trade Agreement between the Government of Canada and the Government of Chile, *supra* note 48; and Free Trade Agreement between the Republic of Chile and the Government of Mexican States, *supra* note 47, Article 18-03, para. 2.

been developed in private international commercial law for dealing with overlaps and conflicts of jurisdictions are also informative. It may be worthwhile to examine whether such rules could be used in situations of multiple jurisdictions of international law tribunals.

Abuse of Process, Abuse of Rights, and Good Faith

In public international law, a state, by initiating a second proceeding on the same matter, may be viewed as abusing its process or procedural rights. A tribunal could decline jurisdiction if it considers that the proceedings have been initiated to harass the defendant or that they were frivolous or groundless. It is not the multiple proceedings that are condemned "but rather the inherently vexatious nature of the proceedings."[50] Such a prohibition against "abuses of rights" could be considered a general principle of law.[51] However, it is unlikely that any adjudicating body, including those of the WTO, would find the allegations that their constitutional treaty has been violated to be "vexatious," especially when, in all probability, the claims would be drafted to capture the specific competence of that tribunal.

One could possibly argue that a state may be bound by its implied commitment to respect a previous ruling and thus may have to refrain from resorting to another forum to challenge the previous ruling. However, at the same time, states may be bound by two different jurisdictions sequentially and this situation happens often in international law. One may also argue that the general obligation of states to enforce their treaty obligations in good faith obliges them to use the most appropriate forum to settle their disputes or to use them in any sequence. However, if states have negotiated the possibility of referring disputes to various fora, it has to be assumed that they intended to retain the possibility of using such fora freely, yet in good faith.

---

50 Lowe affirms that the doctrine of abuse of process is "well established, though occasions for its application are likely to be very rare." Vaughan Lowe, "Overlapping Jurisdictions in International Tribunals" (2000) 20 Australian Y.B. Int'l L. 1 13.

51 Brownlie wrote that "[i]t is not unreasonable to read the principle of abuse of right as a general principle of law." See Ian Brownlie, Principles of Public International Law, 5th ed. (Oxford: 1998), 447-48. See also *United States — Import Prohibition of Certain Shrimp and Shrimp Products*, Appellate Body Report, October 26, 2001, Doc. WT/DS58, at para. 158.

In addition, it may be argued that a WTO panel could consider consultations and the use of the RTA dispute settlement mechanism in an RTA context or the efforts to reach a mutually agreeable solution to the dispute as an evidence of the good faith of its member(s), which may be relevant for the determination of compliance with the WTO provisions. As shown in Table 1, RTAs generally provide for consultation mechanisms. Once consultations have been requested by a party, the other party usually has to respect such a request. Consultations normally take place in a RTA institution composed of representatives of participating member states.

Exhaustion of RTA Remedies

There does not seem to be any rule that demands the exhaustion of one dispute settlement mechanism prior to the initiation of another one. There is a principle in general international law that obliges states to ensure that local remedies have been exhausted before bringing a claim on behalf of a national to international dispute settlement mechanisms, but many would argue that this doctrine does not apply under WTO law.[52] In any case, the dispute settlement mechanism of a RTA does not provide for any "local" remedy, therefore it is difficult to consider that such a principle could be invoked to oblige a state to exhaust RTA remedies before going to the WTO.[53]

Reference to the ICJ

Another solution to address the proliferation of international jurisdictions is to adopt the suggestion of Judge Guillaume and empower the ICJ with some form of reference jurisdiction to be used by international tribunals, possibly through advisory opinion

---

[52] See, for instance, Ernst-Ulrich Petersmann, "Settlement of International Disputes through the GATT: The Case of Anti-Dumping Law," in Ernst-Ulrich Petersmann and Gunther Janicke, *Adjudication of International Trade Disputes in International and National Economic Law* (Fribourg: University Press, 1992), 126;

[53] On the issue of the exhaustion of local remedies in international law and its application in WTO law, see Pieter Jan Kuijper, "The Law of GATT as a Special Field of International Law" (1994) Neth. Y. B. Int'l L. 227; Pieter Jan Kuijper, "The New WTO Dispute Settlement System — The Impact on the European Community" (1995) 29(6) J. World T. 49; and J. Martha Rutsel Silvestre, "World Trade Dispute Settlement and the Exhaustion of Local Remedies Rule" (1996) 30 J. World T. 107.

requests.[54] However, as he points out, it is unrealistic to expect states to empower the ICJ in this way or to expect international tribunals to surrender their judicial power. In addition, states or tribunals may not be able to agree on the type of questions to be referred to the ICJ.

PRINCIPLES OF PRIVATE INTERNATIONAL COMMERCIAL LAW DEALING WITH OVERLAPS AND CONFLICTS OF JURISDICTION

Forum Conveniens *and* Forum Non Conveniens[55]

The *forum conveniens* doctrine is defined as "a court taking jurisdiction on the ground that the local forum is the appropriate forum (or an appropriate forum) for trial or that the forum abroad is inappropriate. It is said to be a positive doctrine, unlike *forum non conveniens* which is a negative doctrine defined as a general discretionary power for a court to decline jurisdiction."[56] However, the objective of both doctrines is the same — that is, to identify which forum is the most convenient one or which forum is not convenient. The criteria to determine which jurisdiction is to be preferred vary with each state. Most states rely on criteria such as connecting factors, expenses, the availability of witnesses, the law governing the relevant transactions, the place where the parties reside or carry on business, the interest of the parties, and the general interest of justice. In some states, courts use the *forum conveniens* doctrine as one of the discretionary criteria on which to base their jurisdiction. Other states explicitly refer to the doctrine and provide when and how such assessment must be performed by national courts and based on what criteria.

In the current state of international jurisdictional law, the doctrine of *forum non conveniens*, or of *forum conveniens*, absent an agreement among states, appears to be inapplicable to an overlap of jurisdictions in public international law tribunals. In domestic jurisdictions, the defendants have usually agreed to subject themselves to any such available jurisdiction, while it may not be the case

---

[54] He referred to the model found in Article 177 of the Treaty Establishing the European Community (consolidated text), Official Journal C 325 of 24 December 2002) [hereinafter EC Treaty] (now Article 234). See, for instance, Guillaume, *supra* note 39 at 242. In contrast, see Higgins, *supra* note 40 at 20.

[55] On this issue, see T. Sawaki, "Battle of Lawsuits — Lis Pendens in International Relations" (1979-80) 23 Japanese Ann. Int'l L. 17.

[56] J.J. Fawcett, *Deciding Jurisdiction in Private International Law* (Oxford: 1995), 5-6 and 10.

with international jurisdictions. The location of evidence, witnesses, and lawyers is usually of minimal importance in international disputes. Although demands of efficiency in the administration of justice may indicate that a specific court should decline to exercise its jurisdiction, "criteria developed in the context of a proper concern for the interest of private litigants make little sense in the context of inter-State proceedings."[57]

Article 23 of the DSU reflects the clear intention of WTO members to ensure that WTO adjudicating bodies can always exercise exclusive jurisdiction on any WTO-related claim. The WTO forum is always a "convenient forum" for any WTO grievance. In fact, it seems to be the exclusive forum for WTO matters. In order to change this situation, members would have to negotiate amendments to Article 23 of the DSU and would risk reopening the debate on the prohibition of unilateral counter-measures, mandated by Article 23 of the DSU.

Lis Alibi Pendens *and* Res Judicata

The rule on *lis alibi pendens* (litispendence) provides that once a process has begun, no other parallel proceedings may be pursued. The object of the *lis alibi pendens* rule is to avoid a situation in which parallel proceedings, which involve the same parties and the same cause of action, simultaneously continue in two different states and with the possible consequence of irreconcilable judgments.[58] The *res judicata* doctrine provides that the final judgment rendered by a court of competent jurisdiction on the merits is conclusive as to the rights of the parties and, as between them, constitutes an absolute bar to a subsequent action involving the same claim, demand, or cause of action.

It is generally difficult to speak of *res judicata* or *lis alibi pendens* between two dispute settlement mechanisms under two different treaties. The parties may be the same and the subject matter may be a related one, but, legally speaking, in the WTO and RTAs, the applicable law would not be the same — certain specific defences may be available only in one treaty or time-limits, procedural rights, and remedies may differ. Therefore, it is difficult to speak of *lis pendens* or *res judicata* between two international law jurisdictions.[59]

---

[57] Lowe, *supra* note 50 at 12.

[58] Fawcett, *supra* note 56 at 26.

[59] As Lowe points out, in most cases, the fact that a state has sought adjudication

However, RTAs such as the Central American Common Market (CACM) and MERCOSUR refer to the effect of *res judicata*. The CACM, for instance, states that the arbitration award has the effect of *res judicata* for *all contracting parties* so far as it contains any ruling concerning the interpretation or application of the provisions of this treaty. Thus, once the interpretive ruling is rendered, all CACM parties are bound by it, even if they are not parties to the dispute. However several questions remain. Does it mean that the WTO panel's ruling, as long as it concerns the interpretation and application of the General Treaty on Central American Economic Integration between Guatemala, El Salvador, Honduras and Nicaragua[60] cannot be challenged (or risk to have it changed) in the WTO forum? How then can it be used? What if a WTO panel, in its assessment of the WTO compatibility of the RTA or one of its specific measure reads a provision of an RTA differently from the CACM formal interpretation? Should the CACM judgment not be considered as a fact — a legal fact — which the WTO panel will have to assess?

In the WTO context, Article 23 of the DSU provides that WTO grievances can only be debated within the parameters of the WTO institutions. It is difficult to see how WTO panels could decline jurisdiction for reasons of *res judicata, lis pendens,* or *forum non conveniens.*[61] This is not to say that the decisions and conclusions of those other RTA jurisdictions would be of no relevance to the WTO process. On the contrary, similar to any other court decision on a similar matter, they will be examined as a judicial interpretation by another international tribunal of a similar provision.

---

under one treaty cannot deprive it of the right to seek a declaration in respect of another treaty. See Lowe, *supra* note 50 at 14.

[60] General Treaty on Central American Economic Integration between Guatemala, El Salvador, Honduras and Nicaragua, December, 1960; Protocol of Tegulcigalpa to the Charter of the Organization of Central American States, December 13, 1991; Protocol of Guatemala to the General Treaty on Central American Economic Integration, October 29, 1993; Convenio del Estatuto de la Corte Centroamericana de Justicia, December 13, 1992, text is available at <http://www.sice.oas.org/cp_disp/English/dsm_II.asp>.

[61] This is not to say that other jurisdictions do not have the capacity to read, take into account, and somehow interpret WTO provisions to the extent that it is necessary to interpret their own treaty.

POSSIBILITY OF INVOKING ARTICLE 13 OF THE DSU TO OBTAIN (EXPERT) EVIDENCE FROM RTA PROCEEDINGS

Article 13 of the DSU allows any WTO panel to request from the parties, or from any source, any relevant information. Arguably, this information could include evidence from the proceedings in another forum. The WTO panel may want to require expert information from a RTA secretariat, or, with the agreement of the parties, it may also want to use the analysis or data collected during a RTA dispute process as expert data. However, how should a WTO panel treat submitted evidence that relates to a RTA's relations? Panels are at all times bound by the provisions of Article 11 of the DSU, which mandates an "objective" assessment of the facts and the law. If the panel respects due process, nothing would limit the right of a panel to inquire about members' actions in another forum dealing with similar claims.

DISCUSSION ON OVERLAPPING DISPUTE SETTLEMENT MECHANISMS

In the absence of any treaty prescription, the state initiating the dispute will make its choice, taking into account the specific facts of the case, which include the expertise of adjudicators of each forum, the need for efficiency and specific remedies, and the procedural aspects of each forum. In addition, there are other factors of a more political nature that may affect the state's choice of forum, such as whether the state will seek a dispute settlement or a systemic declaration or what type, importance, or influence the forum will have, which will affect the state's choice of forum.

Is it conceptually possible that a RTA adjudicating body reach a conclusion contrary to that of the WTO adjudicating body on exactly the same factual allegation? The applicable law — that is, the treaty provision being interpreted and applied— would be different (on the one hand, RTA law and, on the other hand, WTO law), although it may happen that the said provisions of the two treaties are almost identical. Even if WTO members are not faced with a formal conflict between two mutually exclusive jurisdictions, it may be that an RTA jurisdiction and the WTO jurisdiction adjudicate the same dispute or related aspects of the same dispute, and this situation in itself can be problematic.

In the absence of the agreement of the parties to suspend the DSU mechanism, it is most doubtful whether a WTO adjudicating body would terminate its process solely on the ground that a related dispute or aspects of the same dispute are being examined

or have been examined in another forum. Article 23 of the DSU
and the quasi-automaticity of the DSU mechanism do not allow for
such suspension of the DSU mechanism to happen. However, in initiating a WTO process, the RTA member may be in violation of the
RTA and be subject to dispute settlement and possibly retaliation or
other sanctions or countermeasures. It is thus argued that since dispute settlements are inherent to the application of Article XXIV,
countermeasures are necessary instruments for effective RTAs and
are therefore WTO compatible pursuant to Article XXIV.[62]

It is equally wrong to argue for an exclusive allocation in favour
of the WTO forum for any "trade" matter. Could one argue that
Article 23 of the DSU goes as far as denying WTO members the
right to sign RTAs or other treaties with dispute settlement provisions where rights and obligations are parallel to those of the
WTO? Such an argument is rather extreme since RTAs are explicitly permitted (with conditions attached) under Article XXIV of
GATT and Article XIV of the General Agreement on Trade in Services,[63] and such is the practice of states as well.

If an RTA contains an exclusive forum clause, nothing appears to
prevent a WTO panel from proceeding to examine a claim of WTO
violation even if, in initiating the WTO dispute, the WTO complaining party may be in violation of its RTA obligation. As mentioned earlier in this article, in such a case, the WTO member that
is also an RTA state, may, in initiating a parallel WTO dispute, be
found to be violating its obligation under the RTA not to take a dispute outside the RTA and not to trigger a WTO claim regarding a
related violation under the RTA. In these circumstances, the RTA
state that is opposed to the parallel WTO panel could claim before
the RTA panel that the WTO panel initiated by the other RTA party
is impairing some of its benefits under the RTA. The RTA state that
is opposed to a WTO dispute would arguably win this claim before
the RTA dispute settlement body. Theoretically, that RTA state
would then be entitled to some retaliation, the value of which could
probably correspond to (part of) the benefits that the other RTA
party could gain in initiating its WTO panel. In other words, a distinction must be made between the fact that parallel dispute settlement proceedings can be triggered (and arguably cannot be stopped

---

[62] The assumption is that the RTA otherwise respect the prescriptions of Article
XXIV. See the Appellate Body report in *Turkey — Restrictions on Imports of Textile
and Clothing Products*, supra note 4 at para. 48.

[63] GATS, *supra* note 4.

since there is as yet no international agreement on this issue) and the international responsibility of the concerned states, which, in doing so, may be in violation of their treaty obligations.

A large number of difficult issues remain unresolved. Members may consider the possibility of providing for the suspension or the exhaustion of either the WTO or the RTA process in certain circumstances subject to identified criteria. Exchanges of information between RTAs and the WTO Secretariats can also be envisaged. Finally, the relationship between the rulings of RTAs and those of the WTO can also be negotiated. Since there is no "international constitution" regulating the relationship between the dispute settlement procedures of regional and other multilateral agreements, nor any treaty provision on the matter in the WTO or elsewhere, the position taken by the parties to one of these agreements cannot be sufficient to prevent a different forum from adjudicating on a similar matter within its jurisdiction. Hence, there is the potential for tensions in their overlaps and the need to consider that the issue is authentic. At the moment, there is no solution for this matter until a set of common rules is negotiated.

CONCLUSION

There could be overlaps or conflicts of judicial jurisdiction between the dispute settlement mechanism of the WTO and RTAs. The wording of Article 23 and the quasi-automaticity process of the DSU makes it evident that a WTO adjudicating body always has the authority and even the obligation to examine claims of violations of WTO obligations. WTO rights and obligations can be challenged only pursuant to the WTO dispute settlement procedures and only before a WTO adjudicating body (Article 23 of the DSU).[64] In addition, as stated earlier, in the context of a dispute between two WTO members involving situations covered by both a RTA and the WTO Agreement, any WTO member that considers that any of its WTO benefits have been nullified or impaired has the absolute right to trigger the WTO dispute settlement mechanism and to request the establishment of a panel.[65] Such a WTO member cannot be asked, and arguably cannot even agree, to take its WTO dispute to another forum, even if that other forum appears to be more

---

[64] Even an arbitration performed pursuant to Article 25 of the DSU would be a WTO arbitration, hence, covered by the exclusivity provision of Article 23 of the DSU.

[65] See note 8.

relevant or better equipped to deal with the sort of problems at issue. In so doing, the WTO member may be in violation of a RTA, but this matter is not for the WTO adjudicating body (under the existing WTO provisions). However, this WTO member may risk RTA retaliation that could be considered WTO compatible.

There appears to be no legal solution for a situation where two members are faced with two treaties that contain overlapping and potentially conflicting jurisdictions. Members remain obliged at all times to respect both treaties. However, this obligation on states may not suffice to stop a dispute settlement mechanism process triggered by a WTO member contrary to its RTA obligations. Tensions may also arise from the availability of RTA non-compulsory dispute settlement mechanisms with no binding effect even in the absence of strict *de jure* conflicts. It is not clear how members' benefits or their nullification in another forum could be taken by the WTO adjudicating bodies. For the time being, international law does not appear to offer any complete solution. It is therefore for WTO members to negotiate how they want to allocate jurisdiction between RTAs and the WTO and how the dispute settlement mechanism of RTAs and that of the WTO will operate. In the meantime, the general principle of good faith and principles of interpretation call for the "awareness" by jurisdictions and adjudicators of others' jurisdictions.

Sommaire

Chevauchements et conflits de compétences dans les mécanismes prévus par l'OMC et par les accords commerciaux régionaux

Cet article traite de l'attribution horizontale de compétences judiciaires dans le cadre des mécanismes de règlement de différends prévus par les accords commerciaux régionaux et ceux de l'Organisation mondiale du commerce (OMC). Un recoupement de compétences en matière du règlement de différends est possible dans certaines instances. Les recoupements, mais aussi les conflits de compétences sont inévitables, eu égard à la nature quasi automatique et obligatoire des mécanismes de règlement de différends de l'OMC. Afin d'approfondir le sujet, l'article passe en revue une série de principes du droit commercial international en matière de recoupements et de conflits de compétences: les notions de forum conveniens et forum non conveniens, de lis alibi pendens et de res judicata ainsi que les principes généraux du droit international: l'abus de procédure, l'abus des droits et la bonne foi, l'épuisement des recours en vertu des accords commerciaux régionaux, les renvois à la Cour internationale de justice et la possibilité d'invoquer l'article 13 du Mémorandum d'accord sur les règlements des différends afin d'obtenir de la preuve déposée lors d'une procédure en vertu d'un accord commercial régional. Enfin, l'article suggère que dans l'état actuel du droit international, aucune règle ne semble offrir une solution qui permette de résoudre efficacement la question des conflits résultant d'un chevauchement de compétences dans le contexte de l'Accord de l'OMC et des accords commerciaux régionaux. Il appartient donc aux États de décider de l'opération des mécanismes de règlement des différends de l'OMC et des accords commerciaux régionaux ainsi que des interactions entre les deux. En conclusion, l'article suggère de nouvelles pistes de réflexion pour l'avenir.

Summary

Overlaps and Conflicts of Jurisdiction between the World Trade Organization and Regional Trade Agreements

This article addresses the issue of horizontal allocation of judicial jurisdiction between the dispute settlement mechanisms of regional trade agreements (RTAs) and that of the World Trade Organization (WTO). There could be various instances where overlaps of jurisdiction in dispute settlement could occur. Overlaps and even conflicts of jurisdiction are unavoidable due to the quasi-automatic and compulsory nature of the WTO dispute settlement mechanism. With a view to furthering discussions on this issue, the article proceeds to examine a number of principles of international commercial law that deal with overlaps and conflicts: forum conveniens *and* forum non conveniens; lis alibi pendens *and* res judicata *as well as the principle of general international law; abuse of process, abuse of rights, and good faith; the exhaustion of RTA remedies; reference to the International Court of Justice; and the possibility of invoking Article 13 of the DSU to obtain evidence from RTA proceedings. Finally, the article suggests that in the current state of international law, no rules seem to offer any effective answer to resolve conflicts resulting from overlaps of jurisdiction in the context of the WTO Agreement and RTAs. It is thus for states to decide how the dispute settlement mechanisms of the WTO and RTAs should operate and interact with each other. The article concludes by pointing to areas of further discussions.*

Table 1

Dispute Settlement Mechanisms of Regional Trade Agreements[1]

SECTION 1: CONSULTATION, GOOD OFFICES, CONCILIATION, AND MEDIATION

Dispute Settlement Provision	Jurisdiction	Reference to WTO Dispute Settlement (DS) Mechanism	Binding Effect of Decision	Remedy or Other Countermeasures	Potential for Overlap
Asia and the Pacific[2]					
Australia — New Zealand Closer Economic Relations Trade Agreement (ANZCERTA)[3] • In addition to the provisions for consultations elsewhere in the agreement, ministers of the member states shall meet annually or otherwise as appropriate to review the operation of the agreement. • Consultations: The member states shall, at the request of either, promptly enter into consultations with a view to seeking an equitable and mutually satisfactory solution if the party that requested the consultation considers that an obligation under the agreement is not being fulfilled; a benefit conferred upon it by the agreement is being denied; the achievement of any objective of the agreement is frustrated; and a case of difficulty has arisen or may arise.	Non-compulsory	WTO DS mechanism not mentioned	No binding effect	Unilateral safe-guard measures	Low

First Agreement on Trade Negotiations among Developing Member Countries of the Economic and Social Commission for Asia and the Pacific (Bangkok Agreement)[4]	Non-compulsory	WTO DS mechanism not mentioned	Binding effect	Appropriate measures:	Low
• Consultations: If a participating state should consider that another participating state is not duly complying with any given provision under this agreement, and that such non-compliance adversely affects its own trade relations with that participating state, the former may make formal representation to the latter, which shall give due consideration to the representation made to it. • Referral to the Standing Committee:[5] If no satisfactory adjustment is effected between the participating states concerned within 120 days following the date on which such representation was made, the matter may be referred to the Standing Committee, which may, by majority vote, make to any participating state such recommendation as it considers appropriate. • Decision of the Standing Committee: If the participating state concerned does not comply with the recommendation of the Standing Committee, the latter may, by majority decisions authorize any participating state to suspend in relation to the non-complying state, the application of such obligations under this agreement as the Standing Committee considers appropriate.				• The measures considered to be appropriate by the Standing Committee can be taken by the affected party. Unilateral suspension of concessions (safeguard measures): • Suspension of concessions is possible but should be notified to the other party, and the committee shall enter into consultations. • If the consultations fail, the party affected by such suspension shall have the right to withdraw equivalent concession(s)	

Table 1 (continued)

Dispute Settlement Provision	Jurisdiction	Reference to WTO Dispute Settlement (DS) Mechanism	Binding Effect of Decision	Remedy or Other Countermeasures	Potential for Overlap
Agreement on South Asian Association for Regional Cooperation (SAARC) Preferential Trading Arrangement (SAPTA)[6] • Consultations: Each contracting state shall accord sympathetic consideration to, and shall afford adequate opportunity for consultations regarding such representations as may be made by another contracting state with respect to any matter affecting the operation of this agreement. • The Committee of Participants[7] may, at the request of a contracting state, consult with any contracting state in respect of any matter for which it has not been possible to find a satisfactory solution through such consultation. • Agreement between parties: Any dispute regarding the interpretation and application of the provisions of this agreement or any instrument adopted within its framework shall be amicably settled by agreement between the parties concerned. • Referral to committee: In the event of a failure to settle a dispute, it may be referred to the committee by a party to the dispute. The committee shall review the matter and make a recommendation thereon within 120 days from the date on which the dispute was submitted to it.	Non-compulsory	WTO DS mechanism not mentioned	No binding effect	Unilateral suspension of concessions (safeguard measures): • Same as Bangkok Agreement	Low

South Pacific Regional Trade and Economic Agreement (SPARTECA)[8] • Consultations: A party may at any time request consultations on any matter related to the implementation of the agreement. • Director: Any such request shall be submitted in writing to the director of the South Pacific Bureau for Economic Co-operation. On receipt of a request for consultations, the director shall inform the parties accordingly and arrange for consultations between interested parties.	Non-compulsory	WTO DS mechanism not mentioned	No binding effect	Unilateral variation or suspension of obligations (unilateral safeguard measures): • If, after consulting the other party, a mutually satisfactory solution is not available, then the party may vary or suspend its obligations.	Low
Melanesian Spearhead Group[9] • Consultation: Consultation shall take place between the parties, if a party is of the opinion that any benefits conferred on it by this agreement are not being achieved. • Institutional Framework.[10] The consultations shall take place through the institutional framework of the agreement.	Non-compulsory	WTO DS mechanism not mentioned	No binding effect	Unilateral suspension of obligations (safeguard measures): • Same as SPARTECA	Low

Table 1 (*continued*)

Dispute Settlement Provision	Jurisdiction	Reference to WTO Dispute Settlement (DS) Mechanism	Binding Effect of Decision	Remedy or Other Countermeasures	Potential for Overlap
Europe and the Mediterranean					
Central European Free Trade Agreement (CEFTA)[11]	Non-compulsory	WTO DS mechanism not mentioned	No binding effect	Unilateral safeguard measures: • If the party considers that the other party has failed to fulfil its obligations under the agreement, the party may take appropriate measures.	Low
• Exchange of information and consultation within the committee: For the purpose of the proper implementation of this agreement, the parties to it shall exchange information and, at the request of any party, shall hold consultations within a joint committee.					
• Decision-making at the Joint Committee:[12] The Joint Committee is responsible for administration and implementation, keeps under review the possibility of removing further obstacles to trade between the parties. The committee shall/may make decisions in the cases provided for in the agreement and make recommendations on other matters.					
FTAs between European Free Trade Association (EFTA)[13]	Same as CEFTA	Same as CEFTA	Same as CEFTA	Same as CEFTA	Low
• Same as CEFTA					
FTAs between two states[14]	Same as CEFTA	Same as CEFTA	Same as CEFTA	Same as CEFTA	Low
• Same as CEFTA					

FTAs between European Community (EC) and other countries[15] • Same as CEFTA	Same as CEFTA	Same as CEFTA	Same as CEFTA	Same as CEFTA	Low
Association agreements:[16] EC — Cyprus and EC — Malta • Exchange of information and consultation within Association Council:[17] For the purpose of the proper implementation of this agreement, the parties shall exchange information and, at the request of any party, hold consultations. • Decision-making at Association Council: The Association Council is responsible for administration and implementation and shall keep under review the possibility of removing further obstacles to trade between the parties. The council shall make decisions by common agreement in the cases provided for in the agreement. On other matters, the council may make recommendations.	Non-compulsory	WTO DS mechanism not mentioned	No binding effect	Unilateral safeguard measures: • In case of serious difficulties in the economic situation of either party, the party may take the necessary protective measures. Such measures shall be notified to the Association Council.	Low
Cooperation Agreement between the EC and the former Yugoslav Republic of Macedonia (FYROM)[18] • Decision-making at the Cooperation Council:[19] Each party may refer to the cooperation council any dispute relating to the application or interpretation of the agreement. The council may settle the dispute by means of a binding decision.	Non-compulsory	WTO DS mechanism not mentioned	Binding effect	Direct recourse to retaliation: • If a party considers that the other party has failed to fulfil an obligation under the agreement, it may take appropriate measures. Unilateral safeguard measures	Low

Table 1 (*continued*)

Dispute Settlement Provision	Jurisdiction	Reference to WTO Dispute Settlement (DS) Mechanism	Binding Effect of Decision	Remedy or Other Countermeasures	Potential for Overlap
Cooperation agreements:[20] EC — Jordan; EC — Lebanon; and EC — Syria	Non-compulsory	WTO DS mechanism not mentioned	Binding effect	Direct recourse to retaliation Unilateral safe-guard measures: • Same as the Cooperation Agreement between the EC — FYROM	Low
• Referral to Cooperation Council:[21] The parties shall take any general or specific measures to fulfil their obligations under the agreement. If either party considers that the other party has failed to fulfil an obligation under the agreement, it may take appropriate measures. Before so doing, it shall supply the Cooperation Council with all relevant information for a thorough examination of the situation with a view to seeking a solution acceptable to the parties.					
Bilateral Agreement between Kyrgyz and Uzbekistan[22]	Non-compulsory	WTO DS mechanism not mentioned	No binding effect		Low
• Negotiation or other means: Disputes between the parties regarding the interpretation or application of the provisions shall be settled by way of negotiations or by any other way acceptable for the parties.					

America

Latin American Integration Association (ALADI)[23]	Non-compulsory	WTO DS mechanism not mentioned	No binding effect	Low

- Resolution 114:
  — Any member state may request that consultations be held with any member country or countries that, in their view, take measures that are inconsistent with the commitments undertaken by virtue of the provisions of the 1980 Treaty of Montevideo or of relevant resolutions of the association. The request shall also be forwarded to the Committee of Representatives.
  — Consultations: Consultations shall begin within five days after the request is processed and shall conclude ten working days after consultations begin. The member countries agree to respond diligently to requests for consultations and to carry them out without delay in order to reach a mutually satisfactory solution.
  — Referral to the Committee of Representatives:[24] Should no satisfactory solution be achieved between the parties directly involved in the dispute at the end of the consultation period, the member countries may submit the matter to the Committee of Representatives.
  — The committee shall propose to the countries directly involved in the dispute, 15 days after the matter was submitted to its consideration, the formulas deemed most appropriate for settling the dispute.

Table 1 (*continued*)

Dispute Settlement Provision	Jurisdiction	Reference to WTO Dispute Settlement (DS) Mechanism	Binding Effect of Decision	Remedy or Other Countermeasures	Potential for Overlap
• Article 35 of 1980 Treaty of Montevideo: — The Committee has the obligation to propose formulas for the resolution of matters raised by the member states, when the failure to observe some of the rules or principles of the present treaty has been alleged.					
Inter-regional Agreement on the Global System of Trade Preferences among Developing Countries (GSTP)[25] • Consultations: Any dispute that may arise among the participants regarding the interpretation and application of the agreement or any instrument adopted within its framework shall be amicably settled by agreement between the parties through consultation. • Recommendation of Committee:[26] In the event of a failure to settle a dispute through consultations, it may be referred to a committee by a party to the dispute. The committee shall review the matter and make a recommendation within 120 days from the date on which the dispute was submitted to it.	Non-compulsory	WTO DS mechanism not mentioned	No binding effect	Unilateral suspension of concessions: • If a party considers that the value of concessions or any benefit from the agreement is being nullified or impaired, the party may consult the other party.	Low

- If the consultations fail, the matter may be referred to the committee, which may make recommendations.
- If no satisfactory adjustment is made within ninety days after the recommendations, the party may suspend concessions.

Table 1 (*continued*)

SECTION 2: ARBITRATION [27]

Dispute Settlement Provision	Jurisdiction	Reference to GATT/WTO DS Mechanism	Binding Effect of the Decision	Remedy [28]	Potential for Overlap
Asia and the Pacific					
ASEAN Free-Trade Area (AFTA) [29] • Protocol on Dispute Settlement Mechanism: [30] — A member state involved in a dispute can resort to other fora at any stage before the Senior Economic Officials Meeting (SEOM) [31] has made a ruling on the panel report. — Consultations: Members shall accord adequate opportunity for consultations regarding any representation made by other members with respect to any matter affecting the implementation of the agreement. Any differences between the members concerning the interpretation or application of the agreement shall, as far as possible, be settled amicably between the parties. — Good offices, conciliation, or mediation: Member states that are parties to a dispute may at any time agree to good offices, conciliation, or mediation. They may begin at any time and be terminated at any time. Once procedures for good offices, conciliation, or mediation are terminated, a complaining party may then proceed to raise the matter to the SEOM.	Non-compulsory	WTO DS mechanism not mentioned	Binding effect: • Arbitration: The party shall comply with the rulings of the arbitration tribunal within a reasonable time-period. If the party fails to do so, that party may consult with the complaining party. If no mutually satisfactory resolution is reached, the complaining party may request authorization for suspension of benefits from the AEM.	Arbitration award: • Decision by the AEM	High

— Referral to the SEOM: If the consultations fail to settle a dispute within sixty days after the date of receipt of the request for consultations, the matter shall be raised in the SEOM. The SEOM shall establish a panel or, where applicable, raise the matter to the special body in charge of the special or additional rules and procedures for its consideration. However, if the SEOM considers it desirable to do so in a particular case, it may decide to deal with the dispute to achieve an amicable settlement without appointing a panel.

— Establishment of the panel: The SEOM shall establish a panel within thirty days after the date on which the dispute has been raised to it. The SEOM shall make the final determination of the size, composition, and terms of reference of the panel. The panel shall submit its findings to the SEOM.

— Decision by the SEOM: The SEOM shall consider the report of the panel in its deliberations and make a ruling on the dispute within thirty days from the submission of the report.

— Appeal: Parties to the dispute may appeal the ruling by the SEOM to the ASEAN Economic Ministers (AEM)[32] within thirty days of the ruling. The AEM shall make a decision based on a simple majority.

- Appeal with the AEM: The decision of the AEM on appeal shall be final and binding on all parties to the dispute.

Table 1 (*continued*)

Dispute Settlement Provision	Jurisdiction	Reference to GATT/WTO DS Mechanism	Binding Effect of the Decision	Remedy[28]	Potential for for Overlap
Agreement between New Zealand and Singapore on a Closer Economic Relationship (ANZSCEP)[33]	Compulsory	WTO DS mechanism not mentioned. However, the rules and procedures of dispute settlement under the agreement shall apply to the parties in dispute but without prejudice to the rights of the parties to dispute settlement procedures under other agreements to which they are parties.	Binding effect: • The rulings of the arbitral tribunal shall be final and binding on the parties.	• The party shall comply with the rulings of the arbitration tribunal within a reasonable time period. • If the party fails to do so within the time limit, that party may consult with the complaining party. • If no mutually satisfactory resolution is reached, the complaining party may suspend the application of equivalent benefits.	Medium/High

• Consultation: The parties shall consult each other concerning any matter that may affect the operation of the agreement. The parties shall try to reach a mutually satisfactory resolution of any matter through consultations. The parties may at any time agree to good offices, conciliation, or mediation.

• Arbitral stage: If the consultations fail to settle a dispute within sixty days after the date of the receipt of the request for consultations, the complaining party may make a written request to the other party to appoint an arbitration tribunal.

• Composition of the arbitral tribunal: The tribunal consists of three members. Each party shall appoint an arbitrator within thirty days of the receipt of the request, and the two arbitrators appointed shall designate by common agreement the third arbitrator, who shall chair the tribunal. If the chair has not been designated within one month from the appointment of second arbitration, the directorate-general of the WTO, at the request of either party, may select the chair.

Free trade area agreements:[34] EFTA — Morocco and EFTA — PLO	Non-compulsory	WTO DS mechanism not mentioned	Binding effect: • The arbitration award is binding and final upon the parties.	Direct recourse to retaliation: • If a party considers that the other party has failed to fulfil an obligation under the agreement, it may take appropriate measures. Decision of arbitration panel: • However, once the matter is referred to arbitration, the decision of the arbitration panel is binding.	Medium
• Referral to the Joint Committee:[35] For the purpose of the proper implementation of this agreement, the parties to it shall exchange information and, at the request of any party, shall hold consultations within a joint committee. • Decision-making at the Joint Committee: The Joint Committee is responsible for the administration and implementation and shall keep under review the possibility of further removing the obstacles to trade between the parties. The Joint Committee may make decisions in the cases provided for in the agreement. On other matters, the committee may make recommendations. • Arbitral stage: Disputes relating to the interpretation of rights and obligations of the parties, which have not been settled through consultation or the committee within six months, may be referred to arbitration by any party to the dispute by means of a written notification. • Composition of the Arbitral Tribunal: The complaining party will designate one panel member in its notification. Within a month from the receipt of the notification, the other party will designate one member. Within two months from the receipt of the notification, the two members already designated shall agree on the designation of a third member, who will become the president of the Arbitral Tribunal. The tribunal takes its decision by majority vote.					

Table 1 (*continued*)

Dispute Settlement Provision	Jurisdiction	Reference to GATT/WTO DS Mechanism	Binding Effect of the Decision	Remedy[28]	Potential for for Overlap
Free trade area agreements between EFTA and certain countries[36] • Referral to Joint Committee:[37] The parties shall make every attempt through cooperation and consultations to arrive at a mutually satisfactory resolution of disputes. At the request of a party, the consultations shall take place in the Joint Committee if any of the parties so request. • Arbitral stage: Disputes between the parties to this agreement, relating to the interpretation of rights and obligations under this agreement, which have not been settled through direct consultations or in the Joint Committee within ninety days from the date of the receipt of the request for consultations, may be referred to arbitration by any party to the dispute. • Composition of the Arbitral Tribunal: The complaining party will designate one panel member in its notification. Within a month from the receipt of the notification, the other party will designate one member. Within two months from the receipt of the notification, the two members already designated shall agree on the designation of a third member, who will become the president of the Arbitral Tribunal. The tribunal takes its decision by majority vote.	Non-compulsory	WTO DS mechanism not mentioned	Binding effect: • The arbitration award is binding and final upon the parties.	Direct recourse to retaliation: • Same as EFTA — Morocco/ PLO Decision of arbitration panel: • Same as EFTA — Morocco/ PLO	Medium

EFTA — Mexico[38]	Compulsory jurisdiction	Exclusive forum clause: ... Forum election clause:	Binding effect:	Decision of arbitration panel:	Medium
• Consultation: The parties shall at all times endeavour to agree on the interpretation and application of the agreement and shall make every attempt through cooperation and consultations to arrive at a mutually satisfactory resolution of any matter that might affect their operation. • Referral to Joint Committee:[39] Each party may request consultations within the Joint Committee with respect to any matter relating to the application or interpretation of the agreement. The Joint Committee shall convene within thirty days of delivery of the request and shall endeavour to resolve the dispute promptly by means of a decision. That decision shall specify the implementing measures to be taken by the party concerned and the period of time to do so. • Arbitral stage: In case a party considers that a measure applied by the other party violates the agreement and such matter has not been resolved within fifteen days after the Joint Committee has convened or forty-five days after the delivery of the request for a Joint Committee meeting, either party may request in writing the establishment of an arbitration panel.		• Once the dispute settlement provisions of this agreement or the WTO Agreements have been initiated, the procedure initiated shall be used to the exclusion of any other. Forum election clause: • Disputes regarding any matter arising under both this agreement and the WTO Agreement may be settled in either form at the discretion of the complaining party.	• The decision of the arbitration panel is final and binding.	• The party shall comply with the rulings of the arbitration tribunal within a reasonable time period. • If the party fails to do so within the time limit, that party may consult with the complaining party. • If no mutually satisfactory resolution is reached, the complaining party may suspend the application of equivalent benefits.	

Table 1 (*continued*)

Dispute Settlement Provision	Jurisdiction	Reference to GATT/WTO DS Mechanism	Binding Effect of the Decision	Remedy[28]	Potential for for Overlap
• Composition of arbitration panel: The panel consists of three members. Each party shall appoint an arbitrator, and the two arbitrators appointed shall designate by common agreement the third arbitrator, who shall chair the panel. If all three members have not been appointed within thirty days from receipt of notification, any party may request that the directorate-general of the WTO designates the member.		Recourse to DS procedure by a third party: • If a third party wishes to resort to DS procedures as a complainant under this agreement on the same matter, it must inform the notifying party. If these parties cannot agree on a single forum, the dispute normally shall be settled under this agreement.			

Customs Union between the EC and Andorra[40]	Compulsory	WTO DS mechanism not mentioned	Binding effect: • The arbitration award is binding and final upon the parties.	Direct recourse to retaliation: • Same as EFTA — Morocco/ PLO Decision of arbitration panel: • Same as EFTA — Morocco/ PLO	High
• Referral to Joint Committee:[41] Any disputes arising between the contracting parties over the interpretation of the agreement shall be put before the Joint Committee.					
• Arbitral stage: If the Joint Committee does not succeed in settling the dispute at its next meeting, each party may notify the other of the designation of an arbitrator; the other party shall then be required to designate a second arbitrator within two months. The Joint Committee shall designate a third arbitrator. The arbitrator's decisions shall be taken by majority vote.					
Customs Union between the EC and Turkey[42]	Compulsory	WTO DS mechanism not mentioned	Binding effect: • The arbitration award shall be binding on the parties.	Decision of arbitration panel	High
• Consultation: In harmonizing the legislation, each party may consult each other within the Customs Union Joint Committee.[43]					
• Referral to Joint Committee: If a mutually acceptable solution is not found by the committee and if either party considers that discrepancies in the legislation may affect the free movement of goods, deflect trade, or create economic problems, it may refer the matter to the committee, which may make recommendations. If discrepancies cause or threaten to cause impairment of the free movement of goods or the deflection of trade, the party may take the necessary protection measures.					

Table 1 (*continued*)

Dispute Settlement Provision	Jurisdiction	Reference to GATT/WTO DS Mechanism	Binding Effect of the Decision	Remedy[28]	Potential for for Overlap
• Arbitral stage: If the Association Council[44] fails to settle a dispute relating to the scope or duration of protection measures, either party may refer the dispute to arbitration. • Composition of arbitration panel: There shall be three arbitrators, two appointed by each party and a third appointed by common agreement. The panel shall take its decisions by majority.					
Europe Agreements[45] • Referral to Association Council:[46] Each of the two parties may refer to the Association Council any dispute relating to the application or interpretation of the agreement. The Association Council may settle the dispute by means of a decision. Each party shall be bound to take the measures involved in carrying out the decision. • Arbitral stage: If it is impossible to settle the dispute by means of a decision, either party may notify the other of the appointment of an arbitrator; the other party must then appoint a second arbitrator within two months. The Association Council shall appoint a third arbitrator. The arbitrator's decisions shall be taken by majority vote.	Compulsory	WTO DS mechanism not mentioned	Binding effect: • The arbitration award is binding and final upon the parties.	Direct recourse to retaliation: • If a party considers that the other party has failed to fulfil an obligation, it may take appropriate measures. Decision of arbitration panel	High

Association agreements between the EC and certain countries:[47] • Same as Europe Agreements	Compulsory	WTO DS mechanism not mentioned	Same as Europe Agreements	Same as Europe Agreements	High
Cooperation Agreement between the EC and Algeria • Same as Europe Agreements	Compulsory	WTO DS mechanism not mentioned	Same as Europe Agreements	Same as Europe Agreements	High
Bilateral agreements[48] Same as Europe Agreements	Compulsory	WTO DS mechanism not mentioned	Same as Europe Agreements	Same as Europe Agreements	High
EC — Mexico[49] • Consultation: The parties shall endeavour to agree on the interpretation and application of the agreement and shall make every attempt through cooperation and consultations to arrive at a mutually satisfactory resolution of any matter that might affect their operation. • Referral to Joint Committee:[50] Each party may request consultations within the Joint Committee with respect to any matter relating to the application or interpretation of the agreement. The Joint Committee shall convene within thirty days of delivery of the request and shall endeavour to resolve the dispute promptly by means of a decision, which should specify the implementing measure and the period for implementation.	Compulsory	Exclusive forum clause: • Recourse to the dispute settlement provisions of the agreement shall be without prejudice to any action in the WTO framework. However, where a party has instituted a DS proceeding under this agreement or	Binding effect: • Each party shall be bound to take the measures involved in carrying out the final arbitration report.	Decision of arbitration panel	High

Table 1 (*continued*)

Dispute Settlement Provision	Jurisdiction	Reference to GATT/WTO DS Mechanism	Binding Effect of the Decision	Remedy[28]	Potential for for Overlap
• Arbitral stage: In case a party considers that a measure applied by the other party violates the agreement and such matter has not been resolved within fifteen days after the Joint Committee has convened or forty-five days after the delivery of the request for a Joint Committee meeting, either party may request in writing the establishment of an arbitration panel. • Composition of an arbitration panel: The panel consists of three members. Each party shall appoint an arbitrator, and the two arbitrators appointed shall designate by common agreement the third arbitrator, who is the chair of the panel.		the WTO Agreement, it shall not institute a DS proceeding on the same matter under the other forum until the end of the first proceeding. Arbitration proceedings under the agreement will not consider parties' rights and obligations under the WTO Agreement.			

Commonwealth of Independent States (CIS)[51] • Any disputes and disagreements between the members shall be settled in the following manner: conduct immediate consultations through a special conciliatory procedure; in the Economic Court of the CIS; through other procedures provided by international law. • Transition to the subsequent procedure is possible by mutual consent of the disputing parties or by the order of one of them if agreement is not reached within six months from the day of the beginning of the procedure.	Non-compulsory	WTO DS mechanism not mentioned	Binding effect	Medium/High
America[52]				
Central American Common Market (CACM)[53] • General Treaty on Central American Economic Integration: — Agreement: The parties may settle disputes concerning interpretation or application of the agreement amicably through the Executive Council[54] or the Central American Economic Council.[55] — Arbitral stage: If agreement cannot be reached, they shall submit the matter to arbitration. For the purpose of constituting the arbitration tribunal, the secretary-general of the Organization of Central American States and the government representatives in the organization shall select, by drawing lots, one arbitrator for each contracting party from a list containing the names of arbitrators proposed by each member state.	Compulsory	WTO DS mechanism not mentioned	Binding effect: • The award of the arbitration tribunal shall require the concurring votes of not less than three members and shall have the effect of *res judicata* for all the contracting parties so far as it contains any ruling concerning the interpretation	Decision of arbitration panel	High

Table 1 (*continued*)

Dispute Settlement Provision	Jurisdiction	Reference to GATT/WTO DS Mechanism	Binding Effect of the Decision	Remedy[28]	Potential for for Overlap
• Protocol of Tegucigalpa: — Article 35: Any disagreement on the application or interpretation of the provisions contained in this protocol and any other convention, agreement, or protocol between the members (bilateral or multilateral) on Central American integration shall be put before the Central American Court of Justice. — Transitional provisions (Article 3) provides that, for the purposes of what is established in paragraph 2 of Article 35, until the Central American Court of Justice is established, disputes on the application or interpretation of the provisions in the protocol will be submitted to the Central American Judicial Council.			or application of the provisions of this treaty.		
US — Israel FTA[56] • Consultations: The parties shall make every attempt to arrive at a mutually agreeable resolution through consultations whenever: a dispute arises concerning the interpretation of the agreement; a party considers that the other party has failed to carry out its obligations under the agreement; or a party considers that measures taken by the other party severely distort the balance of trade benefits accorded by the agreement or substantially undermine fundamental objectives of the agreement.	Compulsory	WTO DS mechanism not mentioned. However, exclusive forum clause: • If the dispute settlement panel under the agreement or any other international dispute settlement mechanism is	No binding effect: • The panel report is not binding but the Joint Committee will make a final decision taking into account the panel decision.	Appropriate measures: • After a dispute has been referred to a panel and the panel has presented its report, the affected party shall be entitled to take any appropriate measure.	Medium

				Decision of arbitration panel	High

• Referral to Joint Committee:[57] If the parties fail to resolve a matter through consultations within sixty days, either party may refer the matter to the joint committee.
• Arbitral stage: If a matter referred to the joint committee has not been resolved within three months, or within such other period as agreed upon, either party may refer the matter to a dispute settlement panel. The panel shall be composed of three members: each party will appoint one, and two appointees will choose a third.

invoked with respect to any matter, the mechanism shall have exclusive jurisdiction over that matter.

Binding effect:
• The decisions of the tribunal cannot be appealed, and are binding on the parties to the controversies from the moment the respective notification is received and will be deemed by them to have the effect of *res judicata*.

Southern Common Market (MERCOSUR)[58]

There are two tracks of dispute settlement mechanisms to which the parties can resort. Member states can either go straight to the Brasília Protocol, which is faster, or through the Ouro Preto Protocol, which is longer but provides for a technical committee phase and could allow more easily for mutually agreeable solutions.

• Brasília Protocol — Chapter IV:
— Direct negotiations: The state parties to any controversy will first attempt to resolve it through direct negotiations. They will inform the Common Market Group[59] regarding the actions undertaken during the negotiations and their results.

Compulsory:
• The state parties declare that they recognize as obligatory, *ipso facto* and without need of a special agreement, the jurisdiction of the Arbitral Tribunal, which in each case is established in order to hear and resolve all

WTO DS mechanism not mentioned

Table 1 (*continued*)

Dispute Settlement Provision	Jurisdiction	Reference to GATT/WTO DS Mechanism	Binding Effect of the Decision	Remedy[28]	Potential for for Overlap
— Participation of the Common Market Group: if the direct negotiations do not resolve the matter, any of the parties can submit for consideration by the Common Market Group, which will evaluate the situation. At the conclusion of the procedure (not exceeding thirty days), the Common Market Group will formulate its recommendations to the parties. — Arbitral stage: If direct negotiations and inter-vention by the Common Market Group fail, any of the state parties to the controversy can communicate to the Administrative Secretariat its intention to resort to the arbitral procedure. The tribunal shall issue its decision within sixty days, extendable for an additional thirty days, from the time its president is designated. The tribunal will take decision by majority vote. — Composition of the Arbitral Tribunal: Each state party will designate one arbitrator from a pre-existing list of names deposited at the Administrative Secretariat. The third arbitrator will be designated upon common agreement and will reside over the arbitral tribunal. The arbitrators should be named within fifteen days from the date on which the intention of one of the parties to resort to arbitration was communicated to the other parties to the controversy.	controversies that are referred to in the present protocol.				

- Protocol of Ouro Preto — Article 21 + Annex:

— MERCOSUL Trade Commission: The commission receives complaints originating from member states or from private parties. It must consider the complaint in the first subsequent meeting. If no solution is agreed upon, then a technical committee (intergovernmental) is established. There are thirty days to elaborate joint recommendation or individual conclusions. The commission evaluates joint recommendation or conclusions in its next meeting.

— Submission of Complaint to Common Market Group: If there is no consensus, the complaint is submitted to the Common Market Group, which will have thirty days to consider the complaint. If a consensus is reached, a deadline is given to the member state to take measures. If there is no consensus or the member state does not implement measures, Chapter IV of the Brasília Protocol — Ad Hoc Arbitral Tribunal is invoked.

- Protocol of Olivos for the Solution of Controversies:

— The new Protocol of Olivos Protocol was signed in Buenos Aires on 18 February 2002 and changes the mechanism in fundamental ways (Appellate Body, WTO clause, and so on) and will enter into force after ratification and will replace the Brasília Protocol.

Table 1 (*continued*)

Dispute Settlement Provision	Jurisdiction	Reference to GATT/WTO DS Mechanism	Binding Effect of the Decision	Remedy[28]	Potential for for Overlap
North American Free-Trade Agreement (NAFTA)[60] — Cooperation: The parties shall at all times endeavour to agree on the interpretation and application of the agreement and shall make every attempt through cooperation and consultations to arrive at a mutually satisfactory resolution of any matter that might affect its operation. — Consultations: If the matter is not settled through cooperation, either party may request in writing consultations with the other party regarding the interpretation or application of the agreement, or wherever a party considers that an actual or proposed measure of the other party is, or would be, inconsistent with the obligations of this agreement or cause nullification or impairment. — Commission[61] — Good Offices, Conciliation and Mediation: If the parties fail to resolve a matter through consultations within the time limit (thirty days of delivery of a request for consultations, fifteen days of delivery of a request for consultations on matters of urgency, or any other period as they may agree), either party may request in writing a meeting of the commission.	Compulsory	Exclusive forum clause: • Once the dispute settlement provisions of this agreement or the WTO Agreement have been initiated, the procedure initiated shall be used to the exclusion of any other. Forum election clause: • Disputes regarding any matter arising under both this agreement and the WTO Agreement may be settled in either form at the	Binding effect: • On receipt of the final report of a panel, the disputing parties shall agree on the resolution of the dispute, which normally shall conform with the determinations and recommendations of the panel, and shall notify their sections of the Secretariat of any agreed resolution of any dispute.	Suspension of benefits: • If the final panel report determined that a measure is inconsistent with the obligations of the agreement or causes nullification or impairment, and the respondent party has not agreed with the complaining party on a mutually satisfactory solution within thirty days of receiving the final report, the complaining party may	High

— Arbitral stage: If the matter has not been resolved, either party may request in writing the establishment of an arbitral panel within the time limit (thirty days after the commission has convened for the meeting; thirty days after the commission has convened with respect to the matter most referred to it, where proceedings have been consolidated, and such other period as the parties may agree). On delivery of the request, the commission shall establish an arbitral panel. The panel issues the initial report and the parties have the opportunity to submit their comment. The panel issues its final report.

— Composition of arbitration panel: The panel shall comprise three members. Each party shall select one panelist and will agree on a third panelist, who shall serve as chair of the panel.

discretion of the complaining party.

• An exception is made with respect to claims involving environmental, SPS, and technical standards matters, for which the responding party may demand that the matter be settled by a NAFTA panel.

• Recourse to DS procedure by a third party: If a third party wishes to have recourse to NAFTA DS procedures on the same matter and if these parties cannot agree on a single forum, the dispute normally shall be settled under the NAFTA agreement.

suspend the application of benefits of equivalent effect until the measures complained against have been removed or a mutually satisfactory solution is reached.

High

Table 1 *(continued)*

Dispute Settlement Provision	Jurisdiction	Reference to GATT/WTO DS Mechanism	Binding Effect of the Decision	Remedy[28]	Potential for for Overlap
Canada — Israel FTA[62] • Same as NAFTA	Compulsory	Exclusive forum clause Forum election clause: • In the event of any inconsistency between this agreement and the WTO Agreement, this agreement shall prevail to the extent of the inconsistency, except as otherwise provided in the agreement.	Binding effect: • Same as NAFTA.	Suspension of benefits: • Same as NAFTA, except, insert "30 days of receiving the final report if the measure was found to be inconsistent with the agreement or within 180 days if the measure was found to cause nullification or impairment" instead of "30 days of receiving final report."	High

Canada — Chile FTA[63]	Compulsory	Exclusive forum clause:	Binding effect:	Suspension of benefits:	High
• Same as NAFTA		Forum election clause: • If the party claims that its action is subject to Article A-04 (relation to environmental and conservation agreements) and request that the matter be considered under this agreement, then the party has the sole recourse to dispute settlement under the agreement.	• Same as NAFTA	• Same as NAFTA	

Table 1 *(continued)*

Dispute Settlement Provision	Jurisdiction	Reference to GATT/WTO DS Mechanism	Binding Effect of the Decision	Remedy[28]	Potential for for Overlap
Chile — Mexico FTA[64] • Same as NAFTA	Compulsory	Exclusive forum clause: Forum election clause: • If the responding party claims that its action is subject to Article 1-06 (relation to environmental and conservation agreements) and request that the matter be considered under this agreement, the complaining party may have recourse to dispute settlement procedures solely under this agreement.	Binding effect: • Unless the Commission decides otherwise, the final report of the panel shall be published. The final report of the panel is binding on the parties.	Suspension of benefits: • Same as NAFTA	High

Israel — Mexico FTA[65] • Same as NAFTA	Compulsory	Exclusive forum clause Forum election clause	Binding effect: • Same as NAFTA	Suspension of benefits	High
US — Jordan FTA[66] • Consultations: The parties shall make every attempt to arrive at a mutually agreeable resolution through consultations whenever: a dispute arises concerning the interpretation of the agreement; a party considers that the other party has failed to carry out its obligations under the agreement; or a party considers that measures taken by the other party severely distort the balance of trade benefits accorded by the agreement; or substantially undermine fundamental objectives of the agreement. • Referral to the Joint Committee:[67] If the parties fail to resolve a matter through consultations within sixty days, either party may refer the matter to the joint committee. • Arbitral stage: If a matter referred to the joint committee has not been resolved within three months, or within such other period as agreed upon, either party may refer the matter to a dispute settlement panel. The panel shall be composed of three members: each party will appoint one, and two appointees will choose a third.	Compulsory	WTO DS mechanism not mentioned. However, exclusive forum clause: • If the panel under the agreement or any other international dispute settlement mechanism is invoked with respect to any matter, the mechanism shall have exclusive jurisdiction over that matter.	No binding effect: • After the presentation of the panel report, the Joint Committee shall try to resolve the matter taking into account the report. • If the committee does not resolve the dispute within one month, the affected party is entitled to take appropriate measures.	Appropriate measures	Medium

Table 1 (continued)

Dispute Settlement Provision	Jurisdiction	Reference to GATT/WTO DS Mechanism	Binding Effect of the Decision	Remedy[28]	Potential for for Overlap
Inter-regional					
African Caribbean Pacific (ACP) — EC Partnership Agreement • Referral to the Council: Any dispute arising from the interpretation or application of this agreement between one or more member states or the EC and one or more ACP states, shall be submitted to the Council of Ministers.[68] Between the meetings of the Council of Ministers, such disputes shall be submitted to the Committee of Ambassadors. • Arbitral stage: If the Council of Ministers does not succeed in settling the dispute, either party may request settlement of the dispute by arbitration. To this end, each party shall appoint an arbitrator within thirty days of the request for arbitration. In the event of failure to do so, either party may ask the secretary-general of the Permanent Court of Arbitration to appoint the second arbitrator. • The two arbitrators shall in turn appoint a third arbitrator within thirty days. In the event of failure to do so, either party may ask the secretary-general of the Permanent Court of Arbitration to appoint the third arbitrator. • The arbitrators' decisions shall be taken by majority vote within three months.	Non-compulsory	WTO DS mechanism not mentioned	Binding effect: • Each party to the dispute shall be bound to take the measures necessary to carry out the decision of the arbitrators.		

Table 1 (*continued*)

SECTION 3: STANDING TRIBUNAL[69]

Dispute Settlement Provision	Jurisdiction	Binding Effect of the Decision	Potential for Overlap
Europe			
European Economic Area (EEA) Agreement[70]	Compulsory jurisdiction: • The EFTA Court has jurisdiction with regard to EFTA states that are parties to the EEA Agreement (at present Iceland, Liechtenstein, and Norway).	Binding effect Direct effect	High
• Alleged infringement of EEA law by a state party			
• Informal stage			
• Pre 31-Letter sent to the concerned state by the Surveillance Authority			
• The EFTA state submits comments to the authority (within one to two months)			
• Letter of formal notice			
• The EFTA state submits comments to the authority (normally within two months)	Exclusive jurisdiction		
• Reasoned opinion by the authority			
• The EFTA state replies to the opinion (normally within two months)			
• Decision on referral to the EFTA Court Proceedings before the EFTA Court			
• The court is mainly competent to deal with infringement actions brought by the EFTA Surveillance Authority against an EFTA state with regard to the implementation, application, or interpretation of an EEA rule, for the settlement of disputes between two or more EFTA states, for appeals concerning decisions taken by the EFTA Surveillance Authority and for giving advisory opinions to courts in EFTA states on the interpretation of EEA rules.			
Customs Union[71]			

Table 1 (*continued*)

Dispute Settlement Provision	Jurisdiction	Binding Effect of the Decision	Potential for Overlap
• The community court will provide guarantees of uniform enforcement by the parties of this agreement and other agreements between the community members and decisions taken by community institutions. • The court shall also consider economic disputes arising between the parties on issues of implementation of decisions of the community institution and provisions of agreements effective between members, and provide explanations and opinions.	Compulsory jurisdiction Exclusive jurisdiction	Binding effect	High
America Andean Subregional Integration Agreement[72] (Cartagena Agreement) • Action of nullification: It is up to the court to nullify the decisions taken by the commission[73] and the resolutions issued by the Board that violate the rules comprising the legal system of the Cartagena Agreement. When the Board considers that a member state has failed to fulfil the obligations from the Cartagena Agreement, it shall make its observations in writing, to which the member country must reply within two months. The Board shall issue a reasoned opinion. If, in the Board's opinion, the member country failed to fulfil the obligations mentioned above and continues to do so, the Board may request a verdict from the court.	Compulsory jurisdiction Exclusive jurisdiction: • Member countries shall not submit any controversy arising from the application of rules comprising the legal system of the Cartagena Agreement to any court, arbitration system, or proceeding other than those contemplated herein.	Binding effect: • If the court rules finds non-compliance, the member country at fault shall take the necessary steps to execute the judgment within three months after notification.	High

- Action of non-compliance: When a member country considers that another member country has failed to fulfil the obligations from the agreement, it may raise its claim with the Board, stating all of the background of the case, so that the Board can issue a reasoned opinion. If, in the Board's opinion, the member country failed to fulfil its obligations and continues to do so, the Board may request a verdict from the court. Should the Board not file the action within two months after the date of its judgment, the claiming country may appeal directly to the court. Should the Board fail to pronounce judgment within three months from the date the claim was submitted, or rule against the noncompliance, then the claiming country may appeal directly to the court.
- Prejudicial interpretation: It is up to the court to issue a prejudicial interpretation of the rules comprising the legal system of the Cartagena Agreement, in order to ensure its uniform application in the territories of member countries.

Treaty Establishing the Caribbean Community (Caricom) [74]

- Modes of dispute settlement: Disputes shall be settled only by recourse to the following modes: good offices, mediation, consultation, conciliation, arbitration, and adjudication. If a dispute is not settled using one of the modes other than arbitration or adjudication, either party may have recourse to another mode.
- Expeditious settlement of disputes: When a dispute arises between member states, the parties shall proceed expeditiously to an exchange of views to agree on a mode of settlement and a mutually satisfactory implementation method.

- Member countries hereby agree to make use of the procedure established in Article 23 (action for non-compliance) of the Cartagena Agreement only for controversies arising between any one of them and another contracting party of the Montevideo Treaty that is not a member of the agreement.

Compulsory jurisdiction
Exclusive jurisdiction

Binding effect

High

Table 1 (*continued*)

Dispute Settlement Provision	Jurisdiction	Binding Effect of the Decision	Potential for Overlap
• Notification of existence and settlement of dispute: Member states to a dispute shall notify the secretary-general of the existence and nature of the dispute and any mode of dispute settlement agreed upon or initiated. When a settlement is reached, the member states concerned shall notify the secretary-general of the settlement and the mode used in arriving at the settlement.			
• Good offices, mediation, and consultations: Parties to a dispute may agree to employ the good offices of a third party or agree to settle the dispute by recourse to mediation.			
• Consultations: A member state shall enter into consultations upon the request of another member state where the requesting member state alleges that an action taken by the requested member state constitutes a breach of obligations arising from, or under, the provisions of the treaty.			
• Conciliation Commission: Where member states parties to a dispute have agreed to submit the dispute to conciliation, any such member state may institute proceedings by notification addressed to the other party or parties to the dispute. The complaining party chooses one conciliator from a list of conciliators and the other party does the same. Two conciliators will appoint a third conciliator from the list, who will be the chairman. The decision shall be made by majority vote.			
• Arbitration tribunal: A party to a dispute may, with the consent of the other party, refer the matter to an arbitration tribunal. Each of the parties will appoint one arbitrator from the list of arbitrators. The two arbitrators shall appoint a third arbitrator.			

- Judicial settlement: The court has compulsory and exclusive jurisdiction to hear disputes concerning the interpretation and application of the treaty. The court has exclusive jurisdiction on inter-state disputes, disputes between members and the Caricom, referrals from national courts of members, and persons. The court shall have exclusive jurisdiction to deliver advisory opinions concerning the interpretation and application of the treaty.

Africa

Common Market for Eastern and Southern Africa (COMESA)[75]

- The court has jurisdiction to hear the following: disputes between states, disputes between the state and the COMESA institutions, claims from members, the secretary general, and legal and natural persons, claims against COMESA or its institutions by COMESA employees and third parties, and claims arising from arbitration clauses and special agreement.

	Compulsory jurisdiction:	Binding effect	High
	• The court shall have jurisdiction to adjudicate upon all matters that may be referred to it pursuant to the treaty.		

Economic Community of Central African States (CEEAC); Communauté et monétaire de l'Afrique Centrale (CEMAC)[76]

- La Cour de Justice Communautaire comporte deux Chambres: Une Chambre Judiciaire et une Chambre des Comptes.
- La Cour de Judiciaire de la Communauté est régie par une Convention spécifique.

	Compulsory jurisdiction	Binding effect	High
	• La Chambre Judiciaire de la Communauté connaît des litiges liés à la mise en oeuvre de la Convention régissant l'Union Économique de l'Afrique Centrale.		

East African Community (EAC)[77]

- The court can hear claims from members, the secretary general, persons, claims against the EAC or its institutions by EAC employees and third parties, and claims arising from the arbitration clause and special agreement.

	Compulsory jurisdiction:
	• The court shall initially have jurisdiction over the interpretation and application of the treaty.

Table 1 (*continued*)

Dispute Settlement Provision	Jurisdiction	Binding Effect of the Decision	Potential for Overlap
	• The court shall have such other original, appellate, human rights, and other jurisdictions as will be determined by the council at a suitable subsequent date. To this end, the partner states shall conclude a protocol to operationalize the extended jurisdiction.		
Traité de l'Union Economique et Monetaire Ouest Africaine (UEMOA) West African Economic Monetary Union (WAEMU) [78] • La Cour de Justice connaît, sur recours de la Commission ou de tout Etat member, des manquements des Etats membres aux obligations qui leur incombent en vertu du Traité de L'Union. • La Cour de Justice statue à titre préjudicionnel sur l'interprétation du Traité de l'Union sur la légalité et l'interprétation des status des organismes créés par un acte du Conseil. • La Court de justice connaît des litiges relatifs à la réparation des dommages causés par les organes de l'Union, des litiges entre l'Union et ses agents, et des différends entre membres relatifs	Compulsory jurisdiction: • La Cour de Justice veille au respect du droit quant à l'interprétation et à l'application du Traité de L'Union au Traité de l'Union.	Binding effect	High

1 Table 1 is based on the wording of the treaties, but the practices of states may be different. The table does not include regional trade agreements that have not been notified to the World Trade Organization (WTO).

2 The agreements in Table 1 only include the agreements that have been notified to the WTO.

3 The agreement entered into force on 1 January 1983.

4 The agreement is a preferential tariff arrangement that aims at promoting intra-regional trade through exchange of mutually agreed concessions by member countries. The agreement entered into force on 17 June 1976. Current signatories are Bangladesh, China, India, Republic of Korea, Lao People's Democratic Republic and Sri Lanka.

5 A Standing Committee of the participating states members of the Economic and Social Commission for the Asia and the Pacific (ESCAP) Trade Negotiations Group consists of the representatives of the countries participating in the agreement.

6 The agreement entered into force on 7 December 1995. Current signatories are Bangladesh, Bhutan, India, Maldives, Nepal, Pakistan, and Sri Lanka.

7 The Committee of Participants is composed of the contracting states.

8 SPARTECA is a non-reciprocal trade agreement under which the two developed nations of the South Pacific Forum, Australia, and New Zealand offer duty free and unrestricted or concessional access for virtually all products originating from the developing island member countries of the forum. SPARTECA was signed by most forum members at the forum's eleventh meeting in Kiribati on 14 July 1980. It came into effect for most Forum Island countries (FIC) on 1 January 1981. With the joining of new members to the forum, the current list of FIC signatories to SPARTECA includes the Cook Islands, the Federated States of Micronesia, Fiji, Kiribati, Marshall Islands, Nauru, Niue, Papua New Guinea, Solomon Islands, Tonga, Tuvalu, Vanuatu, and Western Samoa.

9 The agreement entered into force on 22 July 1993. The initial members were Papua New Guinea, Solomon Islands, and Vanuatu. Fiji became a formal member of the agreement on 14 April 1998.

10 Under the Melanesian Spearhead Group Institutional Framework, the Annual Summit of Heads of Governments of the Melanesian Spearhead Group provides policy directions with respect to the implementation of the agreement. Trade officials of the parties meet annually prior to the annual summit of heads of governments to jointly review trade matters among the parties. The annual summit of the heads of governments may decide from time to time to establish technical committees to oversee the implementation of specific fields of activity of this agreement.

11 On 21 December 1992, the Former Czechoslovakia, Hungary, and Poland signed the Central European Free Trade Agreement (CEFTA). On 1 March 1993, CEFTA entered into force. Slovenia, Romania, and Bulgaria joined afterwards.

12 The Joint Committee is composed of the representatives of the parties, who act by common agreement.

13 These agreements include the FTAs concerning: EFTA — Czech Republic; EFTA — Hungary; EFTA — Poland; EFTA — Romania; EFTA — Slovak Republic; and EFTA — Turkey. The FTA with the former Czech and Slovak Federative Republic (CSFR) entered into force on 1 July 1992. In the wake of the dissolution, two separate but identical FTAs with the Czech Republic and the Slovak Republic superseded the original one. The FTA with Hungary entered into force on 1 October 1993 and the FTA with Poland entered into force on 1 September 1994. FTAs entered into force on 1 May 1993 for Romania. The FTA with Turkey entered into force on 1 April 1992.

14 Croatia — Hungary, Czech Republic — Estonia, Czech Republic — Latvia, Czech Republic — Turkey, Faroe Islands — Estonia, Faroe Islands — Iceland, Faroe Islands — Norway, Faroe Islands — Poland, Faroe Islands — Switzerland, Hungary — Estonia, Hungary — Latvia, Hungary — Lithuania, Hungary — Slovenia, Hungary — Turkey, Latvia — Estonia, Latvia — Poland, Latvia — Slovak Republic, Romania — Turkey, Slovak Republic — Estonia, Slovenia — Croatia, Slovenia — Estonia, Slovenia — FYROM, Slovenia — Latvia, Slovenia — Lithuania, Turkey — Bulgaria, Turkey — Estonia, Turkey — Latvia, Turkey — Lithuania, Turkey — Slovak Republic, and Ukraine — Estonia.

15 These agreements concern: EC — Faroe Islands; EC — Iceland; EC — Norway; and EC — Switzerland. The agreements entered into force for Faroe Islands on 1 January 1997, for Iceland on 1 April 1973, for Norway on 1 July 1973, and for Switzerland on 1 January 1973.

16 The EC — Cyprus Agreement entered into force on 1 June 1973, and the EC — Malta Agreement entered into force on 1 April 1971.

17 The Association Council consists of the members of the Council and members of the Commission of the EC and of members of the government of the Republic of Cyprus/Malta.

18 The EC — FYROM Agreement entered into force on 1 January 1998.

19 The Cooperation Council is composed of representatives of the EC and its member states and of representatives from the FYROM.

20 The EC — Jordan, EC — Lebanon, and EC — Syria agreements all entered into force on 1 July 1977.

21 The Cooperation Council is composed of representatives of the EC and of its member states and of representatives of Jordan/Lebanon/Syria. The Cooperation Council acts by mutual agreement between the EC and Jordan/Lebanon/Syria.

22 The agreement entered into force on 20 March 1998.

23 The agreement entered into force on 18 March 1981. Argentina, Bolivia, Brazil, Chile, Colombia, Cuba, Ecuador, Mexico, Paraguay, Peru, Uruguay, and Venezuela are current signatories.

24 The committee is the permanent organ of the association and is constituted by one permanent representative from each member state with the right to one vote. Each permanent representative has an alternate.

25 The agreement entered into force on 19 April 1989. Forty-four countries are GSTP participants. See <http://www.g77.org/gstp/#members> for the full list.

26 A Committee of Participants consists of the representatives of the governments of participants. The committee takes decisions by two-thirds majority on matters of substance and a simple majority on matters of procedure.

27 Arbitration is a more judicial and adversarial system, whereas consultations mechanism in a political and diplomatic system. The arbitration procedure is normally used after the consultation mechanism is exhausted.

28 In addition to the remedy provided by the arbitration panel, unilateral safeguard measures adopted by either party are generally available for the agreements in this section (see Section 2: Arbitration).

29 The agreement entered into force on 31 August 1977. Brunei Darussalam, Cambodia, Republic of Indonesia, Malaysia, Myanmar, the Republic of the Philippines, the Republic of Singapore, the Kingdom of Thailand, and Vietnam are the current signatories.

30 The protocol has not been notified to the WTO.

31 The SEOM consists of senior economic officials of the contracting states.

32 The AEM consists of economic ministers of the contracting states.

33 The agreement entered into force on 1 January 2001.

34 The EFTA — Morocco FTA entered into force on 1 December 1999. The interim EFTA — PLO FTA entered into force on 1 July 1999.

35 The Joint Committee consists of the representatives of the parties and acts by common agreement.

36 These agreements concern: EFTA — Bulgaria; EFTA — Croatia; EFTA — Estonia; EFTA — FYROM; EFTA — Israel; EFTA — Jordan; EFTA — Latvia; EFTA — Lithuania; and EFTA — Slovenia. The agreements entered into force for Bulgaria on 1 July 1993, for Croatia on 1 January 2002, for Estonia on 1 October 1997, for FYROM on 19 June 2000, for Israel on 1 January 1993, for Jordan on 21 June 2001, for Latvia on 1 June 1996, for Lithuania on 1 January 1997, and for Slovenia on 1 September 1998.

37 The Joint Committee consists of the representatives of the parties and acts by common agreement.

38 The EFTA — Mexico Agreement entered into force on 1 July 2001.

39 The Joint Committee consists of representatives of the parties and acts by consensus.

40 The agreement entered into force on 1 July 1991.

41 The Joint Committee is composed of representatives of the EC and of representatives of the Principality of Andorra.

42 The agreement entered into force on 31 December 1995.

43 The Joint Committee consists of the representatives of EC and Turkey. It acts by common agreement.

44 The Association Council consists of the members of the Council of the EC and members of the Commission of the EC and of members of the government of Turkey.

45 The Europe Agreements were concluded with respect to: EC — Bulgaria; EC — Czech Rep.; EC — Estonia; EC — Hungary; EC — Latvia; EC — Lithuania; EC — Poland; EC — Romania; EC — Slovak Rep.; and EC — Slovenia. The agreements entered into force for Bulgaria on 31 December 1993, for Czech Republic on 1 March 1992, for Estonia on 1 January 1995, for Hungary on 1 March 1992, for Latvia on 1 January 1995, for Lithuania on 1 January 1995, for Poland on 1 March 1992, for Romania on 1 May 1993, for Slovak Republic on 1 March 1992, and for Slovenia on 1 January 1997.

46 An Association Council consists of the members of the Council of the EC and of members of the Commission of the EC and of members of the governments of participating states.

47 These agreements concern: EC — Israel; EC — Morocco; EC — PLO; and EC — Tunisia. The agreements entered into force for Israel on 1 June 2000, for Morocco on 1 March 2000, for the PLO on 1 July 1997, and for Tunisia on 1 March 1998.

48 These agreements are: Czech Republic — Israel, Israel — Poland, Israel - Slovak Republic, Israel — Slovenia, Israel — Turkey, and Slovenia — Turkey.

49 The EC — Mexico Agreement entered into force on 1 July 2000.

50 The Joint Committee consists of the representatives of the parties and acts by common agreement.

51 The agreement entered into force on 30 December 1994. Azerbaijan Republic, Republic of Armenia, Republic of Belarus, Republic of Georgia, Republic of Kazakstan, Kyrgyz Republic, Republic of Moldova, Russian Federation, Republic of Tajikistan, Republic of Uzbekistan, and Ukraine are the current signatories.

52 The agreements in America, especially in North America, are organized in a chronological manner in order to show the evolution of RTA dispute settlement provisions. Dispute settlement mechanism in Latin American arrangements became more sophisticated with the addition of protocols.

53 The agreement entered into force for Guatemala, El Salvador, and Nicaragua on 4 June 1961, for Honduras on 27 April 1962, and for Costa Rica on 23 September 1963.

54 The Executive Council consists of one titular official and one alternate appointed by each contracting party. Before ruling on a matter, the Executive Council shall determine unanimously whether the matter is to be decided by a concurrent vote of all its members or by a simple majority.

55 The Central American Economic Council is composed of several ministers of economic affairs of several contracting states.

56 The agreement entered into force on 19 August 1985.

57 The Joint Committee is composed of representatives of the parties and shall be headed by the United States trade representatives and Jordan's minister primarily responsible for international trade, or their designees. All the decisions by the Joint Committee are taken by consensus.

58 The Treaty of Asuncion entered into force on 29 November 1991. The members are Argentina, Brazil, Paraguay, and Uruguay.

59 The Common Market Group consists of four members and four alternates for each country, representing the following public bodies: Ministry of Foreign Affairs; Ministry of Economy or its equivalent (areas of industry, foreign trade and/or economic co-ordination); and the Central Bank.

60 The NAFTA agreement entered into force on 4 January 1994.

61 The Free Trade Commission comprises representatives of both parties. The principal representative of each party shall be the cabinet level officer or minister primarily responsible for international trade, or a person designated by the cabinet level officer or minister. All the decisions of the commission is taken by consensus.

62 The agreement entered into force on 1 January 1997.

63 The agreement entered into force on 5 July 1997.

64 The agreement entered into force on 1 August 1999.

65 The agreement entered into force on 1 July 2000.

66 The agreement entered into force on 17 December 2001.

67 The Joint Committee is composed of representatives of the parties and shall be headed by the United States trade representatives and Jordan's minister primarily responsible for international trade, or their designees. All the decisions by the Joint Committee are taken by consensus.

68 The Council of Ministers comprises the members of the Council of the EC and members of the EC Commission, and a member of the government of each ACP state. The council takes its decisions by common agreement of the parties.

69 Standing tribunal is the most sophisticated dispute settlement mechanism to adjudicate disputes within regional trade organizations. One of the most developed regional trade integration systems, the European Communities, is not included here because the European Communities and its member states are treated as one member of the WTO. For the agreements written in French, the original French text was used.

70 The EEA entered into force on 1 January 1994. The EEA Agreement unites fifteen EU member states and three EFTA states (Norway, Iceland, and Liechtenstein) into a single market.

71 The agreement entered into force on 8 October 1997. The members are the Kyrgyz Republic, the Russian Federation, Belarus, and Kazakhstan.

72 The Andean Subregional Integration Agreement entered into force on 25 May 1998. The Customs Union was established in February 1995. On 10 March 1996, the countries signed the Act of Trujillo for the creation of an Andean Community. The members of Andean Community are Bolivia, Colombia, Ecuador, Peru, and Venezuela.

73 The Commission of the Andean Community is comprised of a plenipotentiary representative from each one of the governments of the member countries.

74 The Treaty Establishing the Caricom entered into force on 1 August 1973. Antigua and Barbuda, Bahamas, Barbados, Belize, Dominica, Grenada, Guyana, Haiti, Jamaica, Montserrat, Trinidad and Tobago, St. Kitts and Nevis, St. Lucia, St. Vincent and the Grenadines, and Suriname are Caricom members.

75 The COMESA treaty entered into force in December 1994. Angola, Burundi, Comoros, Democratic Republic of Congo, Djibouti, Egypt, Eritrea, Ethiopia, Kenya, Madagascar, Malawi, Mauritius, Namibia, Rwanda, Seychelles, Sudan, Swaziland, Tanzania, Uganda, Zambia, and Zimbabwe are COMESA members.

76 The CEMAC members are Cameroon, Central African Republic, Congo Republic, Equatorial Guinea, Gabon, and Chad.

77 The EAC treaty was signed on 30 November 1999. Kenya, Uganda, and Tanzania are members.

78 The agreement entered into force on 1 August 1994. Benin, Burkina Faso, Côte d'Ivoire, Guinea Bissau, Mali, Niger, Senegal, and Togo are members.

Environmental Taxes and the WTO — An Analysis of the WTO Implications of Using Fiscal Incentives to Promote Sustainable Forestry in Canada

NATHALIE CHALIFOUR

INTRODUCTION

There is a growing understanding among policy-makers that the environment and the economy are inextricably linked. As many have said before, the economy is really a wholly owned subsidiary of the environment.[1] Unless we make significant changes to the way we do business, we will exceed the carrying capacity of our ecological systems, impacting the health of our air, water, soils, and other systems.[2] The challenge for countries is to address environmental problems while remaining a competitive jurisdiction for investment in a globalizing economy. Domestic regulations, or "command and control" approaches, continue to play a major role in addressing environmental challenges.[3] However, countries are increasingly

---

Nathalie Chalifour, LL.B. (University of Western Ontario), J.S.M. (Stanford University), J.S.D. candidate (Stanford University), is an assistant professor in the Faculty of Law at the University of Ottawa.

[1] For instance, the quote has been attributed to Robert F. Kennedy Jr. (see, for example, Canadian House of Commons, *Labelling of Genetically Modified Foods*, June 12, 2000, 36th Parliament, 2nd Session, Edited Hansard No. 112 at 1205), former US Senator Gaylord Nelson (see, for example, Ernest Partridge, *The State Religion*, January 10, 2002, text available online at <http://www.democraticunderground.com/articles>) and former US Senator Tim Worth (see, for example, Coastal CRC, "Urban Expansion Our Most Pressing Coastal Problem," in *Flotsam and Jetsam*, text available online at <http://www.coastal.crc.org.au/newsletters/f_j_october_2000.html>).

[2] See generally Gretchen C. Daily, ed., *Nature's Services: Societal Dependence on Natural Ecosystems* (San Francisco: 1997). We have arguably exceeded this capacity in many cases to date.

[3] See David Hunter et al., *International Environmental Law and Policy*, 2nd ed. (Washington, DC: 2002).

complementing regulation with economic instruments[4] in order to achieve environmental policy goals, in part because economic instruments are more efficient than traditional regulation and allow countries to meet environmental objectives at a lower overall cost to society.[5]

While economic instruments may be used in discrete circumstances to achieve various policy objectives, a more comprehensive approach to using economic instruments to achieve environmental objectives is to examine and reform a country's *existing* fiscal policy (a significant part of the broader "economic instruments" basket). A government's taxation and expenditure policies create incentives and disincentives that have many environmental implications. Consider, for example, subsidies for coal production or for the capitalization of a commercial fishing industry. These are fiscal policies that could lead to overproduction of coal, or over-fishing, with concomitant environmental impacts.[6] Ecological fiscal reform (EFR) is a comprehensive approach that "goes beyond the selected use of economic instruments."[7] EFR is defined by the National Round Table on the Environment and the Economy as "a coordinated and conscious strategy that aims to redirect a government's taxation and expenditure programs to support sustainable development."[8]

---

[4] Economic instruments are measures that directly influence the price of a product or an activity. Since producers and consumers generally choose the lowest-cost option, economic instruments can be used to affect behaviour by modifying price. The range of economic instruments that can be used to achieve an environmental policy goal is large. Economic instruments range from taxes, charges, and user-fees, to subsidies, tax breaks, and grants, to the creation of a new market for a good or service, such as tradable emission rights. See International Institute for Sustainable Development, *Analysis of Ecological Fiscal Reform Activity in Canada* (Winnipeg: 2000) at 4. See also Organization for Economic Co-operation and Development [hereinafter OECD], Environment Directorate, *Environmentally Related Taxes in OECD Countries: Issues and Strategies* (Paris: 2001) (for a comprehensive discussion of environmental taxes).

[5] See External Advisory Committee on Smart Regulation, *Economic Instruments for Environmental Protection and Conservation: Lessons for Canada* (Ottawa: 2003). See also Charles D. Patterson III, "Environmental Taxes and Subsidies: What Is the Appropriate Fiscal Policy for Dealing with Modern Environmental Problems?" (2000) 24 Wm. & Mary Envtl. L. & Pol'y Rev. 121.

[6] See Patterson, *supra* note 5, for a general discussion of environmental subsidies.

[7] See Allan Howatson, Conference Board of Canada, *Ecological Fiscal Reform* (Ottawa: 1996) at 1.

[8] See National Round Table on the Environment and the Economy, *Towards a Canadian Agenda for Ecological Fiscal Reform: First Steps* (Ottawa: 2002). See also Stephen Barg et al., International Institute for Sustainable Development, *Analysis of Ecological Fiscal Reform Activity in Canada* (Winnipeg: 2000) at 3.

There are numerous ways of approaching EFR. One approach advocates taxing environmental "bads" (such as pollution and waste) and cycling the revenue from such taxation to reduce direct taxes, such as income tax, thereby promoting employment as the principle "good."[9] Using this approach, Germany, for example, has introduced a number of measures, such as taxes on mineral oils and electricity, and applied the revenues from these taxes towards social security and renewable energy.[10] Another EFR approach involves using fiscal measures to impact behaviour within a particular sector, cycling revenue away from activities that are environmentally harmful towards those that are environmentally sound in the same sector.[11] At its core, EFR involves using fiscal policy to shift the incentive structure so that the more environmentally desirable option is increasingly also the more financially desirable.

The readjustment of fiscal policy to achieve environmental policy objectives is an attractive tool available to governments seeking to address environmental issues, in part because it is economically efficient and also because it does not necessitate any overall loss of government revenue. However, the use of economic instruments, and EFR more generally, in various countries around the world is still quite limited, perhaps due to the novelty of the concept to most governments — EFR is largely unchartered territory. The limited use of EFR to date may also be due in part to questions about the effectiveness of EFR measures in achieving environmental goals as well as questions about their economic impacts. Most governments are resistant to reforming taxation — which is their basic source of revenue — or fiscal policy more broadly, to any great extent. Governments have begun testing these approaches, and a body of research is emerging.[12] However, there are still many unknowns,

---

[9] See OECD, *supra* note 4 (for a general discussion of ecological, or green, tax reform).

[10] See Kai Schlegelmilch, *Background Paper on Ecological Fiscal Reform Activities* (Ottawa: 2000) at 13. Two per cent of all taxes imposed in Germany between 1999 and 2003 will have an EFR component (Schlegelmilch at 13). See also OECD, *supra* note 4 at 52.

[11] See S. Ubachs and M. Faure, "Environmental Taxation: A Dutch Treat?" in *Environmental Taxation Conference Abstracts of a Conference Held June 2000* (Vancouver, BC: 2000). The United States has instituted a number of EFR measures, including tax incentives for the development of energy-efficient technologies and a tax on ozone-depleting substances. See Mark Anielski et al., *Analysis of US EFR Activity* (Ottawa: 2000) at 6-14.

[12] See, for example, Barg et al., *supra* note 8; Anielski et al., *supra* note 11; and Schlegelmilch, *supra* note 10.

and it will inevitably take time for governments to gain confidence in the tool.

The limited use of EFR may also be due to real or perceived limitations on the power of governments to implement EFR. At first blush, one might think that a national government is sufficiently sovereign to reform its fiscal policy as it wishes. However, most countries are members of the World Trade Organization (WTO),[13] and the authority of governments to implement measures impacting trade is limited by the rules of this multilateral trading regime. There is very little research examining the extent to which the rules of such trade agreements limit the ability of contracting parties to implement EFR or to apply economic instruments.[14] The research that does exist demonstrates that the WTO's rules are relevant when a country applies environmental taxes and charges to products that enter international trade.[15] The WTO's Trade and Environment Committee has recognized that there are interactions between WTO rules and environmental taxes and charges and that there are unresolved questions with respect to

[13] See Marrakesh Agreement Establishing the World Trade Organization, Legal Instruments — Results of Uruguay Round, April 15, 1994, 33 I.L.M. 1125 (entered into force January 1, 1996) [hereinafter WTO Agreement]. The World Trade Organization [hereinafter WTO] was created in 1994 to be the institutional body governing the General Agreement on Tariffs and Trade, October 30, 1947, 58 U.N.T.S., Can. T.S. 1947 No. 27 (entered into force January 1, 1948) [hereinafter GATT 1947] and several other trade agreements that have been negotiated from the basis of the GATT. See Final Act Embodying the Results of the Uruguay Round of Multilateral Trade Negotiations, April 15, 1994, 33 I.L.M. 1125 (entered into force January 1, 1995); see also John H. Jackson, *The World Trade Organization: Constitution and Jurisprudence* (London: 1998) at 1. 147 countries are currently members of the WTO. See World Trade Organization, "About the WTO," text is available online at <http://www.wto.org/english/thewto_e/thewto_e.htm>. Many countries are also signatories of bilateral and regional trade agreements, such as the North American Free Trade Agreement. North American Free Trade Agreement between the Government of Canada, the Government of Mexico and the Government of the United States, December 17, 1992, Can. T.S. 1994 No. 2, 32 I.L.M. 289 (entered into force January 1, 1994) [hereinafter NAFTA].

[14] The main analyses are Ole Kristian Fauchald, *Environmental Taxes and Trade Discrimination* (New York: 1998); Jan McDonald, "Environmental Taxes and International Competitiveness: Do WTO Rules Constrain Policy Choices?" Critical Issues in Environmental Taxation II" (forthcoming in 2004); and John A. Barrett Jr., "The Global Environment and Free Trade: A Vexing Problem and a Taxing Solution" (2001) 76 Ind. L.J. 829.

[15] The border tax adjustment provisions of the WTO can be important in addressing competitiveness concerns. See Fauchald, *supra* note 14.

these interactions.[16] Given the growing interest in, and use of, environmental fiscal measures around the world, the Committee on Trade and Environment has recommended that work be undertaken to examine the extent to which WTO rules may need to be reviewed to accommodate environmental taxes and charges.[17]

The existing research and the WTO Committee on Trade and Environment's interest in this issue, however, focus on environmental taxes. There is virtually nothing written about the interaction between WTO rules and the other side of the "ecological fiscal reform" coin — fiscal incentives.[18] Fiscal incentives are an important emerging policy option for governments to encourage sustainable industry practices, particularly when those industries are internalizing environmental externalities either in response to regulation or in order to meet a growing demand for sustainable products in the marketplace. The extent to which incentives can be construed as subsidies and subject to countervailing duties is of tremendous importance, particularly for export-led economies such as Canada. The existing research also focuses on environmental taxes aimed at reducing pollution and greenhouse-gas emissions or wastes rather than on the conservation of biodiversity or renewable natural resources.[19]

With the aim of shedding light on these two aspects of the interaction between international trade rules and ecological fiscal reform, this article considers the extent to which trade rules can constrain the policy choices of governments wishing to apply fiscal

[16] See WTO, Committee on Trade and Environment, *CTE Agenda Part 3*, text available online at <http://www.wto.org/english/tratop_e/envir_e/cte03_e.htm>.

[17] See *ibid.*

[18] One article that considers this interaction is a forthcoming publication on the trade legality of incentives proposed under the Kyoto Implementation Plan in Canada from a US perspective. C. Forcese, "The Kyoto Rift: Trade Law Implications of Canada's Kyoto Implementation Strategy in an Era of Canadian-U.S. Environmental Divergence" (forthcoming in 2004).

[19] See Fauchald, *supra* note 14 at 32 (noting that environmental taxes are primarily used to restrict pollution and that there are few examples of taxes on the use of exhaustible natural resources). See Konrad von Moltke, "Environmental Protection and Competitiveness," in Heraldo Munoz and Robin Rosenberg, eds., *Difficult Liaison — Trade and the Environment in the Americas* (Miami: 1993) 5 at 7-10 (noting that little trade and environment research considers natural resources issues). See also Mathis Wackernagel, "Can Trade Promote an Ecologically Secure World? The Global Economy from an Ecological Footprint Perspective" (1998) Buff. Envt'l L.J. 179 at 184 (noting that most of the trade and environment literature focuses on pollution issues).

incentives to encourage biodiversity conservation. In order to provide straw dogs for the purposes of analysis, this article will offer a set of three hypothetical fiscal incentives that could be implemented by the Canadian government to encourage the forest industry to use sustainable forestry practices. These hypothetical measures serve as "straw dogs" against which to understand the implications of trade rules. The article is broken down into two sections. Part 1 provides some background on forest conservation and the forest industry in Canada and sets out the three hypothetical EFR measures against which the analysis of trade rules will be applied. Part 2 analyzes the compatibility of these hypothetical measures with the WTO rules — in particular, the Agreement on Subsidies and Countervailing Measures (SCM Agreement).[20]

PART 1   FISCAL INCENTIVES FOR SUSTAINABLE FORESTRY
          IN CANADA

CANADA'S FORESTS

Canada is home to 418 million hectares of forests, representing 10 per cent of the world's forests.[21] These forests are home to an estimated 90,000 species[22] and provide a variety of ecological services to the country, from purifying water to sequestering carbon from the atmosphere.[23] These forests are also home to over 80 per cent of Canada's Aboriginal peoples.[24] In addition to their ecological and cultural value, Canada's forests are of significant economic value.[25] They support a large forest industry, which directly employed 339,000 Canadians in 1997 and contributed $19 billion, or 2.4 per cent, of Canada's gross domestic product in 1999.[26] Forest products account for over 10 per cent of all of Canada's exports by

---

[20] See Agreement on Subsidies and Countervailing Measures, April 15, 1994, in WTO Agreement, *supra* note 13 [hereinafter SCM Agreement].

[21] This forest heritage includes one-third of the world's boreal forest and one-quarter of the world's temperate coastal forest. See World Wildlife Fund, *Canada's Commitment to Forest Protected Areas* (Toronto: 2000) at 2.

[22] See Global Forest Watch, *Canada at a Crossroads* (Washington, DC: 2000) at 13, 31.

[23] See Daily, *supra* note 2 at 215-35.

[24] See World Wildlife Fund, *supra* note 21 at 2.

[25] See Natural Resources Canada, *The State of Canada's Forests 2002-2003* (Ottawa: 2003) at 26 (describing direct employment and exports attributed to the forest industry). See also Canadian Council of Forest Ministers, *Compendium of Canadian Forestry Statistics* (Ottawa: 2000).

[26] See Natural Resources Canada, *supra* note 25 at 26.

value.[27] These forests also contribute to making Canada a favourite tourist destination for those people seeking wilderness recreational opportunities.[28]

Canadian government policy expressly supports the conservation of this vast wealth of forest heritage, for environmental, social, and economic reasons.[29] The country pursues its conservation objectives through a number of measures. One of the means used is the establishment of protected areas in forests.[30] Another means for pursuing conservation is through the control of commercial industry practices in forests. The majority of forests in Canada are publicly owned.[31] Commercial operators are granted licenses by provincial governments to harvest in these forests.[32] The government controls forest practices both through regulation and through issuing licenses to harvest on public lands.

Canada has an array of forest management and environmental legislation and policy — much of it at the provincial level given the constitutional division of powers over natural resources — which regulates activities in Canada's forest estate.[33] However, as noted earlier, regulation is often not the most efficient way of achieving a

---

[27] See Forest Products Association of Canada, *The Forest Industry in Canada 2002* (Ottawa: 2003) at ii.

[28] One study estimates that wildlife-based activities in Canada contribute $6 billion to the gross domestic product. See Pricewaterhouse Coopers, *Effect of Tax Legislation in Canada on the Sustainability of the Private Woodlot Sector* (Ottawa: 1998) at 8.

[29] See Natural Resources Canada, *supra* note 25 at 66 (describing Canada's new National Forest Strategy, which has sustainable forest management as a core tenet).

[30] Canada's senior governments committed to completing a representative network of protected areas by the year 2000 in the 1992 Tri-Council Statement of Commitment. Despite the commitment, only half of Canada's forested natural regions are even moderately represented by protected areas. See World Wildlife Fund, *Endangered Spaces* (Toronto: 2001) at 17.

[31] Ninety four per cent of the forests in Canada are publicly owned, 71 per cent provincially, and 23 per cent federally. See Natural Resources Canada, *supra* note 25 at 18.

[32] Over 220 million hectares of Canada's forests are held under commercial license agreements. See Global Forest Watch, *supra* note 22 at 44.

[33] The legislation ranges from provincial forest management laws, such as the Forest Practices Code of British Columbia Act, R.S.B.C. 1996, c. 159 and the Ontario Crown Forests Sustainability Act 1994, S.O. 1994, c. 25, to the federal Fisheries Act, R.S. 1985, c. F-14, and the Canadian Environmental Assessment Act, R.S. 1992, c. 37.

desired outcome. Market mechanisms can be an effective complement to regulation to achieve forest management goals. The emergence of independent, third-party forest certification combined with the eco-labeling of forest products from the certified forests, for example, is influencing the management practices of some forest companies that are attempting to capture a market niche for forest products from well-managed forests.[34] Another set of tools for influencing forests — the subject of this article — is fiscal policy.

There is no question that protecting environmental and social values of forests while also deriving economic benefit from the resource is challenging.[35] It is not easy for governments to force the users of forest resources to internalize the environmental costs of the resource use — effectively implementing a "user-pays" principle in commercial forestry — without economic consequences for that industry. There is a growing amount of international competition in forestry,[36] and so it becomes increasingly difficult for any individual government to require internalization of environmental costs by companies without risking a loss of competition. Countries with export-dominated economies, such as Canada, are particularly susceptible to competitiveness losses. Clearly, new tools are needed in the struggle to maintain a competitive forest products industry while also addressing environmental and social concerns.

The Canadian forest industry has faced strong pressure from global market campaigns aimed at ensuring sustainable forest practices. In an effort to demonstrate the sustainability of its forest practices, a large part of the Canadian forest industry has either undergone, or has committed to undergoing, third-party verification of environmental practices.[37] In response to the market campaigns, and in order to satisfy the requirements of the various certification systems, many companies have made significant

---

[34] See generally Virgilio M. Viana et al., eds., *Certification of Forest Products: Issues and Perspectives* (Washington, DC: 1996).

[35] See Hamish Kimmins, *Balancing Act: Environmental Issues in Forestry*, 2nd ed. (Vancouver: 1997) at 3-13.

[36] See Roger A. Sedjo and Kenneth S. Lyon, *The Long-Term Adequacy of World Timber Supply* (Washington, DC: 1990) at 55-56.

[37] The Forest Products Association of Canada (which represents 75 per cent of the Canadian forest industry) has made it a condition of membership that companies have all of their woodlands certified by one of three independent certification systems by 2006. See Forest Products Association of Canada, *Canada's Boreal Forest* (Ottawa: 2003) at 2.

reforms to their forestry practices.[38] Both the process of becoming certified and the resulting changes in forestry practices (especially decreases in wood supply) impact companies' financial bottom lines. While the industry hopes to recapture some or all of these costs though the market benefits of environmentally responsible products, these benefits have yet to materialize. These companies therefore face a potential loss of competitiveness relative to companies operating in jurisdictions without such market pressures.

Given that sustainable forestry practices are a desirable policy objective, one option to address these competitiveness impacts is to use financial incentives to help offset the additional costs that companies are incurring as they internalize environmental costs. Clearly, the long-term goal is for all industries to pay for the environmental costs of their practices, but until this happens, industries at the forefront of cost-internalization should not be penalized for their leadership. Short- to medium-term incentives would provide an interim solution to the potential loss of competitiveness faced by these industry leaders.

USE OF ECOLOGICAL FISCAL REFORM IN CANADA TO ENCOURAGE
SUSTAINABLE FORESTRY

Although Canada has implemented a few EFR measures, the country's use of EFR is really in its infancy.[39] There are very few examples of EFR measures in Canada.[40] One example is a change that was made to the Income Tax Act[41] in the 1990s, allowing a 100 per cent tax deduction for donations of ecologically sensitive lands to a charitable organization or municipality or for the creation of

[38] The forest company Tembec, for example, has made numerous efforts to implement sustainable forestry practices and was recently recognized for its efforts by the Rainforest Alliance with a Lifetime Achievement Award. See "While Its President Receives the Rainforest Alliance Lifetime Achievement Award, Tembec Is Recognized as a Corporate Sustainable Standard-Setter by the Rainforest Alliance," press release (May 20, 2004), text available online <http://www. tembec.com/DynamicPortal?key=web&lng=en-US&page=tpl_press&crit= press_layout&ID_NEWS=1349>.

[39] See generally National Round Table on the Environment and the Economy, *supra* note 8 at 8. See also Barg et al., *supra* note 8, for an overview of EFR in Canada.

[40] See OECD, *supra* note 4 at 51-69. Fauchald posits that Norway may be the most advanced, as it is considering taxes on uses of nature that negatively impact biodiversity. See Fauchald, *supra* note 14 at 17.

[41] Income Tax Act, R.S.C. 1985 (5ᵗʰ Supp.), c. 1.

an easement for such lands.[42] Another federal example is the Permanent Cover Program, which provides funds for converting lands at risk of soil degradation to grassland.[43] Ontario has a fuel tax initiative that is based on taxing fuel inefficient vehicles and rebating fuel-efficient vehicles.[44] Ontario also has a 10 per cent tax on all non-refillable imported alcoholic beverage containers and domestic beer cans that are not deposit returned.[45] British Columbia included three tax-shifting initiatives in its 2000 budget, relating to taxes on beehive burners, aquaculture, and vehicle emissions.[46]

While EFR initiatives have been most common in relation to air quality, emission reduction, and waste reduction, there are some examples of EFR initiatives aimed at influencing forest practices in a number of countries. The United States, for instance, allows reforestation expenses to qualify for amortization and a tax credit and recently proposed increasing the maximum reforestation expences that can qualify for amortization and tax credit from US $10,000 to US $25,000.[47] North Carolina has proposed an initiative to allocate US $1 of every $500 of excise tax that the state levies on profits of the sale of standing timber to the state's Parks and Recreation Trust Fund and Natural Heritage Trust Fund.[48] The Oregon House of Representatives recently proposed offering companies that produce wood products a US $500 income tax credit for each newly hired worker.[49]

There are a handful of examples of EFR initiatives aimed at the forest sector in Canada. One example is British Columbia's wood residue (beehive) burner tax initiative, which taxes burners per unit of emissions and provides a rebate to burner operators for

[42] See Barg et al., *supra* note 8 at 22.

[43] See International Institute for Sustainable Development, *Government Budgets, Replenishing the Prairies: A Canadian Permanent Cover Program,* text is available online at <http://iisd1.iisd.ca/greenbud/replen.htm>.

[44] See International Institute for Sustainable Development, *Green Budget Reform: The Tax for Fuel Conservation in Ontario,* text is available online at <http://www.iisd.org/greenbud/taxfuel.htm.>.

[45] See *ibid.*

[46] See J. Sawicki, "Tax Shifting in B.C. — Stories from the Front Lines," in *Second Annual Global Conference on Environmental Taxation Issues, Experience and Potential* (Vancouver: 2000) at 144.

[47] See Centre for a Sustainable Economy, *Tax News Summary, Forest Tax News,* text available online at <http://www.sustainableeconomy.org/seu/>.

[48] See *ibid.*

[49] See *ibid.*

investments in research and development of value-added alternatives for wood residue disposal.[50] Another example is Ontario's exemption from the sales tax of purchases of tree seedlings for reforestation on woodlots that qualify as farmlands.

However, the use of EFR measures to encourage sustainable forestry (and to conversely discourage unsustainable forestry) is essentially unchartered territory. There is a great deal of potential for advancing the policy agenda in a way that is economically efficient. EFR may also be an important tool for helping companies that are internalizing environmental externalities, but not yet reaping the profits from doing so, to remain competitive in a globalized market, notably in the short to medium term.

STRAW DOG MEASURES

There are countless fiscal incentives that could be used by the Canadian government to bolster forest conservation beyond what is required by law or to help offset the potential competitiveness impacts of forest companies voluntarily internalizing environmental externalities. In order to identify and justify the measures selected, this article briefly discusses some principles of ecologically sustainable forestry and examines the fiscal policies applicable to the Canadian forest industry.

Ecologically Sustainable Forestry

There is no single definition of ecologically sustainable forestry. The key component of such forestry is the maintenance of a forest ecosystem's ecological functions, including maintaining a full complement of ecological diversity (including species, age, and genetic and structural diversity).[51] In practice, sustainable forestry involves a thorough landscape-level forest management plan, including reserving areas needed for ecological representation, harvesting in a way that has the least impact on the forest ecosystem, and managing for restoration of the ecosystem.[52]

[50] See N. Olewiler et al., "The Beehive Burner Operating Permit Fee Tax Shift Pilot Project," in *Second Annual Global Conference on Environmental Taxation Issues, Experience and Potential* (Vancouver: 2000) at 50.

[51] See Jim Drescher, *The Economics of Ecoforestry* (Toronto: 1996) at 232.

[52] The government of Canada's National Forest Strategy has a goal of managing "Canada's natural forest using an ecosystem-based approach that maintains forest health, structure, functions, composition and biodiversity." See National Forest Strategy Coalition, *National Forest Strategy 2003-2008* (Ottawa: 2003) at 10.

Beyond landscape-level planning, how a forest is logged — from which trees are cut, to the rate of cutting, to the equipment used in logging — is probably the most significant factor impacting the forest ecosystem. The harvesting methods chosen, whether selection harvesting or clear-cut harvesting with retention, are critical. However, no single overall harvesting method will be the most ecologically sound in all circumstances. What is ecologically sensitive will vary from site to site, depending on the species, the natural disturbance patterns, the logging history, and other factors.[53]

Some practices are generally universally better for maintaining the health of forest ecosystems than others. For instance, cutting practices that respect the productivity and complexity of the forest, retaining important structures such as snags and coarse woody debris, are better environmentally for the forest than cutting practices that remove all residual structure.[54] Practices that are designed to reduce damage to soils or waterways when accessing a site are better ecologically. Forest harvesting and transportation equipment that minimize soil compaction or bridges that reduce negative impacts on waterways are generally more environmentally sound choices.

Fiscal Policies Applicable to the Forest Industry

Forest companies are subject to numerous fiscal policies — from taxes on profits, to sales tax, to grants for research and development.[55] Tax treatments have a major impact on a company's costs and profits.[56] The current set of economic incentives that is applicable to forest managers through the tax system do little to encourage environmentally sound forest management above the regulatory threshold. In some cases, they actually act as a disincentive to environmentally responsible management. Without changes to the incentive structure created by these tax rules, the additional costs that usually accompany environmental improvements to forestry will continue to act as a disincentive to further environmental improvements.

[53] See generally Kimmins, *supra* note 35.

[54] See Dresher, *supra* note 51 at 56.

[55] The Canadian forest industry paid an estimated $3.5 billion in taxes in 2002. See Forest Products Association of Canada, *supra* note 27 at 11.

[56] See Richard Carson, "Taxation and Accounting Issues," in *Understanding Forestry Taxation in British Columbia* (Canadian Tax Foundation Conference Series, Vancouver: 1998) at 6.

This article identifies three fiscal-incentive measures that could help shift the current incentive structure of fiscal policy in Canada to create incentives for companies to improve their forest practices from an environmental perspective (or help offset the costs for those companies already improving their practices). They are (1) a revision of the allowable depreciation for forest harvesting equipment (Capital Cost Allowance (CCA) Shift); (2) a tax credit for research and development relating to improving forestry practices (R&D Sustainable Forestry Incentive); and (3) a tax credit for training staff to use environmentally sensitive equipment (Training Credit). The economic impacts of these hypothetical measures have not been assessed nor have all of the design options been canvassed. In fact, the measures have been selected somewhat arbitrarily for the purposes of illustration. The following section describes each of these hypothetical measures.

Measure 1 — CCA Shift

As mentioned earlier, ecologically sound logging generally requires some degree of retention, the amount of which depends on the site. Retention includes not only retaining some standing timber but also leaving large snags and, in most cases, coarse woody debris on the site (depending on soil type). Approximately 80 per cent of the forest area harvested annually in Canada is harvested using the clear-cut system,[57] using mechanized harvesters such as feller-forwarders, feller-bunchers, and grapple-skidders. The equipment is designed to remove whole trees from the forest to the roadside or a mill yard for de-limbing.[58] If the tree is de-limbed on a landing on the roadside, the limbs are generally left in a slash pile. Very little downed woody debris is left on the site, resulting in nutrient loss to the site.[59]

A more ecologically sound alternative is to use a different type of mechanized harvester, notably one with a cut-to-length processing head. These harvesters de-limb the tree and cut it to length on the spot, leaving the residual woody structure where the tree is cut. This avoids large slash piles and retains nutrients on the site. It also helps mitigate soil erosion and siltation into nearby waterways. There are other equipment choices that can offer more environmentally

---

[57] See Global Forest Watch, *supra* note 22 at 11.

[58] See Elizabeth May, *At the Cutting Edge: The Crisis in Canada's Forests* (Ottawa: 1998) at 27.

[59] See *ibid.* at 27.

sound forest management. For instance, using equipment that is appropriate to a particular site, given its size, weight and the type of soil.[60] The use of lighter equipment and wider tires, which helps disperse pounds of pressure per square inch on the soils, can reduce impacts on forest soils.[61] Using harvesting equipment that is most appropriate to a particular site and that will reduce damage to the forest environment, however, will likely increase costs, particularly in the short to medium term. Forest managers may have to purchase more expensive equipment and may have to have on hand a wider variety of harvesting equipment.[62] There is currently no incentive in the Income Tax Act to help offset additional costs of such capital investments or, in the case of equal costs, to encourage the purchase of the more environmentally friendly equipment. Most logging equipment is allowed a 30 per cent depreciation rate under the Income Tax Act, regardless of its impact.

This hypothetical EFR measure would increase the allowable depreciation for equipment that qualifies as environmentally sound and decrease allowable depreciation for non-qualifying equipment. For example, equipment such as cut-to-length harvesters and processing heads, lighter and small harvesting equipment, chainsaws, cable-logging systems, wide tires, and central tire inflation could be depreciable at a higher rate than all other logging equipment. There is a precedent for allowing accelerated depreciation for equipment that is environmentally sensitive. For example, there is a provision for accelerated depreciation for water and air pollution control equipment acquired before 1999.[63] There is also a precedent

---

[60] See Kimmins, *supra* note 35 at 227.

[61] Companies manufacture smaller and lighter logging equipment, designed in particular to allow mechanized selection cuts. Central tire inflation is a mechanism used to reduce ground pressure. See May, *supra* note 58 at 31.

[62] For example, a single grip harvester may cost almost twice as much as a regular forwarder. Removable bridges, which are more environmentally benign than permanent bridges, are also more costly. Personal communication with Paul Krabbe, chief economist, Tembec, August 30, 2001.

[63] Class 24 and 27 allow for an allowance of 25 per cent for the year of acquisition, then 50 per cent in year 2, and then the balance in year 3, on a straight line basis to the capital cost of the asset. There is also a special depreciation class for energy conservation equipment (class 34 and 43.1), which also creates this three-year write-off. See Canadian Central Revenue Agency [hereinafter CCRA], "Capital Cost Allowance — Pollution Control Property," Interpretation Tax Bulletin IT-336R (1985). See also *Canadian Tax Master Guide*, 56th ed. (Ottawa: 2001) at 304.

in the United States for giving preferential tax treatment to environmentally sensitive logging equipment. In 1999, the state of Oregon passed a law exempting environmentally sensitive logging equipment and machinery less than eight years old from personal property tax and *ad valorem* taxes.[64]

Measure 2 — R&D Sustainable Forestry Incentive

As noted earlier, defining and identifying ecologically sound forest management is extremely complex. Complex certification systems have been established to verify when a forest is being managed according to numerous environmentally, socially, and economically sound criteria. The Forest Stewardship Council (FSC), which has defined global principles and criteria of environmentally, socially, and economically viable forestry, is generally considered the most rigorous of numerous forest certification schemes.[65] Regional standards of sustainable forestry are developed through a multi-stakeholder process. Products bearing an FSC label are certified to have come from a forest that is certified according to the FSC's standards and are targeted at consumers or retailers concerned about the environmental and social aspects of forestry.

Companies often need to conduct research and attempt new practices in order to find ways of modifying their forest practices in order to meet the certification standards. This hypothetical EFR measure would offer forest companies a credit for the costs of research and development relating to achieving or maintaining the level of management required to be certified.

Measure 3 — Training Credit

As noted earlier, environmentally sound forestry may require using different harvesting equipment on different sites. Most new equipment requires a significant investment in operator training.[66] This proposed measure would allow a tax credit for hiring new, or

---

[64] See Center for a Sustainable Economy, *supra* note 47 at October 5, 1999.

[65] See, for example, Fern, *Behind the Logo: An Environmental and Social Assessment of Forest Certification Schemes* (Boskoop, the Netherlands: 2001); Chris Elliott and Arlin Hackman, *Current Issues in Forest Certification in Canada* (Toronto: 1996). See Forest Stewardship Council, *International Centre*, text available online at <http://www.fscoax.org/.>.

[66] For example, there is a two-year learning curve for operators to learn how to use cut-to-length systems. Personal communications with Paul Krabbe, chief economist, Tembec, August 30, 2001.

training existing, staff in the operation of more environmentally sensitive equipment.

PART 2   COMPATIBILITY OF EFR MEASURES WITH WTO RULES

To a policy-maker unfamiliar with trade law, it is not evident that the straw dog measures described in Part 1 may be inconsistent with international trade rules. They are national measures designed to encourage the more sustainable use of a domestic, renewable natural resource. They are not measures intended to impede trade or achieve environmental goals outside of the country's jurisdiction, nor are they tariffs or export subsidies. A country's sovereign right to manage its natural resources has been reiterated numerous times. For example, the WTO Committee on Trade and Environment has explicitly stated that WTO members maintain the sovereign right to determine the way and extent to which they address the internalization of domestic environmental costs.[67]

Despite this general understanding that WTO members maintain the sovereign right to manage their natural resources and internalize domestic environmental costs, there are circumstances in which WTO rules may interact with EFR measures relating to renewable natural resources. As soon as domestic products made from natural resources enter into international trade, or when similar or "like" products are imported into the country, WTO rules become relevant. This section of the article analyzes the extent, if any, to which the hypothetical EFR measures may be inconsistent with WTO rules. The principal WTO disciplines relevant to this question are found in the SCM Agreement.

"RED HERRING" PHENOMENON

Before turning to the analysis, it is important to note that the *perceived* implication of trade rules on EFR measures can be as important as the *actual* implication. This is particularly the case for a country with an export-led economy such as Canada. Unfettered access to external markets is critical to the Canadian economy. As a result, the government is particularly sensitive to potential violations of trade rules that could result in reduced access (either through trade restrictive policies in an export market or through countervailing action aimed at Canada). In some cases, the fear of

---

[67] See GATT/WTO, *Activities on Trade and Environment 1994-95*, Document PRESS/TE 002, May 8, 1995, at 5.

infringing trade rules is a red herring due to an absence of specific analysis on the implications of trade rules for a particular policy option. These red herring fears, however, unfortunately serve to chill progressive policy-making.

Such red herring fears are fuelled by situations in which policies have been successfully attacked under United States trade law, regardless of their compliance with international law rules. A case in point is the current softwood lumber dispute, under which Canadian softwood lumber exports have been subject to countervailing duties of over 18 per cent by the United States under the application of United States trade law.[68] While Canada has received positive decisions from dispute settlement bodies within the WTO and the North American Free Trade Agreement (NAFTA),[69] the impact of these duties on the Canadian forest industry — which is heavily dependent on the United States market — has already been significant.[70] The dispute serves to increase the hesitation of the Canadian government to implement policies that may trigger further trade disputes. As such, the perceived implication of international and United States trade rules for new policies is a reality that must be taken into account.

The fear of enacting policy measures that could attract countervailing duties or other measures, and/or trigger trade disputes, could be a significant barrier to addressing environmental challenges through progressive fiscal measures in Canada and in other export-dominated economies. Given the potential importance of EFR for helping to achieve economically efficient environmental gains, it is critical to clarify the implications of the trade rules for EFR measures. Such clarification and analysis can help eliminate red herring fears, help governments design EFR measures in a way

[68] See Department of Foreign Affairs and International Trade, *Softwood Lumber,* text available online at <http://www.dfait-maeci.gc.ca/eicb/softwood/menu-en.asp>.

[69] See, for example, *United States — Preliminary Determinations with Respect to Certain Softwood Lumber from Canada* (June 2002), WTO Doc. WT/DS236 (Panel Report); *Final Countervailing Duty Determination with Respect to Certain Softwood Lumber from Canada (Canada v. United States)* (January 2004), WTO Doc. AB/2003-6 (Appellate Body Report). See also generally Department of Foreign Affairs and International Trade, *Softwood Lumber — Canada's Legal Challenges,* text available online at <http://www.dfait-maeci.gc.ca/eicb/softwood/legal_action-en.asp>; and NAFTA, *supra* note 13.

[70] For instance, the British Columbia Lumber Trade Council estimates that 15,000 logging and sawmill jobs have been lost in the province's coastal area and that job losses will likely reach 30,000. See "B.C. Industry Braces for More Cuts," CBC News (March 22, 2002), text available online at <www.cbc.ca>.

that avoids infringing trade law, and can highlight areas of trade law that require clarification and/or reform. Overall, such analysis will help reduce the chill on progressive policy-making.

SCM AGREEMENT

As noted earlier, this article focuses on fiscal incentive measures. Such measures have the potential to come into conflict with the subsidies disciplines of trade law. The rules regulating a WTO member's use of subsidies are essentially contained in the SCM Agreement. An evolution from the Tokyo Round Subsidies Code,[71] the SCM Agreement is more comprehensive and provides clearer disciplines on the use of subsidies. It defines what is a subsidy and introduces the requirement of specificity (which is discussed later in this article). In contrast to the Subsidies Code, to which only some members of the General Agreement on Tariffs and Trade (GATT)[72] were signatories, all WTO members are subject to the SCM Agreement.

The SCM Agreement does not prohibit all subsidies. Instead, it prohibits certain subsidies, allows others, and makes a third category of subsidies "actionable." Prohibited subsidies ("red light" subsidies) are those that are contingent on export performance or the use of domestic versus imported goods.[73] Actionable subsidies ("yellow light" subsidies) are not prohibited, but they may be challenged.[74] For example, members that can show an injury to their domestic industries from subsidies can impose countervailing duties in the amount of the injury caused by the subsidized products.[75] Allowable

---

[71] Agreement on Interpretation and Application of the Articles VI, XVI and XXIII of the General Agreement on Tariffs and Trade, (1980) 26 BISD 56; 31 U.S.T. 513; T.I.A.S. No. 9619.

[72] GATT 1947, *supra* note 13.

[73] There are some exceptions to this rule. Agricultural products, for instance, are not subject to the same stringent rules. Forest products, however, are not considered agricultural products under the WTO. See SCM Agreement, *supra* note 20 at Article 3. See also Jackson, *supra* note 13 at 293-300 (explaining subsidies and countervailing duties under the WTO).

[74] See generally SCM Agreement, *supra* note 20 at Part III.

[75] See *ibid.* at Articles VI and XVI. There are some exceptions to the restrictions on subsidies. Agricultural commodities, which have remained outside the ambit of the GATT for much of its existence, were brought into the fold in the Uruguay Round, but the restrictions on subsidies are not as stringent for agricultural goods. See Jackson, *supra* note 13 at 292, 313.

("green light" subsidies) are permitted.[76] This section of the article considers the extent to which the disciplines of the SCM Agreement apply to the straw dog measures. It focuses on the disciplines relating to actionable subsidies, as these are the most relevant for the measures.[77]

The analysis of whether a subsidy is actionable requires a four-part examination. The first question to be analyzed is whether the measures fall within the definition of subsidies within the agreement. The definition of subsidy requires that the measure in question constitutes a "financial contribution" and "confers a benefit." Second, if the measure falls within the definition of a subsidy, the measure must pass a "specificity" test in order to be actionable. The third part of the analysis involves determining whether the measure causes an "adverse effect" to the domestic industry in the market to which the products that benefited from the subsidy were exported. The fourth and final part of the analysis is an examination of the exemptions found within the SCM Agreement.

Would the Measures Be Considered "Subsidies" within the Meaning of the SCM Agreement?

As noted earlier, subsidies are given a two-part definition in the SCM Agreement. First, the activity must involve "a financial contribution by a government or any public body within the territory of a Member."[78] Second, the measure must confer a benefit in order for the acts to be considered a subsidy.[79]

Financial Contribution

WTO jurisprudence

The Agreement states that a financial contribution exists where there is a financial contribution by a government or any public body, such as where:

i. a government practice involves a direct transfer of funds (e.g. grants, loans and equity infusion), potential direct transfers of funds or liabilities (e.g. loan guarantees);

[76] See SCM Agreement, *supra* note 20 at Article 8. However, the provisions for allowable subsidies have expired under the SCM Agreement. See later in the article for further discussion.

[77] None of the measures are contingent upon export or upon the use of domestic over imported goods, which are both triggers for finding a subsidy prohibited.

[78] SCM Agreement, *supra* note 20 at ss. 1.1 (a)(1).

[79] *Ibid.* at ss. 1.1 (b).

ii. government revenue that is otherwise due is foregone or not collected
(e.g. fiscal incentives such as tax credits);
iii. a government provides goods or services other than general infrastructure, or purchases goods; or,
iv. a government makes payments to a funding mechanism, or entrusts or
directs a private body to carry out one or more of the type of functions
illustrated in (i) to (iii) above which would normally be vested in the
government and the practice, in no real sense, differs from practices
normally followed by governments.[80]

The sub-paragraph of the most relevance to the straw dog measures, which can be loosely categorized as fiscal incentives, is (ii),
which makes explicit reference to fiscal incentives. To date, the
WTO dispute settlement panels have given a broad interpretation
to the meaning of "financial contribution" and notably to "government revenue that is otherwise due is foregone or not collected." In
the case of *United States — Tax Treatment for "Foreign Sales Corporation,"*[81] the European Union challenged the United States's method
of providing a tax exemption to foreign sales corporations for
income from foreign trade. In considering whether the tax exemption was "government revenue that is otherwise due and not collected," within the meaning of Article 1.1(a)(1)(ii) of the SCM
Agreement, the panel first examined the appropriate benchmark
against which to evaluate a particular measure.[82] It noted that the
WTO does not impose an obligation on members to levy direct
taxes at any particular level.[83] The Appellate Body confirmed the
panel's findings[84] that the only appropriate benchmark against
which to compare a measure to determine whether revenue "otherwise due" is "foregone" is the member's existing tax regime.[85] The
Appellate Body held that a measure will qualify as revenue "otherwise due" if it is an exception to the general rules of taxation applicable to taxpayers in comparable circumstances.[86]

---

[80] *Ibid.*

[81] See *United States — Tax Treatment for "Foreign Sales Corporations" (Complaint by the European Community)* (2001), WTO Doc. WT/DS108/RW (Panel Report) [hereinafter *United States — FSC* panel report].

[82] See *ibid.* at paras. 7.41 to 7.48.

[83] See *ibid.* at para. 7.43.

[84] See *United States — Tax Treatment for "Foreign Sales Corporations"(Complaint by the European Community)* (2002), WTO Doc. WT/DS108/AB/R (Appellate Body Report) [hereinafter *United States — FSC* Appellate Body report].

[85] See *ibid.* at paras. 90 to 92.

[86] See *ibid.*

Given this interpretation, it is difficult to imagine any tax exemption or credit not satisfying the "financial contribution" arm of the subsidy definition test. As long as the existing tax regime serves as a benchmark, then any measures that discriminate between taxpayers in otherwise "like" circumstances will constitute a financial contribution. Of course, as noted by the Appellate Body in *Canada —
Measures Affecting the Export of Civilian Aircraft* (*Canada — Aircraft*
case),[87] the "universe of subsidies is vast" and the granting of a subsidy, without more, does not constitute an inconsistency with the agreement.[88] Therefore, as long as the disciplines on subsidies are fair and interpreted reasonably, the broad stroke interpretation of the first arm of the subsidy test is not in and of itself a questionable reach into national sovereignty.

Would the Straw Dog Measures Qualify as a "Financial Contribution"?

Both the R&D Sustainable Forestry Incentive and the Training Credit are programs that would offer a tax break to a subset of taxpayers based on certain activities, such as research and development or training of staff. The interpretation of paragraph 1.1 (a) 1 (ii) of the SCM Agreement by WTO dispute settlement bodies suggests that the ordinary tax rules, absent these two measures, would be the benchmark against which a dispute settlement body would compare the measures to determine whether they constitute revenue otherwise due that is foregone or not collected. Given that the measures both offer an exemption from paying tax based on the defined activities, it seems clear that both measures would qualify as a financial contribution as defined in the SCM Agreement.

Whether the CCA Shift can be considered "foregone revenue," and thereby a financial contribution, is less clear. If the measure offered only an accelerated depreciation on certain types of equipment, above and beyond the rest of the category, it might be considered a financial contribution. Using this analysis, the depreciation allowed generally would serve as the benchmark for comparison, and the accelerated rate of depreciation would be an exception through which revenue was foregone. The CCA Shift as described, however, would raise and lower the depreciation rates in one category equally from their original starting point. In this case, there

---

[87] See *Canada — Measures Affecting the Export of Civilian Aircraft (Complaint by Brazil)*, (1999), WTO Doc. WT/DS70/AB/R (Appellate Body Report) [hereinafter *Canada — Aircraft* case].

[88] See *ibid.* at para. 47.

would be no obvious benchmark against which to compare the accelerated portion of the revised depreciation rates, and it would be more difficult to construe the accelerated depreciation as an exception to a general rule applicable to other taxpayers. Evaluating the measure in sub-components would lead to having one portion of the measure (the accelerated rate) qualify as "revenue otherwise due but foregone" while the portion of the measure lowering depreciation rates would not. In order to avoid this rather strange result, measures should be evaluated as a whole. The panel in *United States — Tax Treatment for "Foreign Sales Corporations"* (*United States — FSC* case) supports this conclusion, holding that its task "is to look at the various exemptions provided by the FSC scheme as a totality."[89]

The CCA Shift is not a discrete program or a specific measure but rather a change in the Income Tax Act. There is therefore no benchmark against which to compare tax liability, other than the Income Tax Act itself, prior to the change. If WTO panels were to use income tax rules prior to any changes to the basis of comparison, it could lead to the absurd result that all changes by a member to direct taxation rules that reduce tax payable could be considered a financial contribution.

Confer a Benefit

Once it is determined that a measure falls within the definition of a subsidy in Article 1.1 (a) of the SCM Agreement, the next question is whether a "benefit is thereby conferred."[90]

WTO jurisprudence

The most helpful discussion of what is meant by conferring a benefit in the WTO jurisprudence is found in the decision of the Appellate Body in *Canada — Aircraft* case.[91] In the original complaint, Brazil had alleged that certain measures used by Canada (such as the activities of the Export Development Corporation and the program known as Technology Partnerships Canada) constituted export subsidies that were inconsistent with the SCM Agreement. Part of Canada's argument was that the cost of the measures

---

[89] See *United States — FSC* panel report, *supra* note 81; *US — FSC* Appellate Body report, *supra* note 84 at para. 7.99.

[90] See SCM Agreement, *supra* note 20 at Article 1.1 (b).

[91] See *Canada — Aircraft* case, *supra* note 87.

to the government should be taken into account in determining whether a measure "conferred a benefit" on the airline industry.[92]

The Appellate Body examined the meaning of the words "confer" and "benefit" and concluded that the words refer to the granting of some sort of advantage to a beneficiary.[93] It noted that paragraph (b) of Article 1.1 is concerned with the recipient of the benefit and not with the government that grants the benefit.[94] As such, the cost of the measure to the government is not relevant in determining whether a benefit is conferred. The Appellate Body also held that the word "benefit" implies a comparison, "for there can be no 'benefit' to the recipient unless the 'financial contribution' makes the recipient 'better off' than it would otherwise have been, absent that contribution."[95] The baseline for comparison is the marketplace.[96] Therefore, the question to be determined in order to ascertain whether a contribution confers a benefit is whether the alleged recipient received a financial contribution on terms more favourable than those available to the recipient in the marketplace.[97] In other words, the question is whether the recipient is in a more advantageous position than it would have been in without the measure.[98]

This approach to paragraph 1.1 (b) of the SCM Agreement was reiterated by the Appellate Body in *United States — Imposition of Countervailing Duties on Certain Hot-Rolled Lead and Bismuth Carbon Steel Products Originating in the United Kingdom,*[99] which considered whether equity infusions by the British government to a state-owned steel company constituted subsidies. Relying on a footnote to Article 10 of the SCM Agreement, the United States argued in this case that "benefit" should be interpreted to refer to a benefit to a company's productive operations rather than to a benefit to legal or natural persons.[100] Confirming the panel's approach, the

---

[92] See *ibid.* at paras. 155-61.

[93] See *ibid* at para. 153.

[94] See *ibid* at para. 154.

[95] See *ibid* at para. 157.

[96] See *ibid.*

[97] See *Canada — Aircraft* case, *supra* note 87 at para. 157.

[98] See *ibid.*

[99] See *United States — Imposition of Countervailing Duties on Certain Hot-Rolled Lead and Bismuth Carbon Steel Products Originating in the United Kingdom (Complaint by European Community)* (1999), WTO Doc. WT/DS138/R [hereinafter *United States — British Steel* case].

[100] See *ibid.* at para. 56.

Appellate Body rejected this argument and reiterated its prior findings that the term "benefit" does not exist in the abstract but that it is something received and enjoyed by a beneficiary.[101]

Would the Straw Dog Measures Confer a Benefit?

Given the WTO dispute settlement bodies' approach to paragraph 1.1(b) of the SCM Agreement, the issue to be determined is whether the three straw dog measures create terms more favourable than those available to the recipient in the marketplace.[102] However, it is difficult to apply this approach to measures under the Income Tax Act since the marketplace is not an appropriate point of comparison (there is no marketplace where the income tax rules do not apply). Perhaps a more appropriate question in cases of measures applying through income tax rules is whether the measure has placed the recipient in a more favourable position than it would have been in without the measure. Using this test, the R&D Sustainable Forestry Incentive and the Training Credit could be said to confer a benefit. These two measures provide a company access to a tax credit that it would not otherwise have had access to, which will most likely confer a financial benefit to the company (assuming that it has income against which to claim the credit).

However, an argument that is untested within the WTO jurisprudence is whether a benefit is indeed conferred if a measure is designed to, and in practice serves only to, offset externalized costs that are being voluntarily internalized by a person or company. Consider the straw dog measures. The aim of all three measures is to create incentives for companies to internalize the environmental costs of their production, which are currently borne by society. Companies that practice environmentally sensitive logging internalize many environmental costs (such as the costs of damage to soil and watershed ecosystems and the impacts on climate cycles). As such, measures that serve to offset these additional costs do not, in effect, confer a benefit. While theoretically, all economic actors should internalize all of their social and environmental costs, it will clearly not happen overnight, and, in the meantime, governments may wish to offer incentives as a means of encouraging companies to begin the process of internalizing environmental costs. This question should be considered by the WTO Committee on Trade and Environment.

[101] See *ibid.* at para. 6.78.

[102] See *Canada — Aircraft* case, *supra* note 87 at para. 157.

Whether the CCA Shift confers a benefit will depend on the type of equipment the alleged recipient uses. If a company uses equipment that qualifies as being more environmentally friendly, then it will have a better depreciation rate. However, if the company is not using environmentally sensitive equipment, it will be in a worse position. Applying the reasoning in the *United States — FSC* case, which suggests that measures should be evaluated as a whole, the CCA Shift would arguably not confer a benefit on "recipients." The impact of the measure would depend on the choices made by a company. Given the lack of clarity on this issue, the WTO Committee on Trade and Environment may want to shed some light on this issue.

Specificity

Determining whether a measure constitutes a subsidy that confers a benefit is only part of the analysis. A subsidy alone is not inconsistent with WTO rules. A subsidy only becomes prohibited or actionable if it is "specific" to an enterprise or industry (or group of enterprises or industries). The rationale is that subsidies should not be allowed to distort the allocation of resources within an economy.[103] Subsidies that are contingent upon export performance or upon the use of domestic over imported goods are deemed to be specific.[104] For other subsidies, Article 2 of the SCM Agreement sets out the principles for determining specificity. It states:

a) where the granting authority, or the legislation pursuant to which the granting authority operates, explicitly limits access to a subsidy to certain enterprises, such subsidy shall be specific.

b) Where the granting authority, or the legislation pursuant to which the granting authority operates, establishes objective criteria or conditions (meaning those that are neutral, which do not favour certain enterprises over others, and which are economic in nature and horizontal in application) governing the eligibility for, and the amount of, a subsidy, specificity shall not exist, provided that the eligibility is automatic and that such criteria and conditions are strictly adhered to. The criteria or conditions must be clearly spelled out in law, regulation, or other official document, so as to be capable of verification.

---

[103] See WTO, *Subsidies and Countervailing Measures Overview*, text available online at <http://www.wto.org/english/tratop_e/scm_e/subs_e.htm>.

[104] See SCM Agreement, *supra* note 20 at Article 2.3. Article 3 of SCM Agreement prohibits the use of such subsidies, except as provided in the Agreement on Agriculture, Final Act Embodying the Results of the Uruguay Round of Trade Negotiations, signed at Marrakesh, April 15, 1994, 33. I.L.M. 1125.

c) If, notwithstanding any appearance of non-specificity ... there are reasons to believe the subsidy may in fact be specific, other factors may be considered. Such factors are: use of a subsidy program by a limited number of certain enterprises, predominant use by certain enterprises, the granting of disproportionately large amounts of subsidy to certain enterprises and the manner in which discretion has been exercised by the granting authority in the decision to grant a subsidy.

Effectively, any subsidy limited to particular enterprises are considered specific, while those that are granted in response to neutral and objective criteria, or conditions that are economic in nature and horizontal in application (that is, the size of the company or the number of employees), are not specific.[105] However, if a subsidy that is offered on neutral and objective criteria is *in practice* used by a specific industry, the subsidy can be considered *de facto* specific and therefore fall within the scope of actionable subsidies.

WTO jurisprudence

Since none of the three straw dog measures are contingent upon export performance or upon the use of domestic over imported goods, this article will not consider the WTO jurisprudence analyzing the meaning of these terms.[106] It will focus on the question of specificity as defined in Article 2. The issue of specificity under Article 2 has not been subject to as much analysis within the WTO dispute settlement bodies as the definitions of a "financial contribution" and "conferring a benefit." The main case to closely examine the meaning of specificity is the recent panel decision in *United States — Final Countervailing Duty Determination with Respect to Certain Softwood Lumber from Canada* (*United States — Softwood Lumber* case).[107] The case involved an investigation, initiated by the United States, to determine whether Canada's system of charging stumpage fees for timber harvested from public land constitutes an actionable subsidy within the meaning of the SCM Agreement.

The panel began its analysis by noting that the specificity test is "concerned with the distortion that is created by a subsidy which

---

[105] See SCM Agreement, *supra* note 20 at Article 2.

[106] Several WTO decisions have considered Article 3 of the SCM Agreement. See, for example, *Canada — Certain Measures Affecting the Automotive Industry (Complaint by Japan)*, WTO Doc. WT/DS139/AB/R (Appellate Body Report).

[107] See *United States — Final Countervailing Duty Determination with Respect to Certain Softwood Lumber from Canada (Complaint by Canada)* (2003) WTO Doc. WT/DS257/R [hereinafter *United States — Softwood Lumber*].

either in law or in fact is not broadly available."[108] It then considered Canada's argument that a subsidy is only specific if a granting authority deliberately limits access to that subsidy to a group of enterprises producing similar products. In examining this argument, the panel considered the meaning of "industry" within the SCM Agreement. It found that the term "industry" is "not used to refer to enterprises producing specific goods or end-products"[109] and that specificity is to be determined "at the enterprise or industry level, not at the product level."[110] Following from this analysis, the panel held that Canada's stumpage program is limited to the "wood products industries," which qualify as an industry or a group of industries.[111]

Would the Straw Dog Measures Be Specific?

Given the *United States — Softwood Lumber* panel's broad interpretation of "specificity," all three of the straw dog measures in this article would be at some risk of being considered specific in law, if not in *de facto* application. The analysis will depend on the design of each measure. The proposed R&D Sustainable Forestry Initiative is clearly targeted through its very title at the forest sector. While the forest sector is comprised of a number of industries, such as the pulp and paper industry, the lumber remanufacturing industry, and the lumber harvesting industry, the *United States — Softwood Lumber* panel decision suggests that the forest sector is sufficiently specific to meet the requirements of Article 2 of the SCM Agreement.

As it is worded in the earlier description, the Training Credit may not be specific *in law* to any particular industry. However, if the credit was designed to be available only to the forest sector, or it was *in practice* used primarily by industries within the forest sector, it would likely be considered specific. Therefore, as will be elaborated upon later in this article, it would be wise for the creators of any such program to design it so that it applies broadly to training for the use of environmentally sensitive production equipment across sectors. A similar analysis applies to the CCA Shift. If the measure is designed in a way that it applies across sectors — in other words, the new depreciable asset classes are not restricted to

---

[108] See *ibid.* at para. 7.116.

[109] See *ibid.* at para. 7.120.

[110] See *ibid.* at para. 7.122.

[111] See *ibid.* at para. 7.121.

logging equipment but apply generally to a cross-sectoral range of environmentally sensitive capital equipment — it should escape the "specificity" label.[112]

Adverse Affect

Once a measure has qualified as an actionable subsidy, it must pass one more threshold in order to be actionable. The measure must cause an adverse effect to another WTO member. The SCM Agreement creates three categories of adverse effect:

a) causing injury to the domestic industry of another Member;
b) nullification or impairment of benefits accruing directly or indirectly to other Members under GATT 1994 in particular the benefits of concessions bound under Article II of GATT 1994; or,
c) causing serious prejudice to the interests of another member.[113]

Countervailing duties are only available when criteria (a) is met.[114] The SCM Agreement provides guidelines for determining whether there has been injury or serious prejudice.[115] However, the determination of the existence of adverse effects will be fact-specific to each case. It is therefore difficult to ascertain whether the straw dog measures would lead to an adverse effect. The WTO jurisprudence on the question of injury is also very fact-specific and thus does not add to the analysis.[116]

---

[112] The revised depreciation classes could still provide specific examples of equipment that would qualify as environmentally sensitive and therefore for the accelerated depreciation rate as long as the examples included equipment from a variety of sectors.

[113] SCM Agreement, *supra* note 20 at Article 5. Serious prejudice is deemed to exist in the case of:
(a) the total ad valorem subsidization of a product exceeding 5 percent;
(b) subsidies to cover operating losses sustained by an industry;
(c) subsidies to cover operating losses sustained by an industry, other than one-time measures that are non-recurrent and cannot be repeated for that enterprise, and which are given merely to provide time for the development of long-term solutions and to avoid acute social problems.
See *ibid.* at Article 6.

[114] See *ibid.* at Article 11.

[115] See, for example, *ibid.* at Articles 6 and 15. The requirement for finding injury before imposing countervailing measures is found in Article 19.1 of the SCM Agreement.

[116] See, for example, *United States — Softwood Lumber, supra* note 107 at 108.

If it could be demonstrated that the measures only offset additional costs borne by producers operating in Canada that are internalizing environmental costs, it could be argued that the measures would not cause injury to the competitor's market but would simply be leveling the playing field between them. This argument is unlikely to find support within the WTO dispute settlement bodies and would require some creative interpretation of the SCM Agreement. However, despite this disadvantage, a WTO member interested in using fiscal measures to promote non-trade distorting, environmentally responsible behaviour may want to test it.

Allowable Measures

To the extent that the straw dog measures qualify as a "subsidy" under Article 1 and are specific as per Article 2, they will be considered "actionable"[117] under the SCM Agreement. Articles 8 and 9 of the SCM Agreement create a category of subsidies that are considered allowable. These subsidies include assistance for research activities conducted by firms, assistance to disadvantaged regions, and assistance to promote the adaptation of existing facilities to new environmental requirements.[118] The exceptions in Article 8, however, applied only for the first five years of the SCM Agreement. While their application could be extended by consensus, no such consensus has been reached and the allowable subsidies provisions of Article 8 (along with a provision establishing a presumption of serious prejudice in respect of certain specified types of actionable subsidies) were no longer valid as of December 31, 1999.[119]

---

[117] This means that a WTO member who can demonstrate that its domestic industry has suffered a material injury as a result of the importation into its market of products that have benefited from such subsidies can apply a countervailing duty on the imported products.

[118] See SCM Agreement, *supra* note 20 at Article 8. Article 8 also states that subsidies that are not specific within the meaning of Article 2 are non-actionable (see Article 8.2). The exception of assistance to promote adaptation of facilities to new environmental regulations was enacted in response to environmental concerns about competitiveness. The provision allows governments to fund or subsidize up to 20 per cent of a one-time capital investment required to satisfy new environmental rules without another country being able to impose a countervailing duty (see Article 8.2.)

[119] Article 31 of the SCM Agreement, *ibid.*, provided for the provisional five-year application of the allowable subsidies categories. See WTO, *Subsidies and Countervailing Measures Overview*, text available online at <http://www.wto.org/english/tratop_e/scm_e/subs_e.htm>.

None of the WTO dispute settlement panels considered the scope and ambit of Article 8 during the five years that it was in force. Given that the allowable subsidy provisions have expired and that the dispute settlement bodies of the WTO never analyzed the provisions, this article will not attempt to analyze whether the straw dog measures could qualify as allowable subsidies. However, to the extent that governments believe that they should be able to enact non-trade distorting measures designed to create incentives for environmentally responsible activities, those governments should encourage the WTO to reopen negotiations on allowable subsidies. And, since those negotiations will likely take a long time, interested governments should consider entering into bilateral or multilateral agreements with trading partners to carve out rules respecting such programs.

CONCLUSION

This article has shown that the straw dog measures put forward for the purposes of analysis could fall within the disciplines of the SCM Agreement. Whether they will so fall will depend greatly on their design. The specificity measures in particular could be determinative in this evaluation. Given that the design of EFR measures can have such a significant influence on the extent to which such measures may come into conflict with the SCM Agreement, it is incumbent upon governments to design and implement measures that are widely available and that will not cause adverse effects to the markets of a competing market. In order to avoid designing measures that qualify as "specific" under the SCM Agreement, measures should be designed to apply widely across sectors and in a way that ensures they are likely to be used by a variety of industry players from different sectors. A dual measure of care would need to be taken in designing measures to ensure that the efforts to conform to WTO disciplines do not dilute their original goal of achieving environmental objectives. Canada would also need to undertake a thorough evaluation of the United State's application of subsidy rules, since it has in practice differed from the WTO rules.

While design will help avoid conflict in some cases, there is still a risk that the SCM Agreement is serving as a deterrent and restriction in implementing EFR, particularly for direct tax measures and particularly in an export-dominated economy such as Canada, which is highly susceptible to potential trade actions. From an innovative policy-making perspective, this "chill" is unfortunate.

The absence of a clear understanding of the subsidies rules and their potential implications for EFR measures could create a "red herring phenomenon," whereby sound policy options are discounted unnecessarily due to a feared conflict with subsidies disciplines.

It is important for governments to commission analysis that will reduce and hopefully eliminate potential "red herring" issues that may lead to a chill on progressive policy-making. WTO members interested in pursuing fiscal reform should initiate a review and clarification within the WTO of the application of its trade rules to EFR measures that legitimately aim to internalize environmental costs and are non-trade distorting. A specific step that could be taken would be to request the WTO Committee on Trade and Environment to follow up on its observations relating to the potential for environmental taxation and to evaluate the subsidies disciplines as they relate to national approaches designed to encourage sustainable behaviour in a non-trade-distorting manner. In addition to initiating a review within the WTO, countries that are beginning to use EFR measures may want to enter into bilateral or multilateral negotiations with trade partners to try to address potential subsidy and countervailing duty conflicts arising from EFR measures ahead of time through agreement. If participating jurisdictions agree to the measures ahead of time, or agree to a set of principles and criteria for designing and implementing EFR measures, potential trade disputes could be avoided altogether.

Clearly, the straw dog measures proposed in this article are only the tip of the iceberg in terms of potential fiscal measures that could be used to encourage environmentally and economically responsible development. Other incentive measures that could be considered include measures relating to property taxes and lower sales or excise tax rates on products that are environmentally sensitive according to objective criteria. In addition, the other side of the EFR coin is that of environmental taxation (versus incentives). WTO disciplines also have the potential to interact with these measures.[120] In sum, the reform of fiscal policy measures to encourage environmentally and economically responsible activities within a country is part of the next wave of innovative policy-making. As more and more countries begin applying these new policy tools, it is incumbent upon governments, academics, non-governmental organizations, policy-makers, and international trade institutions

---

[120] See generally Faucald, *supra* note 14; and McDonald, *supra* note 14.

to begin exploring how to ensure that international trade rules do not impede the use of legitimate, non-trade distorting measures that aim to encourage environmentally responsible economic activities. It would be counterproductive to our common future to do otherwise.

Sommaire

Écotaxes et l'OMC — analyse des répercussions de l'OMC sur l'utilisation de mesures d'incitation financière pour promouvoir la foresterie durable au Canada

Cet article évalue dans quelle mesure les règles du commerce international peuvent limiter les choix politiques des gouvernements qui souhaitent encourager la conservation de la biodiversité par des mesures d'incitation financière. Afin de faciliter l'analyse, l'article propose trois incitatifs fiscaux que le gouvernement du Canada pourrait mettre en œuvre pour encourager l'industrie forestière à recourir à des pratiques de foresterie durable, puis examine l'application de l'Accord sur les subventions et les mesures compensatoires de l'Organisation mondiale du commerce (OMC) en matière de l'utilisation de telles pratiques. En conclusion, l'article énonce que si L'Accord sur les subventions et les mesures compensatoires ne limite pas le choix des gouvernements et le recours aux instruments économiques, il est possible de concevoir pour la réalisation des objectifs environnementaux recherchés des mesures qui ne portent pas atteinte aux règles du commerce. Néanmoins, étant donné la complexité des règles sur les subventions et l'importance des incitatifs économiques en tant qu'instruments politiques dans l'atteinte des objectifs environnementaux, l'article recommande que l'OMC et ses membres poursuivent la réflexion sur le sujet.

Summary

Environmental Taxes and the WTO — An Analysis of the WTO Implications of Using Fiscal Incentives to Promote Sustainable Forestry in Canada

This article examines the extent to which international trade rules can constrain the policy choices of governments wishing to apply fiscal incentives to encourage biodiversity conservation. In order to facilitate the analysis, the article proposes three hypothetical fiscal incentives that could be implemented by the Canadian government to encourage the forest industry to use sustainable forestry practices. It then analyzes the application of the WTO SCM Agreement to the use of such measures. It concludes that while the SCM Agreement does constrain the government's choice and implementation of economic instruments, it is possible to design measures to achieve the desired environmental goals without infringing trade rules. However, given the complexity of the subsidies rules and the importance of economic incentives as policy tools for achieving environmental objectives, the article recommends further consideration of this issue by the WTO and its members.

Bringing Individual Human Rights Issues to the United Nations: John Humphrey and the Quest for Compensation

A.J. HOBBINS AND ANN H. STEWARD

INTRODUCTION

After the Second World War, work began at the United Nations on the creation of an international bill of rights. This effort marked the first time that international law had sought to recognize the individual, which, until this time, had only been recognized by states. The international bill was envisioned to have three parts: a declaration of principles, a convention binding on states, and a means of implementation were envisioned. The first part proved to be relatively simple, and the Universal Declaration of Human Rights (UDHR) was proclaimed by the UN General Assembly on December 10, 1948.[1] A convention proved to be a thornier issue in the politics of the day. Eventually, two conventions were required — one that concentrated on civil and political rights and a second on social, economic, and cultural rights.[2] These conventions were opened for signature in 1966, came into force in 1976, but were binding only on the states that ratified a particular instrument.

A. J. Hobbins, John Humphrey's literary executor, and Ann Hartwell Steward are librarians in the Nahum Gelber Law Library at McGill University. The authors would like to thank Joanne Pelletier and the staff of the McGill University Archives [hereinafter MUA], especially Gordie Burr and Kathi Murphy, for making their materials available.

[1] Universal Declaration of Human Rights, GA Res 217(III), UN GAOR. 3rd Sess., Supp. No. 13, UN Doc. A/810 (1948).

[2] These were the International Covenant on Civil and Political Rights, GA Res. 2200A (XXI), 21 U.N. GAOR Supp. (No. 16) at 52, U.N. Doc. A/6316 (1966), 999 U.N.T.S. 171 (entered into force Mar. 23, 1976) [hereinafter ICCPR]; and the International Covenant on Economic, Social and Cultural Rights, GA Res. 2200A (XXI), 21 U.N. GAOR Supp. (No. 16) at 49, U.N. Doc. A/6316 (1966), 993 U.N.T.S. 3 (entered into force Jan. 3, 1976).

Since this time, other declarations and conventions have been enacted to reflect the evolving concerns of the world.[3] Means of implementation, or enforcement, have always proved to be the most difficult aspect of the international bill of rights. While these means have included armed intervention and sanctions, the more common approach has been the investigation of alleged violations of human rights by various UN bodies, especially the Commission on Human Rights (CHR) and the Office of the High Commissioner for Human Rights (HCHR), followed by a report. Although such reports cannot impose a resolution on an offending state, they are important in molding world opinion to place pressure on an offender. The process, which includes attendant media attention, is sometimes known as the "organization of shame."

One of the first significant steps in implementing rights for individuals was the Optional Protocol of the International Covenant of Civil and Political Rights (ICCPR).[4] By signing this instrument, states agreed to a complaint mechanism whereby cases alleging violations of human rights could be brought before the United Nations by other states and by individuals. The individual rights that may be invoked are found in Articles 6-27 of the ICCPR. In order to hear such cases, the CHR established the Human Rights Committee, which consists of eighteen independent experts who meet three times per year. To begin, a special rapporteur on new communications evaluates the complaints that have been received to determine if they should be registered under the Optional Protocol. The HRC then considers questions of admissibility and the merits simultaneously.[5] The difficulty with this mechanism is that not all states have ratified the ICCPR and not all that have have agreed to the Optional Protocol. What is more, even some that have acceded to the protocol have done so with formal reservations.

---

[3] These would include such items as Declaration on the Granting of Independence to Colonial Countries and Peoples, GA Res. 1514 (XV), 15 U.N. GAOR Supp. (No. 16) at 66, U.N. Doc. A/4684 (1961); and International Convention on the Elimination of All Forms of Racial Discrimination, 660 U.N.T.S. 195 (entered into force Jan. 4, 1969).

[4] Optional Protocol to the International Covenant on Civil and Political Rights, GA Res. 2200A (XXI), 21 U.N. GAOR Supp. (No. 16) at 59, U.N. Doc. A/6316 (1966), 999 U.N.T.S. 302 (entered into force March 23, 1976).

[5] Details of these procedures can be found at the website of the Office of the UN High Commissioner for Human Rights, *Procedure under the Optional Protocol to the International Covenant on Civil and Political Rights* at <http://www.unhchr.ch/html/menu6/2/fs7.htm#ccpr>.

Another mechanism, which is known as Resolution 1503,[6] allows complaints about gross violations of human rights to be brought by individuals against states of which they were not nationals, regardless of whether that state was a party to any convention. Economic and Social Council (ECOSOC) Resolution 1503 was adopted in 1970. It established a working group of the Sub-Commission on the Prevention of Discrimination and the Protection of Minorities to receive complaints. The working group considers the communication and any reply from governments and, if the majority of the group agrees, passes the complaint on to the sub-commission with a recommendation on how to proceed. The sub-commission then reviews any communications received in a confidential session. If the sub-commission considers that the complaint is valid and that it has jurisdiction, the matter is referred to the CHR for disposition. The difficulty with the Resolution 1503 procedure is that the CHR, like most UN organs, is highly political, and many pressures can be brought to bear on members of the sub-commission and the CHR.

At a UN workshop[7] on the Optional Protocol, which was held in Ottawa in 1990, Jan Märtenson, under-secretary-general for human rights, in his opening statement,[8] congratulated the host country, Canada, for being among the first states to sign the protocol and to do so without reservation. Before giving his congratulations, however, Märtenson paid tribute to Canadian human rights activist, John Peters Humphrey, saying:

As to John Humphrey, he demonstrates on the national and international levels an unshakeable will to gain respect for the rights of all people, the same rights that were proclaimed in the *Universal Declaration* in 1948.

A few weeks ago, the Secretary General of the United Nations, Javier Pérez de Cuéllar, paid homage to him in an address at McGill University. This was yet another demonstration of the admiration which the United Nations feels for him, and which he of all people richly deserves.[9]

---

[6] UN Economic and Social Council [hereinafter ECOSOC] Procedure for Dealing with Communications Relating to Violations of Human Rights and Fundamental Freedoms, Resolution 1503 (XLVIII), 1970, UN Doc. E/4832/Add. 1 (1970), text is available at <http://www1.umn.edu/humanrts/procedures/1503.html>.

[7] The workshop, which was jointly sponsored by the UN Centre for Human Rights and the Canadian Department of Justice, was held in Ottawa in June 1990.

[8] The proceedings of the workshop were published in the *Canadian Human Rights Yearbook 1991-1992* (Ottawa: Human Rights Research and Education Centre, University of Ottawa, 1992). Märtenson's opening statement can be found on pages 19-26.

[9] *Ibid.* at 19.

While Humphrey had not been invited to the conference,[10] the tribute was not misplaced. From 1946 to 1966, Humphrey had been the first director of the UN Division of Human Rights — the forerunner of the UN Centre for Human Rights. In this role, he had written the first draft of what became the UDHR and had worked tirelessly on the development of the covenants, including the Optional Protocol. Thirty years before it became a reality, he had advocated his idea for the creation of a high commissioner for human rights.[11] When he retired from international service, he was elected to the Sub-Commission on the Prevention of Discrimination and the Protection of Minorities — a body in which members served in their individual capacity and not as national representatives. Later, as chairman of the sub-commission, he had significant involvement in the drafting of the text that, in amended version, became Resolution 1503.

While Humphrey played as great a role as anyone in the early development of the various components of the international bill of rights, in the twilight of his life he became involved in a number of cases that attempted to use these mechanisms. Using Humphrey's own papers, this article examines some of these cases. They include the initiatives to get compensation for the prisoners of war (POWs), civilian internees, and "comfort women" who suffered at the hands of the Japanese military in the Second World War as well as the challenges to the language laws of Québec on the grounds that they restricted freedom of expression. Since the United Nations is essentially a political body wherein national interest is reflected,

[10] Humphrey was only invited to a *post scriptum* after the workshop ended. Reflecting on this event, he wrote in his diary on August 23, 1990:

> Incidentally I was not invited by the Canadian government to attend a four day [workshop] recently in Ottawa on the Optional Protocol to the Covenant on Civil and Political Rights. Since I am one of the few surviving people who played a part in its adoption I wonder why. It was true that I was invited to a kind of post scriptum conference of one day later. Nor was I invited to a conference in the same city by the Canadian Commission for UNESCO. I sometimes think that I have more enemies in Ottawa than friends. I could make a list.

Humphrey's Diary, McGill University Archives [hereinafter MUA] Manuscript Group [hereinafter MG] 4127, Cont. 20, File 16 [hereinafter Humphrey Diary]. In addition to his diary, Humphrey's extensive collection of papers, of which we cite extensively throughout the footnotes, is housed in the MUA as MG 4127.

[11] See A.J. Hobbins, "Humphrey and the High Commissioner: The Genesis of the Office of the UN High Commissioner for Human Rights" (2001) 3 J. History of Int'l L. 38-74.

these initiatives involved the need to create new international law over such matters as UN jurisdiction and the right to compensation.

WAR AMPUTATIONS OF CANADA

The War Amputations of Canada, which is known generally as the War Amps, was founded after the First World War by Padre Sydney Lambert (himself an amputee) to help disabled veterans.[12] The association provided employment for veterans and raised funds through a number of programs including the innovative Key Tag Service, which was established in 1946.[13] H. Clifford Chadderton took over from Lambert in 1965 as chief executive officer, and, in 1975, he expanded the programs to include child amputees. By the 1980s, the War Amps, in addition to providing support and rehabilitation, began advocating financial compensation for certain disabled groups. The most significant of these groups were the thalidomide victims, who had suffered birth defects from their mothers using an approved drug, and the Hong Kong veterans. The association began lobbying the government of Canada on behalf of the thalidomide victims as well as Japan on behalf of the former POWs. Neither effort was especially successful, so the association decided to take the case of the thalidomide victims to the United Nations under the Optional Protocol. The services of an Ottawa lawyer, Brian Forbes, as association solicitor were secured.

THALIDOMIDE VICTIMS

The case against Canada was based on Article 24(1) of the ICCPR, which states that "[e]very child shall have, without any discrimination ... the right to such measures of protection as are required by his status as a minor, on the part of his family, society and the state."[14] The argument was bolstered by reference to the Convention on the Rights of the Child in which the state is responsible "to ensure appropriate pre-natal and post-natal health care for mothers."[15] The War Amps, jointly with the International

---

[12] The association was established in 1920 as the Amputations Association of the Great War. It changed its name during the Second World War.

[13] This service provides license plate information to be attached to keys and has resulted in a million lost sets of keys being returned to their owners.

[14] ICCPR, *supra* note 2.

[15] Convention on the Rights of the Child, GA Res. 44/25, annex, 44 U.N. GAOR Supp. (No. 49) at 167, U.N. Doc. A/44/49 (1989) (entered into force Sept. 2, 1990) at Article 24(d).

Commission of Health Professionals, maintained that Canada had failed to carry out its obligations for the following reasons:

a) The failure of the government to make itself aware of early contraindications with respect to Thalidomide discovered in other parts of the world;
b) The omission of the government to determine the fact that the American Food and Drug Directorate had rejected the licensing application for Thalidomide on the basis of the same reports received by the Canadian government;
c) Following the withdrawal of the drug Thalidomide in many European countries a three month delay occurred prior to the withdrawal of the drug in Canada;
d) The failure of the Canadian government to provide proper testing and research in its licensing procedures.[16]

The case was accepted and referred to the Human Rights Committee (HRC). Buoyed by this initial success, the War Amps began to consider whether the case for the Hong Kong veterans against Japan could also be brought to the United Nations. Although Japan had signed the ICCPR in 1979, it had never acceded to the Optional Protocol. It was decided therefore to prepare a communication under Resolution 1503.

HONG KONG EXPEDITIONARY FORCE

The situation of the Hong Kong veterans arose from Canada's attempt to do its share for British imperial defence. On September 19, 1941, Great Britain, its troops tied up in European and African theatres of operations, requested Canada to send one or two battalions of infantry to Hong Kong to help protect imperial interests in the Pacific. Such a force was militarily insignificant, but the request was purely political. It was felt that Japan's expansionist ambitions might eventually lead to war and that it was important to demonstrate the intention of holding Hong Kong. Such an act, it was thought, would reassure the potential ally of China, which was then at war with Japan, and serve as a warning to the Japanese. The arrival of fresh troops would also give a boost to the morale of the colony. In the event of war, which was then thought to be far off, the troops could be quickly evacuated either through the friendly offices of the United States Navy, based in Pearl Harbor, or through the

---

[16] International Commission of Health Professionals and War Amputations of Canada, *Joint Statement to the Sub-Commission on Prevention of Discrimination and Protection of Minorities*, August 1989, MUA MG 4127, Cont. 16, File 321.

use of a British fleet, which included the capital ships *Prince of Wales* and *Repulse*, which were then being dispatched to Singapore. Furthermore, China had promised to send ten divisions should Hong Kong be attacked.[17] Canada quickly agreed to the request, sending a battalion from the Québec-based Royal Rifles of Canada and one from the Winnipeg Grenadiers. The 1,985 officers and men — all volunteers for overseas service, who sailed on October 27, 1941 — were neither properly equipped nor fully trained. It was intended that the motorized equipment be sent later in an American vessel and that training could be undertaken in Hong Kong.

Events in the outside world moved faster than had been anticipated. On December 7, 1941, the surprise attack on Pearl Harbor meant not only that the United States Navy could not help in an evacuation but also that the in-transit equipment never arrived. The following day, the *Prince of Wales* and the *Repulse* were both sunk off their China station, and Hong Kong itself was attacked. Cut off from supply, reinforcement, and evacuation, the garrison surrendered on Christmas day. Among the prisoners and civilian internees taken were 1,689 survivors of the Canadian contingent. Japan was not a party to the 1929 Geneva Convention Relative to the Treatment of Prisoners of War[18] and thus for over three years the Canadian POWs were kept in appalling conditions and used as slave labour.[19]

The question of compensation for this treatment came up in the negotiations leading up to the 1952 peace treaty[20] with Japan. The matter had been brought to the Canadian War Claims Commission in 1950. The Japanese government claimed impoverishment and said any assets taken in Canada could be used for reparations.

[17] Great Britain had in fact no intention of accepting this offer since the presence of ten Chinese divisions in Hong Kong might have negatively affected the future of the colony.

[18] Convention Relative to the Treatment of Prisoners of War, with Annex, July 27, 1929, 118 L.N.T.S. 343 [hereinafter Geneva Convention].

[19] This debacle was the subject of a parliamentary enquiry to see if there was any individual culpability for sending the troops in the prevailing circumstances. These facts are taken from Canada, *Report of the Royal Commission to Inquire into and Report upon the Organization, Authorization and Dispatch of the Canadian Expeditionary Force to the Crown Colony of Hong Kong* (Ottawa: King's Printer, 1942).

[20] The treaty was signed in San Francisco on September 8, 1951 and came into force on April 28, 1952. Both years are used in correspondence to refer to this treaty. Treaty of Peace with Japan (with Two Declarations), September 8, 1951, 136 U.N.T.S. 45.

Canada accepted this proposal as did the other allied powers for assets in their countries.[21] From the sale of these assets in Canada, the War Claims Commission paid the Hong Kong veterans $1.50 for each day of captivity, a somewhat trifling sum, and the matter was considered closed. Since Japan experienced a remarkable economic recovery over the next three decades, the War Amps approached them to suggest that they now pay a more reasonable compensation.[22] The Japanese response was always the same — that the 1952 treaty relieved them of any further responsibility in the matter.

Gingras Study

When the War Amps decided to pursue a claim against Japan under Resolution 1503, a world-renowned expert in rehabilitation, Gustave Gingras, was retained to prepare a study on the after-effects of the wartime treatment on the remaining 800 survivors. Chadderton wrote to the minister of veteran affairs, George Hees, to obtain permission for Gingras, who was a resident of Prince Edward Island, to examine service records of the survivors in Charlottetown.[23] Hees agreed, provided that the individual POWs authorized the study. This permission was easily obtained, and Gingras began the study on the basis of the files and some 400 questionnaires.

The following month, Chadderton was inducted into the Knights of Malta. At the ceremony, he met Humphrey, a fellow inductee. On discovering that Humphrey spent each summer in Prince Edward Island, Chadderton asked him if he knew Gingras. Humphrey's answer was an enthusiastic affirmative and when Gingras heard of this chance meeting he wrote to Humphrey to ask him to write a foreword to the report.[24] Humphrey was pleased to comply with Gingras's request and even offered some advice on approaching the United Nations. He felt the sub-commission might ignore the report since it dealt with events from forty years earlier and did not

---

[21] In Article 16 of the treaty, Japan agreed to transfer its assets, and those of its nationals, to create a compensation fund.

[22] At this point, a sum of Cdn $12,000,000 was requested — $12,000 per veteran or widow, there then being about 1,000 potential benefactors.

[23] Letter from Chadderton to Hees (August 5, 1986, MUA MG 4127, Cont. 16, File 331).

[24] Letter from Gingras to Humphrey (November 7, 1986, MUA MG 4127, Cont. 16, File 331).

represent evidence of "persistent patterns of gross violations of human rights." He therefore suggested involving non-governmental organizations (NGOs) with ECOSOC affiliation, such as the World Veterans Federation (WVF), to take the matter up with the CHR and offered to intervene on their behalf with the International Commission of Jurists.[25] When Forbes heard of this collaboration, he immediately recognized the value of involving Humphrey more intimately in the project. He spoke to Humphrey several times on the telephone and subsequently wrote requesting a meeting in which strategies could be discussed and even offered Humphrey a retainer.[26] The strategies that were agreed upon included approaching the Canadian government to gain support for the communication, preparing a declaration on the right to compensation, which could then be adopted by the United Nations, and informing a large number of relevant NGOs about the case and the declaration.

Initial Governmental Response

Chadderton wrote to Joe Clark, Canada's minister for external affairs, to solicit Canadian support in Geneva for the communication. Clark's cautious response indicated the belief that, as Humphrey had warned, the abuses took place too long ago and that the matter had ended with the 1952 treaty. Clark wrote:

Since the U.N. Charter entered into force, the U.N. has developed a variety of mechanisms to examine abuses, primarily of human rights, that have arisen since 1948. You may find that these mechanisms do not meet your claim either because they do not operate retroactively or because none of then make specific mention of reparation.

As you know, the claims of Canadians held prisoner of war by the Japanese government were settled, using funds largely derived from confiscated Japanese property, by the Canadian War Claims Commission in the late 1950s. I recognize that no amount of money could ever compensate for the suffering members of your organization underwent. I only hope that we can prevent such events from ever occurring again.[27]

A franker opinion on the issue was expressed in the British parliament when the War Amps initiative was discussed. David Mellor,

[25] Letter from Humphrey to Gingras (March 7, 1987, MUA MG 4127, Cont. 16, File 331).

[26] Letter from Forbes to Humphrey (May 20, 1987, MUA MG 4127, Cont. 16, File 331).

[27] Letter from Clarke to Chadderton (undated but received June 30, 1987, MUA MG 4127, Cont. 16, File 331).

minister of state responsible for East-West relations and the Middle East, stated in response to a question from Sir Bernard Braine:

My right hon. Friend also mentioned that this claim was submitted under the procedure based on resolution 1503. I have every sympathy for the claimants — I cannot stress that enough — but I am afraid that the chances of success under this procedure cannot, in my judgment, be high. One of the criteria applied under that resolution when judging whether claims are admissible is that the allegation of the violation of human rights must be submitted within a reasonable period, and the 40 years that have elapsed may be held to be not within that proviso.

A second difficulty is that the question may be outside the mandate of the United Nations, since that body was not in existence at the time when the violations took place. All I — [The House adjourned at this point.][28]

It was evident that official circles took a traditional view on international law — that the doctrine of *nulla poena sine lege*[29] applied, that the United Nations had no jurisdiction in the case, and that the 1952 treaty closed the matter. Little help therefore could be expected from the national governments.

Compensation Declaration

Forbes began the drafting of a declaration on compensation with a statement of principle, which he then distributed widely among the relevant NGOs.[30] This declaration stated:

A country which has been identified as having committed a consistent and systematic pattern of acts which represent gross violations of human rights shall indemnify or compensate the victims of such human rights violations with respect to any resultant disability or incapacity suffered by such victims.

He also continued his efforts to make Humphrey a formal part of the team, writing:

[28] Great Britain Parliamentary Debates, July 21, 1988, vol. 137, p. 1423-24.

[29] No punishment unless a law had been broken. Since Japan was not party to the 1929 Geneva Convention, *supra* note 18, it could not be held to have broken a law.

[30] Letter from Forbes to various recipients (December 18, 1987, MUA MG 4127, Cont. 16, File 331). These included Jean-Jacques Surbeck (International Committee of the Red Cross), Berti Ramcharan (UN Human Rights Centre, Geneva), Marc Bossuyt (Chair, Commission on Human Rights [hereinafter CHR]), Adrien-Claude Zoller (International Human Rights Service, Geneva), Niall MacDermot (International Court of Justice), Chris Avery (Amnesty International), and Serge Wourgaft (World Veterans Federation).

We are most grateful to hear that you would have no objection to our employing your name as a contributor or co-author of the Draft declaration as there is little question that your reputation is of extreme significance within the Human Rights community in Geneva. As I mentioned to you by phone a number of NGO representatives have indicated that your name is "legend" within the framework of the Human Rights Commission.
. . .
I am further attaching recent correspondence I received from Niall MacDermot[31] . . . wherein he expresses certain concerns as to the viability of our Communication pursuant to resolution 1503. We have discussed these points by phone and I am satisfied that we must continue to pursue our overall claim with as much complementary publicity as possible in order to sustain our momentum in this regard.

Certainly our presentation of a "Draft Declaration" will be of great assistance in establishing the principle of our Communication vis-a-vis compensation for the Hong Kong veterans.[32]

Humphrey knew this process was likely to be drawn-out, giving the following perspective on the declaration:

Do not forget that what we are trying to do is to get a ball rolling and in the meantime put pressure on the Japanese government. Therefore, while the draft should be as good as you can make it — and you will be getting some help on this from friendly n.g.o.'s in Geneva — the text does not need to be perfect.[33]

Humphrey and Forbes made their final plans for the first of what would prove to be many trips to Geneva. The first visit was at the forty-fourth session of the CHR, where they hoped to familiarize both the diplomats and key NGO representatives with the case. The importance of the declaration grew. Forbes wrote to Humphrey:

I will look forward to having your affirmative response to our request that you attend with me in Geneva during the course of the Human Rights Commission hearings. The War Amputations of Canada would be extremely honoured to have your assistance in this regard as your input would be invaluable to our general pursuit of this matter.

As I had mentioned to you it is the intention of the War Amps to pursue this general Declaration regardless of the outcome of the Human Rights Commission findings in relation to our Resolution 1503 Communication. Indeed we will have to apply our minds to the follow-up strategy we will

---

[31] Secretary-General of the International Commission of Jurists.

[32] Letter from Forbes to Humphrey (January 20, 1988, MUA MG 4127, Cont. 16, File 330).

[33] Letter from Humphrey to Forbes (January 27, 1988, MUA MG 4127, Cont. 16, File 330).

wish to implement as far as the Sub Commission is concerned and potentially the General Assembly.[34]

Forbes also wrote to various NGOs concerning the key elements of the declaration, which stated:

Countries which have committed:
a) war crimes or crimes against humanity or
b) consistent and systematic patterns of gross violations of human rights, during a period of war or armed conflict (as defined by Article 2 and Article 3 of the Geneva Convention Relative to the Treatment of Prisoners-of-War of August 12th, 1949,) shall indemnify or compensate the victims (as defined by Article 3 and Article 4 of the said Geneva Convention of August 12th, 1949) of such crimes or violations for any resultant disability or incapacity suffered by such victims.[35]

While the CHR did not consider the communication, owing to the technicality that the War Amps did not have NGO status,[36] the initial session went well in terms of working with the human rights community. Indeed, Humphrey began to hope that they might "also end up by making some new international law."[37] The only sour note was the attitude of the Canadian delegation. Forbes had written to Michael Cleary of the Department of External Affairs seeking support for the cause, but, as it turned out, the delegation responded with what seemed to be active hostility. After Humphrey read the press release concerning his own remarks, he understood the reason, writing:

Thank you especially for sending me the copies of the press releases. I can now see why Cleary is so upset. The release says that Humphrey "was disappointed with Canada's representatives ..." What disappointed me and you was that the Canadian government was giving us no support in the matter of the Hong Kong veterans. Cleary has obviously interpreted my remark as a personal insult which I never meant it to be. I am therefore writing him a letter of apology which will however repeat my feeling of disappointment that the government is doing nothing to help the veterans.[38]

---

34 Letter from Forbes to Humphrey (February 10, 1988, MUA MG 4127, Cont. 16, File 330).

35 Letter from Forbes to various non-governmental organizations [hereinafter NGOs] (February 11, 1988, MUA MG 4127, Cont. 16, File 330).

36 Letter from Chadderton to Braine (August 16, 1988, MUA MG 4127, Cont. 16, File 330).

37 Letter from Humphrey to Forbes (March 11, 1988, MUA MG 4127, Cont. 16, File 330).

38 Letter from Humphrey to Forbes (March 28, 1988, MUA MG 4127, Cont. 16, File 330).

After each visit to Geneva, Forbes would write Chadderton a lengthy update of what had occurred. The first visit involved liaising with the NGOs wherein "Dr. Humphrey's prominence ... opened a number of doors for us as his significant influence within the human rights community of the U.N. enhanced the credibility of our overall position."[39] Forbes summarized the reaction of the more significant NGOs as follows:

[H]e [MacDermot] was supportive of the principles set out in our draft declaration and initially stated that he was prepared to present the declaration to the current sittings of the Human Rights Commission. However, upon consultation with a number of his executive officers within the ICJ he stated that the issues described in our declaration were considered of such significant importance that the ICJ would prefer to review the declaration at its March executive meeting.

Mr. [Bruno] Zimmerman[40] indicated the ICRC [International Committee of the Red Cross] strongly supported the idea of compensating the victims of gross violations of human rights including the victims of war crimes and crimes against humanity. Significantly he stated that our draft declaration would fill a void with reference to individual claims for disability in that the International Law of Nations generally required the government of the wronged individual to make such claims whereas our declaration proposes a legal mechanism for the individual claimant to do so.

Through the process of our review of the Hong Kong claim and its relationship to the Geneva Conventions Mr. Zimmerman was able to point out that the Japanese position as to the conclusiveness of the 1952 Peace Treaty between the Allied Powers and Japan was indeed erroneous.[41]

Other NGOs were extremely supportive, including Amnesty International (provided the ICRC supported the declaration), the International Federation of Women Career Lawyers, and the International Commission of Health Professionals. Adrien-Claude Zoller offered the assistance of the International Human Rights Service at the approaching sub-commission hearings to coordinate the efforts of the NGOs. Forbes noted that "the Human Rights Community at Geneva was particularly interested as to the position of the World Veterans Federation in that clearly we were advocating an issue which effected [*sic*] veterans as a whole." Serge Wourgaft of the WVF said that he would present the question to the meeting of the association the following month in Austria, at which Chadderton

39 Letter from Forbes to Chadderton (April 7 1988, MUA MG 4127, Cont. 16, File 330).

40 Deputy Chief of the Legal Division of the International Committee of the Red Cross [hereinafter ICRC].

41 Letter from Forbes to Chadderton (April 7, 1988, MUA MG 4127, Cont. 16, File 330).

would be in attendance. Forbes also mentioned Humphrey's suggestion that, should the WVF not be supportive, the War Amps might formally apply to ECOSOC for NGO status. Although the WVF did prove to be supportive,[42] the remarkable idea of a small national lobby group gaining NGO status was not dropped.

The Legal Department of the ICRC provided the War Amps with interpretations of Japan's responsibility in terms of international law. In their opinion, the 1929 Geneva Convention could not be invoked regarding acts perpetrated in the Second World War:

Furthermore, Japan was not party to the 1929 Geneva Convention relative to the treatment of prisoners of war. However, there can be no doubt that most of the acts you describe in your submission were very serious violations of the rules of customary international law applicable at that time and of the very broadly formulated provisions of the 1907 Hague Convention No. IV, to which Japan was party.[43]

Some moderate support was offered for the declaration, as Louise Doswald-Beck continued:

The ICRC does not officially back initiatives for new norms which do not originate from within the Red Cross Movement. However, in spite of the above-mentioned practical reservations which we have made about the expedience of direct claims, we can but support the general goal of your Declaration, namely that victims of violations of international humanitarian law should receive fair and adequate compensation.[44]

Over the next few years, Forbes and Humphrey were extremely active in pursuing their goals despite the initial difficulties. They went to Geneva twice a year for the meetings of the commission and sub-commission, developing strategies to deal with the problems that they encountered. These strategies involved the acquisition of status and allies, dealing with the question of UN jurisdiction, presenting arguments against the principle that the treaty absolved Japan of responsibility, gaining support on the question of the right to compensation, seeking sources of compensation other than the Japanese government, and publicizing their activities as part of the "organization of shame."

[42] Wourgaft wrote to Chadderton on May 8, 1988, stating: "On behalf of our Executive Board, I wish to inform you that the World Veterans Federation fully agrees with the principles set forth in the declaration and is prepared to co-sponsor it should you wish." Letter from Wourgaft to Chadderton (MUA MG 4127, Cont. 16, File 330).

[43] Letter from Louise Doswald-Beck (ICRC) to Forbes (May 10, 1988, MUA MG 4127, Cont. 16, File 330).

[44] *Ibid.*

Acquisition of Status and Allies

Over the summer of 1988, the War Amps initiated the process of applying for NGO status to further their communication, submitting their application to ECOSOC the following January. When this application was successful, the War Amps no longer had to rely on the sponsorship of other NGOs, supportive though these had been. In addition, the new status allowed them to take a leadership position for other POW groups in Great Britain, the United States, Australia, and New Zealand as well as for groups representing civil internees from the Netherlands. NGO status meant that the case could no longer be dismissed for purely technical reasons and that it would have to be considered on its merits. The new status also allowed the War Amps, in a leadership role, to cooperate with another group seeking redress for victims of Japanese war crimes — the so-called "comfort women."

COMFORT WOMEN

Armies throughout history have had camp followers to provide services to the soldiery. The provision of sexual services for the Japanese Imperial Army in the Second World War was a highly organized official activity. "Comfort stations" were created near battlefronts to allow soldiers of all ranks to engage in sexual activity for a fee. The comfort women who served in these stations were of varying backgrounds. A small percentage consisted of Japanese prostitutes, who were encouraged to contribute to the war effort in this way. Some were nationals of captured East Asian countries such as the Philippines, a few were captured civilians of allied combatants, including Dutch and Australian citizens, while the large majority, some 200,000, were from Korea (which was at this time a Japanese colony). Indeed, the exploitation of women of "inferior" races was used as a tactic of war to emphasize the military and racial dominance of Japan. Some of the women were recruited for a salary, often under the misconception they would be working in a factory and with no idea that they would be forced to proffer sexual services. Others were sold in payment of a family debt, while captured civilians were offered no choice. Pregnancies were strongly discouraged both because they cut into productivity and because they threatened racial purity. Therefore, many of the women underwent enforced sterilization.

At the end of war, the comfort women were liberated from the comfort stations. A Dutch military tribunal in Indonesia prosecuted

some members of the Japanese military for using thirty-five Dutch
women as sex slaves in the former Dutch East Indies. Other investigations conducted by the victorious allies came to different conclusions. One secret United States intelligence report, for example,
categorically dismissed a group of twenty Korean women captured
in Burma as "nothing more" than prostitutes, living in "near-luxury,"
attending "sports events ... picnics, entertainments and social din-
ners. They had a phonograph; and in the towns they were allowed
to go shopping."[45] The report continues:

> The interrogations show the average Korean "comfort girl" to be about
> twenty-five years old, uneducated, childish, whimsical, and selfish. She is
> not pretty either by Japanese or Caucasian standards. She is inclined to be
> egotistical and likes to talk about herself. Her attitude in front of strangers
> is demure and quiet, but she "knows the wiles of a woman." She claims to
> dislike her profession and would rather not talk about it or her family.

Attitudes such as this did not allow the true facts surrounding the
comfort women to come to light at this time. The situation of the
majority of these women was simply ignored, and no thought was
given to them during the negotiation of the non-punitive peace
treaty. The matter lay dormant for decades.

After more than forty years of silence caused by shame or fear,
the issue suddenly came to the world's attention. Some of the comfort women decided that their story should be told, and the information began to come out in media articles and documentary films.
Three Korean women filed a landmark lawsuit against the Japanese
government in December 1991. Japanese lawyers, interested in the
issue of the comfort women, went to the sub-commission meetings
in 1992. Humphrey passed this information on to Forbes, who
commented: "There is certainly no lack of media coverage with
regard to the Japanese situation and I have noted your comments
regarding the Gazette story on the Korean 'comfort-women' and
the appalling nature of this 'atrocity.'[46] It was natural that those
groups interested in the comfort women case would discuss the
possibility of potential joint action with the War Amps when
Humphrey and Forbes sought them out in Geneva.

---

[45] US Office of War Information, Psychological Warfare Team, *Japanese Prisoner of
War Interrogation Report no. 49* (October 1, 1944, MUA MG 4127, CC. 02-086,
Box 4, File 106, p. 1-2).

[46] Letter from Forbes to Humphrey (January 27, 1982, MUA MG 4127, Cont. 16,
File 330).

ISSUE OF UNITED NATIONS JURISDICTION

Appeals to UN bodies were pointless if the interpretation that the UN had no jurisdiction over the questions was allowed to stand. The War Amps learned that, under diplomatic pressure from Japan, the sub-commission was leaning towards this conclusion. Forbes informed Adama Dieng of the International Commission of Jurists of this development:

We have since learned from our sources that ... a public announcement has been agreed to by the Sub-Commission ... along the following lines:

"[T]he working group on communications informed the Sub-Commission that it had before it a number of extensively documented communications about alleged gross violations of human rights of thousands of prisoners of war and civilian internees ... United Nations intercession was being sought to obtain compensation ... The working group was of the view that appalling as the events complained of were, the procedure governed by Economic and Social Council Resolution 1503, XLVIII, 27 May 1970, could not be applied as a reparation or relief mechanism in respect of claims of compensation for human suffering or other losses which occurred during the Second World War."

Dr. John Humphrey is totally convinced that the Sub-Commission has overstepped its authority and has made a rather foolish mistake in proposing such a public announcement. John feels quite strongly that the Resolution 1503 procedure was never intended to be so narrowly construed or interpreted, and moreover that violations which amount to war crimes against humanity and/or genocide, are without time limitation.[47]

Humphrey appeared before the full CHR in February 1992 to present his views. His background in the development of human rights instruments, and Resolution 1503, in particular, gave a measure of authority to his intervention, which is worth quoting in full:

Thank you Mr. Chairman for giving me the floor.

For me it is a great honour to address this Commission. I was, for twenty years, the Director — indeed the first Director of what was then called the Division of Human Rights and what we now call the Centre for Human Rights. You can imagine therefore the pleasure I have in participating in this meeting.

What I want to say about the Sub-Commission of which I was once a member and in fact its Chairman gives me far less pleasure. The Sub-Commission has refused to forward to the Commission, under Council Resolution 1503 in the usual manner, a petition emanating from the War Amputations of Canada relating to the consistent pattern of human rights

---

[47] Letter from Forbes to Dieng (September 10, 1991, MUA MG 4127, Cont. 16, File 330).

violations committed against prisoners of war and civilian internees by the Japanese during the Second World War.

Strangely enough, however, the report of the Sub-Commission which we have before us refers to these violations as being "appalling." I think you will probably agree, Mr. Chairman, that whatever else the Sub-Commission may have to say in its report or whatever its intentions may have been, the use of the word "appalling" demonstrates that the Sub-Commission in fact has brought the existence of this pattern of gross violation of human rights to the attention of this Commission. It is therefore the opinion of the War Amputations of Canada that the Commission should deal with this matter in exactly the same way as it deals with other consistent patterns of gross human rights violations.

The Sub-Commission went on to say in its report that it has no jurisdiction to deal with matters relating to the Second World War. This, Mr. Chairman, and I hesitate to use the word, is pure hogwash. I have already said I was a member of the Sub-Commission. It was in this capacity that I had something to do with the origins and indeed the drafting of the original Resolution 1503. This is one reason I can say without hesitation that the Resolution puts no restriction whatsoever on its employment. By saying what it has the Sub-Commission has not only attempted to amend a Resolution of the Economic Council — indeed, without the latter's consent — but it has also done a disservice to what after all is one of the most effective and useful mechanisms for the implementation on human rights in the United Nations. It is for this specific reason, Mr. Chairman, that I feel strongly that this Commission should severely reprimand the Sub-Commission for this action.

I might add, Mr. Chairman, that I am formally authorized by the Secretary-General of the International Commission of Jurists — an organization of which I am a member — to state the ICJ is in full agreement with my statement concerning the position of the Sub-Commission in this regard. Mr. Adama Dieng is fully supportive of this particular position and if not for the fact that the ICJ has already spoken on Agenda Item 12 he would present an intervention at this very point.

I would like to say in the short time left at my disposal that the petitioners are not saying that the Commission on Human Rights has the power in itself to order compensation to be paid to the victims of these consistent patterns of gross violations of human rights. We know that your jurisdiction is limited. What we hope for is that the Commission will agree that Japan is at fault for the commission of these consistent patterns of gross violations of human rights and as a result the Japanese Government will finally decide to do something it should have done years ago — compensate the victims of these gross violations.[48]

Japan's response to this intervention was predictable as Chadderton informed Canadian prime minister, Brian Mulroney:

It is noteworthy in this context that on February 27th, two days after our intervention to the Commission on Human Rights, the Japanese delegation

---

[48] Typescript of speech, MUA MG 4127, Cont. 16, File 333.

in a special intervention found it necessary to actually refer to our submission before the full Commission. With specific reference to our submission the Japanese delegation stated the following:

"My delegation would like to comment on the remarks made by the War Amputations of Canada which refer to the question of claims of the ex-prisoners of war and civilian internees during World War II.

The Government of Japan expressed its view on this issue on several occasions, and it maintains its position. Our position on the procedural aspects of this issue, especially with regard to the 1503 procedure, coincides with the decision 1991/04 of the Sub-Commission on Prevention of Discrimination and Protection of Minorities which was adopted after careful consideration by the Sub-Commission members. Accordingly we express our support for this decision by the Sub-Commission."

Moreover, earlier on the same agenda item the Japanese made further passing reference to their position on human rights violations as relevant to World War II. In this context the Japanese delegation stated the following as a general observation:

a) The history, culture and social values of a country must be considered in reviewing human rights violations committed within individual countries.
b) The Japanese were also calling for a review of the Resolution 1503 procedure as to whether it should be maintained and continued within the human rights community.[49]

Japan therefore not only used the argument that wartime conduct should not be judged by "western" standards because of their different culture but also called into question the entire Resolution 1503 mechanism. This type of diplomatic pressure caused the CHR to delay rendering any hasty decision on the matter.

PEACE TREATY

When Japan claimed that the peace treaty absolved them of further responsibility for compensating prisoners of war, the view was not unsupported. It was the view of most governments, including that of Canada, that such a treaty would end the matter. No government would like to open a Pandora's box, whereby it would become accountable before a world body for the provisions of a bilateral treaty involving its own citizens. Therefore, the War Amps had little formal state support, although a great deal of NGO support, when they put forward the *jus cogens* argument. It suggested that there are certain principles in customary international law that cannot be set

---

[49] Letter from Chadderton to Mulroney (May 7, 1992, MUA MG 4127, Cont. 16, File 330).

aside by an agreement such as the peace treaty. The argument was buttressed by Article 53 of the 1969 Vienna Convention on the Law of Treaties,[50] which provides:

Treaties conflicting with a peremptory norm of general international law (jus cogens).

A treaty is void if, at the time of its conclusion, it conflicts with a peremptory norm of general international law. For the purposes of the present Convention, a peremptory norm of general international law is a norm accepted and recognized by the international community of States as a whole as a norm from which no derogation is permitted and which can be modified only by a subsequent norm of general international law having the same character.

Forbes informed his principal of the intent to challenge the Sub-Commission ruling on this basis, stating:

International law, including the Geneva Conventions and the concept of jus cogens makes clear that the 1952 Peace Treaty does not represent a valid defence to Japan and that both the Allied Governments and the Japanese had no legal authority to release or waive the rights of the Prisoners of War and Civilian Internees.[51]

Although the early Resolution 1503 petitions were rejected, the War Amps were able to use their NGO status to introduce new petitions in succeeding years, based on the earlier judgments, which kept the cause alive.

THE RIGHT TO COMPENSATION

While the War Amps initiatives regarding UN jurisdiction and the potential invalidity of treaties progressed slowly, the advocacy of the right to compensation enjoyed more immediate success. The Canadian Human Rights Foundation, of which Humphrey had been a co-founder and was then honorary president, agreed to sponsor the Ottawa conference on the right to compensation with the Department of the Secretary of State. Erica-Irene Daez, a member of the sub-commission, presented an important paper on the current, unsatisfactory status of the question. Humphrey noted in his diary:

---

[50] Vienna Convention on Law of Treaties, May 23, 1969, UN Doc. A/COF.39/27, text is reprinted in 8 I.L.M. 679 at articles 31(2) and (3).

[51] Letter from Forbes to Chadderton (August 25, 1992, MUA MG 4127, Cont. 16, File 330).

I have been so busy since returning from abroad that I have had no time to make any entry in this journal. The only things of real interest that have happened in the period were however the conference on the right to compensation in Ottawa and the annual meeting of the Human Rights Foundation last night. I gave the luncheon and dinner speeches at both these events, the subject of my talk last night being perestroika at the world level.

The Foundation has I think started the ball rolling in the matter of the right to compensation. The people who started the whole business were however the Hong Kong Veterans and the War Amputees who with my help unsuccessfully invoked the 1503 procedure at the United Nations. Our ambition — I am now an honorary member of the War Amputees — is to get to the General Assembly to adopt a declaration on the question.[52]

Even before the conference, Forbes was able to give Chadderton the glad tidings that the sub-commission, despite rejecting the Resolution 1503 intervention, "has passed a Resolution adopting in substance our Declaration of Principle vis-à-vis the right to compensation for victims of gross violations of human rights."[53] The sub-commission subsequently recommended to the CHR that a special rapporteur be appointed to look into the question. This recommendation was accepted, and Theo van Boven was appointed.[54]

Alternative Sources of Compensation

Since the UN process was a slow one and the veterans were aging, the War Amps began to look at alternative sources of compensation initially on an interim basis. Chadderton wrote Canadian Prime Minister Brian Mulroney requesting some interim compensation be given to the veterans on humanitarian grounds pending the action against Japan. He also pointed out that Canada bore some responsibility for the situation by signing the treaty.[55] It took many follow-up letters to various ministries and over four years to get the official Canadian position. The minister of external affairs, Barbara McDougall, finally told Chadderton:

[I]n signing the 1951 peace treaty with Japan, Canada chose to waive all claims against Japan except as provided for in the Treaty. We are, therefore,

---

[52] Humphrey Diary, *supra* note 10 (June 3, 1989).

[53] Letter from Forbes to Chadderton (September 15, 1988, MUA MG 4127, Cont. 16, File 330).

[54] UN Human Rights Committee [hereinafter HRC], *Report*, 46th Session, UN Doc. E/CN.4/1990/94 at 3 and 96.

[55] Letter from Chadderton to Mulroney (September 23, 1988, MUA MG 4127, Cont. 16, File 330).

not in a position to initiate official claims, nor officially support private claims against the Japanese Government for further reparations.
...
Finally, the question you raise of increased compensation by the Government of Canada is, of course, beyond the mandate of my Ministry. I consulted, therefore, with my colleague, the Honourable Gerald S. Merrithew, Minister of Veterans Affairs ... Mr. Merrithew has advised me that he sees no prospect for further compensation by Canada.[56]

The response did not sit well with Forbes who wrote to Humphrey:

I am certain you will share my disappointment with the rather pathetic position adopted by Ms. McDougall in relation to the United Nations initiative and the responsibility of the Government of Canada.
...
In any event I believe we should discuss the real possibility of initiating an action under the Optional Protocol ... as a direct response to Ms. McDougall's deplorable reaction to our claims within the UN.[57]

Shortly thereafter, the War Amps did indeed initiate a claim against Canada under the Optional Protocol.[58]

Rapporteur's Compensation Study

Van Boven and his assistant, Cees Flinterman, worked closely with the War Amps in preparing the compensation study, exchanging drafts for comment. In part, this joint effort may have been because the War Amps were the moving force behind the study, although Forbes felt that the fact they were the lead NGO for the

---

[56] Letter from McDougall to Chadderton (November 20, 1992, MUA MG 4127, Cont., 16, File 323).

[57] Letter from Forbes to Humphrey (December 21, 1992, MUA MG 4127, Cont., 16, File 323).

[58] Forbes summarized this to Chadderton as follows:

You will note [in a draft letter] that I have formally put the Canadian Government on notice that we have no alternative at this time but to commence proceedings under the Optional Protocol given the present position of the Canadian Government in relation to our general initiative within the United Nations.
...
I would suggest that we will want to give the Prime Minister sufficient time to respond to our demands, as I remain concerned that initiation of the Optional protocol procedure can result in a lengthy and complex proceeding (November 2, 1992, MUA MG 4127, Cont., 16, File 323).

claims of Dutch civil internees may have also added to the warmth of the relationship.[59] Forbes reported to his principal:

I must say at the outset that the War Amputations of Canada were given substantial credit for not only spearheading the Resolution 1503 claims on behalf of Allied groups, but also van Boven himself stated that we should be congratulated for the initiative that we triggered two years ago vis.a.vis [*sic*] the study on the right to compensation.[60]

The War Amps were delighted with the drafts that they received of the preliminary report. Forbes informed Chadderton that

Theo van Boven's preliminary report to the Sub-Commission contains a number of specific references to questions of law that favourably affect our claim for compensation against Japan. In general terms, the van Boven study can be employed in our overall national and international media campaign to refute the constant response of the Japanese that the Peace Treaty terminates their obligation to the former POWs and civilian internees.

The new Resolution 1503 procedures meant the Japanese government would be given five months to respond to the multiple communications which would be part of the formal agenda for the 1991 working group hearings.

While van Boven's final report[61] was somewhat diluted, it contained some proposed basic principles and guidelines that stated, *inter alia,* that victims had a right of reparation, that states had an obligation to make such reparations, and that "[c]laims relating to reparations for gross violations of human rights shall not be subject to a statute of limitations."[62] The CHR accepted van Boven's report[63] and requested the sub-commission to make recommendations regarding these basic principles. At the same time, the CHR called upon the international community to give increased attention to the right of restitution. This request was repeated each year,

---

[59] "Since the involvement of the Dutch civilian internee associations there has been a distinct change in van Boven and Flinterman's attitudes toward the Japanese claim." Letter from Forbes to Chadderton (August 27, 1990, MUA MG 4127, Cont., 16, File 323).

[60] *Ibid.*

[61] UN CHR, Sub-Commission on Prevention of Discrimination and Protection of Minorities, *Study Concerning the Right to Restitution, Compensation and Rehabilitation for Victims of Gross Violations of Human Rights and Fundamental Freedoms,* 45th Session, Item 4, UN Doc. E/CN.4/Sub.2/1993/8 (provisional).

[62] *Ibid.* at 58.

[63] Van Boven produced two revisions of the basic principles (UN Documents E/CN.4/Sub.2/1996/17 and E/CN.4/1997/104).

and, in 1998, Cherif Bassiouni was requested to prepare an independent report on the basic principles with a view to their adoption by the UN General Assembly. While Bassiouni's report[64] reflected changing vocabulary — for example, substituting "violations of human rights and humanitarian law that constitute crimes under international law" for "gross violations of human rights" and "*jus cogens* violations" — the basic principles remained the same. At the time of writing this article, the CHR had requested the secretary-general to distribute the basic principles to all member states and had asked the CHR to hold a consultative meeting with member states, intergovernmental organizations, and NGOs to finalize the text.

ORGANIZATION OF SHAME

The organization of shame required that each initiative be given the greatest possible publicity. The War Amps produced hundreds of press releases and courted the media. While the publicity campaign had some negative consequences, such as Cleary's reaction, noted earlier, and, as will be seen, some consternation by a Japanese lawyer advocating the comfort women case, it was an overall success. The *Toronto Star,* one of Canada's leading newspapers, became interested in the case. In May 1992, Forbes wrote to Humphrey that

> Mr. Don Sellar of the Toronto Star contacted me in confidence approximately two weeks ago to advise that the Prime Minister had attended the Toronto Star to have an "off the record" discussion with their Editorial Board, dealing with current issues affecting the Canadian political scene.
> Sellar advised that he directly queried the Prime Minister as to the Canadian position vis.a.vis the Hong Kong Veterans claim for compensation ... It was quite clear that our Prime Minister was not interested in supporting our claim against the Japanese and saw a "Canadian solution" as a more readily workable resolution of the issue.[65]

Later, Forbes wrote to Chadderton:

> It should in my judgment be our initial objective to have significant impact, hopefully within the media and the public domain, so as to embarrass the Canadian Government into a type of forced settlement with respect to the plight of the Hong Kong Veterans.

---

[64] UN CHR, *Draft Basic Principles and Guidelines on the Right to a Remedy and Reparations for Victims of Violations of International Human Rights and Humanitarian Law,* 56th Sess., Item 11/d, UN Doc. E/CN.4/2000/62 (provisional).

[65] Letter from Forbes to Humphrey (May 12, 1992, MUA MG 4127, Cont., 16, File 323).

I believe the groundwork has been laid over the last number of years and certainly the Toronto Star editorials have become stronger and more aggressive with the passage of time.[66]

The Canadian Broadcasting Corporation (CBC) also produced a documentary of the subject that kept the pressure on the Canadian government. Forbes wrote to Humphrey about his opinion of this production:

I expect you may have seen the CBC production "The Valour and The Horror"[67] shown on Sunday night which described the story of the Canadian Hong Kong Veterans and the ordeal they suffered during World War II. The program not only reflected the atrocities perpetrated by the Japanese and their failure to acknowledge their responsibility in this regard but also represented a strong indictment against the Canadian government.

Our claim for compensation was mentioned prominently throughout the documentary and the authors through the narration were extremely critical of the Canadian Government's refusal to support the United Nations compensation claim against Japan.[68]

CONNECTION WITH THE UN DECADE OF INTERNATIONAL LAW

The General Assembly proclaimed 1990-99 to be the Decade of International Law.[69] Humphrey quickly recognized the potential to add to the publicity of the case by tying it to the UN Decade of International Law. The resolution, among other things, was intended to "encourage the progressive development of international law and its codification" and called upon member states and other organizations to undertake activities in the implementation of the program. In the summer of 1990, Humphrey was attending the Canadian Human Rights Foundation summer course in Prince Edward Island. He invited some of the participants to his summer home at Brackley Beach and the question of what might be done in view of the resolution was discussed. Humphrey noted in his diary:

The other side was the opportunity to renew friendships with Covey and Barbara Oliver, Joe and Françoise Verhoeven, Dan Livermore, Bertie

---

[66] Letter from Forbes to Chadderton (November 2, 1992, MUA MG 4127, Cont., 16, File 323).

[67] *The Valour and the Horror* was actually a series. The item on the Hong Kong veterans was entitled *Savage Christmas*.

[68] Letter from Forbes to Humphrey (January 15,1992, MUA MG 4127, Cont. 16, File 323).

[69] UN General Assembly, *United Nations Decade of International Law*, UN Doc. A/RES/44/23 (1989).

Ramcharan and others who lectured at the course ... And Ron and Mairi Macdonald are at Dalvey.

...

At a luncheon here at our cottage a small group of us decided to form an institution of scholars to promote the decade for international law.[70]

At this time, Humphrey was serving with international lawyers Oliver (from the United States) and Verhoeven (from Belgium) on the International Commission of Inquiry into the 1932-33 Famine in the Ukraine.[71] Ramcharan, a long-service international servant in the human rights area who was currently the deputy high commissioner for human rights, was at the time working as a speechwriter for the secretary-general. Humphrey had known Ronald St. John Macdonald, who was one of Canada's most distinguished legal academics, since the latter had been Canadian representative to the Third Committee in 1965. At this juncture, Macdonald was senior scholar in residence at the University of Toronto and sat as judge on the European Court of Human Rights — the only non-European ever to do so. The following month, Humphrey took his ideas on compensation to Geneva, confiding in his diary:

We returned to Montreal on Monday afternoon after a long stop in Paris. There isn't much to write about the Geneva mission. I spent most of my time — part of it with Brian Forbes — sitting in the lounge at the Palais des Nations, talking to representatives of N.G.O.s about the thalidomide victims, our 1503 petition against Japan and the study on compensation. The most useful of our activities was probably dinner with Theo van Boven and Cees Flinterman on Monday evening, the 13th. Their preliminary report on the right to compensation is excellent. I suggested however that it could be much improved if the whole thing were tied up with the U.N. Decade for the Development of International Law. Van Boven seemed to agree. I also suggested that he might want to accept an invitation to lecture at the Foundation's summer school. He replied that he might be interested in 1992: he will be too busy next summer.[72]

At the same time, he wrote to Forbes:

I think we can agree that the visit was a success and that our interests are proceeding well. I am particularly anxious that the compensation study becomes closely related with the U.N. decade for the development of

---

[70] Humphrey Diary, *supra* note 10 (July 21, 1990).

[71] For full details, see A.J. Hobbins and Daniel Boyer, "Seeking Historical Truth: The International Commission of Inquiry into the 1932-33 Famine in Ukraine" (Fall 2001) 24 Dalhousie L.J. 139-91.

[72] Humphrey Diary, *supra* note 10 (August 22, 1990).

international law. It may well turn out that we have started something very important on the [i.e., this] one.[73]

Forbes conveyed these views to the War Amps, stating:

John Humphrey is extremely excited at the prospect that this initiative may develop a very high profile in the 1990s within the UN human rights system. As I mentioned to you, the 1990s have been designated as the Decade of International Law development within the UN and it is John's view that this particular study could be a centerpiece for such development. As you are aware from our experience at the May, 1989 conference in Ottawa there were a number of legal and human rights experts calling for the development of specific remedies to enforce individual human rights violations. Clearly the overall question of the right to compensation fits squarely within this analysis.[74]

Humphrey had high hopes for the institute, telling Forbes:

I will be happy to let you have my further views on the possible connection between the van Boven study and, hopefully, a declaration of the General Assembly. But I want first of all to discuss the matter of the Institute (of which my friend Judge Macdonald is the chairman) that has just been set up to promote the decade for the development of international law. My intention is to suggest that this question of compensation becomes one of the principal concerns of the Institute.[75]

Several meetings were held in the Canadian legal academic community to discuss the issue. Macdonald recommended that "Canada constitute a national committee on the Decade that would develop and implement Canada's program for the Decade. This program would tackle manageable issues and exploit the expertise of its different regions to develop a constructive approach to the Decade."[76] At one meeting, Humphrey advocated the establishment of a universal court for human rights and an international criminal court.[77] There was, however, little interest in the question of compensation among Humphrey's colleagues and, indeed, nothing much came from these initiatives in Canada. Macdonald enjoyed greater success

---

[73] Letter from Humphrey to Forbes (August 21, 1990, MUA MG 4127, Cont. 16, File 323).

[74] Letter from Forbes to Chadderton (August 27, 1990, MUA MG 4127, Cont., 16, File 323).

[75] Letter from Humphrey to Forbes (September 4, 1990, MUA MG 4127, Cont., 16, File 323).

[76] T. Hopkins and P.D. Paton, "The United Nations Decade of International Law: A Canadian Perspective" (1993) 31 Can. Y.B. Int'l L. 283 at 307.

[77] *Ibid.* at 302

in the United States, where he chaired the UN Decade Interest Group (UNDIG) of the American Society of International Law. He established a newsletter in 1992 under the editorship of William Slomanson to report on US activities, which is still being published under a new title.[78] In the end, however, Humphrey's dream of tying compensation to the Decade of International Law was never realized.

COMFORT WOMEN AT THE UNITED NATIONS

In March 1992, Forbes and Humphrey met with Japanese lawyer, Etsuro Totsuka, who was the East Asian representative for the NGO International Educational Development (IED), which was interested in the case of the comfort women. They discussed the possibilities of a joint submission at the United Nations to place greater pressure on the Japanese government as well as other possible strategies to pursue, including an international conference in Japan the following December. These discussions continued in a lengthy correspondence between Forbes and Totsuka. While it was ultimately decided to make separate submissions, plans were formulated to work together with a variety of NGOs. Unfortunately, the potential of this cooperation was never realized. On August 22, 1992, Forbes held a press conference in advance of the sub-commission hearings, during which he referred, *inter alia*, to what Totsuka was doing. Totsuka was not present, but the content was reported to him and he was given the press release.

Totsuka wrote a long and angry letter to Forbes, protesting that he had been misrepresented. He had always been somewhat ambivalent about his role, writing six months earlier to describe the legal situation of the POWs and the comfort women as being "almost impossible to win" and continuing:

I have no reason to refuse to work for the victims of Japanese war crimes, even if they are too many. This should be the duty of a lawyer to work for human rights, which are not only for Japanese but also for all human beings without any discrimination on the grounds of race, nationality or border. Although this must be a very tough work, I must do my best ... I'll be blamed as a traitor again.[79]

---

[78] The name has now been changed from the *UN Decade of International Law Newsletter* to *UN 21 InterestGroup Newsletter* and is still edited by Slomanson; available online at <http://www.lawschool.cornell.edu/library/asil/>.

[79] Letter from Totsuka to Forbes (March 20, 1992, MUA MG 4127, Cont. 16, File 320).

Now he took exception to Forbes's suggestion that he "represented" a group of comfort women. He stressed that while he had "been advocating and trying to help their demands as much as possible,"[80] he never represented them since he did not have power of attorney from them. He was worried that the press release might reflect negatively on the IED. There was also disagreement over the proposed Asian Women's Fund. It had been advocated in Japan that a fund raised from the private sector could pay compensation to the comfort women, which was a strategy that would allow the Japanese government to avoid an admission of liability. Forbes and Humphrey considered compensation more important than the source of funding and were generally supportive of the idea. Totsuka, however, considered the suggestion a fraud and a trap since it would effectively allow the Japanese government to forestall negotiations and once again escape legal responsibility by means of a nominal cash settlement from unofficial sources.[81]

Totsuka also disagreed with the strategies involved. While he perceived intervention at the UN level to be useful in raising public awareness, he felt that lawsuits needed to be brought in Japan. He urged the War Amps to follow this approach, writing:

Do you think to suit the Japanese Government before the Tokyo District Court will be a very big blow? In Japan, press are allowed to write anything about court cases. It will be said by the people that you did not exhaust local remedy.

If you are interested in this idea, I'll try to organize a group of lawyers, who work for public interested cases. I worked for the biggest civil case (*SMON case*) and the rights of Mental Patients (amendment of the Mental Health Act) in the past, so I have a number of lawyers/friends of that sort.[82]

However, a month later, he was less than optimistic about legal help in Japan, stating:

---

[80] Letter from Totsuka to Forbes (August 22, 1992, MUA MG 4127, Cont. 16, File 320).

[81] The Asian Women's Fund was launched in 1995 with "the aim of expressing a sense of national atonement from the Japanese people to the former 'comfort women' and to work to address contemporary issues regarding the honor and dignity of women." It remains controversial in Japan and most of the "atonement monies" have been paid to Filipina women. See Chunghee Sarah Soh, "Human Rights and Humanity: The Case of the 'Comfort Women.'" *ICAS Lectures*, University of Pennsylvania, December 4, 1998.

[82] Letter from Totsuka to Forbes (March 20, 1992, MUA MG 4127, Cont. 16, File 320).

They are very sympathetic on human rights, as they are some key members of the Lawyers' League against Wars. They have been working for various public interest cases involving human rights. I thought of them, as most ordinary Japanese lawyers might not be prepared to work against Japan. Those lawyers whom I am writing about are critical of the Japanese Imperial Army and militarism ... I asked whether they would help your clients. They seemed a bit reluctant, as they were not confident about succeeding in the case representing the POWs. They raised some difficulties in Japanese law: limitation of time, the difficulties in raising funds for campaigns, litigation and so on.[83]

These views were not especially significant since the War Amps had long since given up any hope of finding a remedy in Japan. However, the press release and Totsuka's reaction ended any meaningful cooperation between the two. Forbes and Totsuka were sundered by seas of misunderstanding, which were largely of a linguistic and cultural nature. Humphrey, however, added the comfort women to his list of causes whether or not his support was wanted. Shortly after receiving Totsuka's letter, he noted in his diary that "I seized the opportunity to support in my intervention on the P.O.W.'s the claims of the Korean 'comfort women.' Margaret and I may go to Tokio in this connection."[84] He did indeed go to Tokyo to attend the International Public Hearing Concerning Post-War Compensation of Japan and the Japanese Bar Association symposium on *War and Human Rights — Legal Analysis on Post-War Settlement,* writing:

On arriving in Japan we were taken from the airport to the Belmonte Hotel. On the 9th there was a meeting at which the chief item was evidence of women, chiefly Koreans, who had been comfort women. The meeting which was well attended was very well reported by the media and therefore a real success because the chief [reason] why I in any event went to Japan was to alert the Japanese people about the bad world image they were acquiring because of the government's failure to compensate these comfort [women]. I also spoke at this meeting.[85]

Following the conference, he continued to make speeches at various Japanese venues, although his audience was less receptive on the issue of the comfort women than he had hoped:

I was invited to give a lecture at Soka University after which they presented me with "the University's highest honour." The next day I gave a lecture at the International Christian University and had lunch with the rector afterwards.

---

[83] Fax from Totsuka to Forbes (April 29, 1992, MUA MG 4127, Cont. 16, File 320).

[84] Humphrey Diary, *supra* note 10 (August 16-23, 1992).

[85] *Ibid.* (January 10, 1993)

I like the Japanese as individuals but find some of their collective attitudes hard to understand — particularly their attitude towards Koreans.[86]

Forbes and Humphrey also continued to press the sub-commission on the issue of comfort women. Humphrey wrote:

It is two weeks since I have made any entry in this diary. There are some good reasons for this, including a meeting in Geneva on behalf of the comfort women and the Hong Kong veterans. I took a strong position against the U.N. Sub-Commission and the Commission on Human Rights. But only Japan responded using as usual its [excuse of] the peace treaty of 1992 [i.e., 1952].

The UN is still seized with the issue of the Comfort Women although its views are far more sympathetic. Many of the legal points urged by the various NGOs have now been accepted and there is strong condemnation of the Japanese position.[87]

QUEBEC LANGUAGE LAWS

Since the 1970s, Québec, a French enclave in English North America, has adopted somewhat controversial legislation designed to protect the French language and culture. Controversy has arisen in part because of prohibitions on the public usage of languages other than French. Successful court challenges to the original Bill 101 brought successive changes to the legislation.[88] In 1988, Bill 178 was enacted and essentially stated that outdoor commercial signs must be only in French, while, indoors, another language could be used provided French predominated.[89] An undertaker, Gordon McIntyre, with the help of Maurice King, president of the Chateauguay Valley English Speakers Association, decided to challenge this law on the grounds that it interfered with freedom of expression[90] and that Québec anglophones were a minority requiring protection.[91] They maintained that there were no internal remedies available since the bill had a "notwithstanding clause," rendering it immune to challenges under the Canadian or Québec charters of

---

[86] *Ibid.* (January 11, 1993).

[87] *Ibid.* (February 28, 1992).

[88] Charter of the French Language, R.S.Q. ch. C-11 (popularly known as Bill 101).

[89] An Act to Amend the Charter of the French Language, Quebec, National Assembly, Thirty-third Legislature, 2nd Session. 1988. Ch. 54. Act amended: Charter of the French Language, R.S.Q., chapter C-11 (popularly known as Bill 178).

[90] ICCPR, *supra* note 2 at Article 19.

[91] *Ibid.* at Article 27.

rights and freedoms.[92] They decided to take the case to the HRC under the Optional Protocol, and, being aware of the War Amps endeavours, they inevitably consulted Humphrey. He wrote in his diary:

> I have just had lunch at the Beaver Club with Maurice King ... and Gordon McIntyre (the petitioner in the case relative to Quebec Bill 178 under the Optional Protocol to the U.N. Covenant on Civil and Political Rights). My advice to them was to find some top lawyer — perhaps Don Johnston to represent them before the Human Rights Committee. He should be committed to the case and a hard worker. The next step should be to make as much noise as possible.[93]

Johnston was legal counsel to the prominent law firm Heenan, Blaikie, having recently retired from federal politics where he had held a number of cabinet posts, including minister of justice. In 1996, he became secretary general of the Organization for Economic Co-operation and Development. Humphrey arranged a meeting, which he describes in his diary:

> Together with Maurice King and [Gordon] McIntyre from the eastern Townships (francophones now call it Estrie) I called on Thursday Morning on Don Johnston to inquire whether he would take over major responsibility for the action under the U.N. Optional Protocol taken by McIntyre at the U.N. Although sympathetic Johnston did not feel that he could take on the job. He suggested the name of Julius Grey.
> Convinced as I am that the Canadian government will do everything in its power to defeat the case it is absolutely necessary to find an experienced lawyer to handle the case.[94]

While Julius Grey did not enjoy quite such a high profile as Johnston, he was a prominent litigator and, in addition, Humphrey's colleague in the McGill Faculty of Law and on the Board of the Canadian Human Rights Foundation. Humphrey was able to arrange a meeting quickly, noting: "Lunch today with Julius Grey and Maurice King. Julius will take on the job of representing McIntyre the case the latter has taken against Canada under the Optional Protocol."[95]

Humphrey was not closely involved with the case beyond this point, although he kept Grey informed of anything that his sources

---

[92] Canadian Charter of Rights and Freedoms, Part 1 of the Constitution Act, 1982, being Schedule B to the Canada Act 1982 (U.K.), 1982, c. 11; Quebec Charter of Human Rights and Freedoms, R.S.Q. Ch. C-12.

[93] Humphrey Diary, *supra* note 10 (March 1, 1990).

[94] *Ibid.* (March 19, 1990).

[95] *Ibid.* (March 21, 1990).

in the United Nations and the federal government told him about. Ultimately, the HRC concluded in a majority decision that the "notwithstanding clause" in Bill 178 rendered domestic remedies inadequate.[96] They further concluded that the legislation contravened Article 19 of the ICCPR concerning freedom of expression and requested Canada to report back in six months with the relevant measures taken to remedy the situation.[97] Nationalists took comfort in the fact that the CHR had found that, while francophones were a minority in Canada, Québec anglophones were not a minority requiring protection as envisioned by Article 27.

Grey was satisfied with this result, which led to a change in the law. He was not interested to the extent that Humphrey was in attempting to embarrass the Québec government over its language policies — the organization of shame. This disagreement became public but did not end the friendship between the two. Humphrey was by now in his eighty-eighth year, and his strong, and often inflexible, opinions were causing him trouble both with his faculty colleagues and in the organizations with which he worked. Grey was aware of these problems and took no personal affront. His friendship with and admiration for Humphrey remained unaltered.

CONCLUSIONS

Humphrey died in March 1995 and did not live to see the results of many of these endeavours aimed at redress and compensation. As he had earlier told Forbes, the process at the United Nations was a long one. His hopes to write new international law may yet bear fruit, as a General Assembly declaration on the right to compensation remains a very real possibility. At this stage, even the declaration's original sponsors, the War Amps, are no longer actively involved, having achieved their goals. In 1990, Canada made an offer to settle the thalidomide victims' case, which the War Amps found inadequate. After making the offer, Canada suggested that the Human Rights Committee should drop the case since it

---

[96] Humphrey had had advance warning of this which he passed on to Grey, writing in his diary: "Short talk with Julius Grey over the telephone. I passed on to him confidentially the information I was given by a member of the U.N. secretariat to the effect that the Human Rights Committee [would] probably find Canada in default in the 'notwithstanding clause' case." *Ibid.* (August 30 1992).

[97] UN HRC, "Ballantyne, Davidson, McIntyre v. Canada," Communications nos. 359/1989 and 385/1989, UN Doc. CCPR/C/47/D/359/1989 and 385/1989/Rev.1 (1993).

was being settled. This tactic did not work. Forbes reported that "[Alfred] de Zayas pointed out the obvious weakness to the Canadian submission is that the Human Rights Committee is not satisfied that a claim is resolved just on the basis of a preliminary proposal of settlement."[98] The case continued and was ultimately dropped when the Canadian government offered a more acceptable compensation package in 1994.

In the Hong Kong veterans' case, the HRC concluded in October 1995 that the War Amps had not yet exhausted all internal remedies, and the matter was placed in abeyance. Chadderton then requested that a parliamentary committee look into the matter. In 1998, this consideration resulted in an offer of Cdn $24,000 to each survivor or widow. This offer was accepted and the case under the Optional Protocol was dropped. The War Amps moved on with equal success and greater expedition to directly securing compensation for Canada's Second World War merchant seamen from the Canadian government. The formal UN processes had proved too tortuous and slow, but the "organization of shame" seemed effective with Canada.

The comfort women continued their UN activity, while various groups also pursued domestic remedies in a number of jurisdictions. In the United States, there are cases still *sub judice*. The South Korean government agreed to pay compensation to the Korean-based comfort women in 1998. In Japan, where many suits were brought, all cases were lost with one exception. Even the victory in that one exceptional case involving three plaintiffs was overturned on appeal.[99] The case before the United Nations was won

---

[98] Letter from Forbes to Chadderton (August 27, 1990, MUA MG 4127, Cont. 16, File 323).

[99] Byoungwook Park provides a legislative history of these cases, noting:

Compare Taihei Okada, The Comfort Women Case: Judgment of Apr. 27, 1998, Shimonoseki Branch, Yamaguchi Prefectural Court, Japan, 8 Pac. Rim. L. & Policy J. 63, 63 (1999) (stating that the Yamaguchi District Court decided in favor of the Korean Comfort Women and awarded them monetary damages); with High Court Reverses Ruling Favoring Comfort Women, Daily Yomiuri, Mar. 30, 2001, at 1 (reporting that the Hiroshima High Court reversed the ruling, which ordered the Japanese government to pay three hundred thousand yen to each of the three plaintiffs by holding that the Japanese government is not legally obliged to apologize or pay monetary compensation in connection with the military's use of Comfort Women).

B. Park, "Comfort Women during WWII: Are U.S. Courts a Final Resort for Justice?" (2002) 17 Am. U. Int'l L. Rev. 403 at note 23.

to the extent that these things can be. In 1998, the sub-commission affirmed Japan's responsibility for the comfort women.[100] Since that time, other UN organs have condemned Japan in ever-stronger language. On the international legal front, the final judgment of the Women's International War Crimes Tribunal of Japan's Military Sexual Slavery was delivered in The Hague on December 4, 2001.[101] The judgment suggested that Japan offer everything that the comfort women had asked for — an apology, an acknowledgment of legal responsibility, compensation, guarantees against recurrence, and so on. However, as with the UN bodies, this tribunal was limited to the exercise of moral authority. Despite this international pressure, Japan remains unmoved on the issue.

During the Second World War, it was a dictate of the Japanese culture that surrender was one of the most shameful things possible. Indeed, many committed suicide or remained hidden long after the armistice to avoid this shame. Also at this time, there were few cultural limitations placed on the treatment that could be accorded to conquered peoples, whether POWs or civilian women. Some of these attitudes may persist today. It certainly seems fruitless to organize shame on the basis of what is shameful to Western eyes but may not be so in other cultures. Therefore, neither the "organization of shame" nor the moral authority of the UN human rights organs are necessarily efficacious in securing justice for the individual whose human rights have been infringed. The right to a remedy needs to become firmly established as *jus cogens,* thus thwarting stonewalling at the national level, before there can be said to be satisfactory mechanisms available to the individual. Humphrey and his allies, and many since, have done a great deal to lay the groundwork to achieve this possibility.

---

[100] The sub-commission accepted the report of the special rapporteur, Gay McDougall, which can be found in UN CHR, Sub-Commission on Prevention of Discrimination and Protection of Minorities, *Report Appendix,* "Contemporary Forms of Slavery: Systematic Rape, Sexual Slavery and Slavery-Like Practices during Armed Conflict," UN Doc. E/CN.4/Sub. 2/1998/13, pp. 38-62.

[101] Text of the judgment can be found at <http://www.korea-np.co.jp/pk/173rd_issue/2001122610.htm>.

Sommaire

Saisir les Nations Unies des plaintes individuelles en matière des droits de la personne: John Humphrey et sa lutte pour l'indemnisation

Lors de la création des Nations Unies, un de ses premiers mandats était le développement d'une charte internationale des droits de la personne, qui allait reconnaître pour la première fois l'individu en droit international. La charte envisagée devait comprendre trois parties: une déclaration, une convention et des mesures de mise en œuvre. Dans ce contexte, un bon nombre de conventions ont depuis été ouvertes à la signature des États. Deux des moyens de mise en œuvre développés sont les poursuites en vertu du Protocole optionnel sur les droits civils et politiques et la résolution 1503 du Conseil économique et social. L'article examine certaines tentatives de la part d'individus et de groupes afin de recourir à ces mécanismes pour demander une indemnisation pour des violations des droits de la personne. L'article s'inspire des travaux du défenseur canadien des droits de la personne John Peters Humphrey. En tant que haut fonctionnaire des Nations Unies, celui-ci a rédigé le premier projet de Déclaration universelle des droits de l'Homme. En outre, il a collaboré à la rédaction des protocoles et il a proposé initialement la résolution 1503. Des années plus tard, en tant que simple citoyen, il a aidé à présenter un certain nombre de dossiers aux Nations Unies en utilisant ces mécanismes. Humphrey et ses alliés ont également cherché à obtenir une déclaration de principe de l'Assemblée générale en matière du droit à l'indemnisation pour les violations des droits de la personne — une question toujours irrésolue.

Summary

Bringing Individual Human Rights Issues to the United Nations: John Humphrey and the Quest for Compensation

When the United Nations was formed, one of its earliest tasks was to develop an international bill of human rights that would recognize the individual in international law for the first time. This bill was envisioned to have three parts: a declaration, a convention, and a means of implementation. A number of conventions have since been opened for signature. Two of the means of implementation that have been developed are actions under the Optional Protocol of the International Covenant of Civil and Political Rights and ECOSOC Resolution 1503. This article examines some attempts on the part of individuals or groups to use these mechanisms to gain compensation for human rights violations. It is based on the papers of Canadian human rights advocate John Peters Humphrey, who as an UN official wrote the first draft of the Universal Declaration of Human Rights, worked on the covenants, and first proposed Resolution 1503. Years later, as a private citizen, he helped bring a number of cases to the United Nations using these mechanisms. Humphrey and his allies also attempted to have a declaration of principle on the right to compensation for human rights violations adopted by the General Assembly — a question that has not yet been resolved.

National Application of International Law: The Statutory Interpretation Perspective

STÉPHANE BEAULAC

INTRODUCTION

There is little doubt that, especially in the last five years, there is no legal issue that has gathered more interest in the international legal community of Canada than that of the national application of international law.[1] It would certainly not be wrong to trace this enthusiasm back to the 1999 decision of the Supreme Court of Canada in *Baker* v. *Canada (Minister of Citizenship and*

Stéphane Beaulac (Ph.D., Cantab.) teaches international law at the Faculty of Law at the University of Montreal. This article is largely based on a paper presented at a Federal Court of Canada seminar on statutory interpretation and administrative law organized by the National Judicial Institute and held in Montebello, Québec, on 10-12 September 2003.

[1] This issue is also very much alive in other common law countries, such as Australia, Great Britain, and New Zealand. See S.A. Riesenfeld and F.M. Abbott (eds.), *Parliamentary Participation in the Making and Operation of Treaties — A Comparative Study* (Dordrecht: Martinus Nijhoff, 1994); S. Donaghue, "Balancing Sovereignty and International Law: The Domestic Impact of International Law in Australia" (1995) 17 Adelaide L. Rev. 213; A. Mason, "The Influence of International and Transnational Law on Australian Municipal Law" (1996) 7 Public L. Rev. 20; B. Conforti and F. Francioni (eds.), *Enforcing International Human Rights in Domestic Courts* (The Hague: Martinus Nijhoff, 1997); K. Keith, "The Application of International Human Rights Law in New Zealand" (1997) 32 Texas Int'l L.J. 401; K. Keith, "The Impact of International Law on New Zealand Law" (1998) 6 Waikato L. Rev. 1; M. Gobbi, "Drafting Techniques for Implementing Treaties in New Zealand" (2000) 21 Statute L. Rev. 71; and B.R. Openkin, "Constitutional Modelling: The Domestic Effect of International Law in Commonwealth Countries — Part I" (2000) Public L. 607. For an general assessment of the situation in some countries on the European continent, see B. Conforti, "Notes on the Relationship between International Law and National Law" (2001) 3 Int'l L. Forum 18.

Immigration),[2] where the majority has been interpreted as opening the door to the use of international treaties unimplemented in the domestic legal system.[3] It might be more accurate, however, to speak of the domestic use of international law not really as a new issue[4] but rather as a "sexy" issue in the contemporary legal literature of the so-called globalized world order.

Karen Knop, for instance, examines *Baker* and opines that it shows that the Supreme Court of Canada is moving away from the traditional model of international law in domestic courts.[5] Developing on Anne-Marie Slaughter's model of transgovernmentalism[6]

---

[2] *Baker* v. *Canada (Minister of Citizenship and Immigration)*, [1999] 2 S.C.R. 817 [hereinafter *Baker*].

[3] See, among others, H.M. Kindred, "Canadians as Citizens of the International Community: Asserting Unimplemented Treaty Rights in the Courts," in S.G. Coughlan and D. Russell (eds.), *Citizenship and Citizen Participation in the Administration of Justice* (Montreal: Thémis, 2002), 263 at 284, who wrote that the "judgement in *Baker* v. *Canada* has carried Canadian courts into new territory" and that, indeed, the "role of unimplemented treaties is [now] better defined."

[4] Indeed, pre-dating *Baker*, the Canadian Council on International Law [hereinafter CCIL] organized in 1998 a congress on the topic. See CCIL, *The Impact of International Law on the Practice of Law in Canada — Proceedings of the 27th Annual Conference of the Canadian Council on International Law, Ottawa, October 15-17, 1998* (The Hague: Kluwer Law International, 1999). Going back further to 1996, one may recall that former Justice Gérard La Forest, in "The Expanding Role of the Supreme Court of Canada in International Law Issues" (1996) 34 Canadian Y.B. Int'l L. 89, at 100, famously wrote that Canadian courts "are truly becoming international courts" and that, already in his 1988 paper, "The Use of International and Foreign Material in the Supreme Court of Canada," in CCIL, *Proceedings of the 1988 Conference of the Canadian Council on International Law* (Ottawa: CCIL, 1988), 230 at 230, the Supreme Court of Canada was one of the most "cosmopolitan of national courts" in regard to the foreign material upon which it relied. Even in the 1970s, Ronald St. J. Macdonald wrote an influential piece entitled "The Relationship between International Law and Domestic Law in Canada," in R. St. J. Macdonald, G. Morris, and D.M. Johnston (eds.), *Canadian Perspectives on International Law and Organization* (Toronto: University of Toronto Press, 1974), 88, in which he examined the doctrine of incorporation in Canada as well as the domestic status of both conventional law and customary law.

[5] See K. Knop, "Here and There: International Law in Domestic Courts" (2000) 32 New York U. J. Int'l L. & Pol. 501.

[6] See A.-M. Slaughter, "Governing the Global Economy through Government Networks," in M. Byers (ed.), *The Role of Law in International Politics — Essays in International Relations and International Law* (Oxford: Oxford University Press, 2000), 177; and A.-M. Slaughter, "A Typology of Transjudicial Communication" (1994) 29 U. Richmond L. Rev. 99.

and Patrick Glenn's comparative law methodology,[7] she argues in favour of a new approach based on the persuasive value of international law. Stephen Toope, for his part, rejects this suggestion of a mere influential role for international norms and argues that we are, in fact, living in a time of changing metaphors, away from national sovereignty and towards transnationalism — "in this in-between time, international law is both 'foreign' and 'part of us.'"[8] Toope develops his thoughts further and writes that "international law is both outside and in."[9] Indeed, he argues that "international law is partly *our* law," which means that the "process of relating international law to domestic law is not a translation of norms from outside."[10]

One of the main characteristics of the discourse about the domestic use of international law in Canada is that the scholarship is written by internationalists and is expressed within the international legal framework[11] — and, arguably, with the underlying objective of promoting the role of international law in the country's judicial decision-making process. The fact that international lawyers participate most actively in the debate is not at all negative — this is not the point. It is rather the lack of serious and substantive doctrinal input from the point of view of the domestic legal

---

[7] See P. Glenn, "Persuasive Authority" (1987) 32 McGill L.J. 261.

[8] S.J. Toope, "The Uses of Metaphor: International Law and the Supreme Court of Canada" (2001) 80 Canadian Bar Rev. 534 at 540. Later, he wrote: "The Supreme Court's telling of the story of international law in Canada will depend upon old and new metaphors, the old metaphor of binding law and the new metaphor of persuasive authority. Both metaphors must be employed, but not usually at the same time or in the same way." *Ibid.*, at 541.

[9] S.J. Toope, "Inside and Out: The Stories of International Law and Domestic Law" (2001) 50 U. New Brunswick L.J. 11 at 11. See also J. Brunnée and S.J. Toope, "A Hesitant Embrace: The Application of International Law by Canadian Courts," in National Judicial Institute, *Federal Court of Canada Education Seminar: Domestic Impact of International Instruments* (conference held in Ottawa on January 31, 2003) [paper on file with author].

[10] *Ibid.*, at 18 [emphasis in original].

[11] For instance, consider the following excerpt from Brunnée and Toope's paper delivered at the Federal Court seminar, where they admit taking the "standpoint of international law" and speak of the "bindingness of international law." They write: "*From the standpoint of international law*, then, the *Baker* decision puts into the spotlight two questions about the *bindingness of international law.* How should courts approach international treaty norms that are binding on Canada, but, absent implementation, not directly applicable in Canada? How should they approach norms that do not bind Canada internationally but that nonetheless reflect important international values" (*supra* note 9 at 45) [emphasis added].

system, in particular, from the statutory interpretation perspective that perhaps ought to be of concern.

Indeed, the two most authoritative works on legislative interpretation — *Driedger on the Construction of Statutes*[12] by Ruth Sullivan and *Interprétation des lois*[13] by Pierre-André Côté — give a comparatively small place to this increasingly important feature of today's approach to the construction of statutes.[14] Sullivan's latest edition of *Construction of Statutes* has noticeably included a separate chapter on the role of international law in legislative interpretation,[15] which examines some questions in more detail (presumptions of compliance implementing legislation) but leaves others unaddressed, such as the different status of treaties and customs, judicial notice of such law, the effect of *jus cogens* norms, and the persuasive force of the argument based on international law. On the other hand, a consultation of a few Canadian textbooks and casebooks in international law — for example, *Public International Law*[16] by John Currie and *International Law*[17] by Hugh Kindred *et al.* — shows how the national application of international law is considered at length.[18]

The purpose of this article is to bring a new and different perspective to the debate over the domestic use of international law —

---

[12] R. Sullivan, *Driedger on the Construction of Statutes*, 3rd ed. (Toronto and Vancouver: Butterworths, 1994).

[13] P.-A. Côté, *Interprétation des lois*, 3rd ed. (Montreal: Thémis, 1999).

[14] In the third edition of *Construction of Statutes* (*supra* note 12), Sullivan had three-and-a-half pages on the "Compliance with International Law" in the chapter entitled "Presumption of Legislative Intent" (*ibid.*, at 330-33), as well as eight pages on the use of international conventions as "extrinsic aids" (at 459-66). In the third edition of Côté (*supra* note 13), international law occupied two-and-a-half pages in a sub-section on norms of a higher level, which are considered as contextual elements of legislative interpretation; *ibid.*, at 466-68.

[15] R. Sullivan, *Sullivan and Driedger on the Construction of Statutes*, 4th ed. (Markham, Ontario and Vancouver: Butterworths, 2002). Chapter 16, entitled "International Law" has twenty pages, three headings, and twelve sub-headings.

[16] J. Currie, *Public International Law* (Toronto: Irwin Law, 2001).

[17] H.M. Kindred *et al.* (eds.), *International Law — Chiefly as Interpreted and Applied in Canada*, 6th ed. (Toronto: Emond Montgomery, 2000).

[18] Both Currie and Kindred *et al.*, *supra* note 16 and 17 respectively, have a separate chapter on the domestic use of international law, of twenty-five pages and eighty pages respectively. Among other important questions, they discuss the interaction of international law and national law, the dualist and monist theories of international law reception, the different status of conventional law and customary law, and the conflicts between international law and domestic statutory law.

one that speaks within the discourse of Canadian internal law and that focuses on the method of legislative interpretation. The argument put forward is that the national application of international law is, as far as Canadian judges and other domestic actors are concerned, a question of statutory interpretation, which must be addressed, rationalized, and understood within that framework. Of course, an exhaustive examination of this issue would look at both conventional norms and customary norms — the two principal sources of international law.[19] The present study, however, is more modest in ambition and, thus, more limited in scope. It concentrates on the domestic use of treaties in Canada, leaving the difficult issue of customary international law for another day. The article begins with a preliminary matter on which is founded the main proposition — the claim that international law "binds" Canada. The hypothesis identified also requires a consideration of the practices of treaty implementation in Canada. Building upon the contextual argument of statutory interpretation, an analytical scheme is then put forward to determine the persuasive force of international law, which is based on the degree of incorporation of treaty norms within the Canadian legal system.

INTERNATIONAL LAW AND CANADIAN JUDGES

It seems that a large part of the polemic among international law scholars revolves around the issue of whether or not "international law" is binding within Canada.[20] The traditional stance that international law is not binding was most clearly reiterated by the Supreme Court of Canada in *Ordon Estate* v. *Grail*,[21] in the context of the interpretation of a statutory provision prescribing a limitation period for maritime negligence claims. In applying the so-called presumption of conformity with international law, Justices Frank Iacobucci and John Major, for the court, wrote that "[a]lthough international law is *not binding* upon Parliament or the provincial legislatures, a court must presume that legislation is intended to comply with Canada's obligations under international instruments

---

[19] Statute of the International Court of Justice, 26 June 1945, U.N.T.S. 961, Can. T.S. 1945 No. 7 (entered into force on 24 October 1945), at Article 38, enunciates the sources of international law [hereinafter ICJ Statute].

[20] See, for instance, G. van Ert, *Using International Law in Canadian Courts* (The Hague: Kluwer Law International, 2002), at 4.

[21] *Ordon Estate* v. *Grail*, [1998] 3 S.C.R. 437.

and as a member of the international community."[22] In an article co-authored with Gloria Chao, Justice Louis LeBel reminds us that "international law is generally non-binding or without effective control mechanisms" and thus warns that domestically "it does not suffice to simply state that international law requires a certain outcome."[23]

However, this traditional position has recently been challenged, presumably following the groundbreaking decision in *Baker* and, it seems, as a result of the suggestion by Karen Knop that, because international law is indeed not binding, the comparative law methodology ought to be useful in conceptualizing the national application of international law.[24] Indeed, Knop writes that the relevance of international law "is not based on bindingness," which means that "the status of international and foreign law becomes similar, both being *external sources of law*."[25] In fact, Knop challenges the binding/non-binding distinction — what she calls the "on/off switches for the domestic application of international law"[26] — and suggests an alternative approach, which she argues springs from the *Baker* case, "where the authority of international law is persuasive rather than binding."[27]

This proposition seemed to "rub"[28] the wrong way some international legal commentators in Canada. One of them is Stephen Toope who, in promoting a more direct role for international law in Canada, opines that "the dichotomy that Knop sets up between a

22   *Ibid.*, at 526 [emphasis added].

23   L. LeBel and G. Chao, "The Rise of International Law in Canadian Constitutional Litigation: Fugue or Fusion? Recent Developments and Challenges in Internalizing International Law" (2002) 16 Supreme Court L. Rev. (2nd) 23 at 62.

24   This proposition has prompted stark, and somehow cavalier, criticism from some authors. See, for instance, G. van Ert, *supra* note 20, at 35: "In my view, Knop's equation of international law with foreign law is simply unsupported by the weight of Anglo-Canadian authority. The rule of judicial notice described above — and much else in this work besides — directly refutes this approach. Knop's mistake is to assume that international law is not binding, and to derive from that assumption the further view that the relevance of international law in Canada is not based on its bindingness. But international law is binding."

25   Knop, *supra* note 5, at 520 [emphasis added].

26   *Ibid.*, at 515.

27   *Ibid.*, at 535.

28   "Rub" is indeed the word Toope himself used in describing the effect that Knop's paper had on him — see Toope, *supra* note 8, at 535.

traditional focus on international law as 'binding' on domestic courts, and international law as 'persuasive authority' is, I think, a false dichotomy."[29] Instead, he argues that "international law can be both"[30] binding and persuasive because "international law is both 'foreign' and 'part of us.'"[31] In another article, Toope further argues that "international law is not merely a story of 'persuasive' foreign law. International law also speaks directly to Canadian law and requires it to be shaped in certain directions. International law is more than 'comparative law,' because international law is partly *our* law."[32] Again, in his presentation with Jutta Brunnée for a Federal Court seminar, he opined:

Our worry is that the majority decision [in *Baker*] places the Supreme Court on a path towards treating all international law as persuasive authority, which the Court *may* use to 'inform' its interpretation of domestic law. In other words, by treating both binding and non-binding international norms in this manner, courts move away from their duty to strive for an interpretation that is consistent with Canada's international obligations. Thus, as appealing as [Knop's] comparative law metaphor may seem at first glance, it too bears risks.[33]

In their final analysis, Brunnée and Toope forcefully conclude that "many international legal rules bind Canada: some are part of Canadian law. They should be treated accordingly."[34]

Whether or not one is in agreement with Knop's comparative law metaphor with respect to all international law norms, strictly speaking, international law does not bind Canada (that is, bind *within* Canada) or bind any sovereign state for that matter.[35] The

---

[29] *Ibid.*, at 536.

[30] *Ibid.*

[31] *Ibid.*, at 540.

[32] Toope, *supra* note 9, at 18 [emphasis added].

[33] Toope and Brunnée, *supra* note 9, at 46 [emphasis in original].

[34] *Ibid.*, at 66 [footnotes omitted].

[35] It is useful to distinguish between, on the one hand, international law as a set of rules regulating the relations between states and, on the other, international law as a set of rules that can have an impact on domestic law that governs people. The former is what could be referred to as "international international law" and the latter "domestic international law." Justice Louis LeBel and Gloria Chao called the former "principles of public international law *qua* binding law," as opposed to "their application in the domestic legal order." See LeBel and Chao, *supra* note 23 at 62. On the binding character of international law on sovereign states, see generally I. Brownlie, *Principles of Public International Law*, 4th ed. (Oxford: Clarendon Press, 1990), at 1-2.

fundamental reason behind this lack of obligatory legal force relates to the so-called Westphalian model of international relations, which very much remains at the centre of the present state system and, hence, the present international law system.

TENETS OF THE INTERNATIONAL LAW SYSTEM

Although some international law scholars have suggested that "national sovereignty" is a dying metaphor[36] — perhaps not dissimilarly to the globalizationist claim of the imminent "end of the nation state"[37] or even the triumphantalist claim of the "end of history"[38] — the matrix in which international affairs are conducted and in which international law operates remains based on the Westphalian model of international relations, at the centre of which is the "*idée-force*"[39] of state sovereignty.[40] As Richard Falk explains, it is "by way of the Peace of Westphalia that ended the Thirty Years' War, that the modern system of states was formally established as the *dominant world order framework.*"[41] Similarly, Mark Janis writes that "[s]overeignty, as a concept, formed the cornerstone of the

[36] See Toope, *supra* note 8, at 540: "To construct the 'foreign,' one must accept the continuing influence of the *dying metaphor of national sovereignty*" [emphasis added].

[37] See K. Ohmae, *The End of the Nation State — The Rise of Regional Economies* (New York and London: Free Press, 1996) and J.-M. Guehenno, *The End of the Nation-State* (Minneapolis and London: University of Minnesota Press, 1995), at 108.

[38] See F. Fukuyama, *The End of History and the Last Man* (New York: Free Press, 1992). The "end of history" thesis holds that the end of the Cold War constitutes compelling evidence that a worldwide consensus has emerged in favour of capitalism and liberal democracy. For a critique of this argument, see J. Derrida, *Specters of Marx — The State of the Debt, the Work of Mourning, and the New International* (New York and London: Routledge, 1994), 56 *ff*. For an interesting parallel between Fukuyama's claim and some international law scholarship, see S. Marks, "The End of History? — Reflections on Some International Legal Theses" (1997) 8 European J. Int'l L. 449.

[39] That is, "idea-force." See A. Fouillée, *L'évolutionnisme des idées-forces* (Paris: Félix Alcan, 1890), at XI.

[40] See, generally, S. Beaulac, "The Westphalian Legal Orthodoxy — Myth or Reality?" (2000) 2 J. History Int'l L. 148.

[41] R.A. Falk, *Law in an Emerging Global Village: A Post-Westphalian Perspective* (Ardsley, US: Transnational Publishers, 1998), at 4 [emphasis added]. See also R. Redslob, *Histoire des grands principes du droit des gens — Depuis l'antiquité jusqu'à la veille de la grande guerre* (Paris: Rousseau, 1923), at 213: "Avec le traité de Westphalie commence une nouvelle époque dans l'histoire du droit des gens" [footnotes omitted].

edifice of international relations that 1648 raised up. Sovereignty was the crucial element in the peace treaties of Westphalia."[42] The international reality consists of a community of sovereign states — sometimes called the society of nations — which are independent from one another and have their own wills and finalities as corporate-like representatives of the peoples living in their territories. The eighteenth-century author Emer de Vattel proposed an international legal framework to regulate the relations between states in his masterpiece *Le Droit des Gens; ou Principes de la loi naturelle appliqués à la conduite & aux affaires des Nations & des Souverains.*[43] His seminal contribution is a scheme in which sovereign states are the sole actors on the international plane and thus the only subjects of international law.[44] It is also based on the formal equality of states and on a notion of national independence that involves non-interference in the domestic affairs of other states.[45] This basic theory is still very much underlying modern international law.[46]

Accordingly, the Westphalian model of international relations, which is governed by the Vattelian legal structure, involves an international realm that is distinct and separate from the internal

[42] M.S. Janis, "Sovereignty and International Law: Hobbes and Grotius," in R. St. J. Macdonald (ed.), *Essays in Honour of Wang Tieya* (Dordrecht: Martinus Nijhoff, 1994), 391, at 393 [emphasis added]. Likewise, see also T.M. Franck, *The Empowered Self — Law and Society in the Age of Individualism* (Oxford and New York: Oxford University Press, 1999), at 5.

[43] E. de Vattel, *Le Droit des Gens; ou Principes de la loi naturelle appliqués à la conduite & aux affaires des Nations & des Souverains*, 2 vols. (London: n.b., 1758). See also the English translation by J. Chitty and E. de Vattel, *The Law of Nations; or, Principles of the Law of Nature, Applied to the Conduct and Affairs of Nations and Sovereigns* (Philadelphia: Johnson Law Booksellers, 1863).

[44] On this point, in the modern context of international law, see W.A. Schabas, "Twenty-Five Years of Public International Law at the Supreme Court of Canada" (2000) 79 Canadian Bar Rev. 174, at 176.

[45] See S. Beaulac, "Emer de Vattel and the Externalization of Sovereignty" (2003) 5 J. History Int'l L. 237.

[46] See, generally, S. Beaulac, *The Power of Language in the Making of International Law — The Word Sovereignty in Bodin and Vattel and the Myth of Westphalia* (Leiden and Boston: Martinus Nijhoff, 2004). However, see P. Allott, "The Emerging Universal Legal System" (2001) 3 Int'l L. Forum 12, at 17: "International social reality has overtaken international social philosophy. The Vattelian mind-world is withering away under the impact of the new international social reality. The reconstruction of the metaphysical basis of international law is now well advanced. The deconstruction of the false consciousness of politicians, public officials, and international lawyers is only just beginning."

realm.[47] John Currie explains thus: "Public international law is not so much an area or topic of the law as it is *an entire legal system, quite distinct from the national legal systems* that regulate daily life within states."[48] As far as the relation between international law and domestic law is concerned, there is no direct connection because the two systems are distinct and separate[49] — "public international law exists outside and independent of national legal systems."[50] With respect to the issue of the national application of international law, these international law/internal law distinct and separate realms are no doubt behind the following comments by LeBel J. and Gloria Chao: "As the heart of the debate is the tension between the democratic principle underlying the *internal legal order* and the search for conformity or consistency with a developing and uncertain *external legal order.*"[51] Appositely, Karen Knop schematically writes that "domestic law is 'here' and international law is 'there.'"[52]

This continuing and continuous distinct and separate reality of our modern state system of international relations explains two fundamental principles of international law. The first one is that, on the international plane, a state is not entitled to invoke its internal law — which includes its constitutional structure[53] — in

---

[47] See S. Beaulac, "On the Saying That International Law Binds Canadian Courts" (2003) 29(3) CCIL Bulletin 1. In fact, even the most forceful advocates of an increased role of international law in Canada acknowledge that "public international law is not a subset of the internal laws of states, but *a separate legal system in its own rights.*" See van Ert, *supra* note 20, at 15 [emphasis added].

[48] Currie, *supra* note 16, at 1 [emphasis added].

[49] It follows that the assertion that the legislative power of a sovereign state like Canada is competent to "violate" international law is a meaningless statement based on a flawed question that wrongly assume some kind of inherent connection between the international plane and the national level — see van Ert, *supra* note 20, at 55 *ff.*

[50] Currie, *supra* note 16, at 1. *Contra,* see G. Palmer, "Human Rights and the New Zealand Government's Treaty Obligations" (1999) 29 Victoria U. Wellington L. Rev. 27, at 59: "For many years international law and municipal law have been seen as two separate circles that never intersect. Increasingly, however, the way to look at them, I suggest, is that they are two circles with a substantial degree of overlap and indeed it can be argued that there is only one circle."

[51] LeBel and Chao, *supra* note 23, at 24 [emphasis added].

[52] Knop, *supra* note 5, at 504.

[53] See R. Jennings and A. Watts, *Oppenheim's International Law,* 9th ed., vol. 1 (London: Longman, 1992), at 254: "Nevertheless, in principle a state which has incurred international obligations cannot rely on its internal constitutional

order to justify a breach of its international obligations.[54] The Supreme Court of Canada accepted this basic principle of international law in *Zingre* v. *The Queen*,[55] where Justice Robert Dickson quoted and endorsed a statement by the Canadian Department of External Affairs stating that "it is a recognized principle of international customary law that a state may not invoke the provisions of its internal law as justification for its failure to perform its international obligations."[56] Fundamentally, a state cannot rely on its domestic law to justify a failure to honour its obligations *vis-à-vis* the international community because these norms and duties are part of two distinct and separate legal systems.

The second core principle of international law springing from the international/internal divide is the need to administer the relationship between the two systems. John Currie refers to this feature as the "international-national law interface"[57] and writes that the relationship "will depend on legal rules that determine, as a matter of law, how one legal system treats another."[58] As in other Commonwealth countries,[59] in Canada the reception rules on how international law is applicable in domestic law are a matter of constitutional law. Francis Jacobs explains:

First, the effect of international law generally, and of treaties in particular, within the legal order of a State will always depend on a rule of domestic law. The fundamental principle is that the application of treaties is

---

arrangements as a justification for any failure to comply with those obligations. In respect of treaties this can lead to federal states being unable to become parties" [footnotes omitted].

[54] The basic authority for this proposition is the arbitration decision in the *Alabama Claims* case (United States/United Kingdom) (1872), Moore, *Arbitrations*, i. 653. This rule was codified in section 27 of the Vienna Convention on the Law of Treaties, 23 May 1969, 1155 U.N.T.S. 331, 8 I.L.M. 679 (1969), Can. T.S. 1980 No. 37 (entered into force on 27 January 1980) [hereinafter Vienna Convention]. See also P. Daillier and A. Pellet (eds.), *Nguyen Quoc Dinh — Droit international public*, 5th ed. (Paris: Librairie générale de droit et de jurisprudence, 1994), at 272.

[55] *Zingre* v. *The Queen*, [1981] 2 S.C.R. 392.

[56] *Ibid.*, at 410.

[57] Currie, *supra* note 16, at 193.

[58] *Ibid.*

[59] See, for instance, the Australian situation with the *Commonwealth of Australia Constitutional Act*, 63 & 64 Victoria, c. 12 (U.K.), and the decision of the Australian High Court in *Minister for Immigration and Ethnic Affairs* v. *Teoh* (1995), 183 C.L.R. 273, at 286-87.

governed by domestic constitutional law. It is true that domestic law may, under certain conditions, require or permit the application of treaties which are binding on the State, even if they have not been specifically incorporated into domestic law. But this application of treaties "as such" is prescribed by a rule of domestic constitutional law. It is not a situation reached by the application of a rule of international law, since such a rule, to have effect, itself depends upon recognition by domestic law. *Indeed international law is generally uninformative in this area since it simply requires the application of treaties in all circumstances. It does not modify the fundamental principle that the application of treaties by domestic courts is governed by domestic law.*[60]

These constitutional rules are unwritten[61] — perhaps amounting to constitutional conventions[62] — and come from the British tradition through the preamble to the Constitution Act, 1867,[63] which provides that Canada shall have "a Constitution similar in principle to that of the United Kingdom." As Peter Hogg has explained, "Canada's constitutional law, derived in this respect from the United Kingdom, does not recognize a treaty as part of the internal (or 'municipal') law of Canada."[64]

Indeed, it has become an orthodoxy[65] in Canada that an international treaty[66] is not part of the law of the land until it has been incorporated domestically, which must be accomplished "by the enactment of a statute which makes the required change in the law."[67] The basic authority for this proposition undoubtedly remains

[60] F.G. Jacobs, "Introduction," in F.G. Jacobs and S Roberts (eds.), *The Effect of Treaties in Domestic Law* (London: Sweet and Maxwell, 1987), xxiii, at xxiv [emphasis added].

[61] As Chief Justice Antonio Lamer confirmed in *Re Provincial Court Judges*, [1997] 3 S.C.R. 3, at 68, "the general principle [is] that the Constitution embraces unwritten, as well as written rules."

[62] Constitutional conventions were considered by the Supreme Court of Canada in *Re Resolution to Amend the Constitution*, [1981] 1 S.C.R. 753. See also A. Heard, *Canadian Constitution Conventions: The Marriage of Law and Politics* (Toronto: Oxford University Press, 1991).

[63] Constitution Act, 1867, 30 & 31 Victoria, c. 3 (U.K.), reprinted in R.S.C. 1985, Appendix II, No. 5.

[64] P.W. Hogg, *Constitutional Law of Canada*, 3rd (student) ed. (Scarborough, ON: Carswell, 1992), at 285.

[65] Stephen Toope referred to this principle as "trite law." See Toope, *supra* note 9, at 12.

[66] It must be emphasized that the present article does not examine the situation with regard to customs.

[67] Hogg, *supra* note 64, at 285. The suggestion recently made that international treaty norms could be implemented through non-legislative means such as government policy measures, albeit virtuous (perhaps), is unsupported by authority

the decision of the Judicial Committee of the Privy Council in the notorious case *Attorney General for Canada* v. *Attorney General for Ontario* (*Labour Conventions* case).[68] The implementation requirement for treaties has been reiterated and applied at the Supreme Court of Canada[69] — Justice Claire L'Heureux-Dubé reaffirmed the rule in the 1999 *Baker* case: "International treaties and conventions are not part of Canadian law unless they have been implemented by statute."[70] Again, in *Suresh* v. *Canada* (*Minister of Citizenship and Immigration*),[71] in 2002, the Supreme Court wrote: "International treaty norms are not, strictly speaking, binding [*sic*] in Canada unless they have been incorporated into Canadian law by enactment."[72]

INTERNATIONAL LAW IS NOT AND CANNOT BE "BINDING" IN CANADA

Going back to the two distinct and separate realms of the international and the internal, it is understood of course that each of these legal systems has its own judiciary. At the international level, Article 92 of the Charter of the United Nations[73] provides that "[t]he International Court of Justice shall be the principal judicial organ of the United Nations" — it was created with the adoption of the Statute of the International Court of Justice (ICJ Statute).[74]

— see E. Brandon, "Does International Law Mean Anything in Canadian Courts?" (2001) 11 J. Environmental L. & Prac. 399, at 407: "Thus a treaty that has been brought into Canadian law through other measures — such as policy — should be of equal status to treaties implemented by specific legislation."

[68] *Attorney General for Canada* v. *Attorney General for Ontario*, [1937] A.C. 326, at 347 [hereinafter *Labour Conventions*].

[69] See, for instance, *Francis* v. *The Queen*, [1956] 618, at 621; *Capital Cities Communications Inc.* v. *Canada* (*C.R.T.C.*), [1978] 2 S.C.R. 141, at 172-73 [hereinafter *Capital Cities*]; *Operation Dismantle Inc.* v. *R.*, [1985] 1 S.C.R. 441, at 484.

[70] *Baker*, *supra* note 2 at 861.

[71] *Suresh* v. *Canada* (*Minister of Citizenship and Immigration*), [2002] 1 S.C.R. 3 [hereinafter *Suresh*]. See also S. Beaulac, "The *Suresh* Case and Unimplemented Treaty Norms" (2002) 15 Rev. québécoise d. int'l 221.

[72] *Suresh*, *supra* note 71 at 38.

[73] Charter of the United Nations, June 26, 1945, Can. T.S. 1945 No. 7 (entered into force on 24 October 1945); not published in the U.N.T.S.

[74] ICJ Statute, *supra* note 19. Its predecessor was the Permanent Court of International Justice of the League of Nations, created pursuant to Article 415 of the Treaty of Versailles, concluded on 28 June 1919 — see the English text of the treaty in C. Parry (ed.), *Consolidated Treaty Series*, vol. 225 (Dobbs Ferry, US: Oceana Publications, 1969), at 189. There has been a proliferation of courts and tribunals at the international level, especially in the past fifteen years, with

At the national level, to take Canada as an example, there exists a whole judicial structure of domestic courts and tribunals,[75] both provincial and federal, at the pinnacle of which is the Supreme Court of Canada, established pursuant to section 101 of the Constitution Act, 1867[76] and created in 1875 (along with the ancestor of the Federal Court) with the adoption of the Supreme and Exchequer Courts Act, 1875.[77]

The more important point is that both sets of courts have their own sets of legal norms — that is, the ICJ and the other international courts and tribunals apply international law and the Supreme Court of Canada and the other Canadian courts and tribunals (or any domestic courts of sovereign states) apply their domestic law.[78] This assertion may sound trite, but, in the present debate over the issue of the internal use of international law, some truisms might need to be recalled from time to time.[79] Of course, it does not mean that international judicial bodies cannot take into consideration domestic law, which is in fact an explicit source of international law under Article 38(1) of the ICJ Statute[80] or that

---

over a dozen international judicial or quasi-judicial bodies established. See C. Brown, "The Proliferation of International Courts and Tribunals: Finding Your Way through the Maze" (2002) 3 Melbourne J. Int'l L. 453, at 455-56.

[75] On the Canadian judiciary, in general, see G.L. Gall, *The Canadian Legal System*, 4th ed. (Scarborough, ON: Carswell, 1995), at 181 *ff.*

[76] Constitution Act, 1867, *supra* note 63.

[77] Supreme and Exchequer Courts Act, 1875, S.C. 1875, c. 11. Now, it is the Supreme Court Act, R.S.C. 1985, c. S-26, which provides for the Supreme Court of Canada.

[78] For the sake of completeness, it must be added that, of course, Canadian private international law can dictate that foreign domestic law will apply to a particular situation. This does not change the basic proposition, however, because Canadian courts fundamentally resort, even in such cases, to Canadian domestic law in the first instance.

[79] For instance, see the following statement that appears to run in the face of the general tenets of international law: "The tendency to look to explicitly international forums, such as the International Court of Justice, for the exclusive enforcement of international law is a mistake. International jurisdiction is not confined to internationally constituted courts in the way that jurisdiction over Japan is reserved to Japanese courts. Rather, international and domestic courts share jurisdiction. *Indeed, to distinguish between international and domestic courts is a false dichotomy.*" Van Ert, *supra* note 20, at 5 [emphasis added].

[80] ICJ Statute, *supra* note 19. Sub-paragraph b of Article 38(1) provides, as a source of international law, "the general principles of law recognized by civilized nations." On general principles of law, see M. Shaw, *International Law*, 4th ed. (Cambridge: Cambridge University Press, 1997), at 77 *ff.*

domestic case law does not influence their decisions as a secondary source of international law[81] and even as evidence of international customs.[82] Conversely, Bill Schabas rightly points out that Canadian judicial organs may use "international law to the extent that it is also part of the 'Laws of Canada.'"[83]

The mutual influence, however, does not modify the basic situation that the international judiciary applies the legal norms of its realm and that national judiciaries apply the legal norms of their realms. The international reality is distinct and separate from the internal reality and, consequently, the actualization of international law through judicial decision-making is distinct and separate from the actualization of domestic law through judicial decision-making. Although this aspect is not usually dwelled upon in judicial decisions, the Supreme Court of Canada has had such an opportunity to consider its role *vis-à-vis* the international legal system in *Reference re Secession of Quebec*.[84] The *amicus curiae* argued that the court had no jurisdiction to answer questions of "'pure' international law."[85] The response, which is significant for the present purposes, was that the "Court would not, in providing an advisory opinion in the context of a reference, be purporting to 'act as' or substitute itself for an international tribunal."[86] Thus, as LeBel J. and Gloria Chao observe, "the key limits to the [Supreme] Court's use [of these norms] is that it has never seen itself as a final arbiter of international law."[87]

The acknowledgment that the international legal reality is distinct and separate from the national legal reality, including with

---

[81] Sub-paragraph c of Article 38(1) of the ICJ Statute provides that judicial decisions, including those of domestic courts, are a subsidiary source of international law. It may be going too far, however, to argue that, through its decisions, "the Supreme Court of Canada not only applies and interprets public international law, *it may also create it*" — see W.A. Schabas, *supra* note 44, at 176 [emphasis added].

[82] See Brunnée and Toope, *supra* note 9, at 7, where the authors appositely wrote: "Especially in the context of customary international law, domestic courts participate in the continuous weaving of the fabric of international law." See also A.E. Roberts, "Traditional and Modern Approaches to Customary International Law: A Reconciliation" (2001) 95 American J. Int'l L. 757.

[83] Schabas, *supra* note 44, at 176.

[84] *Reference re Secession of Quebec*, [1998] 2 S.C.R. 217.

[85] *Ibid.*, at 234.

[86] *Ibid.*

[87] LeBel and Chao, *supra* note 23, at 59.

respect to their judicial instances, does not mean that the former may not have any effect on the latter.[88] In *Reference re Secession of Quebec,*[89] an argument was also made that the court had no jurisdiction to "look at international law"[90] in order to decide the questions at issue. "This concern is groundless" was the reply: "In a number of previous cases, it has been necessary for this Court to look to international law to determine the rights or obligations of some actor within the Canadian legal system."[91] Therefore, treaty norms of the distinct and separate international legal system may have an effect within the Canadian domestic legal system.[92] It is important to acknowledge, however, that such a legal effect will not at all be automatic or obligatory. Rather, because the two legal systems exist independently, the impact that one can have on the other will be decided by the latter system — that is, by the legal rules of reception already explained earlier in this article with respect to international treaties.

Put another way, domestic courts (such as Canadian courts) interpret and apply domestic law (such as Canadian law), and it is to the extent that the constitutional and other domestic legal rules allow international law to be part of domestic law — and that it has in effect become part of that domestic law — that international treaty norms may have an impact on the interpretation and application of domestic law by domestic courts. In this sense, international law *qua* international law can never "bind" a sovereign state such as Canada, or, more accurately, international law can never be *stricto sensu* "binding" *within* the Canadian legal system because Canadian domestic courts have jurisdiction over Canadian law, not international law.[93] What international law can do, and, indeed, should do as much as possible, is to "influence" the interpretation and application of domestic law — the degree of which will depend,

---

[88] The position defended here is thus reconcilable with La Forest J.'s comments (*supra* note 4, at 100-1) about the internationalization of our courts.

[89] *Reference re Secession of Quebec, supra* note 84.

[90] *Ibid.,* at 235.

[91] *Ibid.*

[92] The Supreme Court of Canada referred to the *Reference re Powers to Levy Rates on Foreign Legations and High Commissioners' Residences,* [1943] S.C.R. 208; *Reference re Ownership of Offshore Mineral Rights of British Columbia,* [1967] S.C.R. 792; and *Reference re Newfoundland Continental Shelf,* [1984] 1 S.C.R. 86.

[93] See S. Beaulac, "Arrêtons de dire que les tribunaux au Canada sont 'liés' par le droit international" (2004) 38 Rev. jur. Thémis, forthcoming.

in the words of Schabas, on the extent that international law "is also part of the 'Laws of Canada.'"[94]

The "influence" of international law on the interpretation and application of Canadian law can also be put in terms of the determination of the "persuasive force" of international law or the evaluation of the "weight" of the international law argument. This approach to the domestic use of international law is not an endorsement of the proposition put forward by Karen Knop based on the transgovernmental model and the comparative law methodology.[95] The approach shares, however, the belief that international law, by definition, cannot "bind" the courts of sovereign states. The reason suggested in this article why international law can only be "influential" or "persuasive" is different from Knop's and boils down to the two distinct and separate realities of international law and national law. Canadian courts interpret and apply Canadian law and, with respect to treaties, in order to know what influence the written norms of international law found in them can have on the written norms of Canadian domestic law found in statutes, it is now appropriate to bring the debate within the discourse of legislative interpretation.

INTERNATIONAL LAW AS A CONTEXTUAL ELEMENT OF STATUTORY INTERPRETATION

The argument at the heart of this article is that the use of international law is, as far as Canadian judges and other domestic actors are concerned, a question of statutory interpretation, which must be addressed, rationalized, and understood within this framework. This hypothesis now requires an examination of the general discourse of statutory interpretation and, in particular, the contextual argument, which is considered in some detail. Only then can the main proposal be properly explained, namely, the analytical scheme to decide the persuasive force of international law, which considers the matter in which treaties were implemented and is thus based on the degree of incorporation of treaty norms within the Canadian legal system.

TREATY IMPLEMENTATION PRACTICES

The implementation of treaties is required to bridge the international and the national distinct and separate realms and to give

[94] Schabas, *supra* note 44, at 176.
[95] See Knop, *supra* note 5.

legal effect to such international norms at the domestic level.[96] It will be argued that the manner in which treaty norms are incorporated within the Canadian legal system by the competent legislative authority should determine the persuasive force of the international law argument of contextual interpretation of domestic statutes. Accordingly, it is first necessary to examine in some detail the different legislative practices that are followed to implement international conventions.

Ruth Sullivan identifies two techniques used by legislative authorities to give legal effect to international treaty law in Canada: (1) incorporation by reference and (2) harmonization.[97] The first technique directly implements the treaty, either by reproducing its provisions in the statute itself or by including the text as a schedule and somehow indicating that it is thus part of the statute.[98] "When a legislature implements an international convention through harmonization," on the other hand, "it redrafts the law to be implemented in its own terms so as to adapt it to domestic law."[99]

---

[96] For the same of completeness, one must mention that it is the very large majority of international treaties that require legislative implementation, but not in any way all of them — see Hogg, *supra* note 64, at 285: "Many treaties do not require a change in the internal law of the states which are parties. This is true of treaties which do not impinge on individual rights, nor contravene existing laws, nor require action outside the executive powers of the government which made the treaty. For example, treaties between Canada and other states relating to defence, foreign aid, the high seas, the air, research, weather stations, diplomatic relations and many other matter, may be able to be implemented simply by the executive action of the Canadian government which made the treaty" [footnotes omitted]. Moreover, treaties relating to war and peace as well as treaties pertaining to territory transfers do not require implementation through legislation. See Brownlie, *supra* note 35, at 48; and R. St. J. Macdonald, "International Treaty Law and the Domestic Law of Canada" (1975) 2 Dalhousie L.J. 307 at 308-10 and 313-14.

[97] See Sullivan, *supra* note 15, at 430.

[98] Indeed, it has become clear with the majority reasons of Iacobucci J. in *Re Act Respecting the Vancouver Island Railway*, [1994] 2 S.C.R. 41, that scheduling an international treaty is not sufficient to directly incorporating it domestically. Using two opinions expressed in *Ottawa Electric Railway Co.* v. *Corporation of the City of Ottawa*, [1945] S.C.R. 105, Iacobucci J. wrote: "Although divided in the result, I discern a common thread in the judgments of Rinfret C.J. and Kerwin J., namely, that statutory ratification and confirmation of a scheduled agreement, standing alone, is generally insufficient reason to conclude that such an agreement constitutes a part of the statute itself" (at 109). See also *Winnipeg* v. *Winnipeg Electric Railway Co.*, [1921] 2 W.W.R. 282 (Manitoba C.A.), at 306.

[99] Sullivan, *supra* note 15, at 434.

Following this classification, one must realize that these practices are not mutually exclusive — that is, international norms in a treaty can be implemented not only by using one or the other technique but also by using a combination of both, where part of the treaty would be directly incorporated in the statute while another part would be incorporated through harmonization. The federal Immigration Act[100] is such a piece of hybrid legislation that it both directly implements and harmonizes Canadian law in view of the Convention Relating to the Status of Refugees.[101]

Another challenge regarding the implementation of treaties, which is this time due to Canada's federal nature, is that the same treaty — the subject matter of which falls within provincial power — is not necessarily implemented the same way across the country. *Thomson* v. *Thomson*[102] is an illustration of such a situation, where Justice Gerard La Forest identified the various ways in which the provinces had implemented the Hague Convention of the Civil Aspects of International Child Abduction[103] — all of the provincial acts, with the exception of Quebec, directly implemented the convention by reference (New Brunswick, Nova Scotia, Saskatchewan, and Alberta incorporated the exact scheme, while Manitoba, Ontario, British Columbia, Prince Edward Island, and Newfoundland incorporated the treaty along with other legislative provisions).[104] As for Canada's civil law jurisdiction, it did not "adopt the integral wording thereof," as L'Heureux-Dubé J. pointed out later in *W. (V.)* v. *S. (D.)*,[105] hence, implementing the treaty through harmonizing legislation and, thus, "ensuring that the new rules can be applied effectively within the institutional framework of domestic law."[106]

---

100 Immigration Act, R.S.C. 1985, c. I-2.

101 Convention Relating to the Status of Refugees, 28 July 1951, 189 U.N.T.S. 150, Can. T.S. 1969 No. 6 (entered into force on 22 April 1954).

102 *Thomson* v. *Thomson*, [1994] 3 S.C.R. 551, at 601-2 [hereinafter *Thomson*].

103 Hague Convention of the Civil Aspects of International Child Abduction, 25 October 1980, 1343 U.N.T.S. 89, Can. T.S. 1983 No. 35 (entered into force on 1 December 1983).

104 See M. Bailey, "Canada's Implementation of the 1980 Hague Convention on the Civil Aspects of International Child Abduction" (2000) 33 New York U. J. Int'l L. & Pol. 17 at 17-19.

105 *W. (V.)* v. *S. (D.)*, [1996] 2 S.C.R. 108, at 133.

106 Sullivan, *supra* note 15, at 434.

Parliamentary Intention and Implementation

Given the formal requirement of having legislation transform international treaty norms within the Canadian domestic legal system,[107] the deciding factor in knowing whether or not such incorporation has occurred is the "intention of Parliament." Relying on Iacobucci J.'s reasons in *Re Act Respecting the Vancouver Island Railway*,[108] Justice J. François Lemieux at the Federal Court in *Pfizer Inc. v. Canada*[109] explained that "whether an agreement is legislated so as to become endowed with statutory force is a matter of *discovering Parliament's intention*."[110] Thus, when the statute explicitly declares that a certain international convention has "force of law in Canada,"[111] the implementing requirement is most likely fulfilled.[112] Although the language that is used in the act is important, "all of the tools of statutory interpretation can be called in aid to determine whether incorporation is intended."[113] The old view that "courts should be able to say, on the basis of the expression of the legislation, that it is implementing legislation,"[114] therefore, appears to be obsolete.

Such an assessment of legislative intention led the Federal Court to hold in *Pfizer*[115] that the whole of the Marrakesh Agreement Establishing the World Trade Organization (WTO Agreement)[116] was not incorporated in Canada through the World Trade Organization Agreement Implementation Act,[117] which even scheduled

---

[107] See Hogg, *supra* note 64 and accompanying text.

[108] *Re Act Respecting the Vancouver Island Railway, supra* note 98, at 110.

[109] *Pfizer Inc. v. Canada,* [1999] 4 F.C. 441 (F.C.T.D.) [hereinafter *Pfizer*].

[110] *Ibid.,* at 458 [emphasis added].

[111] For instance, see section 3 of the United Nations Foreign Arbitral Awards Convention Act, R.S.C. 1985, c. 16 (2nd supp.); and section 3(1) of the Foreign Missions and International Organizations Act, S.C. 1991, c. 41.

[112] Such clear intention to implement, however, is not necessarily conclusive — see *Antonsen* v. *Canada (Attorney General),* [1995] 2 F.C. 272 (F.C.T.D.), at 305-6.

[113] *Re Act Respecting the Vancouver Island Railway, supra* note 98, at 110. See also *Cree Regional Authority* v. *Canada (Federal Administrator),* [1991] 3 F.C. (F.C.A.), at 546-47 and 551-52.

[114] *MacDonald* v. *Vapor Canada Ltd.,* [1977] 2 S.C.R. 134, at 171, *per* Chief Justice Boris Laskin.

[115] *Pfizer, supra* note 109.

[116] Marrakesh Agreement Establishing the World Trade Organization, 15 April 1994, 1867 U.N.T.S. 3 [hereinafter WTO Agreement].

[117] World Trade Organization Agreement Implementation Act, S.C. 1994, c. 47.

the relevant international documents. Justice Lemieux reached the following conclusion:

When Parliament said, in section 3 of the WTO Agreement Implementation Act, that the purpose of that Act was to implement the Agreement, Parliament was merely saying the obvious; it was providing for the implementation of the WTO Agreement as contained in the statute as a whole including Part II dealing with specific statutory changes. When Parliament said in section 8 of the WTO Agreement Implementation Act that it was approving the WTO Agreement, Parliament did not incorporate the WTO Agreement into federal law. Indeed, it could not, because some aspects of the WTO Agreement could be only implemented by the provinces under their constitutional legislative authority pursuant to section 92 of the *Constitution Act, 1867*... What Parliament did in approving the Agreement is to anchor the Agreement as the basis for its participation in the World Trade Organization, Canada's adherence to WTO mechanisms such as dispute settlement and the basis for implementation where adaptation through regulation or adjudication was required.[118]

In short, as in any case in the determination of the intention of Parliament, the statute should be read as a whole, in light of the language used, the objective pursued, and the context, both immediate and extended (including the preamble), of the enactment under examination.[119]

Passive Incorporation Is Not Implementation

The next important aspect of the implementation requirement question is whether or not what some have called "passive incorporation"[120] of treaties actually constitutes the transformation of international norms within the Canadian domestic legal system.[121] Such passive incorporation could be said to have occurred where the federal government concludes and ratifies an international agreement on the basis of existing domestic law that already conforms with Canada's new international obligations. In the context of international human rights law, Irit Weiser has considered the issue and attempted to elucidate the effect of such passive

---

[118] *Pfizer, supra* note 109, at 460.

[119] See *R. v. Crown Zellerbach Canada Ltd.*, [1988] 1 S.C.R. 401 [hereinafter *Crown Zellerbach*]; and *R. v. Hydro-Quebec*, [1997] 3 S.C.R. 213.

[120] Also known as "incorporation by complacence."

[121] See J. Ebbesson, *Compatibility of International and National Environmental Law* (London: Kluwer Law International, 1996), at 206.

246 Annuaire canadien de Droit international 2003

incorporation on statutory interpretation.[122] In the context of international environmental law, Elizabeth Brandon writes that, "[g]iven the common government practice of assessing Canada's legislative framework prior to signing a treaty, significance can be attached to legislative inaction by the government following signature."[123] She opines that "such inaction signals that the existing legislative or policy framework has been deemed adequate to fulfil the treaty obligations."[124] Similarly, Jutta Brunnée and Stephen Toope argue that, "[i]n cases where there was no specific legislative transformation but Canadian law is in conformity with a treaty due to prior statutory, common law, or even administrative policy, we suggest that the treaty is also implemented for the purposes of domestic law."[125]

The contention that passive incorporation actually constitutes the domestic transformation of international treaty norms can be attractive given the claim that the federal government has made on occasion in its reports to international treaty bodies that Canada's human rights commitments, for instance, have been met on the basis of prior conformity.[126] This contention would be an error, however, especially in view of the three rationales — separation of powers, federalism, democracy — that underlie the implementation requirement of international treaties. First, it would allow the executive branch of government to determine, in effect, the legal effect of international treaty law within the domestic realm of Canada in blatant violation of the separation of powers in our parliament system of government. Second, it would be the federal government, which is deemed to have sole treaty-making power and

---

[122] See I. Weiser, "Effect in Domestic Law of International Human Rights Treaties Ratified without Implementing Legislation," in CCIL, *The Impact of International Law on the Practice of Law in Canada — Proceedings of the 27th Annual Conference of the Canadian Council on International Law, Ottawa, October 15-17, 1998* (The Hague: Kluwer Law International, 1999), 132, at 137-39.

[123] Brandon, *supra* note 67, at 418.

[124] *Ibid.*

[125] Brunnée and Toope, *supra* note 9, at 29.

[126] See, for instance, Canada's report to the United Nations Human Rights Committee, sitting under the first Optional Protocol to the International Covenant on Civil and Political Rights, 16 December 1966, 999 U.N.T.S. 171, 6 I.L.M. 368 (1967), Can. T.S. 1976 No. 47 (entered into force on 23 March 1976) — Human Rights Committee, *Consideration of Reports Submitted by States under Article 40 of the Covenant: Fourth Periodic Report of States Parties Due in 1995: Canada,* U.N. C.C.P.R.O.R., 1995, U.N. Doc. CCPR/C/103/Add.5.

international personality, that could indirectly transform treaties in Canada through such passive incorporation, with no apparent restriction in regard to the constitutional division of legislative authority. Third, allowing for the incorporation of treaty norms without the participation of the elected assembly of the competent government would create a real democratic deficit, which, in a way, would see the international legal realm, in which citizens have no participation, dictate the democratically legitimate national legal realm.[127]

These may have been some of the considerations that the Ontario Court of Appeal had in mind when considering the argument based on the International Covenant on Civil and Political Rights[128] in *Ahani v. Canada (Attorney General).*[129] The question at issue was whether the Optional Protocol[130] to this convention was part of the laws of the land. The fact that there is no legislation in Canada transforming these human rights commitments, directly or

---

[127] Compare these arguments with the following ones by Brunnée and Toope: "Two considerations suggest that the [passive incorporation] approach is both correct and compatible with legitimate concerns over the proper roles of the executive, legislators, and the judiciary. First, where a treaty does not actually affect domestic law, the concern that the authority of Parliament or the provincial legislature could be usurped by federal executive action seems misplaced. In any event, it remains open to Parliament or provincial legislatures to deviate from treaty provisions through explicit statutory action. Second, where no legislative action is required to bring domestic law in line with Canada's treaty commitments, it seems absurd to insist on explicit statutory implementation. This applies with even greater force when Canada, in international forums, reports its implementation of treaty commitments, as it does regularly, for example, in the human rights context." Brunnée and Toope, *supra* note 9, at 30-31.

[128] International Covenant on Civil and Political Rights, *supra* note 126.

[129] *Ahani v. Canada (Attorney General)* (2002), 58 O.R. (3d) 107 [hereinafter *Ahani*]. The *Ahani* case was considered with the *Suresh* case at the Supreme Court of Canada, the decisions in which were handed down on 11 January 2002. Unlike the latter, the petitioner Ahani was not given a new deportation hearing and, having exhausted all domestic remedies, he petitioned the United Nations Human Rights Committee under the Optional Protocol to the International Covenant of Civil and Political Rights, *supra* note 126. The international instance requested Canada to stay the deportation until the full consideration of Ahani's case, which was refused by the federal government. The second Canadian judicial proceeding, which reached the Ontario Court of Appeal (the Supreme Court of Canada refused leave to appeal), was asking for an injunction to suspend his deportation order, which was refused.

[130] Optional Protocol, *supra* note 126. See, on petitions under the Optional Protocol in general, Schabas, *supra* note 44, at 193-95.

through harmonization, is well documented in legal literature.[131] Both the majority and the dissent reached the inescapable conclusion that these international norms have no legal effect within the Canadian domestic legal system: "Canada has never incorporated either the Covenant or the Protocol into Canadian law by implementing legislation. Absent implementing legislation, neither has any legal effect in Canada."[132] It would lead to an "untenable result," the majority further wrote, to "convert a non-binding request, in a Protocol which has never been part of Canadian law, into a binding obligation enforceable in Canada by a Canadian court."[133] Justice Marc Rosenberg, in dissent, agreed with the federal government and, thus, the majority of the court on this point.[134]

This clear judicial pronouncement from the authoritative Ontario Court of Appeal will hopefully put to rest the argument that the passive incorporation of a treaty constitutes the transformation of international norms. Yet the legal community of Canada, and especially the judiciary, ought to remain vigilant that the basic rule requiring domestic transformation of international conventions through domestic legislation not be furtively changed through the backdoor with this unsound doctrine.[135]

---

[131] See, for instance, Kindred, *supra* note 3, at 265: "Yet nowhere to date is there legislation explicitly implementing within Canada such fundamental international human rights conventions as the *International Covenant on Civil and Political Rights*, the *International Covenant on Economic, Social and Cultural Rights* and the *Convention on the Rights of the Child*" [footnotes omitted]. This is the generally accepted view in Canada, which contrasts with that expressed by van Ert, *supra* note 20, at 186: "It is true that there is no such thing as the ICCPR Implementation Act. To conclude from this, however, that Canadian law does not implement the ICCPR is, at best, an oversimplification and, at worst, simply wrong."

[132] *Ahani, supra* note 129, at para. 31, *per* Laskin J.

[133] *Ibid.*, at para. 33.

[134] See Justice Rosenberg's reasons, *ibid.*, at para. 73, which read as follows: "On the legal side, they [the federal government *et al.*] invoke the established principle that international conventions are not binding in Canada unless they have been specifically incorporated into Canadian law. The Covenant, while ratified, has never been incorporated into Canadian domestic law and therefore does not create legal obligations enforceable in Canada."

[135] See B.R. Openkin, "Constitutional Modelling: The Domestic Effect of International Law in Commonwealth Countries — Part II" (2001) Public L. 97, at 109, who wrote: "A concern that judges should not be seen to be implementing treaties by the 'back door' has been expressed in other cases as well. It demonstrates a judicial sensitivity to the primacy of parliament and the corresponding

STATUTORY INTERPRETATION AND THE CONTEXTUAL ARGUMENT

The different ways in which international treaties can be transformed in Canada through legislation will inform the proposed analytical scheme. The premise here is that international treaty law must be considered in terms of persuasive force (as opposed to being "binding") within the Canadian domestic legal system — that is, as being influential on the interpretation and application of legislative norms. Therefore, the most appropriate discourse to address, rationalize, and understand the national application of international law is that of the construction of statutes and, specifically, the contextual argument.

If there is a consensus on anything at the Supreme Court of Canada (as well as in lower courts) it is that, when it comes to statutory interpretation, the proper approach is that expressed by Elmer Driedger in his second edition of his celebrated book *Construction of Statutes:* "Today there is only one principle or approach, namely, the words of an act are to be read in their entire context in their grammatical and ordinary sense harmoniously with the scheme of the Act, the object of the Act and the intention of Parliament."[136] It has now become known as the "modern principle" of legislative interpretation in Canada and, as Iacobucci J. wrote in *Bell ExpressVu Limited Partnership* v. *Rex,* it "has been repeatedly cited by this Court as the *preferred approach* to statutory interpretation across a wide range of interpretive settings."[137] Even in the context of taxation, the principle applies, as Major J. pointed out in *Will-Kare Paving & Contracting Ltd.* v. *Canada:* "The modern approach to

---

need for caution in superintending the relationship between the external and internal legal order" [footnotes omitted]. See also R. Higgins, "The Relationship between International and Regional Human Rights Norms and Domestic Law" (1992) 18 Commonwealth L. Bulletin 1268, at 1274-75.

[136] E.A. Driedger, *Construction of Statutes,* 2nd ed. (Toronto: Butterworths, 1983), at 87.

[137] *Bell ExpressVu Limited Partnership* v. *Rex,* [2002] 2 S.C.R. 559, at 580 [emphasis added]. Iacobucci J. cited the following cases: *Stubart Investments Ltd.* v. *The Queen,* [1984] 1 S.C.R. 536, at 578; *Québec (Communauté urbaine)* v. *Corp. Notre-Dame de Bon-Secours,* [1994] 3 S.C.R. 3, at 17; *Rizzo & Rizzo Shoes Ltd. (Re),* [1998] 1 S.C.R. 27, at 40-41; *R.* v. *Gladue,* [1999] 1 S.C.R. 688, at 704; *R.* v. *Araujo,* [2000] 2 S.C.R. 992, at 1006-7; *R.* v. *Sharpe,* [2001] 1 S.C.R. 45, at 74-75 [hereinafter *Sharpe*]; and *Chieu* v. *Canada (Minister of Citizenship and Immigration),* [2002] 1 S.C.R. 84, at 101-2.

statutory interpretation has been applied by this Court to the interpretation of tax legislation."[138]

In *R.* v. *Ulybel Enterprises Ltd.*, Iacobucci J. further opined that the
"famous passage from Driedger 'best encapsulates' our court's preferred approach to statutory interpretation."[139] Likewise, according to Justice Charles Gonthier in *Barrie Public Utilities* v. *Canadian
Cable Television Assn.*: "The starting point for statutory interpretation in Canada is Driedger's definitive formulation."[140] The modern principle has recently been reformulated in *R.* v. *Jarvis*,[141] where
Iacobucci and Major JJ. paraphrased Driedger and wrote: "The
approach to statutory interpretation can be easily stated: one is to
seek the intent of Parliament by reading the words of the provision
in context and according to their grammatical and ordinary sense,
harmoniously with the scheme and the object of the statute."[142]

Of course, this modern approach to the construction of legislation contrasts with the old restrictive "plain meaning rule,"[143] which
was adopted at a time when it was seriously believed that "Parliament
changes the law for the worse"[144] and that a statute was an "alien
intruder in the house of the common law."[145] The plain meaning
rule is now generally considered obsolete in common law jurisdictions because courts realized that legislative language cannot be
read in isolation:[146] "The most fundamental objection to the rule
is that it is based on a false premise, namely that words have plain,

---

[138] *Will-Kare Paving & Contracting Ltd.* v. *Canada*, [2000] 1 S.C.R. 915, at 934.
Major J. cited the following two cases: *65302 British Columbia Ltd.* v. *Canada*,
[1999] 3 S.C.R. 804, at 810-11 and 832; and *Stubart Investments Ltd.* v. *The
Queen*, [1984] 1 S.C.R. 536, at 578.

[139] *R.* v. *Ulybel Enterprises Ltd.*, [2001] 2 S.C.R. 867, at 883.

[140] *Barrie Public Utilities* v. *Canadian Cable Television Assn.*, [2003] 1 S.C.R. 476, at
para. 20.

[141] *R.* v. *Jarvis*, [2002] 3 S.C.R. 757.

[142] *Ibid.*, at para. 77.

[143] On the "plain meaning rule" (or "literal rule") in general, see P.-A. Côté, *supra*
note 13, at 357-86.

[144] F. Pollock, *Essays in Jurisprudence and Ethics* (London: Macmillan, 1882), at 85.

[145] H. Stone, "The Common Law in the United States" (1936) 50 Harvard L. Rev.
4, at 15.

[146] See, on this point, S. Beaulac, "Le *Code civil* commande-t-il une interprétation
distincte?" (1999) 22 Dalhousie L.J. 236, at 251-52; and S. Beaulac, "Parliamentary Debates in Statutory Interpretation: A Question of Admissibility or of
Weight?" (1998) 43 McGill L.J. 287, at 310-12.

ordinary meanings apart from their context."[147] In England,[148] the House of Lords acknowledged this shift in favour of a purposive and contextual construction of legislation in *Pepper* v. *Hart*,[149] where Lord Griffiths said:

> The days have long passed when the courts adopted a strict constructionist view of interpretation which required them to adopt the literal meaning of the language. The courts now adopt a purposive approach which seeks to give effect to the true purpose of legislation and are prepared to look at much extraneous material that bears upon the background against which the legislation was enacted.[150]

British author Francis Bennion very recently reiterated the danger of the plain meaning rule — what he called the "first glance approach": "The informed [that is, modern] interpretation rule is to be applied no matter how plain the statutory words may seem at first glance."[151] Bennion went further and argued that, "*[w]ithout exception,* statutory words require careful assessment of themselves and their context if they are to be construed correctly."[152]

In Canada, L'Heureux-Dubé J. at the Supreme Court of Canada was one of the main proponents of a liberal approach to the interpretation of statutes. Already in *Hills* v. *Canada (Attorney General)*,[153] for which she wrote the majority decision in 1988, her views on the matter were well settled. Later in *2747-3174 Québec Inc.* v. *Quebec (Régie des permis d'alcool)*,[154] she wrote an impressive dissenting opinion in which she made an exhaustive historical and doctrinal

---

[147] M. Zander, *The Law-Making Process*, 4th ed. (London: Butterworths, 1994), at 121.

[148] See A. Lester, "English Judges as Law Makers" (1993) Public L. 269, at 272, who explains the old English approach thus: "Yet they [courts] decided that, to avoid 'making laws,' they were compelled to give effect to the 'plain and unambiguous' language of a statute, no matter that words are rarely plain or unambiguous in real life, and no matter how absurd might be the result of such a literal interpretation."

[149] *Pepper* v. *Hart*, [1993] A.C. 593 [hereinafter *Pepper*].

[150] *Ibid.*, at 617.

[151] F.A.R. Bennion, *Statutory Interpretation — A Code*, 4th ed. (London: Butterworths, 2002), at 500.

[152] *Ibid.* [emphasis added].

[153] *Hills* v. *Canada (Attorney General)*, [1988] 1 S.C.R. 513.

[154] *2747-3174 Québec Inc.* v. *Quebec (Régie des permis d'alcool)*, [1996] 3 S.C.R. 919 [hereinafter *Régie des permis d'alcool*].

review of the methodology of statutory interpretation. Her conclusion captured the essence of the modern approach:

> What Bennion calls the "informed interpretation" approach is called the "modern interpretation rule" by Sullivan and "pragmatic dynamism" by Eskridge. All these approaches reject the former "plain meaning" approach. In view of the many terms now being used to refer to these approaches, I will here use the term "modern approach" to designate a synthesis of the contextual approaches that reject the "plain meaning" approach. According to this "modern approach," consideration must be given at the outset not only to the words themselves but also, *inter alia*, to the context, the statute's other provisions, provisions of other statutes *in pari materia* and the legislative history in order to correctly identify the legislature's objective.[155]

She is obviously not alone anymore in openly holding that a proper interpretation and application of a statute must consider the context and purpose as well as the language of the enactment. One of the latest examples is found in *Harvard College* v. *Canada (Commissioner of Patents)*,[156] where Justice Michel Bastarache, for the majority, wrote: "This Court has on many occasions expressed the view that statutory interpretation cannot be based on the wording of the legislation alone."[157]

At the outset of the second edition of *Construction of Statutes*, Elmer Driedger forcefully expresses the view that in fact "[w]ords, when read *by themselves* in the abstract can hardly be said to have meanings."[158] In the latest edition of *Construction of Statutes*, Ruth Sullivan points out that "Driedger's modern principle is sometimes referred to as the *words-in-total-context approach*, a characterization that is apt."[159] Developing on the idea that words need to be read in context to identify their meanings,[160] she writes:

---

155 *Ibid.*, at 1002.

156 *Harvard College* v. *Canada (Commissioner of Patents)*, [2002] 4 S.C.R. 45.

157 *Ibid.*, at para. 154. Bastarache J. refered to the opinion of Iacobucci J. in *Rizzo & Rizzo Shoes Ltd. (Re)*, *supra* note 137, at 41. In addition, to the same effect, see the dissenting opinion by Bastarache and LeBel JJ. in *Macdonell* v. *Quebec (Commission d'accès à l'information)*, [2002] 3 S.C.R. 661, at 698, which reads: "[T]he interpretation of an Act cannot be based simply on its wording."

158 Driedger, *supra* note 136, at 3 [emphasis in original].

159 Sullivan, *supra* note 15, at 259 [emphasis added].

160 See also R. Sullivan, "Some Implications of Plain Language Drafting" (2001) 22 Statute L. Rev. 145, at 147-49. The author wrote: "Virtually everyone who studies language and communication agrees that, contrary to these assumptions, different readers bring different levels of competence and different contexts to their reading" (at 149) [footnotes omitted].

The meaning of a word depends on the context in which it is used. This basic principle of communication applies to all texts, including legislation. It has been repeatedly confirmed by linguists, linguistic philosophers, cognitive psychologists and others — by virtually anyone who studies communication through language. And it has long been recognized in law.[161]

A similar position, albeit more qualified, was taken by Pierre-André Côté in *Interpretation des lois*.[162] Randal Graham, using Derrida's deconstruction,[163] opines likewise:

By far the most important of these [interpretative] tools is often referred to as "the context." In ascertaining the meaning of a word or a written passage, we appeal to the context to guide our interpretation.[164]

In order to address, rationalize, and understand the national application of international law within the framework of statutory interpretation, treaties ought to be considered within this *modern approach* — that is, within the *words-in-total-context approach*. Ruth Sullivan, who now has a whole chapter on international law,[165] provides a list of contextual elements that includes, significantly, such norms:

Under Driedger's modern principle, the words to be interpreted must be looked at in their *total context*. This includes not only the Act as a whole and the statute book as a whole but also the legal context, consisting of case law, common law and *international law*. The primary significance

---

[161] Sullivan, *supra* note 15, at 259. This proposition was again recently affirmed by Bastarache and Lebel JJ., dissenting, in *Macdonell* v. *Quebec (Commission d'accès à l'information)*, *supra* note 157, at 698: "The plain meaning of the words will not be of much value if the court considers it without regard to the context of the statutory provision and the purposes of the Act."

[162] See Côté, *supra* note 13, at 355, where the author wrote: "Sans aller jusqu'à prétendre que les mots n'ont pas de sens en eux-mêmes, on doit admettre cependant que leur sens véritable dépend partiellement du context dans lequel ils sont employés" [footnotes omitted]. A similar somewhat qualified position was expressed by the American author W.N. Eskridge Jr., "The New Textualism" (1990) 37 U.C.L.A. L. Rev. 621, at 621: "The statute's text is the most important consideration in statutory interpretation, and a clear text ought to be given effect. Yet the meaning of a text critically depends upon its surrounding context."

[163] The French author Jacques Derrida has developed his ideas on deconstruction in several books, including J. Derrida, *Positions* (Paris: Minuit, 1972); J. Derrida, *Marges de la philosophie* (Paris: Minuit, 1972); and J. Derrida, *De la grammatologie* (Paris: Minuit, 1967).

[164] R.N. Graham, *Statutory Interpretation — Theory and Practice* (Toronto: Emond Montgomery, 2001), at 62-63.

[165] See Sullivan, *supra* note 15, at 421-39.

of legal context is that it supplies a set of norms that affect interpretation at every stage. These norms influence the intuitive process by which ordinary meaning is established; they are also relied on in textual, purposive and consequential analysis. Whether or not they are acknowledged, these norms are part of the mindset that lawyers and judges unavoidably bring to interpretation.[166]

This point is confirmed in the international legal literature where, for instance, Hugh Kindred writes that "where the context of the legislation includes a treaty of other international obligation, the statute should be interpreted in light of it."[167] The last section of this article will develop this idea and suggest guidelines to assist in determining the interpretative value and weight of international law as a contextual element in the construction of Canadian domestic statutes.

INTERNATIONAL TREATY NORMS AS CONTEXTUAL ELEMENTS OF INTERPRETATION

The argument defended throughout this article is that, fundamentally, the national application of international law is a question pertaining to the construction of statutes. Indeed, the legislative interpretation framework reflects that, far from being binding in Canada, international treaty law can only be influential or persuasive within the domestic legal system. Now, informed by the treaty implementation practices and in light of the modern approach to statutory interpretation, the main contribution consists in proposing an analytical scheme of the persuasive force of international law, which is based on the degree of incorporation of treaty norms within the Canadian legal system. However, first, it is necessary to briefly consider the so-called presumption of conformity with international law and the correlative ambiguity requirement.

CONTEXT RATHER THAN PRESUMPTION AND AMBIGUITY

Given the recent developments in regard to the methodology of statutory interpretation in Canada, especially with the modern principle that recognizes the proper role of context and remembering that it is more appropriate to consider international law as

---

[166] *Ibid.*, at 262 [emphasis added]. See also J. Simard, "L'interprétation législative au Canada : la théorie à l'épreuve de la pratique" (2001) 35 Rev. jur. Thémis 549, at 583 *ff.*

[167] Kindred, *supra* note 3, at 271.

an element of persuasion rather than an all-or-nothing "binding" factor, the old way in which courts were able to resort to norms from the international legal order should be reformulated in a more contemporary fashion.[168] The relevant presumption of conformity — which is similar to those regarding the conformity with the constitution or fundamental legal principles[169] — is a rule of interpretation according to which domestic statutes ought to be read, whenever possible, consistently with international law.[170] British author Peter Maxwell gives an early formulation of this rule when he writes that "every statute is to be so interpreted and applied, as far as its language admits, as not to be inconsistent with the comity of nations, or with the established rules of international law."[171] This

---

[168] This black-or-white approach to the domestic use of international law is illustrated by the decision of the Judicial Committee of the Privy Council in *Chung Chi Cheung* v. *The Queen*, [1939] A.C. 160, at 168, where Lord Atkin expressed the following view: "The Courts acknowledge the existence of a body of rules which nations accept amongst themselves. On any judicial issue they seek to ascertain what the relevant rule is, and, having found it, they will treat it as incorporated into domestic law, so far as it is not inconsistent with rules enacted by statutes or finally determined by their tribunals." In Canada, see the reasons of Justice Andrew MacKay of the Federal Court in *José Periera E. Hijos, S.A.* v. *Canada (Attorney General)*, [1997] 2 F.C. 84, at 100 (F.C.T.D.), who wrote that "[i]n construing domestic law, whether statutory or common law, the courts will seek to avoid construction or application that would conflict with the accepted principles of international law."

[169] See Côté, *supra* note 13, at 465: "L'interprète doit favoriser l'interprétation d'un texte qui permet de le concilier avec les textes qui énoncent des règles de niveau hiérarchique supérieur. On présume que le législateur n'entend pas déroger à ces règles, qu'il s'agisse de règles du droit international (1), de règles qui conditionnent la validité du texte (2) ou de règles énoncées dans certains textes de nature fondamentale (3)."

[170] See Sullivan, *supra* note 15, at 421: "Although international law is not binding on Canadian legislatures, it is presumed that the legislation enacted both federally and provincially is meant to comply with international law generally and with Canada's international law obligations in particular." In international legal literature, see also D.C. Vanek, "Is International Law Part of the Law of Canada?" (1960) 8 U. Toronto L.J. 251, at 259-60; Toope, *supra* note 8, at 538; and H.M. Kindred, *supra* note 3, at 269-70.

[171] P.B. Maxwell, *On the Interpretation of Statutes* (London: Sweet and Maxwell, 1896), at 122. See also, in England, *Corocraft* v. *Pan American Airways*, [1968] 3 W.L.R. 1273, at 1281 (C.A.), where Lord Denning wrote that there is a "duty of these courts to construe our legislation so as to be in conformity with international law and not in conflict with it." In international legal literature, see also H. Lauterpacht, "Is International Law a Part of the Law of England?" (1939) Transactions Grotius Society 51.

rule was enunciated clearly in Canada by Justice Louis-Philippe Pigeon in *Daniels* v. *White and The Queen:*

I wish to add that, in my view, this is a case for the application of the rule of construction that Parliament is not presumed to legislate in breach of a treaty or in any manner inconsistent with the comity of nations and the established rules of international law. It is a rule that is not often applied, *because if a statute is unambiguous, its provisions must be followed even if they are contrary to international law.*[172]

Very recently, the Supreme Court of Canada again referred to this presumption and, indeed, relied on this excerpt in *Schreiber* v. *Canada (Attorney General).*[173]

When examined closely, this passage from Pigeon J.'s opinion provides the reason why the presumption of conformity with international law does not any longer correspond to the statutory interpretation approach favoured in Canada. Namely, the preliminary requirement of the utilization of international law through such a presumption, which is to find that the statutory provision is *ambiguous.*[174] This precondition was considered by Justice Willard Estey in *Schavernoch* v. *Foreign Claims Commission,*[175] where he explained:

If one could assert an ambiguity, either patent or latent, in the Regulations it might be that a court could find support for making reference to matters external to the Regulations in order to interpret its terms. Because, however, there is in my view no ambiguity arising from the above-quote excerpt from these Regulations, there is no authority and none was drawn to our attention in argument entitling a court to take recourse either to an underlying international agreement or to textbooks on international law with reference to the negotiation of agreements or to take recourse to reports made to the Government of Canada by persons engaged in the negotiation referred to in the Regulations.[176]

---

[172] *Daniels* v. *White and The Queen,* [1968] S.C.R. 517, at 541 [emphasis added].

[173] *Schreiber* v. *Canada (Attorney General),* [2002] 3 S.C.R. 269, at 293-94. See also, on the *Schreiber* case, S. Beaulac, "Recent Developments on the Role of International Law in Canadian Statutory Interpretation" (2004) 25 Statute L. Rev. 19.

[174] See also the decision of the Judicial Committee of the Privy Council in *Collco Dealings* v. *Inland Revenue Commissioners,* [1962] A.C. 1, at 19, where Viscount Simonds said: "My Lords, the language that I have used is taken from a passage of p. 148 of the 10th edition of 'Maxwell on the Interpretation of Statutes' which ends with the sentence: 'But if the statute is unambiguous, its provisions must be followed even if they are contrary to international law.'"

[175] *Schavernoch* v. *Foreign Claims Commission,* [1982] 1 S.C.R. 1092 [hereinafter *Schavernoch*].

[176] *Ibid.,* at 1098. See also, to the same effect, the reasons by Chief Justice Boris Laskin in *Capital Cities, supra* note 69, at 173.

The main problem with such an ambiguity requirement is that it perpetuates the empty rhetoric of the plain meaning rule.[177] Another concern is how difficult it is to determine whether or not the legislation is ambiguous or unambiguous.[178] As Lord Oliver of Aylmerton pointed out in *Pepper:* "Ingenuity can sometimes suggest ambiguity or obscurity where none exists in fact."[179]

The truth of the matter is that, when judges hold that a statutory provision is clear or that it is ambiguous, they have in fact already construed the legislation.[180] L'Heureux-Dubé J., dissenting in *Régie des permis d'alcool*, considered this point and appositely observed that, "[i]n reality, the 'plain meaning' *can be nothing but* the result of an *implicit process* of legal interpretation."[181] Indeed, rather than being something *a priori*, legislative ambiguity is a conclusion — can really be only a conclusion — that is reached at the end of the process of interpretation. Ambiguity is in effect a determination that can be made only after a full assessment of the intention of Parliament, using canons and tools of statutory interpretation, including international law as a contextual element.

It is illogical and thus erroneous to require that legislation be ambiguous as a preliminary threshold test to the interpretation of legislation either in general or specifically with respect to the use of international law as an aid to the construction of statutes. This was the conclusion reached by Gonthier J. in *National Corn Growers Assn. v. Canada (Import Tribunal)*,[182] where he effectively narrowed down Estey J.'s statement in *Schavernoch*[183] and wrote that "it is

---

[177] On this point, see S. Beaulac, "Recent Developments at the Supreme Court of Canada on the Use of Parliamentary Debates" (2000) 63 Saskatchewan L. Rev. 581, at 602.

[178] See, generally, C.B. Nutting, "The Ambiguity of Unambiguous Statutes" (1940) 24 Minnesota L. Rev. 509.

[179] *Pepper, supra* note 149, at 620.

[180] See, on this general issue, Zander, *supra* note 147, at 121-27; W.N. Eskridge, *Dynamic Statutory Interpretation* (Cambridge, MA: Harvard University Press, 1994), at 38-41; N.J. Singer, *Statutes and Statutory Construction*, vol. 2A, 5th ed. (New York: Clak Boardman Callaghan, 1992), at 5-6; V. van de Kerchove, *L'interprétation en droit — Approche pluridisciplinaire* (Brussels: Facultés universitaires St-Louis, 1978); F.E. Horack Jr., "In the Name of Legislative Intention" (1932) 38 West Virginia L.Q. 119, at 121; and M. Radin, "Statutory Interpretation" (1930) 43 Harvard L. Rev. 863, at 869.

[181] *Régie des permis d'alcool, supra* note 154, at 997 [emphasis in original].

[182] *National Corn Growers Assn. v. Canada (Import Tribunal)*, [1990] 2 S.C.R. 1324 [hereinafter *National Corn Growers*].

[183] *Schavernoch, supra* note 175, at 1098.

reasonable to make reference to an international agreement *at the very outset* of the inquiry to determine if there is any ambiguity, even latent, in the domestic legislation."[184] Ruth Sullivan also notes the problems with the reasoning behind the ambiguity requirement and agrees that no such preliminary condition is necessary before resorting to international law.[185]

The new position that holds that domestic courts in Canada do not have to find an ambiguity or an obscurity in the statutory provision before construing it as having a regard to international law falls squarely within Driedger's modern principle of legislative interpretation. This words-in-total-context approach also commands that the old way to resort to international law, by invoking the presumption of conformity, be reformulated in terms of the purposive and contextual method of statutory interpretation. Indeed, international treaty law ought to be considered in all cases — not only when one artificially concludes that there is an ambiguity — as an *element of context* that, as Dickson J. wrote in *R. v. Zingre*, would allow for "a fair and liberal interpretation with a view to fulfilling Canada's international obligations."[186]

Ruth Sullivan accurately noticed that the recent trend at the Supreme Court of Canada — in decisions such as *Baker, Suresh, R. v. Sharpe,*[187] and *114957 Canada Ltée (Spraytech)* v. *Hudson (Town)*[188] — is an increased open "reliance on international law as legal context."[189] In this regard, it is interesting to point out that in *Baker*[190] Justice L'Heureux-Dubé relied on an excerpt of the third edition of the *Construction of Statutes,* where Sullivan writes:

---

184 *National Corn Growers, supra* note 182, at 1371 [emphasis added]. Similarly, see M. Hunt, *Using Human Rights Law in English Courts* (Oxford: Hart, 1997), at 40, where the author writes: "So instead of asking if there is ambiguity which can be resolved with the 'assistance' of international law, on this approach the court should ask, having automatically considered the international law alongside the national law, whether the domestic law is unambiguously (in the sens of irreconcilably) in conflict with the international norms."

185 See Sullivan, *supra* note 15, at 437-38.

186 *R. v. Zingre,* [1981] 2 S.C.R. 392, at 409-10.

187 *Sharpe, supra* note 137.

188 *114957 Canada Ltée (Spraytech)* v. *Hudson (Town),* [2001] 2 S.C.R. 241 [hereinafter *Spraytech*].

189 Sullivan, *supra* note 15, at 426.

190 *Baker, supra* note 2 at 861.

Second, the legislature is presumed to respect the values and principles enshrined in international law, both customary and conventional. *These constitute a part of the legal context in which legislation is enacted and read.* In so far as possible, therefore, interpretations that reflect these values and principles are preferred.[191]

Justice L'Heureux-Dubé thus endorsed Sullivan's view on the relevance of international law as a *contextual element of interpretation.* It is certainly meaningful that her ladyship did not refer to — and thus did not endorse — what Sullivan writes about the presumption of compliance, which is in the preceding two sentences.[192] Therefore, an argument can be made that *Baker* stands as an authority for the proposition that the appropriate way to consider international law is now as an element of context and not through a presumption of conformity.[193]

In *Rahaman* v. *Canada (Minister of Citizenship and Immigration)*,[194] Justice Kerry P. Evans of the Federal Court of Appeal referred to *Baker* and *Suresh* and opined that "[n]owadays, there is no doubt that, even when not incorporated by Act of Parliament into Canadian law, international norms are *part of the context* within which domestic statutes are to be interpreted."[195] He further wrote, quite significantly, that, "[o]f course, the *weight* to be afforded to international norms that have not been incorporated by statute into Canadian law will depend on all the circumstances of the case."[196] There is no reason why these remarks do not equally apply to international law that *has been* implemented within the Canadian domestic legal system. Given that such legal norms are authoritative and persuasive — and not binding — the national application of

---

[191] Sullivan, *supra* note 12, at 330 [emphasis added].

[192] This passage, at *ibid.*, reads: "First, the legislature is presumed to comply with the obligations owed by Canada as a signatory of international instruments and more generally as a member of the international community. In choosing among possible interpretations, therefore, the court avoid interpretations that would put Canada in breach of any of its international obligations."

[193] See S. Beaulac, "L'interprétation de la *Charte:* Reconsidération de l'approche téléologique et réévaluation du rôle du droit international," in G.-A. Beaudoin and E. Mendes (eds.), *The Canadian Charter of Rights and Freedoms*, 4th ed. (Toronto: Carswell, 2004, forthcoming). This is an aspect of the *Baker* case that Jutta Brunnée and Stephen Toope also noticed, but which they used to argue that the majority should have resorted to the old approach of the presumption of conformity with international law. See Brunnée and Toope, *supra* note 9, at 42-43.

[194] *Rahaman* v. *Canada (Minister of Citizenship and Immigration)*, [2002] 3 F.C. 537.

[195] *Ibid.*, at 558 [emphasis added].

[196] *Ibid.* [emphasis added].

international law should always be considered as a question of *weight*, as Evans J. put it.

ANALYTICAL SCHEME OF PERSUASIVE FORCE OF TREATY NORMS

Now that all the building blocks have been laid down, it is possible to put forward an analytical scheme to determine the persuasive force of international law in interpreting statutes. These issues had to be examined first, however, starting with the fundamental proposition that international law in our Westphalian system is not "binding" within a sovereign state such as Canada, then moving to the treaty implementation techniques that ought to inform the statutory interpretation framework, which is the most appropriate to use in order to address, rationalize, and understand the national application of international law. It was also seen that today's legislative interpretation discourse endorses Driedger's modern principle. Away from the plain meaning rule or any preliminary threshold of ambiguity, this approach advocates the construction of enactments in context — an element of which is, of course, international treaty law.

International Treaty Norms as an Element of Internal Context

The proposed analytical scheme of the persuasive force of treaty norms, as an element of the contextual interpretation of Canadian legislation, is based on their degree of incorporation within the domestic legal system. Simply put, the clearer it is that the parliamentary authority intended to give effect to international law through the transformation of the convention, the more weight a court should recognize and attribute to such norms in the process of ascertaining the meaning of the statutory provision.[197] There is obviously quite a spectrum of different levels of domestic incorporation of international treaties. Based on the two techniques of legislative implementation examined earlier in this article — incorporation by reference and harmonization[198] — the main categories of implementation are as follows:

---

[197] See, however, Brandon, *supra* note 67, at 443, who wrongly dissociated, on the one hand, the way in which the parliamentary authority implemented an international treaty law and, on the other, the intention of Parliament in regard to the transformation of such norms in the domestic legal system. She writes: "It is contended that the method of implementation is less important than are indications of an intention to implement."

[198] See footnotes 97-106 and accompanying text.

- directly through reference or reproduction of treaty norms in statute;
- directly by scheduling treaty and intention to thus implement;
- indirectly through the adoption of a statute based on treaty; and
- indirectly by amending or repealing existing legislation.[199]

In terms of contextual interpretation, the first two categories of incorporated treaty norms form part of the "internal-immediate-context" — they are *internal* in the sense that the statute incorporates them within itself, thus embodying and giving direct effect domestically to such international norms, and they are *immediate* in that they are so intrinsically intertwined with the legislation that to construe the domestic legal norms amounts to construing the international legal norms.[200] This is why, in such situations, courts must use the "wording of the Convention and the rules of treaty interpretation,"[201] which are found in Articles 31 and 32 of the Vienna Convention on the Law of Treaties,[202] as the majority of the Supreme Court of Canada wrote in *Pushpanathan v. Canada (Minister of Citizenship and Immigration)*. To this extent, therefore, Bill Schabas is right to say: "Hence, the exercise is one of treaty

---

[199] These categories borrow, in part, from the following excerpt in Macdonald, *supra* note 96, at 311: "A treaty may be implemented by legislation in one of three ways: first, Parliament may translate the treaty into a number of statutes or amendments to existing statutes; second, it may enact a general law which uses the key terms of the treaty; finally, it may directly enact the treaty, with an appropriate preamble, into English law."

[200] See Sullivan, *supra* note 15, at 430, where she writes: "Although it becomes part of domestic legislation it retains its identity as an instrument of international law. It carries its international law baggage with it."

[201] *Pushpanathan v. Canada (Minister of Citizenship and Immigration)*, [1998] 1 S.C.R. 982, at 1019-20, *per* Bastarache J. [hereinafter *Pushpanathan*]. See also *R. c. Parisien*, [1988] 1 S.C.R. 950, at 958; *Crown Forest Industries Ltd. v. Canada*, [1995] 2 S.C.R. 802, at 827; and *R. v. Palacio* (1984), 7 D.L.R. (4th) 112, at 120 (Ontario C.A.). In *Thomson v. Thomson*, *supra* note 102, at 577, La Forest J., for the majority, wrote that, except for *travaux préparatoire*: "By and large, international treaties are interpreted in a manner similar to statutes." On this point, see also Kindred *et al.*, *supra* note 17, at 202.

[202] Vienna Convention, *supra* note 54. It is interesting that in *Canada (Attorney General) v. Ward*, [1993] 2 S.C.R. 689, at 713 *ff.*, La Forest J. appears to use the rules of treaty interpretation (in particular, those concerning *travaux préparatoires*), without mentioning the Vienna Convention in order to assist in interpreting the Immigration Act (*supra* note 100).

interpretation and not statutory interpretation,"[203] This type of international law context should have the most persuasive force.[204]

An illustration of the first category, which is where there is direct implementation through the reference or reproduction of treaty norms in the legislation, is in *Pushpanathan*,[205] where section 2(1) of the Immigration Act[206] incorporated by Reference Article 1F of the Convention Relating to the Status of Refugees.[207] An example of the second category, where there is direct implementation because the treaty is reproduced in a schedule and there is an intention to thereby incorporate the conventional norms, is the situation in *Thomson* v. *Thomson*,[208] where Manitoba's Child Custody Enforcement Act[209] had the Hague Convention of the Civil Aspects of International Child Abduction[210] in a schedule and had an express provision (section 17) indicating a clear legislative intention to implement the corresponding international norms.

The last two categories of incorporated treaty norms form part of the "internal-extended-context" — they are also *internal* in the sense that they have direct effect on the interpretation of the statute but they are *extended* (not immediate) in that the parliamentary authority did not accept them as international legal norms but rather changed them into domestic legal norms through the process of transformation. This second group of incorporated treaty law, unlike the previous one, is really only domestic in nature and, although due regard should be given to its international filiation, such internal legislation must be interpreted according to the

---

[203] Schabas, *supra* note 44, at 178. See also, interestingly, Sullivan, *supra* note 15, at 430-31: "In interpreting an incorporated provision, the court appropriately looks to international law materials and to interpretations of the incorporated provision by international courts or by courts in other jurisdictions."

[204] Having said that, like any other interpretative argument, a contextual element such as international law can never be "determinative" on the construction of a statutory provision. Accordingly, the following statement by Brunnée and Toope, *supra* note 9, at 26, appears questionable: "When a treaty has been explicitly transformed into Canadian law, its provisions should be *determinative* in the interpretation of domestic legislation" [emphasis added].

[205] *Pushpanathan, supra* note 201.

[206] Immigration Act, *supra* note 100.

[207] Convention Relating to the Status of Refugees, *supra* note 101.

[208] *Thomson, supra* note 102.

[209] Child Custody Enforcement Act, S.M. 1982, c. 27 (now R.S.M. 1987, c. C360).

[210] Hague Convention of the Civil Aspects of International Child Abduction, *supra* note 103.

principles of statutory interpretation.[211] Ruth Sullivan writes that, for such implementing statutes, "the court still looks to international law materials and interpretations but it considers the domestic context as well and in particular *it relies on domestic rules and techniques of interpretation.*"[212] This type of international law context, nevertheless, has substantial persuasive force.

An illustration of the third category, where there is indirect implementation through the adoption of legislation based on the intentional convention, is the situation in *W. (V.)* v. *S. (D.)*,[213] where Québec's Act Respecting the Civil Aspects of International and Interprovincial Child Abduction[214] was based on the Hague Convention of the Civil Aspects of International Child Abduction[215] and, accordingly, did not integrate *per se* the treaty norms. An example of the fourth category, where there is indirect implementation because of the amendment or the repeal of existing legislation, is the situation in *Pfizer*,[216] where Part II of the World Trade Organization Agreement Implementation Act[217] amended and repealed several statutory provisions of federal legislation to bring them into line with Canada's international obligations, but was deemed not to incorporate the WTO Agreement,[218] which was scheduled in the said implementing statute.[219]

---

[211] See *Schavernoch, supra* note 175, at 1098, where Estey J. wrote: "Here the regulations fall to be interpreted according to the maxims of interpretation applicable to Canadian law generally." See also *Crown Zellerbach, supra* note 119, where the Supreme Court of Canada interpreted the federal statute at issue as a domestic piece of legislation, although it was indirectly implementing an international agreement. See also, at the Federal Court of Canada, *R.* v. *Seaboard Lumber Sales Co.*, [1994] 2 F.C. 647 (F.C.T.D.).

[212] Sullivan, *supra* note 15, at 431 [emphasis added].

[213] *W. (V.)* v. *S. (D.), supra* note 105.

[214] Act Respecting the Civil Aspects of International and Interprovincial Child Abduction, R.S.Q., c. A-23.01.

[215] Hague Convention of the Civil Aspects of International Child Abduction, *supra* note 103.

[216] *Pfizer, supra* note 109.

[217] World Trade Organization Agreement Implementation Act, *supra* note 117.

[218] WTO Agreement, *supra* note 116.

[219] See also the following decision, in similar circumstances and to the same effect, by the Quebec Court of Appeal, *UL Canada Inc.* v. *Procureur du Québec*, 500-09-008256-992, 1 October 2003.

International Treaty Norms as an Element of External Context

International norms that do not meet the implementation requirement examined earlier[220] are not, strictly speaking, part of Canadian law; but Pigeon J., dissenting in *Capital Cities Communications Inc.* v. *Canada (C.R.T.C.)*, was right in saying that it "is an over-simplification to say that treaties are of no legal effect unless implemented by legislation."[221] Thus, although their potential influence on the construction of a statute is greatly reduced — especially in light of the separation of powers, federalist and democratic arguments — there are four other categories of international treaty norms that must be considered for the present purposes. They are:

- treaty norms that are unimplemented by statute;
- unimplemented treaty norms created after the adoption of a statute;
- unratified and even unsigned international treaties; and
- "soft-obligation" treaties (and perhaps other "soft-law" instruments).

In terms of contextual interpretation, all of these international norms form part of the "external context." They are *external* in the sense suggested by Ruth Sullivan: "The external context of a provision is the setting in which the provision was enacted, its historical background, and the setting in which it operates from time to time."[222] She notices that the Supreme Court of Canada has referred to these elements as social context, which "encompasses any facts that are judged to be relevant to the *conception* and *operation* of legislation, whether social, political, economic, cultural, historical or institutional."[223]

The international norms of these four categories — and, arguably, international customs and general principles, although these are beyond the scope of the present discussion,[224] — are relevant to the interpretation and application of statutes even though they

---

[220] See footnotes 57-72 and 107-35 and accompanying text.

[221] *Capital Cities, supra* note 69, at 188.

[222] R. Sullivan, *supra* note 15, at 457.

[223] *Ibid.* [emphasis added].

[224] As stated at the outset of the present article, no position is taken with regard to the domestic role of international customary law nor, for that matter, of the general principles of international law.

are *not* part of the laws of Canada.[225] These norms were privy to the original conception or are relevant to the contemporary operation of the enactment and, to borrow from the *Baker* case,[226] the "values" they represent and enshrine ought to legitimately inform legislative interpretation. Therefore, unimplemented treaty norms, as well as unimplemented treaty norms created after the adoption of the statute, form part of the "external-immediate-context" — they are *immediate* in that, although external to the statute *per se,* the norms have been given some authority, through ratification, by an organ of government (that is, the executive branch) as the expression of an international consensus. An undeniable degree of persuasive force should thus be recognized and attributed to such international legal norms as a valuable element of context to the construction of statutes.

The first category of treaty norms that are unimplemented by legislation is of course the situation in the *Baker* case, where the majority, *per* L'Heureux-Dubé J., used the values associated with the notion of the "best interest of the child" in Article 3(1) of the Convention on the Rights of the Child,[227] which had not been transformed through legislation in Canada, as a contextual element to interpret the discretionary power of an immigration officer granted pursuant to section 114(2) of the Immigration Act.[228] The second category of unimplemented treaty norms created after the adoption of the legislation under scrutiny was also the situation in *Baker* because, to be precise about it, the Immigration Act[229] was adopted in 1976 while the Convention on the Rights of the Child[230] entered into force in 1990 and was actually ratified by Canada in 1992, thus post-dating the legislative provision at issue.

The last two categories of international norms form part of the "external-extended-context" — they are *extended* as well as external

---

[225] See footnote 94 and accompanying text.

[226] In *Baker, supra* note 2 at 861, L'Heureux-Dubé J. famously wrote: "I agree with the respondent and the Court of Appeal that the Convention has not been implemented by Parliament. Its provisions there have no direct application within Canadian law. Nevertheless, the *values* reflected in international human rights law may help inform the contextual approach to statutory interpretation and judicial review" [emphasis added].

[227] Convention on the Rights of the Child, 20 November 1989, 1577 U.N.T.S. 3, 28 I.L.M. 1448, Can. T.S. 1992 No. 3 (entered into force on 2 September 1990).

[228] Immigration Act, *supra* note 100.

[229] *Ibid.*

[230] Convention on the Rights of the Child, *supra* note 227.

because they represent no more than the opinion of government representatives, or other actors on the international plane, with respect to legal norms relevant to the conception or operation of the Canadian statute. In *Re Canada Labour Code*,[231] Justice La Forest referred to an unratified treaty (the North Atlantic Treaty Status of Forces Agreement[232]) and wrote that "[it] has no legal effect in Canada, as it has not been ratified by domestic legislation. [*sic*] Inasmuch as it might influence the interpretation of the Act, a contrary interpretation is demanded by Article I of the Leased Bases Agreement."[233] Ruth Sullivan refers to this excerpt after explaining that "[t]he body of international conventions, including conventions to which Canada may not be a signatory, forms part of the legal context in which legislation *is drafted* and *operates*."[234]

In regard to "soft-obligation" treaties,[235] Jutta Brunnée and Stephen Toope agree that international instruments such as declarations, codes of conduct — and, presumably, unratified and unsigned treaties — have a place as secondary elements of contextual interpretation: "There is no reason why Canadian courts should not draw upon these types of norms," they write, "so long as they do so in a manner that recognizes their non-binding [that is, less persuasive] quality."[236] An illustration of such external-extended-context is the situation in *Spraytech*,[237] where L'Heureux-Dubé J. referred to the Bergen Ministerial Declaration on Sustainable Development in the ECE Region[238] as a non-binding international instrument to which Canada is a signatory, as evidence of the

---

[231] *Re Canada Labour Code*, [1992] 2 S.C.R. 50.

[232] North Atlantic Treaty Status of Forces Agreement, Can. T.S. 1953 No. 13.

[233] *Re Canada Labour Code*, *supra* note 231.

[234] Sullivan, *supra* note 12, at 464 [emphasis added].

[235] For a definition of "soft-law," see C.M. Chinkin, "The Challenge of Soft Law: Development and Change in International Law" (1989) 38 Int'l & Comp. L.Q. 850, at 851: "Soft law instruments range from treaties, but which include only soft obligations ('legal soft law'), to non-binding or voluntary resolutions and codes of conduct formulated and accepted by international and regional organisations ('non-legal soft law'), to statements prepared by individuals in a non-governmental capacity, but which purport to lay down international principles" [footnotes omitted].

[236] Brunnée and Toope, *supra* note 9, at 62.

[237] *Spraytech*, *supra* note 188.

[238] Bergen Ministerial Declaration on Sustainable Development in the ECE Region, 6 August 1990, Doc. A/CONF.151/PC/10, reprinted in (1990) 1 Y.B. Int'l Environmental L. 429.

so-called precautionary principle in international environmental law, which her ladyship used to confirm the interpretation given to a municipal by-law adopted pursuant to section 410(1) of the Quebec's Cities and Towns Act.[239]

CONCLUSION

To recall the hypothesis that is central to this article, it is argued that the national application of international law is, as far as Canadian judges and other domestic actors are concerned, an issue pertaining to statutory interpretation, which must thus be addressed, rationalized, and understood within this framework. In order to prepare the ground for the main proposition, the erroneous claim that international law "binds" Canada (that is, binds *within* Canada) had to be rebutted, having regard to the general tenets of our international law system. Then, after considering the practices followed by parliamentary authorities to implement international treaties, Driedger's modern principle was examined in detail, including the important role of context in ascertaining the meaning of legislation. Finally, a set of directives was put forward to assist in the determination of the persuasive force of the international law argument.

The proposed analytical scheme speaks within the discourse of statutory interpretation and considers the matter in which conventions were implemented in Canada and, accordingly, is based on the degree of incorporation of treaty norms within the domestic legal system. It follows that, all things being otherwise equal, the weight of the different types of international law contexts (grouping the eight categories of treaty norms identified earlier) can be ranked thus in a decreasing order of authority:

• internal-immediate-context;
• internal-extended-context;
• external-immediate-context; and
• external-extended-context.

That being said, the flexibility of any guidelines meant to help in the construction of statutes is crucial in order to allow the consideration of the particular circumstances of each enactment and of each interpretative situation. Therefore, the hierarchy of the persuasive force of international law as a contextual element suggested in this article is by no means absolute.

[239] Cities and Towns Act, R.S.Q., c. C-19, as amended.

Sommaire

L'application du droit international en droit interne: la perspective de l'interprétation législative

Bien que l'application du droit international en droit interne ait suscité beaucoup d'intérêt depuis quelques années, le point de vue national dans le débat n'a pas été considéré adéquatement. L'auteur soutient que le recours au droit international est, pour le juge canadien et les autres intervenants nationaux, une question d'interprétation des lois qui doit être abordée, rationalisée et comprise dans cette optique. Tout d'abord, on rappelle la validité du principe selon lequel les tribunaux canadiens ne sont pas liés par les normes internationales, y compris celles issues de traité, et ce malgré certains prononcés judiciaires et doctrinaux qui laissent entendre le contraire. Le droit international ne peut être contraignant puisque notre modèle "westphalien" de relations internationales, régi par la structure juridique "vattelienne," postule l'existence d'un domaine international qui est distinct et séparé des sphères nationales. De là l'exigence de mettre en œuvre par voie législative les conventions internationales. Nos tribunaux interprètent et appliquent le droit canadien; le droit international peut les influencer dans la mesure où ce droit issu de traité fait partie du droit interne, mais il ne peut jamais les lier. La seconde partie, et c'est l'apport principal du texte, présente un modèle d'analyse de la force persuasive du droit international. À cette fin, il faut examiner la pratique en matière de mise en œuvre de traité et comment elle est liée à l'intention du parlement — indiquant l'impossibilité de l'incorporation passive. Il faut aussi tenir compte de la méthode moderne d'interprétation des lois de Driedger, qui favorise le recours au droit international comme élément contextuel dans tous les cas plutôt que comme présomption de conformité liée à l'exigence préliminaire, et artificielle, d'ambiguïté. En bout d'analyse, il est démontré que le poids de l'argument de droit international dépendra du degré d'incorporation des normes conventionnelles dans le système juridique canadien. À cet égard, il y aurait quatre types de contexte dans lesquels tomberaient les catégories de normes issues de traité. Dans l'ordre décroissant de leur autorité persuasive: (a) le contexte interne immédiat, (b) le contexte interne élargi, (c) le contexte externe immédiat et (d) le contexte externe élargi.

Summary

National Application of International Law: The Statutory Interpretation Perspective

In recent years, although the national application of international law has gathered much interest, the domestic point of view on the issue has not been adequately considered. The argument defended in this article is that the domestic use of international law is, as far as Canadian judges and other domestic actors are concerned, a question of statutory interpretation, which must be addressed, rationalized, and understood within this framework. First, the author refers to the principle according to which Canadian courts are not bound by international norms, including treaty norms, which is still valid even though some judicial and doctrinal statements seem to challenge it. International law cannot be binding upon national courts because the "Westphalian" model of international relations, regulated by the "Vattelian" legal structure, postulates the existence of an international plane that is distinct and separate from the internal spheres. Hence, the requirement that international conventions be implemented through the adoption of domestic legislation. Our courts interpret and apply Canadian law and, to the extent that international treaty law is part of domestic law, it may have an influence on them, but without ever binding them. The second part, and the main contribution of the article, consists of an analytical scheme of the persuasive force of international law. The practices of treaty implementation and how it relates to parliamentary intent — showing also that passive incorporation is impossible — as well as Driedger's modern approach to statutory interpretation, which favours recourse to international law as a contextual element in all cases over a presumption of conformity involving the preliminary and artificial requirement of ambiguity are discussed in the article. In the final analysis, it is shown that the weight of the international law argument shall be based on the degree of incorporation of treaty norms within the Canadian legal system. In this regard, there would be four types of context in which fall the categories of treaty norms. In decreasing order of persuasive authority: (1) internal-immediate context; (2) internal-extended context; (3) external-immediate context; and (4) external-extended context.

Notes and Comments /
Notes et commentaires

Les transferts de populations quatre-vingts ans après la Convention de Lausanne

L e droit international des réfugiés s'est inscrit dès ses origines dans une tradition pragmatique, contrairement à la protection internationale des droits de l'homme qui est profondément inspirée par un idéalisme néo-kantien. Le Haut Commissaire pour les réfugiés nommé par la Société des Nations à la suite de la Première Guerre mondiale, le Docteur Fridtjof Nansen,[1] a dû faire face aux limites de l'action humanitaire en plein milieu d'un conflit armé dès 1922 quand la nouvelle armée nationaliste turque a vaincu l'expédition militaire grecque en Anatolie. La crise en Asie Mineure a effectivement mis en lumière les dilemmes liés aux conflits ethniques caractérisés par des transferts de populations. Ces dilemmes continuent à affecter de nombreuses personnes en zone de conflit et à poser des problèmes quasiment insolubles pour les institutions internationales.

Bien que la forme de cette pratique varie à travers l'histoire,[2] le déplacement forcé des populations ennemies constitue depuis des siècles une stratégie utilisée par des belligérants pour renforcer leur mainmise politique sur un territoire. Le XXe siècle connaît de nombreux exemples de déplacement forcé et prémédité ayant pour objectif de consolider le pouvoir politique. La séparation des populations en Europe, au Moyen Orient et sur le sous-continent

---

[1] Voir Jon Sörensen, *The Saga of Fridtjof Nansen*, New York, Norton Publishers, 1932 à la p. 282. Voir aussi la lettre du Dr Nansen, 1er septembre 1921, Doc. SDN C.337.M.239.1921. Nansen a occupé le poste à partir du 20 août 1921.

[2] Voir, par exemple, Walter Schätzel, "Les transferts internationaux de populations: Réponses," AIDI, vol. 44, t. II, avril 1952 à la p. 182: "Les temps ne sont pas trop éloignés où, en Europe même, des États s'imaginaient qu'il était de l'intérêt public de se débarrasser des hommes d'une autre religion ou confession."

indien figurent parmi les exemples les plus notoires de cette forme de violence au XXe siècle.

Hélas, les gouvernements non-occidentaux ne sont pas les seuls à contempler de telles mesures en temps de conflit armé. Les déportations massives des populations allemandes ont été discutées ouvertement dans les parlements britannique et américain à la fin de la Seconde Guerre mondiale.[3] Les transferts de populations menés par les forces armées occidentales lors des opérations de contre-insurrection et lors des luttes coloniales dans les années 1950 et 1960 sont également des exemples de déplacements qui ont pour but d'accroître le contrôle territorial en temps de conflit. Qu'il s'agisse des "camps de regroupement" établis par les militaires français en Algérie,[4] des programmes de *"villagisation"* mis en œuvre par les soldats britanniques au Kenya[5] ou des *"strategic hamlets"* supervisés par les troupes américaines dans le Vietnam du Sud,[6] il est clair que le déplacement prémédité des populations civiles est parfois considéré comme une option stratégique dans la conduite contemporaine des conflits armés.

---

[3] Le premier ministre Sir Winston Churchill: "The transference of several millions of people would have to be effected from the East to the West or North, as well as the expulsion of the Germans — because that is what is proposed: the total expulsion of the Germans from the area to be acquired by Poland in the West and the North." 406 Parliamentary Debates, House of Commons (5e sér.) 1713 (1944).

[4] Michel Cornaton, *Les Camps de regroupement de la guerre d'Algérie*, Paris, L'Harmattan, 1998.

[5] Frank Furedi, *The Mau Mau War in Perspective*, Oxford, James Currey Publishers, 1989. Pour des informations sur les abus commis par les troupes britanniques lors de la rébellion Mau Mau, voir l'épisode "Mau Mau" de l'émission *"Secret History"* (Channel Four) diffusé le 24 août 1999. Voir aussi l'étude de Sir Robert Thompson, *Defeating Communist Insurgency: The Lessons of Malaya and Vietnam*, New York, Praeger, 1966.

[6] "People were forcibly uprooted from their homes and ancestral graves and herded into unprepared compounds where they were instructed to build a new hamlet and construct defences from sharpened bamboo poles and barbed wire." T. Louise Brown, *War and Aftermath in Vietnam*, London, Routledge, 1991 aux pp. 216-17. Voir aussi Milton E. Osborne, *Strategic Hamlets in South Vietnam: A Survey and Comparison*, Ithaca (NY), Cornell University Press, 1965, et Richard A. Falk, *"Son My: War Crimes and Individual Responsibility,"* dans Richard Falk (dir.), *The Vietnam War and International Law*, vol. 3, Princeton, Princeton University Press, 1972 à la p. 329. Sur un problème distinct qui soulève certaines questions similaires, voir *Hirabayashi v. United States* (320 U.S. 81 (1943)) et *Korematsu v. United States* (323 U.S. 214 (1944)) où la majorité des juges de la Cour suprême des États-Unis ont estimé que la réinstallation des Américains d'origine japonaise pendant la Seconde Guerre mondiale était justifiée par la nécessité militaire.

Cet article explore les dilemmes qui résultent quand une population habitant un territoire multiethnique est expulsée ou évacuée afin d'empêcher une continuation de la violence interethnique. Le droit international doit lutter contre le nettoyage ethnique[7] s'il veut préserver son autorité morale. Cependant, si l'application des normes juridiques n'arrive pas à prévenir le nettoyage ethnique, la possibilité de réglementer par traité certains aspects du transfert de populations ne devrait pas être écartée dans la mesure où cette approche permet de promouvoir la paix et éviter des massacres.[8] L'argumentation présentée dans cet article provient de la constatation que les conflits contemporains continuent d'être caractérisés par le nettoyage ethnique et les transferts *de facto*, malgré les nouvelles normes des droits de l'homme qui ont caractérisé le développement du droit international au XXe siècle.

---

[7] Le terme est utilisé pour désigner "le fait d'obliger les personnes appartenant à une race ou un groupe ethnique particulier à quitter une région afin de provoquer un changement durable de la situation démographique de la région." Georges Abi-Saab *et al.*, *Avis relatif aux problèmes juridiques liés à certains transferts et déplacements de population sur le territoire de la République de Chypre*, Law Office of the Republic of Cyprus, 30 juin 1999 au par. 13.

[8] Voir Henri Rolin, "Les transferts internationaux de populations: Réponses," AIDI, vol. 44, t. II, avril 1952 à la p. 174: "Il ne semble pas qu'on puisse *a priori* rejeter comme inadmissible l'intervention de législateurs étatiques instituant le transfert obligatoire pour des raisons d'ordre public ou de bien-être général. L'appréciation des considérations de nature à justifier un transfert de populations me paraît incontestablement entrer dans la compétence de l'État." Voir aussi Alfred von Verdross, "Les transferts internationaux de populations: Réponses," AIDI, vol. 44, t. II, avril 1952 à la p. 186: "D'après le droit international général, les États peuvent conclure des traités sur un objet quelconque. Nulle règle ne leur interdit de stipuler des accords sur un transfert de populations. Un tel accord pourrait être attaqué seulement dans des cas extrêmes s'il viole les principes élémentaires de l'humanité." Pour un point de vue plus extrême, voir J. Spiropoulos, "Les transferts internationaux de populations: Réponses," AIDI, vol. 44, t. II, avril 1952 aux pp. 185-86: "C'est à l'autorité qui conclut l'accord qu'il incombe de déterminer librement les intérêts qu'il convient de protéger ... Du point de vue du droit international, il existe, en cette matière, liberté d'action absolue des États pourvu que les lois sur l'humanité ne soient pas violées." *Contra.* Max Huber, "Les transferts internationaux de populations: Observations," AIDI, vol. 44, t. II, avril 1952 à la p. 164: "le transfert ne se prête guère à une réglementation." Pour un autre point de vue qui nie toute possibilité d'un transfert de population, voir Georges Scelle, "Les transferts internationaux de populations: Observations," AIDI, vol. 44, t. II, avril 1952 à la p. 176: "Il paraît difficile de formuler des règles juridiques s'appliquant à des opérations politiques qui constituent la négation même des principes élémentaires et fondamentaux du Droit des gens."

La Convention concernant l'échange des populations grecques et turques signée à Lausanne le 30 juillet 1923 constitue un des premiers et plus controversés traités sur ce sujet.[9] À la suite de la défaite de l'armée grecque en Asie Mineure en 1922, les Turcs victorieux ont imposé la signature de ce traité qui a effectivement légalisé le nettoyage ethnique des populations "ennemies" dans l'État turc émergeant et en Grèce. Une cohabitation multiethnique de plusieurs siècles sous les Ottomans a dû subitement céder aux dures réalités d'exclusion qui accompagnent la création des États monoethniques.

L'incapacité des instances internationales à prévenir la violence qui mène au nettoyage ethnique oblige les diplomates à explorer parfois des options désagréables afin de créer des conditions favorables à l'établissement de la paix. Dans le contexte difficile d'un conflit armé interethnique, le transfert de populations demeure malheureusement une option qui doit être évaluée en termes des conséquences sur la paix et la sécurité internationales, aussi bien que sur les droits individuels de la personne humaine.[10]

Les questions délicates soulevées par les transferts de populations reflètent le caractère particulièrement controversé de ce sujet.[11] De nombreux commentateurs sont outragés par la suggestion que l'identité ethnique puisse être utilisée pour installer de

---

[9] *Recueil des Traités de la Société des Nations*, n° 807, vol. XXXII, 1925. Ci-après "Convention de Lausanne."

[10] "[L]e transfert international des populations n'est jamais un moyen de protection des droits de l'homme; tout au contraire, il est un moyen de satisfaction de certains droits que les États invoquent et qu'ils s'accordent à se reconnaître … il ne faut jamais perdre de vue que les États, dans des conventions de ce genre, poursuivent leurs propres intérêts, et non ceux de leurs sujets." Giorgio Balladore Pallieri, "Les transferts internationaux de populations: Rapport," AIDI, vol. 44, t. II, avril 1952 aux pp. 140-41. *Contra*. Baron F. van Asbeck, "Les transferts internationaux de populations: Observations," AIDI, vol. 44, t. II, avril 1952 à la p. 157: "Quand, dans un État pluriforme, multi-national, multi-racial ou multi-religieux, une partie de la population est menacée de mort par une autre, le transfert du groupe menacé dans son pays d'origine peut apparaître comme la seule solution équitable et juste, comme le seul moyen de préserver la vie de milliers d'être humains. Dans un cas pareil, cette mesure-là constituerait peut-être la seule véritable protection des droits de l'homme, et en même temps il pourrait s'avérer que le transfert était exigé par le maintien de la paix."

[11] "Among most international organizations, western leaders, and scholars, population exchanges and partition are anathema." Chaim Kaufmann, "Possible and Impossible Solutions to Ethnic Civil Wars," *International Security*, vol. 20, n° 4, 1996 à la p. 170.

force des populations civiles en dehors de leur pays d'origine afin de rétablir la paix:

> On comprend donc mal comment des juristes pourraient discuter de sang-froid sur l'existence de compétences gouvernementales aboutissant à décréter de pareilles horreurs. Il devrait s'agir bien plutôt des devoirs d'intervention susceptibles d'y mettre fin ... La seule utilité que puisse présenter l'inscription de ce sujet à l'ordre du jour de notre Compagnie semble être de lui fournir l'occasion d'une condamnation absolue et solennelle des pratiques criminelles de plusieurs gouvernements.[12]

Même plusieurs décennies après la crise d'Asie Mineure, l'actuel Haut Commissariat pour les réfugiés continue d'être troublé par le précédent créé avec la "solution" élaborée lors de la Conférence de Lausanne.[13] Lord Curzon, le ministre britannique des affaires étrangères qui a présidé la Commission militaire et territoriale établie pendant la Conférence de Lausanne, illustre le sentiment d'indignation dans sa description de la proposition d'échanger les populations grecques et turques: "a thoroughly bad and vicious solution for which the world will pay a heavy penalty for a hundred years to come."[14]

Néanmoins, Lord Curzon a accepté en fin de compte cette solution et il a même justifié son caractère obligatoire. Le premier ministre Venizelos de la Grèce à l'époque de la Conférence de Lausanne avait accepté la solution d'un échange de populations avant d'ajuster sa position à cause des réactions publiques.[15] Le fait qu'il a aussi signé une entente acceptant *de jure* le nettoyage ethnique suggère qu'il puisse avoir une divergence considérable entre les déclarations destinées au public et les positions confidentielles

---

[12] Scelle, *supra* note 8 aux pp. 177-78. Voir aussi Stelio Séfériadès, "L'échange des populations," RCADI, t. 24, 1928 à la p. 372; C.G. Tenekides, "Le statut des minorités et l'échange obligatoire des populations gréco-turques," R.G.D.I.P. t. XXXI, 1924 aux pp. 72-88; Christa Meindersma, "Population Exchanges: International Law and State Practice — Part I," IJRL, vol. 9, 1997 aux pp. 338-51. *Contra* Sir John Hope Simpson, "The Refugee Problem," *International Affairs*, vol. 17, 1938 aux pp. 607, 628; et Dorothy Thompson, "Refugees: A World Problem," *Foreign Affairs*, vol. 16, n° 3, 1938 à la p. 381.

[13] Adam Roberts, "More Refugees, Less Asylum: A Regime in Transformation," *Journal of Refugee Studies*, vol. 11, n° 4, 1998 à la p. 391: "the question of compulsory population transfers has been a virtual taboo subject in UNHCR because of unhappy memories of the League of Nations involvement in Greek-Turkish population exchanges."

[14] Conférence de Lausanne, *Livre jaune*, t. I, 1923 à la p. 176.

[15] Sur la politique du premier ministre Venizelos concernant l'échange de populations, voir Séfériadès, *supra* note 12 à la p. 373.

dans les négociations diplomatiques. Les approches réalistes aux problèmes du nettoyage ethnique doivent être explorées afin d'examiner toutes les options disponibles aux acteurs internationaux.[16] La crise d'Asie Mineure montre de manière particulièrement frappante une des approches historiques aux dilemmes suscités par le phénomène du transfert de populations. La réaction internationale a contribué pendant plusieurs décennies à établir le ton au travail du Haut Commissariat pour les réfugiés et son approche humanitaire dans des situations hautement politisées.

Conformément à la position du Haut Commissaire Fridtjof Nansen, cet article aborde la question des transferts de populations avec une approche pragmatique afin de reconnaître la complexité des crises humanitaires où des décisions rapides peuvent avoir des conséquences dramatiques sur la survie des minorités menacées. Des arguments d'ordre moral qui sous-tendent certains principes juridiques sont également abordés car une politique humanitaire viable doit être fondée sur des principes cohérents. Bien que les relations internationales soient affectées de manière fondamentale par les développements positifs en matière des droits de l'homme,[17] nous croyons que cette nouvelle perspective politico-juridique dominante[18] ne répond pas de façon satisfaisante aux problèmes soulevés par les diplomates lors de la Conférence de Lausanne. L'analyse qui suit ne cautionne aucunement les transferts de populations: elle ne fait que reconnaître la réalité de ce phénomène et s'efforce d'aborder de manière pragmatique certaines de ses conséquences.

I   LES DÉPLACEMENTS MASSIFS ET LES EFFORTS DE PAIX

La Convention de Lausanne ne représente pas la première tentative de formaliser une séparation de populations afin d'atténuer les tensions régionales.[19] Le traité de paix de 1913 entre la Bulgarie

[16] Myron Weiner, "The Clash of Norms: Dilemmas in Refugee Policies," *Journal of Refugee Studies*, vol. 11, n° 4, 1998 à la p. 449.

[17] Voir, par exemple, Bertrand Badie, *La diplomatie des droits de l'homme*, Paris, Fayard, 2002; Jack Donnelly, *Universal Human Rights in Theory and Practice*, 2ᵉ éd., Ithaca, Cornell University Press, 2003; et David P. Forsythe, *Human Rights in International Relations*, Cambridge, Cambridge University Press, 2000.

[18] Voir la section intitulée "Hegemony and Settled Norms" dans Donnelly, *ibid.* aux pp. 38-40.

[19] Awn Shawkat Al-Khasawneh et Ribot Hatano, *Les transferts de populations, y compris l'implantation de colons et de colonies, considérés sous l'angle des droits de l'homme*, Rapport préliminaire à la Sous-Commission de la lutte contre les mesures discriminatoires et de la protection des minorités, E/CN.4/Sub.2/1993/17, 6 juillet 1993

et l'empire ottoman[20] contient dans son annexe un protocole qui comprend un "échange facultatif mutuel des populations bulgare et musulmane.[21] Le Traité de paix de Neuilly-sur-Seine comprend également une convention qui prévoit "l'émigration réciproque et volontaire des minorités ethniques, de religion ou de langue en Grèce et en Bulgarie."[22] Des arrangements juridiques de ce genre ont été encouragés également par des gouvernements fascistes et totalitaires au début de la Seconde Guerre mondiale.[23] En effet,

au par. 115: "Les accords relatifs aux échanges d'entre les deux guerres ne préconisaient pas de transferts massifs de populations mais ouvraient aux intéressés la possibilité d'émigrer volontairement vers l'État auquel les rattachait leur identité ethnique, en atténuant le fardeau financier qui en résulterait pour eux. Cette possibilité a d'abord été offerte et exercée dans les Balkans mais uniquement comme un complément de protection et non pas en lieu et place de protection."

[20] Traité de paix signé à Constantinople le 16 septembre 1913. *Recueil général de traités*, 3ᵉ série, t. VIII, Leipzig, 1914 à la p. 78.

[21] Protocole n° 1 signé à Constantinople le 16 septembre 1913. *Recueil général de traités*, 3ᵉ série, t. VIII, Leipzig, 1914 à la p. 85. Au sujet du caractère réellement "volontaire" auquel fait allusion ce traité, voir Pallieri, *supra* note 10 à la p. 144: "On laisse toujours une liberté, plus ou moins illusoire, à l'individu; et, d'autre part, on exerce toujours une pression plus ou moins dissimulée sur lui. Prenons comme exemple le Traité turco-bulgare du 16/29 septembre 1913 où il est stipulé que l'échange des populations sera facultatif mais "aura lieu par villages entiers." Cela signifie que la majorité de la population de chaque village peut imposer sa volonté à la minorité. Peut-on encore parler dans ces conditions, et du point de vue individuel, de transfert volontaire? Je crois devoir le nier." La Bulgarie et la Turquie ont par la suite négocié une Convention d'établissement, signée à Angora le 18 octobre 1925. *Recueil général de traités*, 3ᵉ série, t. XX (1920), Leipzig, 1929 à la p. 349.

[22] Convention entre la Grèce et la Bulgarie, relative à l'émigration réciproque, signée le 27 novembre 1919 à Neuilly-sur-Seine, R.T.S.N., n° 1, vol. 1, septembre 1920 à la p. 67. Al-Khasawneh et Hatano, *supra* note 19 au par. 116: "[O]n estime à 37 000 Grecs en Bulgarie et quelque 150 000 Bulgares en Macédoine et en Thrace (grecques) le nombre des personnes auxquelles elles se sont appliquées. En vertu de la Convention de Neuilly, les émigrants pouvaient traverser la frontière avec leurs biens mobiliers en franchise de droits tandis que la valeur de leurs biens immobiliers devait leur être remboursée lors de la liquidation de ces biens. Les États ont réciproquement accepté de faciliter ce processus par le truchement d'une Commission mixte."

[23] Voir les exemples cités dans Al-Khasawneh et Hatano, *supra* note 19 aux par. 128-37. Il est intéressant de noter que le Soviet suprême a adopté le 14 novembre 1989 une déclaration reconnaissant le caractère "illégal" et "criminel" des déportations forcées menées par Joseph Staline. Voir Izvestia, "*Deklaracija Verhovnogo Soveta Sojuza Sovetskih Socialicticheskih Respublik o priznanii nezakonnimi i prestupnimi repressivnih aktov protiv narodov, podvergshihsja nasilstvennomu pereseleniju, i obespechenii ix prav*" (Déclaration du Soviet suprême de l'Union des républiques soviétiques socialistes relative à la reconnaissance du caractère

Hitler a annoncé dans le Reichstag le 6 octobre 1939 qu'il y aurait un nouvel ordre ethnographique et une réinstallation de nationalités afin d'obtenir de meilleures "lignes de division."[24] Parallèlement à l'agression et la terreur générées par le régime nazi, une série d'"arrangements d'option" a été conclue dans la période 1939-1941 entre l'Allemagne et l'Estonie, la Lettonie, la Croatie, la Roumanie, l'Italie et l'Union soviétique[25] impliquant de nombreux transferts volontaires.[26]

L'expulsion d'environ seize millions d'Allemands dans la période 1944-1949 représente peut-être l'exemple le plus dramatique de ce genre de déplacement dans le contexte européen. Bien que sanctionnées par le Protocole de Potsdam,[27] les expulsions ont été

---

illégal et criminel des actes répressifs contre les peuples, soumis à l'émigration forcée, et garantissant leurs droits), 24 novembre 1989 à la p. 1.

[24] "Parmi les tâches qu'impose une conception élevée de la vie européenne, figurent les transferts de populations, qui permettront d'écarter en partie les causes de conflits européens." Discours de Hitler cité dans Robert Ginesy, "L'Organisation internationale des réfugiés," R.G.D.I.P., t. 52, 1948 à la p. 455. Voir aussi Hedwig Wachenheim, "Hitler's Transfers of Population in Eastern Europe," *Foreign Affairs*, vol. 20, n° 4, 1942 à la p. 705.

[25] Joseph B. Schechtmann, "The Option Clause in the Reich's Treaties on the Transfer of Population," AJIL, vol. 38, 1944 à la p. 357.

[26] "On the whole, it may be asserted that the transfer of some 600,000 Volksdeutsche from Eastern Europe to the Reich pursuant to the option treaties was legally unobjectionable, insofar as each transfer was on a voluntary basis and no physical abuse was connected with the resettlement. It was not an expulsion." Alfred de Zayas, "International Law and Mass Population Transfers," HarvILJ, vol. 16, 1975 à la p. 249. Pour un point de vue plus sceptique sur le caractère "volontaire," voir Al-Khasawneh et Hatano, *supra* note 19 au par. 137: "D'ailleurs, étant donné les circonstances et le grand intérêt qu'avaient les États à organiser ces transferts, il est probable que la plupart des personnes transférées sont parties moins de leur plein gré que poussées par le désespoir et la peur. Les accords bilatéraux successifs prévoyant un "droit d'option" allaient éroder les structures communautaires de base et la confiance fragile que la communauté avait dans son droit à une protection en tant que minorité. Le caractère volontaire des transferts devenait, dans ces conditions, tout à fait relatif." *Contra* Schechtmann, *supra* aux pp. 358-59: "Nevertheless, to speak of a forced evacuation of the German Baltic minorities would be inaccurate and unjustified. Both from the legal point of view and in practice these minorities were given the right as well as the possibility to choose freely."

[27] Protocol of the Proceedings of the Berlin (Potsdam) Conference, 2 août 1945, dans US Senate Committee on Foreign Relations and State Department, *A Decade of American Foreign Policy: Basic Documents 1941-1949*, Washington, Government Printing Office, 1950. Plusieurs auteurs ont tenté de justifier cet accord en invoquant des arguments discutables aussi bien sur le plan du positivisme

menées dans des conditions violentes qui ont entraîné la mort d'environ deux millions d'Allemands.[28] Albert Schweitzer a condamné les Alliés victorieux pour cette pratique quand il a reçu le prix Nobel de 1952.[29] Peu importe que l'objectif immédiat des auteurs soit de sauver des minorités menacées en leur permettant de se réinstaller dans un autre pays ou de débarrasser des groupes minoritaires gênants de certains territoires, l'histoire récente apporte de nombreux exemples où des expulsions de populations ont été proposées pour améliorer la sécurité régionale.

Bien que la SDN ait demandé à son Haut Commissaire pour les réfugiés de s'occuper de la crise en Asie Mineure, les personnes déplacées d'origine grecque ou turque n'étaient pas considérées comme des "réfugiés" selon le droit international des réfugiés naissant. Avant le début de la Conférence de Lausanne, Nansen a notifié le Conseil de la SDN que la délégation grecque lui avait demandé d'arranger un échange de populations.[30] Nansen a éventuellement été invité à assister une sous-commission de la Conférence dans la rédaction d'une convention d'échange. Quand la

---

juridique que celui de l'éthique. Voir Pallieri, *supra* note 10 aux pp. 145-46: "On n'a pas appliqué aux Allemands, au lendemain de la dernière guerre, les principes généraux de la communauté internationale. Il fallait réparer les torts qu'ils avaient causés et, à cette fin, il fallait faire usage contre eux des mêmes méthodes qu'ils avaient employées." Voir aussi Bohdan Winiarski, "Les transferts internationaux de populations: Réponses," AIDI, vol. 44, t. II, avril 1952 à la p. 192: "L'accord de Potsdam, du 2 août 1945, constitue, à mon avis, une de ces opérations exceptionnelles mais nécessaires. L'assentiment de l'Allemagne est donné par le fait qu'elle a accepté la capitulation sans condition; le consentement de la Pologne, de la Tchécoslovaquie et de la Hongrie était acquis expressément. Cet accord est l'aboutissement naturel des quelque quinze Traités, Conventions et Accords conclus par l'Allemagne de 1939 à 1943, avec l'intention de concentrer des masses ethniquement allemandes, venues des divers pays en territoire polonais." D'autres auteurs, par contre, considèrent que les dispositions de l'accord de Potsdam "inspirées par des visées d'ordre purement politique ne peuvent être considérées comme légitimes du point de vue du droit international." Fernand De Visscher, "Les transferts internationaux de populations: Observations," AIDI, vol. 44, t. II, avril 1952 à la p. 190.

[28] Voir les statistiques dans Al-Khasawneh et Hatano, *supra* note 19 au par. 138 et dans de Zayas, *supra* note 26 à la p. 238. Sur les tentatives de contrôler ces mouvements, voir Malcolm J. Proudfoot, *European Refugees: A Study in Forced Population Movement*, Illinois, Northwestern University Press, 1956 aux pp. 372-74.

[29] Discours de remerciement prononcé à l'Université d'Oslo le 4 novembre 1954 (plus d'un an après la remise du prix).

[30] Lettre de Nansen au Conseil de la SDN, doc. A/48/24318/24318 (16 octobre 1922). *Cf.* Tenekides, *supra* note 12 à la p. 83.

rédaction a été complétée, la Convention de Lausanne prévoyait que les "émigrants perdront la nationalité du pays qu'ils abandonnent, et ils acquerront celle du pays de destination dès leur arrivé sur le territoire de ce pays."[31] Le régime particulier pour les Grecs et les Turcs accordait aux personnes transférées de nouvelles nationalités et conséquemment il n'était pas nécessaire d'introduire une protection internationale pour remplacer la protection étatique découlant de la nationalité. Les quelques cas d'apatridie résultant des évènements en Asie Mineure concernent uniquement les déplacés qui ont trouvé un refuge dans des pays tiers, tels les déplacés grecs qui ont fui en Égypte.[32]

En examinant les réactions internationales possibles au nettoyage ethnique, il faut considérer que les interventions militaires motivées par des raisons humanitaires se sont montrées peu fiables au cours des siècles. Étant donné que la France, le Royaume-Uni et l'Italie n'allaient pas intervenir militairement contre l'armée turque pour sauver les populations grecques à Smyrne (Izmir) en septembre-octobre 1922 malgré la présence de leurs troupes dans la région,[33] une solution alternative était nécessaire. Si des puissances étrangères ne veulent pas envoyer leurs soldats pour prévenir le nettoyage ethnique et refusent d'examiner d'autres possibilités, on peut s'attendre à une aggravation des épreuves des populations victimes. Comme Lord Curzon l'avait dit en 1923:

I believe that an exchange of populations, however well it were carried out, must impose very considerable hardships, perhaps very considerable impoverishment, upon great numbers of individual citizens of the two countries who are exchanged. But I also believe that these hardships, great though they may be, will be less than the hardships which will result for these same populations if nothing is done.[34]

Dans des situations de nettoyage ethnique, le fait de refuser une option indésirable à cause d'une profonde indignation peut être contestable si cela mène à l'inaction.

[31] Art. 7 de la Convention de Lausanne.

[32] Voir Tenekides, *supra* note 12 à la p. 85.

[33] Les troupes alliées se trouvaient en Thrace orientale, dans la péninsule de Constantinople et dans la péninsule de Gallipoli. Voir les articles III, IX et XII de la Convention militaire signée à Moudania le 11 octobre 1922, *Recueil général de traités*, 3ᵉ série, t. XIII (1924-1925), Leipzig, 1924 à la p. 336.

[34] Lausanne Conference on Near Eastern Affairs, *Discussions on the Exchange Convention*, 1923 à la p. 114. Il est clair que les échanges de populations au début du XXᵉ siècle ont été proposés en partie sur la base de considérations humanitaires, contrairement à la suggestion dans Kaufmann, *supra* note 11 à la p. 137.

Les pertes de vie en Asie Mineure ont été minimisées à la suite de la signature de la Convention de Lausanne, contrairement à la situation des Allemands expulsés en 1944-1949 ou à la situation des *Cherokees* qui ont été transférés de force à travers l'Amérique au XIXe siècle.[35] Quelques années avant la crise d'Asie Mineure, les acteurs internationaux n'ont pas pu aider les populations arméniennes qui n'avaient pas réussi à fuir la violence et intégrer un nouvel État d'accueil.[36] Leur émigration s'est avérée généralement difficile et le résultat a été des massacres à grande échelle perpétrés par les autorités turques. D'un point de vue humanitaire, il est préférable d'avoir une population expulsée plutôt que tuée en masse. Le sort des Juifs dans l'Allemagne nazie deux décennies plus tard souligne ce point.[37]

Malgré les épreuves humaines terribles créées par les transferts de populations, il ne faut pas ignorer les conséquences sur la stabilité régionale. La séparation des populations en Asie Mineure a contribué à faire cesser les hostilités et à pacifier les nations belligérantes.[38] Elle a rendu possible la signature quelques mois plus tard du Traité de Lausanne qui constitue un plan de paix pour la région.[39]

Toutefois, les conséquences négatives de cette approche à la fois réaliste et odieuse aux problèmes du nettoyage ethnique ne peuvent pas être ignorées. La Convention de Lausanne demeure un

[35] De Zayas, *supra* note 26 aux pp. 223, 251.

[36] "The most tragic of the target groups were the Armenians, who must figure prominently in any account such as this, not only because many of them became refugees, but also because most did not—a fate that befell also most European Jews two decades later." Aristide R. Zolberg, Astri Suhrke et Sergio Aguayo, *Escape from Violence*, Oxford, Oxford University Press, 1989 à la p. 15.

[37] "In the cases of the Armenians and the Jews in Nazi-controlled Europe, as with many other minorities before them and after them, the objective was to rid the land of their presence. Turkey initially sought to achieve this by terrorizing the Armenians into flight. In Germany, the Nazis similarly sought at first to rid themselves of the Jews by a combination of expulsion (foreign Jews) and the imposition of conditions that would cause them to leave (German Jews). In both cases, when external conditions made emigration impossible, the persecutor resorted to mass murder. Among these external conditions, particularly with respect to the Jews, was the refusal of other States to accept the target population as refugees." *Ibid.* à la p. 16.

[38] "The regrouping of populations [grecques et turques] helped end the international conflict and the violence." *Ibid.* à la p. 14.

[39] Traité de paix signé à Lausanne le 24 juillet 1923. *Recueil général de traités*, 3e série, t. XIII (1924-1925), Leipzig, 1924 à la p. 342.

exemple brutal du pouvoir de l'État sur l'individu.[40] Dans la mesure où elle reflète une "commodification" de l'être humain,[41] elle est difficile à concilier avec les développements récents en matière des droits de l'homme. Elle implique clairement la domination des intérêts étatiques sur les droits de la personne humaine. Les échanges de populations "récompensent" indirectement l'usage de la force et établissent un précédent dangereux pour les belligérants qui voudront dans l'avenir profiter des "faits accomplis" sur le terrain.[42] Toutefois, dans la mesure où ces intérêts étatiques concernent la protection des populations civiles et la cessation des hostilités, il ne faut pas nécessairement les considérer comme illégitimes.

En considérant ces facteurs, il est manifeste que la relation entre la paix et le respect des droits de l'homme est plus complexe que communément admise. Ces deux missions humanistes peuvent même être parfois en conflit ou en contradiction à court terme. À long terme, la paix et les droits de l'homme sont sans doute intimement liés. Un ordre juridique international préoccupé par la paix et les droits de l'homme devrait chercher un équilibre approprié en ce qui concerne les solutions envisagées pour les conflits armés. Par son action pendant la crise d'Asie Mineure, Nansen nous donne un exemple d'une approche qui propose un équilibre judicieux entre les principes humanitaires et le pragmatisme diplomatique.

II   LES CONTROVERSES JURIDIQUES SUR LES ÉCHANGES DE POPULATIONS

A   ÉCHANGES VOLONTAIRES OU OBLIGATOIRES?

Si le Haut Commissaire pour les réfugiés et les diplomates considèrent qu'un arrangement sur l'échange de populations puisse faire éviter des massacres et promouvoir la paix, une question qui

---

[40] Patrick Thornberry, *International Law and the Rights of Minorities*, Oxford, Clarendon Press, 1991 à la p. 51.

[41] Pour une critique générale de la "commodification" des personnes déplacées, voir Deborah Anker, Joan Fitzpatrick et Andrew Shacknove, "Crisis and Cure: A Reply to Hathaway/Neve and Schuck," Harv.Hum.Rts.J., vol. 11, 1998 à la p. 295.

[42] "Realistically speaking, following armed conflict and victory, it is very difficult to deny the victorious state the benefits of the success of arms, one of which is formulating the peace terms ... Kemal Atatürk defeated the Greeks and provided for their expulsion from Asia Minor ... This is the old might makes right positivism." de Zayas, *supra* note 26 à la p. 224.

doit être abordée concerne le caractère volontaire ou obligatoire de l'échange. La Convention de Lausanne représente un exemple unique et frappant dans le sens qu'il implique un échange explicitement obligatoire. Pour plusieurs observateurs, c'est particulièrement cet aspect qui le rend inacceptable en tant que mesure d'assistance aux minorités menacées: "Il est obligatoire, ce qui le rend si odieux."[43] Ils préfèrent, par exemple, l'approche du Traité de Neuilly-sur-Seine qui comportait un échange volontaire entre la Bulgarie et la Grèce.[44] Le caractère absolument obligatoire de l'échange prévu dans la Convention de Lausanne a été comparé à d'autres conventions comprenant des échanges volontaires et à la tendance générale sous la SDN de vouloir protéger les minorités à l'intérieur de leur pays d'origine.[45]

La notion d'échange obligatoire est devenue tellement embarrassante que l'origine même de l'idée lors de la Conférence de Lausanne est contestée. Bien que Nansen encourageait une telle approche avant le début de la Conférence,[46] il n'est pas clair si le premier ministre Venizelos avait l'intention que sa proposition d'échanger les populations soit obligatoire. Aussitôt que les déplacés grecs ont commencé à protester contre l'idée d'un échange obligatoire et que les musulmans ont indiqué qu'ils ne voulaient pas quitter leur résidence en Grèce, les opinions publiques en Occident ont manifesté un sentiment d'indignation.[47] Les politiciens ont alors commencé à rejeter la responsabilité pour la suggestion d'un échange obligatoire.[48] Cette sous-section démontre que le caractère volontaire ou obligatoire de l'échange est pertinent principalement dans la mesure où il affecte la question critique du retour des personnes transférées.

En évaluant les implications d'un arrangement d'échange obligatoire, il faut constater que les instruments internationaux sur ce sujet sont généralement signés après qu'une partie substantielle du nettoyage ethnique ait déjà eu lieu. Bien que l'autorisation officielle pour le transfert des populations allemandes ait suivi la

---

[43] Tenekides, *supra* note 12 à la p. 85.

[44] *Idem.*

[45] Voir, par exemple, Meindersma, *supra* note 12 à la p. 348.

[46] *Ibid.* à la p. 338. Voir aussi Tenekides, *supra* note 12 à la p. 83.

[47] Meindersma, *supra* note 12 à la p. 341. Voir aussi Tenekides, *supra* note 12 à la p. 86.

[48] Séfériadès, *supra* note 12 à la p. 373.

conférence de Potsdam tenue du 17 juillet au 2 août 1945,[49] la réalité sur le terrain indique que les Allemands étaient déjà expulsés de façon systématique depuis la Prusse orientale, la Poméranie, le Brandebourg oriental, la Silésie, la Haute Silésie et les Sudètes sous des conditions considérées comme inhumaines par le CICR.[50] Peu après, l'Inde et le Pakistan ont signé le 8 avril 1950 l'Accord de New Delhi[51] qui cherchait à réglementer certains aspects de l'échange *de facto* de plusieurs millions de personnes d'origine hindoue, musulmane et sikhe qui affectait le sous-continent indien depuis son partage en 1947.[52]

Même en ce qui concerne l'échange obligatoire prévu par la Convention de Lausanne, les statistiques de Lord Curzon indiquent que la population grecque en Asie Mineure comptait 1 600 000 personnes avant la Première Guerre mondiale et que celle-ci avait déjà était réduite à environ 500 000 personnes à la fin de 1922.[53] De façon similaire, la moitié des 800 000 musulmans

---

49 Art. 13 du Protocole de Potsdam: "Les trois gouvernements [R.-U., É.-U. et U.R.S.S.], après avoir examiné la question sous tous ses aspects, reconnaissent qu'il y aura lieu de procéder au transfert en Allemagne des populations allemandes restant en Pologne, en Tchécoslovaquie et en Hongrie." Traduction dans Pallieri, *supra* note 10 à la p. 145. Pour un examen de la conférence, voir Charles L. Mee, *Meeting at Potsdam,* New York, M. Evans & Company, 1975, 370 p.

50 "Close on fourteen million people affected by these measures were thus forced to abandon their homes at short notice, and those who had to leave them for a time because of the fighting, were prevented from returning. The ICRC at once received a great number of appeals, drawing its attention to the alarming conditions of food and health in which a great number of these people were living, after hasty expulsion from their homes and assembly in provisional camps, and also to the often deplorable conditions of their transfer to Germany. Had it been borne in mind that the repatriation of some 1,500,000 Greeks from Asia Minor, after the first World War, had taken several years and required large-scale relief schemes, it would have been easy to foresee that the hurried transplanting of fourteen million human beings would raise a large number of problems from the humanitarian standpoint, especially in a Europe strewn with ruins and where starvation was rife." *Report of the International Committee of the Red Cross on its Activities during the Second World War,* 1er septembre 1939-30 juin 1947, 1948 à la p. 675. Cité dans de Zayas, *supra* note 26 à la p. 235.

51 Accord entre le Pakistan et l'Inde signé à New Delhi le 8 avril 1950, R.T.N.U., vol. 131, 1950 à la p. 5.

52 Voir Gopal Das Khosla, *Stern Reckoning: A Survey of the Events Leading Up To and Following the Partition of India,* Delhi, Oxford University Press, 1949. Entre 1 et 2 millions de personnes ont trouvé la mort lors de ces mouvements. Voir Al-Khasawneh et Hatano, *supra* note 19 au par. 141.

53 *Lausanne Conference on Near Eastern Affairs, supra* note 34 à la p. 114.

en Grèce avait fui avant 1922.[54] La Commission mixte établie par la Convention de Lausanne[55] a transféré sous ses auspices 189 916 personnes d'origine grecque vers la Grèce et 355 635 musulmans vers la Turquie pendant la période 1923-1926.[56] Bien que la Convention de Lausanne a été signée le 30 janvier 1923 et que l'échange devait commencer officiellement le 1er mai 1923,[57] le transfert des personnes "échangeables" avait commencé en fait plus tôt que prévu.[58] Les deux gouvernements concernés avaient accéléré les départs, contribuant ainsi à l'atmosphère de transferts désordonnés. Dans de telles conditions, le caractère volontaire ou obligatoire des échanges perd sa pertinence en termes du départ effectif des populations affectées.

La question controversée en ce qui concerne les échanges de populations n'est pas nécessairement l'obligation imposée sur certaines personnes qui doivent quitter leur résidence, car la signature des instruments internationaux intervient d'habitude après le déplacement. Le problème du caractère volontaire ou obligatoire affecte plutôt le retour éventuel des personnes déplacées, comme décrit dans la prochaine sous-section.

L'adoption d'un arrangement sur un échange de populations à caractère obligatoire s'explique par plusieurs facteurs. On peut s'attendre à ce que les États victorieux dans un conflit armé soient en position avantageuse pour négocier les conditions de paix. Tel était le cas en octobre 1922 quand la délégation turque s'est présentée à la Conférence de Lausanne[59] et a insisté éventuellement

[54] Statistiques citées dans Zolberg, Suhrke et Aguayo, *supra* note 36 à la p. 14.

[55] Art. 11.

[56] Meindersma, *supra* note 12 à la p. 346. Voir aussi Al-Khasawneh et Hatano, *supra* note 19 au par. 125.

[57] Art. 1. En termes d'obligation juridique internationale, la Convention est entrée en vigueur le 25 août 1923 après la ratification par la Grèce (la Turquie a ratifié le 23 août 1923).

[58] Meindersma, *supra* note 12 à la p. 344.

[59] "Unlike previous conferences such as the Congress of Berlin [en 1878], the Conference of Lausanne found itself confronted, not by an abject conquered Sick Man, but by an invigorated re-awakened nation determined at all costs to maintain what it believes to be the sovereign rights of the Turkish people. The result has been that it was found necessary at Lausanne to seek a conciliatory adjustment of the Western and Eastern questions. The pretensions of the European Powers both among themselves and as against Turkey have naturally assumed a less important place than the claims of the Turks who felt that they had everything to gain and little to lose by an unyielding belligerent attitude." Philip Marshall Brown, "The Lausanne Conference," AJIL, vol. 17, 1923 à la p. 290.

que les Grecs acceptent un échange obligatoire de populations.[60] L'argument selon lequel un échange obligatoire permettrait un transfert rapide a aussi été présenté à Lausanne: l'objectif était d'éviter un processus prolongé qui pourrait résulter d'un échange volontaire.[61] Dès que le principe d'échange de populations ait été accepté à la Conférence de Lausanne, il est devenu clair qu'il était dans l'intérêt des gouvernements grec et turc que l'échange soit complété aussi vite que possible.

Malgré le malaise considérable à défendre publiquement cette approche, la décision de rendre l'échange obligatoire peut possiblement se comprendre si l'accent doit être mis sur un achèvement rapide du processus de nettoyage ethnique, atténuant ainsi les souffrances des personnes déplacées. Il est possible, par exemple, que le refus international d'accepter formellement la partition territoriale en Bosnie-Herzégovine dans les années 1990[62] a simplement prolongé les souffrances et a facilité l'échange *de facto* de populations sans changer le résultat: la création de territoires ethniquement homogènes. Les négociateurs à la Conférence de Lausanne, contrairement aux déclarations de plusieurs diplomates impliqués dans la crise en Bosnie-Herzégovine soixante-dix ans plus tard, parlaient ouvertement de l'équilibre qu'ils espéraient atteindre en termes de *realpolitik*:

The conference had only ceded to the demand that the exchange should be compulsory because all those who had studied the matter most closely seemed to agree that the suffering entailed, great as it must be, would be repaid by the advantages which would ultimately accrue to both countries from a greater homogeneity of population and from the removal of old and deep rooted causes of quarrel.[63]

---

[60] Vers la fin du mois, la délégation insistait sur un "total and enforced exchange of populations." Rapport de Nansen au Conseil de la SDN, doc. C.736/M447, 5. Voir aussi Tenekides, *supra* note 12 à la p. 83.

[61] Lord Curzon a déclaré: "If the exchange were left on a voluntary basis, months might pass before it was carried out, whereas what was wanted was firstly to get the Turkish population back into Eastern Thrace so that they might till the soil early next year; and, secondly, to provide for accomodation in Greece of the refugees pouring in from other parts." Lausanne Conference on Near Eastern Affairs, *supra* note 34 à la p. 114.

[62] Nous ne partageons pas l'analyse selon laquelle l'Accord de Dayton constitue en réalité un simple arrangement de partition telle que proposée dans Radha Kumar, "The Troubled History of Partition," *Foreign Affairs*, vol. 76, n° 1, janvier-février 1997 à la p. 22.

[63] Lausanne Conference on Near Eastern Affairs, *supra* note 34 à la p. 412 (Lord Curzon).

Les négociateurs dans un tel contexte doivent faire face à un autre problème connexe: les expériences du XXe siècle suggèrent que les échanges volontaires ont tendance à se transformer *de facto* en transferts obligatoires.[64] L'adoption d'instruments juridiques qui ne peuvent pas être respectés contribue à saper la crédibilité du droit international. Dans une situation de conflit armé, il est peut-être plus approprié de reconnaître certaines dures réalités, plutôt que d'expérimenter avec des positions progressistes fondées sur l'idéalisme. Même des juristes opposés aux échanges obligatoires reconnaissent que des arrangements "quasi volontaires" puissent jouer un rôle important s'ils encouragent des transferts plus humains et ordonnés.[65]

Si les échanges de populations sont obligatoires, la mise en œuvre de la Convention de Lausanne indique que l'identification des personnes "échangeables" puisse être compliquée et qu'elle comprenne des conséquences à long terme pour les individus déplacés et les populations restantes. La Convention de Lausanne prévoit qu'il "sera procédé dès le 1er mai 1923 à l'échange obligatoire des ressortissants turcs de religion grecque orthodoxe établis sur les territoires turcs et des ressortissants grecs de religion musulmane établis sur les territoires grecs."[66] Cette disposition est suivie par une exception: "Ne seront pas compris dans l'échange prévu à l'article premier: a) les habitants grecs de Constantinople; b) les habitants musulmans de la Thrace occidentale."[67] Afin d'aborder la situation

---

[64] Voir De Visscher, *supra* note 27 à la p. 188: "La distinction entre transferts obligatoires et transferts volontaires est vaine et le plus souvent trompeuse. En de telles matières l'élément volontaire n'est jamais invoqué que pour dissimuler les mesures de contrainte directe ou indirecte qui répondent aux visées réelles de l'État." Voir aussi Christa Meindersma, "Population Exchanges: International Law and State Practice — Part II," IJRL, vol. 9, 1997 à la p. 652: "Experience with earlier exchange provisions had indicated that, if left truly voluntary, few persons would avail themselves of the rights to emigrate and those exchanges had in fact become largely compulsory."

[65] Voir, par exemple, de Zayas, *supra* note 26 à la p. 250: "Those who want to stay should be given the right of option, but in extreme cases of irreconcilable hostility it may be preferable to be transferred under compulsion than to be left and exterminated. This, however, is an exception to the rule of voluntary transfers and should not be abused."

[66] Art. 1.

[67] L'art. 2 contient également la précision suivante: "Seront considérés comme habitants grecs de Constantinople tous les Grecs déjà établis avant le 30 octobre 1918 dans les circonscriptions de la préfecture de la ville de Constantinople, telles qu'elles sont délimitées par la loi de 1912. Seront considérés comme

précaire des populations qui avaient fui avant la signature de la Convention de Lausanne, l'article 3 stipule que les "Grecs et les musulmans, ayant déjà quitté depuis le 18 octobre 1912 les territoires dont les habitants grecs et turcs doivent être respectivement échangés, seront considérés comme compris dans l'échange prévu."

L'application *ratione personae* de la Convention de Lausanne n'est pas claire dans le sens qu'elle puisse inclure tous les coreligionnaires dans les transferts. En conséquence, il était nécessaire de clarifier que la Convention s'appliquerait uniquement aux coreligionnaires présumés de partager le sentiment national du pays d'accueil.[68] Par exemple, les Albanais musulmans en Grèce ne devaient pas être inclus dans l'échange et transférés vers la Turquie. Cependant, le sentiment national de certaines populations n'était pas facile à identifier. Certains groupes avec une affiliation douteuse au pays d'accueil ont donc été inclus dans l'échange. Le transfert des Crétois musulmans vers la Turquie illustre le problème.

Les populations minoritaires non comprises dans l'échange ont été autorisées à rester dans leur pays d'origine et devaient bénéficier du système des minorités de la SDN. En effet, le Traité de Paix avec la Turquie signé six mois après la Convention de Lausanne comprenait un régime de protection des minorités qui s'appliquait aux minorités non-musulmanes restantes en Turquie et aux minorités musulmanes en Grèce.[69]

B   LES OPTIONS: RETOUR OU COMPENSATION?

Étant donné que le premier ministre Venizelos a admis avoir signé la Convention de Lausanne pour assurer le départ des musulmans résidant en Grèce parce que la Turquie avait déjà expulsé la

---

habitants musulmans de la Thrace occidentale tous les musulmans établis dans la région à l'est de la ligne-frontière établie en 1913 par le Traité de Bucarest." Voir aussi l'avis consultatif de la Cour permanente de justice internationale concernant l'interprétation du terme "établis" à l'art. 2: "La limitation ainsi apportée au principe de l'échange a été déterminée par plusieurs raisons. En ce qui concerne les habitants grecs de Constantinople, il y a eu, entre autres, celle d'éviter à cette ville la perte qui aurait été la conséquence de l'exode d'une population qui constitue l'un des plus important facteurs économiques et commerciaux." Cour permanente de justice internationale, *Recueil des avis consultatifs*, série B, n° 10, 21 février 1925 à la p. 18.

[68]   Sur ce point, voir Stephen P. Ladas, *The Exchange of Minorities: Bulgaria, Greece and Turkey*, New York, MacMillan Company, 1932 à la p. 380 et Charles B. Eddy, *Greece and the Greek Refugees*, London, George Allen & Unwin Ltd., 1931 à la p. 203.

[69]   Art. 37-45.

majorité de sa population grecque,[70] la motivation de l'approbation de la délégation turque peut paraître peu claire. La réponse se trouve dans le deuxième paragraphe du premier article: "Ces personnes [échangeables] ne pourront venir se rétablir en Turquie, ou, respectivement, en Grèce, sans l'autorisation du Gouvernement turc ou respectivement, du Gouvernement hellénique." Même si de nombreux Grecs ayant fui l'Asie Mineure voulaient retourner dans leur maison à la suite d'une entente de paix, la Convention de Lausanne leur refusait ce droit. La délégation turque à la Conférence de Lausanne avait réussi à obtenir une disposition qui justifiait *de jure* l'interdiction du retour. Bien qu'une interdiction de retour pour les réfugiés représente actuellement un aspect fondamental de la politique officieuse de plusieurs factions en Bosnie-Herzégovine et du gouvernement israélien dans sa lutte contre les groupes armés palestiniens, il est improbable qu'une telle disposition explicite soit acceptable aujourd'hui compte tenu des développements en matière des droits de l'homme.

Cette question stratégique met l'accent sur une autre considération importante concernant la rédaction des arrangements d'échange de populations: la réparation offerte aux victimes du déplacement.[71] Les documents internationaux qui abordent la détresse des populations déplacées offrent d'habitude le choix entre le retour ou la compensation. Par exemple, dans sa résolution 194(III) concernant les réfugiés palestiniens, l'Assemblée générale

décide qu'il y a lieu de permettre aux réfugiés qui le désirent, de rentrer dans leurs foyers le plus tôt possible et de vivre en paix avec leurs voisins,

---

[70] Ladas, *supra* note 68 à la p. 465.

[71] Pour une approche libérale qui reconnaît quelques possibilités de transfert des populations en même temps que la nécessité de restreindre la liberté des États, particulièrement par le biais de la compensation, voir Pallieri, *supra* note 10 aux pp. 149-50: "En résumé, nous estimons qu'il n'y a rien à opposer au transfert de populations et que, dans certaines circonstances, les efforts faits dans ce sens doivent même être encouragés par le droit international: le légitime désir de tout État moderne d'avoir des citoyens loyaux, l'aspiration de l'humanité entière à sauvegarder la paix, nous donnent autant de raisons pour favoriser, le cas échéant, le transfert de populations. Mais on ne doit jamais oublier qu'on a affaire à des hommes et qu'on leur demande de grands sacrifices, comme celui d'abandonner le territoire où ils sont nés et où ils ont vécu. Le seul moyen admissible pour réaliser ce résultat, est d'obtenir leur libre consentement par des avantages d'un autre genre qui, à leur avis, soient suffisants pour les indemniser du sacrifice qu'on leur demande. L'opération pourra devenir très onéreuse et coûteuse pour les États intéressés; mais c'est à eux de décider d'y recourir, ou de s'en abstenir parce qu'ils n'ont pas un intérêt assez vif à le faire."

et que des indemnités doivent être payées à titre de compensation pour les biens de ceux qui décident de ne pas rentrer dans leurs foyers et pour tout bien perdu ou endommagé lorsque, en vertu des principes du droit international ou en équité, cette perte ou ce dommage doit être réparé par les Gouvernements ou autorités responsables.[72]

Cet instrument tente formellement d'atténuer certaines conséquences du nettoyage ethnique et à rendre justice aux populations déplacées, tout en reconnaissant les complexités concernant la paix et la sécurité régionales après un déplacement massif de population.[73]

Les réactions au nettoyage ethnique qui favorisent le droit au retour découlent généralement du désir de renverser le nettoyage ethnique.[74] Bien que louable, cette position doit être évaluée par rapport aux problèmes rencontrés dans le retour des réfugiés. Ces problèmes sont considérables quand la paix résulte de la création effective de territoires homogènes. Dans ces conditions, le retour des populations déplacées représente une menace directe à l'entité politique qui a consolidé son pouvoir par l'exclusion extrême des minorités.[75] Du point de vue de la protection des droits de l'homme, la résolution des tensions entre divers droits individuels s'avère difficile même dans des conditions de paix car les droits de propriété des personnes déplacées qui retournent après une absence

---

[72] 11 décembre 1949, par. 11. Les résolutions du CSNU sur la situation des Palestiniens ne contiennent pas de dispositions similaires. Contrairement aux résolutions du CSNU, les résolutions de l'AGNU ne sont pas contraignantes sur le plan juridique (sauf pour certaines questions budgétaires et pour son propre règlement interne). Voir art. 10 et 25 de la Charte des Nations Unies.

[73] Voir aussi l'art. I(1) et (4), Accord sur les réfugiés et les personnes déplacées, Annexe VII de l'Accord-cadre général négocié à Dayton et signé à Paris le 14 décembre 1995 (source: Conférence de Paris, traduction du ministère des Affaires étrangères, République française).

[74] Voir, par exemple, Meindersma, *supra* note 64 à la p. 639: "the obligation to cease and reverse the consequences of ethnic cleansing is not only incumbent on the violating State; a duty to ensure this outcome rests on the entire community of nations."

[75] Sergio Vieira de Mello, "Forcible Population Transfer and Ethnic Cleansing," *Refugee Survey Quarterly*, vol. 16, 1997 à la p. vi: "Ethnic cleansing poses particular difficulties regarding the effective enjoyment of the right to return without causing further displacement or exposing returnees to renewed violence ... Such return is, however, particularly difficult in conditions where peace may have been brought about in part because the state was successful in its ethnic cleansing policies."

prolongée ont souvent été assumés par de nouveaux "colons." Ces derniers peuvent être également des déplacés.[76]

Si le retour des personnes déplacées ne représente pas toujours une option réaliste dans une situation de conflit caractérisée par le nettoyage ethnique,[77] plusieurs exemples du XXᵉ siècle suggèrent que les mécanismes de compensation semblent impossibles à mettre en application. Pourtant la possibilité d'indemniser les populations "échangées" paraît comme une option attrayante pour les commentateurs qui ont émis les critiques les plus sévères de la Convention de Lausanne.[78]

L'expérience de la Commission mixte établie en vertu de la Convention de Lausanne est révélatrice. Même si elle était responsable de l'évaluation et de la liquidation des biens immobiliers et mobiliers des personnes déplacées[79] afin d'assigner au pays d'immigration une dette à l'encontre des propriétaires destitués,[80] elle n'a pas pu procéder à des évaluations individuelles des biens.[81]

[76] Sur la situation palestinienne, voir ci-dessous. Sur l'exemple du Rwanda, voir Chaloka Beyani, "A Political and Legal Analysis of the Problem of the Return of Forcibly Transferred Populations," *Refugee Survey Quarterly*, vol. 16, 1997 à la p. 21.

[77] Pour un avis juridique qui considère que les victimes du nettoyage ethnique doivent avoir un choix véritable entre le droit au retour ou la *restitutio in integrum*, voir Georges Abi-Saab *et al.*, *supra* note 7 au par. 22: "Face à la violation d'une norme impérative, la responsabilité première qui incombe aux États concernés selon le droit international est la restitution aux victimes de leurs propriétés. L'indemnisation n'a lieu d'être que si la restitution s'avère irréalisable ou si les victimes y renoncent." Voir aussi par. 32.

[78] Voir, par exemple, Tenekides, *supra* note 12 à la p. 87.

[79] Art. 13 de la Convention de Lausanne: "La Commission mixte aura tout pouvoir pour faire procéder à l'estimation des biens mobiliers et immobiliers qui doivent être liquidés en vertu de la présente Convention, les intéressés étant entendus ou ayant été dûment convoqués pour être entendus. La base de l'estimation des biens qui doivent être liquidés sera la valeur de ces biens en monnaie d'or."

[80] Art. 14: "La Commission remettra au propriétaire intéressé une déclaration constatant la somme qui lui est due du chef des biens dont il a été dépossédé, biens qui resteront à la disposition du Gouvernement sur le territoire duquel ils sont situés. Les montants dus sur la base de ces déclaration constitueront une dette du Gouvernement du pays où la liquidation aura eu lieu envers le Gouvernement dont relève l'émigrant. Celui-ci devra en principe recevoir, dans le pays où il émigre, en représentation des sommes qui lui sont dues, des biens d'égale valeur et de même nature que ceux qu'il aura abandonnés."

[81] Sur les problèmes encourus, voir, par exemple, Tenekides, *supra* note 12 à la p. 85: "La convention ne dit pas, ce qui pourtant est essentiel, à quel moment et sur quelle base aura lieu l'estimation." Plusieurs actes ont été signés en 1925-1927

Les déclarations publiques de certains politiciens grecs suggérant qu'une annulation réciproque des dettes était envisagée entre Athènes et Ankara ont mené à des manifestations de la part de nombreux Grecs "échangés." Les gouvernements concernés ont néanmoins signé une entente en 1930 qui a remplacé le mécanisme d'indemnisation prévu dans la Convention de Lausanne.[82] Le nouvel arrangement a simplement transféré la propriété des biens au gouvernement du pays où ils se trouvaient.[83]

L'expérience de la Commission de conciliation pour la Palestine établie par la résolution 194(III) ne donne pas plus de raisons pour être optimiste concernant l'efficacité des mécanismes internationaux de compensation. Même si elle s'est concentrée sur le paiement de la compensation,[84] elle s'est vite rendue compte qu'il serait peu probable de pouvoir indemniser individuellement les

---

afin de clarifier certaines dispositions de la Convention de Lausanne: Accord relatif aux biens des Turcs en Grèce et des Hellènes en Turquie, signé à Angora le 21 juin 1925, suivi d'un Procès-Verbal de signature, de deux Protocoles et Projets de résolutions signés à la date du même jour et d'une Résolution de la Commission mixte d'échange des populations grecques et turques prise par l'Assemblée plénière le 19 mars 1927, Accord afin de faciliter l'application de certaines dispositions du Traité de Lausanne et de la Déclaration n° IX, signé à Athènes le 1er décembre 1926, suivi de plusieurs Protocoles signés à la date du même jour. *Recueil général de traités*, 3e série, t. XX (1920), Leipzig, 1929 aux pp. 86 et ss.

[82] Convention sur la liquidation définitive des questions découlant de l'application du Traité de Lausanne et de l'Accord d'Athènes au sujet de l'échange des populations, signée à Ankara le 10 juin 1930. *Recueil général de traités*, 3e série, t. XXVIII, Leipzig, 1934 à la p. 654.

[83] Jusqu'à ce moment, les biens laissés par les musulmans en Grèce avaient été pris en charge par un office autonome d'établissement des réfugiés créé par le Protocole relatif à l'établissement des réfugiés en Grèce et à l'institution, à cet effet, d'un office autonome d'établissement des réfugiés, R.T.S.N., vol. XX, 1923 à la p. 503. Signé à Genève le 29 septembre 1923 et ratifié par la Grèce le 2 novembre 1923. L'office a été dissous en 1930. Al-Khasawneh et Hatano, *supra* note 19 au par. 122: "Tous les travaux de la Commission mixte devaient se ressentir de l'hostilité mutuelle entre les principaux États. La Commission avait totalement échoué à superviser les dédommagements, tandis que les gouvernements respectifs confisquaient carrément les biens immobiliers des émigrants, souvent avant que ceux-ci aient pu obtenir un certificat en attestant la valeur. Les deux gouvernements étaient en faveur de l'annulation de tout le plan d'indemnisation. Avec la Convention d'Angora ils renvoyèrent la question aux membres neutres de la Commission qui dénoncèrent les dispositions pertinentes de la Convention et décidèrent que le dédommagement devait être effectué par les États d'accueil."

[84] Voir par. 11 de la résolution 194(III) de l'AGNU datée du 11 décembre 1948.

réfugiés.[85] La magnitude du problème est décrite dans le commentaire suivant:

Of the first 370 Jewish settlements established after 1948, 350 were on former Arab property. Whole Arab cities — such as Jaffa, Acre, Lydda, Ramle, Baysan and Majdal — 388 towns and villages, and large parts of other cities, containing nearly a quarter of all buildings standing in Israel during 1948, were abandoned by the refugees.[86]

Si l'indemnisation individuelle est difficile à réaliser immédiatement à la suite d'un conflit interethnique comme le suggère l'expérience de la Commission mixte établie par la Convention de Lausanne, le cas palestinien indique qu'elle est presque impossible à réaliser quand une longue période de temps s'est écoulée.[87] Compte tenu de la spécificité des conflits interethniques, les tentatives d'indemniser individuellement les victimes déplacées peuvent paraître illusoires.[88] Le commentaire suivant illustre le paradoxe de la situation:

Theoretically, the Convention of Lausanne was drawn up with scrupulous regard to the rights of exchangeables, but practically the rights so granted were of no real value. No Convention of the sort could be put in practice in a satisfactory manner unless, coincident with the departure of an emigrant, he received the value of the property abandoned by him. In order that this should be possible, the two contracting countries must be at peace, and no pressure to bring about an exchange must exist. In other words, the scheme would only work at a time when it is improbable that anyone would think of putting it into practice.[89]

---

[85] Lex Takkenberg, *The Status of Palestinian Refugees in International Law*, Oxford, Clarendon Press, 1998 à la p. 339.

[86] Don Peretz, *The Middle East Today*, Westport Praeger, 6ᵉ éd., 1994 à la p. 335.

[87] "After almost fifty years it will be very difficult to identify and evaluate abandoned property. Since most refugee property was absorbed into Israel's economy, it has been transformed, often beyond recognition. In many cases it has passed through several successive owners of Israeli government agencies and has been classified and reclassified under a variety of laws. Much land that was once agricultural has become urban; in many cases where there were once Palestinian Arab farms, orchards, or orange groves, there are now Jewish high-rise apartments or office buildings. Moveable property such as vehicles, household goods, farm animals, and personal property has long since disappeared without any record of its disposition." Takkenberg, *supra* note 85 à la p. 340.

[88] La compensation est plus compliquée que la présomption simpliste évoquée dans Kaufmann, *supra* note 11 à la p. 168.

[89] Eddy, *supra* note 68 à la p. 228.

La question du caractère volontaire ou obligatoire des échanges de populations soulevée dans la sous-section précédente est affectée de façon fondamentale par le dilemme qui résulte de l'inefficacité des mécanismes de compensation individuelle. Pour que des échanges involontaires soient acceptables sur le plan politique, il faut au moins accorder une compensation individuelle aux personnes déplacées. Mais l'expérience de la Commission mixte de Lausanne et de la Commission de conciliation pour la Palestine suggère que les personnes transférées peuvent tout au plus s'attendre à une compensation sous forme de montant global.[90] Même si cela représenterait une réussite considérable dans le contexte difficile du nettoyage ethnique,[91] il devient clair que des individus n'accepteront pas de participer volontairement à un arrangement d'échange parce qu'il est peu probable qu'ils obtiennent une compensation individuelle.

III LES PRINCIPES HUMANITAIRES ET LE PRAGMATISME FACE AU NETTOYAGE ETHNIQUE

De toute évidence, les transferts de populations et le nettoyage ethnique portent atteinte aujourd'hui à un vaste éventail des droits de l'homme.[92] En tant qu'actes illicites, ils engagent la responsabilité des États et la responsabilité pénale des individus.[93] Pour les

---

[90] Pour une position optimiste dans le contexte palestinien, voir Takkenberg, *supra* note 85 à la p. 339: "to be expected that payment of compensation will benefit the rehabilitation and rehousing of the refugees at large."

[91] Par exemple, une telle compensation augmenterait la capacité d'absorption de la nouvelle entité territoriale pour les réfugiés palestiniens. *Ibid.* aux pp. 336, 341.

[92] Dans le contexte du conflit armé en Bosnie-Herzégovine, le CSNU a condamné les violations du droit international qu'implique la pratique d'"épuration ethnique" dans sa résolution 771 du 13 août 1992 (par. 2) et il a affirmé que le nettoyage ethnique est illégal dans sa résolution 808 du 22 février 1993 (préambule) et sa résolution 820 du 17 avril 1993 (préambule, par. 6). L'AGNU considère de façon générale que le nettoyage ethnique "constitue une violation grave et sérieuse du droit international humanitaire" dans sa résolution 46/242 du 25 août 1992 et sa résolution 47/80 du 15 mars 1993. Le Comité pour l'élimination de la discrimination raciale considère que tout transfert involontaire est contraire au droit international. Voir sa décision 2(47) relative à la Bosnie-Herzégovine du 17 août 1995, doc. A/50/18, au par. 26: "toute tentative visant à changer ou valider la modification de la composition démographique d'une région sans le consentement des habitants originaires, par quelque moyen que ce soit, est une violation du droit international."

[93] Awn Shawkat Al-Khasawneh, *Droits de l'homme et transferts de population*, Rapport final, Commission des droits de l'homme (Sous-Commission de la lutte contre

personnes transférées, il est clair que les circonstances entourant le nettoyage ethnique sont caractérisées par des souffrances terribles. La situation est pourtant compliquée par le fait que les transferts ont généralement lieu dans des circonstances où il y va des intérêts vitaux des États.

Il y a au moins deux questions distinctes qu'il ne faut pas confondre dans l'évaluation des réactions internationales au nettoyage ethnique. La première concerne la réaction politique face aux auteurs des violations des droits de l'homme qui entourent généralement les transferts forcés. Cette réaction peut comporter, par exemple, des mesures coercitives contre les auteurs en conformité aux principes établis du droit international. Mais une fois les violations déjà commises, la réponse humanitaire pour aider les victimes déplacées constitue une question distincte. Les deux questions sont certes liées et il est possible que la réponse politique à la première puisse apporter une solution humanitaire à la deuxième. Cependant, une position éthique qui refuse de trouver une solution concrète et durable au sort des personnes déplacées si cela laisserait les violations des droits de l'homme impunis demeure discutable. Quel que soit l'action prise à l'encontre des auteurs du nettoyage ethnique, il est impératif d'aborder aussi vite que possible la situation des populations déplacées de façon réaliste. Un moralisme absolu inspiré par une éthique de conviction qui refuse de trouver une solution durable au déplacement si les violations des droits de l'homme n'ont pas été sanctionnées paraît inapproprié dans le contexte difficile des conflits armés. Telle est la leçon implicite de l'expérience du Haut Commissaire Nansen en Asie Mineure.

Bien que la plupart des observateurs soient d'accords que la condamnation du nettoyage ethnique n'est pas suffisante, il peut être utile de reconnaître que les auteurs des abus sont rarement arrêtés pendant qu'ils sont en train de poursuivre leurs crimes. Dans cette perspective, il est dangereux de suggérer que le renversement du nettoyage ethnique constitue la seule solution moralement acceptable car cela entraîne presque inévitablement le recours à la force. Le risque d'inaction augmente si les États perçoivent peu de flexibilité quant aux solutions possibles. À titre d'illustration, il est peu probable que la crise au Moyen Orient puisse être résolue si les acteurs internationaux insistent sur le renversement du nettoyage

---

les mesures discriminatoires et de la protection des minorités), E/CN.4/Sub.2/1997/23, 27 juin 1997 aux par. 12-17, 60.

ethnique et rejettent tout plan de paix qui comporte une compensation aux réfugiés palestiniens qui ne peuvent pas exercer leur droit au retour.

Même dans les rares occasions où les puissances occidentales sont disposées à intervenir militairement pour influencer un conflit interethnique, l'expérience récente du Kosovo illustre comment il est difficile de prévenir le nettoyage ethnique par des moyens militaires. En effet, le Kosovo s'est transformé depuis l'intervention de l'OTAN en territoire presque ethniquement homogène,[94] malgré une présence imposante de l'ONU, de l'OSCE et d'une force militaire sous le contrôle de l'OTAN.[95]

Les problèmes difficiles décrits ci-dessus sont parmi ceux que les participants à la Conférence de Lausanne ont dû aborder il y a quatre-vingts ans. Étant donné qu'une intervention militaire pour prévenir les déplacements n'était pas envisagée par les membres de la SDN, le pragmatisme suggérait qu'un échange de populations représentait la seule façon de minimiser les souffrances des populations civiles. En conséquence, le Haut Commissaire Nansen a participé à l'évacuation et la réinstallation des déplacés grecs et turcs. Bien que l'analyse de cet article suggère que de tels échanges soient problématiques à plusieurs égards, les négociations diplomatiques

---

[94] Pour une autocritique publiée par un *leader* albanais au Kosovo, voir Veton Surroi, "Victims of the Victims," *The New York Review of Books*, 7 octobre 1999. Voir aussi Agence France Presse, *Les civils serbes font leurs valises*, 15 juin 1999; Tim Butcher, "Serbs take refuge as revenge killings grow," *The Daily Telegraph*, 25 juin 1999; Susan Milligan, "A reversal in roles: Serbs become targets," *The Boston Globe*, 9 juillet 1999; BBC World News Online, *Kosovo reprisals horrify UN*, 17 juillet 1999; Tom Walker, "Vengeful KLA turns on nuns and Gypsies," *The Times*, 21 juillet 1999; Agence France Presse, *La minorité turque du Kosovo priée de "s'albaniser,"* 23 août 1999; Agence France Presse, *Zorica, 20 ans, a identifié son mari parmi les cadavres du site d'Ugljare*, 29 août 1999; Agence France Presse, *Le Kosovo d'après-guerre reste une terre de déplacements forcés de populations*, 30 août 1999; Milovan Mracevich, "Targets of terrorism, Pristina's Jews forced to flee," *The Globe and Mail*, 31 août 1999, p. A16.

[95] Agence France Presse, *L'ONU appelle les Serbes à rester — sans garantie*, 30 juin 1999: "La communauté internationale a appelé mercredi les Serbes à prendre le risque de rester au Kosovo, tout en admettant n'avoir pas les moyens de les protéger contre les violences des Albanais." Voir aussi Agence France Presse, *Les Tziganes reprochent à l'ONU et l'OTAN de ne pas les protéger au Kosovo*, 6 septembre 1999; *Situation des droits de l'homme en Bosnie-Herzégovine, dans la République de Croatie et dans la République fédérale de Yougoslavie (Serbie et Monténégro)*, Doc. NU S/1999/1000/Add.1, A/54/396/Add.1, 3 novembre 1999 au par. 34; Reuters, *Dernier appel de Kouchner à l'arrêt des violences au Kosovo*, 12 janvier 2001; BBC News Online, *UN "failed" Kosovo Serbs*, 12 janvier 2001.

à l'époque indiquent qu'ils représentaient la seule option réaliste qui pouvait être acceptée par les belligérants.

Nansen considérait l'échange négocié pendant la crise d'Asie Mineure comme un succès par rapport à ses autres opérations humanitaires, car au moins dans celle-ci il y avait une supervision internationale et la possibilité de compensation pour les personnes déplacées. Les Arméniens, par exemple, n'avaient pas de véritable appui international et selon Nansen leur sort était pire que celui des Grecs transférés.[96]

Au cours de la Conférence de Lausanne, les participants n'ont même pas considéré la possibilité de permettre aux populations envisagées pour l'échange de rester dans leur pays d'origine et de bénéficier du système des minorités de la SDN. Le système des minorités était considéré comme réalisable uniquement après que le gros des populations "indésirables" ait été échangé, de la sorte qu'il a été inclus dans le Traité de Lausanne pour les populations restantes. La cohérence de cette approche se comprend si on reconnaît que la prévention des massacres représente l'objectif primordial de tout système de protection des minorités, ainsi que la seule justification d'un transfert de populations. Il est sans doute plus facile d'introduire un système de protection des minorités dans l'État turc naissant ou d'établir un cadre juridique de protection des droits de l'homme en Bosnie-Herzégovine ou au Kosovo après l'achèvement du processus de nettoyage ethnique, que d'affronter le nettoyage ethnique pendant qu'il se déroule.[97] En examinant les réactions internationales possibles, il peut être utile de reconnaître que les transferts de populations sont parfois inévitables[98] même s'ils présentent de nombreux aspects difficilement acceptables. Il s'agit alors d'une option de dernier recours qui ne devrait pas être adoptée sans résistance considérable.

Comme indiqué dans l'analyse concernant le droit au retour et le droit à la compensation, le droit international reconnaît qu'il

---

[96] Claudena Skran, "Profiles of the First Two High Commissioners," *Journal of Refugee Studies*, vol. 1, n° 3/4, 1988 aux pp. 287-88.

[97] Ce point essentiel est sous-estimé dans Meindersma, *supra* note 12 à la p. 348: "Compared to the protection guaranteed to minorities under the Lausanne Peace Treaty, the Exchange Convention begs the question why the populations selected to be forcibly exchanged were denied the rights and protection afforded to other, and remaining, minority groups in Turkey and Greece."

[98] Voir le point de vue exprimé dans Kaufmann, *supra* note 11 à la p. 137: "Stable resolutions of ethnic civil wars are possible, but only when the opposing groups are demographically separated into defensible enclaves."

puisse y avoir conflit entre certaines revendications liées aux droits de l'homme. La recherche du remède approprié en situation de transfert de populations soulève souvent la tension fondamentale entre paix et justice: est-ce que la *restitutio in integrum* constitue toujours le remède sur lequel il faut insister? De la perspective de l'individu lésé, la *restitutio in integrum* est sans doute le remède le plus juste car il cherche à annuler le préjudice initial. Cependant, la paix est souvent l'aboutissement d'un compromis qui reflète le rapport des forces entre les parties au conflit et il n'est donc pas toujours fondé sur des principes de justice.[99] Après tout, la paix constitue l'objectif ultime de l'ONU et une approche absolutiste fixée uniquement sur l'illégalité des transferts de populations peut se heurter aux droits des personnes de vivre dans la paix et la sécurité.

Les successeurs du Haut Commissaire Nansen reconnaissent depuis de nombreuses années que le rapatriement volontaire ne constitue qu'une des trois solutions durables au drame des réfugiés: les deux autres sont l'intégration dans le pays de premier asile et la réinstallation dans un pays tiers. Cette approche admet implicitement que la *restitutio in integrum* sous forme de rapatriement puisse être irréalisable dans certaines situations. Elle reflète le caractère historiquement pragmatique du droit international des réfugiés en suggérant qu'une réponse humanitaire soit nécessaire même s'il n'y a pas eu de réparation concernant les violations des droits de l'homme.

Dans ce contexte, l'histoire récente suggère que la justice n'est pas nécessairement une condition requise pour une paix efficace. Par exemple, il est difficile de concilier la pratique des Alliés décrite dans cet article avec le fait que les condamnations du Tribunal militaire international de Nuremberg concernant la déportation de populations civiles ont visé uniquement les autorités allemandes.[100]

---

[99] Voir, par exemple, Al-Khasawneh, *supra* note 93 au par. 63.

[100] Voir, par exemple, le procès en 1946 du juriste nazi Hans Frank qui est devenu le gouverneur général du Gouvernement Général en Pologne (*Procès des Grands Criminels de Guerre devant le Tribunal Militaire International*, vol. 1, 1947 aux pp. 315-18). Voir aussi la condamnation à dix-huit ans de prison prononcée par un tribunal militaire britannique à Hambourg contre le maréchal von Manstein pour son rôle dans la déportation de populations civiles lors de la retraite de l'Ukraine du Groupe Armée Sud sous son commandement: Re von Lewinski, A.D.I.L., 1949 aux pp. 521-23. La capitulation inconditionnelle de l'Allemagne est parfois invoquée pour justifier le recrutement de travailleurs allemands qui ont été utilisés pour des travaux de reconstruction menés par l'autorité suprême des Alliés et pour justifier la déportation d'Allemands en Union soviétique pour du travail forcé. Voir, par exemple, John H.E. Freid,

Bien que l'occupation et la restructuration de l'État allemand à la suite de la Seconde Guerre mondiale soient difficilement conciliables avec le respect de la souveraineté de l'Allemagne,[101] elles ont toutefois contribué à l'établissement d'une paix effective en Europe. Ce point de vue concernant le lien entre la paix et la justice n'est généralement pas partagé par la plupart des juristes qui ont mené récemment des recherches sur les transferts de populations sous l'égide du Haut Commissaire pour les réfugiés. Ces derniers adoptent une approche axée exclusivement sur les droits de l'homme.[102]

Sous certaines conditions, une cessation durable des hostilités et l'établissement de la paix doivent être prioritaires malgré certaines conséquences indésirables à court terme. Étant donné la réalité des conflits armés interethniques où les populations civiles sont directement menacées, la réalisation d'une paix "juste" où le nettoyage ethnique est renversé et les droits des victimes sont respectés peut s'avérer illusoire. Il est préférable de favoriser la survie immédiate des populations et essayer de créer des conditions qui vont permettre d'aborder les questions de justice en temps utile.

Le point de vue des juristes qui travaillent au sein des organisations internationales a changé considérablement à la suite de la Seconde Guerre mondiale.[103] L'analyse de cet article suggère que

"*Transfer of Civilian Manpower from Occupied Territory,*" AJIL, vol. 40, 1946 aux pp. 326-30.

[101] Cette question controversée dépend de la constatation que l'Allemagne a cessé temporairement d'être une entité gouvernementale parce qu'elle a été "subjuguée" par les Alliés. Une réponse affirmative permet le transfert légal de la souveraineté aux Alliés. Pour une opinion en faveur du caractère légal de l'opération, voir Ian Brownlie, *International Law and the Use of Force,* Oxford, Clarendon Press, 1963 à la p. 408.

[102] Voir, par exemple, Beyani, *supra* note 76 à la p. 15: "there cannot be meaningful peace without justice" et Meindersma, *supra* note 64 à la p. 636: "From the perspective of human rights law, it is questionable whether human rights can be neglected in the interest of peace. The normative structure of human rights law and the very objective of establishing a lasting peace rally against that. If peace is to embrace more than the short-term goal of ending war, respect for the human rights of the people concerned must constitute the basis of a lasting settlement. Without a solid human rights foundation, a durable peace is hard to conceive."

[103] Le titre de l'article suivant reflète les points de vue récents: Maria Stavropoulou, "The Right Not to Be Displaced," Am.U.J.Int'l L.&Pol'y, vol. 9, 1994 à la p. 689. Pour un point de vue moins récent, voir Freid, *supra* note 99 à la p. 304: "Under special circumstances — or, to be more exact, for particularly important purposes — international law recognises the right of governments to organise compulsory migration." Les opinions juridiques rassemblées par

l'idéalisme du mouvement des droits de l'homme a encouragé les juristes à prendre depuis plusieurs années une position moraliste sur ce sujet délicat sans trop d'égard pour les problèmes d'application sur le terrain ou le lien avec l'établissement d'une trêve durable.[104] Les juristes qui considèrent que la paix ne devrait pas être négociée "à n'importe quel prix"[105] assument une responsabilité considérable. Les problèmes fondamentaux liés au respect des droits de l'homme peuvent être abordés dans une perspective à plus long terme. En distinguant entre les objectifs à court terme et ceux à long terme, on arrive à concilier possiblement les différences doctrinales au sujet de la relation compliquée entre la paix et la justice.[106] Malheureusement, les développements récents

---

l'Institut de Droit International en 1952 démontrent une "presque unanimité à reconnaître du moins quelques possiblités de transferts de populations; il y a également unanimité à reconnaître la nécessité de restreindre la liberté des États en cette matière." Giorgio Balladore Pallieri, "Les transferts internationaux de populations: Remarques complémentaires du rapporteur," AIDI, vol. 44, t. II, avril 1952 à la p. 195.

[104] Voir, par exemple, Association de Droit International, *Déclaration des principes de droit international sur les expulsions massives*, 1986, principe 14: "Tout transfert ou échange forcé de population, fondé sur la race, la religion, la nationalité ou l'appartenance à un groupe social particulier ou l'opinion publique, est intrinsèquement inadmissible [sic], qu'il découle de traités ou d'une expulsion unilatérale." Le texte original se trouve dans International Law Association, *Report of the Sixty-Second Conference Held at Seoul*, 1986 aux pp. 13-18. Traduction française reproduite dans Al-Khasawneh et Hatano, *supra* note 19 au par. 356. Voir aussi Abi-Saab *et al.*, *supra* note 7 au par. 9: "Nous sommes convaincus qu'aujourd'hui de tels actes sont indiscutablement contraires au droit international tel qu'il a évolué." Cependant, il n'est pas clair de quels actes il s'agit car cet avis juridique amalgame et mélange des termes qui désignent des situations distinctes: "déplacement massif," "échange forcé" et "transfert forcé." Voir par. 5 et 9. En conséquence, la distinction importante entre un échange volontaire et un échange involontaire n'est pas reconnue.

[105] Meindersma, *supra* note 64 à la p. 636.

[106] Pour un exemple d'une approche réaliste, voir Henry A. Kissinger, "Peace and Justice," *Does America Need a Foreign Policy?*, New York, Simon & Schuster, 2001 aux pp. 234-82; et David P. Forsythe, "The United States and International Criminal Justice," Hum.Rts.Q., vol. 24, 2002 aux pp. 974-91. Pour un exemple d'une approche qui s'oppose à ce réalisme, voir Juan E. Mendez, "National Reconciliation, Transnational Justice, and the International Criminal Court," *Ethics & International Affairs*, vol. 15, 2001 à la p. 32: "seeking peace between warring factions should be guided by ... long-term goals and not simply by the more immediate need to persuade the actors to lay down their arms. A promise of impunity may well lead to a cease-fire; but a lasting peace can only be built over a foundation of truth, justice, and meaningful reconciliation."

concernant le droit pénal international et les commissions de vérité n'apportent pas de réponse claire aux dilemmes abordés dans cet article.

D'une certaine façon, c'est le rôle et la pertinence du droit international qui sont remis en cause. Après tout, si des idées de justice ou des principes juridiques émergeant se heurtent aux réalités du droit, ce légalisme ne peut pas être utile aux décideurs politiques qui doivent prendre des décisions rapides dans des conditions difficiles de conflit interethnique. Dans la mesure où la logique affreuse des transferts de populations a souvent dominé la conduite des belligérants pendant l'histoire moderne, une alternative fiable et efficace doit être proposée par les juristes qui considèrent que ce genre de déplacements n'a pas de place dans le contexte actuel des droits de l'homme. Nous croyons que, malgré leur contribution et leur influence majeures par rapport aux relations internationales, les droits de l'homme n'offrent pas une solution aux problèmes soulevés par les diplomates à Lausanne.

CONCLUSION

Du point de vue du droit international, l'illégalité des activités liées au nettoyage ethnique et aux transferts de populations semble être une position largement acquise. Les dilemmes se manifestent plutôt quand on considère la réaction internationale appropriée aux conflits caractérisés par ce genre d'abus et de violence. Cet article suggère que certaines présomptions et positions dominantes dans le milieu des droits de l'homme ne sont pas partagées par nombreux spécialistes des relations internationales.[107] Les droits de l'homme sont en pleine évolution depuis quelques décennies et ils semblent avoir encouragé une orientation partiellement problématique concernant les dilemmes abordés dans cet article. Notamment, l'éthique de conviction qui inspire la plupart des défenseurs des droits de l'homme paraît discutable dans le sens qu'elle semble parfois détachée des considérations pragmatiques concernant la réalité sur le terrain et la flexibilité nécessaire pour les solutions diplomatiques.

L'analyse ci-dessus suggère que le réalisme manifesté lors de la Conférence de Lausanne ne devrait pas être écarté facilement. Si

---

[107] Voir, par ex., Kissinger, *supra* note 105; Weiner, *supra* note 16; Zolberg, Suhrke et Aguayo, *supra* note 38; Kaufmann, *supra* note 98; Al-Khasawneh, *supra* note 106; Vieira de Mello, *supra* note 75; de Zayas, *supra* note 65; Takkenberg, *supra* note 87.

les principes humanitaires contemporains sont détachés de la réalité sur le terrain ou s'ils servent à brouiller des solutions possibles et à divertir des ressources limitées, il n'est pas clair qu'ils soient défendables. Selon une approche éthique que Max Weber qualifierait de verantwortungsethisch,[108] c'est-à-dire une approche axée sur la responsabilité et non sur la conviction morale, ils seraient problématiques. On peut comparer la logique de protection décrite dans cet article, qui reflète les origines du droit international des réfugiés, à la logique militante du mouvement des droits de l'homme. Cette dernière est dominée par la pureté morale des intentions de l'intervenant et dans ce sens elle se rapproche de la gesinnungsethisch.[109] Or, les problèmes de protection que les praticiens doivent confronter sur le terrain sont parfois mieux abordés dans une perspective qui concilie l'idéalisme avec une approche pragmatique. Une éthique qui met l'accent sur la responsabilité permet une telle conciliation dans le contexte difficile des conflits interethniques.

Telle est la logique de l'approche proposée au début de la dernière section. Elle suggère qu'il est parfois utile de distinguer les droits individuels de la personne déplacée par rapport aux violations initiales des droits de l'homme qui ont provoqué le déplacement. Dans la mesure où les acteurs internationaux ont accès aux personnes qui ont dû fuir les zones de conflit, il est impératif d'améliorer avant tout le sort de ces victimes déracinées. C'est-à-dire, il faut aborder les nouveaux défis relatifs aux droits de l'homme dans un contexte d'exil. La prévention du déplacement est un problème distinct pour lequel, malheureusement, la pratique internationale laisse toujours à désirer. En d'autres termes, la "commodification" de l'être humain qu'on trouve dans la Convention de Lausanne est déplorable et elle doit être résistée autant que possible et autant que cela n'augmente pas les souffrances des personnes déplacées. Cependant, l'alternative illustrée par les massacres de populations civiles au XXᵉ siècle est encore moins acceptable.

MICHAEL BARUTCISKI
Collège Glendon, Université York

---

[108] Max Weber, *Le savant et le politique*, Paris, Libraire Plon, 1959 aux pp. 186-95.
[109] *Idem.*

Summary

Population Transfers Eighty Years after the Lausanne Convention

This article examines the Asia Minor crisis and the dilemmas raised by population transfers. Contemporary conflicts continue to be characterized by ethnic cleansing and de facto transfers despite the new human rights norms that have influenced the development of international law. The international instruments that deal with the displaced populations generally offer the option of return or compensation. Yet various examples from the twentieth century indicate that these two approaches are difficult to implement. The analysis suggests that the relationship between peace and respect for human rights is more complex than commonly assumed. The pragmatism demonstrated by the High Commissioner for Refugees during the Asia Minor crisis should not be dismissed if it provides a realistic approach to avoiding massacres of civilian populations.

Sommaire

Les transferts de populations quatre-vingts ans après la Convention de Lausanne

Cet article examine la crise d'Asie Mineure et les dilemmes suscités par le phénomène du transfert de populations. Les conflits contemporains continuent d'être caractérisés par le nettoyage ethnique et les transferts de facto, malgré les nouvelles normes des droits de l'homme qui ont influencé le développement du droit international. Les instruments internationaux qui abordent la détresse des populations déplacées offrent d'habitude le choix entre le retour ou la compensation. Pourtant plusieurs exemples du XXe siècle indiquent que ces deux approches sont difficiles à mettre en application. L'analyse suggère que la relation entre la paix et le respect des droits de l'homme est plus complexe que communément admise. Le pragmatisme manifesté par le Haut Commissaire pour les réfugiés lors de la crise d'Asie Mineure ne devrait pas être écarté s'il représente une option réaliste afin d'éviter les massacres de populations civiles.

Canada–United States "Safe Third Country" Agreement: To What Purpose?

INTRODUCTION

The Agreement between the Government of Canada and the Government of the United States of America for Cooperation in the Examination of Refugee Status Claims from Nations of Third Countries (STCA),[1] which was initialed in August 2002 by Canada and the United States, is regarded by many as one more *non-entrée* mechanism[2] adopted by the countries of the North in response to the increasing numbers of refugees from the South.[3] Whatever the stated objectives of this agreement are, the most immediate impact of the STCA will be to significantly diminish the number of refugee claimants in Canada. In order for asylum-seekers to obtain refuge in Canada, they must have access to Canadian territory and access to the procedures for claiming refugee status.[4] The STCA permits the United States and Canada to return asylum-seekers arriving at

---

[1] Agreement between the Government of Canada and the Government of the United States of America for Cooperation in the Examination of Refugee Status Claims from Nations of Third Countries, August 30, 2002, text is available online at <http://www.cic.gc.ca/english/policy/safe-third.html> [hereinafter STCA].

[2] *Non-entrée* mechanisms include visa requirements, interdiction at sea, refusal to accept claims made in so-called "international zones," and so on. See James C. Hathaway, "The Emerging Politics of *Non-Entrée*" (1992) 91 Refugees 40.

[3] See, for example, David Matas and Ilana Simon, *Closing the Doors: The Failure of Refugee Protection* (Toronto: Summerhill Press, 1989).

[4] Asylum-seekers may obtain refugee status in Canada either through the Refugee and Humanitarian Resettlement Program for people seeking protection from outside Canada or through the In-Canada Refugee Protection Process for persons making refugee protection claims from within Canada. For details regarding these processes, see Citizenship and Immigration Canada, which is accessible at <http://www.cic.gc.ca/english/index.html>.

land border ports of entry to the country of last presence for the determination of a refugee status claim. From a Canadian perspective, this regulation means that if an asylum-seeker at any one of the entry points on the Canada-United States border does not fall within one of the exceptions in the STCA, he or she will not be permitted to seek refugee status in Canada and will be sent back into the United States and *vice versa*. The categories of asylum-seekers who may be exceptions to the rule of being removed to the United States ("the country of last presence") are: persons who have in Canada at least one family member who has refugee status or other legal status; persons who have at least one adult family member who has a refugee status determination pending; unaccompanied minors; and persons who arrived in Canada with valid visas or were persons who did not require visas.[5] The regulations implementing the provisions of the STCA have added two additional categories: persons who have been charged outside Canada with an offence that could subject them to the death penalty and persons who are nationals or residents of a country on which the minister has imposed a stay on enforcement of removal orders.[6]

Although the right of a state to expel non-nationals has long been accepted in international law,[7] Canada as a signatory to the 1951 Convention Relating to the Status of Refugees[8] (Refugee Convention) has undertaken to be bound by the principle of *non-refoulement* (not returning refugees to a country where they may face danger to their safety and lives), which is found in Article 33 of the Refugee Convention. The 1951 Refugee Convention provides no criteria for the constitution of national asylum procedures and no mechanism for monitoring compliance with the obligation of *non-refoulement*.[9] Thus, any rules pertaining to the entry into a

---

[5] STCA, *supra* note 1 at section 4.

[6] Regulations Amending the Immigration and Refugee Protection Act, S.O.R. 02-326, s. 159.6, text is available online at <http://canadagazette.gc.ca/partI/2002/20021026/html/regle-e.html#36> [hereinafter IRPA Regulations].

[7] See, for example, Guy S. Goodwin-Gill, *International Law and the Movement of Persons between States* (Oxford: Clarendon Press, 1978) at 202-5. The notion that states have an unrestricted right to determine issues of admissibility has not gone unchallenged. See, for example, James A.R. Nafziger, "The General Admission of Aliens under International Law" (1983) 77 Am J. Int'l L. 804.

[8] Convention Relating to the Status of Refugees, July 28, 1951, 189 U.N.T.S. 150 (entered into force April 22, 1954) [hereinafter Refugee Convention].

[9] James C. Hathaway, "A Reconsideration of the Underlying Premise of Refugee Law" (1990) 31 Harv. Int'l L.J. 129 at 167.

state's territory and decisions relating to the granting of refugee status are regarded as being within the domestic jurisdiction of a state subject only to the laws of that state and any relevant customary international law. The Refugee Convention's failure to explicitly provide what should happen if a state where an individual seeks protection decides to send the refugee to another country (other than the alleged state of persecution) has permitted the development of the so-called "safe third country" principle. The underlying assumption of the STCA is that the United States is a "safe third country" for refugees, and, therefore, in sending asylum-seekers back to the United States, Canada would not be in breach of its obligation of *non-refoulement*. To determine the extent of the obligation of *non-refoulement* in relation to the application of a "safe third country" agreement then, one must examine the provisions of the convention itself as well as state practice, the work of eminent scholars, and judicial decisions. It is submitted that the United Nations High Commission for Refugees (UNHCR), with its worldwide presence and significant body of expertise on this subject is also an authoritative, albeit non-binding, source of legal interpretation. Many of the conclusions adopted by the Executive Committee of the UNHCR refer to the rights of asylum-seekers. While these conclusions are not binding on states per se, they consistently affirm the basic principles and may be regarded as a measure against which the actions of states may be reviewed as a factor influencing state practice.[10]

The first part of this note examines the concept of "third safe country" in the context of the obligations of states parties to the Refugee Convention, while the second part analyzes, in particular, the provisions of the STCA between Canada and the United States that have given rise to concerns. Finally, this analysis is undertaken with a view to building a case against the advisability of this agreement in light of Canada's international obligations, Canada's commitment to the protection of human rights, and its humanitarian traditions. The US regulations regarding the implementation of the STCA have recently been made available, and it is not yet clear

---

[10] The United Nations High Commission for Refugees [hereinafter UNHCR] role in influencing the development of the law has been particularly noted in relation to the protection of women refugees. See Nancy Kelly, "Gender-related Persecution" (1993) 26 Cornell Int'l L.J. 626 at 633; Audrey Macklin, "Cross-Border Shopping for Ideas: A Critical Review of United States, Canadian, and Australian Approaches to Gender-Related Asylum Claims" (1998) 13 Geo. Imm. L.J. 25 at 28-30.

if they will soften the potential impact of some of the provisions under criticism.[11] The fact remains that the very nature of the STCA, regardless of the manner of its implementation, is troubling when viewed in light of international refugee law and the Canadian Charter of Rights and Freedoms.[12]

"SAFE THIRD COUNTRY" AND THE REFUGEE CONVENTION

The concept of "safe third country" originated in Europe from a combination of goals but was primarily designed to create a system whereby one state could be said by all involved to be the one responsible for assessing a claim for asylum.[13] It was a direct response to the dramatic rise in the number of requests in Europe for refugee status in the late 1980s and early 1990s.[14] The system was designed to ensure that all of the states involved would know where the asylum-seeker should lodge his/her claim and that all asylum-seekers would be guaranteed that one state should assess their claim. "Safe third country" has been described as meaning a country other than the country of origin or the one where the applicant is seeking asylum, which is "safe" in that the applicant would not "face treatment contrary to Article 33 of the 1951 United Nations Convention Relating to the Status of Refugees, or other violations of human rights."[15] The concept was enshrined in the Convention Determining the State Responsible for Examining Applications for Asylum Lodged in One of the Member States of

---

[11] The US regulations may be found online at <http://uscis.gov/graphics/lawsregs/04-5077.pdf>.

[12] Canadian Charter of Rights and Freedoms, Part I of the Constitution Act, 1982, being Schedule B to the Canada Act 1982 (U.K.), 1982, c. 11 [hereinafter Charter].

[13] Joanne van Selm, "Access to Procedures: 'Safe Third Countries,' 'Safe Countries of Origin' and 'Time Limits,'" paper commissioned by the UNHCR and the Carnegie Endowment for International Peace (2001), text available online at <http://www.unhcr.ch/cgi-bin/texis/vtx/home/+-wwBmewzEd_wwwwmww wwwwwhFqA72ZogRfZNtFqupGdBnqBAFqA72ZRogRfZNcFqJwqqn55aBdap Gdqnm1Gn5euG4nwhnaBrGomaqd1DBGon5Dzmxwwwwwww/opendoc.pdf>.

[14] In 1983, the number was 65,400; in 1992, it was 692,686. Germany alone in 1992 received 79 per cent of the asylum-seekers in Europe. See Nazaré A. Abell "The Impact of International Migration on Security and Stability" (1996) 4 Can. Foreign Policy 83 at 93-97.

[15] United Kingdom Delegation to Geneva, "Sending Asylum Seekers to 'Safe Third Countries'" (1995) 7 Int'l J. Ref. L. 120.

the European Communities (Dublin Convention)[16] and the Convention Implementing the Schengen Agreement on the Gradual Abolition of Checks at Their Common Borders (Schengen Convention),[17] whose objects were to move asylum seekers to the country that, according to the rules of the agreements, should assess their claim.

The Dublin and Schengen Conventions were premised on the assumption that all of the states involved already implement the provisions of the Refugee Convention. However, there were no provisions in the Dublin and Schengen Conventions to ensure that all states parties would maintain the common standards of procedural and substantive rules regarding refugee claims. The practice of the European states thus far indicates that there is little consistency either in the interpretation of the term "safe third country" or on the point during protection procedures at which the concept is applied.[18] In many European countries, the concept of "safe third country" is in fact interpreted as a mixture of the concept of "first country of asylum" and "safe third country." The former refers to a country in which an asylum-seeker had earlier received protection and in which the level of protection had remained satisfactory and the latter refers to a place with which the asylum-seeker has some connection —for instance, transit — and which the state applying the principle believes is the appropriate state in which asylum should be sought. It has been noted that in the Dublin Convention and in European practice, even just the potential for protection elsewhere is enough to justify the return to a transit state.[19] In other words, even if protection in the other state was not sought or offered, as long as it was possible, the asylum-seeker can

---

[16] Convention Determining the State Responsible for Examining Applications for Asylum Lodged in One of the Member States of the European Communities, 2144 U.N.T.S. 492 (it was signed by eleven member states on June 15, 1990 and was signed and ratified by the twelfth state, Denmark, on June 12, 1991; it came into force on September 1, 1997) [hereinafter Dublin Convention].

[17] Convention Implementing the Schengen Agreement on the Gradual Abolition of Checks at Their Common Borders, Official Journal of the European Communities, text is available online at <http://europa.eu.int/eur-lex/pri/en/oj/dat/ 2000/l_239/l_23920000922en00010473.pdf> (it was concluded in June 1990, entered into force between Belgium, France, Germany, Luxembourg, the Netherlands, Portugal, and Spain on March 26, 1995).

[18] S. Lavenex, *Extending the EU Asylum and Immigration Policies to Central and Eastern Europe* (Budapest: Central European University Press, 1999).

[19] Van Selm, *supra* note 13 at 16.

be returned to that country. In fact, Article 3(5) of the Dublin Convention expressly reserves to each member state "the right ... to send an applicant for asylum to a third state" and, the safe third country concept only comes into operation when there is no other non-European Union state to which the claimant may be sent by a member state, "pursuant to its national laws."[20] Thus, under the Dublin Convention, the "safe third country" concept applies only if it has been determined that the asylum applicant cannot be sent to a third country.

An issue that troubles many is whether the application of the "safe third country" concept, which permits a sending state to remove asylum-seekers to "safe" countries where they have, or could have, applied for asylum, is consistent with the obligation of *non-refoulement* found in the Refugee Convention.[21] The duty of states parties to the Refugee Convention to comply with the principle of *non-refoulement* has long been regarded as the cornerstone of the convention, allowing for no derogation from the rule.[22] The obligation of states not to expel, return, or *refoule* refugees to territories where their life or freedom would be threatened has come to be considered a rule of customary international law binding on all states.[23] It is found in Article 33(1), which states:

No Contracting State shall expel or return (*"refouler"*) a refugee in any manner whatsoever to the frontiers of territories where his life or freedom would be threatened on account of his race, religion, nationality, membership of a particular social group or political opinion.[24]

Contracting states are thus clearly prohibited from returning refugees to a place where they might face danger on the grounds of belonging to one of the earlier-mentioned groups. The only exception to the duty of *non-refoulement* is found in Article 33(2), which

---

[20] Guy S. Goodwin Gill, *The Refugee in International Law*, 2nd ed. (Oxford: Clarendon Press, 1996) at 336.

[21] See, for example, Nazare. A. Abell, "The Compatibility of Readmission Agreements with the 1951 Convention Relating to the Status of Refugees" (1999) 11 Int'l J. Ref. L. 60.

[22] Reinhard Marx, "Non-Refoulement, Access to Procedures, and Responsibility for Determining Refugee Claims" (1995) 7 Int.'l J. Ref. L. 383 at 388.

[23] Goodwin Gill, *Refugee in International Law, supra* note 20 at 30; see also Kathleen Keller, "A Comparative and International Law Perspective on the United States (Non) Compliance with Its Duty of Refoulement," text is available online at <http://www.yale.edu/yhrdlj/vo102/keller_Kathleen_note.htm>.

[24] Refugee Convention, *supra* note 8 at Article 33(1).

specifies that the benefit of *non-refoulement* may not "be claimed by a refugee whom there are reasonable grounds for regarding as a danger to the security of the country in which he is, or who, having been convicted by a final judgment of a particularly serious crime, constitutes a danger to the community of that country."[25]

It is submitted therefore that conceptually speaking and in practical terms, the concept of "safe third country" is fraught with difficulty in view of the letter and spirit of the Refugee Convention and of refugee law generally. The very purpose of the Refugee Convention was to ensure that persons who had fled their country for fear of persecution would be given the opportunity to seek protection in another country.[26] Although the Refugee Convention stops short of requiring states to recognize refugees, it does seek to achieve its goal of protection for asylum-seekers through the principle of *non-refoulement*. It has been held that this principle applies as soon as an asylum-seeker claims protection and applies independently of any formal determination of refugee status.[27] Otherwise, as the UNHCR has pointed out, the principle of *non-refoulement* would not provide effective protection for refugees because applicants might be rejected at borders or otherwise returned to the country from which they fled on the grounds that their claim had not been established.[28] Although there was a time when there was some question as to whether the *non-refoulement* principle applied to refugees presenting themselves at the frontier,[29] more recently, most

[25] Refugee Convention, *supra* note 8 at Article 33(2). For a discussion on how this provision has been used to justify automatic exclusion of certain groups, see James C. Hathaway and Colin J. Harvey, "Framing Refugee Protection in the New World Disorder" (2001) 34 Cornell Int'l L.J. 257.

[26] The definition of refugee in the Refugee Convention states that the term "refugee" applies to any person who because of a "well-founded fear" of persecution on grounds of race, religion, nationality, political opinion, or membership in a social group, are unwilling or unable to return to their home countries. Refugee Convention, *supra* note 8 at Article 1, para. A (2).

[27] Marx, *supra* note 22 at 383.

[28] UNHCR Executive Committee, *Note on International Protection* (document issued at the forty-fourth session of the Executive Committee of the High Commissioner's Program, Doc. A/AC.96/815, 1993), text is available online at <http://www.unhcr.ch/cgi-bin/texis/vtx/home/+uwwBme8UZ6gwwwwwwwwwwwwwh FqhokgZTtFqnnLnqAFqhokgZTcFqHDdBnadDaoDBnGDwBodDwcapGdBn qBodDDzmxwwwwwww1FqmRbZ/opendoc.pdf> [hereinafter UNHCR, *Note on International Protection*].

[29] Saddrudin A. Khan, "Legal Problems Relating to Refugees and Displaced Persons" (1976) 149 Recueil des Cours 287 at 318.

commentators have held, and state practice has confirmed, that *non-refoulement* applies at the border.[30] One noted expert in refugee law, Guy Goodwin Gill, has observed that "[a]s a matter of fact, anyone presenting themselves at a frontier post, port or airport will already be within state territory and jurisdiction"[31] and thus entitled to the benefit of *non-refoulement*. A recent US Supreme Court decision confirmed the application of the principle to all asylum-seekers within the border when it held that the principle of *non-refoulement* did not apply to the actions of the United States on the high seas but that it did not deny that the principle applied to refugees at the borders of the United States.[32] Thus, the very notion of turning asylum-seekers away from one's borders would appear to be contrary to the objectives of the Refugee Convention of providing protection for those whose lives or safety might be threatened.[33]

Although there is nothing in the Refugee Convention that directly prohibits returning asylum-seekers to a third country, such a return, without ensuring that *refoulement* would not occur, places the returning state in a position of potential breach of the *non-refoulement* obligation. According to many experts in this field, while the 1951 Refugee Convention does not obligate contracting states to recognize persons as refugees, the duty not to *refoule* implies the individual appraisal of each and every asylum application.[34] It implies that *prima facie* refugees within the territory of a state cannot be expelled by that state without a complete examination of their claim to refugee protection. The UNHCR has pointed

---

30 Kay Hailbronner, "*Non-refoulement* and 'Humanitarian' Refugees: Customary International Law or Wishful Legal Thinking?" (1985) 26 Va. J. Int'l L. 857 at 862-63; Robert C. Sexton, "Political Refugees, *Non-refoulement* and State Practice: A Comparative Study" (1985) 18 Vand. J. Transn'tl L. 731 at 739; and European Consultation on Refugees and Exiles, *Asylum in Europe: A Handbook for Agencies Assisting Refugees*, 3rd ed. (European Consultation on Refugees and Exiles, 1983) at 17.

31 Goodwin Gill, *Refugee in International Law, supra* note 20 at 123.

32 *Sale* v. *Haitian Centers Council*, 509 U.S. 155 (1993).

33 The Vienna Convention on the Law of Treaties supports the approach of examining the objectives of a treaty in treaty interpretation. Article 31(1) of the treaty states: "A treaty shall be interpreted in good faith in accordance with the ordinary meaning to be given to the terms of the treaty in their context and in light of its object and purpose." 1969 Vienna Convention on the Law of Treaties, May 23, 1969, 1155 U.N.T.S. 331 (entered into force January 27, 1980).

34 Cornelis D. de Jong, "The Legal Framework: *The Convention Relating to the Status of Refugees* and the Development of Law Half a Century Later" (1980) 10 Int'l J. Ref. L. 688 at 689.

out that every refugee is initially an asylum-seeker and that all asylum-seekers should, in principle, have access to individual refugee status determination procedures.[35] Without a thorough examination of each claim for refugee status, any action precipitating the return of such persons to another country leaves open the possibility of *refoulement*.

It is arguable that the very generalized designation of a "safe country" is itself incompatible with the obligation of *non-refoulement*. What does the "safe" in "safe third country" refer to? If it is a reference to the general condition of the country, then it is not of any assistance to the asylum-seeker. The UNHCR has often asserted that the question of whether a particular third country is "safe" for the purpose of returning an asylum-seeker is not a generic question, which can be answered for any asylum-seeker in any circumstances.[36] A country may be "safe" for asylum-seekers of a certain origin and "unsafe" for others of a different origin. From his or her point of view, the country must be "safe" for the particular asylum-seeker. This conclusion would require that prior to sending the asylum-seeker to the so-called "safe third country" there would have to be a determination that the country is "safe" *vis-à-vis* the particular asylum-seeker. The earlier in the asylum process that this principle is employed, the less likely a state is to have considered an asylum application on the merits of its relevance to the Refugee Convention, meaning that the assessment of another state as "safe" for the individual concerned might not be based on the full facts of the individual case.[37]

The "safe third country" approach to receiving asylum-seekers, which is designed to deal with categories of persons to which the concept applies rather than individual claims, makes it virtually impossible to ensure that an individual's claim will be examined in detail. A couple of examples will illustrate this point. Asylum applicants at the German-Polish border will normally be met by a border control official who will establish that the asylum applicant has

---

[35] See UNHCR Executive Committee, "Note on International Protection" (1999) 18 Ref. Survey Quart. 85 at 88 [hereinafter UNHCR, "Note on International Protection"].

[36] UNHCR, *The Application of the "Safe Third Country" Notion and its Impact on the Management of Flows and on the Protection of Refugees* (May 2002), available online at <http://www.unhcr.bg/global_consult/background_paper2_en.htm> [hereinafter UNHCR, *Application of the Safe Third Country Notion*]; see also UNHCR, "Note on International Protection," *supra* note 35

[37] Van Selm, *supra* note 13 at 9.

transited through Poland and, therefore, that he or she could have asked for asylum in Poland, which is considered "safe." An asylum-seeker in this situation will only have access to the regular protection procedures if he or she can provide evidence of a well-founded fear of persecution in Poland. Otherwise, he or she will be sent to Poland.[38] In Austria, border guards have the authority to deny entry to refugees who do not come directly from the state in which they claim to fear persecution (which is not a likely scenario); who have been persecuted for reasons other than their political opinion; or who fear, but have not actually suffered, persecution. Again, this decision is made on the basis of limited evidence and no guidelines.[39] This type of response to an asylum claim would appear to conflict with the "essential premise that states must assume responsibility to avoid the *refoulement* of refugees within their ambit of effective jurisdiction."[40] In effect, the "safe third country" principle that allows for the return of asylum-seekers to another state (be it the first country in which they could have sought asylum or any transit country in which they could have sought protection) prior to an effective assessment of their claim would result in a transference of the responsibility to accord protection. The inappropriate application of the "safe third country" notion could lead to asylum-seekers being denied the opportunity to have their claims properly assessed.

A breach of *non-refoulement* in the "safe third country" context can also be indirect. The obligation of *non-refoulement* encompasses any action attributable to a state that has the effect of returning an asylum-seeker to a place where his or her life or freedom would be threatened. In other words, if an asylum-seeker is sent to a "safe third country," which in turn returns the claimant to a country in which he or she fears persecution, the precipitating removal by the first state is said to constitute a breach of the *non-refoulement* obligation.[41] Support for this argument is found not only in the work of eminent scholars but also in the *travaux preparatoires* of the Refugee

---

[38] De Jong, *supra* note 34 at 692

[39] James C. Hathaway and Johan A. Dent, *Refugee Rights: Report on a Comparative Survey* (Toronto: York Lanes Press, 1995) at 15.

[40] E. Wiederin, "IACL National Report for Austria," as cited in Hathaway and Dent, *supra* note 39 at 7-8.

[41] Marx, *supra* note 22 at 393; see also Patricia Hyndman, "The 1951 Convention and Its Implications for Procedural Questions" (1994) 6 Int'l J. Ref. L. 252; see also UNHCR, *Application of the Safe Third Country Notion*, *supra* note 36.

Convention. During the negotiations preceding the convention, an attempt to expressly prohibit the avoidance of responsibility by sending refugees to an intermediate state was rejected.[42] European case law also supports the position that a state cannot abrogate its responsibilities on the matter of *refoulement* by laying the responsibility for a case in the hands of a "safe third country" alone — it still has a duty to ensure that the state to which it sends an applicant really will not send the person back to a situation where life and freedom could be threatened.[43] In *T.I* v. *United Kingdom*, a case involving the return of an asylum-seeker to Germany as a "safe third country," the European Court of Human Rights stated that the indirect removal to an intermediary country, which was also a contracting state (to the Dublin Convention), did not affect the responsibility of the United Kingdom to ensure that the applicant was not, as a result of its decision to expel, exposed to danger and that the United Kingdom could not rely automatically on the arrangements made in the Dublin Convention.[44] It has been argued that the practice of sending asylum-seekers on to another state just because that state may have obligations in relation to a particular refugee is one of the three heresies related to the Refugee Convention.[45] Clearly, more than one state can have responsibility in relation to a refugee, but the obligations of the second state do not absolve the first state from its obligations to comply with the principle of *non-refoulement*.

The extent to which indirect or chain *refoulement* is occurring in Europe and elsewhere[46] where the "safe third country" concept is utilized is unclear. The UNHCR has claimed awareness of actual situations of *refoulement:*

UNHCR is aware of a number of instances where asylum-seekers have been refused admission and returned to a country through which they had passed, only to be summarily sent onwards from there, without examination of their claim, either to their country of origin, or to another, clearly

---

[42] Abell, *supra* note 14 at 71.

[43] T. Einarsen, "The European Convention on Human Rights and the Notion of an Implied Right to *de facto* Asylum" (1990) 2 Int.'l J. Ref. L. 362 at 372.

[44] *T.I.* v. *United Kingdom* (2000), Application no. 43844/98, Eur. Ct. H.R.

[45] J. Crawford and Patricia Hyndman, "Three Heresies in the Application of the Refugee Convention" (1989) 1 Int.'l J. Ref. L. 155 at 171.

[46] European states and North American states are not the only ones that have established "safe third country" rules. African states and some Central Asian states have also applications for asylum on this basis. Van Selm, *supra* note 13 at 19.

unsafe country. Where asylum-seekers are returned to third\countries this needs to be implemented with due regard to the principle of *non-refoulement*. Without prior consent and the co-operation of the country in which an asylum-seeker is returned, there is a grave risk that an asylum-seeker's claim may not receive a fair hearing there and that a refugee may be sent on, directly or indirectly to persecution, in violation of the principle of *non-refoulement* and of Article 33 of the 1951 Convention.[47]

It may be argued that Article 31 of the Refugee Convention also places some limitation upon the right of states to expel asylum-seekers. Article 31(1) states:

The Contracting States shall not impose penalties, on account of their illegal entry or presence, on refugees who, coming directly from a territory where their life or freedom was threatened in the sense of Article 1, enter or are present in their territory without authorization, provided they present themselves without delay to the authorities and show good cause for their illegal entry or presence.[48]

This limitation is not without ambiguity. The use of the phrase "coming directly" has been interpreted strictly by those who see it as an endorsement of the right of a state to send an asylum-seeker to a third state that may be more appropriately responsible to determine the issue of protection — the so-called "safe third country."[49] This argument may be particularly appealing if the asylum-seeker transited through a third country in which he or she might have been able to seek asylum. Case law does not support this narrow approach to Article 31 protection. In the British case, *R. v. Uxbridge Magistrate Court and Another ex parte Adimi*,[50] there was an attempt to argue that the applicant must claim asylum where it was first

---

[47] UNHCR, "Note on the Principle of Non-Refoulement — EU Seminar on the Implementation of the 1995 EU Resolution on Minimum Guarantees for Asylum Procedures" (November 1997), cited in Van Selm, *supra* note 13. Amnesty International reported several cases of asylum-seekers who, after being returned from the United Kingdom on safe third country grounds, ended up being sent to their country of origin. See Amnesty International U.K., *Afghanistan: International Responsibility for Human Rights Disaster* (November 29, 1995), text available online at <http://web.amnesty.org/library/Index/ENGASA110091995?open &of=ENG-369>.

[48] Refugee Convention, *supra* note 8 at Article 31(1).

[49] Guy S. Goodwin Gill, *The Protection of Refugees and the Safe Third Country Rule in International Law in Asylum Law* (London: First International Judicial Conference, 1995) at 90.

[50] *R. v. Uxbridge Magistrate Court and Another ex parte Adimi*, [1999] I.N.L.R. 490; Van Selm, *supra* note 13 at 48.

possible and that the Article 31 protection did not apply to him as he did not come directly to Britain. The court rejected this argument, stating: "A literal construction of 'directly' would contravene the clear purpose of the Article ... this condition can be satisfied even if the refugee passes through intermediate countries on his way to the United Kingdom." The UNHCR position on this is similar:

> The expression "coming directly" in Article 31(1) covers the situation of a person who enters the county in which asylum is sought directly from the country of origin, or from another country where his protection, safety and security could not not be assured. It is understood that this term covers a person who transits an intermediate country for a short period of time without having applied for, or received, asylum there. No strict time limit can be applied to the concept "coming directly" and each case must be judged on its own merits.[51]

While debate on the subject of the concept of safe third country *vis-a-vis* the principle of *non-refoulement* has been extensive and is ongoing,[52] it is clear that states have accepted that "the fundamental criterion when considering resort to the notion [of safe third country] was protection against *refoulement*."[53] The European Community ministers responsible for immigration have also specifically recognized the importance of guarding against *refoulement* by proposing some fundamental requirements as a precondition to the identification of a state as one to which asylum-seekers may be returned: (1) the applicant's life or freedom must not be threatened in the country in question within the meaning of Article 33 of the Refugee Convention; (2) he or she must not be exposed to torture or inhuman or degrading treatment; (3) either the applicant must already have been granted protection or have had a previous opportunity to contact the country's authorities to seek protection; and (4) the applicant must be afforded effective protection in the host third country against *refoulement* within the meaning of the Refugee Convention.[54] The foregoing authoritative

---

51 UNHCR, *Guidelines on Applicable Criteria and Standards Relating to the Detention of Asylum-Seekers* (February 10, 1999) at para. 4, cited in Van Selm, *supra* note 13 at 49.

52 See, for example, Abell, *supra* note 14; van Selm, *supra* note 13.

53 *Report of the Sub-Committee of the Whole on International Protection*, 1991, UN Doc. A/AC.96/781 at para. 34.

54 Ministers of the Member States of the European Communities Responsible for Immigration Resolution on a Harmonized Approach to Questions Concerning Host Third Countries, cited in European Council on Refugees and Exiles,

statements regarding the pre-conditions for returning an asylum-seeker to a "safe third country" would seem to indicate that in order to protect against the breach of the *non-refoulement* obligation there must be a determination in each case that the asylum-seeker will have access to effective procedures for the determination of his/ her claim for protection in the third country.

Goodwin-Gill points out that formal effectiveness may be preju-diced by restrictions on access, and he concludes that actual return is likely to satisfy a best practice standard only if the receiving state is able to provide guarantees that include the following: (1) the willingness to readmit asylum-seekers; (2) the acceptance of responsibility to determine claims of refugee status, notwithstand-ing departure from the country in question or the circumstances of initial entry; (3) the treatment of applicants during the determina-tion process in accordance with generally accepted standards; and (4) some provision with respect to subsistence and human dignity issues, such as social assistance or access to the labour market in the interim, family unity, education of children, and so forth.[55] Although the STCA between Canada and the United States has not been implemented, it appears at this point to be highly unlikely that it will have the potential to satisfy a best practice standard with regard to accessibility.

CANADA-UNITED STATES STCA

Provisions for returning asylum-seekers to a so-called "safe coun-try" have existed in Canadian law since 1989 but have not been called into force prior to 2003. According to section 101(1)(e) of Canada's current immigration legislation, the Immigration and Refugee Protection Act (IRPA), a claim for refugee protection is ineligible to be referred to the Immigration and Refugee Board (IRB) if the claimant came directly or indirectly to Canada from a country designated by the minister and may be returned to that country to make their claim for protection.[56] With the signing of the STCA,[57] the United States will be the first country given the

---

Safe Third Countries: Myths and Realities (February 1995), text is available online at <http://www.ecre.org/positions/s3c.pdf> at appendix C.

[55] Goodwin Gill, *Refugee in International Law, supra* note 20 at 343.

[56] Immigration and Refugee Protection Act, S.C. 2001, c.27, s. 101 (1)(e) [here-inafter IRPA].

[57] STCA, *supra* note 1.

designation of a "safe third country." Regulations to implement the terms of the STCA, pursuant to section 101(1)(e) of the IRPA, that will make persons entering Canada from the United States ineligible to make a claim for refugee status have been published,[58] but it is unclear exactly when they will be put into effect. Canada has been trying for a number of years to interest the United States in such an agreement, and it was only in the aftermath of September 11 and the heightened sense of insecurity in North America that an agreement was reached.[59] The STCA is part of the Smart Border Declaration's thirty-point action plan, which was agreed upon by Canada and the United States.[60] It is anticipated that the agreement will be implemented sometime in 2005. Considering the significance of this agreement on Canada's protection system and its potential impact on Canada's reputation as a country with a strong humanitarian tradition *vis-à-vis* refugees,[61] it is not surprising that interested groups in Canada have been vocal on the subject of the STCA.[62]

[58] IRPA Regulations, *supra* note 6.

[59] It has been alleged that despite an absence of evidence linking global terrorism with refugees, the security threat has been used as a cover to cut down on the entry of refugee claimants to Canada through the proposed STCA, *supra* note 1. See Howard Adelman, "Refugees and Border Security Post September 11" (2002) 20 Refuge 5 at 11. See also International Civil Liberties Monitoring Group, "In the Shadow of the Law," a report in response to Justice Canada's first annual report on the application of the Anti-Terrorism Act (Bill C-36), text is available online at <http://www.cba.org/cba/news/pdf/shadow.pdf>. This report views the STCA with the United States as a serious negative outcome of the government's anti-terrorism initiatives and calls for the repeal of the STCA. See also Sharryn J. Aiken, "Of Gods and Monsters: National Security and Canadian Refugee Policy" (2001) 14 Rev. Que. D. Int.'l 7.

[60] For a description of the specific actions taken to implement the Shared Border Accord of 1995 and the Border Vision of 1997, see Citizenship and Immigration Canada, *Joint Statement on Cooperation on Border Security and Regional Migration Issues,* text is available online at <http://www.cic.gc.ca/english/press/01/0126-pre.html#statement>.

[61] Canada's historical treatment of refugees has not been without blemish. See Ninette Kelley, "History of Canadian Immigration and Refugee Policy," in Jesuit Centre for Faith and Social Justice, *Borders and Barriers* (Toronto: Jesuit Centre for Faith and Social Justice, 1988).

[62] See, for example, Amnesty International's position at <http://www.amnesty.ca/Refugee/unsafethird.htm>; see also Canada Council for Refugees, "Ten Reasons Why the US-Canada Refugee Deal Is a Bad Idea," text is available online at Canadian Council for Refugees <http://www.web.net/%7Eccr/10reasons.html>. For opposition in the United States, see, for example, Lawyers Committee for Human Rights, Media Alert, "U.S. Canada 'Safe Third Country' Agreement

The stated objectives of the STCA from the Canadian perspective are: (1) to reinforce refugee protection by establishing rules for the sharing of responsibility for hearing refugee claims between Canada and the United States; (2) to reduce the misuse of the respective asylum systems and to restore public confidence; and (3) to reduce backlogs and improve the efficiency of Canada's refugee determination system.[63] The stated objectives do not stand up even to superficial scrutiny. The flow of refugees between the two countries is very uneven, with approximately one-third of all refugee claims made in Canada in one year being made by persons who come via the United States whereas only a few hundred refugee claims in the United States are made by persons who went there via Canada. Thus, the STCA appears to be not so much a question of apportioning responsibility as of reducing the flow of asylum-seekers coming into Canada via the United States. It is not quite clear what is meant by the two other objectives, but the underlying assumptions of those objectives will be addressed in the third part of this note. Regardless of the stated objectives, the consequences are clear: asylum-seekers coming to a Canadian border point of entry will be sent back to the United States unless they fall within one of the stated exceptions. Questions have been raised as to whether the real objective was simply to reduce the overall number of refugees to Canada.[64] On at least one occasion, officials from the Ministry of Citizenship and Immigration have stated openly that the purpose of the STCA is to reduce the number of claimants before the IRB, particularly those coming into Canada via the United States.[65]

The Canadian government has made it a point to underscore the fact that the UNHCR does not in principle oppose agreements

---

will Hurt Asylum-Seekers" (December 4, 2002), text is available online at <http://www.lchr.org/media/2002_alerts/1204a.htm>. For support of the STCA, see James Bissett, "A Defense of the 'Safe Country' Concept for Refugees" (2002) Policy Options 36, text is available online at <http://www.irpp.org/po/archive/sep02/bissett.pdf>.

[63] *Government Response to the Report of the Standing Committee on Citizenship and Immigration on Safe Third Country Regulations* (May 2003), text is available online at <http://www.cic.gc.ca/english/pub/safe-third.html> [hereinafter *Government Response*].

[64] *Report of the Standing Committee on Citizenship and Immigration on Safe Third Country Regulations* (December 2002), text is available online at <http://www.parl.gc.ca/InfoComDoc/37/2/CIMM/Studies/Reports/cimmrp01/cimmrp01-e.pdf> [hereinafter *Report of the Standing Committee*].

[65] *Ibid.* at 12.

utilizing the "safe third country agreement," but it has also acknowledged the position of the UNHCR that states are entitled to enter into agreements to share responsibility for determining asylum requests provided it is explicit that return can be effected *only when* the claimant will be able to access fair asylum procedures in the receiving countries.[66] This determination is the crux of the issue for Canadians. Does returning asylum-seekers to the United States ensure access to fair asylum procedures? The Canadian government has repeatedly acknowledged the importance of compliance with its international obligations regarding *refoulement* in the Refugee Convention in the context of the STCA.[67] However, the government's view is that *refoulement* is not an issue since the STCA is built on the foundation that both Canada and the United States maintain refugee protection programs that meet international standards and that both have mature legal systems that offer procedural safeguards.[68] The government's position has not gone unchallenged. Some have argued that the agreement itself is contrary to Canada's international obligations and humanitarian traditions, while others, including representatives of the UNHCR, have indicated that portions of the agreement could jeopardize access to refugee protection, contrary to international norms.[69]

The view that refugee claimants receive comparable treatment on both sides of the Canada/United States border is not universally shared.[70] While Canada has often received high praise for its asylum procedures,[71] the United States has come under considerable

[66] *Government Response, supra* note 63 at 8.

[67] IRPA Regulations, *supra* note 6 (see the Regulatory Impact Analysis Statement at 3241).

[68] *Government Response, supra* note 63 at 1.

[69] UNHCR, *Comments on the Draft Agreement between Canada and the United States of America for "Co-operation in the Examination of Refugee Status Claims from Nationals of Third Countries"* (July 2002), text is available online at <http://web.net/ %7Eccr/safethird.htm> [hereinafter UNHCR, *Comments on the Draft Agreement*].

[70] See, for example, Amnesty International Canada, *Regulating for Safety*, Submission to the Standing Committee on Citizenship and Immigration (November 2002), text is available online at <http://www.amnesty.ca/Refugee/safe_third_country.htm>.

[71] In 1986, the UNHCR awarded the Canadian people the Nansen Medal for their outstanding efforts on behalf of refugees. In the decade prior to 1986, Canada had resettled over 150,000 refugees from camps overseas. See Valerie Knowles, *Strangers at Our Gates* (Toronto: Dundurn Press, 1997) at 181; see also Inter-American Commission on Human Rights, *Report on the Situation of Human Rights of Asylum-Seekers within the Canadian Refugee Determination System* (February 28,

criticism for its failure to respect the letter and the spirit of the Refugee Convention.[72] During the debate in the Standing Committee on Citizenship and Immigration, Member of Parliament Yvon Charbonneau quoted James Hathaway of the Harvard Law School as stating that the United States had a troubling relationship with international law and that the United States Supreme Court jurisprudence is notably out of sync with the rest of the industrialized world because it does not take into account whatsoever the fundamental obligations that have been established by international law.[73] Other Canadian critics of the STCA have highlighted some of the significant differences between the asylum procedures in the two countries and the aspects of the STCA that could lead to asylum-seekers being denied their rights under the Refugee Convention.[74] The Standing Committee on Citizenship and Immigrations attempted to address some of these issues, but many of their recommendations to protect the rights of asylum seekers were rejected by the government.[75]

While it may well be true that the United States asylum procedures and those in Canada have much in common, one factor that sets the two countries apart is the United States's propensity to permit foreign policy considerations to markedly influence decisions on refugee admissions.[76] The probability of obtaining refugee status in the United States may well depend not so much on whether

---

2000), text is available online at <http://www.cidh.oas.org/countryrep/Canada2000en/table-of-contents.htm>.

[72] See, for example, Keller, *supra* note 23.

[73] Standing Committee on Citizenship and Immigration, *Debates* (November 19, 2002), text is available online at <http://www.parl.gc.ca/InfoComDoc/372/cimm/meetings/evidence/cimmev03-e.htm>.

[74] See, for example, Canadian Council for Refugees, *Comments to the Standing Committee on Citizenship and Immigration on the Proposed Safe Third Country Regulations* (November 14, 2002), text is available online at <http://www.web.net/~ccr/s3cregscommentsstandcomm.html>.

[75] *Government Response, supra* note 63

[76] Sexton, *supra* note 30 at 779; Norman L. Zucker and Naomi F. Zucker, *The Guarded Gate: The Reality of American Refugee Policy* (California: Harcourt Brace Jovanovich, 1987). This concern was also raised by the New Democratic party in its dissenting opinion to the Safe Third Country Regulations Report of the Standing Committee on Citizenship and Immigration, *Government Response, supra* note 63. For the influence of the Cold War on Canadian refugee policy, see Reg Whitaker, "Refugees: The Security Dimension" (1998) 2 Citizenship Studies 413.

one meets the criteria of the Refugee Convention for refugee status but rather on the relationship between the United States and the source country. A generous admissions policy towards persons from a particular country could be a reflection of US dissatisfaction with the government of that country and, conversely, a denial of refugee status might imply support for the government of the state from which the asylum-seekers fled. It has been said that foreign policy considerations explain, for example, the different treatment accorded by the United States to Salvadoreans and Haitians, as opposed to Cubans, Indo-Chinese, and Nicaraguans.[77] The United States history of linking inappropriately its foreign policy objectives to its decision-making in refugee assessment makes the United States a highly suspect candidate for the label of "safe third country" — at least for those asylum-seekers coming from countries that are at odds with the United States government.

Another aspect of the US asylum procedures that has no counterpart in the Canadian system is the United States's system of expedited removals. Under the illegal 1996 Immigration Reform and Immigrant Responsibility Act, a US immigration officer who believes that a foreign national has arrived at a port of entry without proper documents and is illegally in the country can order the person removed without further hearing or review.[78] Even when a foreign national without proper travel documents makes a claim to asylum at the port of entry or if a claim to asylum is made when the foreign national has previously entered the country without being inspected at an official port of entry, the claimant can still be removed if the asylum official believes that he or she does not have "a credible fear" of persecution. Observers of the immigration scene in the United States believe that expedited removal has already had an enormous impact on the face of immigration law and on the issue of observing the *non-refoulement* obligation. Between August 1997 and the end of January 1998, 1,300 individuals with fraudulent or non-existent documents expressed a fear of return to their home country, 1,066 of them were deported through expedited removal.[79] Given that the UNHCR has stressed the need for greater procedural guarantees to ensure that bona

---

[77] Gil Goescher and Laila Monahan, eds. *Refugees and International Relations* (Oxford: Clarendon Press, 1990) at 15.

[78] Illegal Immigration Reform and Immigrant Responsibility Act, 18 U.S.C. para. 1546 (1996).

[79] Keller, *supra* note 23.

fide refugees are not inadvertently removed to a country of feared
persecution (*refoulement*); that they have all "necessary facilities" to
present their asylum claim; and that they are treated in a humane
manner while their applications are pending,[80] it is perhaps not
surprising that the UNHCR has expressed concern about how the
US expedited removal process functions.

Asylum-seekers being returned to the United States run the risk
of being removed prior to receiving a full and effective hearing. It
is unclear whether persons being returned pursuant to the STCA
will be treated as "arriving aliens," which is the only category of
persons subjected to expedited removal. At this point, there has
been no written commitment that persons subject to the STCA will
be exempt from expedited removal proceedings. The Canadian
government appears satisfied with assurances from "senior U.S.
officials" that US implementing regulations would not treat persons returned under the agreement as "arriving aliens."[81] The government chose not to accept the recommendation of the Standing
Committee on Citizenship and Immigration that it seek assurances
from the United States that the persons under this agreement will
not face expedited removal proceedings.[82] The failure to define the
term "adjudication" in the STCA leaves open the possibility that
it could be used to refer to a pre-hearing determination with the
potential of excluding access to a full hearing to determine refugee
status and with the further potential of *refoulement*.[83] If the United
States elects to apply the expedited removal proceedings to asylum-
seekers sent back to the United States, pursuant to the STCA, it will
effectively negate Article 3 of the STCA, which requires adjudication of a refugee claim in one of the two countries.[84]

---

[80] UNHCR, *Issues to Be Considered in the Context of Discussions Regarding a Responsibil-
ity-Sharing Agreement between Canada and the United States* (January 29, 2002), text
is available online at <http://www.web.net/~ccr/safethirdunhcr.html>.

[81] *Government Response, supra* note 63.

[82] *Report of the Standing Committee, supra* note 64 at 14.

[83] The UNHCR has noted that if the term "adjudicate" is used to mean "determine
eligibility to apply for asylum," this could lead to a worst case scenario of
·refugees in orbit and/or *refoulement*. See *Comments on the Draft Agreement, supra*
note 69.

[84] *STCA, supra* note 1, Article 3(1) states: "In order to ensure that refugee status
claimants have access to a refugee status determination system, the Parties shall
not return or remove a refugee status claimant referred by either Party under
the terms of Article 4 to another country until an adjudication of the person's
refugee status claim has been made."

There is also considerable concern over the possibility that asylum-seekers turned back to the United States will face detention for unknown periods of time. Representatives of the UNHCR appearing before the Standing Committee on Citizenship and Immigration have pointed out that detention of asylum-seekers in the United States is common even though Article 31 of the Refugee Convention specifies that no refugee should be subject to detention because he or she is present in a country without authorization.[85] The Standing Committee on Citizenship and Immigration has noted that American detention practices differ from Canadian practices but has concluded that the United States is in compliance with international law.[86] No recommendations have been made in this regard. In light of recent practice, this issue should not be lightly dismissed. During the recent surge in asylum-seekers at the United States-Canada border in June 2002, the United States indicated that it would retain the right to detain any person in unlawful status who was "directed back" from Canada to the United States.[87] There is no guarantee that the position would be different for claimants returned to the United States under the STCA.

Another potential cause for creating a *refoulement* situation for asylum-seekers being returned to the United States is the one-year time requirement for filing asylum claims in the United States. While the United States is not alone in having introduced time limits for asylum claims, Canada does not have any such requirement. The US one-year filing deadline denies admissibility to asylum procedures to any alien unless the alien demonstrates by clear and convincing evidence that the application has been filed within one year after his or her arrival in the United States.[88] The UNHCR has been clear in its opposition to time limits, suggesting that they are contrary to accepted asylum and refugee principles.[89] With specific reference to the STCA, the UNHCR has pointed out that refugee claimants subject to a US statutory bar, which has no equivalent under Canadian law and is contrary to the 1951 Refugee Convention, may be returned under the agreement to the United States, where they would not be eligible for asylum and/or *non-refoulement* protection. Under these circumstances, the UNHCR noted, they

[85] *Ibid.*

[86] *Report of the Standing Committee, supra* note 64 at 14.

[87] *Comments on the Draft Agreement, supra* note 69.

[88] Immigration and Naturalization Act, 8 U.S.C. § 208 (a)(2)(B).

[89] UNHCR, *Note on International Protection, supra* note 28 at para 18.

may well be denied rights that, except for the operation of the STCA, would be available to them.[90] In spite of urging from the UNHCR[91] and the Standing Committee on Citizenship and Immigration[92] that the Canadian government seek to exempt claimants returned under the STCA from the one-year requirement, the Canadian government has indicated that it is "satisfied" that claimants returned to the United States will not be precluded from a fair protection decision.[93] The US legislation does provide exceptions to the deadline requirement, but these are not likely to be of assistance to those whose delay in making the application was caused by ignorance, fear, or the impact of trauma.

Apart from the procedural differences between the asylum systems in the two countries, there exists the very real possibility that because of substantive differences in approaching the definition of a refugee, an asylum-seeker who may qualify for refugee status in Canada will not necessarily be recognized as such in the United States. One area of significant difference between the two countries relates to gender-based claims for refugee status. Canadian practice regarding gender-based claims for protection differs significantly from United States practice. In 1993, Canada's IRB became the first country to issue guidelines on refugee women claimants fleeing gender-related persecution,[94] such as domestic violence, "honour" crimes, and dowry deaths. Since that time, claims of this description within Canada have generally been accepted, whereas the US record of granting status to women fearing such abuses has been described as mixed at best.[95] While acknowledging these differences, the Canadian government has rejected the suggestion that women claiming refugee status on the basis that they are victims of domestic violence be exempt from the impact of the STCA until such time as the American regulations regarding

[90] UNHCR, *Comments on the Proposed Regulations Amending the Immigration and Refugee Protection Regulations Relating to the Agreement between the Government of Canada and the Government of the United States of America for Cooperation in the Examination of Refugee Status Claims from Nationals of Third Countries* (November 14, 2002), text is available online at <http://www.web.net/~ccr/regula_11.html>.

[91] UNHCR, *Comments on the Draft Agreement, supra* note 69.

[92] *Report of the Standing Committee, supra* note 64.

[93] *Government Response, supra* note 63.

[94] Immigration and Refugee Board, *Guidelines on Women Refugee Claimants Fearing Persecution* (February 1993), text is available online at <http://www.cisr-irb.gc.ca/en/about/tribunals/rpd/compendium/compendium_e.pdf>.

[95] Amnesty International, *supra* note 70.

gender-based persecution are consistent with Canadian practice.[96] Given Canada's reputation as a leader in the recognition of gender-based persecution, it is entirely possible that women who have sought consciously to seek protection in Canada and were merely in transit in the United States will nevertheless be returned to the United States without having been given an opportunity to seek asylum in Canada.

As noted earlier, the obligation of *non-refoulement* encompasses a duty to fully ascertain the potential for danger in relation to each individual asylum-seeker. This process entails a careful examination of the circumstances of each asylum-seeker at a Canada-United States border to determine whether the potential for *refoulement* exists if the asylum-seeker is returned to the United States. At this point, it is not entirely clear what sort of process will be established at the Canadian land ports of entry to administer the provisions of the STCA. Citizenship and immigration officials have indicated that two officers would review claims by people who indicated that they meet one of the exceptions under the regulations.[97] The decision to place the burden of proof on the asylum-seeker [98] appears designed to make it extremely difficult, if not impossible, to make such claims successfully. Asylum-seekers do not generally appear at the border aware of their rights and accompanied by lawyers prepared to make the claim that they fall within one of the exceptions. The physical, emotional, and psychological conditions of persons fleeing persecution often make the preparation of a claim both difficult and time-consuming.[99]

The lack of explicit procedural safeguards in the decision-making (as to whether one of the exceptions is applicable) is all the more disturbing because of the absence of an effective appeal mechanism.

[96] *Government Response,* supra note 63.

[97] *Ibid.*

[98] IRPA Regulations, *supra* note 6 at section 159.5.

[99] See, for example, Glenn Randall and Ellen L. Lutz, *Serving Survivors of Torture: A Practical Manual for Health Professionals and Other Service Providers* (Washington, DC: American Association for the Advancement of Science, 1991) at 29 and 42-44, where the authors discuss the psychological impact of traumatic human rights violations and added consequences of being a refugee; see also F. Allodi et al., "Physical and Psychiatric Effects of Torture: Two Medical Studies," in Eric Stover and Elena Nightingale, eds., *The Breaking of Bodies and Minds: Torture, Psychiatric Abuse, and the Health Professions* (New York: Freeman, 1985) at 58-78, where the authors analyze results of studies of torture survivors in the United States and Canada.

While any decision by an immigration officer is subject to judicial review by the federal court, judicial review entails making an application for leave within fifteen days and leave is not easily attainable. An application for leave and judicial review to the federal court must be filed within fifteen days of the decision.[100] It is not likely that most asylum-seekers would be able to obtain the necessary legal assistance in a timely manner and, even if they do, judicial review may not provide the relief they seek. Thus far, the only tangible protection for the rights of the asylum-seekers in this process can be found in the vague provisions in the Statement of Principles to the STCA. In addition to providing that two different port of entry officers be involved in the decision-making process, it also provides that the applicant be provided with the opportunity to understand the basis for the proposed decision and that the applicant have an opportunity to provide corrections or additional relevant information, *provided it does not unduly delay the process*.[101] There does not appear to be any plans for an effective and transparent internal review mechanism as recommended by the Standing Committee on Citizenship and Immigration.[102]

IMPLICATIONS OF THE STCA FOR CANADA

Canada's commitment to its international obligations and its humanitarian tradition is clearly stated in section 3 of the IRPA.[103] Its specific commitment to the principle of *non-refoulement* is stated in section 115.[104] By signing the STCA, Canada has opened itself to being in breach of international law and to allegations of acting contrary to the principles of fundamental justice. As discussed in the second part of this note, refugee law and the principle of *non-refoulement* do not compel Canada to accept refugees, but they do require that Canada ensure that asylum-seekers are not returned to a place where their lives would be endangered. The lack of a clear requirement to offer asylum has formed the basis of some claims

---

[100] IRPA, *supra* note 56 at section 3.

[101] STCA, *supra* note 1, Statement of Principles [italics added].

[102] The *Report of the Standing Committee* states: "The Committee recommends that the regulations provide for an effective and transparent internal review mechanism before returning someone to the United States to make a claim," *Report of the Standing Committee, supra* note 64, recommendation 15.

[103] IRPA, *supra* note 56 at section 3.

[104] *Ibid.* at section 115.

that the principle of *non-refoulement* does not prohibit the application of the "safe third country" principle.[105] Others take the position that prohibition against a return to the country of persecution cannot be replaced by agreements among a group of countries because this could lead to asylum-seekers being bounced around from state to state and perhaps eventually being sent back to the place from which they fled in the first place.[106] The latter view is consistent with the underlying objective of the *non-refoulement* obligation in the Refugee Convention. Even during the 1951 Conference of Plenipotentiaries on the Convention Relating to the Status of Refugees, there was an agreement that this principle meant that no refugee should be sent to a country where he or she would be in danger of persecution whether it was the country from which the refugee came or any other country.[107] Logically, this prohibition regarding *refoulement* extends to any country where there is a danger that he or she might be compelled to return to the country of persecution. Given that Canada has committed itself to sending to the United States any asylum-seeker who came from the United States and who does not fall within one of the stated exceptions to the STCA, what then is the extent of Canada's obligations regarding *non-refoulement* in this context?

It would appear that the concept of *non-refoulement* has developed into a rule of customary international law that is not limited to a simple prohibition of return to the alleged state of persecution. Born out of the convention's objective of providing protection, the prohibition of *non-refoulement* is now said to include the obligation of not denying to those within one's borders the right to claim refugee status, to provide access to one's refugee procedures, and to avoid taking any action that could lead to *non-refoulement*. This view of *non-refoulement* has led legal scholars to describe the rule as encompassing a positive duty on the part of the receiving state to apply the principle of *non-refoulement* to those within its territory irrespective of whether or not they have been formally recognized as refugees.[108] The receiving state is obliged to identify its obligation

---

[105] This has been the position taken by the United Kingdom. Goodwin Gill, *Refugee in International Law, supra* note 20 at 334.

[106] This was the position taken by Argentina. *Ibid.*

[107] UN Conference of Plenipotentiaries on the Convention Relating to the Status of Refugees, UN Doc. A/CONF 2/SR.16 at 9.

[108] De Jong , *supra* note 34. See also UNHCR Executive Committee, *Non-refoulement*, Conclusion no. 6, 28ᵗʰ Sess. (1977), text is available online at <http://www.

by determining which asylum-seekers are subject to the *non-refoulement* obligation. There appears to be no prohibition against sharing responsibility through an agreement with another state, but such an agreement would require that any actions taken in this context be taken with a view to not contravening the *non-refoulement* obligations. In relevant conclusions,[109] as well as in specific statements regarding the STCA, the UNHCR has stipulated that the application of the "safe third country" principle, without sufficient guarantee against *refoulement,* may lead to violations of the principle.[110] Thus, while there can be a sharing of responsibility regarding the acceptance of asylum claims, obligations regarding *non-refoulement* are not transferable.[111] If responsibility for responding to asylum-seekers is shared through a "safe third country" agreement, according to the UNHCR[112] and refugee law expert Goodwin-Gill,[113] there must be guarantees regarding (1) admission; (2) protection against *refoulement;* and (3) access to asylum procedures that must conform to international procedures. The STCA will be examined in light of these safeguards against *non-refoulement.*

Admission into the United States for asylum-seekers being sent there pursuant to the STCA is unlikely to be an issue since that is exactly what the STCA was designed to do. However, there is nothing in the STCA that prevents the United States from returning asylum-seekers to yet another "third" state.[114] As noted earlier, there

---

unhcr.ch/cgi-bin/texis/vtx/home/+lwwBmemkZ69wwwweIqwwwwwww hFqhokgZTtFqnnLnqAFqhokgZTcFq7oLnq1BoVnagdMMoBBnnagdDqc150 dDaNdeIGYdaWKssDzmxwwwwwww/opendoc.htm> at para. (c).

[109] UNHCR Executive Committee, *Refugees without an Asylum Country,* Conclusion no. 15, 30th Sess. (1979), text is available online at <http://ca.search.yahoo. com/search/ca?p=%22Refugees+Without+an+Asylum+Country%22&vm=i& n=20&fl=0&x=wrt&vc=> [hereinafter UNHCR Executive Committee Conclusion no. 15]. UNHCR Executive Committee, *The Problem of Refugees and Asylum-seekers Who Move in an Irregular Manner from a Country in Which They Had Already Found Protection,* Conclusion no. 58, 40th Sess. (1989), text is available online at <http://www.unhcr.bg/bglaw/en/_15a_excom58en.pdf> [hereinafter UNHCR Executive Committee Conclusion no. 58].

[110] UNHCR, *Issues to be Considered, supra* note 80.

[111] See Crawford and Hyndman, *supra* note 45.

[112] UNHCR, *Note on International Protection, supra* note 28 at 19.

[113] Goodwin Gill, *The Protection of Refugees, supra* note 49.

[114] The STCA does appear to prohibit either state party from sending an asylum-seeker sent by the other state to a third state pursuant to another "safe third country" agreement: "The Parties shall not remove a refugee status claimant

is no guarantee that returning asylum-seekers will not be subject to the expedited removal system in the United States.[115] One way for Canada to guard against the possibility of *non-refoulement* by the United States would be to assess the possibility of *refoulement* for each asylum-seeker. In the context of the STCA, it would imply that prior to sending back an asylum-seeker to the United States, there would have been a determination in Canada by a competent decision-maker that the individual in question did not fall within one of the exceptions (permitting a claim in Canada) *and* that there did not appear to be a danger that the person would be *refouled* from the United States. Without a full prior assessment in Canada as to the danger of *refoulement* from the United States, returning an asylum-seeker to the United States places Canada in potential breach of Article 33 of the Refugee Convention.

The STCA makes reference to the *non-refoulement* obligation,[116] but the provisions for the implementation of the STCA at a Canadian border do not appear to include effective decision-making regarding the possibility of *refoulement*. The STCA and the Canadian regulations to implement the STCA make provisions only for the review of claims that fall within the exemptions to the STCA. *Prima facie*, the STCA falls short of the necessary guarantees to protect against *non-refoulement*. Even the arrangements for the review of those asylum-seekers who wish to claim an exemption under the STCA are questionable. Applicable international law leaves the choice of procedural means for dealing with asylum-seekers to national authorities. However, given the interests involved and the particularly critical assessment regarding *refoulement*, a competent decision-maker in this context would be one that has independence and expertise in refugee issues. In another similar context, arguing for decision-making to be made by those with expertise in the area, the Inter-American Commission on Human Rights noted that the UNHCR has stated that eligibility determinations are best made by those persons tasked with interpreting and applying refugee law

---

returned to the country of last presence under the terms of this Agreement to another country pursuant to any other safe third country agreement or regulatory designation" (section 3(2)) However, this does not provide a full proof guarantee against deportation on other grounds prior to a full hearing for refugee status.

[115] See the previous section of this article, entitled Canada-United States STCA.

[116] STCA, *supra* note 1, preamble.

and policy.[117] This view is held by a number of individuals and entities dealing with refugee issues, including Amnesty International.[118] Determination regarding the applicability of the exceptions in the STCA may well be a primarily factual matter but assessing compliance with the *non-refoulement* obligation would require experience and knowledge of refugee issues. Immigration officers, who are the persons currently designated as the decision-makers implementing the STCA, are employees of the Department of Citizenship and Immigration Canada — persons who generally deal with broader issues of control and law enforcement as well as issues relating to who is admissible or removable from Canada and detention reviews. Expertise in decision-making in refugee law may be found in members of the IRB who have received training and who operate at arms length from the Ministry of Citizenship and Immigration. The UNHCR has emphasized the "critical importance" of having a careful and sympathetic examination of refugee claims completed by a qualified, knowledgeable, and impartial decision-maker.[119]

Making provisions in Canada for an effective and complete examination of each asylum-seeker's claim regarding the danger of *refoulement* from the United States would undoubtedly entail a commitment of resources and time.[120] As obvious as it may seem, however, it is important that any discussion of the costs of asylum procedures be placed in the context of what is at stake in a decision that has the potential for *refoulement*. In the 1985 Supreme Court of Canada decision, *Singh* v. *Canada (M.E.I.)*,[121] Justice Bertha Wilson,

[117] UNHCR Executive Committee, *The Problem of Manifestly Unfounded or Abusive Applications for Refugee Status or Asylum*, Conclusion no. 30, 34th Sess. (1983), text is available online at <http://ca.search.yahoo.com/search/ca?p=UNHCR+ Executive+Committee+Conclusion+No.+6%2C+1977&vm=i&n=20&fl=0&x= wrt&vc=> at para. 97(2)(e).

[118] Amnesty International has frequently called on the government of Canada to put eligibility decision-making in the hands of the independent and expert Immigration Refugee Board. See Amnesty International, "Refugee Protection in Canada," presentation before the Inter-American Human Rights Commission (October 20, 1997) at 5, cited in Inter-American Commission on Human Rights, *supra* note 71

[119] UNHCR, *Note on International Protection, supra* note 28.

[120] The Standing Committee on Citizenship and Immigration did recommend that additional resources be provided to the department to meet the demands that will result from implementation of the STCA. The government's response was that it does not anticipate the need for any additional resources. See *Report of the Standing Committee, supra* note 64.

[121] *Singh* v. *Canada (M.E.I.)*, [1985] 1 S.C.R. 177, 17 D.L.R. (4th) 422 [hereinafter *Singh*].

in commenting upon the applicability of the Canadian Charter of Rights and Freedoms (Charter) to the examination of refugee determination procedures, made reference to the potential consequences for the asylum-seekers of a denial of refugee status if they are in fact persons with a "well founded fear of persecution."[122] In response to the issue of expense that would be involved in altering the procedures, Wilson pointed out that the guarantees of the Charter would be illusory if they could be ignored because it was administratively convenient to do so.[123] The obligation to provide protection by *non-refoulement* from Canada would also be illusory if Canada, for reasons relating to cost, abrogated its responsibilities under the Refugee Convention. A comprehensive examination of each asylum-seeker's claim with a view to guarding against *refoulement* would not be as much of a guarantee against *refoulement* as a clear commitment from the United States, but it would certainly mitigate against the possibility of such an occurrence.

The next condition for a legitimate transfer of asylum-seekers pursuant to a "safe third country" is that the asylum-seeker being transferred to the "safe third country" have access to refugee determination procedures that conform with international standards. As noted in the second part of this note, the differences between Canadian and United States asylum procedures are not insignificant. Asylum-seekers may seek protection in a particular state precisely because of that state's asylum procedures. Differences in the manner or basis in which claims are decided in different states may result in a greater likelihood of protection in one than in the other for a particular individual. For instance, the government of Canada has acknowledged that there are significant differences between Canada and the United States in the treatment of gender-based refugee claims,[124] but it has nevertheless failed to seek an exemption for this category of asylum-seekers. It is not unlikely that women asylum-seekers would seek refuge in Canada precisely because of Canada's leading role in the area of gender-based persecution. If they are unfortunate enough to be making their way into Canada via the United States, they will most likely be returned to the United States. Women and children make up more than 51 per cent of the world's 25.5 million refugees,[125] but they have not

[122] *Ibid.* at 210. Canadian Charter of Rights and Freedoms, *supra* note 12.

[123] *Ibid.* at para. 218.

[124] *Government Response, supra* note 63.

[125] Canada and the United Nations General Assembly Special Session Beijing +5: *Status of Women Fact Sheet,* June 2000, text is available online at <http://www.swc-cfc.gc.ca/pubs/b5_factsheets/b5_factsheets_2_e.html>.

always formed a proportionate percentage of the total number of refugees accepted into Canada.[126] The provisions of the STCA will most likely lead to a further reduction of women refugees in Canada because they will be kept out of Canada unless they fall within one of the exceptions to the STCA. Their likelihood of obtaining refugee status will be determined by their choice of a travel route, if indeed there has even been a choice in the matter. Given Canada's geographical location, it is not unlikely that asylum-seekers coming to Canada were merely in transit in the United States and had never intended to utilize the asylum procedures of that country. The future prospects of an asylum-seeker should not be determined by where they happen to first land.[127]

Given that the Canada-United States STCA, as currently framed, does not appear to conform with the best practice international standards regarding *non-refoulement*, can an asylum-seeker find any protection within Canada's domestic laws regarding protection of human rights and rules of fundamental justice? The legal framework for pursuing this avenue exists, but, given the legal history of Charter challenges relating to immigration and refugees, the outcome of such a pursuit is unclear. Notwithstanding the 1985 Supreme Court of Canada decision of *Singh*,[128] which declared that every human being who is physically present in Canada is by virtue of such presence amenable to Canadian law, Canadian courts have been notoriously ambivalent about the application of the Charter to non-nationals.[129] Supreme Court of Canada decisions have reiterated the almost entirely unlimited right of the Canadian government to set the terms and conditions of entry and departure from Canadian soil on the basis that only nationals have unrestricted right to enter Canada.[130] The Supreme Court of Canada decision

---

[126] For instance, from 1981 to 1991, Canada admitted nearly twice as many men as women into Canada as refugees within the meaning of the Refugee Convention. Monica Boyd, *Canada's Refugee Flows: Gender Inequality,* text is available online at <www.statscan.ca/english/ads/11-008-XIE/refugees.html>.

[127] In the European context, the use of the principle of first asylum has led to Turkey bearing a disproportionate share of the responsibility for asylum-seekers. Turkey has taken a position against "safe third country" returns. See UN Doc. A/AC.96/SR.430 (1988) at para. 66.

[128] *Singh, supra* note 121.

[129] See, for example, F. Pearl Eliadis, "The Swing from *Singh:* The Narrowing Application of the Charter in Immigration Law" (1995) 256 Imm. L. R. 130.

[130] See, for example, *Chiarelli* v. *Canada (M.E.I.),* [1992] 1 S.C.R. 711 at 714, where the Supreme Court of Canada rejected the notion that the Charter applied to

of *Suresh* v. *Canada (M.C.I.)*[131] may however have opened the door to Charter application to non-nationals a little wider. Among other things, *Suresh* dealt with the question of whether the IRPA, which permitted the deportation of a refugee on the grounds of his or her being a danger to the security of Canada, infringed sections 7(2)(b) and (d) of the Charter. While upholding the minister's discretion to deport a refugee even to a place where he or she may face torture, the court stated that the process involving deportation, which is a deprivation of section 7 rights, must be in accordance with the principles of fundamental justice.[132] It concluded that determining whether the deprivation is in accordance with the principles of fundamental justice in this case required balancing the nature of the Canadian interests (combating terrorism) with the interests of the Refugee Convention (avoiding return to a place of torture). Furthermore, the court stated that inquiry into the principles of fundamental justice is informed not only by Canadian experience and jurisprudence but also by international law and Canada's international obligations and values as expressed in various international instruments and fora.[133] The approach taken by the Supreme Court of Canada has potential for a Charter challenge regarding the return of asylum-seekers to the United States without a guarantee involving *non-refoulement.*

Canada's interest in controlling the entry of asylum-seekers into Canada, at least to the extent of being permitted to send back those arriving from the United States, must be balanced with the implications for the asylum-seeker of being denied access to Canada's asylum procedures and with the international obligations that Canada has undertaken in this regard. This approach would require that consideration be given to the consequences for the asylum-seeker of the denial of the opportunity to claim refugee status in Canada; to the objective of the principle of *non-refoulement* (preventing persecution of refugees); to Canada's commitment to *non-refoulement* in its domestic legislation (IRPA); to Canada's commitment to this

---

the deportation in question and reiterated the long-standing position of Canadian courts that the most fundamental principle of immigration law is that non-citizens do not have an unqualified right to enter or remain in the country and that at common law an alien has no right to enter or remain in the country.

[131] *Suresh* v. *Canada (M.C.I.)*, [2002] S.C.R. 1, 208 D.L.R. (4th) 1 [hereinafter *Suresh*].

[132] *Ibid.* at para. 77-78.

[133] *Ibid.* at para. 59.

principle as expressed by the ratification of the Refugee Convention; to the customary law rule prohibiting *refoulement;* and so on. Even if it is deemed to be entirely within Canada's prerogative to return asylum-seekers to a "safe third country," there nevertheless is the question of whether such a return without a guarantee of *non-refoulement* from the United Sates or without an effective inquiry in Canada as to the possibility of *non-refoulement* from the United States entails a breach of section 7 Charter rights.

The Canadian government may well attempt to argue that its act of returning an asylum-seeker to the United States per se would not constitute *refoulement* and therefore would not entail a breach of section 7 rights. The argument may not succeed as it could be argued that it would be an act of the Canadian government that would have paved the way for the possibility of *refoulement* at a later date. In *Suresh,* the Supreme Court of Canada addressed the question of whether section 7 of Canada's Charter applied in a situation where the actions contrary to section 7 might occur in another country and would be carried out by the government of another country. Specifically, if Canada deported an individual to a country where there was the possibility that he may face torture, something prohibited both by domestic law (and international treaties that Canada has ratified), is the Canadian government culpable? The court was clear:

[T]he governing principle was a general one — namely that the guarantee of fundamental justice applies even to deprivations of life, liberty or security effected by actors other than our government, if there is a sufficient causal connection between our government's participation and the deprivation ultimately effected ... At least where Canada's participation is a necessary precondition for the deprivation and where the deprivation is an entirely foreseeable consequence of Canada's participation, the government does not avoid the guarantee of fundamental justice merely because the deprivation in question would be effected by someone else's hand.[134]

It would follow then that if an asylum-seeker sent to the United States was eventually *refouled,* something that is "entirely foreseeable" in at least some situations, this action would constitute a failure of the guarantee of the principles of fundamental justice.

Respect for other human rights that Canada has traditionally promoted is also in danger of being diminished by the manner in which asylum-seekers are treated in the STCA. Ultimately, refugee

---

[134] *Ibid.* at para 54.

protection is about individuals, and individuals should have the right to seek asylum in the country of their choice.[135] Asylum-seekers may target a particular country because of family connections, cultural ties, or climate. The fact that one is desperate for protection does not diminish the importance of any of these other factors. The UNHCR Executive Committee has stated that "the intentions of the asylum-seeker as regards the country in which he wishes to request asylum should as far as possible be taken into account.[136] Canada and the United States have endorsed Conclusion 15 of the UNHCR Executive Committee, which states, *inter alia:* "The intentions of the asylum-seeker as regards the country in which he wishes to request asylum should as far as possible be taken into account."[137] Determination of refugee status based on the travel route as opposed to personal choice also has the effect of inhibiting integration into society.[138]

Not only does the STCA appear to be moving Canada in a direction contrary to its international and Charter obligations, but there is no evidence to indicate that the agreement will meet its stated objectives. In stating that one of the objectives of the STCA was the reduction of misuse of the asylum systems in Canada and the United States, the minister of immigration noted that many refugee claimants who arrive in Canada pass up the opportunity to seek protection in other countries, such as the United States, which have asylum systems that meet the same high standards as Canada's own determination process, and that this practice was undermining public confidence in the integrity of our refugee determination system.[139] The government appears to have taken the position that

---

[135] Although the Universal Declaration of Human Rights proclaims that "[e]veryone has the right to seek and to enjoy in other countries asylum from persecution," this right has developed into a rule of customary international law binding upon states. Universal Declaration of Human Rights, GA. Res. 217 (III), UN GAOR, 3d Sess., supp. No. 13, U.N. Doc. A/810 (1948) 71. See generally Steering Committee of the Judicial Conference on Asylum Law, *Asylum Law* (first International Judicial Conference, Inner Temple, London, December 1-2, 1995).

[136] UNHCR Executive Committee Conclusion no. 15, *supra* note 109 at para. (h) iii, iv.

[137] UNHCR, *Issues to Be Considered*, *supra* note 80.

[138] Van Selm, *supra* note 13 at 53.

[139] Citizenship and Immigration Canada, "Minister Coderre Seeks Government Approval of Safe Third Country Agreement," News Release 2002-26 (September 10, 2002), text is available online at <http://www.cic.gc.ca/english/press/02/0226-pre.html>.

asylum-seekers are obliged to seek asylum in the first country where it is possible to do so.[140] There is nothing in the Refugee Convention that supports such a conclusion and there has been no endorsement of the principle by the UNHCR. The Executive Committee of the UNHCR has adopted two conclusions[141] that set out a clear distinction between the notions of a "first country of asylum" — a country where a person has already been granted some legal status allowing him/her to remain in the territory either as an asylum-seeker or as a refugee, with all of the guarantees that international standards attach to such status — and a "safe third country" — a country where the person could have found protection. According to the Executive Committee, access to a substantive procedure can legitimately be denied to a person who has already found protection in a first country of asylum, provided that such protection continues to be available, but the fact that the asylum-seeker has been in a third state where he or she could have sought asylum does not, in and by itself, provide sufficient grounds for the state in whose jurisdiction the claim has been submitted to refuse considering his or her asylum claim.[142] Discussions on the subject of the notion of "first country of asylum" involving representatives from a variety of states indicates a clear lack of consensus on the question of whether an asylum-seeker should be obliged to seek asylum at the first country where it was possible to seek asylum.[143]

Another anticipated benefit of the STCA that does not seem to have a basis in experience is that it will reduce the backlog and improve the efficiency of the refugee system. The European experience indicates that *non-entrée* mechanisms such as the "safe third country" agreement are likely to encourage illegal entry into a country and have little impact on reducing the overall numbers of asylum-seekers. Austria acknowledged that since a refugee who attempts to enter the country legally runs the very real risk of being

[140] For a discussion regarding the Canadian government's long-standing position on "country of first asylum," see Matas and Simon, *supra* note 3 at 252.

[141] See UNHCR Executive Committee Conclusion no. 15, *supra* note 109; see UNHCR Executive Committee Conclusion no. 58, *supra* note 109.

[142] UNHCR Global Consultations on International Protections, *Asylum Processes (Fair and Efficient Asylum Procedures)*, May 31, 2001, text is available online at <http://www.unhcr.ch/cgi-bin/texis/vtx/home/+mwwBme1zzd_wwwwAww wwwwwhFqA72ZRogRfZNtFqrpGdBnqBAFqA72ZRogRfZNcFq+E50c1Ma7G dqn55n5aeN8xwoGawDmaohhoqonDBaE50c1Ma7Gdqnm1Gn5eZX3qmxw wwwwww/opendoc.pdf>.

[143] Goodwin Gill, *Refugee in International Law*, *supra* note 20 at 339.

denied access to the determination process at the border itself, there is a strong incentive to enter the country illegally.[144] The government's Standing Committee on Citizenship and Immigration was informed about the German attempt in 1993 to cut down on the number of asylum-seekers through the use of the "safe third country" principle. While the numbers of asylum-seekers at the border dried up, every year since then, 100,000 persons have sought asylum from within Germany.[145] The incentive for asylum-seekers to enter Canada illegally is very strong since those who apply for refugee status from within Canada are not being caught in the STCA web.

CONCLUSION

It was the need to protect every refugee from situations of peril that led to the formulation of the obligation of *non-refoulement*, which is the heart of the provisions of the Refugee Convention. While there may be some debate about the finer points regarding the content of the obligation, the principle itself is so highly regarded that it is considered a rule of customary international law binding upon all states. Nevertheless, the lack of either a clear obligation to receive asylum-seekers or a clear prohibition against returning asylum-seekers to a "safe" country has permitted the proliferation of "safe third country" agreements. There is no dispute about the fact that these agreements without appropriate safeguards can lead to *non-refoulement*. State practice, legal scholars, and the UNHCR are consistent in the view that *non-refoulement* is not just about not returning an asylum-seeker to the country of alleged persecution but rather about the obligation of not denying access to asylum-procedures so as to determine whether the asylum-seeker can claim the protection afforded by the Refugee Convention. How then can states interested in sharing responsibility for asylum-seekers protect against *refoulement*? Presumably if two states with similar asylum procedures, meeting international standards for protection, enter into a bilateral agreement, both states will bind themselves to not enter into a "safe third country" agreement with any other state and will thereby guarantee access to asylum procedures in at least one of the two states. In this way, the obligation of *non-refoulement*, as it is currently understood, would be met.

[144] Wiederin, *supra* note 40 at 9.

[145] *Report of the Standing Committee*, *supra* note 64 at 16.

Such an agreement would have to include a very clear commitment that every asylum-seeker would be granted access to procedures for seeking refugee status and that there would be provisions for appeal from such procedures. The STCA falls short of these requirements.

While the sheer size of the refugee situation in the world is daunting, and concerns about the current backlog in Canada are legitimate, cost-based approaches to the obligation of providing protection to asylum-seekers are in direct contradiction to Canada's humanitarian traditions as well as to the principles of fundamental justice and Canada's obligations under international law. In 2001, 34 per cent of refugee claimants in Canada came through the United States — 95 per cent of them arriving through land border ports of entry.[146] If the STCA (and its accompanying regulations) is implemented in its current form, there will be a dramatic reduction in the numbers of asylum-seekers permitted to enter Canada through the United States.

EMILY CARASCO
Faculty of Law, University of Windsor

---

[146] These figures were provided by Joan Atkinson, assistant deputy minister, Policy and Program Development, Department of Citizenship and Immigration, to the chair of the Standing Committee on Citizenship and Immigration (November 19, 2000), text is available online at <http://www.parl.gc.ca/InfoComDoc/37/2/cimm/meetings/evidence/cimmev03-e.htm>.

Sommaire

Entente sur les tiers pays sûrs entre les États-Unis et le Canada: sa raison d'être

L'auteur analyse l'Entente sur les tiers pays sûrs entre les États-Unis et le Canada à la lumière des dispositions de la Convention sur les réfugiés de 1951, et plus particulièrement de l'obligation de non-refoulement. Il soulève certaines questions quant à sa conformité avec les traditions humanitaires et les obligations du Canada en droit international.

Summary

Canada-United States "Safe Third Country" Agreement: To What Purpose?

The author analyzes the Agreement between the Government of Canada and the Government of the United States of America for Cooperation in the Examination of Refugee Status Claims from Nations of Third Countries in light of the provisions of the 1951 Convention Relating to the Status of Refugees and particularly the obligation of non-refoulement, and raises questions about the consistency of the agreement with Canada's humanitarian traditions and its obligations under international law.

Bouzari v. *Iran:* Testing the Limits of State Immunity in Canadian Courts

INTRODUCTION

State immunity is a doctrine of international law aimed at regulating the adjudicative and enforcement jurisdiction of municipal courts in proceedings involving foreign states or their representatives. Grounded in the principle of sovereign equality, the doctrine generally operates to limit the ability of national courts to sit in judgment of foreign government actions. Though once supposed to be absolute, state immunity is now widely accepted as being restrictive, or relative, and only applicable to "sovereign" or "public" acts of state. Legal scholars and judges have spent the last century delineating a workable scope for the restrictive doctrine of state immunity, attempting to reconcile its rationale and purposes with the imperatives of a changing international legal order. In particular, the growing salience of human rights, the notion of peremptory norms, and the development of international criminal law since the Second World War has intensified the debate regarding the proper extent of state immunity in a world where the individual occupies an increasingly important role.

Over the last twenty years, the rise of transnational human rights litigation in the United States has resulted in the further re-evaluation of the doctrine of state immunity as individuals bring civil claims in domestic courts against foreign states and their officials for human rights violations committed abroad.[1] Internationally, the last five years have been particularly eventful with important

The author gratefully acknowledges James Crawford, Philip Allott, Christine Gray, Mark Power, Don McRae, and Yves LeBouthillier for their careful reading of, and incisive comments on, earlier drafts of this case comment.

[1] *Filártiga* v. *Peña-Irala,* 630 F.2d 876 (C.A. 2nd Cir. 1980).

343

judicial pronouncements on immunity by the House of Lords in
R. v. *Bow Street Metropolitain Sitpendiary Magistrate,* ex parte *Pinochet*
(1999/2000),[2] the French Cour de cassation in the *Qaddafi* case
(2001),[3] the European Court of Human Rights (ECHR) in *Al-
Adsani* v. *United Kingdom* (2001),[4] and the International Court of
Justice (ICJ) in *Case Concerning the Arrest Warrant of 11 April 2000
(Republic of the Congo* v. *Belgium)* (2002).[5] While these decisions
appear harmonious in their results — each (with the exception of
Pinochet) upheld immunity against competing claims of *jus cogens*
and human rights — they in fact disclose a persistent and unresolved controversy surrounding the scope of restrictive immunity.

The decision of the Ontario Superior Court of Justice in *Bouzari*
v. *Islamic Republic of Iran* (2002) is a Canadian contribution to this
debate.[6] Mr. Bouzari brought a civil action against Iran claiming
damages for torture in relation to events that occurred in that
country in 1993-94. The issue was "whether the Superior Court
of Justice has jurisdiction over this proceeding, both under the
common law rules respecting conflicts of law and under the State
Immunity Act" (SIA).[7] The plaintiff further challenged the constitutionality of the SIA under the Canadian Charter of Rights and
Freedoms.[8] After first concluding that the claim presented no real
and substantial connection to Canada, Justice Katherine Swinton
went on to dismiss the matter under the SIA, holding that the
court had "no jurisdiction over the Islamic Republic of Iran."[9] The

---

[2] *R.* v. *Bow Street Metropolitain Sitpendiary Magistrate,* ex parte *Pinochet* (No. 3),
[1999] 2 W.L.R. 827 (H.L.) [hereinafter *Pinochet*].

[3] Cour de Cassation, 13 March 2001, Judgment No. 1414, in (2001) 105
R.G.D.I.P. 473.

[4] *Al-Adsani* v. *United Kingdom* (2001), 34 E.H.R.R. 273; *Al-Adsani* v. *Government of
Kuwait and Others* (1994), 103 I.L.R. 420 (Q.B.); (1996) 107 I.L.R. 536 (C.A.);
leave to appeal to the House of Lords denied 27 November 1996 [hereinafter *Al-
Adsani*].

[5] *Case Concerning the Arrest Warrant of 11 April 2000 (Republic of the Congo* v. *Belgium),*
Judgment 14 February 2002, International Court of Justice [hereinafter *Arrest
Warrant*]. See also *Case Concerning Certain Criminal Proceedings in France (Republic of
the Congo* v. *France),* hearing on the indication of a provisional measure concluded
29 April 2003, decision forthcoming.

[6] *Bouzari* v. *Islamic Republic of Iran,* [2002] O.J. No. 1624 (S.C.J.), per Swinton J.;
aff'd by [2004] O.J. No. 2800 (C.A.) [hereinafter *Bouzari*].

[7] *Ibid.* at para. 2. State Immunity Act, R.S.C. 1985, c. S-18.

[8] Canadian Charter of Rights and Freedoms, Part 1 of the Constitution Act, 1982,
being Schedule B to the Canada Act 1982 (UK), 1982, c. 11.

[9] *Bouzari, supra* note 6 at para. 90.

constitutionality of the SIA was also upheld. *Bouzari* is the first Canadian case in which a plaintiff has sought to obtain civil redress from a foreign state for acts of extraterritorial torture. Along with *Al-Adsani*,[10] it is the second such case in the Commonwealth.

The issue of the constitutionality of the SIA exceeds the scope of this case comment, which will analyze the *Bouzari* decision in relation to the doctrine of state immunity. It will be argued that the court's decision was reasonable given the language of the SIA but that the act is not the sole basis for the determination of immunities. There exists a Canadian common law of state immunity. Under the common law, the characterization of state acts should take into account the entire context in which the claim has arisen, including the peremptory status of the torture prohibition. It will be further argued that the peremptory prohibition of torture overrides any protection it might otherwise derive from its characterization as a governmental act and *ipso facto* disentitles a respondent state to immunity.

BOUZARI DECISION

FACTUAL BACKGROUND

Houshang Bouzari, an Iranian national, worked as a consultant in the oil and gas industry, helping foreign companies find projects in Iran. In 1991, a consortium for the South Pars project, an offshore site in the Persian Gulf, hired him. The consortium sought to provide exploration and drilling technology as well as pipeline and refinery construction to the state-owned National Iranian Oil Company (NIOC). The South Pars project was worth US $1.8 billion from which Mr. Bouzari was to collect a 2 per cent commission. In 1992 and 1993, Mr. Bouzari was approached by Mehdi Hashemi Bahramani, the son of the president of Iran, who offered his father's help in bringing the South Pars project to fruition. In return for his familial influence, Bahramani demanded a US $50 million commission from Mr. Bouzari. He refused.

In June 1993, three plain-clothed police officers forcefully entered Mr. Bouzari's home in Tehran. At gunpoint, Mr. Bouzari was made to drive to a detention centre operated by the Ministry of Information where he was incarcerated for several months. During this period, Mr. Bouzari claims to have been tortured: he was beaten, had his head plunged into a toilet filled with excrement,

[10] *Al-Adsani, supra* note 4.

was subject to mock executions, was hung by the shoulders for extended durations, and was beaten around the ears with slippers. His captors demanded and were paid a US $3 million ransom for his release in January 1994. In Mr. Bouzari's opinion, his torture was aimed at his removal from the South Pars project. The NIOC terminated the contract with the consortium in the summer of 1993. In 1996, Bahramani created another state-owned company, which contracted with the consortium for the exploitation of South Pars.

Mr. Bouzari and his family came to Canada in July 1998 as landed immigrants. He brought an action in Ontario, seeking both compensatory and punitive damages against Iran for torture. Mr. Bouzari's injuries included post-traumatic stress disorder, chronic pain in his back and shoulders, and deafness. Iran did not defend and was accordingly noted to be in default. Under the Ontario Rules of Civil Procedure, Iran is also deemed to have admitted the truth of Mr. Bouzari's allegations.[11] On May 1, 2002, Swinton J. held that the court had no jurisdiction in the matter and dismissed the action.

THE ISSUE BEFORE THE COURT

Swinton J. stated the issue as follows: "[W]hether the Superior Court of Justice has jurisdiction over this proceeding, both under the common law rules respecting conflicts of law and under the *State Immunity Act.*"[12] On its face, this formulation seems problematic as it suggests that both Canadian conflicts rules and the SIA are determinative of the court's ability to assert jurisdiction over a given matter. This premise is not entirely accurate. While conflicts rules and the doctrine of state immunity can both *in effect* cause the plaintiff's claim to be dismissed, it is conceptually imprecise to meld their distinct legal nature and operation, as was recently emphasized by the ICJ in the *Arrest Warrant* case.[13]

In its most general sense, jurisdiction "relates to the power of a state to affect the rights of a person ... by legislative, executive or judicial means."[14] In its narrower judicial meaning, jurisdiction refers to the power of a court over particular claims (*ratione materiae*)

---

[11] Rules of Civil Procedure, R.R.O. 1990, Reg., Rule 19.02(1)(a).

[12] *Bouzari, supra* note 6 at para. 2.

[13] *Arrest Warrant, supra* note 5.

[14] *Ibid.*, separate opinion of Judge Koroma at para. 5.

and particular parties (*ratione personae*) within particular geographical limits (*ratione loci*) as well as the authority to make determinations of law and of fact in the course of its proceedings. By contrast,
the doctrine of state immunity is a procedural plea that "prevents
the subjection of an independent state to proceedings in another
country relating to a dispute about its exercise of governmental
power."[15] Insofar as state immunity is a personal plea "based on
the status of the defendant as a sovereign state," it directly limits
the jurisdiction *ratione personae* of national courts by exempting foreign states from their legal process.[16] In this sense, immunity can
indeed be conceived as an inherent aspect of jurisdiction. However,
in a manner similar to the *forum non conveniens* rule, the doctrine of
state immunity is more precisely concerned with *declining* jurisdiction once it has been properly asserted.[17] As stated by the court
in the *Arrest Warrant* case, "it is only where a state has jurisdiction
under international law in relation to a particular matter that there
can be any question of immunities in regard of the exercise of that
jurisdiction."[18] In other words, immunity is distinct from, and ana-
lytically dependent upon, the existence of jurisdiction.

In the *Arrest Warrant* case, the ICJ discussed the relationship
between the exercise of universal jurisdiction and the immunities
of foreign ministers. After acknowledging immunity's conceptual
subordination to jurisdiction, the majority regrettably declined
to articulate its views on jurisdiction, invoking the *non ultra petita*
principle. This omission was strongly criticized by the concurring
judges who felt that the court had improperly "given the impression
that immunity is a free-standing topic of international law. It is
not. 'Immunity' and 'jurisdiction' are inextricably linked."[19] However, despite their interconnection, immunity and jurisdiction stem
from distinct rationales. Jurisdiction is concerned with the exercise
of power and immunity with its control. Indeed, the concurring
judges continued: "[W]hile the notion of immunity depends, conceptually, upon pre-existing jurisdiction, there is a distinct corpus

---

[15] H. Fox, *The Law of State Immunity* (Oxford: Oxford University Press, 2002) at 11.

[16] *Ibid.* at 18.

[17] The comparisons between the doctrines of state immunity and *forum non conveniens* should not be taken too far given the inherently discretionary nature of
the latter.

[18] *Arrest Warrant, supra* note 5 at para. 46.

[19] *Ibid.*, joint separate opinion of Judges Higgins, Koojimans, and Buergenthal at
para. 3.

of law that applies to each. What can be cited to support an argument about the one is not necessarily relevant to the understanding of the other. In bypassing the issue of jurisdiction, the Court has encouraged a regrettable current tendency ... to conflate the two issues."[20]

Thus, to avoid undue conceptual conflation, the issues in *Bouzari* could have been more accurately formulated as follows: (1) whether the court has jurisdiction over the present proceedings under conflicts of law rules; and (2) if so, whether jurisdiction should be declined on the basis of the SIA. Despite an ambiguously worded statement of issues, Swinton J. properly went on to consider the questions of jurisdiction and immunity separately.

JURISDICTION OF THE COURT

While jurisdiction and immunity are inextricably linked, an indepth analysis of the jurisdictional aspects of *Bouzari* exceeds the scope of this comment on state immunity. However, the intriguing nature of the court's decision on jurisdiction warrants brief commentary. Summarizing the law, Swinton J. stated that "[u]nder the common law, a Canadian court has jurisdiction over a tort where there is a real and substantial connection between the subject matter of the litigation and the forum."[21] On the basis of the facts as alleged, Swinton J. held:

[16] ... If one were to apply Canadian conflicts rules with respect to jurisdiction in the normal fashion, the logical conclusion would be that there is no real and substantial connection between the wrongdoing that gave rise to the litigation and Ontario, and therefore, Ontario courts have no jurisdiction. A similar result would come with a *forum non conveniens* analysis, given that events occurred in Iran; Iranian law would apply; and there was no link to Canada at the time of these events.

[17] However, the plaintiff is here seeking damages for torture. Clearly, he cannot bring such an action in Iran, given the facts alleged. Given this reality, I do not feel it appropriate to decide this case on conflicts rules alone. It may be that the Canadian courts will modify the rules on jurisdiction and *forum non conveniens* where an action for damages for torture is brought with respect to events outside the forum. Therefore, I turn to the issue of state immunity.

These passages call for comment. First, as stated earlier, the assertion of jurisdiction precedes and determines any subsequent enquiry

---

[20] *Ibid.* at para. 4.

[21] *Bouzari, supra* note 6 at para. 15.

into the existence of a more suitable alternative forum or the application of immunities. Arguably, the court's decision on jurisdiction is the operative *ratio decidendi* of the case, and the remaining portion of the judgment (paragraphs 18-90) is *obiter dicta*. In deciding that it had no jurisdiction, the court effectively ruled out the possibility of jurisdiction being declined on the basis of *forum non conveniens* or immunity. Although the court did "not feel it appropriate to decide this case on conflicts rules alone," the analytical priority of jurisdiction over these doctrines has arguably resulted in it doing so. Nevertheless, this being a first instance decision, Swinton J. was entirely justified in pursuing her analysis.

After ruling that the court had no jurisdiction, Swinton J. stated at paragraph 17 that it was appropriate to turn to the immunity issue, surmising that Canadian courts might eventually "modify the rules on jurisdiction and *forum non conveniens* where an action for damages for torture is brought with respect to events outside the forum." One can only hypothesize as to the intended meaning of this last statement. Was the court of the view that the special nature of the torture prohibition warrants the recognition of universal jurisdiction in civil proceedings? Did Swinton J. feel that any development of the rules of jurisdiction was for a higher court to initiate? Given that courts might eventually modify the rules of jurisdiction in civil proceedings for extraterritorial torture, did Swinton J. accept *arguendo* that the court had *prima facie* jurisdiction in this matter before turning to the question of immunity? Such speculation goes beyond the scope of this comment on the issue of state immunity, to which I now turn.

STATE IMMUNITY IN CIVIL PROCEEDINGS FOR TORTURE

In deciding the issue of state immunity, Swinton J. considered the various provisions of the SIA, which codifies the doctrine of restrictive immunity. As drafted, the SIA provides for the jurisdictional immunity of foreign states (section 3), then goes on to enumerate certain exceptions (sections 4-8). In *Bouzari*, the plaintiff argued that the commercial activity (section 5) and local tort exceptions (section 6) were applicable. He further argued that a new exception should be read into the SIA in light of international law. The court rejected these arguments, concluding that it had no jurisdiction over Iran in these proceedings. The remainder of this comment will discuss the decision of the court with respect to the SIA and its treatment of the relevant international legal principles.

CANADIAN STATE IMMUNITY ACT

Brief History of State Immunity

It is useful to situate the SIA in the wider context of the international law of state immunity before discussing its application in civil proceedings for extraterritorial torture. In Canada, as in other common law countries with similar legislation, the SIA was enacted to codify the restrictive theory of state immunity developed by courts in the twentieth century.[22] Before this time, courts adhered to the notion that states, being equal in sovereignty and dignity, could not be subjected to the judicial process of other states without their consent — a principle expressed by the maxim *par in parem non habet imperium*.[23] The rule of absolute immunity prevailed in most of the common law world until the middle of the last century when it was jettisoned by the relative theory.

The emergence of the absolute theory of state immunity appears to be linked to the historical immunities enjoyed by monarchs and their representatives.[24] While the personal sovereign enjoyed immunity on the basis of his independence and dignity, ambassadors were granted a functional immunity predicated upon the freedom necessarily required in the course of their duties. "Ils sont la parole du prince qui les envoie, et cette parole doit être libre. Aucun obstacle ne doit les empêcher d'agir," explained Montesquieu.[25] While in power or on duty, sovereigns and diplomats were deemed inviolable and immune. As Sir Ian Sinclair speculated, this inviolability of the personal sovereign may have been transposed to the nation state during the seventeenth and eighteenth centuries, "when more and more, the monarch came to personify

---

[22] H.L. Molot and M.L. Jewett, "The State Immunity Act of Canada" (1982) 20 Can. Y.B. Int'l L. 79; *Re Canada Labour Code*, [1992] S.C.R. 50 at para. 30 [hereinafter *Re Labour Code*].

[23] *The Cristina*, [1938] A.C. 485 at 490 (H.L.) [hereinafter *Cristina*]; and *I Congreso del Partido*, [1983] A.C. 244 at 262 (H.L.) [hereinafter *I Congreso*].

[24] Fox, *supra* note 15 at 101-3; I. Sinclair, "The Law of Sovereign Immunity: Recent Developments" (1980-II) 167 R.C. 113 at 198; H. Lauterpacht, "The Problem of Jurisdictional Immunities of Foreign States" (1951) 28 B.Y.I.L. 220 at 228; and I. Brownlie, *Principles of Public International Law*, 5th ed. (Oxford: Oxford University Press, 1998) at 329.

[25] Montesquieu, *De l'esprit des lois*, XXVI, c. 21. This functional immunity is expressed by the maxim: "Non datur actio adversus legatum, ne ab officio suscepto legationis avocetur, ne impediatur legatio."

the state. It was Louis XIV of France who is alleged to have remarked: "L'État, c'est moi."[26] This equation of the state with the monarch is also signalled by the language used to describe their common attributes — sovereignty, dignity, and independence — which hitherto had solely been associated with the personal sovereign. By the end of the nineteenth century, sovereignty, dignity, and independence, the hallmarks of Westphalian statehood, came to be seen as the normative bedrock of absolute state immunity.[27]

The restrictive doctrine's triumph in the twentieth century involves over 200 years of judicial history that has been extensively described by others.[28] It is unnecessary to revisit every phase of the recessive history of state immunity to understand the implications of the restrictive doctrine in the context of civil claims for extraterritorial torture. A broad sketch of the law's evolution will suffice for this purpose. For P.D. Trooboff, the shift to the restrictive doctrine of immunity can be attributed to five factors: (1) the growing accountability of governments before their own courts; (2) the increase of international trade; (3) the questionable rationale of defending immunity in relation to commercial activity; (4) a growing state practice of waiving immunity in the course of business; and (5) the unfairness to private parties of shielding states from court process.[29] Responding to these concerns, early nineteenth-century courts in the United States and the United Kingdom attempted to distinguish between the private and public acts of state, upholding immunity only with respect to the latter. In 1824, Chief Justice Marshall held that "when a government becomes a partner in any trading company, it divests itself, so far as concerns the transactions of that company, of its sovereign character and takes that of a private citizen."[30] Early cases in the United Kingdom

---

[26] Sinclair, *supra* note 24 at 198. *Schreiber* v. *Canada*, [2002] 3 S.C.R. 269 at para. 13 [hereinafter *Schreiber*].

[27] Fox, *supra* note 15 at 24-25.

[28] *Ibid.* at 101-23; S. Sucharitkul, "Immunities of Foreign States before National Authorities" (1976-I) 149 R.C. 86; P.D. Trooboff, "Foreign State Immunity: Emerging Consensus on Principles" (1986-V) 200 R.C. 245; Sinclair, *supra* note 24; I. Pingel-Lenuzza, *Les immunités des états en droit international* (Bruxelles: Éditions Bruylant, 1997). See also *The Philippine Admiral*, [1977] A.C. 373 at 391-401 (P.C.) [hereinafter *Philippine Admiral*].

[29] Trooboff, *supra* note 28 at 266-67.

[30] *Bank of the United States* v. *Planters' Bank of Georgia*, 22 U.S. 904 at 907 (1824). This case is not about foreign state immunity. Marshall C.J. used the public/private distinction in ruling that the state of Georgia's participation in a corporation

also reveal the pale outline of the restrictive theory with courts distinguishing between the private and public nature of state acts. In 1851, the immunity of a foreign sovereign was upheld with respect to actions performed "in his public capacity."[31] Similarly, in 1873, Justice Phillimore found immunity inapplicable in proceedings against the property of a sovereign used in trade, although his decision was reversed on appeal.[32]

Despite this apparent early willingness to restrict state immunity to public acts and property, the absolute theory rigidly gripped the common law world for nearly a century after having been definitively established by the landmark case of the *Parlement Belge* (1880)[33] and later authoritatively supported by Lord Atkin in *The Cristina* (1938).[34] The *Parlement Belge* is the "first clear formulation of a rule of state immunity in English law" and was treated for over fifty years "as authority ... for an absolute doctrine of immunity."[35] The Court of Appeal's ruling on "the exemption of every sovereign from the jurisdiction of every court"[36] relied largely on Marshall C.J.'s classic decision in *The Schooner Exchange* v. *McFaddon*.[37] However, as many commentators have observed, the ratio of the *Schooner Exchange* concerned not the absolute immunity of states but rather their unlimited territorial jurisdiction.[38] Far from adopting absolute immunity, Marshall C.J.'s decision heralded the restrictive theory of immunity insofar as it distinguished between private and public "pursuits."[39] This being so, one is tempted to suppose

---

did not exempt that corporation from being sued in US courts. Georgia's sovereign privileges and prerogatives did not extend to the corporation.

[31] *De Haber* v. *Queen of Portugal* (1851), 17 Q.B. 171 at 206.

[32] *The Charkieh* (1873), 4 L.R. (Adm. & Ecc.) 59 [hereinafter *Charkieh*].

[33] *Parlement Belge* (1880), 5 P.D. 197 (C.A.).

[34] *Cristina, supra* note 23.

[35] Fox, *supra* note 15 at 104.

[36] *Parlement Belge, supra* note 33 at 207.

[37] *The Schooner Exchange* v. *McFaddon*, 11 U.S. (7 Cranch) 116 (1812) [hereinafter *Schooner Exchange*].

[38] G. Badr, *State Immunity: An Analytical and Prognostic View* (The Hague: Martinus Nijhoff, 1984) at 11-14; H. Lauterpacht, *supra* note 24 at 229; Sinclair, *supra* note 24 at 122; and Trooboff, *supra* note 28 at 256.

[39] *Schooner Exchange, supra* note 37 at 144. Marshall C.J. held that the immunity of warships should not extend to "merchant vessels [that] enter for the purposes of trade" for such vessels "are not employed by [a foreign sovereign], nor are they engaged in national pursuits."

that the doctrine of absolute state immunity might have been the result of an historic jurisprudential misunderstanding. Indeed, as Trooboff put it, "with the benefits of later developments, we can see today that some of the earlier cases [on state immunity] were probably read to stand for propositions that, on analysis, their authors did not necessarily intend."[40] Be that as it may, the absolute doctrine was notionally adopted in the common law and followed as a matter of *stare decisis* for nearly a century.

On the other hand, the doctrine was never literally "absolute." Despite their adherence to a strict principle of immunity, courts nevertheless developed certain exceptions under which immunity was denied.[41] Therefore, given its uncertain origins and uneven application by national courts, it is doubtful whether the absolute doctrine of state immunity ever formed part of customary international law, notwithstanding Swinton J.'s contrary assertion in *Bouzari*.[42] Indeed, the restrictive doctrine was consistently employed in civil law jurisdictions as early as the 1880s, notably by Italy and Belgium, and is still today applied by many European courts without the benefit of legislation or codification.[43]

In the United States, courts upheld the immunity of foreign states, following a mixed application of absolute immunity and "suggestions" from the executive branch.[44] In 1952, with the so-called "Tate Letter," the Department of State announced its adoption of the restrictive theory of state immunity.[45] The policy of direct in-

---

[40] Trooboff, *supra* note 28 at 257.

[41] As pithily summarized by Finlayson J.A. in *Jaffe* v. *Miller* (1993), 13 O.R. (3rd) 745 (C.A.) [hereinafter *Jaffe*], in common law there was no immunity "in respect of (1) land situate in the host state, (2) trust funds or moneys lodged for the payment of creditors, (3) debts incurred for service of its property in the host state and (4) commercial transactions entered into with a trader in the host state." See also *Thai-Europe Tapioca Service Ltd.* v. *Government of Pakistan, infra* note 47.

[42] "Historically, in accordance with customary international law, foreign states were granted absolute immunity from proceedings in the courts of other states." *Bouzari, supra* note 6 at para. 18. Contrast with H. Lauterpacht, *supra* note 24 at 221: "[I]nsofar as the actual practice of states can be said to be evidence of customary international law, there is no doubt that the principle of absolute immunity forms no part of international custom."

[43] *Guttieres* v. *Elmilik* (1886), Foro. It. 1886-I, 913 (Corte di Cassazione di Firenze); *S.A. des chemins de fer Liégeois-Luxembourgeois* c. *l'État Néerlandais*, Pasicrisie Belge, 1903. Cited in Fox, *supra* note 15 at 119-20.

[44] *Ex parte Peru*, 318 U.S. 578 (1943); and Fox, *supra* note 15 at 183-85.

[45] *Changing Policy Concerning the Granting of Sovereign Immunity to Foreign Governments,*

tervention of the government in judicial proceedings involving
foreign states continued until the enactment of the Foreign State
Immunity Act (FSIA) in 1976, which codified the restrictive theory
and left its application entirely to the courts.[46] In the United Kingdom, the absolute doctrine of immunity gradually lost ground in
the 1950s, partly due to the influence of Lord Denning.[47] It was
he, with the concurrence of Shaw L.J., who finally adopted the
restrictive doctrine in 1977 in *Trendtex* v. *Central Bank of Nigeria*,[48]
although the Privy Council had already adopted the restrictive rule
with respect to actions *in rem* in *The Philippine Admiral*.[49] Finally,
drawing on the provisions of the European Convention on State
Immunity (ECSI),[50] the United Kingdom adopted the State Immunity Act (UK SIA).[51]

The Supreme Court of Canada adhered to the absolute rule until
the enactment of the SIA in 1982, although lower courts were not
insensitive to the rise of the restrictive doctrine. In *Dessaulles* v.
Republic of Poland in 1944, the plaintiff lawyer sued his client, the
Polish consulate, to recover fees for professional services. Justice
Robert Taschereau held for the court: "Il ne fait pas de doute
qu'un état souverain ne peut être poursuivi devant les tribunaux
étrangers. Ce principe est fondé sur l'indépendance et la dignité
des états, et la courtoisie internationale l'a toujours respecté. La
jurisprudence l'a aussi adopté comme étant la loi domestique de
tous les pays civilisés."[52]

Letter to US Acting Attorney-General, 19 May 1952, (1952) 26 US Department
of State Bulletin 984 at 985.

[46] Foreign State Immunity Act, 28 U.S.C. § 1330 [hereinafter FSIA].

[47] In 1952, the Privy Council did "not consider that there had been finally established in England any absolute rule": *Sultan of Johore* v. *Abubakar Tunku Aris Bren-
dahar*, [1952] A.C. 318 at 343 (P.C.); *Rahimtoola* v. *Nizam of Hyderabad*, [1958]
A.C. 379 (H.L.), where Denning L.J. objected to the absolute theory; *Thai-Europe
Tapioca Service Ltd.* v. *Government of Pakistan*, [1975] 1 W.W.R. 1485 at 1490-91
(C.A.) [hereinafter *Thai-Europe*], where Denning M.R. recognized a commercial
exception to immunity but held it inapplicable to the facts of the case.

[48] *Trendtex* v. *Central Bank of Nigeria*, [1977] 2 W.L.R. 356 (C.A.) [hereinafter
Trendtex].

[49] *Philippine Admiral*, *supra* note 28.

[50] European Convention on State Immunity, E.T.S. No. 074 [hereinafter ECSI].
Fox, *supra* note 15 at 133.

[51] State Immunity Act, 1978, c. 33 [hereinafter UK SIA].

[52] *Dessaulles* v. *Republic of Poland*, [1944] S.C.R. 275 at para. 1.

The first signs of the restrictive doctrine in Canada appeared in 1958, when, in concurring reasons, Justices Charles Locke and John Cartwright would have upheld the immunity of US leaseholds from taxation by local authorities in New Brunswick insofar as the property was destined to a "public use."[53] Similarly, in *Flota Maritima Browning de Cuba S.A.* v. *The Canadian Conqueror* in 1962, an action *in rem* against Cuban-owned ships, the court was satisfied that the vessels in question were "public ships" and, for this reason, immune from legal process. Significantly, Justice William Ritchie, for the majority, explicitly refused "to adopt that part of Lord Atkin's judgment in *The Cristina* in which he expressed the opinion that property of a foreign sovereign state only used for commercial purposes is immune from seizure under the process of our courts."[54]

The clearest pre-SIA consideration of the restrictive theory of immunity by the Supreme Court of Canada was in *Congo* v. *Venne* in 1971, in which an architect sued the Congo for unpaid fees regarding the design of its pavilion for the 1967 World Fair in Montréal (Expo 67). Québec courts denied the Congo's immunity plea on the basis of the restrictive doctrine.[55] A majority of the Supreme Court of Canada reversed these judgments without deciding whether the restrictive theory was part of Canadian law. The majority held that the hiring of an architect to design a national pavilion in the context of Expo 67 was a sovereign act that could not be impugned in Canada, "even if the so-called doctrine of restrictive sovereign immunity had been adopted in our courts."[56] With characteristic erudition and clarity, Justices Bora Laskin and Emmett Hall dissented, unequivocally holding that "the [absolute immunity] doctrine is spent." Québec courts remained unwavering and stated the following year that "it is open for this Court to reaffirm its belief in the existence in Canada of a doctrine of restrictive immunity."[57] Ontario courts also came to accept the restrictive theory as

---

[53] *Saint John (City)* v. *Fraser-Brace Overseas Corp.*, [1958] S.C.R. 263 [hereinafter *Fraser-Brace*].

[54] *Flota Maritima Browning de Cuba S.A.* v. *The Canadian Conqueror,* [1962] S.C.R. 598 at 608.

[55] *Congo* v. *Venne*, [1968] R.P. 6 (Q.B.), affirmed [1969] B.R. 818 (Qué. C.A.) [hereinafter *Venne*]. Later that year, the Court of Appeal confirmed its *Venne* ruling in *Penthouse Studios* v. *Republic of Venezuela* (1969), 8 D.L.R. (3d) 686 (Qué. C.A.) [hereinafter *Penthouse Studios*].

[56] *Congo* v. *Venne*, [1971] S.C.R. 997.

[57] *Zodiak International Products Inc.* v. *Polish People's Republic* (1978), 81 D.L.R. (3d) 656 at 659 (Qué. C.A.) [hereinafter *Zodiac*].

part of the common law.[58] Before the Supreme Court of Canada could have another say in the matter, Parliament codified the restrictive theory of immunity in 1982 with the enactment of the SIA.

Framework and Operation of the SIA

It is in the context outlined earlier that the SIA was enacted to implement the restrictive doctrine of state immunity in Canadian law. Much like the ECSI and other national statutes on immunity, the SIA, as drafted, first establishes the immunity of foreign states (section 3) and then subjects this immunity to a series of exceptions, namely waiver (section 4), commercial activity (section 5), torts in Canada (section 6), maritime law (section 7), and property in Canada (section 8). The rest of the act (sections 9-18) deals with procedure, relief, and general matters of application. Under the restrictive theory and the SIA, the grant of state immunity hinges upon the nature of the proceedings rather than on the identity of the defendant as a state. If the subject matter of a claim is properly cognizable by Canadian courts and falls within the terms of the listed exceptions, the SIA prevents the immunity plea from being received and the matter proceeds, notwithstanding the character of the defendant as a "foreign state" within the meaning of the act.[59] In *Bouzari*, Swinton J. held that the action for damages for extraterritorial torture did not fall within the commercial activity or tort exceptions of the SIA. Iran's immunity was consequently upheld. This portion of her judgment will now be analyzed with respect to the relevant international law principles.

Commercial Activity Exception

Section 5 of the SIA (commercial activity) codifies the oldest exception to state immunity under the restrictive doctrine and, in a

---

[58] *Smith* v. *Canadian Javelin* (1976), 12 O.R. (2d) 244 (H.C.) [hereinafter *Smith*] (accepted the rule of "qualified immunity" developed in *Thai-Europe, supra* note 47, but it did not apply to the facts of the case); *Corriveau* v. *Cuba* (1979), 26 O.R. (2d) 674 (H.C.) [hereinafter *Corriveau*] (refused to apply absolute doctrine as the "law is evolving on the subject"); and *Khan* v. *Fredson Travel Inc. (No. 2)* (1982), 36 O.R. (2d) 17 (H.C.) [hereinafter *Khan*] (held that the absolute "doctrine had been abandoned in commercial matters in Ontario").

[59] Under section 2, a "foreign state includes (a) any sovereign or other head of the foreign state or of any political subdivision of the foreign state while acting as such in a public capacity; (b) any government of the foreign state or of any political subdivision of the foreign state, including any of its departments, and any agency of the foreign state; and (c) any political subdivision of the foreign state."

manner of speaking, embodies the essence of restrictive immunity by distinguishing between public (*jure imperii*) and private (*jure gestionis*) acts of states, denying immunity with respect to the latter. As states increased their trading activity, behaving more like private corporations than public sovereigns, it became common ground among the courts of trading nations that states should not be able to escape liability by merely invoking their sovereign independence and dignity — a view vividly expressed by Justice Robert Phillimore in *The Charkieh:*

> No principle of international law, and no decided case, and no dictum of jurists of which I am aware, has gone so far as to authorize a sovereign prince to assume the character of a trader, when it is for his benefit; and when he incurs an obligation to a private subject to throw off, if I may so speak, his disguise, and appear as a sovereign, claiming for his own benefit, and to the injury of a private person, for the first time, all the attributes of his character.[60]

The commercial activity exception was thus developed in part to prevent the denial of justice to private parties injured in their business dealings with sovereign states. Moreover, it was acknowledged that no affront to the dignity and independence of foreign states resulted from their involvement in legal proceedings connected to non-sovereign activity in which they had willingly engaged.[61]

Distinguishing between sovereign and non-sovereign state acts is not free of difficulties, as has been notably shown by H. Lauterpacht[62] and J. Crawford.[63] Insofar as the distinction is reflective of the separation of public and private law at the municipal level, courts have arrived, through varying methods, at disparate conclusions as to what constitutes *acta jure imperii* and what does not, precisely because the respective limits of public and private spheres vary from state to state. To give but one example, the purchase of army boots by a foreign government was held to be a sovereign act in France and a commercial act in Italy.[64] In addition, depending on whether courts focus on the nature or the purpose of state

---

[60] *Charkieh, supra* note 32 at 99-100. See also *Thai-Europe, supra* note 47 at 1491.

[61] *Rahimtoola, supra* note 47 at 422; *Trendtex, supra* note 48 at 386.

[62] Lauterpacht, *supra* note 24 at 222-26.

[63] J. Crawford, "International Law and Foreign Sovereigns: Distinguishing Immune Transactions" (1983) 54 B.Y.I.L. 75.

[64] *Gouvernment espagnol* c. *Cassaux,* S. 1849-I-81, Cour de Cassation; *Governo Rumeno* v. *Trutta,* Annual Digest, vol. 3, 1925-26. Both cited in Sinclair, *supra* note 24 at 211.

activity, different characterizations may result. Pursuant to section 2 of the SIA, "commercial activity" is defined as "any particular transaction, act or conduct or any regular course of conduct that by reason of its nature is of a commercial character." Despite the act's insistence on the "nature" of the transaction, the Supreme Court of Canada counsels a broader enquiry: "[T]he proper approach to characterizing state activity is to view it in its entire context. This approach requires an examination predominantly of the nature of the activity, but its purpose can also be relevant."[65]

In *Bouzari*, Swinton J. properly reminded herself of the contextual approach adopted by the Supreme Court of Canada in *Re Canada Labour Code*.[66] Turning to the facts of the case, she identified the impugned state acts: "kidnapping, false imprisonment, assault, torture and death threats." For the purpose of the motion, Swinton J. accepted the plaintiff's allegations that he "was abducted and held because he refused to pay monies ... and [that] the imprisonment and torture were aimed at extracting an advance payment from him on the commission that he had refused to pay Mehdi [in reference to the South Pars project]."[67] Ultimately, however, Swinton J. did not find these acts to be of a "commercial character" within the meaning of the SIA. She stated:

[27] Here, the activity or conduct that gives rise to the litigation was imprisonment by agents of the foreign state and acts of torture performed by them in a state prison. Even if the motive behind these acts was to obtain funds from Mr. Bouzari by way of ransom or to remove him from the South Pars project, the acts were those of state officials, and the funds paid were deposited to bank accounts of the state.
[28] In my view, regardless of the state's ultimate purpose, the exercise of police, law enforcement and security powers are inherently exercises of governmental authority and sovereignty.

Swinton J. cited *Saudi Arabia* v. *Nelson* as authority for this last proposition. There, a plaintiff sought damages against Saudi Arabia for wrongful imprisonment, battery, and torture inflicted by police officers as retaliation against the plaintiff for reporting safety defects in his work place, a public hospital. The majority of the US Supreme Court held that the "conduct boils down to abuse of the power of its police by the Saudi government," upholding the latter's immunity on the basis that "a foreign state's exercise of the

---

[65] *Re Labour Code, supra* note 22 at 70.

[66] *Ibid.*

[67] *Bouzari, supra* note 6 at para. 25.

power of its police has long been understood for the purposes of the restrictive theory as particularly sovereign in nature."[68] It bears emphasis that, contrary to the Canadian contextual approach, US courts characterize state acts exclusively by reference to their "nature," without regard to their "purpose," as required by paragraph 1603(d) of the FSIA.

Mindful as she was of the differing Canadian and US approaches,[69] Swinton J.'s characterization of the impugned state acts appears inconsistent with the Canadian test and more in line with the US criterion, as she held the impugned acts to be inherently *jure imperii* "regardless of the state's ultimate purpose."[70] Swinton J. held that, even if one assumed the conduct to be financially motivated and related to the South Pars project, the fact that "the acts were those of state officials, and the funds paid were deposited to bank accounts of the state" effectively brought them within the realm of *acta jure imperii*. The court's analysis discloses an undue fixation on the identity of the actors as state functionaries and offers little assessment of the acts themselves or of the context in which they arose. As mentioned earlier in this comment, the distinguishing feature of the restrictive theory of immunity is precisely the relative unimportance it places on state participation in a given activity, the emphasis having been shifted to the activity itself. It cannot be the case that the mere involvement of police officers in a given activity results, without more involvement, in the classification of that activity as *acta jure imperii*. Without commenting on the correctness of the court's ultimate characterization of the impugned acts, it is submitted that it misapprehended or misapplied the Canadian contextual approach.

In *Re Labour Code,* Justice Gerard La Forest observed that section 5 of the SIA,

in combination with the definition of "commercial activity" in s. 2, raises two basic questions. First, what is the "nature" of the activity in question. [In *Bouzari*, does kidnapping, imprisonment and torture constitute a commercial activity?] Second, are the proceedings in this case [in *Bouzari*, an action in damages for torture] "related" to that activity?

If a commercial aspect emerges from the context of the activity, the enquiry involves whether "the commercial realm is sufficiently

---

[68] *Saudi Arabia* v. *Nelson,* 507 U.S. 349 at 361 (1993) [hereinafter *Nelson*].

[69] *Bouzari, supra* note 6 at para. 29.

[70] *Ibid.* at para. 28.

strong as to form a 'nexus' so that it can truly be said that the proceedings 'relate' to commercial activity."[71] As mentioned earlier, the impugned state activity must be viewed in its entire context — that is, with proper regard to its ontological and teleological aspects — and not with sole reference or undue emphasis on the fact that the state or its agents are involved in the activity. In *Bouzari,* the context might have been framed as follows: (1) in themselves, kidnapping, imprisonment, and torture are not acts of a commercial nature;[72] and (2) the accepted immediate purpose of the acts — that is, to obtain funds or to remove Mr. Bouzari from the South Pars Project — relates to a commercial enterprise. Thus, the only commercial aspect that emerges from this context is Iran's interest in the South Pars project. Therefore, as the present claim concerns compensatory and punitive damages for torture, it cannot be said that the proceedings are "related" to commercial activity to the proximate degree required in Canadian law. As La Forest J. says at paragraph 46 of *Re Labour Code,* "it is not enough that the proceedings merely 'touch on' or 'incidentally affect'" the commercial activity. Rather, a "more substantial connection is needed." The present case is substantially a civil claim for torture. It is not premised on the (vague) commercial relationship between Mr. Bouzari and the state of Iran. It follows that the commercial activity exception codified in section 5 of the SIA does not apply.

Perhaps counter-intuitively, the supreme illegality of torture does not alter the assessment of its non-commercial character in this case for the purposes of the SIA section 5 analysis. To the contrary, the decision to torture and to violate international law (not to mention the law of the forum, torture being illegal in Iran[73]) remains a governmental act. In *Letelier* v. *Chile,* the court stated that "a decision calculated to result in injury or death to a particular individual ... made for whatever reason, would be one most assuredly involving policy judgment."[74] In this case, however, immunity was ultimately denied since the events occurred on US soil and it was held that, despite the governmental nature of political assassinations, "there is no discretion to commit, or to have one's

---

[71] *Re Labour Code, supra* note 22 at para. 22.

[72] See, however, the dissent of White and Blackmun JJ. in *Nelson, supra* note 68 at 366-67, where it was supposed that torture could have been viewed as "commercial" had the state hired "thugs" to carry it out instead of using police officers.

[73] Constitution of Iran, 28 July 1989, Article 38, text is available at <www.oefre. unibe.ch/law/icl/ir00000_.html> (last visited: 15 March 2003).

[74] *Letelier* v. *Chile,* 488 F. Supp 665 at 673 (D.C. Dist. Ct., 1980) [hereinafter *Letelier*].

officers or agents commit, an illegal act."[75] This result is to be contrasted with the one in *Jaffe* v. *Miller*, where the Ontario Court of Appeal held that the illegal and malicious conduct of state functionaries acting in the scope of their duties did not deprive them of the protection of the SIA.[76] While it may be that the unlawfulness of a governmental act might give rise to a new exception to state immunity (as will be discussed later in this comment), illegality does not alter the character of an act once it has been classified as *jure imperii* or *gestionis* for the purposes of the statutory commercial activity exception. As J. Crawford suggests, if a "transaction can fairly be classified as a 'commercial transaction' … then the transaction will not lose that character or classification because extraneous facts or aspects surrounding the individual transaction suggest or would attract a different classification."[77] It is submitted that if an exception to state immunity is to emerge in relation to unlawful acts, it should do so on its own merits and for its own reasons and not by artificially shoe-horning illegal governmental conduct into the commercial activity exception.

Tort Exception

After holding section 5 of the SIA to be inapplicable, Swinton J. considered whether Mr. Bouzari's claim fell within the tort exception codified in section 6, which reads as follows:

6. A foreign state is not immune from the jurisdiction of a court in any proceedings that relate to (a) any death or personal or bodily injury, or (b) any damage to or loss of property that occurs in Canada.

As Swinton J. correctly observed, this exception is relatively recent, given that it was previously unavailable in common law prior to its inclusion in the various national statutes on jurisdictional immunities.[78] Though the exception is generally thought to have first appeared in the ECSI (Article 11), Fox notes that the Institut de droit international "proposed [an] exception for delictual or quasi-delictual acts committed within the forum state" in its 1891 Resolution.[79] Originally meant to remove immunity in claims for

---

[75] *Ibid.*

[76] *Jaffe, supra* note 41.

[77] Crawford, *supra* note 63 at p. 96.

[78] *Bouzari, supra* note 6 at para. 31.

[79] Fox, *supra* note 15 at 309. See 1891 Resolution, I.D.I. II (1885-1891) Hamburg at 1215.

personal injuries resulting from the negligent use of motor vehicles by foreign officials in the forum state, the exception was ultimately widened to apply to all non-commercial torts committed by the foreign state in the forum territory.[80] Endorsed by the International Law Commission, the purpose of the tort exception is to allow injured parties to access justice and recover their losses in cases where the foreign state is bound to make reparation under the *lex loci delicti commissi*. The exception generally covers insurable risks as well as intentional, indeed criminal, misconduct occurring in the forum state.[81] The requirement of a territorial connection to the forum state is a feature shared by the various national statutes on immunity.[82] As held by Swinton J., it is precisely the lack of a Canadian territorial connection that causes section 6 to be inapplicable in *Bouzari* where the torture occurred in Iran.[83]

The language of section 6 is clear: the exception applies only to a tort "that occurs in Canada," with the result that proceedings against a foreign state in relation to an extraterritorial tort will be barred by the SIA even if, as in *Bouzari*, the effects of the tort are felt in Canada. This territorial restriction exceeds the ties typically required by Canadian rules for service *ex juris* where it is sufficient for the damage to be continued in the forum province. For example, the Ontario Rules of Civil Procedure permit the service of originating process in proceedings "in respect of damage sustained in Ontario arising from a tort ... wherever committed."[84] In addition to its corrective justice goals, the tort exception can be viewed as striking a balance between the principles of territorial jurisdiction and state independence, allowing the forum state to exercise unimpeded authority over persons (including other states), things, and events within its territory, without going so far as to permit it to sit in judgment of foreign delictual state conduct.

Significantly, the tort exception applies regardless of the nature of the tortious act of state, be it *jure gestionis* or *imperii*. This exception was recently confirmed by the Supreme Court of Canada in

---

[80] Fox, *supra* note 15.

[81] Commentary on Article 12 of the Draft Articles on Jurisdictional Immunities of States and Their Property, in *Report of the ILC on the Work of Its 43rd Session*, 1991, Doc. A/46/10(Supp) at 113-18.

[82] See, for example, the UK SIA, *supra* note 51 at s. 5 and the US FSIA, *supra* note 46 at s. 1605(a)(5).

[83] *Bouzari*, *supra* note 6 at paras. 32-34.

[84] Rules of Civil Procedure, R.R.O. 1990, Reg. 194 Rule 17.02(h).

Schreiber v. *Canada*, where a Canadian citizen sued Germany for personal injuries suffered in the course of his arrest and detention in Canada. The plaintiff alleged having suffered mental distress, denial of liberty, and damage to his reputation, all of which were held not to be "personal injuries" within the meaning of section 6 as they did not result from a bodily or physical injury as required by the SIA. The United States intervened in the proceedings, urging the Supreme Court of Canada to read section 6 as applying solely to non-governmental acts.[85] However, on a plain reading of that section and relying on various international authorities, the court held "that the 'death or personal injury' restriction to immunity is applicable to both *jure imperii* and *jure gestionis* acts."[86]

This particular feature of the tort exception indicates that it hinges solely on notions of geography and territoriality and not on the character of the state act. The elementary principle of the restrictive theory — that sovereign acts are immune — is rejected. In this case, it is the *situs* of the act that is determinative of its justiciability and not its sovereign or non-sovereign character. In this sense, the tort exception represents a further restriction on state immunity. The exception is consistent with the principle noted in the *Schooner Exchange*, which holds that "the jurisdiction of a nation within its own territory is necessarily exclusive and absolute" but that this "full and absolute territorial jurisdiction ... [is] incapable of conferring extraterritorial power."[87] Moreover, the exception is consistent with the notion of redress — that is, insofar as there exists a principled basis for doing so, the law commands that wrongs be righted and that justice be done.[88] To exclude the tortious governmental conduct of foreign states from the jurisdiction of national courts, when authority over such cases can otherwise be asserted, would seriously compromise the forum state's ability to do justice in its own territory. This is perhaps what the Supreme Court of Canada had in mind in *Schreiber* when, in refusing to apply a *jure imperii/gestionis* distinction to the tort exception, it stated:

---

[85] The position advocated by the US State Department in *Schreiber* has not been accepted by US courts. See particularly *Letelier, supra* note 74.

[86] *Schreiber, supra* note 26 at para. 36.

[87] *Schooner Exchange, supra* note 37 at 136-37.

[88] As stated by Bingham M.R., "that wrongs be remedied" is the rule of public policy "which has first claim on the loyalty of the law." *X* v. *Bedfordshire County Council,* [1995] 2 A.C. 633 at 663 (C.A.).

[T]he interpretation advanced by the United States would deprive the victims of the worst breaches of basic rights of any possibility of redress in national courts. Given the recent trends in the development of international humanitarian law enlarging this possibility in cases of international crime ... such a result would jeopardize at least in Canada a potentially important progress in the protection of the rights of the person.[89]

Civil claims for extraterritorial torture, such as in *Bouzari*, will continue to be barred by section 6 of the SIA as long as the territorial requirement of this provision is maintained. Given the clear language of section 6 and its adherence to the principle of territoriality, no convincing basis can be asserted in defence of a judicial extension of its ambit to include extraterritorial torts absent parliamentary intervention.

INTERPRETING THE SIA IN LIGHT OF INTERNATIONAL LAW

If none of the statutory exceptions applied, the plaintiff submitted that the SIA should be interpreted in light of contemporary international law, which, he argued, does not require the grant of state immunity in civil proceedings for extraterritorial torture. In Canada, "Parliament is not presumed to legislate in breach of a treaty or in any manner inconsistent with the comity of nations and the established rules of international law."[90] Relying on this interpretative presumption of international legality, the plaintiff argued that Canada's treaty obligations under the Convention against Torture and Other Cruel, Inhuman or Degrading Treatment or Punishment (CAT)[91] and the International Covenant on Civil and Political Rights (ICCPR)[92] obligate it to provide victims of torture with a civil recourse. To interpret the SIA as barring his claim, the plaintiff contended, would place Canada in violation of its treaty obligations. In addition, Mr. Bouzari submitted that the peremptory status of the torture prohibition also required the availability

---

[89] *Schreiber, supra* note 26, at para. 37.

[90] *Daniels* v. *White and the Queen*, [1968] S.C.R. 517 at 541 [hereinafter *Daniels*]. For a detailed discussion of the presumption of international legality, see G. van Ert, *Using International Law in Canadian Courts* (The Hague: Kluwer, 2002), c. 4.

[91] Convention against Torture and Other Cruel, Inhuman or Degrading Treatment or Punishment, 10 December 1984, UN Doc. A/39/51 (1985), 1465 U.N.T.S. 85 (entered into force 26 June 1987) [hereinafter CAT].

[92] International Covenant on Civil and Political Rights, 16 December 1966, UN Doc. A/6136 (1966), 999 U.N.T.S. 171 (entered into force 23 March 1976) [hereinafter ICCPR].

of civil remedies in Canada against foreign states — a proposition that entails, he argued, the denial of immunity in proceedings for extraterritorial torture. The court rejected these arguments.

Treaty Obligations

Under the CAT, to which Canada is a party but to which Iran is not, states agree to criminalize torture under their criminal law (Article 4) and to prosecute or extradite all torturers present in their jurisdiction (Article 5) regardless of where the torture occurred. Article 14 of the CAT obligates a state party to "ensure in its legal system that the victim of an act of torture obtains redress and has an enforceable right to fair and adequate compensation," without indicating, however, whether such a remedy is to be made available with respect to extraterritorial torture. In the opinion of Ed Morgan, one of the two international law experts testifying before the court, the absence of territorial language in Article 14 means that the provision has no geographical constraints and is applicable to torture wherever committed. The opposite view was taken by the second expert, Christopher Greenwood, who argued that state practice belied such an interpretation. Following the interpretative principles set out in Article 31 (contextual approach) of the Vienna Convention on the Law of Treaties (VCLT),[93] Swinton J. held that the "text of the treaty [did] not provide clear guidance" as to the proper meaning of Article 14.[94] Resort was thus made to Greenwood's survey of the state practice in relation to the CAT to conclude that "both at the time the treaty was signed and since . . . no state interprets Article 14 to require it to take civil jurisdiction over a foreign state for acts committed outside the forum state."[95]

Reasonable people can disagree as to the meaning of Article 14. Unfortunately, as Swinton J. noted, the surrounding provisions do very little to clarify its scope. Its position among other articles containing territorial restrictions can suggest both that it too should

---

[93] Vienna Convention on the Law of Treaties, 23 May 1969, 1155 U.N.T.S. 331, 8 I.L.M. 679 (1969), Can. T.S. 1980 No. 37 (entered into force 27 January 1980).

[94] *Bouzari, supra* note 6 at para. 49.

[95] *Ibid.* at para. 50. At para. 55, the court also accepted Greenwood's evidence that, to date, Article 14 of the ICCPR (access to justice) has not been interpreted "to require a state to provide access to its courts with respect to sovereign acts committed outside its jurisdiction." Insofar as the court's decision focused almost entirely on the CAT, the following discussion will correspondingly be restricted to that treaty.

apply solely to torture committed within the jurisdiction of a party state or, alternatively, that the drafters deliberately omitted geographical language to capture torture wherever committed. Following a purposive interpretation as directed by the VCLT, this second possibility resonates with the aim of the CAT, as expressed in its preamble: "[T]o make more effective the struggle against torture ... throughout the world." However, proponents of this interpretation eventually face the task of justifying why the putative grant of universal civil jurisdiction was not formulated in a manner resembling the grant of universal criminal jurisdiction under Article 5. The enigma deepens when one considers the drafting history of Article 14, which reveals that, at one point, following a Netherlands proposal, it contained the words "committed in any territory under its jurisdiction." While the decision to include the phrase is documented, its ultimate exclusion remains inexplicable, except perhaps, as supposed by some, as the result of a mistaken omission.[96]

As evidence of state practice, the court relied on an uncontested "understanding" entered by the United States "that Article 14 requires a state party to provide a private right of action for damages only for acts of torture committed in territory under the jurisdiction of that state party."[97] According to Greenwood, to this day, none of the implementation reports filed with the Committee against Torture disclose that Article 14 has been given an extraterritorial reach and the committee has issued no disapproving statements.[98] Internal Canadian practice, however, may be evidence of a possible wider construction of Article 14. In 1988, with the enactment of the Torture Prohibition Act, the Yukon legislature explicitly created a civil tort of torture. After recognizing in the preamble that Canada is a party to the CAT, the act provides that "every public official, and every person acting at the instigation of or with the consent or acquiescence of a public official, who inflicts torture on any other person commits a tort and is liable and renders his or her employer liable to pay damages to the victim of the torture."[99]

---

[96] For a detailed account of Article 14's history and a learned discussion of its scope, see A. Byrnes, "Civil Remedy for Torture Committed Abroad: An Obligation under the Convention against Torture," in C. Scott, ed., *Torture as Tort* (Oxford: Hart Publishing, 2001) at 542-49.

[97] *Ibid.* at 546, citing *Declarations and Reservations to the Convention against Torture*, Point II(3) of the United States' Statement of Declarations and Reservations, (1990) 136 Congressional Record S17, 492.

[98] *Bouzari, supra* note 6 at para. 51.

[99] Torture Prohibition Act, S.Y. 1988, c. 26, s. 1.

Section 5 of the act defines a "public official" as "any person in the public service of the Yukon (a) who is authorized to do or enforce the doing of any act or thing or to exercise any power, or (b) upon whom any duty is imposed by or under any act." While it is clear that the act only contemplates the civil liability of Yukon public officials who commit torture, it does not place any territorial restrictions on the torture itself. Under the act, it is thus possible to sue the Yukon for torture committed by its officials, whether in Whitehorse, Washington, or Wellington. As such, the Yukon legislation cannot be said to be inconsistent with Article 14 of the CAT, which, if nothing else, underscores this provision's ambiguity.

Absent the express grant of universal civil jurisdiction by Parliament, Canadian courts should refrain from asserting jurisdiction over civil proceedings for extraterritorial torture on the sole basis of the CAT. Moreover, insofar as the assertion of jurisdiction precedes the determination of immunity, if the CAT does not confer civil jurisdiction over extraterritorial torture, it cannot, *a fortiori*, serve as a basis for refusing immunity under the SIA. While treaties such as the CAT may serve in the interpretation of statutes, as suggested by the Supreme Court of Canada in *Baker* v. *Canada*,[100] they cannot be used by courts to alter legislation enacted by Parliament without violating the principle of legislative supremacy in the process.[101] Moreover, having regard to the principle of international legality, as Swinton J. concluded, the clear words of the SIA do not appear inconsistent with the scope of the CAT as defined by the practice of states.

Peremptory Norms

Finally, the plaintiff submitted that as a peremptory norm, the prohibition against torture includes a concomitant obligation to provide victims with a civil remedy against foreign states for torture committed within their own territory and that the SIA should be interpreted accordingly. The argument is one of normative hierarchy — *jus cogens* rules are said to "trump" incompatible international norms, such as state immunity, which can be waived by states or overridden by the exceptions developed under the restrictive theory. By contrast, *jus cogens* norms

---

[100] *Baker* v. *Canada*, [1999] 2 S.C.R. 817.

[101] W. Adams, "In Search of a Defence of the Transnational Human Rights Paradigm: May *Jus Cogens* Norms Be Invoked to Create Implied Exceptions in Domestic State Immunity Statutes?" in Scott, *supra* note 96 at 263.

cannot be derogated from by States through international treaties or local or special customs or even general customary rules not endowed with the same normative force. Clearly, the *jus cogens* nature of the prohibition against torture articulates the notion that the prohibition has now become one of the most fundamental standards of the international community.[102]

It will be recalled that Article 53 of the VCLT defines *jus cogens* as

a norm accepted and recognized by the international community of States as a whole as a norm from which no derogation is permitted and which can be modified only by a subsequent norm of general international law having the same character.

Relying on the opinion of both Morgan and Greenwood and on *dicta* from the House of Lords in *Pinochet*[103] and the Supreme Court of Canada in *Suresh* v. *Canada (Minister of Citizenship and Immigration)*,[104] Swinton J. readily accepted that the torture prohibition is a peremptory norm. After reviewing various decisions of national courts, as well as decisions from the ECHR and the ICJ, Swinton J. held that there is no "general state practice which provides an exception from state immunity for acts of torture committed outside the forum state" and that "there is no conflict between the [SIA] as written, with its limited exceptions, and customary international law." She added in the same paragraph:

Were I to accept the suggestion of the plaintiff and find [a *jus cogens*] exception, not only would I be interpreting the legislation incorrectly, but also, in Mr. Greenwood's view, putting Canada in violation of customary international law.[105]

Swinton J. therefore concluded that the action was barred by the SIA.

---

[102] *Prosecutor* v. *Furundzija*, 10 December 1998, IT-95-17/1-T at paras. 153-54 (ICTY) [hereinafter *Furundzija*].

[103] *Pinochet, supra* note 2.

[104] *Suresh* v. *Canada (Minister of Citizenship and Immigration)*, [2002] 1 S.C.R. 3. The Supreme Court of Canada did not explicitly hold the prohibition of torture to be *jus cogens*, but commented that the fact that torture is prohibited in numerous international instruments and "that it is considered by many academics to be an emerging, if not established peremptory norm, suggests that it cannot be easily derogated from" (at para. 65). Commentators have criticized the court's conservatism in not expressly recognizing the *jus cogens* status of the torture prohibition. C. Johnson and M.C. Power, "*Suresh*: Some Aspects of Public International Law" (2002) 28(1) Canadian Council on International Law Bulletin 11.

[105] *Bouzari, supra* note 6 at para. 73.

Before discussing the relationship between customary norms and national legislation, Swinton J.'s review of the case law warrants comment. Following its survey of the relevant cases, the court concluded: "[T]here is an ongoing rule of customary international law providing immunity for acts torture committed outside the forum state."[106] There are serious reasons to doubt the accuracy of this proposition. While judicial decisions are evidence of state practice for the purposes of finding custom, it is highly unlikely that the scant judgments in civil proceedings for extraterritorial torture against foreign states have resulted in the crystallization of a customary norm upholding state immunity in such cases. *Bouzari*, after *Al-Adsani*, is the second case of this nature in the Commonwealth. Even in the United States, where transnational human rights litigation began, there have only been a handful of cases in which damages were sought against foreign states for extraterritorial torture. Moreover, each of these decisions ultimately turned on judicial precedent and on the particularities of the forum's own immunity legislation, not on a general interpretation of customary law. Most notably, in the United States, judicial development in the area of *jus cogens* and state immunity was arrested by the Supreme Court of Canada's decision in *Argentina* v. *Amerada Hess*, where the FSIA was held to be "the sole basis for obtaining jurisdiction over a foreign state," with the result that "immunity is granted in those cases involving alleged violations of international law that do not come within one of the FSIA's exceptions."[107] In *Siderman de Blake* v. *Argentina*, which was considered by Swinton J., the court stated: "[A]s a matter of international law, the [*jus cogens*] argument carries much force." "Unfortunately," the court continued, "we do not write on a clean slate ... We must interpret the FSIA through the prism of *Amerada Hess*."[108] By contrast, as will be discussed later

---

106 *Ibid.* at para. 63.

107 *Argentina* v. *Amerada Hess*, 488 U.S. 428 at 434-36 (1989) [hereinafter *Amerada Hess*]. In this case, the plaintiffs sued Argentina for damages to their ship caused by military aircraft during the Falklands War.

108 *Siderman de Blake* v. *Argentina*, 965 F.2d 699 at 718 (9th Cir. 1992) [hereinafter *Siderman*]. Also bound by *Amerada Hess* were the decisions in *Sampson* v. *Germany*, 975 F. Supp 1108 (Dist. Ct. 1997) (Germany immune for mass murder of plaintiff's family and detention in Nazi concentration camp); *Smith* v. *Libya*, 101 F.3d 239 (2d Cir. 1996) (Libya immune in relation to the bombing of Pam Am 103 over Lockerbie); *Princz* v. *Germany*, 26 F.3d 1166 (D.C. Cir. 1994) [hereinafter *Princz*] (Germany immune in connection to slave labour in Nazi concentration camps); *Nelson*, *supra* note 68 (Saudi Arabia was immune in a claim for torture by police officers).

in this comment, neither Canada nor the United Kingdom has adopted the rigid approach of *Amerada Hess* with respect to their immunity statutes. Accordingly, the jurisprudential progeny of the US Supreme Court's restrictive interpretation of the FSIA in *Amerada Hess* does not afford much guidance in determining what effect, if any, *jus cogens* norms should have on state immunity under Canadian law.

The decisions of the ICJ in the *Arrest Warrant* case and of the ECHR in *Al-Adsani* are instructive *vis-à-vis* the interplay of immunity and *jus cogens* but remain ultimately inconclusive as to the requirements of customary law. In the *Arrest Warrant* case, the ICJ upheld the immunity of foreign ministers (not the state) from criminal (not civil) proceedings, in relation to war crimes and crimes against humanity. The court held the immunity of incumbent ministers to be absolute on the functional basis that ministers ought to be able to perform their duties without impediments (*ne impediatur legatio*) — a rationale that is quite different from that of state immunity (*par in parem not habet imperium*).[109] Surprisingly, the court side-stepped the issue of *jus cogens* and normative hierarchy (the words do not even appear in the judgment, save in a quotation of Lord Millet from *Pinochet*), referring instead only to "serious crimes." This decision is therefore of little use in the present enquiry. By contrast, the dissenting opinions of Judge Al-Khasawneh and Judge *ad hoc* van der Wyngaert take into account the tension between immunity and peremptory norms, holding that the latter should prevail in case of conflict insofar as they are reflective of the common and vital interests of the international community.[110]

The *Al-Adsani* case is similar to *Bouzari:* a Kuwaiti national sued Kuwait in the British courts for the torture that he suffered in that country. The High Court held that the applicant's claim did not fall within the exceptions of the UK SIA. The Court of Appeal agreed that none of the exceptions to immunity applied and that no new exception could be created. The House of Lords denied leave to appeal.[111] At the ECHR, Mr. Al-Adsani argued that the United Kingdom had effectively denied his rights under the European Convention of Human Rights[112] to be free from torture (Article 3) and to access justice (Article 6). The ECHR unanimously held that

---

[109] *Arrest Warrant, supra* note 5 at paras. 53-58.

[110] *Ibid.*, dissenting opinion of Al-Khasawneh J. at para. 7.

[111] *Al-Adsani, supra* note 4.

[112] European Convention of Human Rights, 1950 E.T.S. No. 5.

the United Kingdom had not caused or contributed to the torture of Mr. Al-Adsani in Kuwait, thus dismissing the Article 3 claim. The court then queried whether, by upholding Kuwait's immunity, the United Kingdom had deprived Mr. Al-Adsani of his right to bring a civil claim and seek redress under Article 6, an issue that eventually split the court nine to eight. Although the majority recognized the peremptory status of the torture prohibition, it refused to give effect to the consequences of that characterization in terms of normative hierarchy. Acknowledging that the *jus cogens* nature of the torture prohibition entailed the removal of immunity of individuals in criminal trials, the majority observed that no such rule had emerged with respect to the immunity of states in the context of civil proceedings.[113] Eight judges strongly disagreed with the majority's distinction between criminal and civil proceedings in deciding how peremptory norms should be applied with respect to state immunity. In their view, such a distinction is

not consonant with the very essence of the operation of the *jus cogens* rules. It is not the nature of the proceedings which determines the effects that a *jus cogens* rule has upon another rule of international law, but the character of the rule as a peremptory norm and its interaction with a hierarchically lower rule.[114]

The court's decision in *Al-Adsani* begs more questions than it answers. If one accepts, as did the ECHR and Swinton J., that peremptory norms enjoy "a higher rank in the international hierarchy than treaty law and even 'ordinary' customary rules,"[115] on what basis can this normative anteriority be disregarded in relation to state immunity? To what extent do criminal trials differ from civil proceedings with respect to immunity? In answering the question of whether state immunity *ought to* be denied in civil claims for torture, it is not enough merely to observe that no state has *yet* done so. The absence of state practice is not the sole determinant of the law's future path. Clear and convincing reasons must be articulated before pursuing or abandoning legal developments. In this respect, the majority decision in *Al-Adsani* is unsatisfactory, showing the majority to be more preoccupied with past state practice

---

[113] *Al-Adsani, supra* note 4 at para. 66.

[114] *Ibid.* See the dissenting opinions of Judges Rozakis and Calflisch, joined by Judges Wildhaber, Costa, Cabral Barreto, and Vajiæ. Judges Ferrari Bravo and Loucaides each issued separate dissenting reasons along similar lines.

[115] *Ibid.* at para. 60.

and comity and less concerned with prospective legal coherence and normative integrity.

Returning to the central problem of this discussion, it must be determined what effect, if any, the peremptory status of the prohibition of torture should have on the interpretation of the SIA in a civil claim against a foreign state. As stated earlier, international law (treaties and custom) may serve in the interpretation of national statutes, especially when such legislation is, like the SIA, the domestic codification of customary law. That being said, international norms cannot displace "a community's power and practice of determining its beliefs, status and future for itself" through "the deliberative, representative, public and participatory decision making model that is the parliamentary process."[116] This principle of self-determination is embodied in the constitutional doctrine of parliamentary supremacy. For the same reasons that international treaties should not be used by courts to redraft democratically enacted legislation, parliamentary supremacy would be made nugatory if customary law could, by mere incantation, transform the intended will of the legislature. The judicial presumption of international legality stands until rebutted by the clear and supreme intention of the legislature.[117] Parliament's omnipotence is such that it can also legislate in violation of international law, provided it expresses its "clear and unmistakable" intention to do so.[118] Indeed, Parliament can even legislate in violation of *jus cogens* rules since, as customary law (albeit of a higher form), they are incorporated into the common law and thus "take on the common law's great frailty: its subordination to statute."[119] However, as will be argued later in this comment, such legislation should not receive international recognition. In short, as stated by the Federal Court in *Suresh*, "while principles of customary international law may be recognized and applied in Canadian courts as part of the domestic law, this is true only insofar as those principles do not conflict with domestic law."[120]

[116] van Ert, *supra* note 90 at 9.

[117] *Chung Chi Cheung* v. *The King*, [1939] A.C. 160 at 168 (P.C.).

[118] *Daniels, supra* note 90 at 541.

[119] van Ert, *supra* note 90 at 168. As the author points out, however, countries that so legislate would likely incur international responsibility. See *Commentary to the Draft Articles on Responsibility of States for Internationally Wrongful Acts*, Report of the International Law Commission on the Work of its Fifty-Third Session, Doc. A/56/10(Supp.), Chapter III, Articles 40 and 41.

[120] *Suresh* v. *Canada (Minister of Citizenship and Immigration)* (2000), 183 D.L.R. (4ᵗʰ) 629 at 659 (F.C.A.).

The SIA was enacted to codify the restrictive theory of state immunity in Canadian law, which was also part of the common law.[121] The SIA was not then, nor is it now, inconsistent with Canada's treaty obligations. Nor was the SIA enacted in a manner inconsistent with customary law since, after all, the statute is the "domestic implementation of international legal principles that have evolved on a state-by-state basis."[122] However, as cautioned by Lord Wilberforce in *I Congreso,* one should not take the SIA as evidence of the precise requirements of international law for these are "still in course of development and in many respects uncertain."[123] Nevertheless, it can be said that the SIA reflects the historical practice of states to afford each other a certain measure of immunity from the jurisdiction of their courts. Indeed, the rules of immunity are the product of customary law.[124] However, as a written statute, the SIA represents a frozen snapshot of state practice as understood by Canada in 1982, if indeed not earlier, and, as such, it may not faithfully reflect prevailing or emerging state practice.[125] It is also the case that pre-1982 principles of immunity provided no exception on the basis of peremptory norms. Therefore, courts should not look for *jus cogens* between the lines of the SIA — that would be an exercise in futility. Nor should the words of the SIA be contorted to comply with emerging principles of international law — that would be an unacceptable exercise of judicial legislation. In short, even if the *jus cogens* prohibition of torture required the denial of immunity in civil proceedings such as *Bouzari,* courts could not extrapolate such a result from the limited exceptions of the SIA without effectively rewriting the statute. It is submitted, however, that if an exception to state immunity predicated on the peremptory prohibition of torture is to be found, Canadian courts would be well advised to look for it in the common law.

[121] This proposition is defended in the next section of this comment.

[122] M.L. Jewett and H.L. Molot, "State Immunity Act: Basic Principles" (1983) 61 Can. B. Rev. 843 at 854; and *Re Labour Code, supra* note 22 at para. 30.

[123] *I Congreso, supra* note 23 at 260.

[124] *Schreiber, supra* note 26 at para. 1; *Holland* v. *Lampen-Wolfe,* [2000] 1 W.L.R. 1573 at 1583 (H.L.) [hereinafter *Lampen-Wolfe*]; Sucharitkul, *supra* note 28 at 206. See also Yearbook of the ILC, 1980, vol. II-1 at para. 90.

[125] Arguably, insofar as the Canadian SIA was modeled partly on the FSIA (1976) and the UK SIA (1978), which in turn incorporated the terms of the ECSI (1972), *supra* note 50, the act is perhaps more representative of the custom of the 1970s. See Molot and Jewett, *supra* notes 22 and 122. See Debates of the House of Commons, 32nd Legislature, 1st session, Vol. X, at 10902-04.

COMMON LAW OF STATE IMMUNITY

While the US Supreme Court has taken the position in *Amerada Hess* that the FSIA is the "the sole basis for obtaining jurisdiction over a foreign state in [US] courts," Canadian courts have not adopted an exclusive or exclusionary view of the SIA.[126] There still exists in Canada, as in the United Kingdom, a common law principle of restrictive immunity that operates parallel to the SIA and applies to those matters not covered by the statute. It will be argued that the SIA has not evacuated the common law of state immunity, which remains a fertile ground for the incorporation of customary norms in the law of Canada. On this basis, it is finally argued that the evolving Canadian common law of state immunity might eventually come to admit an exception to state immunity predicated on the peremptory prohibition of torture.

COMMON LAW AND THE SIA

Before the enactment of the immunity statutes, English and Canadian courts had already recognized restrictive immunity as part of the common law. In the United Kingdom, as outlined earlier, the restrictive theory had been partially introduced by the Privy Council, fully adopted by the Court of Appeal, and ultimately endorsed by the House of Lords in, respectively, *Philippine Admiral, Trendtex,* and *I Congreso*.[127] In Canada, on the authority of the English cases, the lower courts of Québec and Ontario found the principle of restrictive immunity to be part of the common law despite the Supreme Court of Canada's inconclusive decision in *Venne*.[128] Similarly, in pre-SIA proceedings involving the commercial activity of Iran, the Federal Court of Appeal held that "the law of Canada at the time of the institution of the suit . . . did not permit

---

[126] *Amerada Hess, supra* note 107.

[127] *Philippine Admiral, supra* note 28; *Trendtex, supra* note 48; and *I Congreso, supra* note 23. Although *I Congreso* came after the enactment of the UK SIA, the case was decided on the basis of the common law. See Fox, *supra* note 15 at 157-58.

[128] Québec: *Venne* and *Penthouse Studios, supra* note 55; *Zodiak, supra* note 57. Ontario: *Smith, Corriveau,* and *Khan, supra* note 58. However, see *Tritt* v. *U.S.A* (1989), 68 O.R. (2d) 284 (H.C.), where in proceedings initiated before the SIA came into force, Steele J. upheld the immunity plea "because the acts [were] those of a foreign state." That judgment is to be contrasted with his decision in *Carrato* v. *U.S.A.* (1982), 40 O.R. (2d) 459 (H.C.) [hereinafter *Carrato*], where, noting the existence of the restrictive doctrine in Canada, Steele J. upheld the immunity plea because the claim concerned "public acts." One must conclude that *Tritt* was wrongly decided or the reasons improperly explained.

Iran to assert a claim of sovereign immunity."[129] In *Re Labour Code*, the Supreme Court of Canada also recognized that the restrictive doctrine of immunity was part of the common law prior to its codification.[130]

In one scholar's opinion, as "legislation purporting to implement an area of customary international law," the effect of the SIA is to "arrest the development of the common law as a reflection of evolving customary international law on [state immunity]."[131] This view is predicated upon the assumption that the SIA is a "complete code," which has ousted the common law. Admittedly, at first glance at least, the SIA does appear to cover the entire field of jurisdictional immunities. Section 3 provides: "Except as provided by this Act, a foreign state is immune from the jurisdiction of any court in Canada." As supported by the Canadian rules of statutory interpretation and judicial precedent, it is submitted that this formulation reflects a legislative drafting technique (that is, a statement of the rule and its exceptions) rather than Parliament's intention to evacuate the common law of state immunity.[132] Several principles lend support to this conclusion. First, pursuant to the principle of stability in the law, Canadian legislation is presumed not to interfere with the common law, unless otherwise stated with "irresistible clearness."[133] Indeed, when Parliament wishes to preclude recourse to the common law it does so unequivocally, as it did for example in section 6.1 of the Extradition Act.[134] This section provides: "Despite any other Act or law, no person who is the subject of a request for surrender ... may claim immunity under common law or by statute from arrest or extradition under this Act." In addition to evincing Parliament's practice and ability of clearly defining its statutes' relationship to the common law, section 6.1 of the Extradition Act is also evidence that in Canada immunities continue to be governed

---

[129] *Lorac Transport Ltd.* v. *The Atra*, [1987] 1 F.C. 108 at para. 30 (C.A.).

[130] *Re Labour Code, supra* note 22 at para. 25. Cory J., dissenting on another point, agreed at para. 92 that the restrictive doctrine existed in Canada prior to codification, although its evolution had not been as "clear-cut" as in England or the United States.

[131] J.H. Currie, *Public International Law* (Toronto: Irwin Law, 2001) at 336.

[132] R. Sullivan, *Driedger on the Construction of Statutes*, 3rd ed. (Toronto: Butterworths, 1994) at c. 13.

[133] *Goodyear Tire & Rubber Co. of Canada* v. *T. Eaton Co.*, [1956] S.C.R. 610 at 614.

[134] Extradition Act, S.C. 1999, c. 18. Section 6.1 was enacted by S.C. 2000, c. 43, s. 48.

in part by the common law. Second, far from providing an exhaustive regulation of jurisdictional immunities in Canada, the SIA
expressly provides for its own inapplicability in criminal proceedings (section 18) and in case of conflict with other legislation (section 17).[135]

Third, in the absence of conflict between the statute and the
common law, both are said to coexist and apply. In *R. v. Amato*, the
Supreme Court held:

Where a statute might be read as displacing the common law the appropriate canon of interpretation is a preference for that construction which
preserves the rule of common law where it can be done consistently with
the statute. By analogy the common law would be allowed to develop
defences not inconsistent with the provisions of the Code if the construction adopted was prospective.[136]

Similarly, where the objectives of the statute are furthered by maintaining the common law, the latter should be preserved. This is what
the majority of the Supreme Court of Canada ruled in *Rawluk* v.
Rawluk when it maintained the common law doctrine of constructive trust despite the existence of competing legislation on matrimonial property division.[137] Not only did the common law doctrine
of constructive trust not conflict with the statute, it allowed judges
a desirable measure of discretion in achieving greater and indi-
vidualized justice and fairness. Likewise, it is submitted that, insofar as the SIA is meant to implement the restrictive principle of state
immunity in Canadian law, the common law doctrine of state
immunity should be allowed to evolve and develop in a manner
consistent with the spirit of the SIA — that is, by upholding immunity solely with regard to *acta jure imperii*. A fourth relevant factor is
the area of law in which the common law and statute intersect. As
a statute dealing with an area of the law that was historically developed by courts — that is, state immunity — the SIA is presumed to
allow judges, as "custodians of the common law," to continue to

---

135 The SIA does not apply to the extent that its provisions conflict with those of the
Extradition Act, *ibid.*; the Visiting Forces Act, R.S.C. 1985, c. V-2; or the Foreign
Missions and International Organizations Act, S.C. 1991, c. 41.

136 *R. v. Amato*, [1982] 2 S.C.R. 418 at 443 (per Laskin C.J., Estey, McIntyre, and
Lamer JJ, dissenting) [hereinafter *Amato*]. The majority did not dispute this
statement of principle.

137 *Rawluk* v. *Rawluk*, [1990] 1 S.C.R. 70 at paras. 36-56. See *Hernandez* v. *1206625
Ontario Inc.* (2002), 61 O.R. (3d) 584 at paras. 38-44, where the Court of
Appeal for Ontario upheld the common law right of action for a taverner's neg-
ligence to the extent that it did not nullify the purpose of competing legislation.

shape the law of state immunity to reflect "the emerging needs and values of our society."[138]

Finally, and perhaps most importantly, the common law of state immunity should properly be regarded as a special strain of common law insofar as it is a product of ongoing state practice, namely customary international law. The international customary ascendance of the common law of state immunity, it is submitted, attracts particular considerations in the face of competing legislation. Indeed, if the SIA were deemed to have evacuated the pre-existing common law of state immunity, the adoption of new customary international law on state immunity would be statute-barred in Canada. Such an interpretation of the SIA would not only prevent Canadian courts from giving effect to emerging customary international law, but it would also cause Canada to stand in breach of its international customary obligations. Conversely, just as customary international law is incorporated into the common law, the Canadian common law contributes to the ongoing formation of customary international law. The judgments of Canadian courts on the law of state immunity form part of the state practice that can eventually give rise to new customary law. If the SIA is interpreted as barring further curial developments in the law of state immunity in Canada, Parliament will have effectively excluded Canada from the international process and dialogue through which the customary law of state immunity is formed. It is submitted that Parliament did not intend such a result by enacting the SIA. Rather, given the erratic jurisprudence that followed the *Venne* decision — with some courts clinging to absolute immunity and others applying the restrictive doctrine, sometimes inconsistently — the SIA was adopted to clarify the Canadian position and keep pace with international developments.[139] The Supreme Court of Canada recognized this fact when it properly characterized the SIA as "a codification ... intended to clarify and continue the theory of restrictive immunity, rather than to alter its substance."[140] The "substance" of the restrictive theory, as stated earlier, is its applicability to sovereign acts of state only.

Likewise, in the United Kingdom, the SIA has not entirely displaced the common law.[141] The House of Lords recently recognized

---

[138] *R.* v. *Salituro*, [1991] 3 S.C.R. 654 at 667 and 678.

[139] Molot and Jewett, *supra* notes 22 and 122. See also Debates of the House of Commons, *supra* note 125.

[140] *Re Labour Code, supra* note 22 at para. 30.

[141] Fox, *supra* note 15 at 136.

that unlike the US FSIA, the UK SIA is not the exclusive source of the law relating to state immunity:

Immunity which is accorded by English law to foreign states in civil proceedings is the subject of two separate regimes. The first is that laid down by Part I of the State Immunity Act 1978 ... The second regime is that under the common law. It applies to all cases that fall outside the scope of Part I of the Act.[142]

In so stating, the House of Lords effectively rejected the view taken by the Court of Appeal in *Al-Adsani* that the UK SIA is a "comprehensive code."[143] The common law applies to "all cases" that are not explicitly covered in the SIA. Under the common law analysis, as concisely summarized by Lord Millet, "the question is whether, in accordance with the law laid down in *I Congreso* ... the act complained of was *jure imperii* or *jure gestionis*. This must be judged against the background of the whole context in which the claim is made."[144]

The existence in Canada and England of a common law regime of state immunity operating in tandem with the SIA affords these jurisdictions considerable flexibility and responsiveness to changing customary law. Indeed, under Canada's reception system, customary norms are immediately incorporated into the common law. Treaties, by contrast, must be implemented by statute.[145] The ancient authority of Lord Mansfield in *Heathfiled* v. *Chilton*[146] was endorsed by the Supreme Court of Canada in *Saint John (City)* v. *Fraser-Brace Overseas Corp.*, where Justice Ivan Rand —ironically, in defence of absolute immunity —lauded the incorporation of international custom as the touchstone of the "inherent adaptability which has maintained the life of the common law."[147] He stated:

---

[142] *Lampen-Wolfe, supra* note 124 at 1575-76. Section 16(2) of the UK SIA provides for the act's own inapplicability in claims involving visiting forces. In *Lampen-Wolfe*, a claim involving an allegedly defamatory performance report produced by a US military education services officer, section 16(2) was held to result in the SIA's inapplicability and the immunity issues were resolved under the common law.

[143] *Al-Adsani* (C.A.), *supra* note 4 at 538-47.

[144] *Lampen-Wolfe, supra* note 124 at 1485.

[145] Van Ert, *supra* note 90 at 49.

[146] *Heathfiled* v. *Chilton*, (1767), 4 Burr. 2015.

[147] *Fraser-Brace, supra* note 53 at 269. See van Ert, *supra* note 90 at 142-50, for an outline of the incorporation doctrine in Canada.

If in 1767 Lord Mansfield ... could say 'The law of nations will be carried as far in England, as anywhere,' in this country, in the 20th century, in the presence of the United Nations and the multiplicity of impacts with which technical developments have entwined the entire globe, we cannot say anything else.[148]

Accordingly, if international state practice gave rise to further exceptions to state immunity, these would be valid in Canada by virtue of the common law. Indeed, the SIA applies exclusively with respect to the exceptions it codifies but does not preclude the application in Canada of further exceptions forged by state practice and received in the common law. It is not suggested that the common law can be used to circumvent the written words of the SIA in relation to the areas covered therein, such as commercial activity or local torts. As statutory enactments, they prevail over inconsistent customary international norms and common law.[149] However, the common law acts as a conduit for the reception and application of emerging customary exceptions *consistent with but not already contained* within the four corners of the SIA, such as violations of *jus cogens*.[150] In addition, beyond the SIA, it is open to courts, pursuant to their inherent jurisdiction to change the common law, to develop new exceptions to state immunity, which in their view reflect emerging international law. Such developments constitute state practice that could eventually, if imitated, give rise to new customary norms.

After reviewing contemporary state practice, the ECHR and Swinton J. both concluded that states currently still grant each other immunity in civil claims for extraterritorial torture, despite

---

[148] *Fraser-Brace, supra* note 53 at at 268-69.

[149] *Re Regina and Palacios* (1984), 17 D.L.R. (4th) 112 (Ont. C.A.). In this case, the Court of Appeal for Ontario recognized the continued salience of the common law of diplomatic immunity after the enactment of the Diplomatic and Consular Privileges and Immunities Act, S.C. 1976-77, c. 31, which implemented the terms of the Vienna Convention on Diplomatic Relations, 500 U.N.T.S. 95 (18 April 1961) a codification of the rules of customary international law on the matter. After first acknowledging that the customary law of diplomatic immunity was incorporated into the common law (at 118), Blair J.A. noted that the statutory provisions prevailed "wherever they differ from it" (at 119). The court thus implicitly recognized that the statute did not extinguish the pre-existing common law of diplomatic immunity and that new customary norms could be received in the common law to the extent of their consistency with the act.

[150] In *Amato, supra* note 136, Estey J. recognized that the "common law would be allowed to develop defences not inconsistent with the provisions of the Code" (at 443).

the peremptory status of the torture prohibition.[151] This finding is not surprising given the relative novelty of transnational human rights litigation as well as the conceptual uncertainty of, and judicial unfamiliarity with, *jus cogens*. No doubt, there is wisdom in not rushing to remove state immunity in proceedings such as *Bouzari*, given the indeterminate effects such a decision would have on the world order. Apocalyptic visions of flooded courtrooms, embarrassed sovereigns, and envenomed international relations come to mind.[152] However, this comment is not the place for a conjectural assessment of the consequences of denying torturer states the protection of immunity.

ACTA JURE IMPERII AND JUS COGENS

Assuming that the *Bouzari* claim is properly cognizable by Ontario courts, on what basis — applying the common law rules described earlier — should immunity be upheld or denied? At first glance, following the principles of *I Congreso*, the problem presents itself as whether the torture of Mr. Bouzari can be characterized as an act *jure imperii*. Under one view, given the definitional requirement under the CAT that torture be "inflicted by or at the instigation of or with the consent or acquiescence of a public official or other person in an official capacity,"[153] torture will always be an *acta jure imperii* and, thus, always entitled to immunity. Obviously, this conclusion fails to distinguish between acts performed by public officials and the character of those acts — that is, whether they represent the exercise of legitimate sovereign authority. As Judges Higgins, Koojimans, and Burgenthal stated in the *Arrest Warrant* case, the notion of *acta jure imperii* is continually evolving, "reflecting the changing priorities of society."[154] In this connection, given the growing salience of peremptory norms and human rights, it seems, intuitively at least, that the peremptory illegality of torture should somehow be factored into its characterization as a sovereign or non-sovereign act or, at the very least, in the ultimate grant or denial of immunity. This has not been the case in Canada, where,

[151]   *Al-Adsani, supra* note 4 at para. 61; *Bouzari, supra* note 6 at para. 73.

[152]   See R. Garnett, "The Defense of State Immunity for Acts of Torture" (1997) Australian Y.B. Int'l L. 97 at 124-26. In contrast, see A. Bianchi, "Denying State Immunity to Violators of Human Rights" (1994) 46 Austrian J. Pub. Intl. L. 195.

[153]   CAT, *supra* note 91, article 1.

[154]   *Arrest Warrant, supra* note 5, joint separate opinion at para. 72.

before *Bouzari*, mere illegality did not result in the loss of immunity under the SIA.[155] The decision in *Bouzari* holds that the violation of peremptory prohibitions is equally inconsequential in the determination of immunities under the SIA. The House of Lords reached a similar conclusion in *Kuwait Airways Corporation* v. *Iraqi Airways Co.* in 1995.[156]

However, illegal state conduct does not attract immunity everywhere and in every circumstance. A 1996 amendment to the FSIA has removed the immunity of designated states in lawsuits initiated by US nationals for extraterritorial "sovereign acts which are repugnant to the United States and the international community," including torture, extra-judicial killing, aircraft sabotage, and hostage taking.[157] The distinction created by the FSIA between torture in Cuba and torture in, for instance, Canada, is dubious to say the least. Notwithstanding the political motives of solely depriving its enemies of immunity, it is significant that the United States reserves these extreme measures only for acts of extreme international illegality. The FSIA also provides for the removal of immunity in claims related to "property taken in violation of international law."[158] In *Letelier*, a civil action for damages relating to events occurring in the United States, the court expressly recognized the governmental nature of political assassinations but added that there is "no discretion to perpetrate conduct ... that is clearly contrary to the precepts of humanity as recognized in both national and international law," thus preventing Chile from availing itself of the discretionary act exception under the FSIA.[159] In a case where the acts of foreign officials performed in the scope of their duties only violated US law, the court stated that "it cannot be said that every conceivable illegal

[155] *Jaffe, supra* note 41: "The illegal and malicious nature of the acts alleged do not of themselves move the actions outside the scope of the official duties of the responding defendants." See also *Carrato, supra* note 128. No peremptory norms were violated in these cases.

[156] *Kuwait Airways Corporation* v. *Iraqi Airways Co.*, [1995] 1 W.L.R. 1147 (H.L.) (Iraq's invasion of Kuwait, though illegal, was held to be an immune *acta jure imperii*.)

[157] *Flatow* v. *Iran*, 999 F. Supp. 1 at 12 (D.C. Dist. Ct.) See Antiterrorism and Effective Death Penalty Act, 1996, 28 U.S.C.A, para. 1605. Cuba, Iran, Iraq, Libya, North Korea, Syria, and Sudan have been designated state sponsors of terrorism by the US Department of State.

[158] FSIA, *supra* note 46 at s. 1605(a)(3). See also *Thai-Europe, supra* note 47.

[159] *Letelier, supra* note 74 at 673. See also *Liu* v. *Republic of China*, 892 F.2d 1419 (9th Cir. 1989) (no discretion to violate foreign law prohibiting murder).

act is outside the scope of discretionary function," distinguishing the illegality in that case (tortious interference with a court order) from the egregious acts in *Letelier*.[160]

In New Zealand, in the famous wine box case, *Controller and Auditor-General* v. *Sir Ronald Davison*, the Court of Appeal suggested that state violations of international policy might eventually cause immunity to be withdrawn. As stated by the majority, "one might speculate that the law may gradually but steadily develop, perhaps first excepting from sovereign immunity atrocities or the use of weapons of mass destruction, perhaps going on to except acts of war not authorized by the United Nations."[161] The only express denial of immunity for governmental acts performed in violation of peremptory norms was in *Prefecture of Voiotia* v. *Germany*, a claim arising from the Nazi occupation of Greece during the Second World War.[162] The court held that Germany's violations of *jus cogens* amounted to an implied waiver of its immunity — an argument that hitherto had not been well received on the basis that the waiver ultimately hinges upon some indication from the foreign state of "its amenability to suit."[163] It is observed that the claim in *Voiotia* would have succeeded under the SIA by virtue of the tort exception insofar as the alleged mass murders occurred in the forum state. Whether the decision of basing the denial of immunity in the peremptory illegality of sovereign acts is viewed as following "a well-established [Greek] tradition of innovation" or "as an acute case of judicial activism,"[164] it remains — like the ECHR dissent in *Al-Adsani* — evidence of shifting curial attitudes as to the role of *jus cogens* in the determination of immunities.

What role then, if any, should the peremptory illegality of torture play in characterizing state conduct as *jure imperii*? The answer to this question requires a theory of the state and of the power it wields as well as a theory of international law as a whole. Under the view that states are the ultimate embodiment of social power,

---

160 *Risk* v. *Haloversen*, 936 F.2d 393 at 396 (9th Cir. 1991).

161 *Controller and Auditor-General* v. *Sir Ronald Davison*, [1996] 2 N.Z.L.R. 278 at 290 (C.A.). Richardson J. also forcefully argued (at 306) in favour of a public policy exception to state immunity. It is to be noted that New Zealand has no immunity statute and operates solely on the basis of the common law.

162 *Prefecture of Voiotia* v. *Germany*, 4 May 2000, Case 11/2000, Areios Pagos (Hellenic Supreme Court) [hereinafter *Prefecture of Voiotia*]. The decision is summarized at (2001) 95 A.J.I.L. 198.

163 *Siderman*, *supra* note 108; and *Princz*, *supra* note 108; Fox, *supra* note 15 at 269.

164 *Prefecture of Voiotia*, *supra* note 162 at 198 and 204.

including the power to make and break laws, torture — that is, the extraordinary use of social power directed against one member of society — can be conceived as the sovereign act par excellence. Under this worldview, described by Marshall C.J. in *Schooner Exchange*, the planet is inhabited by equal and independent sovereigns, owing nothing to each other but that which they politely concede. However, through constant and deliberate practice, in their mutual interest and for that of their members, states have outlawed torture, imbuing this prohibition with the full force of their combined sovereignties, elevating it among those rules that govern the formation of all others. In so restricting their respective sovereignties, nations have permanently excluded torture from the panoply of possible policies that they may pursue, *ipso facto* gaining in protection what they have lost in prerogative. In a manner of speaking, the sovereign discretion to torture has been reallocated to the empowerment of its peremptory prohibition. Thus, every time and everywhere torture is ordered, it is never an exercise of social power but simply the utterance of words — just words, not law; mere *flatus vocis*, not *acta jure imperii*. Following this conception of things, the supreme illegality of torture becomes a decisive component of the contextual characterization of state acts resulting in its *ab initio* removal from the ambit of immunity.

Under the restrictive doctrine, it is the character of the impugned act that is determinative of its justiciability. As a peremptory norm, torture is internationally illegitimate and thus never an *acta jure imperii*.[165] For this reason, immunity should not be granted. The dignity of states is irrelevant, although in cases of torture, to quote H. Lauterpacht, "the dignity of a foreign state might suffer more from an appeal to immunity than from a denial of it."[166] Moreover, the dignity of the forum state might be lessened, as suggested by J. Paust, if immunity is upheld, as the decision could amount to a tacit approval of the foreign criminality.[167] In the final analysis, immunity is a function of sovereignty: "[I]t derives from the sovereign nature of the exercise of the state's adjudicative powers and the basic principle of international law that all states are equal."[168]

---

[165] *Furundzija, supra* note 102 at para 155.

[166] Lauterpacht, *supra* note 24 at 232.

[167] J. Paust, "Federal Jurisdiction over Extraterritorial Acts of Terrorism and Non-Immunity for Foreign Violators of International Law" (1983) 23 Virgina J. Intl. L. 191.

[168] *Lampen-Wolfe, supra* note 124 at 1583.

A non-sovereign act, bereft of any international legitimacy, torture cannot attract immunity. In other words, the forum will exercise its sovereignty in claims where the foreign state did not.

CONCLUSION

As the first civil claim for extraterritorial torture in Canada, the *Bouzari* decision is an important first step, representing a sound, cautious application of the evolving principles of state immunity. Despite occasionally ambiguous reasoning, the court's ultimate interpretation of the SIA appears to be on the mark: neither the commercial nor tort exceptions apply directly to the facts of this case. Moreover, given the SIA's apparent conformity with Canadian international obligations under treaty and customary law, its provisions should not be contorted to accommodate claims for extraterritorial torture in the absence of further Parliamentary intervention. Emerging customary norms relating to immunity, however, may fail to be reflected in the frozen provisions of the SIA, particularly with respect to *jus cogens* human rights violations, such as torture. These were not contemplated as a possible ground for denying state immunity at the time the SIA was enacted. It is suggested therefore that, instead of reading the SIA in a manner contrary to Parliament's intent, courts that are inclined to give effect to emerging custom should look to the common law. The SIA has not displaced the Canadian common law of state immunity, which remains a fertile ground for the reception of international customary norms. As incorporated custom, the peremptory prohibition of torture is part of the common law and part of the contextual characterization of state acts in the determination of immunities under the common law. If torture cannot be said to be an *acta jure imperii,* state immunity should accordingly be denied in civil claims where the jurisdiction of the court is otherwise properly established.

Both in *Bouzari* and *Al-Adsani,* the courts recognized the peremptory status of the torture prohibition but refused to give effect to the consequence of that finding on the basis that there is no established state practice of denying immunity in civil proceedings for extraterritorial torture. Be that as it may, it is no answer to the proposition that such a step should be taken in a given case. The customary law of restrictive immunity is the product of judicial innovation that necessarily required a first bold step. There must be, as it were, a *Trendtex* moment, where Denning M.R. first acknowledged the restrictive theory of immunity as part of the common law.

The denial of immunity in civil claims for extraterritorial torture, should it be pursued, will also require such a bold first step. "Whenever a change is made, some one some time has to make the first move. One country alone may start the process. Others may follow. At first a trickle, then a stream, last a flood."[169]

FRANÇOIS LAROCQUE
Ph.D. candidate, Faculty of Law, University of Cambridge

---

[169] *Trendtex, supra* note 48 at 367.

Sommaire

Bouzari c. *Iran*: évaluation des limites de l'immunité des États étrangers devant les tribunaux canadiens

L'immunité étatique limite-t-elle la compétence des tribunaux canadiens dans le cadre de poursuites civiles portant sur des actes de torture extraterritoriaux? Telle était la question soulevée dans l'affaire Bouzari c. Islamic Republic of Iran. *La Cour supérieure de justice de l'Ontario a conclu qu'en vertu de la* Loi sur l'immunité des États *(LIE), l'Iran jouissait de l'immunité au Canada relativement à la torture commise sur son territoire. Dans cet article portant sur l'immunité des États, la décision précitée est analysée à la lumière du droit international contemporain et de la jurisprudence pertinente. L'auteur fait valoir que la LIE n'a pas évacué la common law canadienne en matière d'immunité étatique, laquelle continue à s'appliquer aux instances exclues par la loi. En common law, soutient finalement l'auteur, la torture ne saurait être qualifiée d'*acta jure imperii.

Summary

Bouzari v. *Iran*: Testing the Limits of State Immunity in Canadian Courts

Does state immunity limit the jurisdiction of Canadian courts in the context of civil proceedings relating to acts of extraterritorial torture? Such was the issue in Bouzari v. Islamic Republic of Iran. *The Ontario Superior Court of Justice held that, pursuant to Canada's State Immunity Act (SIA), Iran was entitled to immunity in Canada for torture committed within its own borders. In this article on the law of state immunity, the decision in* Bouzari *is analyzed in light of contemporary international law and relevant jurisprudence. It is argued that the SIA has not evacuated the Canadian common law of state immunity, which continues to apply to all matters not covered by the statute. At common law, it is finally argued, torture cannot be considered an* acta jure imperii.

L'invocabilité des traités de libre-échange en droit interne: nouveau regard sur l'arrêt *Project Blue Sky* v. *Australian Broadcasting Authority* de la Haute Cour d'Australie

I INTRODUCTION

La Cour suprême du Canada entendra prochainement la cause de la société multinationale Unilever contre la réglementation québécoise sur la couleur de la margarine, ce qui mettra un terme au dernier acte du différend qui oppose le Québec aux fabricants de ce produit depuis plus de cinquante ans.[1] Dans cette affaire, Unilever allègue entre autres que le Québec viole l'*Accord de libre-échange nord-américain*[2] (ALÉNA) ainsi que l'*Accord instituant l'Organisation mondiale du commerce*[3] (Accord sur l'OMC), deux traités conclus par le Canada et auxquels la province a donné son assentiment suivant sa constitution interne.[4] La Cour d'appel du Québec a jugé que la société plaignante ne pouvait pas invoquer ces traités devant une juridiction interne, puisqu'ils n'avaient pas été dûment incorporés dans l'ordre juridique canadien par les législateurs compétents aux termes du partage des compétences, et ce malgré l'adoption de lois de mise en œuvre pour chacun de ces accords.[5]

Cette note a été réalisée avec l'aide financière du Conseil de recherches en sciences humaines du Canada. Les opinions exprimées n'engagent que l'auteur.

[1] *U.L. Canada inc.* c. *Québec (Procureur général)*, [2003] R.J.Q. 2729 (C.A. Qué.), confirmant [1999] R.J.Q. 1720 (C.S. Qué.); demande d'autorisation de pourvoi à la Cour suprême du Canada accueillie le 6 mai 2004.

[2] Canada–États-Unis–Mexique, 17 décembre 1992, R.T. Can. (1994) n° 2, 32 I.L.M. 289 (entrée en vigueur: 1ᵉʳ janvier 1994).

[3] 15 avril 1994, 1867 R.T.N.U. 3, 33 I.L.M. 1144 (entrée en vigueur: 1ᵉʳ janvier 1995).

[4] Voir le décret 985-94, 6 juillet 1994, G.O.Q. 1994.II.4298; *Loi concernant la mise en œuvre des accords de commerce international*, L.R.Q. c. M-35.2, art. 2.

[5] *Supra* note 1 aux par. 72–86. Voir la *Loi concernant la mise en œuvre des accords de*

La jurisprudence récente indique que les personnes privées tentent de plus en plus d'invoquer ces traités de libre-échange devant les tribunaux canadiens — toujours sans succès[6] — ce qui n'est probablement pas étranger à leur incapacité de porter plainte contre le Canada auprès de l'Organe de règlement des différends de l'OMC ou devant la Commission du libre-échange nord-américain. En outre, le caractère exécutoire du jugement rendu par un tribunal national, par opposition au caractère souvent aléatoire de l'exécution de la décision obligatoire d'une instance internationale, est certainement un autre facteur expliquant l'attrait des juridictions nationales pour les personnes privées affectées par la violation présumée d'un traité de libre-échange.

L'état du droit canadien sur ces questions est relativement clair. Conformément à la tradition dualiste à laquelle il appartient, tout traité conclu par le Canada doit être incorporé par une loi afin que celui-ci fasse partie de son ordre juridique interne. Cette loi doit être adoptée par le législateur compétent aux termes du partage des compétences, et seul le traité dûment incorporé peut être invoqué comme source de droit positif devant les tribunaux canadiens.[7] La jurisprudence constante veut que pour qu'un traité

---

commerce international, *ibid.; Loi de mise en œuvre de l'Accord de libre-échange nord-américain*, L.C. 1993, c. 44.

[6] Voir par ex. *Baker Petrolite Corp.* c. *Canwell Enviro-Industries Ltd.*, [2003] 1 C.F. 49 (C.A.F.); *Pellikaan* c. *Canada*, [2002] 4 C.F. 169; *Industries Hillenbrand Canada ltée* c. *Québec (Bureau de normalisation)* (15 août 2002), Montréal 500-05-071484-024, J.E. 2002-1805 (C.S. Qué.), conf. par (10 mai 2004) Montréal 500-09-091 2689-022 (C.A. Qué.); *Apotex Inc.* c. *Wellcome Foundation Ltd.*, [2001] 1 C.F. 495 (C.A.F.); *Pfizer Inc.* c. *Canada*, [1999] 4 C.F. 441, conf. par (14 octobre 1999) Ottawa A-469-99 (C.A.F.); *Entreprises de rebuts Sanipan* c. *Québec (Procureur Général)*, [1995] R.J.Q. 821 (C.S. Qué.); *Antonsen* c. *Canada (Procureur général)*, [1995] 2 C.F. 272.

[7] Un traité conclu par le Canada, mais non incorporé par le législateur compétent, pourrait cependant servir de source interprétative du droit interne canadien. Voir notamment l'arrêt *Baker* c. *Canada (Ministre de la Citoyenneté et de l'Immigration)*, [1999] 2 R.C.S. 817 au par. 70. Concernant plus spécifiquement l'utilisation des traités de libre-échange non incorporés comme source interprétative du droit interne, voir les arrêts *Harvard College* c. *Canada (Commissaire aux brevets)*, [2002] 4 R.C.S. 45; *Canada (Sous-ministre du Revenu national)* c. *Mattel Canada Inc.*, [2001] 2 R.C.S. 100; *National Corn Growers Assn.* c. *Canada (Tribunal des importations)*, [1990] 2 R.C.S. 1324. Pour des études récentes sur les relations entre l'ordre juridique international et l'ordre juridique canadien, voir généralement J. Brunnée et S.J. Toope, "A Hesitant Embrace : The Application of International Law by Canadian Courts" (2002) 40 A.C.D.I. 3; G. Van Ert, "Using Treaties in Canadian Courts" (2000) 38 A.C.D.I. 3.

soit incorporé par le législateur, celui-ci doit avoir exprimé une intention "claire et non ambiguë" à cet effet.[8]

Si pour le moment cette intention ne semble pas avoir été manifestée dans la législation fédérale ou québécoise, à l'exception notable d'une disposition réglementaire en matière de passation des marchés publics,[9] d'autres pays partageant les mêmes règles constitutionnelles ont eu recours à de telles incorporations législatives de traités de libre-échange. Par exemple, c'est au moyen d'un tel procédé que le Royaume-Uni a pu se conformer à l'acquis communautaire et permettre l'effet direct du *Traité instituant la Communauté européenne*[10] (traité CE) et des règlements communautaires dans son ordre juridique interne.[11]

L'Australie a, elle aussi, eu recours à ce procédé. Contrairement au Canada, le législateur australien a incorporé dans son ordre juridique interne le traité de libre-échange liant l'Australie et la Nouvelle-Zélande, l'*Australia New Zealand Closer Economic Relations Trade Agreement*[12] (ANZCERTA). Cette incorporation n'a cependant

---

[8] *U.L. Canada inc.* c. *Québec (Procureur général)* (C.S. Qué.), *supra* note 1 au par. 87. Voir aussi le jugement de la Cour d'appel dans la même affaire, *supra* note 1 aux par. 78 et 84.

[9] Une disposition réglementaire fédérale enjoint le Tribunal canadien du commerce extérieur à vérifier la conformité des décisions de l'administration fédérale, concernant la passation des marchés publics, avec l'ALÉNA et l'*Accord sur les marchés publics* figurant en annexe de l'Accord sur l'OMC. *Règlement sur les enquêtes du Tribunal canadien du commerce extérieur sur les marchés publics*, D.O.R.S./93-602, art. 11 (modifié par D.O.R.S./95-300, D.O.R.S./96-30 et D.O.R.S./2000-395). Cette disposition permet aux personnes privées d'invoquer ces traités de libre-échange devant le Tribunal, de même que devant la Cour fédérale, en contrôle judiciaire. Voir par ex. *Canada (Procureur Général)* c. *McNally Constructions Inc.*, [2002] 4 C.F. 633; *Siemens Westinghouse Inc.* c. *Canada (Ministre des Travaux publics et des Services gouvernementaux)*, [2002] 1 C.F. 292; *Canada (Procureur général)* c. *Symtron Systems Inc.*, [1999] 2 C.F. 514; *Wang Canada Ltd.* c. *Canada (Ministre des Travaux publics et des Services gouvernementaux)*, [1999] 1 C.F. 3.

[10] 25 mars 1957, 294 R.T.N.U. 16 (entrée en vigueur: 1er janvier 1958; modifié pour la dernière fois par le *Traité de Nice modifiant le traité sur l'Union européenne, les traités instituant les Communautés européennes et certains actes connexes*, 26 février 2001, [2001] J.O.C.E. n° C 80, entré en vigueur le 1er février 2003; version consolidée publiée dans [2002] J.O.C.E. n° C 325) (ci-après *Traité CE*). Voir *NV Algemene Transport- en Expeditie Onderneming van Gend en Loos* c. *Administration fiscale néerlandaise*, C-26/62, [1963] Rec. C.J.C.E. 3.

[11] Voir *European Communities Act 1972* (R.-U.), 1972, c. 68, art. 2(1).

[12] 28 mars 1983, Austr. T.S. 1983 n° 2, 22 I.L.M. 948 (entrée en vigueur: 1er janvier 1983).

pas été réalisée par une loi d'application générale, mais plutôt par une série de législations sectorielles, permettant l'invocation du traité devant les tribunaux australiens pour les fins prévues par ces lois.[13] De cette manière, les personnes privées sont invitées à contribuer au respect de ses obligations internationales par l'Australie.

Les effets juridiques d'une de ces clauses d'incorporation législative sectorielle, dans le domaine des activités de télédiffusion, ont fait l'objet d'une décision importante de la Haute Cour d'Australie. L'arrêt *Project Blue Sky* v. *Australian Broadcasting Authority*,[14] rendu en 1998, offre une perspective intéressante sur la problématique de l'invocation des traités de libre-échange par les personnes privées, particulièrement au vu de la cause d'Unilever actuellement devant la Cour suprême du Canada. Même si la Haute Cour a pris acte de l'invocabilité du traité, son arrêt sibyllin laisse transparaître un certain inconfort face à l'application des traités de libre-échange par de tels renvois législatifs. Cet arrêt, qui constitue à ce jour la seule décision de la plus haute juridiction australienne sur l'ANZCERTA, jette un éclairage utile sur le débat qui s'ouvre maintenant à la Cour suprême du Canada, et qui mènera vraisemblablement à la première décision de la plus haute juridiction du pays sur l'invocabilité des traités de libre-échange en droit interne canadien, aussi est-il justifié de s'y intéresser à nouveau.

II LES DONNÉES DU LITIGE

L'Australian Broadcasting Authority (ABA) était l'organisme public chargé de la régulation des activités de radio et de télédiffusion en Australie. Sa loi constitutive, la *Broadcasting Services Act 1992*,[15] lui confiait notamment la responsabilité de développer des normes applicables aux émissions de télévision, et de surveiller le

---

[13] Voir par ex. *Air Services Act 1995* (Cth), art. 9(3); *Australian Postal Corporation Act 1989* (Cth), art. 28c); *Chemical Weapons (Prohibition) Act 1994* (Cth), art. 22, 95; *Civil Aviation Act 1988* (Cth), art. 11; *Customs Act 1901* (Cth), art. 269SK; Customs (Prohibited Exports) Regulations 1956 (Cth), reg. 13CA(2); *Endangered Species Protection Act 1992* (Cth), art. 171; Extradition (Ships and Fixed Platforms) Regulations, regs. 6(2), 7(2); Hazardous Waste (Regulation of Exports and Imports) Regulations, reg. 7(2); *Navigation Act 1912* (Cth), art. 422; *Nuclear Non-Proliferation (Safeguards) Act 1987* (Cth), art. 70(1); *Ozone Protection Act 1989* (Cth), art. 45(5); *Sea Installations Act 1987* (Cth), art. 13; *Telecommunication Act 1997* (Cth), art. 366.

[14] (1998), 194 C.L.R. 355; 153 A.L.R. 490 (Haute Cour d'Australie).

[15] (Cth), 1992, c. 110.

respect de ces normes par les détenteurs de permis de télédiffusion. Parmi les objectifs poursuivis par la loi, l'un d'eux était d'assurer que le contrôle des services de télédiffusion les plus influents fût exercé par des Australiens, alors qu'un autre était de promouvoir le rôle de ces services dans le développement et la mise en valeur de l'identité australienne. Une disposition de la loi (la disposition de renvoi), au cœur du litige, enjoignait l'ABA à exercer ses fonctions de manière compatible avec les obligations de l'Australie, découlant de toute convention à laquelle celle-ci était une partie, ou de tout accord entre elle et un État étranger.[16] La même disposition renvoyait aussi aux objectifs de la loi, aux politiques gouvernementales, ainsi qu'aux directives du ministre responsable.

Une autre disposition de la loi (la disposition habilitante) donnait à l'ABA le pouvoir d'adopter des normes relatives au contenu australien des émissions de télévision, mais ces normes ne devaient pas être incompatibles avec la loi.[17] L'ABA a adopté une telle norme de contenu australien le 15 décembre 1995, qui était censée entrer en vigueur le 1er janvier 1996, et prévoyait que les émissions australiennes devaient constituer au moins 50 % de la programmation télévisuelle produite sans le soutien des fonds publics et diffusée entre 6h00 et 24h00; à compter du 1er janvier 1998, cette proportion devait passer à 55 %. La norme définissait une "émission australienne" comme une émission qui était produite sous le contrôle créatif d'un citoyen ou d'un résident permanent australien, assurant une perspective australienne, et qui n'était pas financée par les fonds publics australiens.

Six sociétés privées néo-zélandaises oeuvrant dans l'industrie de la télévision ont immédiatement contesté la validité de cette norme de contenu australien, au motif qu'elle était incompatible avec l'ANZCERTA, et plus particulièrement avec son protocole relatif au commerce des services,[18] en raison de la préférence accordée aux émissions de télévision australiennes. La question de la conformité de la norme avec le Protocole n'était pas litigieuse, puisque toutes les parties s'entendaient sur le fait qu'elle était incompatible,

[16] La disposition originale se lisait comme suit: "The ABA is to perform its functions in a manner consistent with: … Australia's obligations under any convention to which Australia is a party or any agreement between Australia and a foreign country." *Ibid.*, art. 160(d).

[17] *Ibid.*, art. 122(2)(b), (4).

[18] *Protocol on Trade in Services to the Australia New Zealand Closer Economic Relations Trade Agreement*, 18 août 1988, Austr. T.S. 1988 n° 20 (entrée en vigueur: 1er janvier 1989).

ce qui signifiait que la véritable question en litige était celle de savoir quels étaient les effets juridiques de la disposition de renvoi aux obligations internationales de l'Australie. La norme violait-elle la disposition de renvoi? Dans l'affirmative, la norme était-elle invalide?

Le juge de première instance de la Cour fédérale a déclaré que la norme était invalide en raison de son incompatibilité avec le Protocole et, qu'à défaut d'être mise en conformité avec celui-ci, elle serait abrogée à compter du 31 décembre 1996. En appel devant un banc complet de la Cour fédérale,[19] la majorité des juges a renversé cette décision en raison du conflit irréconciliable qu'elle percevait entre la disposition habilitante et la disposition de renvoi, lorsqu'appliquée à l'ANZCERTA et au Protocole, décidant que ce conflit devait être résolu en faveur de la disposition habilitante. Le juge dissident a refusé de voir un conflit irréconciliable entre ces dispositions; il a jugé que l'ABA n'avait pas respecté ses obligations au titre de la disposition de renvoi, et que par conséquent, la norme de contenu australien était invalide.

III   La validité de la norme de contenu australien au
      regard de la disposition habilitante

La majorité (quatre) des juges de la Haute Cour a d'abord conclu que selon une interprétation littérale de la disposition habilitante, la norme de contenu australien avait été adoptée validement par l'ABA, puisqu'une norme de contenu australien antérieure à la loi avait été maintenue en vigueur comme si elle avait été adoptée par l'ABA en vertu de la disposition habilitante, ce qui illustrait qu'une telle norme pouvait être adoptée par l'ABA.[20] Mais en poussant plus loin son interprétation, la majorité a jugé que lorsque la disposition habilitante était lue en conjonction avec la disposition de renvoi, il apparaissait que l'ABA était obligé de s'assurer que les normes qu'il adoptait n'étaient pas incompatibles avec l'ANZCERTA et le Protocole.[21]

La majorité de la Haute Cour a refusé de voir un conflit irréconciliable entre les deux dispositions, contrairement à la majorité de la Cour fédéral en appel, qui y avait vu un conflit entre une

---

[19] *Australian Broadcasting Authority* v. *Project Blue Sky Inc.* (1996), 141 A.L.R. 397 (Cour fédérale d'Australie).

[20] *Project Blue Sky* v. *Australian Broadcasting Authority, supra* note 14 aux par. 72 et 77.

[21] *Ibid.* au par. 80.

disposition générale (la disposition de renvoi) et une disposition particulière (la disposition habilitante), qui devait être résolu en faveur de la dernière. La Haute Cour a aussi refusé de voir dans la disposition habilitante une obligation d'accorder un traitement préférentiel aux ressortissants australiens.[22] Elle en est venue à la conclusion que le pouvoir conféré par la disposition habilitante devait être exercé dans le cadre posé par la disposition de renvoi, c'est-à-dire en respectant les obligations posées par l'ANZCERTA et le Protocole.[23]

Le juge en chef Brennan a été en désaccord avec la majorité sur cette question de la validité de la norme de contenu australien au regard de la disposition habilitante. Pour trancher le litige, il a arrêté son analyse avant même d'avoir à examiner l'articulation entre la disposition habilitante et la disposition de renvoi. Il a jugé que la disposition habilitante n'autorisait pas l'ABA à adopter une norme classant les émissions de télévisions selon leur provenance ou leur origine, comme l'organisme l'avait fait en l'espèce; le pouvoir d'adopter des normes relatives au contenu australien des émissions de télévision se référait plutôt à leur classement selon leur objet ou la matière dont elles traitaient.[24]

Le juge dissident a néanmoins poursuivi son analyse dans un long *obiter dictum*, pour examiner la question de la compatibilité de la norme avec la disposition de renvoi aux obligations internationales de l'Australie, ainsi que celle des effets juridiques de la violation de cette disposition, puisqu'il était également en désaccord avec les juges de la majorité sur cette dernière question, qui nous intéresse au premier titre. Il a convenu que la disposition de renvoi interdisait effectivement que le pouvoir statutaire soit exercé de manière incompatible avec les obligations internationales de l'Australie.[25]

IV   La compatibilité de la norme de contenu australien avec la disposition de renvoi à l'anzcerta

Poursuivant son raisonnement, la majorité de la Haute Cour, appuyée sur ce point par le juge en chef Brennan, a donc jugé que la disposition habilitante interdisait à l'ABA d'adopter une norme

---

[22] *Ibid.* aux par. 87-89.

[23] *Ibid.* au par. 81.

[24] *Ibid.* au par. 26.

[25] *Ibid.* au par. 31.

qui était incompatible avec l'ANZCERTA et le Protocole.[26] Elle a d'abord rappelé que, même si le traité de libre-échange n'était pas nommé explicitement dans la disposition de renvoi, les travaux préparatoires de la loi et le sens littéral de la disposition indiquaient clairement que celui-ci était visé.

Même si toutes les parties au litige s'entendaient sur l'incompatibilité de la norme de contenu australien avec le Protocole, la majorité a tout de même procédé à un examen rapide de cette compatibilité.[27] Elle a jugé que la norme protégeait le marché en faveur des émissions australiennes à hauteur de 50 % du temps de télédiffusion quotidien, et que les émissions néo-zélandaises devaient concurrencer avec les émissions provenant des autres États étrangers et de l'Australie pour la partie restante du temps de télédiffusion quotidien. La norme violait donc les articles 4 et 5 du Protocole, aux termes desquels l'Australie s'est engagée à garantir aux ressortissants néo-zélandais un accès à son marché des services égal à celui de ses ressortissants, ainsi qu'un traitement égal à celui accordé à ses ressortissants une fois sur le marché des services australiens.

Dans son *obiter dictum*, le juge en chef Brennan a aussi examiné la compatibilité de la norme avec les articles 4 et 5 du Protocole, pour constater leur incompatibilité pour les mêmes motifs.[28] D'une manière analogue à l'examen de l'effet direct d'une disposition du traité CE par la Cour de justice des Communautés européennes, ou du caractère *self-executing* d'une disposition d'un traité conclu par les États-Unis d'Amérique par les juridictions américaines, il a souligné que ces deux dispositions imposaient une obligation claire à l'Australie quant au traitement à accorder aux fournisseurs de services néo-zélandais.

V   LA CONSÉQUENCE JURIDIQUE DE LA VIOLATION DE LA DISPOSITION DE RENVOI À L'ANZCERTA

Puisque la majorité de la Haute Cour avait jugé que la norme de contenu australien avait été adoptée en violation de la disposition de renvoi aux obligations internationales de l'Australie, il lui restait à déterminer quelle en était la conséquence juridique. C'est ici que l'inconfort de la majorité face à l'application du traité de

---

[26] *Ibid.* aux par. 31, 82.

[27] *Ibid.* au par. 84.

[28] *Ibid.* aux par. 30-31.

libre-échange est apparu, celle-ci ayant refusé d'aller au bout de son raisonnement juridique en introduisant une distinction spécieuse entre illégalité et invalidité. Elle a affirmé d'entrée de jeu qu'un acte posé en violation d'une condition d'exercice d'un pouvoir statutaire n'était pas nécessairement invalide; cela dépendait de l'intention du législateur.[29] Elle a proposé un nouveau test en droit administratif australien, qui consistait à rechercher l'intention du législateur pour répondre à la question de savoir si la conséquence de la violation de cette condition d'exercice devait être l'invalidité de l'acte résultant de l'exercice du pouvoir statutaire.[30] L'introduction de ce nouveau test visait à remplacer le test traditionnel qui consistait à établir une distinction entre les actes posés en violation d'une condition préliminaire d'exercice d'un pouvoir statutaire, qui était obligatoire et dont la violation entraînait l'invalidité de l'acte, et les actes posés en violation d'une condition procédurale d'exercice d'un pouvoir statutaire, qui était seulement indicatrice (*"directory"*) et dont la violation n'entraînait pas l'invalidité de l'acte.

Appliquant son nouveau test, la majorité de la Haute Cour a jugé que la norme de contenu australien, bien qu'adoptée en violation de la disposition de renvoi à l'ANZCERTA, n'était pas invalide.[31] Elle a dégagé l'intention du législateur à cet égard de cinq éléments distincts. Premièrement, elle a observé — en référence au test traditionnel qu'elle voulait pourtant remplacer par un autre — que la disposition de renvoi visait l'exercice d'un pouvoir déjà conféré par la disposition habilitante, ce qui signifiait qu'il ne s'agissait pas d'une condition préliminaire d'exercice d'un pouvoir statutaire.[32]

Deuxièmement, elle a relevé que la disposition de renvoi se référait aussi à des instructions de nature beaucoup moins juridiques que les obligations internationales conventionnelles de l'Australie, comme par exemple les objectifs de la loi, la politique australienne de régulation de la télédiffusion, les politiques générales du gouvernement, ainsi que les directives du ministre responsable de l'ABA. La majorité en a tiré la conclusion que lorsque les conditions d'exercice d'un pouvoir statutaire relevaient davantage du politique que du juridique, il s'agissait d'une indication que

---

[29] *Ibid.* au par. 91.

[30] *Ibid.* au par. 93.

[31] *Ibid.* au par. 99.

[32] *Ibid.* au par. 94.

l'on visait l'exercice du pouvoir plus que la validité de l'acte qui en résultait.[33]

Troisièmement — cachant mal son inconfort face aux traités internationaux — la majorité a souligné que plusieurs traités étaient rédigés en termes peu clairs ou en fonction d'objectifs à atteindre plutôt que de règles à observer; elle a soulevé du même souffle les problèmes que le grand nombre de traités conclus par l'Australie poseraient si la conséquence juridique interne de leur inobservance par l'ABA devait être l'invalidité de ses actes.[34]

Quatrièmement, la majorité a avancé que les inconvénients pour le public que poserait l'invalidité d'un acte posé par l'ABA en violation de la disposition de renvoi, sur lequel plusieurs personnes se seraient fondées de bonne foi, indiquaient que cela ne pouvait être l'intention du législateur.[35]

Finalement, exprimant à nouveau son inconfort face aux traités internationaux, la majorité de la Haute Cour a estimé qu'il était difficile de croire, au vu des autres pouvoirs confiés à l'ABA, comme l'octroi de permis de télédiffusion, que l'intention du législateur était que la validité d'un tel permis dépendait en bout de ligne d'une décision judiciaire sur sa compatibilité avec des traités, dont même des internationalistes chevronnés avaient de la difficulté à déterminer l'étendue exacte des obligations.[36]

Mais la majorité de la Haute Cour ne s'est pas arrêtée là. Même si elle a jugé que la norme de contenu australien n'était pas invalide (*"invalid"*), elle a cependant déclaré qu'elle était illégale (*"unlawful"*)![37] Ainsi, une personne justifiant d'un intérêt juridique suffisant pourrait-elle demander un jugement déclaratoire concernant l'exercice illégal de son pouvoir par l'ABA et, s'il y avait lieu, obtenir une injonction pour empêcher l'ABA de prendre toute autre action sur la base de son action illégale [*sic*].[38] La majorité a

---

[33] *Ibid.* au par. 95.

[34] *Ibid.* au par. 96.

[35] *Ibid.* au par. 97.

[36] *Ibid.* au par. 98.

[37] *Ibid.* au par. 100.

[38] *Ibid.* au par. 101. Le passage original du jugement de la Haute Cour dit ceci: "Although an act done in contravention of s. 160 is not invalid, it is a breach of the Act and therefore unlawful. ... [A] person with sufficient interest is entitled to sue for a declaration that the ABA has acted in breach of the Act and, in appropriate case, obtain an injunction restraining that body from taking any further action based on its unlawful action."

été avare de détails sur la justification de cette distinction, mais elle a expliqué que celle-ci importerait uniquement pour les actions déjà posées par l'ABA, ou prises en s'étant fié sur la conduite de l'ABA. Dans le dispositif de son arrêt, la Haute Cour d'Australie a donc déclaré que la norme de contenu australien avait été adoptée illégalement.

Dans son *obiter dictum*, le juge en chef Brennan n'a pas du tout retenu la distinction spécieuse opérée par la majorité entre illégalité et invalidité. Il a clairement déclaré que la conséquence juridique de l'exercice illégal de son pouvoir statutaire par l'ABA était nécessairement que la norme de contenu australien qui en avait résulté était invalide (dans l'hypothèse où il aurait conclu que la norme avait été validement adoptée aux termes de la disposition habilitante).[39] Puisque l'ABA a exercé son pouvoir d'adopter des normes relatives au contenu australien des émissions de télévision de manière incompatible avec la disposition de renvoi, du fait de la violation du protocole de l'ANZCERTA sur le commerce des services, la norme ainsi adoptée était invalide. La disposition de renvoi délimitait l'étendue du pouvoir confié par la loi à l'ABA, ce qui voulait dire que l'organisme n'avait pas le pouvoir d'adopter une norme de contenu australien qui fût incompatible avec le Protocole. Le juge en chef Brennan a donc pris acte de la volonté du législateur australien que l'ABA respectât les obligations internationales de l'Australie dans l'exercice de ses pouvoirs statutaires, n'ayant pas éprouvé le même inconfort que la majorité de la Haute Cour face à l'application d'un traité de libre-échange en droit interne.

VI Conclusion

L'arrêt *Project Blue Sky* illustre les craintes qu'éprouvent parfois les tribunaux nationaux face à l'applicabilité directe des traités de libre-échange, particulièrement dans les États appartenant à la tradition dualiste, pourrait-on penser, et ce malgré une disposition législative d'incorporation. Même dans une situation juridique relativement claire, où un renvoi aux obligations internationales de l'Australie avait été prévu par le législateur, les tribunaux ont hésité à leur donner leur plein effet juridique en droit interne. Peut-être ces craintes pourraient-elles s'estomper quelque peu si un mécanisme de renvoi préjudiciel auprès d'une juridiction internationale

---

[39] *Ibid.* au par. 42.

spécialisée était prévu, à l'instar de la Communauté européenne,[40] ou encore un renvoi auprès des parties au traité comme le prévoit l'ALÉNA?[41]

Il est intéressant de noter qu'une modification législative postérieure est venue calmer les appréhensions de la Haute Cour, concernant le grand nombre de traités conclus par l'Australie et les difficultés que posait la disposition de renvoi à cet égard. Le législateur australien a effectivement modifié cette disposition, afin d'en réduire la portée et de la limiter exclusivement au protocole de l'ANZCERTA sur le commerce des services.[42] En outre, l'ABA a également abrogé sa norme de contenu australien, pour la remplacer par une nouvelle norme rédigée de manière à être cette fois entièrement compatible avec le Protocole.[43]

Le procédé utilisé par le législateur australien serait juridiquement transposable au Canada, puisque ces deux États partagent des règles constitutionnelles semblables en ce qui a trait aux rapports entre leur ordre juridique interne et l'ordre juridique international. D'ailleurs, la disposition réglementaire fédérale évoquée précédemment, en matière de passation des marchés publics, qui est passée relativement inaperçue dans la doctrine, semble même en être un exemple en droit canadien.

Cela ne veut pas dire que l'état du droit est limpide à cet égard. Un jugement récent de la Cour supérieure du Québec illustre les difficultés d'application des règles concernant l'incorporation de traités de libre-échange par des clauses de renvoi sectoriel. Dans l'affaire *Hypertec Systèmes inc. c. Commission scolaire de la Capitale*,[44] la Cour supérieure avait à interpréter une disposition de la loi québécoise sur l'instruction publique, qui enjoignait les commissions scolaires à passer leurs marchés publics "dans le respect d'un accord intergouvernemental de libéralisation du commerce."[45] La Cour a d'abord souligné que si un accord intergouvernemental de libéralisation du commerce s'appliquait, la commission scolaire

---

[40] Voir le *Traité CE*, *supra* note 10, art. 234.

[41] Voir l'ALÉNA, *supra* note 2, art. 2020.

[42] Voir *Broadcasting Services Amendment Act (No. 3) 1999* (Cth), 1999, c. 198, sched. 2.

[43] Voir *Broadcasting Services (Australian Content) Standard 1999*, en ligne: ABA <http://www.aba.gov.au/tv/content/ozcont/std/index.htm#1> (date d'accès: 15 juillet 2004).

[44] *Hypertec Systèmes inc. c. Commission scolaire de la Capitale* (31 mai 2001), Québec 200-05-012028-994 (C.S. Qué.) [non rapporté] (ci-après *Hypertec Systèmes*).

[45] *Loi sur l'instruction publique*, L.R.Q. c. I-13.3, art. 266.

devait en "tenir compte" dans sa procédure d'appel d'offre.[46] Puis, soulignant l'existence de tels accords conclus par le Québec avec le Nouveau-Brunswick et l'Ontario, elle a conclu que ceux-ci ne pouvaient pas être sanctionnés par les tribunaux, puisqu'il s'agissait d'"accords politiques entre gouvernements dont les écarts de conduite sont réglés par une procédure de règlement des différends prévue à ces accords."[47] La question de savoir si cette disposition de renvoi vise également les traités de libre-échange conclus par la Canada, et auxquels le Québec a donné son assentiment, se pose. De plus, ne faudrait-il pas voir dans cette disposition une incorporation législative sectorielle similaire à la disposition réglementaire fédérale précitée, ainsi qu'à la disposition de renvoi en cause dans l'arrêt *Project Blue Sky*? Dans l'affirmative, la Cour supérieure aurait-elle appliqué un peu trop rondement la règle concernant l'incorporation des traités?

On le voit, l'application des règles sur l'incorporation des traités en droit interne canadien est complexe, voire confuse. Dans un autre jugement, la Cour supérieure du Québec a poussé plus loin la confusion en affirmant que le jugement dans l'affaire *Hypertec Systèmes inc.* constituait une application de la règle dégagée dans son jugement dans l'affaire *U.L. Canada inc.*, concernant l'incorporation des traités de libre-échange, alors que la première affaire ne mettait pas en cause de tels traités internationaux.[48] La question tombe donc à point devant la Cour suprême du Canada, qui, espérons-le, saura clarifier l'état du droit en la matière, y apporter toutes les nuances requises, et, contrairement à la Haute Cour d'Australie, ne pas inhiber les dispositions de renvoi sectoriel, de façon à ce que ce procédé puisse être utilisé par les législateurs, si tel devait être leur souhait.

CHARLES-EMMANUEL CÔTÉ
Doctorant, Faculté de droit, Université McGill

---

[46] *Hypertec Systèmes, supra* note 44 à la p. 17.

[47] *Ibid.* à la p. 18.

[48] *Industries Hillenbrand Canada ltée* c. *Québec (Bureau de normalisation), supra* note 6 au par. 191.

Summary

Direct Effect of Free Trade Agreements in Domestic Law: A Look Afresh at *Project Blue Sky* v. *Australia Broadcasting Authority* of the High Court of Australia

In 1998, the High Court of Australia rendered its first and only decision dealing with the Australia New Zealand Closer Economic Relations Trade Agreement (ANZCERTA) in Project Blue Sky *v.* Australian Broadcasting Authority. *In this case, the High Court had to determine the legal effects of a legislative provision that enjoined an administrative body to use its statutory powers in a manner consistent with this treaty. While the administrative body did adopt a standard inconsistent with the ANZCERTA, the majority of the High Court preferred not to invalidate the standard, despite the fact that it had found it to be unlawful. The dissenting chief justice, speaking in a dictum, rejected this distinction between invalidity and unlawfulness and found that a standard inconsistent with the treaty had to be invalid, giving their full internal legal effects to provisions of sectoral legislative incorporation of treaties. The forthcoming hearing of the challenge of* Unilever Corporation *against Québec's margarine coloration regulation, by the Supreme Court of Canada, is likely to bring new interest into the* Project Blue Sky *judgment, since it will raise the question of the direct effect of free trade agreements in Canadian law. In settling the question, it is to be hoped that the Supreme Court of Canada will not follow the reasoning of the majority of the High Court of Australia and will not inhibit such provisions of sectoral legislative incorporation of treaties, in order to leave this legal technique available to Parliament and the legislatures.*

Sommaire

L'invocabilité des traités de libre-échange en droit interne: nouveau regard sur l'arrêt *Project Blue Sky* v. *Australian Broadcasting Authority* de la Haute Cour d'Australie

La Haute Cour d'Australie rendait en 1998 son premier et seul arrêt concernant le traité de libre-échange liant l'Australie et la Nouvelle-Zélande, l'Australia New Zealand Closer Economic Relations Trade Agreement (ANZCERTA), dans l'affaire Project Blue Sky *v.* Australian Broadcasting Authority. *Dans cette affaire, la Haute Cour avait à déterminer les effets juridiques d'une disposition législative qui enjoignait un organe administratif à exercer ses pouvoirs statutaires de manière compatible avec ce traité. L'organe administratif en question avait certes adopté une norme incompatible avec l'ANZCERTA, mais les juges de la majorité ont préféré ne pas invalider la norme, même si elle était illégale. Le juge en chef dissident a rejeté cette distinction entre invalidité et illégalité, dans un long obiter dictum, et jugé invalide la norme incompatible avec le traité, afin de donner leurs pleins effets juridiques internes à ces dispositions de renvoi sectoriel au droit international conventionnel. L'audition prochaine par la Cour suprême du Canada de la cause de la société multinationale Unilever, qui s'attaque à la réglementation québécoise sur la couleur de la margarine, invite à s'intéresser à nouveau à cet arrêt de la Haute Cour d'Australie, puisqu'elle soulèvera la question de l'invocabilité des traités de libre-échange en droit interne canadien. Dans sa clarification du droit applicable en la matière, il est à souhaiter que la Cour suprême du Canada ne suivra pas le raisonnement de la majorité dans l'arrêt* Project Blue Sky, *et n'inhibera pas les dispositions de renvoi sectoriel, de façon à ce que ce procédé puisse être utilisé par les législateurs, si tel devait être leur souhait.*

Chronique de Droit international économique en 2002 / Digest of International Economic Law in 2002

I Commerce

préparé par
RICHARD OUELLET

I Introduction

Entre deux Conférences ministérielles de l'OMC, entre deux Sommets des Amériques, on aurait pu croire que l'année 2002 serait une année où le commerce international connaîtrait peu de rebondissements. Il est vrai que les négociations commerciales, tant au plan hémisphériques qu'à l'OMC, n'ont pas amené de chambardement ni de progrès spectaculaires. Il n'en demeure pas moins que l'activité n'a pas manqué.

II Le commerce canadien aux plans bilatéral et régional

A Les négociations commerciales aux plans bilatéral et régional

1 Le projet de la ZLÉA

Le projet partagé par trente-quatre des trente-cinq États de l'Hémisphère et devant mener à la création d'une Zone de libre-échange des Amériques (ZLÉA) n'a connu que des avancées timides pendant l'année 2002. La Septième Réunion des Ministres du commerce des Amériques tenue le 1ᵉʳ novembre 2002 à Quito, en Équateur, devait être un moment fort des négociations conduisant à la mise en place de la ZLÉA en 2005. Or, bien que la

---

Richard Ouellet est professeur à la Faculté de droit et à l'Institut québecois des hautes études internationales, Université Laval.

Déclaration ministérielle rendue publique à l'issue de la réunion ait amené son lot de progrès et de bonnes nouvelles,[1] le contexte entourant son adoption en aura laissé plus d'un sceptiques quant à l'avènement de la ZLÉA dans les délais et selon la forme prévus à l'origine.

Parmi les principaux éléments de la Déclaration ministérielle, on note d'abord le rappel des échéances fixées par les chefs d'État et de Gouvernement lors du Troisième Sommet des Amériques tenu à Québec en avril 2001, à savoir que les négociations doivent "prendre fin au plus tard en janvier 2005 ... pour s'efforcer que la ZLÉA entre en vigueur aussitôt que possible, mais, dans tous les cas, au plus tard en décembre 2005 ..."[2] Dans cette perspective, les Ministres du commerce ont confirmé l'ambitieux calendrier de négociations élaboré par le Comité des négociations commerciales (CNC-ZLÉA) et imposé aux groupes de négociation devant traiter des questions d'accès aux marchés. Ce calendrier prévoit l'échange d'offres initiales entre le 15 décembre 2002 et le 15 février 2003, l'examen des offres et la soumission des demandes de bonification entre le 16 février et le 16 juin 2003 et la présentation des offres révisées et la négociation sur la bonification à partir du 15 juillet 2003.[3] Les Ministres ont aussi convenu qu'il sera procédé à un bilan des négociations commerciales lors de la réunion devant se tenir pendant le quatrième trimestre de 2003 à Miami.[4] Il sera intéressant de vérifier si ce calendrier que plusieurs observateurs ont qualifié d'optimiste pourra être respecté et mener en bout de piste à la mise en place de la ZLÉA en 2005.

Les Ministres du commerce de l'Hémisphère ont aussi réaffirmé deux objectifs fondamentaux directement inspirés des principes et disciplines de l'OMC: la prise de décisions par consensus et le *single undertaking,* principe qui veut que le résultat des négociations se traduise par une entente unique et globale qui prévoit les mêmes droits et obligations pour tous les pays membres.[5] Les Ministres ont également réitéré "l'engagement hémisphérique d'éliminer les subventions aux exportations qui affectent le commerce des produits

---

[1] On peut trouver le texte intégral de la Déclaration ministérielle de la Septième Réunion des Ministres du commerce de l'Hémisphère tenue à Quito le 1er novembre 2002 sur le site WEB de la ZLÉA à l'adresse <http://www.alca-ftaa.org/ministerials/quito/Quito_f.asp> (dernière visite le 25 juin 2004).

[2] *Ibid.* au par. 1.

[3] *Ibid.* aux par. 4 et 21.

[4] *Ibid.* aux par. 22 et 40.

[5] *Ibid.* au par. 5.

agricoles dans l'hémisphère et de développer des disciplines à être adoptées pour le traitement de toutes les autres pratiques qui créent des distorsions dans le commerce des produits agricoles."[6] Liant le succès des négociations agricoles dans la ZLÉA à celui des négociations tenues sous l'égide de l'OMC, les Ministres ont indiqué qu'ils devraient "considérer les pratiques des pays tiers qui créent des distorsions dans le commerce mondial des produits agricoles"[7] pour que les négociations hémisphériques apportent des résultats significatifs.

La Déclaration ministérielle comporte aussi l'approbation par les Ministres du commerce du Programme de coopération hémisphérique[8] qui prévoit qu'une aide technique et financière sera consentie aux gouvernements des économies de petite taille pour les aider "à se préparer aux négociations, à mettre en œuvre leurs engagements commerciaux, à relever les défis de l'intégration hémisphérique et à tirer le plus grand parti possible de cette intégration."[9] L'efficacité de ce programme reste tributaire des engagements concrets et chiffrés que doivent prendre les gouvernements les mieux nantis.

Les Ministres du commerce ont aussi convenu de devancer la publication de la deuxième version de l'avant-projet d'Accord de la ZLÉA et de rendre ces textes publics dans les quatre langues officielles de la ZLÉA soit le français, l'anglais, l'espagnol et le portugais.[10] Cette publication s'est faite notamment à l'instigation du Canada, dont on peut dire sans craindre d'être accusé de chauvinisme, qu'il est l'un des principaux promoteurs de la culture de transparence qui prévaut aujourd'hui dans le processus d'intégration des Amériques. L'étude de cette deuxième version a permis de constater que beaucoup de travail restait à accomplir que plusieurs consensus restaient à trouver avant d'en arriver à un accord de libre-échange pour les Amériques.

---

[6] *Ibid.* au par. 15.

[7] *Ibid.*

[8] On peut trouver le texte intégral du Programme de coopération hémisphérique à l'annexe III de la Déclaration ministérielle sur le site WEB de la ZLÉA à l'adresse <http://www.alca-ftaa.org/Popup/PopQuitoHCP_f.htm> (dernière visite le 28 juin 2004).

[9] *Supra* note 1 au par. 18.

[10] On trouve le texte de la deuxième version de l'avant-projet d'Accord de la ZLÉA sur le site WEB de la ZLÉA à l'adresse <http://www.alca-ftaa.org/ftaadraft02/draft_f.asp> (dernière visite le 28 juin 2004).

C'est aussi avec la Réunion ministérielle de Quito que s'est achevée la troisième phase de négociations de la ZLÉA présidée par la République de l'Équateur. La présidence de la quatrième et dernière phase des négociations était dès lors confiée conjointement au Brésil et aux États-Unis. Cette cession de la présidence du processus de négociation à ces deux géants des Amériques n'était pas la meilleure nouvelle pour les tenants d'une intégration hémisphérique rapide, inclusive et couvrant un maximum de secteurs d'activités économiques. On sait que les relations entre le Brésil et l'administration américaine ne sont pas à leur meilleur depuis l'élection à la présidence brésilienne, le 27 octobre 2002, de Luiz Inacio Lula da Silva qui doit assumer ses fonctions présidentielles à compter du 1er janvier 2003. En plus des tensions entre les deux gouvernements co-présidents, chacun d'eux risquent fort de consacrer peu d'énergie au progrès des négociations. Le président brésilien nouvellement élu a déjà qualifié le projet de ZLÉA d'"annexion économique" de l'Amérique latine par les États-Unis et semble plus enclin à renforcer le Mercosur que la ZLÉA. Quant à l'actuelle administration américaine, bien qu'elle ait obtenu le *Trade Promotion Authority*,[11] elle montre bien peu d'empressement à assumer le rôle de promoteur d'accords commerciaux multilatéraux et régionaux qu'a joué l'administration précédente.

2   *Les autres développements aux plans bilatéral et régional*

Le gouvernement du Canada a profité de la Réunion ministérielle de Quito pour tenir, en marge de cette réunion, des rencontres bilatérales et annoncé d'importants développements relatifs à des accords commerciaux le liant. Les ministres du Commerce canadien et costaricien ont procédé, le 31 octobre, à un échange de notes marquant l'entrée en vigueur dès le lendemain de l'*Accord de libre-échange entre le Canada et le Costa Rica* et de deux accords distincts sur la coopération en matière d'environnement et de travail.[12]

---

[11] Le *Trade Promotion Authority* est, pour l'essentiel, l'équivalent du *Fast Track Authority*. Sans entrer dans les nuances du droit américain, nous dirons ici qu'il s'agit d'un pouvoir conféré par le Congrès des États-Unis à l'administration en vue d'accélérer la négociation d'accords commerciaux internationaux et de faciliter leur réception et leur mise en œuvre en droit interne américain.

[12] Ces accords ont été signés en avril 2001. Ils sont brièvement décrits dans la chronique "Commerce" de l'année 2001 de cet annuaire. On peut trouver le texte intégral de ces accords sur le site WEB du Ministère canadien du commerce international à l'adresse <http://www.dfait-maeci.gc.ca/tna-nac/Costa_Rica_toc-fr.asp> (dernière visite le 29 juin 2004).

Le même jour, se tenait la quatrième réunion de la Commission de *l'Accord de libre-échange Canada-Chili* (ALECC). Cette réunion fut l'occasion, pour le ministre canadien du Commerce international et la ministre chilienne des Relations extérieures de souligner le cinquième anniversaire de l'ALECC et procéder à la signature de notes d'interprétation visant à clarifier certaines dispositions de l'ALECC portant sur l'investissement et directement inspirées des notes d'interprétation déjà signées le 31 juillet 2001 dans le cadre de l'ALÉNA.[13] Les ministres canadien et chilienne ont rappelé l'importance de l'ALECC et indiqué que les échanges commerciaux entre leur deux pays étaient évalués à 839 millions de dollars américains pour l'année 2001.[14]

Une autre relation commerciale de grande importance pour le Canada, celle avec le Mexique, a connu d'intéressants développements pendant l'année 2002. En tout début d'année, les partenaires de l'ALÉNA ont convenu de devancer d'un an l'élimination de tarifs douaniers applicables à plusieurs produits d'importance pour le commerce nord-américain. Le Mexique a ainsi convenu d'éliminer dès le 1er janvier 2002 les tarifs applicables notamment à la plupart des véhicules motorisés, à certaines pâtes de bois et au matériel ferroviaire. Le Canada a, pour sa part, éliminé les tarifs sur les véhicules motorisés provenant du Mexique.[15] En juin, le ministre canadien du Commerce international a conduit une importante mission commerciale à Mexico et à Monterrey et a rencontré le président du Mexique et le secrétaire mexicain à l'économie pour discuter notamment des moyens d'intensifier les échanges

---

[13] *Accord de libre-échange entre le Canada et le Chili*, Quatrième réunion de la Commission du libre-échange Canada-Chili, Notes d'interprétation de certaines dispositions du chapitre G, Quito, Équateur, le 31 octobre 2002. On trouve le texte de ces notes d'interprétation sur le site WEB du Ministère canadien du commerce international à l'adresse <http://www.dfait-maeci.gc.ca/tna-nac/ccftacommission-fr.asp> (dernière visite le 29 juin 2004).

[14] *Accord de libre-échange entre le Canada et le Chili*, Quatrième réunion de la Commission du libre-échange Canada-Chili, Déclaration conjointe des ministres, Quito, Équateur, le 31 octobre 2002, au par. 2. On trouve le texte de cette Déclaration sur le site WEB du Ministère canadien du commerce international à l'adresse <http://www.dfait-maeci.gc.ca/tna-nac/fourth_meet-fr.asp> (dernière visite le 29 juin 2004).

[15] Les États-Unis et le Mexique ont aussi convenu de l'élimination accélérée de certains tarifs. Quant au commerce entre le Canada et les États-Unis, faut-il rappeler que, sauf de rares — mais parfois importantes — exceptions, les marchandises circulant entre ces deux pays le font en franchise de droits depuis le 1er janvier 1998.

commerciaux entre le Canada et ce partenaire de l'ALÉNA qui est son sixième marché d'exportation.[16]

Enfin, le Canada a lancé en 2002 deux grands chantiers devant mener à des accords de libre-échange avec des partenaires de l'hémisphère américain. Il a amorcé en août des pourparlers avec les pays de la Communauté andine (Bolivie, Colombie, Équateur, Pérou, Venezuela). Plus tard, à l'automne, le gouvernement canadien a annoncé la tenue de consultations publiques sur ce projet de libre-échange et sur un autre projet d'accord cette fois avec la République Dominicaine. Dans ce deuxième cas, les premières rencontres exploratoires entre représentants canadiens et dominicains sont prévues pour 2003.[17]

B   LES DIFFÉRENDS LIÉS À L'ALÉNA

Pendant l'année 2002, aucun rapport de groupe spécial mandaté en vertu du chapitre 20 pour examiner un différend entre deux parties à l'ALÉNA quant à l'interprétation ou à l'application de l'ALÉNA n'a été rendu. Les rapports et décisions rendus relevaient du chapitre 11 portant sur l'investissement[18] ou du chapitre 19 portant sur le règlement des différends en matière de droits antidumping et compensateurs. Les sept décisions rendues en application du chapitre 19 opposaient le Canada aux États-Unis. Deux de ces décisions portaient sur le commerce d'appareils ménagers au Canada en provenance des États-Unis[19] tandis que les cinq autres décisions

---

[16] Ministère des Affaires étrangères et du Commerce international, Cabinet du ministre du Commerce international, Communiqué de presse n° 63, le 5 juin 2002.

[17] On peut connaître l'avancement des négociations touchant ces initiatives bilatérales et régionales en allant sur le site WEB du Ministère canadien du Commerce international à l'adresse <http://www.dfait-maeci.gc.ca/tna-nac/reg-fr.asp> (dernière visite le 29 juin 2004).

[18] Ces décisions sont traitées dans cet annuaire dans la chronique "Investissement."

[19] Accord de libre-échange nord-américain, Examen par un groupe spécial binational institué en application de l'art. 1904 de l'Accord de libre-échange nord-américain dans l'Affaire de certains réfrigérateurs, lave-vaisselle et sécheuses originaires ou exportés des États-Unis, Dossier du Secrétariat n° CDA-USA 2000-1904-04, Décision du Groupe spécial, 16 janvier 2002; Accord de libre-échange nord-américain, Examen par un groupe spécial binational institué en application de l'art. 1904 de l'Accord de libre-échange nord-américain dans l'Affaire de certains réfrigérateurs électriques avec compartiment de congélation dans la partie supérieure, lave-vaisselle électriques de type ménager et sécheuses au gaz ou électriques originaires ou exportés des États-Unis, Dossier du Secrétariat n° CDA-USA 2000-1904-03, Décision du Groupe spécial sur l'examen de la décision définitive rendue par le Commissaire des droits et du Revenu, 15 avril 2002.

portaient sur le commerce de magnésium aux États-Unis en provenance du Canada.[20] Ces sept décisions, techniques et spécifiques aux branches de production touchées, ne nous apparaissent pas justifier des développements dans la présente chronique.

Par ailleurs, quelques tensions dans les relations commerciales entre le Canada et les États-Unis, sans entraîner de rapports ou de décisions de la part de groupes spéciaux, ont marqué l'année 2002.

En septembre, des producteurs de blé américains ont déposé auprès des autorités américaines des requêtes alléguant que le gouvernement du Canada, par le biais de la Commission canadienne du blé, versait des subventions visant la production et l'exportation de blé dur et de blé de force roux du printemps canadiens. À la suite de la décision du département du commerce des États-Unis (DOC) de mener les enquêtes demandées, le gouvernement canadien a vivement réagi en rappelant que neuf enquêtes et études antérieures ont montré que le Canada et la Commission canadienne du blé respectaient les règles et disciplines du commerce international. Les divergences de vue entre le Canada et les États-Unis quant au commerce du blé remontent déjà à plusieurs années et il est à craindre qu'un peu comme pour le bois d'œuvre, elles ne perdurent. Nous reviendrons d'ailleurs sur cette question plus bas, dans la section sur les différends impliquant le Canada à l'OMC.

---

[20] Accord de libre-échange nord-américain, Examen par un groupe spécial binational institué en application de l'art. 1904 de l'Accord de libre-échange nord-américain dans l'Affaire du magnésium pur en provenance du Canada, Dossier du Secrétariat n° USA-CDA-2000-1904-06, Décision du Groupe spécial, 27 mars 2002; Accord de libre-échange nord-américain, Examen par un groupe spécial binational institué en application de l'art. 1904 de l'Accord de libre-échange nord-américain dans l'Affaire du magnésium pur en provenance du Canada, Dossier du Secrétariat n° USA-CDA-2000-1904-06, Décision du Groupe spécial, 15 octobre 2002; Accord de libre-échange nord-américain, Examen par un groupe spécial binational institué en application de l'art. 1904 de l'Accord de libre-échange nord-américain dans l'Affaire du magnésium pur et alliage de magnésium en provenance du Canada, Dossier du Secrétariat n° USA-CDA-2000-1904-07, Décision du Groupe spécial, 27 mars 2002; Accord de libre-échange nord-américain, Examen par un groupe spécial binational institué en application de l'art. 1904 de l'Accord de libre-échange nord-américain dans l'Affaire du magnésium pur et alliage de magnésium en provenance du Canada, Dossier du Secrétariat n° USA-CDA-2000-1904-07, Décision du Groupe spécial, 15 octobre 2002; Accord de libre-échange nord-américain, Examen par un groupe spécial binational institué en application de l'art. 1904 de l'Accord de libre-échange nord-américain dans l'Affaire du magnésium en provenance du Canada, Dossier du Secrétariat n° USA-CDA-2000-1904-09, Décision du Groupe spécial, 16 juillet 2002.

Dans le secteur du bois d'œuvre, précisément, les différends entre le Canada et les États-Unis ont continué de plus belle pendant l'année 2002. Le 22 mars, le département du commerce des États-Unis (DOC) a rendu des déterminations finales de subventionnement et de dumping à l'issue d'enquêtes sur le bois en provenance du Canada. Le DOC a estimé que les programmes gouvernementaux canadiens, fédéraux comme provinciaux, conféraient des subventions devant faire l'objet de droits compensateurs de l'ordre de 19,34 %. Il a aussi statué que les producteurs et exportateurs canadiens de bois d'œuvre faisaient du dumping en vendant leur bois d'œuvre à un prix inférieur à sa valeur normale. Selon les compagnies sous enquête, les marges de dumping déterminées par le DOC allaient de 2,26 % à 15,83 %. Dans les jours qui ont suivi l'annonce de ces déterminations, le gouvernement du Canada a officiellement requis qu'il soit procédé à l'examen de celles-ci conformément au chapitre 19 de l'ALÉNA.[21] Le 2 mai, la Commission du commerce international des États-Unis (USITC) a déterminé à l'unanimité que le secteur du bois d'œuvre américain était menacé d'un préjudice grave en raison de l'importation de bois d'œuvre canadien qui, d'après le DOC, était subventionné et faisait l'objet de dumping. Les rapports des groupes spéciaux appelés à examiner les déterminations américaines sont attendues au cours de l'année 2003. D'autres procédures relatives au différend canado-américain sur le bois d'œuvre feront l'objet de quelques développements plus loin quand il sera question des litiges impliquant le Canada à l'OMC.

Finalement, il convient de mentionner que les importations d'acier au Canada ont donné lieu à une enquête de sauvegarde devant le Tribunal canadien du commerce extérieur. Cette enquête a, en partie, été rendue nécessaire à la suite des décisions des autorités américaines par lesquelles elles restreignaient l'entrée de produits de l'acier sur le territoire des États-Unis et imposaient des droits de douane très élevés, pouvant aller jusqu'à 30 %, sur ces

---

[21] Accord de libre-échange nord-américain, Examen par un groupe spécial binational institué en application de l'art. 1904 de l'Accord de libre-échange nord-américain dans l'Affaire de certains produits de bois d'œuvre résineux du Canada (Décision définitive du département du Commerce sur la vente à un prix inférieur à la juste valeur), Dossier du Secrétariat n° USA-CDA-2002-1904-02; Accord de libre-échange nord-américain, Examen par un groupe spécial binational institué en application de l'art. 1904 de l'Accord de libre-échange nord-américain dans l'Affaire de certains produits de bois d'œuvre résineux du Canada (Décision définitive positive du département du Commerce en matière de droits compensateurs, Dossier du Secrétariat n° USA-CDA-2002-1904-03.

produits. Le gouvernement canadien, inquiet de ce que les produits d'acier qui se voyaient coupés du marché américain ne soient détournés vers le marché canadien, a confié au Tribunal canadien du commerce extérieur (TCCE) le mandat d'effectuer une enquête sur la hausse des importations des produits d'acier au Canada et sur les éventuels préjudices causés par ces hausses aux producteurs canadiens d'acier. Dans un rapport déposé en août 2002, le TCCE a conclu que l'importation de plusieurs produits de l'acier menaçait de causer un préjudice grave aux producteurs canadiens d'acier. Le TCCE a suggéré l'instauration d'un contingent tarifaire dont une partie serait réservée aux États-Unis. À ce contingent, s'ajoute un tarif hors-contingent très élevé visant à restreindre voire empêcher les importations au-delà du contingent fixé.[22]

III LE COMMERCE CANADIEN ET L'OMC

A   LES NÉGOCIATIONS COMMERCIALES MULTILATÉRALES

En soi, l'année 2002 a amené peu de progrès substantiels dans les négociations commerciales multilatérales. Il est vrai qu'à la suite de la Conférence ministérielle de Doha et de l'adoption d'un programme de grande envergure, il faut laisser le temps aux Membres de l'OMC de préparer leurs positions de négociations et leurs stratégies.[23] Certains faits, sans être directement reliés aux négociations, sont tout de même dignes de mention.

Deux postes extrêmement importants ont changé de titulaire pendant l'année 2002. Le 31 août, le directeur général de l'OMC, Mike Moore, voyait son mandat se terminer et cédait la place au Dr Supachai Panitchpakdi. Plus tôt, le 15 février 2002, l'ambassadeur du Canada auprès de l'OMC, M. Sergio Marchi était nommé président du Conseil général de l'OMC. Monsieur Marchi sera ainsi notamment amené à superviser les négociations lancées à Doha. Le Conseil général a d'ailleurs approuvé l'accession de deux nouveaux Membres au cours de l'année 2002, l'Arménie et l'Ex-République yougoslave de Macédoine. Ces deux États deviendront officiellement Membres au cours de l'année 2003.

---

[22] On peut trouver le texte de ce rapport sur le site WEB du Tribunal canadien du commerce extérieur à l'adresse <http://www.citt-tcce.gc.ca/safeguar/global/finalrep/gc2b001_f.asp> (dernière visite le 30 juin 2004).

[23] On notera d'ailleurs que le Canada a fait connaître en juillet 2002 ses demandes en vue des négociations sur les services. On peut trouver le texte de ces demandes à l'adresse <http://www.dfait-maeci.gc.ca/tna-nac/TS/service_neg-fr.asp> (dernière visite le 30 juin 2004).

B   LES DIFFÉRENDS DEVANT L'OMC IMPLIQUANT LE CANADA

1   *Canada — Mesures concernant les exportations de blé et le traitement
des grains importés*

En plus des demandes d'enquêtes déposées par les producteurs
de blé américains en vue de l'imposition de droits compensateurs par les autorités américaines,[24] les autorités américaines ont
amorcé une autre procédure de règlement des différends, cette fois
devant l'OMC. Les États-Unis ont en effet demandé, en décembre
2002,[25] l'ouverture de consultations avec le gouvernement du
Canada au sujet de l'exportation de blé par la Commission canadienne du blé et au sujet du traitement accordé par le Canada aux
grains importés sur le territoire canadien.

Les États-Unis sont d'avis que les actions du gouvernement canadien et de la Commission canadienne du blé liées aux exportations
de blé sont incompatibles avec le paragraphe 1a) de l'article XVII
du GATT de 1994 qui impose aux entreprises d'État l'obligation
de se conformer, dans leurs achats ou leurs ventes se traduisant par
des exportations, aux principes généraux de non-discrimination
prescrits par le GATT. Les États-Unis prétendent aussi que les
actions de la Commission canadienne du blé sont incompatibles
avec le paragraphe 1b) de l'article XVII du GATT de 1994 qui exige
des entreprises d'État qu'elles ne s'inspirent que de considérations
d'ordre commercial lors des achats et des ventes auxquels elles
procèdent et qu'elles offrent aux entreprises des autres Membres de
l'OMC des possibilités adéquates de participer à ces ventes ou à ces
achats dans des conditions de libre concurrence et conformément
aux usages commerciaux ordinaires.

Quant au traitement des grains importés aux États-Unis, les États-
Unis soutiennent que la loi et la réglementation canadienne, qui
interdisent le mélange du blé importé avec des grains de production
nationale reçus à une installation ou qui en sont déchargés, sont
incompatibles avec l'article III du GATT de 1994 et avec l'article 2
de l'*Accord sur les mesures concernant les investissements et liées au commerce.* Enfin, les États-Unis font valoir que la loi canadienne fixe un
niveau maximal pour les recettes que les compagnies de chemins de
fer peuvent tirer de l'expédition de grains canadiens de production

---

[24] Nous avons brièvement traité de cette demande d'enquête plus haut, dans la section 1B portant sur les différends liés à l'ALÉNA.

[25] Canada — Mesures concernant les exportations de blé et le traitement des
grains importés, Demande de consultation présentée par les États-Unis, OMC/
WT/DS276/1, le 19 décembre 2002.

nationale, mais pas pour les recettes qu'elles peuvent tirer de l'expédition de grains importés. Les autorités américaines sont d'avis que ces dispositions législatives canadiennes sont incompatibles avec la règle du traitement national prévue à l'article III du GATT de 1994 et avec l'article 2 de l'*Accord sur les mesures concernant les investissements et liées au commerce*. Il est à prévoir qu'un Groupe spécial sera formé au cours de l'année 2003 pour étudier cette affaire.

2   *États-Unis — Article 129C)1) de la Loi sur les Accords du Cycle d'Uruguay*

Le Groupe spécial chargé de cette affaire a rendu son rapport le 15 juillet 2002.[26] On se rappellera que, dans cette affaire, le Canada demandait que l'article 129C)1) de la Loi américaine sur les Accords du Cycle d'Uruguay soit déclaré incompatible avec certaines dispositions du GATT de 1994, de l'*Accord antidumping*, de l'*Accord sur les subventions et mesures compensatoires* et de l'Accord sur l'OMC. Le Canada prétendait notamment que l'article 129C)1) prescrivait aux autorités américaines compétentes en matière de droits antidumping ou compensateurs, d'entreprendre certaines actions incompatibles avec les règles de l'OMC ou, selon le cas, de ne pas entreprendre certaines actions requises par les règles de l'OMC. Après analyse du texte de l'article 129C)1), de l'Énoncé des mesures administratives se rapportant à la *Loi sur les Accords du Cycle d'Uruguay* et à l'application qui avait été faite jusqu'alors par les autorités américaines de l'article 129C)1), le Groupe spécial a jugé que le Canada n'avait pas établi que l'article 129C)1) était incompatible avec les dispositions invoquées. À sa réunion du 30 août 2002, l'Organe de règlement des différends a adopté le Rapport du Groupe spécial.[27] Cette affaire est donc terminée.

3   États-Unis — Loi de 2000 sur la compensation pour continuation du dumping et maintien de la subvention (CDSOA)

En septembre 2001, un Groupe spécial avait été mandaté pour entendre des plaintes déposées par plusieurs Membres de l'OMC[28]

---

[26] États-Unis — Article 129C)1) de la *Loi sur les Accords du Cycle d'Uruguay*, Rapport du groupe spécial, OMC/WT/DS221/R, le 15 juillet 2002.

[27] États-Unis — Article 129C)1) de la *Loi sur les Accords du Cycle d'Uruguay*, Rapport du groupe spécial, Dispositions prises par l'Organe de règlement des différends, OMC/WT/DS221/7, le 4 septembre 2002.

[28] L'Australie, le Brésil, le Chili, les Communautés européennes, la Corée, l'Inde, l'Indonésie, le Japon et la Thaïlande étaient les parties plaignantes dans l'affaire

contre plusieurs dispositions de la CDSOA aussi connue sous le vocable "Amendement Byrd." Le Rapport du Groupe spécial a été mis en distribution le 16 septembre 2002.[29] Après une longue étude des dispositions en cause, le Groupe spécial a jugé que la CDSOA était une mesure particulière visant à neutraliser ou à empêcher le dumping ou le subventionnement des produits entrant aux États-Unis. Du fait de cette qualification, la CDSOA doit respecter les termes de l'*Accord antidumping* et de l'*Accord sur les subventions et mesures compensatoires* (Accord SMC). Or, l'attribution de subventions aux producteurs américains qui appuient des requêtes en vue d'imposer des droits antidumping et compensateurs, ainsi que le prévoit la CDSOA, n'est autorisée ni par l'Accord antidumping ni par l'Accord SMC. Le Groupe spécial a donc conclu que la CDSOA était incompatible avec plusieurs dispositions de l'Accord anti-dumping et de l'Accord SMC ainsi qu'avec l'article VI:2 et VI:3 du GATT de 1994 et avec l'article XVI:4 de l'Accord sur l'OMC. En octobre 2002, les États-Unis ont notifié à l'Organe de règlement des différends qu'ils en appelaient du rapport du Groupe spécial.[30]

4   *Le différend canado-brésilien sur les aéronefs régionaux*

Sans que l'on ne parvienne à aplanir toutes les divergences entre le Canada et le Brésil, sans non plus que l'on ne trouve de solution qui satisfasse pleinement Bombardier et Embraer, on est parvenu pendant l'année 2002 à apaiser un peu le climat entre les protagonistes dans ce dossier. Le 28 janvier, le Groupe spécial chargé d'examiner divers crédits à l'exportation et garanties de prêts consentis sous diverses formes par les gouvernements du Canada et du Québec a rendu son rapport.[31] Le Groupe spécial y a évalué la

---

WT/DS217. Le Canada et le Mexique étaient les parties plaignantes dans l'affaire WT/DS234. Un seul Groupe spécial a été formé et mandaté pour entendre conjointement les deux affaires.

[29] États-Unis — Loi de 2000 sur la compensation pour continuation du dumping et maintien de la subvention, Rapport du Groupe spécial, OMC/WT/DS217/R et OMC/WT/DS234/R, le 16 septembre 2002.

[30] États-Unis — Loi de 2000 sur la compensation pour continuation du dumping et maintien de la subvention, Notification d'un appel des États-Unis présentée conformément au par. 4 de l'art. 16 du Mémorandum d'accord sur les règles et procédures régissant le règlement des différends, OMC/WT/DS217/8 et OMC/WT/DS234/16, le 22 octobre 2002.

[31] Canada — Crédits à l'exportation et garanties de prêts accordés pour les aéronefs régionaux, Rapport du Groupe spécial, OMC/WT/DS222/R, le 28 janvier 2002.

compatibilité de chacune de ces formes de crédits et de garanties de prêts avec les termes de l'Accord SMC. Le Groupe a jugé que la plainte du Brésil devait être rejetée à l'égard des programmes de financement suivants: Compte du Canada, Compte de la société du gouvernement du Canada, Investissement Québec, Investissement Québec (Financement des transactions particulières d'Atlantic Coast Airlines, d'Air Littoral, de Midmay, de Mesa Air Group, d'Air Nostrum et d'Air Wisconsin), Compte de la société du gouvernement du Canada (Financement des transactions particulières d'Atlantic Southeast Airlines, de Kendell Airlines, d'Air Nostrum et de Comair).[32] Le Groupe spécial a par contre accueilli les plaintes du Brésil à l'égard des financements suivants: Compte de la société du gouvernement du Canada (Financement de trois transactions particulières passées avec Comair), Compte du Canada (Financement des transactions particulières avec Air Nostrum et avec Air Wisconsin).[33] Dans le cas du financement de cette dernière transaction, le Canada a tenté de se prévaloir de ce qu'il est convenu d'appeler la clause du refuge et qui se trouve au deuxième paragraphe du point k de la Liste exemplative des subventions à l'exportation figurant à l'annexe I de l'Accord SMC. Le Canada prétendait être en droit de financer Air Wisconsin dans sa transaction avec Bombardier à des conditions en deçà de celles du marché. Le Canada prétendait pouvoir agir de la sorte puisque ce faisant, il alignait son offre de financement sur celle qu'avait faite le Brésil et qu'un tel "alignement sur dérogation" était autorisé par l'*Arrangement de l'OCDE relatif à des lignes directrices pour les crédits à l'exportation bénéficiant d'un soutien public*.[34] Le Groupe spécial n'a pas adhéré aux arguments du Canada. Il a indiqué que les termes de l'Arrangement de l'OCDE ne peuvent être incorporés à l'Accord SMC sans en respecter les règles et les principes généraux. Le Groupe spécial a donc déterminé que l'alignement sur dérogation ne pouvait pas entrer dans le champ d'application de la clause du refuge.[35]

Le Canada s'est déclaré satisfait de la décision du Groupe spécial et l'Organe de règlement des différends a adopté le rapport.[36]

---

[32] *Ibid.* au par. 8.1.

[33] *Ibid.*

[34] Cet arrangement de l'OCDE répond aux critères mentionnés au deuxième paragraphe du point k de la Liste exemplative figurant à l'annexe I de l'Accord SMC.

[35] *Supra* note 31, aux par. 7.176 et 7.180.

[36] Canada — Crédits à l'exportation et garanties de prêts accordés pour les aéronefs régionaux, Rapport du Groupe de travail [*sic*], OMC/WT/DS222/6, le 27 mars 2002.

Le Canada n'ayant pas procédé au retrait des subventions pro-
hibées dans les délais prescrits, le Brésil a demandé à l'Organe
de règlement des différends l'autorisation de prendre des contre-
mesures contre le Canada pour un montant de 3,36 milliards de
dollars américains.[37] Ce sont finalement des contre-mesures de 248
millions de dollars américains qui seront autorisées. En fin d'année
2002, les gouvernements canadien et brésilien ont déclaré vouloir
désormais axer leurs relations commerciales sur le dialogue et la
négociation. Il sera intéressant de voir s'ils y parviendront.

5   *Canada — Mesures visant l'importation de lait et l'exportation de
    produits laitiers*

À la toute fin de l'année 2001, les États-Unis et la Nouvelle-
Zélande avaient institué un deuxième recours selon l'article 21:5
du Mémorandum d'accord sur le règlement des différends afin de
voir si le Canada avait correctement mis en œuvre les recommandations émises par l'Organe d'appel dans son rapport du 13
décembre 1999. C'est le 26 juillet 2002 que le rapport du Groupe
spécial chargé d'évaluer ce deuxième recours a été rendu public.[38]
Le Groupe spécial a notamment décidé que:

> le Canada, du fait du régime LEC [lait d'exportation commerciale] et du
> maintien de la classe spéciale de lait 5d), a agi d'une manière incompati-
> ble avec ses obligations au titre des articles 3:3 et 8 de l'*Accord sur l'agricul-
> ture*, en octroyant des subventions à l'exportation au sens de l'article 9:1c)
> de l'*Accord sur l'agriculture* en dépassement des niveaux de ses engagements
> en matière de quantités spécifiés dans sa Liste pour les exportations de
> fromages et d'"autres produits laitiers."[39]

Le Groupe spécial a aussi estimé que le Canada n'avait pas agi en
conformité avec les articles 10:1 et 8 de l'*Accord sur l'agriculture*. Le
Canada en a appelé de cette décision qui a, pour l'essentiel, été

---

[37] Canada — Crédits à l'exportation et garanties de prêts accordés pour les
aéronefs régionaux, Recours du Brésil à l'art. 4.10 de l'Accord sur les subventions et mesures compensatoires et à l'art. 22:2 du Mémorandum d'accord sur
les règles et procédures régissant le règlement des différends, OMC/WT/
DS222/7, le 24 mai 2002.

[38] Canada — Mesures visant l'importation de lait et l'exportation de produits
laitiers, Deuxième recours des États-Unis et de la Nouvelle-Zélande à l'art. 21:5
du Mémorandum d'accord, Rapport du Groupe spécial, OMC/WT/DS103/
RW2 et OMC/WT/DS113/RW2, le 26 juillet 2002.

[39] *Ibid.* au par. 6.1.

confirmée par l'Organe d'appel.[40] Reste maintenant au Canada, aux États-Unis et à la Nouvelle-Zélande à se mettre d'accord sur la mise en œuvre et l'application de ces décisions.

6 *Le bois d'œuvre résineux*

Si d'autres différends semblent se diriger lentement vers une solution négociée, il en va tout autrement dans le dossier du bois d'œuvre. Les procédures se sont en effet multipliées pendant l'année 2002 et rien ne laisse espérer un rapprochement des positions canadienne et américaine.

Le Canada a fait des gains importants dans l'affaire *États-Unis — Déterminations préliminaires concernant certains bois d'œuvre résineux en provenance du Canada*. Le rapport du Groupe spécial, distribué le 27 septembre 2002,[41] a confirmé la position canadienne sur des questions majeures relatives au subventionnement et à l'application de droits compensateurs. Le Groupe spécial a indiqué que pour vérifier si une contribution financière du gouvernement canadien confère un avantage, il faut se référer aux conditions existantes sur le marché canadien et non à celles prévalant sur le marché américain. Le Groupe spécial a aussi donné raison au Canada et jugé que les États-Unis avaient eu tort de supposer que les présumés avantages tirés de la récolte du bois sous les programmes gouvernementaux de droits de coupe sont transférés lorsque les producteurs en amont vendent des billes ou du bois d'œuvre aux producteurs en aval qui s'en servent pour fabriquer les biens visés par l'enquête en subventionnement. Troisièmement, le Groupe spécial a clairement rappelé que le département du commerce américain (DOC) n'avait pas le droit d'imposer rétroactivement des mesures provisoires à la suite d'une détermination préliminaire de circonstances critiques. Des mesures rétroactives ne peuvent être appliquées qu'après une détermination finale. Ce rapport très favorable au Canada fut adopté par l'ORD le 1er novembre.

Trois autres procédures de règlement des différends liées au commerce canado-américain du bois d'œuvre ont été amorcées par

---

[40] Canada — Mesures visant l'importation de lait et l'exportation de produits laitiers, Deuxième recours des États-Unis et de la Nouvelle-Zélande à l'art. 21:5 du Mémorandum d'accord, Rapport de l'Organe d'appel, OMC/WT/DS103/AB/RW2 et OMC/WT/DS113/AB/RW2, le 20 décembre 2002.

[41] États-Unis — Déterminations préliminaires concernant certains bois d'œuvre résineux en provenance du Canada, Rapport du Groupe spécial, MC/WT/DS236/R, le 27 septembre 2002.

le Canada en 2002. En mars, le Canada a demandé l'ouverture
de consultations relativement à des mesures antidumping provisoires.[42] En mai, il a demandé l'ouverture de consultations au sujet
de la détermination finale en matière de droits compensateurs
publiée par les autorités américaines le 25 mars 2002.[43] Le Groupe
spécial chargé de cette affaire a été constitué et a reçu son mandat
en novembre.[44] Finalement, en septembre, le Canada a demandé
l'ouverture de consultations sur la détermination finale de l'existence d'un dumping annoncée le 22 mai 2002.[45] En décembre, le
Canada a demandé la constitution d'un Groupe spécial dans ce
même dossier.[46]

Rare geste d'accommodement à travers cette vague de procédures formelles, la Commission internationale du commerce des
États-Unis (ITC) a accepté le 16 mai 2002 de rembourser aux producteurs canadiens les cautions perçues jusqu'à cette date sur les
expéditions de bois d'œuvre à destination des États-Unis.

IV CONCLUSION

À la fin de l'année 2002, l'observateur des questions reliées
au commerce international et au phénomène d'intégration économique doit attendre. Attendre de voir si le projet de ZLÉA peut continuer de progresser malgré une conjoncture défavorable. Attendre
de voir ce qu'il adviendra des chantiers lancés à Doha et qui ont
peu avancé pendant l'année 2002. Attendre enfin de voir si les systèmes de règlement des différends de l'ALÉNA et de l'OMC que

[42] États-Unis — Mesure antidumping provisoire appliquée aux importations de
certains bois d'œuvre résineux en provenance du Canada, Demande de consultations présentée par le Canada, OMC/WT/DS247/1, le 12 mars 2002.

[43] États-Unis — Détermination finale en matière de droits compensateurs concernant certains bois d'œuvre résineux en provenance du Canada, Demande de consultations présentée par le Canada, OMC/WT/DS257/1, le 13 mai 2002.

[44] États-Unis — Détermination finale en matière de droits compensateurs concernant certains bois d'œuvre résineux en provenance du Canada, Constitution du
Groupe spécial établi à la demande du Canada, OMC/WT/DS257/4, le 12
novembre 2002.

[45] États-Unis — Détermination finale de l'existence d'un dumping concernant
certains bois d'œuvre résineux en provenance du Canada, Demande de consultations présentée par le Canada, OMC/WT/DS264/1, le 19 septembre 2002.

[46] États-Unis — Détermination finale de l'existence d'un dumping concernant
certains bois d'œuvre résineux en provenance du Canada, Demande d'établissement d'un Groupe spécial présentée par le Canada, OMC/WT/DS264/2,
le 9 décembre 2002.

l'on croyait arrivés au bout de leurs possibilités ne s'avéreront pas beaucoup plus utiles, efficaces et solides que ce que les événements de l'année 2001 avaient pu laisser croire. Les acteurs du système commercial multilatéral arrivent à la croisée des chemins. Il sera intéressant de voir si cette année où l'on a assisté à plus de consolidation que de progrès annonce une période de stagnation ou prépare au contraire des temps plus fébriles.

II Le Canada et le système financier international en 2002

préparé par
BERNARD COLAS

L a lutte contre le terrorisme et le blanchiment d'argent, les scandales financiers[1] et le ralentissement marqué de l'économie mondiale sont les événements qui ont retenu l'attention de la communauté internationale en 2002. C'est donc tout naturellement que la communauté internationale a consacré ses travaux à la consolidation du système financier international, à l'intensification de la lutte contre le terrorisme et le blanchiment d'argent et au renforcement de la surveillance des entreprises. Ces travaux ont été menés de concert par le Groupe des vingt (I), les institutions financières internationales (II) et les organismes de contrôle des établissements financiers (III), le Groupe d'action financière (IV) et le Forum de stabilité financière (V) au sein desquels le Canada joue un rôle de premier plan.

I LE GROUPE DES VINGT

À l'occasion de leur réunion annuelle tenue à New Delhi en Inde le 23 novembre 2002, le Groupe des vingt (G-20) a réaffirmé que la réduction de la pauvreté et l'augmentation du niveau de vie des populations des pays les plus pauvres passent par une intégration accrue de l'économie mondiale.[2] Pour le G-20, les effets de la

---

Bernard Colas est Avocat de l'étude Gottlieb et Pearson (Montréal), Docteur en droit, Commissaire, Commission du droit du Canada, Président de la Société de droit international économique (SDIE). L'auteur remercie Xavier Mageau, LL.M., de la même étude pour son importante contribution à la préparation de cet article.

[1] Au cours de l'année 2002, les scandales financiers ont été au cœur de l'actualité. Citons par exemple *Enron*, *Worldcom*, etc.

[2] *Delhi Communiqué, G-20 Finance Ministers' and Central Bank Governors' Meeting dated November 23, 2002*, au par. 6 (*Communiqué du G-20*).

mondialisation doivent profiter à tous et peuvent être maximisés en poursuivant des politiques économiques nationales appropriées dans un environnement extérieur sain. Dans ce contexte, la suppression des subventions et l'élimination des obstacles au commerce peuvent contribuer à l'expansion des bénéfices de la globalisation notamment au profit des pays en développement.[3]

Le G-20 a également insisté sur l'importance de renforcer la capacité de la communauté internationale à prévenir les crises financières et à développer des réponses rapides, efficaces, socialement et économiquement acceptables dès la survenance des crises financières. Pour le G-20, la prospérité et la croissance économique dépendent largement de l'adoption de politiques macroéconomiques fortes et de la mise en place d'institutions fortes et d'une bonne gouvernance.[4] Ces trois éléments peuvent également contribuer à limiter la vulnérabilité de certains pays aux crises financières. Sur la base de ce constat, le G-20 a prôné la mise en place de systèmes financiers nationaux sains, une supervision effective de ces systèmes financiers nationaux ainsi qu'une gouvernance d'entreprise qui soit en adéquation avec les meilleures pratiques.

Au cours de sa réunion annuelle tenue à Ottawa en 2001, le G-20 avait convenu de dresser rapidement un bilan de la mise en œuvre du plan d'action adopté en 2001 pour remédier aux conséquences économiques engendrées par les attentats mais également pour lutter contre le terrorisme. Lors de sa réunion annuelle de 2002, le G-20 a analysé l'application de ce plan d'action du point de vue du gel des avoirs terroristes, de l'application des standards internationaux, de l'échange d'informations et de la fourniture d'une assistance technique à certains États. Le G-20 a convenu de poursuivre ses efforts en vue d'éliminer les abus du système financier et plus particulièrement le blanchiment d'argent. En outre, le G-20 a réaffirmé son engagement dans la lutte au terrorisme et la lutte contre ceux qui le financent.[5]

---

[3] *Communiqué du G-20, supra* note 2 au par. 7.

[4] *Communiqué du G-20, supra* note 2 au par. 3.

[5] La perpétration de nouveaux attentats à Bali et à Moscou en 2002 a été à l'origine de la réaffirmation de l'engagement du G-20, *Communiqué du G-20, supra* note 2 au par. 9.

II LES INSTITUTIONS INTERNATIONALES

A FONDS MONÉTAIRE INTERNATIONAL (FMI)

Au cours de l'année 2002, de nombreux pays ont souffert du ralentissement de l'économie mondiale amorcé en 2001. Outre les pays déjà éprouvés en 2001 comme l'Argentine et la Turquie,[6] d'autres pays comme l'Uruguay et le Brésil sont venus s'ajouter à la liste des pays bénéficiaires du soutien du FMI.[7]

Les travaux relatifs à la réforme du FMI se sont poursuivis au cours de l'année 2002. Ces travaux ont porté principalement sur le renforcement de la surveillance, la mise en œuvre des normes et des codes internationaux, les mécanismes du FMI et le renforcement de la régie du FMI.

En ce qui concerne le renforcement de la surveillance et de la prévention des crises, le FMI a terminé l'examen de surveillance détaillé en 2002. Suite à cet examen, le FMI a modifié la nature et la portée de ses travaux de surveillance pour insister davantage sur la politique macro-économique, sur les mouvements de capitaux et sur les enjeux structurels ayant une incidence sur la stabilité macro-économique. Au cours de l'année 2002, le FMI a développé de nouveaux outils d'analyse pour mieux évaluer la vulnérabilité externe du secteur financier mais aussi pour aider les pays à surveiller et à gérer leur dette de manière à éviter les crises financières. Le FMI a également poursuivi ses travaux en matière de transparence

---

[6] Suite à la suspension du programme du FMI pour l'Argentine en 2001, l'Argentine a engagé en 2002 des négociations avec le FMI pour convenir des modalités d'un nouveau programme visant à stabiliser la situation financière du pays. À la fin de l'année 2002, l'Argentine avait d'importants arriérés de paiement auprès de la Banque mondiale et de la Banque interaméricaine de développement. Quant à la Turquie, le FMI a obtenu un accord de confirmation de 16,3 milliards de dollars américains en février 2002. La situation économique de la Turquie s'est considérablement améliorée en 2002. En effet, la hausse du PIB a été deux fois plus importante que prévue et l'inflation a atteint son niveau le plus bas depuis 20 ans. Toutefois, la Turquie reste très vulnérable aux fluctuations brusques de la confiance des marchés en raison de son fort taux d'endettement intérieur. *Rapport sur les opérations effectuées en vertu de la Loi sur les accords de Bretton Woods et des accords connexes 2002* (ci-après *Bretton Woods 2002*) à la p. 11.

[7] L'Uruguay, voisin de l'Argentine, a été considérablement affecté par la crise sévissant en Argentine. Dans ce contexte, l'Uruguay a reçu un total de 2,8 milliards de dollars américains aux termes d'accord de confirmation. En ce qui concerne le Brésil, l'incertitude liée à l'élection présidentielle a contribué à l'affaiblissement de sa monnaie et a accru le risque de crédit à partir du mois d'avril 2002. Le FMI a approuvé en septembre 2002 un accord de confirmation de 30 milliards de dollars américains, *Bretton Woods 2002, supra* note 6 aux pp. 10 et 11.

et de circulation de l'information relative aux politiques menées par les membres du FMI.[8]

Les travaux du FMI sur la mise en œuvre et l'évaluation des normes et des codes internationaux ont abouti à la mise en place d'une méthode par modules pour évaluer la conformité des membres aux normes internationales. Cette évaluation se fait par le biais de rapports pour chaque module.[9] Le Canada a d'ailleurs été le premier pays à publier les résultats de l'évaluation de sa conformité aux normes internationales. Cette évaluation a été publiée sous la forme d'un rapport sur l'observation des normes et des codes internationaux. Suite à la publication de ce premier rapport, le Canada a entamé la préparation de nouveaux rapports sur la surveillance des banques et des compagnies d'assurance, sur la transparence des politiques budgétaires, sur la transparence des politiques financières et monétaires, des systèmes de paiements et de la réglementation des valeurs mobilières. À la fin de l'année 2002, près de la moitié des 184 pays membres du FMI avait terminé au moins un rapport.

Au cours des dernières années, le FMI est fréquemment intervenu pour soutenir certains de ses membres et mettre fin aux crises financières auxquels ils sont confrontés. Suite à ces interventions, le FMI a jugé utile de redéfinir les politiques d'accès aux ressources du FMI.[10] Ainsi, depuis septembre 2002, les conditions posées pour accéder aux ressources du FMI ont été restreintes. Désormais, l'accès exceptionnel aux ressources du FMI ne sera ouvert qu'aux membres du FMI qui, lorsqu'ils sont confrontés à une crise du compte capital, satisfont aux nouvelles conditions minimales approuvées par le conseil d'administration du FMI.

Le membre du FMI qui souhaite bénéficier de ce soutien doit tout d'abord démontrer que sa balance des paiements exerce des tensions exceptionnelles sur son compte capital. Une analyse rigoureuse doit démontrer que la dette restera viable et que le membre a de bonnes chances d'avoir, à nouveau, accès aux marchés de capitaux privés avant le remboursement complet des crédits du FMI. De plus, le programme stratégique du membre doit offrir des chances raisonnables de succès. Le processus décisionnel à l'égard des demandes d'accès exceptionnel aux ressources du FMI a également été considérablement renforcé.

[8] *Bretton Woods 2002, supra* note 6 à la p. 5.

[9] *Bretton Woods 2002, supra* note 6 à la p. 16.

[10] *Bretton Woods 2002, supra* note 6 à la p. 19.

En septembre 2002, le Bureau d'évaluation indépendant du FMI (BEI) a publié sa première évaluation relative à l'utilisation prolongée des ressources du FMI définie comme l'utilisation des ressources du FMI pendant plus de sept années. Il ressort de cette évaluation que l'utilisation prolongée des ressources du FMI peut avoir un impact sur le caractère renouvelable des ressources du FMI mais également sur la capacité du FMI à consentir des prêts.[11]

Le BEI a formulé diverses recommandations afin de rendre l'utilisation prolongée des ressources du FMI moins attrayante, d'améliorer l'efficacité des programmes et d'en atténuer les conséquences négatives. Le FMI s'est engagé à effectuer un suivi des recommandations du BEI au cours de l'année 2003.

Cette évaluation effectuée par le BEI complète la nouvelle méthode de mesure des liquidités du FMI dont l'objet est de mieux évaluer l'ampleur des ressources régulières du FMI disponibles pour l'attribution de nouveaux prêts. Cette nouvelle méthode, adoptée en 2002, s'inscrit dans le cadre du renforcement de la transparence et de la responsabilisation du FMI.

Le FMI a adopté en 2001 un plan d'actions pour lutter contre le blanchiment de capitaux et le financement du terrorisme. En novembre 2002, le FMI a ajouté les recommandations du Groupe d'action financière sur le blanchiment de capitaux (GAFI) portant sur la lutte contre le blanchiment de capitaux et le financement des activités terroristes à la liste des normes et des codes visés par les rapports sur l'observation des normes et codes dans le contexte du cadre Programme d'évaluation du secteur financier. Le FMI a également approuvé un projet pilote de douze mois sur l'évaluation des mesures de lutte contre le blanchiment de capitaux et le financement des activités terroristes, sur l'élaboration de rapports connexes et sur l'observation des normes et des codes.[12]

B BANQUE MONDIALE

La lutte contre la pauvreté a fait l'objet d'une attention particulière de la part de la Banque Mondiale au cours de l'année 2002.

Au début de l'année 2002, la Banque Mondiale et le FMI ont procédé à un examen exhaustif du processus des documents de stratégie pour la réduction de la pauvreté. Outre qu'il confirme l'utilité de ces documents de stratégie, l'examen a mis en évidence

---

[11] *Bretton Woods 2002, supra* note 6 aux pp. 14 et 22.

[12] *Bretton Woods 2002, supra* note 6 à la p. 17.

la nécessité d'accroître la participation des intervenants, d'améliorer le lien entre les documents de stratégie pour la réduction de la pauvreté et les processus nationaux d'élaboration des politiques mais aussi la nécessité de renforcer la coordination et l'harmonisation de l'aide des donateurs.[13]

En 2002, la Banque Mondiale a adopté la nouvelle stratégie de développement rural. Cette nouvelle stratégie reconnaît l'importance de l'agriculture comme source principale de croissance économique générale et de réduction de la pauvreté dans de nombreux pays pauvres. Dans ce contexte, le financement de la Banque Mondiale au secteur agricole augmentera annuellement de plus de 20 % au cours des deux prochaines années. La Banque Mondiale espère ainsi améliorer l'infrastructure et les services financiers et sociaux destinés aux pauvres des régions rurales.[14]

Au cours de l'année 2002, les engagements de la Banque Mondiale en matière d'éducation ont atteint 1,4 milliards de dollars américains.[15] Depuis l'année 2002, la Banque Mondiale accorde des aides accélérées aux pays qui se dotent de stratégies judicieuses en matière d'éducation.[16] Le Canada a accru son aide aux programmes d'éducation, et en particulier en faveur de la promotion de l'égalité des sexes en Tanzanie et au Mozambique. En outre, le Canada s'est également engagé à fournir une contribution additionnelle de 10 millions de dollars.

Le mandat du Groupe consultatif d'assistance aux plus pauvres (GAPP) créé en 1995 a été renouvelé pour la troisième fois en 2002. Le GAPP a consacré 7,8 millions de dollars américains à l'élargissement des opérations de micro-crédits dans les pays les plus pauvres.[17] Le Canada a appuyé fortement les efforts du GAPP pour élargir la portée du micro-crédit. Le processus de développement du micro-crédit entre dans sa troisième phase. À ce stade, il s'agit de promouvoir la diversité des institutions financières qui aident les pauvres, de faciliter l'accès des pauvres à un large éventail de services financiers souples et pratiques, d'améliorer la disponibilité et la qualité de l'information sur le rendement des institutions

---

[13] *Bretton Woods 2002, supra* note 6 à la p. 38.

[14] *Bretton Woods 2002, supra* note 6 à la p. 46.

[15] Ces engagements prennent tantôt la forme de prêts tantôt la forme de travaux consultatifs analytiques et stratégiques.

[16] En juin 2002, la Banque Mondiale a présenté une liste de 18 pays pouvant recevoir une aide accélérée, *Bretton Woods 2002, supra* note 6 aux pp. 47-49.

[17] *Bretton Woods 2002, supra* note 6 à la p. 50.

de micro-crédit et de promouvoir un cadre politique et juridique solide pour le micro-crédit.

Concernant l'allègement de la dette des pays pauvres très endettés (PPTE), des progrès encourageants ont été accomplis au cours de l'année 2002. En décembre 2002, vingt-six pays ont profité de l'allègement de la dette aux termes de l'initiative en faveur des PPTE, parmi lesquels six ont bénéficié d'un allègement irrévocable de leur dette.[18] Ils ont donc profité d'un allègement de la dette de 40 milliards de dollars américains dans le cadre de l'initiative en faveur des PPTE ainsi que de mesures additionnelles et le fardeau de la dette a été ou sera réduit en moyenne des deux tiers. Le Canada favorise également l'allègement de la dette des PPTE. À ce titre, dans le cadre de l'initiative canadienne d'effacement de la dette, le Canada a, au cours l'année 2002, annulé toutes les dettes de la Tanzanie et de la Bolivie.

III   Organismes de contrôle des établissements
      financiers

L'année 2002 aura été marquée en grande partie par la révélation de scandales financiers importants. Face à ces scandales financiers, le Comité de Bâle sur le contrôle bancaire a concentré les travaux sur les mesures à prendre pour éviter la répétition de ces scandales dans le futur.

A   COMITÉ DE BÂLE SUR LE CONTRÔLE BANCAIRE

En 2002, le Comité de Bâle sur le contrôle bancaire a poursuivi ses travaux portant sur la révision de l'Accord de Bâle sur les fonds propres qui sert maintenant de fondement à la réglementation d'une centaine de pays. Au cours du quatrième trimestre de l'année 2002, le Comité de Bâle a mené auprès des banques une troisième étude quantitative en vue d'évaluer l'impact des propositions complétées et modifiées. Sur la base de cette troisième étude quantitative, le Comité de Bâle doit lancer une dernière consultation au courant du second trimestre de l'année 2003. Cette consultation permettra au Comité de Bâle de décider si des modifications doivent être apportées avant la mise en consultation du troisième et dernier projet.

---

[18] *Bretton Woods 2002, supra* note 6 à la p. 73.

La réglementation définitive doit être publiée au dernier trimestre de l'année 2003.[19] À partir de la publication de la réglementation définitive, les pays membres disposeront de trois années pour transposer à l'échelon national cette norme minimale intitulée Bâle II avant l'entrée en vigueur de la réglementation définitive prévue à la fin de l'année 2006.[20]

Au cours du mois de juillet 2002, le Comité de Bâle a annoncé d'autres modifications stratégiques telles que l'addition d'une fonction supplémentaire de pondération des risques permettant de gérer certaines expositions renouvelables dans le segment clientèle privée plus sensible au risque, notamment les encours sur les cartes de crédit. En outre, il a été prévu que les banques qui souhaitent adopter l'approche de notation interne complexe devront tenir compte de la durée résiduelle d'un crédit dans le calcul des exigences en matière de fonds propres. L'écart entre les exigences de fonds propres dans les deux variantes de la méthode de notation interne de crédits (la méthode simple et la méthode complexe) a été restreint de façon à éviter une trop forte réduction lorsque c'est la méthode complexe qui est appliquée.[21]

En janvier 2002, le Comité de Bâle a publié la version finale du document actualisé "The relationship between banking supervisors and the bank's external auditors."[22] Ce document a été préparé en collaboration avec l'*International Auditing Practices Committee*. Pour ce qui est de la révision interne, l'Accounting Task Force du Comité de Bâle a effectué un sondage auprès de soixante et onze banques pour vérifier l'état d'avancement de l'application des principes édictés par le Comité en 2001.

Au cours de l'année 2002, l'"Electronic Banking Group" du Comité de Bâle sur le "E-Banking" a concentré ses efforts sur l'élaboration d'un rapport sur l'e-banking frontalier. En octobre 2002, le Comité de Bâle a mis en consultation le rapport "Management and Supervision of Cross-Border E-Banking Activities." Le rapport mis en consultation précise qu'il incombe aux banques de procéder à un examen adéquat des risques avant d'entreprendre des activités d'*e-banking* transfrontalières et d'intégrer ces affaires

---

[19] *Rapport annuel de la Commission bancaire et financière 2002-2003* à la p. 167 (ci-après *Commission bancaire*).

[20] *Rapport de gestion de la Commission fédérale des Banques 2002* à la p. 92 (ci-après *Commission fédérale*).

[21] *Commission fédérale, supra* note 20 à la p. 94.

[22] *Commission fédérale, supra* note 20 à la p. 96 et *Commission bancaire, supra* note 19.

dans leur gestion globale des risques. Le rapport souligne également l'importance d'une surveillance efficace par l'autorité du pays d'origine et d'une collaboration entre les autorités de surveillance.[23] Le rapport conclut d'ailleurs que la surveillance prudentielle par l'autorité du pays cible est superflue si ces deux éléments sont présents.

En matière de surveillance transfontalière, le *Working Group on Cross-Border Banking* composé des représentants du Comité de Bâle et du groupement des autorités de surveillance des places financières offshore a poursuivi ses travaux dans le domaine de la surveillance transfrontalière. Le groupe de travail a concentré ses efforts sur le devoir de diligence en matière de prévention du blanchiment de capitaux, sur la surveillance mondiale et sur la limitation des risques juridiques et de réputation.[24]

B   ORGANISATION INTERNATIONALE DES COMMISSIONS
     DE VALEURS (OICV)

La conférence annuelle de l'OICV a été placée sous le thème "La Mondialisation: possibilités et défis."[25] La mondialisation offre de nouvelles possibilités aux investisseurs et aux prestataires de services financiers en même temps qu'elle place les autorités de surveillance devant de nouveaux défis. Cette conférence a permis l'étude approfondie de thèmes tels que la réglementation et la surveillance dans le contexte des marchés financiers mondialisés, les lacunes et les défis des procédures transfrontalières, les conflits d'intérêt dans l'analyse financière et le *Corporate Governance.*[26]

Le comité présidentiel de l'OICV a adopté un Protocole d'accord multilatéral (Protocole) dont l'objet est l'échange mondial d'informations et la coopération lors de procédures d'enquête.[27] Ce Protocole découle du constat qu'il n'existe aucun accord mondial d'échange d'informations entre les régulateurs boursiers mondiaux. Les seuls accords existant sont des accords régionaux ou bilatéraux. Ce Protocole résulte des travaux du Special Project Team créé à Rome en 2001 suite aux événements du 11 septembre

---

[23] *Commission fédérale, supra* note 20 à la p. 97.

[24] *Commission fédérale, supra* note 20 à la p. 98.

[25] L'OICV a organisé sa conférence annuelle à Istanbul, Turquie en mai 2002.

[26] *Commission fédérale, supra* note 20 à la p. 102.

[27] *Commission fédérale, supra* note 20 aux pp. 102-3 et *Rapport annuel 2002 de la Commission des Opérations de Bourse* aux pp. 253 et 255 (ci-après COB).

2001. Ce groupe s'était alors vu confier la mission d'explorer les actions à prendre par les régulateurs boursiers pour élargir la coopération et l'échange d'informations en matière de lutte contre les infractions boursières.

Les régulateurs boursiers qui souhaitent devenir signataires de ce Protocole doivent tout d'abord répondre à un questionnaire détaillé qui vise à déterminer leur capacité à obtenir des informations et à les échanger avec leurs homologues. Les réponses apportées au questionnaire sont analysées par un *Screening Group* qui vérifie les dispositifs législatifs et réglementaires des commissions candidates et propose, le cas échéant, leur acceptation. Un mécanisme de vérification et de sanction du non-respect des obligations découlant du Protocole a été mis en place.

En octobre 2002, le Comité technique de l'OICV a adopté trois rapports du Comité spécial pour réfléchir aux mesures à proposer à la suite des faillites de plusieurs grandes entreprises. Les rapports portent respectivement sur la supervision des commissaires aux comptes, l'indépendance des commissaires aux comptes et l'information périodique et permanente. Concernant la supervision des commissaires aux comptes, le Comité spécial dresse une liste des principes menant à la création d'une structure de supervision des commissaires aux comptes. Sur la question de l'indépendance des commissaires aux comptes, le rapport souligne que l'indépendance des commissaires aux comptes nécessite la réunion de trois conditions, soit l'existence de normes relatives à l'indépendance, la supervision des auditeurs par un organisme indépendant et l'existence au sein des entreprises d'un comité d'audit en charge de superviser le processus de sélection et de nomination des auditeurs externes ainsi que la conduite des audits. Le dernier rapport sur l'information périodique et permanente reprend les principes de diffusion de l'information adoptés par l'OICV en 1998 sur l'information à diffuser lors d'une offre publique.[28]

IV   GROUPE D'ACTION FINANCIÈRE SUR LE BLANCHIMENT DE CAPITAUX (GAFI)

Au cours de l'année 2002, le GAFI a poursuivi la révision de ses quarante recommandations. Cette révision a été rendue nécessaire par la complexité croissante des techniques utilisées pour blanchir les fonds d'origine criminelle. La révision a pris la forme d'une

---

[28] COB, *supra* note 27 à la p. 256.

large consultation ouverte aux membres et observateurs du GAFI, aux pays non membres, aux différents secteurs impliqués (financiers ou autres) et à toute partie concernée. Ces consultations tenues dans le cadre des travaux du GAFI ont pour objectif la formulation, en 2003, de nouvelles propositions concernant les recommandations.[29]

En matière de financement du terrorisme, le GAFI a travaillé à compter du mois de juin 2002 à la mise en place d'un processus destiné à identifier les lacunes des initiatives prises à l'échelle mondiale dans la lutte contre le financement du terrorisme.

Suite aux attentats du 11 septembre 2001, des recommandations spéciales ont été adoptées sur le financement du terrorisme. En 2002, des directives d'interprétation ont été publiées concernant certaines de ces recommandations spéciales comme la recommandation spéciale VIII sur les organismes à but non lucratifs. La directive publiée dans le cas de la recommandation spéciale VIII tend de la meilleure façon qui soit à protéger la collecte de dons charitables contre une utilisation abusive comme couverture de financement du terrorisme. Comme les directives publiées ne concernent pas toutes les recommandations spéciales, d'autres directives devraient être publiées au cours de l'année 2003.[30]

Suite à l'adoption des recommandations spéciales en 2001, le GAFI a entrepris d'évaluer dans quelle mesure ces recommandations spéciales étaient appliquées par les pays membres en mettant au point un mécanisme d'évaluation. En 2002, le GAFI a entrepris de procéder à la même évaluation auprès des pays non membres. En octobre 2002, quelques cent pays non membres du GAFI ont répondu à ce questionnaire dont les résultats doivent être connus en 2003.[31] À la fin de l'année 2002, la liste des pays considérés comme non-coopératifs dans la lutte contre le blanchiment de capitaux comprend quinze pays ou territoires.[32]

Au cours de l'année 2002, le GAFI a accru sa coopération avec d'autres organisations internationales comme le Comité de Bâle. Cette coopération a conduit à la mise au point d'une méthodologie commune pour évaluer le respect des normes de lutte contre le

---

[29] *Rapport annuel du GAFI 2002-2003* à la p. 5 (ci-après *Rapport GAFI*).

[30] *Rapport GAFI, supra* note 29 à la p. 8.

[31] *Rapport GAFI, supra* note 29 à la p. 9.

[32] Les Îles Cook, la Dominique, l'Égypte, Grenade, le Guatemala, l'Indonésie, les Îles Marshall, Myanmar, Nauru, le Nigéria, Niue, les Philippines, la Russie, Saint Vincent et les Grenadines font partie de la liste dressée au mois de décembre 2002.

blanchiment de capitaux et le financement du terrorisme. La méthodologie élaborée repose sur les recommandations du GAFI, les
principes du Comité de Bâle et de l'OICV.[33]

V LE FORUM DE STABILITÉ FINANCIÈRE

Les travaux du Forum de stabilité financière ont porté principalement sur l'impact des turbulences politiques, économiques
et financières sur le marché et sur les réponses qui peuvent être
apportées pour restaurer la confiance des investisseurs et consolider les fondations des marchés financiers.

Les travaux du Forum de stabilité financière ont porté sur trois
points:

- La révision des principes du gouvernement d'entreprise par
  l'OCDE favorablement accueillie par le Forum de stabilité
  financière;
- L'accélération des travaux portant sur la convergence des normes
  comptables internationales et l'élaboration de standards internationaux pour favoriser la transparence et la comparabilité des
  documents;
- La mise en place de standards internationaux en matière d'audit.

Les membres du Forum de stabilité financière ont rappelé aux cen-
tres financiers peu coopératifs la nécessité de renforcer leur pratique en matière de surveillance, de régularisation, d'échange des
informations et de coopération afin de consolider le système financier international dans son ensemble et de contribuer à accroître
l'efficacité globale de lutte contre le financement du terrorisme. Le
Forum de stabilité financière a également invité ses membres à renforcer la coopération technique avec les pays qui ont des difficultés
pour mettre en œuvre les standards internationaux en raison de
leur capacité financière limitée.

Ainsi, en 2002, les acteurs du système financier international
ont concentré leurs efforts sur l'intensification de la lutte contre
le blanchiment de capitaux et contre le financement du terrorisme
et sur l'élaboration des mesures appropriées pour renforcer la
surveillance des entreprises et consolider le système financier
international.

---

[33] *Rapport GAFI, supra* note 29 à la p. 11.

III Investissement

préparé par
CÉLINE LÉVESQUE

INTRODUCTION

La chronique de l'année 2002 porte sur les travaux de la CNUDCI sur les projets d'infrastructure à financement privé, sur la sentence évaluant les dommages dans l'affaire *Pope & Talbot* rendue sous le régime du Chapitre 11 de l'ALÉNA, et sur l'adoption aux États-Unis du *Trade Promotion Authority Act* de 2002.

I ACHÈVEMENT DES TRAVAUX DE LA CNUDCI SUR LES PROJETS D'INFRASTRUCTURE À FINANCEMENT PRIVÉ

En 1996, la Commission des Nations Unies pour le droit commercial international (CNUDCI) a entrepris des travaux sur les projets d'infrastructure à financement privé. En 2000, elle a adopté un guide législatif portant sur ces projets.[1] Un an plus tard, la Commission a décidé de confier à un groupe de travail l'élaboration de dispositions législatives types afin de faciliter la mise en oeuvre des recommandations du *Guide législatif.* Les travaux du groupe de travail ont abouti à l'automne 2002 avec l'approbation d'un projet d'additif au *Guide législatif.*[2] Ce projet devait

---

Céline Lévesque, professeure agrégée, Faculté de droit, Université d'Ottawa.

[1] *Guide législatif de la CNUDCI sur les projets d'infrastructure à financement privé,* Nations Unies, New York, 2001, en ligne: <http://www.uncitral.org/french/texts/procurem/pfip-index-f.htm> (ci-après: *Guide législatif* ou *Guide*).

[2] Voir Projet d'additif au Guide législatif de la CNUDCI sur les projets d'infrastructure à financement privé — Note du secrétariat et annexe, Doc. A/CN.9/522 et A/CN.9/522/Add.1 respectivement, en ligne: <http://www.uncitral.org/french/sessions/unc/unc-36/acn9-522-f.pdf> (ci-après: Additif (Note)); <http://www.uncitral.org/french/sessions/unc/unc-36/acn9-522-addl-f.pdf> [ci-après: Additif (Annex)].

ensuite être soumis à la Commission pour examen et adoption en 2003.[3]

Ces travaux, dont l'achèvement aura requis une période d'environ sept ans, méritent d'être soulignés. D'abord, leur aboutissement coïncide avec l'intérêt accru porté à ce genre de projets dans plusieurs forums internationaux. On se rappellera notamment le "Consensus de Monterrey" (atteint en mars 2002 suite à la Conférence internationale sur le financement du développement) ainsi que le Plan d'action du Sommet mondial pour le développement durable (adopté à la suite du Sommet à Johannesburg en septembre 2002), qui tous deux soulignent l'importance pour le développement des partenariats entre les secteurs public et privé.[4] Aussi, en réponse au Nouveau Partenariat pour le développement de l'Afrique (NEPAD), le G-8 a adopté au Sommet de Kananaskis en 2002 un Plan d'action qui vise à encourager l'investissement direct étranger à destination de l'Afrique, notamment à travers des partenariats entre les secteurs public et privé.[5] Il est à noter que l'expression "partenariats public-privé," souvent utilisée dans le contexte de projets d'infrastructure à financement privé, est un euphémisme pour privatisation.

Par ailleurs, ces projets ont connu une croissance phénoménale dans les années 1990. Selon des données de la Banque mondiale, quelque 2 500 projets impliquant la participation du secteur privé dans les infrastructures de plus de 132 pays en développement ont été exécutés de 1990 à 2001. Ces projets ont mobilisé des investissements de quelque 750 milliards de dollars (US).[6]

---

[3] Le projet de dispositions a effectivement été adopté, sans changements substantiels notables, par la Commission à l'été 2003. Voir Rapport de la Commission des Nations Unies pour le droit commercial international sur les travaux de sa trente-sixième session, 30 juin-11 juillet 2003, AG NU, Doc. off., 58e session, supp. n° 17. Doc. A/58/17, en ligne: <http://www.uncitral.org/french/sessions/unc/unc-36/36-index-f.htm>.

[4] Voir, par exemple, Nations Unies, Conférence internationale sur le financement du développement, Adoption du Consensus de Monterrey, Doc. A/CONF.198/3, par. 20–21, en ligne: <http://www.un.org/french/esa/ffd/docs/aconf1983f.pdf>; et Plan d'application du Sommet mondial pour le développement durable, Doc. A/Conf.199/20, par. 47–50, en ligne: <http://www.agora21.org/johannesburg/rapports/plan-action.pdf>.

[5] Voir G-8, Plan d'action pour l'Afrique du G-8, Sommet Kananaskis, Canada 2002, Partie III, Section 3.1, en ligne: <http://www.g8.gc.ca/2002Kananaskis/kananaskis/afraction-fr.asp>.

[6] Voir World Bank, *Private Participation in Infrastructure—Trends in Developing Countries*, Washington, D.C., 2003, en ligne: <http://rru.worldbank.org/PPIbook/>.

Le *Guide législatif,* ainsi que les dispositions types, ont pour objet "d'aider à la mise en place d'un cadre juridique favorable à l'investissement privé dans les infrastructures publiques."[7] Avant de procéder à l'étude des préoccupations et valeurs sous-jacentes de ce guide et de son additif, il est utile de s'attarder aux types de projets visés ainsi qu'à la méthode d'intervention choisie par la CNUDCI.

De façon générale, le type d'arrangement visé par cette initiative est la "concession." Il prendra souvent la forme d'un contrat liant une entreprise privée à une autorité publique en vertu duquel la partie privée s'engage à faire certains investissements et à offrir un service public en contre-partie du droit de recevoir des redevances pour le service offert (payées directement par les usagers ou par l'État).[8] Les infrastructures publiques, dans ce contexte, sont définies comme des installations matérielles qui fournissent des services essentiels à la population notamment dans les secteurs de l'électricité, des télécommunications, de l'eau, de l'assainissement et des transports.[9]

La CNUDCI, dont le mandat est de faire avancer l'harmonisation et l'unification progressives du droit commercial international, fait appel à la méthode jugée la plus appropriée pour atteindre ses objectifs compte tenu de la matière.[10] Dans le cas des projets d'infrastructure à financement privé, il a été jugé qu'un guide législatif, accompagné de dispositions types, était plus approprié qu'une convention internationale, par exemple. Le *Guide législatif* adopté comporte soixante et onze recommandations, qui sont suivies de près de 250 pages d'explications et d'informations.[11] La lourdeur du Guide n'est probablement pas étrangère à la décision de la Commission de formuler par la suite des "orientations plus concrètes

---

[7] *Guide législatif, supra* note 1, Introduction, au par. 4. Voir aussi Additif (Annexe), *supra* note 2, avant-propos, p. 5.

[8] Voir, pour une définition plus complète, *Guide législatif, supra* note 1 aux pp. 3 et 30.

[9] *Ibid.* à la p. 4.

[10] En général, voir CNUDCI, *Un monde du commerce : vers un droit commercial unique,* en ligne: <http://www.uncitral.org/french/commiss/geninfo-f.htm>.

[11] La liste des sujets couverts par le *Guide, supra* note 1, comprend: Introduction et informations générales sur les projets d'infrastructure à financement privé; I. Cadre législatif et institutionnel général; II. Risques de projet et appui des pouvoirs publics; III. Sélection du concessionnaire; IV. Construction et exploitation de l'infrastructure: cadre législatif et accord de projet; V. Durée, prorogation et résiliation de l'accord projet; VI. Règlement des différends; VII. Autres domaines pertinents du droit.

sous forme de dispositions législatives types."[12] Ces dispositions types, au nombre de cinquante et une, ne couvrent pas tous les sujets abordés dans le *Guide*. L'accent est placé sur la sélection du concessionnaire et sur le contrat de concession. Somme toute, il s'agit d'un instrument souple, qui a soin de ne pas imposer à un système juridique (de droit civil ou de Common Law, par exemple) des notions qui lui seraient étrangères ou même antinomiques.

La lecture du *Guide*, et de son additif, révèle une sensibilité à certaines préoccupations de forme et de fond. Quant à la forme, on reconnaît que ces instruments font nécessairement partie d'un ensemble plus large. Bien que l'intégration des dispositions types à des textes visant spécifiquement les projets d'infrastructure à financement privé soit visée, on admet que le succès de tels projets dépend non seulement de l'adéquation du cadre juridique général du pays hôte de l'investissement, mais aussi de ses moyens organisationnels, des compétences des autorités publiques, ainsi que de la stabilité de l'économie, pour ne mentionner que ces facteurs.[13] Parmi les domaines du droit ayant un effet potentiel sur ces projets, on mentionne notamment la promotion et la protection des investissements (dont les traités bilatéraux), le droit des biens (dont la garantie des droits de propriété privée) et le droit des sûretés (dont la protection juridique des créanciers).

Quant au fond, ces instruments témoignent d'une orientation "pro-concurrence" et de recherche d'équilibre entre les intérêts des investisseurs, d'une part, et l'intérêt général du pays, d'autre part. Le penchant pour la concurrence prend différentes formes. On le reconnaît dans les conseils liés aux structures de marché et aux réformes sectorielles,[14] mais aussi dans les procédures de sélection des concessionnaires. À cet égard, le *Guide législatif* "exprime une préférence pour l'emploi de procédures de sélection avec mise en compétition, tout en reconnaissant que des concessions peuvent parfois être attribuées sans recourir à ce type de procédure, conformément à la tradition juridique du pays concerné."[15] Il est toutefois clair, dans le *Guide* comme dans l'additif, que l'attribution de concessions sans procédure de mise en compétition devrait être réservée à des cas exceptionnels.[16]

[12] Additif (Note), *supra* note 2 à la p. 2, para. 2.

[13] Additif (Annexe), *supra* note 2, Avant-propos, p. 5.

[14] Voir *Guide législatif, supra* note 1 aux pp. 7-14.

[15] *Ibid.* à la p. 67.

[16] *Ibid.* aux pp. 95-96. Voir aussi, Additif (Annexe), *supra* note 2, disposition type 18.

Les conseils donnés dans ces instruments visent à concilier l'intérêt des investisseurs et l'intérêt général.[17] Aussi, guidés par plusieurs valeurs, dont la transparence, l'équité et la viabilité à long terme, ces instruments cherchent à répondre aux préoccupations des parties prenantes à la relation d'investissement.[18] La promotion de la transparence, qui profite non seulement aux investisseurs mais à la population de façon générale, est omniprésente dans les procédures de sélection des concessionnaires. De nombreuses obligations de publicité et de partage d'information font foi de cette valeur.[19] Le souci d'équité se reflète à diverses étapes des projets d'infrastructure, de la sélection du concessionnaire jusqu'à la conclusion du contrat de concession. À titre d'exemple, il est prévu que le contrat de concession énoncera "selon qu'il convient, l'étendue des obligations imposées au concessionnaire pour assurer: a) la modification du service afin de répondre à la demande de ce service; b) la continuité du service; c) la fourniture du service dans des conditions essentiellement identiques pour tous les usagers;" etc.[20] Enfin, les procédures de révision des contrats de concession illustrent la recherche de viabilité à long terme de ce type de projet. Il n'est pas rare que les projets d'infrastructure à financement privé se déroulent sur une période de dix, vingt ou même trente ans. Dans ces conditions, on tente d'assurer à la fois la stabilité, mais aussi la flexibilité de la relation d'investissement.[21]

Il est évidemment trop tôt pour évaluer le succès de cette initiative de la CNUDCI. Toutefois, on peut penser qu'elle possède un bel avenir, compte tenu des efforts pour faire du *Guide* et de l'additif des instruments souples, offrant une approche ouverte, globale et équilibrée.

II L'AFFAIRE *POPE & TALBOT:* LA SUITE

En mai 2002, le Tribunal dans l'affaire *Pope & Talbot* a rendu une sentence dans laquelle il ordonne au Gouvernement du Canada de payer à l'investisseur un montant d'un peu plus de 460 000 $ à titre

---

[17] Voir, notamment, *Guide législatif, supra* note 1 à la p. 2.

[18] Voir Additif (Annexe), *supra* note 2, disposition type 1 (préambule).

[19] Voir, à titre d'illustration, les dispositions types 6 et 13, Additif (Annexe), *supra* note 2.

[20] Additif (Annexe), *supra* note 2, disposition type 38.

[21] Voir *ibid.*, disposition type 40.

de dommages et intérêts.[22] Dans cette affaire, le Tribunal formé sous le régime du Chapitre 11 de l'ALÉNA avait rendu deux sentences sur le fond, en 2000 et 2001.[23] Dans cette dernière sentence, il avait déclaré que le Canada avait agi en violation de ses obligations en vertu de l'article 1105 de l'ALÉNA portant sur la norme minimale de traitement.

On se souviendra des faits dans cette affaire.[24] L'investisseur, Pope & Talbot, s'est plaint de la façon dont le Canada avait mis en oeuvre l'Accord sur le bois d'oeuvre résineux entre le Canada et les États-Unis. En vertu de cet Accord, un système de quotas à l'exportation avait été établi, en échange duquel les États-Unis s'étaient engagés à ne pas entreprendre certaines actions contre le Canada. Finalement, le Tribunal a retenu un seul des arguments présentés par Pope & Talbot, ayant trait à ce qu'il a appelé le "Verification Review Episode."[25] Après avoir décrit en détails cet épisode, le Tribunal a conclu, notamment que Pope & Talbot avait été l'objet de menaces en ce qui concerne l'obtention de quotas, qu'on lui avait refusé des demandes raisonnables d'informations, qu'elle avait été obligée de faire des dépenses inutiles et avait subi des perturbations en se pliant aux exigences du gouvernement.[26] Ce traitement, selon le Tribunal, dépassait de loin les erreurs et les accrocs auxquels on pouvait s'attendre d'un processus administratif et constituait "nothing less than a denial of the fair treatment required by NAFTA Article 1105."[27] Sur cette base, le Tribunal a conclu que le Canada était responsable des dommages subis par l'investisseur.

Ce qui est notable dans la sentence rendue en 2002 est moins le montant ou même le calcul des dommages accordés, que l'analyse et les remarques faites par le Tribunal. En effet, la sentence présente un intérêt certain quant aux pouvoirs d'interprétation de la

---

[22] *Pope & Talbot Inc.* v. *Canada*, Award in respect of damages (2002), 41 I.L.M. 1347 (sentence rendue le 31 mai 2002), en ligne: http://www.dfait-maeci.gc.ca/tna-nac/documents/damage_award.pdf (ci-après: Sentence — dommages).

[23] *Pope & Talbot Inc.* c. *Canada*, Interim Award (2001), 40 I.L.M. 258 (sentence rendue le 26 juin 2000) et Award on the Merits of Phase II (2001), (sentence rendue le 10 avril 2001), en ligne, respectivement: <http://www.dfait-maeci. gc.ca/tna-nac/pubdoc7.pdf> et <http://www.dfait-maeci.gc.ca/tna-nac/ Award_Merits-e.pdf>.

[24] Voir C. Lévesque, "Chronique de Droit international économique en 2000 — Investissement" (2002) 39 A.C.D.I. 463 aux pp. 465-66.

[25] Voir *Pope & Talbot Phase II, supra* note 23 aux par. 156-81.

[26] *Ibid.* au par. 181.

[27] *Ibid.*

Commission du libre-échange, quant à l'existence des travaux préparatoires de l'ALÉNA, et quant au seuil "minimal" permettant de conclure à une violation de l'article 1105.

En vertu de l'article 1131(2) de l'ALÉNA, "[u]ne interprétation faite par la Commission [du libre-échange] d'une disposition du présent accord liera un tribunal établi en vertu de la présente section." Le 31 juillet 2001, la Commission a notamment interprété l'article 1105.[28] Sans que le texte en fasse mention, il est évident que l'interprétation a été fortement motivée par un mécontentement face à la sentence rendue en avril 2001 dans l'affaire *Pope & Talbot*. Aussi, les Parties à l'ALÉNA ont choisi, à ce moment, "d'éclaircir et de réaffirmer la signification de certaines dispositions de l'Accord," dont l'article 1105.[29]

Une première difficulté découle du fait que cette note d'interprétation a été émise entre la sentence concluant à la violation de l'article 1105 et la sentence évaluant les dommages découlant de cette violation dans l'affaire *Pope & Talbot*. Ensuite, l'interprétation de la Commission contredit résolument celle du Tribunal, ce qui mène ce dernier à se poser la question de savoir s'il s'agit véritablement d'une "interprétation" ou plutôt d'un amendement irrégulier de l'ALÉNA par les Parties. À travers un raisonnement sinueux, le Tribunal en arrive à la conclusion qu'il n'a pas à trancher cette question, mais que s'il avait eu à le faire, il aurait conclu qu'il s'agissait d'un amendement au Traité.[30] Le Tribunal a donc procédé comme si une "interprétation" avait été émise et s'est ensuite demandé si cette dernière avait un effet rétroactif. Il a décidé que l'interprétation était obligatoire même pour ce Tribunal.[31]

Quant à l'existence des travaux préparatoires, d'aucuns seront surpris d'apprendre qu'ils existent après tout! À la recherche de la "véritable" interprétation de l'article 1105, le Tribunal avait lors des procédures dans cette affaire demandé à ce que ces documents soient produits. Le Canada, selon le Tribunal, avait alors nié l'existence de travaux préparatoires notamment au sujet de l'article 1105.[32] Suite à l'obtention de certaines informations, le Tribunal a

---

[28] Commission du libre-échange de l'ALÉNA, *Notes d'interprétation de certaines dispositions du chapitre 11*, en ligne: <http://www.dfait-maeci.gc.ca/tna-nac/NAFTA-Interpr-fr.asp> (ci-après: Notes d'interprétation).

[29] *Ibid.*

[30] Sentence — dommages, *supra* note 22 au par. 47.

[31] *Ibid.* au par. 51.

[32] Voir *ibid.* aux par. 28 et s.

de nouveau demandé au Canada de produire ces travaux. Finalement, le 12 avril 2002, le Canada produisait quelque 1 500 pages
de documents, comportant plus de quarante versions de l'article
1105.[33] Il va sans dire que le Tribunal ne s'est pas privé d'exprimer
son mécontentement.[34]

Le dernier tour de force du Tribunal a été d'interpréter à nouveau l'article 1105, compte tenu de l'interprétation de la Commission, de façon à confirmer que le Canada avait tout de même violé
cet article.[35] Ce faisant, le Tribunal a réussi à maintenir sa position selon laquelle le "seuil" de la norme minimale de traitement
n'était pas aussi élevé que le Canada le prétendait. Le Tribunal a
fini par conclure que même en appliquant les normes suggérées
par le Canada, il serait arrivé à la même conclusion.[36]

Les rebondissements dans cette affaire ont été nombreux. Somme
toute, des dommages relativement mineurs ont été accordés à l'investisseur pour une violation du Traité qui s'est produite après
la notification par l'investisseur de son intention de soumettre une
plainte à l'arbitrage.[37] Des années et plusieurs milliers de dollars
ont été dépensés pour arriver à une conclusion qui est à tout le
moins discutable.[38] Cette affaire a malheureusement laissé plus de
questions en suspens qu'elle en a réglé.

III   ADOPTION DU *TRADE PROMOTION AUTHORITY ACT* AUX
      ÉTATS-UNIS

L'adoption aux États-Unis du "Bipartisan Trade Promotion Authority Act of 2002"[39] (TPA) est digne de mention. Connue précédemment sous le nom de "fast-track," cette législation facilite la
négociation par l'administration d'accords commerciaux en permettant uniquement au Congrès d'accepter ou de rejeter dans
l'ensemble le résultat des négociations. Le TPA fixe toutefois certains objectifs de négociation qui méritent examen.

---

[33] *Ibid.* au par. 38.

[34] *Ibid.* aux par. 39-42.

[35] Voir *ibid.* aux par. 52 et s.

[36] *Ibid.* aux par. 65-69.

[37] Voir *Pope & Talbot Phase II, supra* note 23 aux par. 156 et s.

[38] Voir notamment, C. Lévesque, *supra* note 24 aux pp. 466-67 où est présentée une
critique de l'interprétation faite par le Tribunal.

[39] *Bipartisan Trade Promotion Authority Act of 2002*, Trade Act of 2002, P.L. 107-210,
Aug. 2, 2002, en ligne: <http://www.sice.oas.org/Trade/tradeact/act7.asp>.

En matière d'investissement étranger, le TPA énonce:

Recognizing that United States law on the whole provides a high level of protection for investment, consistent with or greater than the level required by international law, the principal negotiating objectives of the United States regarding foreign investment are to reduce or eliminate artificial or trade-distorting barriers to foreign investment, *while ensuring that foreign investors in the United States are not accorded greater substantive rights with respect to investment protections than United States investors in the United States,* and to secure for investors important rights *comparable to* those that would be available under United States legal principles and practice, by . . .[40]

Cette disposition prévoit ensuite en plus de détails les moyens à utiliser pour atteindre ces objectifs, par exemple en matière d'expropriation et de traitement "juste et équitable." Dans ces cas, l'idée dominante de la référence à des standards proprement américains revient.

Ces développements chez nos voisins du Sud sont notables pour plusieurs raisons. D'abord, les objectifs du TPA se refléteront dans les positions de négociation des Américains dans le cadre de la Zone de libre-échange des Amériques (ZLÉA) et, éventuellement, de l'Organisation mondiale du commerce (OMC).[41] Ensuite, on sait déjà que le TPA a influencé les négociations bilatérales américaines avec le Chili et Singapour. Les accords de libre-échange en cours de négociation avec ces pays en 2002 comportaient des dispositions sur l'investissement reflétant les objectifs précités.[42] Aussi, on peut s'attendre à ce que le "model BIT" (bilateral investment treaty) américain, en cours de révision, suive les grandes lignes tracées par le TPA et développées dans les accords de libre-échange avec le Chili et Singapour.[43] Compte tenu du fait que le Canada suit le "modèle ALÉNA" dans le cadre de son programme de traités d'investissement bilatéraux, et que le Chapitre 11 de l'ALÉNA avait largement été inspiré par le modèle bilatéral américain, ce

---

[40] *Ibid.* à l'art. 2102(b)(3) (notre souligné).

[41] Sur la négociation d'accords couvrant les investissements dans ces forums, voir C. Lévesque, "Chronique de Droit international économique en 2001 — Investissement" (2003) 40 A.C.D.I. 453.

[42] Ces deux accords ont effectivement été conclus en 2003, voir US-Chile Free Trade Agreement, en ligne: <http://www.ustr.gov/new/fta/Chile/final/index. htm>; et US-Singapore Free Trade Agreement, en ligne: <http://www.mti.gov. sg/public/FTA/frm_FTA_Default.asp?sid=36>.

[43] Voir Inside U.S. Trade, Vol. 20, No. 39, 27 septembre 2002, Introduction et pp. 18 et s.

développement soulèvera plusieurs interrogations pour le Canada. Finalement, on peut se questionner quant aux répercussions indirectes que ces développements pourraient avoir sur l'interprétation de l'ALÉNA.

CONCLUSION

Les questions diverses posées par les instruments, décisions et lois qui ont fait l'objet d'une description dans cette chronique auront un intérêt pour le Canada durant plusieurs années à venir. Reste à voir de quelle façon le Canada choisira de relever les défis de l'harmonisation, du règlement des différends internationaux investisseur-État et de la tendance américaine à vouloir imposer des normes nationales dans l'arène internationale.

Canadian Practice in International Law /
Pratique canadienne en matière de
droit international

At the Department of Foreign Affairs and International Trade in 2002-3 / Au ministère des Affaires étrangères en 2002-3

compiled by / préparé par
COLLEEN SWORDS

INTERNATIONAL ENVIRONMENTAL LAW

Legal Status of Decisions Made by Multilateral Environmental Agreement (MEA) Conference of the Parties (COPs)

In November 2002, the Legal Bureau wrote:

Prima facie, decisions made by consensus or vote of Conferences of Parties [COPs] created by MEAs [multilateral environmental agreements] do not fit within the framework of recognized sources of international law (treaty or customary international law) and, hence, as a technical matter do not create legally enforceable obligations on states. Decisions of COPs may provide influential understandings of the wording of a constitutive treaty and, therefore, as subsequent acts of states concerning a treaty will be of considerable importance in treaty interpretation and application.

While the *prima facie* situation is against decisions of COPs having direct legal status, where a constitutive treaty provides direct authority to the COP to amend or add to the legal obligations contained in the

Colleen Swords, Legal Advisor, Department of Foreign Affairs and International Trade, Ottawa. The extracts from official correspondence contained in this survey have been made available by courtesy of the Department of Foreign Affairs and International Trade. Some of the correspondence from which the extracts are given was provided for the general guidance of the enquirer in relation to specific facts that are often not described in full in the extracts within this compilation. The statements of law and practice should not necessarily be regarded as definitive.

constitutive treaty then the actions taken by the COP pursuant to this grant of authority would create legal responsibilities. It is not uncommon for some constitutive treaties to provide for the addition of species or substances to endangered or hazard lists in treaty annexes by COP decisions or similar mechanisms. Such actions by COPs, mandated by the constitutive treaty, would have binding effect on all parties to the constitutive treaty subject to any opt-out authority or ratification process that may exist respecting such actions.

Meaning of "Voluntary Participation" in the Kyoto Protocol

In May 2003, the Legal Bureau wrote:

[W]hat do the words "voluntary participation" mean in the context of Art 12 of the Kyoto Protocol, and in particular, what obligations [does] Art 12(5)(a) imposes on ... [States] in approving projects under the Clean Development Mechanism.

Article 12 of the Kyoto Protocol establishes the "clean development mechanism" (CDM), one of three mechanisms created under the Protocol to allow Annex I Parties to obtain credit for the reduction of greenhouse gas emissions abroad. Article 12(2) reads:

> The purpose of the clean development mechanism shall be to assist Parties not included in Annex I in achieving sustainable development and in contributing to the ultimate objective of the Convention, and to assist Parties in Annex I in achieving compliance with their quantified emission limitation and reduction commitments under Article 2.

The CDM thus allows Annex I Parties ... to implement projects in non-Annex I Parties (developing countries) that will lead to reduced greenhouse gas emissions (presumably at lower cost than at home). These projects may be implemented by private and/or public entities, and are subject to guidance by the Executive Board. The "certified emission reductions" (CERs) that are generated by such projects can then be used by Annex I Parties to meet their greenhouse gas emission reduction obligations. In return the developing country Party that is the "host country" of the project has the benefit of a project that helps it meet its sustainable development goals.

Art. 12(5)(a) provides that participation in a CDM project is "voluntary." Art. 12(5) reads as follows:

> Emission reductions resulting from each project activity shall be certified by operational entities to be designated by the Conference of the Parties serving as the meeting of the Parties to this Protocol, *on the basis of:*
> (a) *Voluntary participation approved by each Party involved;*
> (b) Real, measurable, and long-term benefits related to the mitigation of climate change; and
> (c) Reductions in emissions that are additional to any that would occur in the absence of the certified project activity. (emphasis added)

Although at first glance it might appear that the use of word "voluntary" is unnecessary, in the sense that no State could be forced to accept a project contrary to its domestic policy or law, it is helpful to bear in mind the negotiating history of this provision. It is generally understood that the origins of Article 12(5) can be traced to a Brazilian proposal that would have imposed financial penalties on Annex I Parties that failed to comply with their emission reduction obligations. The Brazilian proposal would have allowed the funds so acquired to be accessed "on a voluntary basis" by non-Annex I Parties for climate change projects. This text appears to have been inserted to address a concern of a number of developing countries, as expressed during negotiation of the Kyoto Protocol, that the CDM would be used as a mechanism to force developed country priorities on them, instead of as a means to allow developing countries to meet their own sustainable development priorities. As a result, the texts make it abundantly clear that it is open to either Party participating in a CDM project to establish the conditions for approving "voluntary participation" that it views as appropriate.

Modalities and Procedures

Although the Protocol establishes the basic features of the Clean Development Mechanism, detailed elaboration was left for further negotiation. These negotiations culminated in the various decisions and draft decisions that compose the Marrakesh accords. The "modalities and procedures" for the clean development mechanism are to be found in Decision 17/CP.7, and the draft decision CMP.1. The "voluntary" nature of host country participation in CDM projects is reflected in these texts. Decision 17/CP.7 affirms "that it is the host Party's prerogative to confirm whether a clean development mechanism project activity assists it in achieving sustainable development." Section F of draft decision CMP.1 reiterates in paragraph 28 that "participation in a CDM project activity is voluntary."

In addition to the criteria of "voluntary participation," paragraph 33 of the draft decision referred to above also provides that a Party that authorizes private and/or public entities to participate in Article 12 projects shall ensure that such participation is consistent with the Annex to CMP.1. In addition, paragraph 40 effectively requires project participants to provide "written approval of voluntary participation from the designated national authority of each Party involved, including confirmation by the Host Party that the project activity assists it in achieving sustainable development" to the "designated operational entity."

Meaning of "State Not Party to This Protocol" in the Montreal Protocol

In September 2003, the Legal Bureau wrote:

The question has arisen whether a Party to the Beijing amendment may import and export HCFCs to and from a State that is not Party to both the Beijing and Copenhagen amendments and, if so, under what circumstances . . . The Montreal Protocol on Substances That Deplete the Ozone

Layer is an international agreement aimed at reversing the damage done to the stratospheric ozone layer that protects the earth from harmful solar ultraviolet radiation. The Protocol was adopted in 1987 and came into force on 1 January 1989, and currently has 184 Parties. The focus of the Protocol is the control of production and consumption of ozone depleting substances. The Protocol can be tightened or "adjusted" by amendment as the scientific evidence strengthens. The control provisions of the Protocol have been adjusted through amendments adopted in London (1990), Copenhagen (1992), Vienna (1995), Montreal (1997) and Beijing (1999).

Two amendments impose control measures on HCFCs. HCFCs are the less-ozone depleting replacement for CFCs that have almost been phased out under the Montreal Protocol.

The 1992 Copenhagen Amendment introduced HCFCs to the list of substances subject to control, specifically by imposing control measures on the *consumption* of HCFCs. The 1999 Beijing Amendment imposed further control measures on HCFC *production* beginning in 2004. The Beijing Amendment also bans trade of HCFCs with non-Parties as provided in Article 4 paragraph 1 quin and paragraph 2 quin, which respectively read as follows:

> Paragraph 1 quin: As of 1 January 2004, each Party shall ban the *import* of the controlled substances in Group 1 of Annex C [i.e. HCFC's where the control measures are applicable to both production and consumption] from any State not party to this Protocol.
> Paragraph 2 quin: As of 1 January 2004, each Party shall ban the *export* of the controlled substances in Group 1 of Annex C [i.e. HCFC's where the control measures are applicable to both production and consumption] to any State not party to this Protocol.

The term "State not party to this Protocol" is defined in Article 4(9), which reads:

> For the purpose of this Article, the term "State not party to this Protocol" shall include, with respect to a particular controlled substance, a State or regional economic integration organization that has not agreed to be bound by the control measures in effect for that substance.

As a result, when an amendment imposes control measures for a particular substance, a State that "has not agreed to be bound" by that amendment is to be treated as a non-Party under the Protocol as regards trade in that particular substance. Canada is Party to both the Copenhagen and Beijing Amendments ... Our legal analysis supports [that] ... the correct interpretation of Article 4(9) of the Montreal Protocol ... [is that] "Any State not a party to this Protocol" as used in Article 4 paragraph 1 quin and paragraph 2 quin of the Beijing Amendment and defined in Article 4(9) is a State that is not a Party to the Beijing Amendment. The result of this is that a Beijing Party can only import/export HCFCs from other Beijing Parties and a non-Beijing Party can only import/export HCFCs from non-Beijing Parties.

Article 4(9) directs that, for the purposes of trade measures under Article 4 of the Montreal Protocol, a non-Party is one "which has not agreed to be bound by the control measures in effect" for a particular substance. Both the Copenhagen Amendment and the Beijing Amendment create "control measures." The use of the wording "*the* control measures," as opposed to "*a* control measure," indicates that all control measures are to be accepted for a State to avoid non-Party status. Moreover, the phraseology in 4(9) indicates that control measures are those "in effect" for particular substances. The phrase "in effect" is tied to "to be bound" (which is a legal consideration) and, thus on its face means in effect legally at the international level. Therefore, in our opinion, "has not agreed to be bound by the control measures in effect" in Article 4(9) can only mean that a non-Party is a State which has not agreed to *all* the control measures internationally legally applicable ("in effect"). A State not a Party to the Beijing Amendment "has not agreed to be bound by the control measures in effect" and, therefore, for the purposes of the trade ban in the Beijing Amendment, must be considered a "State not Party to this Protocol."

Because "not a Party to this Protocol" is defined in Article 4(9), it is unnecessary to have recourse to the general international law of treaties. However, the above result does accord with the international law of treaties which provides that a non-Party to an instrument (e.g. an amendment) is a State which has not ratified, acceded or otherwise consented to the instrument ... Parties to the Beijing Amendment are legally required to ban trade in HCFCs with States that are "not party" to the Protocol. States not Party to the Protocol are defined as including States that have "not agreed to be bound by the control measures in effect" for HCFCs. As both the Copenhagen and Beijing amendments create "control measures" for HCFCs and both these amendments are "in effect," it is our opinion that Parties to Beijing may not trade in HCFCs with States that are not Party to both Beijing and Copenhagen.

Are Manufactured Products Covered by the Rotterdam Convention?

In January 2004, the Legal Bureau wrote:

The Rotterdam Convention makes prior informed consent procedures for certain industrial chemicals and pesticides legally binding. Since the late 1980s, there has been a voluntary prior informed consent procedure pursuant to the FAO International Code of Conduct and the UNEP London Amended Guidelines. When the Rotterdam Convention was adopted in 1998, a Resolution on Interim Arrangements that modified the FAO/UNEP voluntary prior informed consent procedure to bring it into conformity with the Convention regime was also adopted. Thus, since 1999 the Convention regime on prior informed consent has been operating, albeit on a voluntary basis.

There is no explicit reference in the operative wording of the Rotterdam Convention to goods, products or manufactured products. All relevant references are to "chemicals." In an early draft of the Rotterdam Convention, the term "products" was used but in all cases the term was either dropped or changed to "chemicals."

However, the second preambular paragraph reads:

Recalling the pertinent provisions of the Rio Declaration ... and Chapter 19 of Agenda 21 on 'Environmentally sound management of toxic chemicals, including prevention of illegal international traffic in toxic and dangerous *products* (emphasis added).

The negotiating text that emerged from the third INC had a footnote that "chemical products" might have to be defined in the definitions section. The completed text does not contain such a definition.

Article 3(1) of the Rotterdam Convention provides that the Convention applies to: banned or severely restricted chemicals and severely hazardous pesticide formulations. It has been noted that these two categories of chemicals were what was covered by the UNEP Amended London Guidelines and the FAO International Code of Conduct. Certain types of chemicals are excluded from the Rotterdam Convention pursuant to Article 3(2). The Article 3(2) exclusion also covers "radioactive materials," "chemical weapons," "pharmaceuticals" and "food," which are not types of chemicals *per se* but products wherein chemicals may be a component. However, Article 3(2) can be read as ensuring that the Rotterdam Convention does not deal with substances dealt with elsewhere and significantly different than the industrial chemicals and pesticides that are the aim of the Convention.

Regarding the two categories covered by the Rotterdam Convention: a "banned chemical" is defined in Article 2(b), a "severely restricted chemical" in Article 2(c) and a "severely hazardous pesticide formulation" in Article 2(d). The common element in all three definitions is that reference is made to a "chemical" that is defined in Article 2(a) as:

a substance whether by itself or in a mixture or preparation and whether manufactured or obtained from nature, but does not include any living organism. It consists of the following categories: pesticide (including severely hazardous pesticide formulations) and industrial.

Prima facie, unless "a mixture or preparation" can be interpreted to stretch to products or goods containing a chemical, manufactured products containing a listed chemical are not be covered by the Rotterdam Convention. The key wording in the definition of a chemical, "a substance whether by itself or in a mixture or preparation and whether manufactured or obtained from nature," is virtually identical to the definition of wording in the UNEP Amended London Guidelines. Products containing a chemical were not covered by the UNEP Amended London Guidelines.

The obligations on the exporter outlined in Article 11 as regards prior informed consent relate only to "chemicals listed in Annex III" and the obligations in Article 12 regarding export notification relate only to "a chemical." Moreover, the obligation on importers in Article 10 relates only to "chemicals listed in Annex III." There is nothing in these provisions that can be said to create obligations that extend beyond what is defined as a chemical in Article 2(a). Quite clearly, the negotiators could have included language indicating that the prior informed consent regime applies to products containing a certain chemical but did not do so.

Note should also be made of Article 13(1) that directs the Conference of the Parties to encourage the assignment of customs codes to chemicals listed in Annex III. This points strongly to the conclusion that what is covered by the Rotterdam Convention is the trade in the chemical itself (which is to be assigned a customs code) and not products containing the chemical that would have other customs codes. Moreover, there is no wording in the Convention suggesting that a good or product should be labelled or documented to indicate that it contains (or may contain) an Annex III listed chemical. Such a provision would be expected if manufacturing goods containing Annex III listed chemicals were covered by the Convention.

In the absence of clear language including manufactured products in the Rotterdam Convention:

- the removal of all references to "products" in the negotiating documents;
- the non-inclusion of "products" in the UNEP Amended London Guidelines and the FAO International Code of Conduct;
- the practice during the interim period of only dealing with chemicals and not products containing such chemicals; and
- the definition of a chemical in Article 2(a) and the use of chemical throughout the Convention;

all support the conclusion that manufactured goods containing chemicals listed in Annex III are not covered by the Rotterdam Convention and the obligations in the Rotterdam Convention regarding prior informed consent do not apply when a manufactured product containing a chemical listed in Annex III is traded internationally.

INTERNATIONAL DISPUTE RESOLUTION

Dispute Settlement Procedures under the Madrid Protocol on Environmental Protection

In March 2003, the Legal Bureau wrote:

Articles 18-20 [of the Madrid Protocol on Environmental Protection] deal with the issue of dispute resolution. Article 18 provides that any dispute regarding the interpretation or application of the Protocol shall be resolved between the disputing Parties themselves through an initial request for consultations by one of the Parties, with a view to employing mediation, conciliation, etc., as those disputing Parties themselves deem appropriate. Article 20 stipulates that any dispute dealing with particular enumerated provisions of the Protocol that has not been resolved within twelve months of the initial request for consultations shall be referred, should any disputing Party so request, to the dispute resolution procedure outlined under Article 19 (4) and (5).

Article 19 provides that at the time of signature or ratification of the Protocol, or any time afterwards, a Party may indicate its preference to have disputes with another Party arising under the Protocol dealt with in the International Court of Justice and/or the Arbitral Tribunal established under the Protocol. Articles 19(4) and (5) then set out a somewhat complicated formula that results in either the ICJ or the Tribunal having binding jurisdiction to resolve disputes not settled between the Parties, if one or both Parties so choose. It should be noted that this is a more robust dispute settlement provision than is common to most multilateral environmental agreements.

[E]ven if [a State Party] ... does not elect a dispute resolution procedure at the time of ratification, it may do so at any time afterwards, by depositing a declaration with the depositary. Accordingly, even if a dispute arose between ... Parties regarding the interpretation or application of the protocol, nothing in the Protocol prevents ... [a State Party], at that time, from making such an election. In other words, as long as a decision was made prior to the expiry of the twelve month deadline for consultations ... [a State Party] would not be prejudiced in any way by delaying its decision regarding forum election. The "deadline" for ... [a State Party] to select a forum would be before the expiration of twelve months following the request for consultations to or by ... [a State Party] in a particular matter. Once the twelve month period is up, the other disputing Party may refer the matter for resolution to either the Arbitral Tribunal or the ICJ, in accordance with paragraphs 4 and 5 of Article 19.

If the parties to a dispute have not accepted the same means for the settlement of a dispute, or if they have both accepted both means, the dispute may be submitted only to the Arbitral Tribunal, "unless the parties otherwise agree." Art. 19(3) provides that the default forum would be the Tribunal if ... [a State Party] had not made a choice by that time.

The Schedule to the Protocol sets out in detail how the Arbitral Tribunal shall function. Each Party (regardless of the forum they select) is entitled to designate up to three Arbitrators to be registered on the list of Arbitrators. Importantly, Article 2 of the Schedule states that at least one of these must be designated within three months of the entry into force of the Protocol for the Party. When struck, the Arbitral Tribunal is to be composed of three members — one appointed by each Party (who can be their own national) and a third "outsider" to be mutually agreed upon.

INTERNATIONAL CRIMINAL TRIBUNAL FOR THE FORMER
YUGOSLAVIA: APPLICATION FOR ORDERS TO NATO AND STATE FOR
PRODUCTION OF INFORMATION

In February 2003, Canada submitted the following to the International Criminal Tribunal for the Former Yugoslavia in the case *The Prosecutor* v. *Nikola Sainovic and Dragoljub Ojdanic* (Case no. IT-99-37-PT):

1. On 15 November 2002, counsel for Dragoljub Ojdanic ("the Applicant") filed "General Ojdanic's Application for Orders to NATO and States for Production of Information" ("the Application"). The Application requested the Trial Chamber to issue an order directing NATO, its member States other than Norway and Portugal, the Republic of Croatia, Bosnia and Herzegovina, the Republic of Albania, the Former Yugoslav

Republic of Macedonia, Bulgaria and Romania ("the States concerned") to produce:

(A) All recordings, summaries, notes or text of any intercepted communications (electronic, oral or written) during the period 1 January through 20 June 1999, to which General Dragoljub Ojdanic was a party;

(B) All recordings, summaries, notes or text of any intercepted communications (electronic, oral or written) during the period 1 January through 20 June 1999, originating in the Federal Republic of Yugoslavia, and relating to Kosovo, in which General Dragoljub Ojdanic was mentioned or referred to in the communication; and

(C) All correspondence, memoranda, reports, recordings or summaries of any statements made by General Dragoljub Ojdanic during the period 1 January through 20 June 1999 to any representative of your organization, including sources of information working on your behalf...

OVERVIEW

3. The Government of Canada has been and remains a strong supporter of the International Criminal Tribunal for the former Yugoslavia ("the Tribunal"). Canada has cooperated consistently with the Tribunal and fully accepts the need for a robust, independent Tribunal with the power necessary to fulfill the mandate accorded to it. In furtherance of this mandate, Canada recognizes and supports the power of the Tribunal to issue orders to States for the production of evidence.

Security Council Resolution 827 (1993)

Statute of the Tribunal, Article 29

Rules of Procedure and Evidence, Rule 54 *bis*

4. At the same time, Canada also supports the conclusion of the Appeals Chamber in *Prosecutor* v. *Blaskic,* which indicated that the power of the Tribunal to issue orders for the production of evidence is not unlimited. Various grounds of objection may properly be raised to the issuance of such orders. Canada submits that, for sound reasons of judicial economy and to prevent abuse of its processes, the Tribunal should rigorously scrutinize applications to ensure *inter alia* that issuance of an order to States is necessary for a fair determination of a matter in issue, that orders are not unduly onerous, that orders are confined in scope to specific and relevant information, and that legitimate national security interests are respected.

Prosecutor v. *Tihomir Blaskic,* Judgement of the Appeals Chamber on the Request of the Republic of Croatia for Review of the Decision of Trial Chamber II of 18 July 1997 (*"Blaskic* Subpoena Decision"), paragraphs 32 and 67

Rule 54 *bis*

5. Canada submits that the Applicant has not satisfied the requirements for the issuance of an order. The order sought is not necessary for a fair

determination of a matter in issue, it is a classic "fishing expedition," and it would be extraordinary and unprecedented in terms of the "unduly onerous" burden it imposes on States, given the number of States affected, the breadth of the order, and the sensitive nature of the information sought. Alternatively, if an order is granted, it should be limited to specific, relevant information likely to assist the Applicant, and legitimate national security concerns should be addressed.

I. *The order sought is not necessary for a fair determination and should not be granted*

6. Rule 54 *bis* indicates that, for an order for production of evidence to be granted, it must be "necessary for a fair determination of a matter in issue in the proceedings." The necessity requirement was also affirmed by the Appeals Chamber in the *Blaskic* decision, where it held that "resort to mandatory compliance powers expressly given by Article 29(2) should be reserved for cases in which they are really necessary." Canada submits that rigorous scrutiny of the necessity of orders is essential for the efficient administration of justice, as well as to preserve Tribunal control over its processes.

Rule 54 *bis* (A) (ii) and (B) (i)

Prosecutor v. *Tihomir Blaskic,* Judgement of the Appeals Chamber on the Request of the Republic of Croatia for Review of the Decision of Trial Chamber II of 18 July 1997 (*"Blaskic* Subpoena Decision"), paragraph 31

7. In considering the necessity requirement, it is important to distinguish between the disclosure obligation incumbent upon the Prosecutor and orders to States for production of information. The broad principles relating to the former cannot be transposed to the latter. Given the Prosecutor's unique role as a party to the proceedings and a "minister of justice assisting in the administration of justice" (*Kordic and Cerkez*), and in order to promote equality of arms and transparent prosecutions, the Prosecutor's obligation of disclosure applies without an inquiry into necessity. Conversely, States are not an arm of the prosecution, they are third parties to the proceedings, and it cannot be presumed that they possess relevant information. Recognizing these distinctions, Rule 54 *bis* strikes an appropriate balance by requiring a determination of whether an order is necessary for a fair determination of a matter in issue in the proceedings.

Rule 54 *bis* (A) (ii) and (B) (i)

Blaskic Subpoena Decision, paragraph 31

Prosecutor v. *Kordic and Cerkez,* Decision on Motions to Extend Time for Filing Appellant's Briefs, 11 May 2001, paragraph 14

8. With respect to orders against States for production of evidence, mere speculation that relevant evidence might exist is insufficient. Concrete substantiation is needed to demonstrate the necessity of an order. As noted in the Appeals Chamber decision in *Delalic,* Separate Opinion of Judge David Hunt:

A party is not entitled to have an order made to produce material . . . simply because he says that the material is relevant to an issue in the trial or appeal. He is not entitled to conduct a fishing expedition — in the sense that he wishes to inspect the material in order to discover whether he has any case at all to make. An order to produce is not the same as obtaining discovery against a party.

Accordingly, a party seeking an order must show "that the party already has a case, and is not 'fishing' in the hope of establishing one." An applicant must demonstrate that the access sought "is likely to materially assist the case of the party seeking access, or that there is at least a good chance that it will give that assistance."

Prosecutor v. *Delalic,* Separate Opinion of Judge David Hunt on Motion by Esad Landzo to Preserve and Provide Evidence (*"Delalic,* Separate Opinion of Judge Hunt"), paragraphs 4 and 7

9. The Application is a classic "fishing expedition" as described in the passages quoted above. The Applicant has not established that there were any particular communications that could materially assist the defence. Instead, the Applicant is seeking a sweeping "discovery" process in the hopes of finding "whether he has any case at all to make." The Applicant has failed to establish the existence of specific information that is likely to materially assist the defence, and has failed to establish that the States concerned are likely to possess the information sought.

10. In addition, the Applicant has not shown why the evidence sought is not accessible to the defence without resort to an order against States. For example, the Applicant is in the best position to know what statements he made and what conversations he had. The Applicant has not shown why evidence of conversations to which General Ojdanic was a party cannot be introduced by other means, such as calling as witnesses the participants to those conversations.

Prosecutor v. *Kordic and Cerkez,* Decision on Motions to Extend Time for Filing Appellant's Briefs, 11 May 2001, paragraphs 9 & 21

Prosecutor v. *Blaskic,* Decision on the Appellant's Motion for the Production of Material, etc., 26 September 2000, paragraphs 38-39

11. In the context of the foregoing submissions, Canada wishes to emphasize that the right to a fair trial is in no way prejudiced by a denial of this order. The requirements of a fair trial are fully protected and respected in the Statute, Rules and practice of the Tribunal. While a fair trial entails a search for truth and the best evidence, this search is subject to a variety of reasonable limitations. The prohibition on fishing expeditions and the requirement that an applicant demonstrate the necessity of an order to States are appropriate limitations.

12. For all of these reasons, the necessity of resorting to an order against States has not been shown.

II. *The order sought is "unduly onerous" and should not be granted*

13. Tribunal jurisprudence also affirms that an order must not be "unduly onerous." This requires an assessment of the burden imposed and whether that burden is "disproportionate" or "not strictly justified by the exigencies of the trial." Thus, in addition to the basic necessity test for any order, an order that would impose an onerous burden on States requires particular justification. This requirement helps ensure that orders issued are appropriate, focused and effective in each given case. In this case, the burden that would be imposed by the order sought is unusually heavy, and no justification is offered.

Blaskic Subpoena Decision, paragraph 32

Prosecutor v. *Kordic and Cerkez,* Decision on the Request of the Republic of Croatia for Review of a Binding Order, 9 September 1999, paragraph 41

14. With respect to the burden imposed, the order sought is extraordinary in several respects:

(A) The order sought refers to broad categories, not specific documents.

(B) The order sought is directed against numerous States, thus multiplying the total resource demands that would be imposed by the order.

(C) Certain headings of the order sought are directed at information of the highest sensitivity, such as intercepted communications and human intelligence, which is particularly difficult to access, collate, and even to handle and to discuss internally.

(D) The order sought is directed against "concerned bystander" States that are not implicated in the activity under investigation.

The Appeals Chamber in *Blaskic* accepted the relevance of the distinction between "concerned bystanders" and States implicated in the activity under investigation. Bystander States are less likely to be the sole source of relevant information, and are even further removed from the proceedings, which is a further factor rendering recourse to mandatory compliance powers more exceptional. Canada submits that a very high level of justification is required for an order that is broad in scope, directed against numerous States that are not implicated in the activity under investigation, and targeting information of the highest sensitivity.

Blaskic Subpoena Decision, paragraphs 30, 32, 67

15. In assessing whether the burden imposed is justified, the Tribunal should also consider the precedent-setting effect of granting this extraordinary order. Given that the Application is based on mere speculation that the States concerned might have relevant information, any defendant will be able to make the same argument and therefore seek the same remedy. The resulting proliferation of orders of this nature would hamper the expeditious functioning of the Tribunal and would have extreme resource implications for States, straining their capacity to cooperate with Tribunal requests. It is therefore necessary and appropriate that such extraordinary orders only be granted where strictly justified.

16. The Applicant has not provided a justification for an order of this extraordinary nature, or indeed for any order, and therefore the order should not be granted.

III. *If an order is granted, its scope should be narrowed to specific, relevant information likely to materially assist the Applicant*

17. In the alternative, Canada submits that the scope of the order sought is inappropriately broad and should be narrowed. The order sought extends well beyond the grounds of relevance identified in the Application. The Applicant argues that evidence of statements made by or to General Ojdanic may be "directly relevant to show whether he in fact participated in any of the crimes, or in the joint criminal enterprise ... whether war crimes were reported to him or brought to his attention ... and to show his state of mind concerning the events occurring in Kosovo and the prevention and punishment of war crimes." However, the order sought, as worded, would encompass material bearing no relation to any of these grounds of relevance. For example, heading (B) requests intercepts of any conversation where General Ojdanic was "*mentioned,*" even in passing, and whether or not it has any bearing on the identified grounds of relevance.

Rule 54 *bis (A)*(i) and (ii)

Application, paragraph 15

18. Appropriately focused orders enable prompt cooperation from States and spare them from the expense, labour and delay of gathering and analyzing information that is ultimately not relevant to the proceedings. This is particularly important where an order may relate to national security information, as in the present case.

19. Canada submits that, in the event that an order is granted, it should (1) correspond to the grounds of relevance identified in paragraph 15 of the Application and (2) be limited to information likely to materially assist the defence. Canada submits that, in order to satisfy the requirement of specificity, the order should be further narrowed, by identifying particular pertinent conversations, communication or information.

Rule 54 *bis* (A) (i) and (ii)

Blaskic Subpoena Decision, paragraph 32 (*"Delalic,* Separate Opinion of Judge Hunt"), paragraphs 4 and 7

IV. *If an order is granted, legitimate national security interests must be addressed*

20. Canada accepts that States may not avoid their obligation to cooperate by a unilateral blanket assertion that national security is at stake; a State must identify, as far as possible, the basis on which its national interests would be prejudiced. At the same time, Tribunal jurisprudence has repeatedly affirmed the need to respect legitimate State concerns related to national security.

Blaskic Subpoena Decision, paragraphs 61, 65 and 67

Rule 54 *bis* (F)

Prosecutor v. *Milosevic*, Public Version of the Confidential Decision on the Prosecutor's Motion to Grant Specific Protections Pursuant to Rule 70 ("Rule 70 Decision"), Trial Chamber, paragraph 17 (overturned on other grounds)

Prosecutor v. *Milosevic*, Public Version of the Confidential Decision on the Interpretation and Application of Rule 70, Appeals Chamber, paragraph 19

21. Canada respectfully submits that, as a threshold test, before the Tribunal requests States to submit sensitive material for evaluation under Rule 54 *bis* (F) and (G), the Tribunal should consider whether the applicant has made a case for production that could in principle overcome the particular national security concerns identified. In particular, where a State (1) has provided compelling reasons for which its national security interests would be prejudiced by production, (2) has a history of *bona fide* cooperation with the Tribunal, and (3) is a bystander to the activity under investigation, the Tribunal should assess whether the applicant has demonstrated that the State is the best source or only source of information that is potentially critical for the adjudication of the guilt or innocence of the accused. Where this has not been demonstrated, the process of disclosing and examining sensitive information, even in *ex parte, in camera* proceedings, would seem unnecessary and should not be engaged.

(a) Objection in relation to intercepted communications and human intelligence

22. Canada objects in principle to production of some of the types of information sought in the Application, which are of particular sensitivity even within the general category of information whose disclosure could prejudice national security interests. With respect to headings (A) and (B) of the order sought, Canada emphasizes the extreme sensitivity of information relating to the existence or non-existence of intercepted communications. To disclose whether such information does or does not exist would cause serious prejudice to national security interests by potentially revealing the existence and capabilities of any intelligence programs, by jeopardizing methods and sources, or by potentially revealing which areas and subjects are or are not of surveillance interest. Similarly, if the last clause of heading (C) of the order sought ("including sources of information working on your behalf") is intended to include human intelligence, then the same considerations would apply, and discussion of such matters could put lives at risk and jeopardize a State's future capacity to collect information.

23. For these reasons, and without limiting consideration of other categories, production of information relating to intercepted communications or human intelligence would cause serious prejudice to national security interests. Such information is among the most sensitive forms of national security information, warranting a very circumspect approach, even in the context of *ex parte, in camera* hearings.

24. Canada does not lightly invoke national security concerns. Canada submits that its history of *bona fide* co-operation and assistance to the Tribunal and its consistent support for the work of the Tribunal are factors which should be taken into account in assessing its assurances. As an additional assurance, Canada is committed to the fundamental principle of the right to a fair trial, and, in the event that Canada were to possess information responsive to an order or a properly framed request, particularly if it were of an exculpatory character, Canada would explore means to share the necessary information and prevent a miscarriage of justice, without prejudicing its national security interests.

Blaskic Subpoena Decision, paragraph 68

25. Canada is a "bystander" to the activity under investigation, a factor which should give greater weight to the foregoing assurances. Bystanders are less likely to hold instructions, reports and other important evidence, and their assurances are likely more reliable, as they have little incentive to conceal information unless legitimate national security interests are indeed prejudiced.

Blaskic Subpoena Decision, paragraph 30

26. In the light of these specific concerns and assurances, Canada submits that the Applicant has not satisfied the threshold test for production of sensitive national security information.

(b) Objection in relation to third party information

27. Canada respectfully requests the Tribunal to provide additional guidance with respect to information provided in confidence by a third party ("third party information"). In this connection, Canada submits that the Tribunal should adopt the sound approach reflected in Article 73 of the Rome Statute of the International Criminal Court. While the Tribunal is not bound by the rules of the International Criminal Court, "it can seek guidance from those rules, where appropriate" (*Milosevic*). Article 73 of the Rome Statute provides particular clarification with respect to the problem of third party information, recognizing that a State cannot disclose such information without the consent of the originator. Adopting the same approach would promote consistency of international jurisprudence and would recognize that this approach was developed by the international community as a whole, following careful deliberation on the best balance between national security interests and the needs of effective international criminal justice.

Rome Statute of the International Criminal Court, Articles 72 and 73

Prosecutor v. *Milosevic*, Rule 70 Decision, Trial Chamber, paragraph 17 (overturned on other grounds)

Prosecutor v. *Furundzija*, Trial Judgment, paragraph 227

Prosecutor v. *Tadic*, Appeal Judgment, paragraph 223

Prosecutor v. *Kupreskic,* Appeal Judgment, paragraph 47

28. This approach to third party information is an intrinsically sound and practical approach. Under the well-established principle of "originator control," third party information cannot be released or discussed by the recipient State without the consent of the originator. To release or discuss third party information in any circumstance would breach this trust and cause the gravest injury to national security interests, as it would jeopardize the State's future ability to benefit from sharing of sensitive information. For countries such as Canada, this ability is of paramount importance for its national security capabilities. In addition, this approach is also appropriate for other practical reasons. It recognizes that the receiving State is in no position to assess the sensitivity of information, as only the originator is aware of the full sensitivities and risks entailed. The approach also avoids unnecessary duplication of efforts where originators of information are recipients of the same order.

29. Accordingly, adoption of the approach reflected in Article 73 of the Rome Statute with respect to third party information would provide a helpful and appropriate clarification.

INTERNATIONAL ECONOMIC LAW

NAFTA: Interpretation of Articles 1116 and 1117

In a submission to a North American Free Trade Agreement (NAFTA) tribunal dated July 19, 2002, the Legal Bureau wrote:

The NAFTA Chapter Eleven Tribunal in Pope & Talbot did not properly appreciate the fact that where an Investor bases its claim on Article 1116 ("Claim by an Investor of a Party on Its Own Behalf"), the Investor cannot recover damages incurred by its enterprise. Those damages can only be recovered where an Investor bases its claim on Article 1117 ("Claim by an Investor of a Party on Behalf of an Enterprise"). Canada had argued that the Investor could have filed its claim under both Article 1116 and 1117, but had chosen not to do so. Accordingly, it was precluded from recovering damages incurred by the enterprise investment arising out of the breach.

The Pope & Talbot Tribunal held that "Article 1117 is permissive, not mandatory" because it uses the language "may submit to arbitration," and because Article 1121(1), which sets the conditions precedent to the submission of a claim, includes a reference to claims under Article 1116 involving a "claim for loss or damage to an interest in an enterprise."

In finding that the language of Article 1117 "is permissive," the Tribunal reasoned that the Investor was not required to bring its claim for damages incurred under Article 1117. The interpretation makes Article 1117 redundant. Nor does the "permissive language" that appears in both Articles 1116 and 1117 offer support for such a conclusion. Articles 1116 and 1117 provide that an investor of a Party "may submit to arbitration under this Section a claim that another Party has breached an obligation under Section A" of Chapter Eleven or Articles 1503(2) or 1502(3). The use of "may" in Articles 1116 and 1117 does not allow investors to claim under either 1116 or 1117 regardless of whether the damages complained of were suffered by the investment or the investor.

The Pope & Talbot Tribunal's second argument, based on the language of Article 1121(1), ignores the actual wording of that provision. Article 1121(1) refers to "a claim for loss or damage to an interest in an enterprise." It was Canada's position that the damages sought by the Investor for harm caused to the investment could only be claimed under Article 1117, because many of the Investor's claims were made on behalf of the investment, not with respect to the Investor's interest therein. The Tribunal's analysis suggests that, despite the separate legal personality of the investor and the investment, damage to the investment is damage to the investor.

Article 1121 mirrors the distinction between direct and derivative claims for loss and simply requires that in either case, the appropriate waivers must be filed and claims for loss may not be pursued simultaneously before a domestic court and a NAFTA Chapter Eleven tribunal.

The NAFTA Parties carefully drafted Chapter 11 to distinguish claims by an Investor on its own behalf from claims by an Investor on behalf of an enterprise. This distinction is adhered to in Articles 1116, 1117, 1119, 1121 and 1135 and should not be rendered meaningless by a Chapter Eleven tribunal.

"Pass Through" of a Subsidy Analysis under the Agreement on Subsidies and Countervailing Measures

In a submission to a World Trade Organization panel dated December 19, 2002, the Legal Bureau wrote:

In accordance with the SCM Agreement, where the recipient of a subsidy (whose products are not subject to the investigation) enters into transactions with other entities, an investigating authority may not *presume* that those other entities have benefited from the alleged subsidy. An investigating authority must always establish that both elements of the subsidy definition in Article 1 exist.

The Appellate Body stressed this principle in paragraph 68 of *United States — Countervailing Duties on Hot-Rolled Steel from the United Kingdom* (*United States — Lead and Bismuth II*), where it explained that:

The question of whether a "financial contribution" confers a "benefit" depends, therefore, on whether the *recipient has received* a "financial contribution" on terms more favourable than those available *to the recipient* in the market ... UES and BSplc/BSES paid fair market value for all the productive assets, goodwill, etc., they acquired from BSC and subsequently used in the production of leaded bars imported into the United States in 1994, 1995 and 1996. We, therefore, see no error in the Panel's conclusion that, in the specific circumstances of this case, the "financial contributions" bestowed on BSC between 1977 and 1986 *could not be deemed to confer a "benefit"* on UES and BSplc/BSES.

As the Appellate Body further held at paragraph 62 in *United States — Lead and Bismuth II*, an administering authority must establish that a benefit has been conferred upon the recipient of the alleged subsidy. It may not irrebuttably presume that the benefit has been passed through in a subsequent transaction.

This analysis is even more apt in respect of original determinations where an investigating authority has the duty to establish each element of a subsidy. (See paragraph 63 of *United States — Lead and Bismuth II*.) In particular, for transactions that take place in the market and at arm's length, the applicable presumption is that fair market value has been paid. The original recipient of a subsidy is presumed to have retained the benefit to the extent that it could, and it is therefore presumed that no advantage has been conferred onto the purchaser in the market when compared to the market benchmark for the input, as provided for in Article 14(d) of the Agreement.

Standard of Review under Article 17.6 of the Anti-Dumping Agreement

In a submission to a World Trade Organization panel dated April 11, 2003, the Legal Bureau wrote:

Article 17.6 of the *Anti-Dumping Agreement* sets out the standard of review to be applied by a panel in reviewing the initiation and subsequent investigation by the investigating authority. Article 17.6(i) of the *Anti-Dumping Agreement* establishes the standard that must be applied in reviewing questions of fact (*e.g.*, was there "sufficient evidence" to justify the initiation of the investigation?), while Article 17.6(ii) establishes the standard that must be applied in reviewing questions of law (*i.e.*, the interpretation of the words in the relevant provisions of the *Anti-Dumping Agreement*).

Regarding questions of law, in *US — Hot Rolled Steel*, the Appellate Body, at paragraphs 59 to 60, held that pursuant to Article 17.6(ii) of the *Anti-Dumping Agreement*, "panels are obliged to determine whether a measure rests upon an interpretation of the relevant provisions of the *Anti-Dumping Agreement* which is *permissible under the rules of treaty interpretation* in Articles 31 and 32" of the *Vienna Convention*.

Article 17.6(i) of the *Anti-Dumping Agreement* provides as follows:

in its assessment of the facts of the matter, the panel shall determine whether the authorities' establishment of the facts was proper and whether their evaluation of those facts was unbiased and objective. If the establishment of the facts was proper and the evaluation was unbiased and objective, even though the panel might have reached a different conclusion, the evaluation shall not be overturned.

A determination of whether decisions made by the investigating authority during the course of the investigation are consistent with the basic rules for determining dumping will require a review by the Panel of the establishment and evaluation of the facts that were before the investigating authority at the time the decisions were made. Article 17.6(i) requires panels to make an active review or examination of the pertinent facts, to be carried out in an objective manner. In *US — Stainless Steel Plate*, the panel held as follows at paragraph 6.18:

[Article 17.6(i)] speaks not only to the establishment of the facts, but also to their evaluation. Therefore, the Panel must check not merely whether the national authorities have properly established the relevant facts but also the value or weight attached to those facts and whether this was done in an unbiased and objective manner. This concerns the according of a certain weight to the facts in their relation to each other; it is not a legal evaluation.

In *US — Hot-Rolled Steel,* the panel stated as follows in paragraph 7.26 regarding the obligation of panels in assessing factual determinations:

> Whether the facts were properly established involves determining whether the investigating authorities collected relevant and reliable information concerning the issue to be decided — it essentially goes to the investigative process. Then, assuming that the establishment of the facts with regard to a particular claim was proper, we consider whether, based on the evidence before the US investigating authorities at the time of the determination, an unbiased and objective investigating authority evaluating that evidence could have reached the conclusions that the US investigating authorities reached on the matter in question. In this context, we consider whether all the evidence was considered, including facts which might detract from the decision actually reached by the investigating authorities.

The Appellate Body, in reviewing the Report of the panel in *US — Hot-Rolled Steel,* made a similar finding regarding the proper application of the standard or review enunciated in Article 17.6(i). The Appellate Body stated as follows at paragraphs 55 and 56:

> [T]he text of both provisions [Article 11 of the DSU and Article 17.6(i) of the ADA] requires panels to "assess" the facts and this, in our view, clearly necessitates an active review or examination of the pertinent facts ... Article 17.6(i) of the *Anti-Dumping Agreement* also states that the panel is to determine, first, whether the investigating authorities' "*establishment* of the facts was *proper*" and, second, whether the authorities' "*evaluation* of those facts was *unbiased and objective.*" Although the text of Article 17.6(i) is couched in terms of an obligation on *panels* — panels "shall" make these determinations — the provision, at the same time, in effect defines when *investigating authorities* can be considered to have acted inconsistently with the *Anti-Dumping Agreement* in the course of their "establishment" and "evaluation" of the relevant facts ... Thus, panels must assess if the establishment of the facts by the investigating authorities was *proper* and if the evaluation of those facts by those authorities was *unbiased and objective.* If these broad standards have not been met, a panel must hold the investigating authorities' establishment or evaluation of the facts to be inconsistent with the *Anti-Dumping Agreement.*

In *US — Cotton Yarn,* a review of a safeguard determination under Article 11 of the DSU, the Appellate Body stated as follows at paragraph 74 regarding the meaning to be attributed to "objective assessment":

> [p]anels must examine whether the competent authority has evaluated all relevant factors; they must assess whether the competent

authority has examined all the pertinent facts and assessed whether an adequate explanation has been provided as to how those facts support the determination; and they must also consider whether the competent authority's explanation addresses fully the nature and complexities of the data and responds to other plausible interpretations of the data.

The panel in *Korea — Dairy* found that the "objective assessment" requirement is not to be interpreted by the reviewing panel to mean "total deference." The panel stated as follows at paragraph 7.30:

> We consider that for the Panel to adopt a policy of total deference to the findings of the national authorities could not ensure an "objective assessment" as foreseen by Article 11 of the DSU. This conclusion is supported, in our view, by previous panel reports that have dealt with this issue ... For us, an objective assessment entails an examination of whether the KTC had examined all facts in its possession or which it should have obtained in accordance with Article 4.2 of the Agreement on Safeguards (including facts which might detract from an affirmative determination in accordance with the last sentence of Article 4.2 of the Agreement on Safeguards), *whether adequate explanation had been provided of how the facts as a whole supported the determination made*, and, consequently, whether the determination made was consistent with the international obligations of Korea.

In considering an anti-dumping determination, the panel, in *Egypt — Rebar,* stated at paragraph 7.14 that, in conducting an objective assessment, "we deem it necessary to undertake a *detailed review* of the evidence submitted to the [investigating authority] to be able to determine whether an *objective and unbiased investigating authority* could have reached the determinations that Turkey challenges in this dispute."

It is clear that panels must conduct a thorough examination of how investigating authorities arrived at their conclusions to properly apply the standard of review under Article 17.6, and ultimately to determine whether their actions are inconsistent with the relevant provisions of the *Anti-Dumping Agreement.*

Indeed, in the context of panels' determining whether the "establishment" of facts by an investigating authority is "proper," the Appellate Body, in *Thailand - Steel,* stated at paragraph 116 that the ordinary meaning of "proper" in Article 17.6(i) is "accurate" or "correct." The Appellate Body further stated that: "the ordinary meaning of 'establishment' suggests an action to place beyond dispute: ascertain, demonstrate, prove."

To determine whether the investigating authority's evaluation of the facts was "unbiased and objective," a panel must, at the very least, examine: (1) whether the authority has given proper weight to the facts; (2) whether it has collected relevant and reliable information concerning the issue to be decided; and (3) whether all the evidence was considered, including facts that might detract from the decision actually reached by the investigating authority. In the end, the panel must determine whether an unbiased and objective investigating authority evaluating all of the evidence could properly have made the determination that was reached by the investigating authority on the matter in question.

Breach of Contract in NAFTA Chapter Eleven Disputes

In a submission to a NAFTA tribunal dated July 19, 2002, the Legal Bureau wrote:

Pursuant to NAFTA Articles 1116 and 1117, an Investor of a NAFTA Party can bring a claim that another NAFTA Party has breached an obligation in Section A of Chapter Eleven or certain parts of Chapter 15. The jurisdiction of a NAFTA Tribunal established under Chapter Eleven is limited to examining whether there has been a breach of the obligations listed in Articles 1116 or 1117 as alleged by the Investor.

A NAFTA Tribunal does not have jurisdiction to determine contractual claims. A mere breach by a State of its contractual obligations with an investor, does not, in and of itself, constitute a breach of the minimum standard of treatment or an expropriation.

As the *Azinian* Tribunal has recognized at paragraph 87, "NAFTA does not ... allow investors to seek international arbitration for mere contractual breaches. Indeed, NAFTA cannot possibly be read to create such a regime, which would have elevated a multitude of ordinary transactions with public authorities into potential international disputes."

The Tribunal's analysis should therefore be based on the specific NAFTA provisions at issue in the claim, and not simply on the question of whether or not there was a breach of contract. To find a breach of the minimum standard of treatment under Article 1105, a Tribunal would have to conclude that the State's actions fell below the customary international law standard. To find an expropriation under Article 1110, the Tribunal would have to conclude that the State's actions have all the attributes of an expropriation, including a substantial deprivation or substantial interference with the alleged investment. For example, tribunals have found expropriations in certain cases where there has been a taking of assets or an interference with the management of a company so severe that it amounts to a taking.

INTERNATIONAL LIABILITY FOR DAMAGE CAUSED BY
SPACE OBJECTS

In February 2003, the Legal Bureau wrote:

Until the mid-1980s, space activities were the exclusive domain of States and inter-governmental organizations. Sensing the potential commercial applications of space technologies, private corporations have become increasingly involved in space activities, particularly in the launching of space objects, such as commercial-use satellites. This privatization poses unique challenges as regards liability, given the inadequacies of the current international legal regime, domestic tort law and the absence of specific legislation in a number of space-faring countries, including Canada.

The international legal regime is focussed on States and the absolute liability of launching States in relation to damage caused by space objects. Absent domestic legislation addressing the issue, private entities involved in the launch of space objects are not liable for damage caused by their space objects. Ambiguities in the international regime, particularly as regards the definitions of "launching" State, "space object," "damage," make it very difficult for States to determine with clarity their degree of exposure to liability. Some space-faring nations, in particular the United States, have attempted to mitigate their exposure by establishing a domestic legal regime allowing the State to recover, at least partly, compensation costs from private entities concerned. The following analysis sets out the international legal regime for damages caused by space objects and its shortcomings, elements of the US *Commercial Space Launch Act* and policy issues related to liability that need to be addressed in the context of RADARSAT-II.

I. The International Liability Regime for Damages Caused by Space Objects

A. *Customary International Law*

Customary international law establishes two fundamental principles, applicable to a State's conduct in the international sphere, including its space activities: 1) a State, in conducting its activities, should strive not to harm the interests of other States; and 2) reparation must occur for damage caused by activities violating international law.

B. *International Treaties*

1. The Outer Space Treaty

The *Treaty on Principles Governing the Activities of States in the Exploration and Use of Outer Space, including the Moon and Other Celestial Bodies* (the "Outer Space Treaty") was adopted by the United Nations General Assembly in 1967 and was ratified by Canada, along with 95 other States.

Article VI of the Outer Space Treaty provides that:

> States Parties to the Treaty shall bear international responsibility for national activities in outer space, including the moon and other celestial bodies, whether such activities are carried out by governmental agencies or by non-governmental entities. The activities of non-governmental entities in outer space, including the moon and other celestial bodies, shall require authorization and continuing supervision by the appropriate State Party to the Treaty.

Some have argued that "international responsibility" is different from international "liability." Article VII of the Outer Space Treaty further provides, however, that:

> Each State Party to the Treaty that launches or procures the launching of an object into outer space, including the moon and other celestial bodies, and each State Party from whose territory or facility an object is launched, is internationally liable for damage to another State Party to the treaty or to its natural or juridical persons by such object or its component parts on the Earth, in air or in outer space, including the moon and other celestial bodies.

These provisions combined place third-party liability risks squarely on the so-called "launching State," including for activities of national non-governmental entities.

2. The Liability Convention

The *Convention on the International Liability for Damages Caused by Space Objects* (the "Liability Convention") was adopted in 1972 and ratified by Canada in 1975. The Liability Convention was meant to deal with a specific aspect of the Outer Space Treaty, namely damages caused by space objects. It therefore completes and expands the regime established by the Outer Space Treaty. It retains a fundamental premise of the Outer Space Treaty, i.e. that States should be held liable and accountable for space activities. The Convention was, after all, adopted at a time where privatization of space activities had yet to occur and was not even envisaged.

(a) Scope of Application

The Liability Convention only deals with third-party liability, rather than inter-party liability which is left to domestic law (contracts and torts law).

It does not apply in case of damage caused to nationals of a launching State by a space object of that launching State or to foreign nationals participating in the launch. It does not apply either to damage caused to a space object by a space object from the same launching State.

The scope of the Liability Convention is limited to damage caused by space objects on the surface of the Earth or to aircraft in flight, or to other space objects elsewhere than on the surface of the Earth.

(b) Liability Regime

The Liability Convention establishes a two-tiered liability regime for the launching State: (1) absolute liability for damage occurring on the surface of the Earth or to aircraft in flight; and (2) fault- or negligence-based liability for damage to another space object or persons or property therein elsewhere than on the surface of the Earth.

Exoneration of the launching State is limited to situations where damage is caused by gross negligence or an act or omission done with the intent to cause damage by the claimant State. The burden of proof rests with the launching State and exoneration is limited to the damage actually caused by the negligence or fault of the claimant State.

(c) Claims Process

Claimants and respondents are exclusively States Parties to the Liability Convention. Major space-faring nations, including the United States, have ratified the Convention.

A claim can only be filed against a "launching State." A launching State is: (1) the State that actually launches the space object; (2) the State that procures the launching of the object; (3) the State from whose territory the object is launched; or (4) the State that owns the facility from which the object is launched. Given today's cooperative launching projects, it is highly likely that more than one State would qualify as a launching State for the purposes of the Convention. In cases of joint launches, States are held jointly and severally liable. In the absence of an agreement among the States concerned in relation to apportionment of liability, apportionment is made to the extent that the State is "at fault" or, if this cannot be determined, liability is apportioned equally.

A claimant can only be a State. A State can make a claim: (1) for damage to its nationals, territory or property; (2) for a foreign national suffering damage on its territory, if the State of nationality has failed to make a claim; or (3) for a foreign national permanently resident in its territory if no claim has been filed by either the State of nationality or the State on the territory of which the damage occurred.

Claims are dealt with through diplomatic channels. Claims are assessed in accordance with "international law and the principles of justice and equity, in order to provide such reparation in respect of the damage as will restore" the claimant to its former condition (Article XII). If a claim is not settled within one year of submission, a Claims Commission is established at the request of either State involved. However, the determinations of the Claims Commission are not binding on the parties.

II. Shortcomings of the International Legal Regime

Given modern realities of space activities, particularly space launch activities, the international legal regime presents fundamental inadequacies. Many of them are linked to the absence of definition of key terms/ concepts that renders the application of the Convention uncertain and unpredictable.

First, the international liability regime does not deal with the conduct of space activities by private entities rather than States. Under the Liability Convention, a State could be held liable for incidents involving private entities exclusively. This stems to a large extent from the confusion surrounding the notion of "launching State" and the particular notion of "procuring a launch." The degree of involvement of a State in a launch for it to qualify as a "launching State" is not specified. It has been argued that "procuring" means anything from providing financial backing to inducing another State to launch a space object in exchange for certain benefits.

Ambiguities also exist in relation to proof of damage. The Liability Convention establishes liability for damage caused by a space object. However, neither "damage" nor "space object" are clearly defined. Article I(a) of the Convention stipulates that "damage means loss of life, personal injury or impairment of health, or loss of or damage to property." As the liability provisions of the Convention have never been tested, the extent of situations covered remains unclear. For example, would psychological impairment be covered? What about pure economic loss or loss of profits? The term "space object" is not defined at international law. Article I(d) of the Convention does state that the term includes "component parts of a space object as well as its launch vehicle and parts thereof." Do space debris constitute space objects? What about parts affixed to a space object after it has been launched?

In addition, the basis for the assessment of compensation is unclear. As noted above, compensation is to be assessed on the basis of "international law and the principles of justice and equity" and the principle of restoration. The vagueness of this construction, and the absence of liability limits, creates an unpredictable environment.

Finally, in the case of damage to another space object, the application of concepts such as "fault" and "negligence" to space activities is not clear. Traditional concepts of "fault" may prove difficult to apply in the space context where it may argued that there is no clear standard of behaviour (as that of the "reasonable person" in civil law) for the conduct of space activities.

HUMAN RIGHTS

Legal Status of "General Comments of the Committee on Economic, Social and Cultural Rights"

In February 2004, the following statement was made by the Head of the Canadian Delegation to the Open-Ended Intergovernmental Working Group for the Elaboration of a Set of Voluntary Guidelines to Support the Progressive Realization of the Right to Adequate Food in the Context of National Food Security:

Let me take this opportunity to make clear Canada's position on the legal status of General Comments of the Committee on Economic, Social and Cultural Rights regarding the implementation of obligations of States Parties to the *International Covenant on Economic, Social and Cultural Rights*. Canada does not consider that the General Comments, including General Comment No. 11 and General Comment No. 15, to be authoritative interpretations of *Covenant* obligations, legal or otherwise. Rather the General Comments merely represent the views or interpretations of Committee members in their independent capacities. The General Comments have not been endorsed by Canada or other States Parties to the *Covenant* and they do not enjoy any status in law.

INTERNATIONAL COURT OF JUSTICE

Request for an Advisory Opinion by the UN General Assembly Regarding the Israeli Wall

In January 2004, the Government of Canada submitting the following written statement to the International Court of Justice:

Pursuant to the provisions of Article 66(2) of the Statute of the International Court of Justice, and in response to the invitation addressed to the Government of Canada by the Registrar of the International Court of Justice in its Order of 19 December 2003, the Government of Canada wishes to submit certain general comments on the request for an Advisory Opinion submitted to the Court through Resolution A/RES/ES-10/14, in which the General Assembly of the United Nations asked the Court to respond to the following question:

What are the legal consequences arising from the construction of the wall being built by Israel, the occupying Power, in the Occupied Palestinian Territory, including in and around East Jerusalem, as described in the report of the Secretary-General, considering the rules and principles of international law, including the Fourth Geneva Convention of 1949, and relevant Security Council and General Assembly resolutions?

Canada has made clear its position regarding Israel's actions in constructing the barrier, emphasizing, in particular, the importance of a political solution to resolve the on-going conflict in the Middle East. Canada voted in favour of General Assembly Resolution ES-10/13, which was adopted on October 21, 2003 and offered the following Explanation of Vote:

> Canada has voted in favour of this resolution. Canada affirms the right of Israel to assure its own security. Neither terrorism nor support for terrorists who target the innocent — in whatever form to advance whatever cause — can ever be justified. Israel has the right to take necessary measures to protect the security of its citizens and its borders from attacks by Palestinian terrorist groups, including by restricting access to its territory.
>
> While we respect Israel's right and obligation to defend its citizens, Canada opposes all unilateral actions which could pre-determine the outcome of final status negotiations, including the construction of an extensive security barrier by Israel on land inside the occupied territory of the West Bank. Canada considers the expropriation of land to facilitate the construction of this barrier to be unacceptable.
>
> We are moreover concerned with the highly prejudicial impact this barrier may have on the already-flagging prospects for peace. Further its adverse effect on the ever dire humanitarian and economic situation in the Occupied Territories is worrisome. We fear that the scope and location of the barrier being constructed further undermines the hopes of the many who yet yearn for peace.
>
> While such unilateral actions outside of the territory of the state of Israel raise serious matters of international law, Canada believes that ultimately this tragic ongoing conflict can only be resolved politically. A just, lasting and comprehensive peace in the Middle East remains possible. The Road Map is still a viable instrument for achieving this goal. Canada calls on the parties to acquit their obligations and to return to the negotiating table.

At the time Resolution A/RES/ES-10/14 was adopted by the General Assembly, Canada abstained from the resolution with the following Explanation of Vote:

> While Canada agrees that there could be legal questions regarding the construction of this extensive barrier within the Occupied Palestinian Territories on which the International Court of Justice could usefully provide guidance, we nevertheless question whether this request for an advisory opinion is a useful step at this time, in this highly charged environment. In addition, the General Assembly has already expressed its opposition to the construction of this barrier

and has called for construction to cease and for the sections of its route in deviation from the Armistice Line of 1949 to be reversed. This conflict needs to be resolved through negotiation. A unilateral re-partition of land through the establishment of this barrier will not lead to lasting peace.

The reference to the question of the usefulness of this request for an advisory opinion "at this time" was understood by Canada as having regard to ongoing efforts at a negotiated settlement of all issues pertaining to the Middle East Peace Process, including through the implementation of the "Roadmap" endorsed by the Security Council in its resolution S/RES/1515(2003).

The "legal questions" Canada refers to are the legal implications or consequences of the barrier for the rights and obligations of Israel as the occupying power pursuant to international humanitarian and human rights law. Canada's view, however, is that in light of the resolutions at the United Nations Security Council and the General Assembly which encourage the parties and the international community to proceed by way of the "Roadmap" to a negotiated solution, these issues would be more effectively addressed in a broader negotiation context rather than within the procedural limitations of a judicial hearing. Canada respectfully requests that the Court exercise its discretion and decline to respond to the request for an Advisory Opinion at this time.

DIPLOMATIC PROTECTION: CORPORATIONS AND SHAREHOLDERS

In October 2003, Canada made the following statement in the Sixth Committee of the Fifty-Eighth General Assembly during the debate on the report of the International Law Commission:

In regard to the report [of the International Law Commission] ... on the diplomatic protection of shareholders and corporations, the rapporteur has proposed that the rule from *Barcelona Traction* be adopted. The issue is whether this rule is an accurate statement of customary international law or whether international law has evolved since that decision.

The International Court of Justice in *Barcelona Traction* held that shareholders had no right to take action on behalf of the corporation; if the corporation was injured, the corporation alone could act despite the fact that a damage done to the company undoubtedly affected the company's shareholders.

Canada, for its part, has relied upon the *Barcelona Traction* rule in past litigation as being a correct statement of the current state of customary international law.

One area of interest is the implications of the development of various investment treaties on the *Barcelona Traction* rule. The issue is whether the development and prevalence of bilateral investment treaties and multilateral investment treaties have moved customary international law away from the *Barcelona Traction* rule to a point where the state of the shareholder has a right of action. As noted by the Special Rapporteur, investment treaties were treated as *lex specialis* by the Court in *Barcelona Traction*. Canada suggests that although bilateral investment treaties have become quite prevalent, they have not become customary international law and continue to be treated as *lex specialis*. Indeed, it could be argued that it is by virtue of the fact that the *Barcelona Traction* rule is still considered by tribunals as a true statement of customary international law which is driving force behind the desire of states to enter into investment treaties.

Canada thus agrees with the approach taken by the Rapporteur in developing these articles on diplomatic protection of shareholders and corporations.

Parliamentary Declarations in 2002-3 / Déclarations parlementaires en 2002-3

compiled by / préparé par

ALIAKSANDRA LOGVIN

A STATEMENTS MADE ON THE INTRODUCTION OF LEGISLATION /
   DÉCLARATIONS SUR L'INTRODUCTION DE LA LÉGISLATION

I *Bill S-2: Tax Conventions Implementation Act, 2002 (An Act to
    Implement an Agreement, Conventions and Protocols Concluded
    between Canada and Kuwait, Mongolia, the United Arab Emirates,
    Moldova, Norway, Belgium and Italy for the Avoidance of Double
    Taxation and the Prevention of Fiscal Evasion and to Amend the
    Enacted Text of Three Tax Treaties) / Loi S-2: La Loi de 2002 pour
    la mise en oeuvre de conventions fiscales (Loi mettant en oeuvre un
    accord, des conventions et des protocoles conclus entre le Canada et le
    Koweït, la Mongolie, les Émirats Arabes Unis, la Moldova, la
    Norvège, la Belgique et l'Italie en vue d'éviter les doubles impositions
    et de prévenir l'évasion fiscale et modifiant le texte édicté de trois
    traités fiscaux)*

Mr. Bryon Wilfert (Parliamentary Secretary to the Minister of
Finance):

The bill relates to Canada's ongoing effort to update and modernize its
network of income tax treaties with other countries ... At present, Canada
has tax treaties in place with over 75 countries. Passage of the bill will, of
course, see the number increase. The bill would enact tax treaties that
Canada has signed with seven countries. Of these seven treaties, three represent updates to existing tax treaty arrangements and four of the treaties
establish bilateral tax arrangements with countries for the first time.

    More specifically, the treaties with Kuwait, Moldova, Mongolia and
the United Arab Emirates are all new treaties that have recently been
signed ... The new treaties will provide individuals and businesses, both in
Canada and in the other countries concerned, with more predictable and

Aliasksandra Logvin is in the Faculty of Law at the University of Ottawa.

equitable tax results in their cross-border dealings. What is more, our arrangements with Belgium, Italy and Norway are updated to ensure that our bilateral arrangements are consistent with current Canadian tax policy ... Bilateral tax treaties or ... income tax conventions, are an integral part of our tax system. Basically, they are arrangements signed between countries that are primarily aimed to protect taxpayers from double taxation and to assist tax authorities in their efforts to prevent fiscal evasion.

Canada benefits significantly from having tax treaties in force with other countries. Our tax treaties, for example, assure us of how Canadians will be taxed abroad. At the same time they assure our treaty partners of how their residents will be treated here in Canada.

Tax treaties also impact on the Canadian economy, particularly because they help facilitate international trade and investment by removing tax impediments to cross-border dealings ... Canada's economy relies significantly on international trade. In fact, Canadian exports account for more than 40% of our annual GDP.

What is more, Canada's economic wealth depends on direct foreign investment to Canada as well as inflows of information, capital and technology. In other words, by eliminating tax impediments and by creating more predictable tax results for traders, investors and other taxpayers with international dealings, our tax treaties promote opportunities at home and in international trade and investment abroad.

Since Canada's economy is likely to become more intertwined in the world economy, eliminating administrative difficulties and unnecessary tax impediments with respect to cross-border dealings will remain important.

(House of Commons Debates, November 1, 2002, pp. 1175-77)
(Débats de la Chambre des Communes, le 1er novembre 2002, pp. 1175-77)

2   *Bill C-4: An Act to Amend the Nuclear Safety and Control Act / Loi C-4: Loi modifiant la Loi sur la sûreté et la réglementation nucléaires*

Hon. Herb Dhaliwal (Minister of Natural Resources):

Bill C-4 ... is a one clause bill with the same provision as that contained in Bill C-57 introduced in the House in May 2002.[1]

The amendment clarifies the wording in subsection 46(3) of the act which has had the consequence of extending the obligation for site remediation beyond the owners and managers to private sector lending institutions. This is an anomaly that must be corrected.

Under the current wording of subsection 46(3), the Canadian Nuclear Safety Commission has the authority to order the owner or occupant or any other person with a right to or an interest in to take prescribed measures to reduce the level of radioactive contamination. This proposed

---

[1] On May 31, 2002, Hon. Claudette Bradshaw (for the Minister of Natural Resources) moved for leave to introduce Bill C-57, an Act to Amend the Nuclear Safety and Control Act. See *House of Commons Debates*, May 31, 2002, p. 11997.

amendment clarifies the subsection by deleting the words "person with a right or interest in" and replacing them with the words "person who has the management and control" ... The amendment serves to clarify the risk for institutions lending to companies in the nuclear industry. A lender who goes into management and control of a nuclear facility would be within the reach of this subsection ... This amendment ... is not, and should not be misconstrued as, a measure to provide favourable treatment to the nuclear industry. All the stringent mechanisms embodied in the Nuclear Safety and Control Act and regulations, which are designed to ensure that nuclear facilities are managed in a safe and environmentally sound manner, are still in place and unaffected by this provision ... The bill [C-4] ... will not in any way weaken Canada's stringent licensing and regulatory regime, which is designed to protect human health, safety and security and the environment ... It demonstrates the government's commitment to ... "achieve the public good" and at the same time enhance "the climate for investment and trust in markets."

(House of Commons Debates, October 10, 2002, pp. 550-51)
(Débats de la Chambre des Communes, le 10 octobre 2002, pp. 550-51)

3   *Bill C-9: An Act to Amend the Canadian Environmental Assessment Act / Loi C-9: Loi modifiant la Loi canadienne sur l'évaluation environnementale*

Hon. David Anderson (Minister of the Environment):

The purpose of an environmental assessment is to ensure that the environmental effects of a proposed development are identified, assessed and that, as far as possible, mitigation is done early in the planning phase of the project. It is a precautionary tool that is now used in more than 100 countries ... [A] renewed federal assessment process [incorporated in the Bill] brings a greater measure of certainty, predictability and timeliness of all participants ... [T]he renewed process must produce high-quality environmental assessments that contribute to better decisions in support of sustainable development ... [T]he process must provide opportunities for meaningful public participation ... [T]he improvements in Bill C-9 will lead to the achievement of [these] goals.

The Government of Canada will be investing some $51 million over the next five years to implement the renewed act. This new funding and the legislative changes made by Bill C-9 will ensure that decision makers, both inside and outside the government, have better information about the environmental effects of proposed projects. Better information will mean better decisions that promote progress on the environmental priorities, including clean air, clean water, protection of Canada's biodiversity and climate change.

(House of Commons Debates, April 30, 2003, pp. 5647-49)
(Débats de la Chambre des Communes, le 30 avril 2003, pp. 5647-49)

4   *Bill C-14: Export and Import of Rough Diamonds Act (An Act*
Providing for Controls on the Export, Import or Transit across
Canada of Rough Diamonds and for a Certification Scheme for the
Export of Rough Diamonds in Order to Meet Canada's Obligations
under the Kimberley Process) / Loi C-14: Loi sur l'exportation et
l'importation des diamants bruts (Loi concernant le contrôle de
l'exportation, de l'importation et du transit au Canada des diamants
bruts et établissant un processus de certification pour leur exportation
en vue de l'exécution par le Canada de ses obligations découlant du
Processus de Kimberley)

M. Benoît Serré (secrétaire parlementaire du ministre des Ressources naturelles):

La communauté internationale s'inquiète encore vivement du lien qui existe entre le commerce illicite des diamants bruts et le financement de conflits armés, particulièrement en Angola, en Sierra Leone et en République démocratique du Congo.

Bien que les diamants de la guerre ne constituent qu'une faible partie du commerce international des diamants, ils ont cependant de lourdes répercussions sur la paix, la sécurité et le développement durable des pays touchés.

With leadership from Canada, the United Nations has taken several initiatives to address this problem. In 1998 the Security Council imposed sanctions prohibiting the import of rough diamonds from Angola that were not controlled through an official certificate of origin scheme.

During its term on the UN Security Council in 1999 and 2000, Canada played a key role as chair of the Angola sanctions committee in pressing for measures to strengthen implementation of these sanctions. These measures laid the foundation for the adoption of additional sanctions on Sierra Leone which placed similar restrictions on rough diamond imports from that country ...

L'ONU démontre un intérêt soutenu pour le problème des diamants de la guerre. En décembre 2000, puis en mars 2002, l'Assemblée générale des Nations Unies a adopté des résolutions, coparrainées par le Canada, réclamant l'élaboration d'un programme international de certification des diamants bruts, afin de resserrer les mesures de contrôle du commerce des diamants et de prévenir l'entrée des diamants de la guerre sur les marchés légitimes.

Le G-8 porte aussi un grand intérêt à la question ... Au Sommet d'Okinawa, en juillet 2000, le premier ministre [canadien], de concert avec les dirigeants des autres pays du G-8, a souligné que le commerce des diamants de la guerre constitue pour le G-8 une question prioritaire dans la prévention des conflits armés.

À cette occasion, les dirigeants des pays du G-8 ont réclamé que soit étudiée la possibilité de formuler un accord international sur la certification des diamants bruts.

Au Sommet de Kananaskis, en juin 2002, dans le cadre du Plan d'action du G-8 pour l'Afrique, les dirigeants ont de nouveau accordé leur appui aux efforts internationaux visant à cerner le lien qui existe entre l'exploitation des ressources naturelles et les conflits en Afrique, y compris les mesures de contrôle des diamants élaborées en vertu du Processus de Kimberley dirigé par l'Afrique du Sud...

The Kimberley process is the principal international initiative established to develop practical approaches to the conflict diamond problem. Launched in May 2000, the process was initiated by several southern African countries in response to growing international pressure to address peace and security concerns as well as to protect several national economies in the sub-region, including Namibia, Botswana and South Africa, that depend on the diamond industry.

The process, which is chaired by South Africa, now includes 48 countries involved in producing, processing, importing and exporting rough diamonds. These countries account for 98% of the global trade in and production of rough diamonds and they include all of Canada's major diamond trading partners. For example, the United States, the European Union, Japan, Russia, Israel and India are all participating in the Kimberley process.

En mars 2002, le Canada était l'hôte de la plus récente rencontre du processus, qui a abouti à un consensus sur les propositions du programme...

Le projet de programme international de certification comprend plusieurs engagements clés, y compris une exigence selon laquelle tous les diamants bruts importés au Canada ou exportés vers d'autres pays doivent répondre aux critères du programme de certification. Il comporte aussi des restrictions commerciales qui interdisent le commerce de diamants bruts avec des pays qui ne participent pas au programme.

La mise en oeuvre du programme au Canada exige la création de méthodes de certification des diamants bruts et de mesures de contrôle des importations et des exportations. Il faudra donc que soient mises en place les autorités législatives, comme le prévoit le projet de loi C-14...

Consistent with the scheme and other country's processes, the bill is designed to ensure that natural rough diamonds in transit from one country to another across Canadian territory will be limited to trade between Kimberley process participants. Canada will not be a conduit for conflict diamond trade.

Passage of Bill C-14 will put in place all of the authorities required for Canada to meet its commitment under the international Kimberley process. The early passage of Bill C-14 will ensure that these authorities are in place by year end, when the process is planned for international implementation.

(House of Commons Debates, October 21, 2002, pp. 651-52)
(Débats de la Chambre des Communes, le 21 octobre 2002, pp. 651-52)

5   *Bill C-17: An Act to Amend Certain Acts of Canada, and to Enact Measures for Implementing the Biological and Toxin Weapons Convention, in Order to Enhance Public Safety / Loi C-17: Loi modifiant certaines lois fédérales et édictant des mesures de mise en oeuvre de la convention sur les armes biologiques ou à toxines, en vue de renforcer la sécurité publique*

M. André Harvey (secrétaire parlementaire du ministre des Transports):

Les gouvernements n'ont d'autres choix que de se doter d'outils importants pour faire face à des situations d'urgence. Des menaces extrêmes, absolument insoupçonnées peuvent survenir. On l'a vécu et on le vit encore quotidiennement depuis le 11 septembre ... Les gouvernements ont maintenant un agenda prioritaire qui s'appelle "la sécurité de leurs concitoyens." Tous les gouvernements responsables n'ont maintenant d'autre choix que de se doter d'outils leur permettant de réagir rapidement ... Notre gouvernement a pris ses responsabilités ... Plusieurs ministères ont été mis à contribution pour essayer ... d'ériger un mur contre le terrorisme international ... [L]oi C-17 ... est la continuité du projet de loi C-55[2] ... [L]a loi C-17 modifie ... des éléments importants qui sont les délais [relatifs aux arrêtés d'urgence] ayant été prescrits dans l'ancienne loi C-55. Les délais ... ont été normalisés ... pour fixer des délais plus brefs ... [T]rois nouvelles parties ont été ajoutées au projet de loi. Les deux premières, les parties 5 et 11, ont été ajoutées afin de permettre le partage des renseignements dans des situations identifiées en vertu de la Loi sur le ministère de la Citoyenneté et de l'Immigration et de la Loi sur l'immigration et la protection des réfugiés.

La troisième nouvelle partie, la partie 17, consiste dans une modification corrélative à la Loi sur la protection des renseignements personnels et les documents électroniques, pour permettre le fonctionnement du régime de partage des données fixé dans les articles 4.82 et 4.83 proposés pour ce qui est de la Loi sur l'aéronautique ... [Les] changements concernant les mandats [qui sont mentionnée dans l'article 4.82 de la Loi sur l'aéronautique] permettent de protéger le public, tout en respectant la vie privée des passagers individuels sauf ... pour des infractions extrêmement graves [comme le meurtre ou l'enlèvement] ... [L]es zones militaires d'accès contrôlé ... sont maintenant extrêmement limitées à trois endroits stratégiques ... [Les] arrêtés d'urgence ... sont aussi très bien encadrés dans des secteurs d'activités extrêmement graves.

(House of Commons Debates, November 5, 2002, pp. 1265-67)
(Débats de la Chambre des Communes, le 5 novembre 2002, pp. 1265-67)

---

2   As for the introduction of Bill C-55 at the House of Commons, see "Parliamentary Declarations in 2001-2002" (2002) 40 Canadian Yearbook of International Law 499 at 511-12.

Mrs. Marlene Jennings (Parliamentary Secretary to the Solicitor General of Canada):

Bill C-17 is a necessary tool to improve the safety and security of Canadians, of our neighbours and of global air travel ... [The Bill] struck[s] the right balance between public safety and respect for the privacy of individuals ... [T]he types of offences we are referring to [in the Bill] ... are: terrorism offences, transportation security offences, serious violent offences, serious drug offences, and organized crime offences.

(House of Commons Debates, May 27, 2003, pp. 6550-51)
(Débats de la Chambre des Communes, le 27 mai 2003, pp. 6550-51)

6 *Bill C-18: Citizenship of Canada Act (An Act Respecting Canadian Citizenship) / Loi C-18: Loi sur la citoyenneté au Canada (Loi concernant la citoyenneté canadienne)*

Hon. Denis Coderre (Minister of Citizenship and Immigration):

[C]itizenship is a fundamental issue. Deciding who is a full member of society is one of the most important powers of the modern state ... The [introduced] legislation has a number of aims. First, it would ensure that our citizenship rules more clearly reflect the fundamental values of Canadian society. Deuxièmement, reconnaître et protéger la valeur même de la citoyenneté canadienne. Troisièmement, mieux faire valoir aux Canadiens et aux nouveaux arrivants que la citoyenneté est un partenariat, c'est-à-dire que les citoyens et l'État ont tous les deux des droits ainsi que des responsabilités. Fourth, it would change how we make decisions so that we can obtain fair results but in a more efficient manner ...
Le projet de loi est évidemment fidèle à la Charte des droits et libertés qui n'existait pas avant que la loi actuelle n'ait été adoptée. Présentement par exemple, des centaines d'enfants adoptés chaque année à l'étranger par des parents canadiens doivent arriver au Canada à titre d'immigrants, pas comme des citoyens ... The new bill would correct this form of discrimination ...
We would no longer allow Canadian citizenship to be transmitted indefinitely from generation to generation among people who have never lived in Canada. However, to honour our tradition of openness and balance, persons born in Canada would continue to have an automatic right to citizenship ... As for the right to challenge decisions, the proposed procedure would be straightforward and accessible in clear-cut cases. Applicants would be able to request administrative review of decisions where an error in decision making has occurred. Applicants would also have access to the Federal Court ...
Seule la Cour fédérale évidemment aura le pouvoir de révoquer la citoyenneté. En même temps, elle pourrait ordonner le renvoi du Canada de terroristes, de criminels de guerre et de membres du crime organisé qui ont été naturalisés canadiens.

In black and white cases the minister would have limited power to annul citizenship. In exceptional situations the governor in council could refuse applications from individuals who do not respect the values of our free and democratic society ...
The Canadian system currently handles approximately 190,000 citizenship applications a year. It is therefore understandable that we would want a system that would be efficient and produced fair decisions.

(House of Commons Debates, November 7, 2002, pp.1421-23)
(Débats de la Chambre des Communes, le 7 novembre 2002, pp. 1421-23)

7   *Bill C-33: International Transfer of Offenders Act (An Act to Implement Treaties and Administrative Arrangements on the International Transfer of Persons Found Guilty of Criminal Offences) / Loi C-33: Loi sur le transfèrement international des délinquents (Loi de mise en oeuvre des traités ou des ententes administratives sur le transfèrement international des personnes reconnues coupables d'infractions criminelles)*

Hon. Wayne Easter (Solicitor General of Canada):

The Transfer of Offenders Act authorizes the implementation of treaties between Canada and other countries, including multilateral conventions for international transfer of offenders ... There is no doubt that most states wish to cooperate with one another on matters of criminal justice ... Modern technology and global travel have led to increased opportunities for the commission of crimes in countries other than one's own. Therefore, states have a common interest in cooperating to prevent and respond to criminal conduct. This actually protects the sovereignty of states by preventing offenders from escaping justice, and this is exactly what the transfer of offenders scheme allows states to do ...
[T]here is a clear need for legislative flexibility in Canada to further the humanitarian objective of transfers. There is a clear need for international cooperation in matters of criminal justice and there is a clear need for public protection with the safe and gradual reintegration of offenders into society.
Bill C-33 would respond to those needs by incorporating traditional international treaty principles, closing identified gaps and ensuring consistency with other legislative provisions. Bill C-33 would further contribute to these objectives by expanding the class of offenders who may be transferred and of jurisdictions with which Canada could enter into transfer arrangements.

(House of Commons Debates, April 29, 2003, pp. 5560-62)
(Débats de la Chambre des Communes, le 29 avril 2003, pp. 5560-62)

8   Bill C-42: An Act Respecting the Protection of the Antarctic Environment / Loi C-42: Loi concernant la protection de l'environnement en Antarctique

Mr. Alan Tonks (Parliamentary Secretary to the Minister of the Environment):

Bill C-42 is enabling legislation that will allow Canada to ratify the Protocol on Environmental Protection to the Antarctic Treaty, commonly known as the Madrid protocol.

Since signing the protocol in 1991, Canada has been committed to its ratification. By doing so, Canada will be joining the other 29 nations that have ratified the protocol. It will commit the country to the protection of this unique ecosystem, from which we can learn a great deal about the world's environment . . .

The challenge that nations operating in the Antarctic face is to manage activities in a way that balances the benefits of access with the need for environmental protection. The Madrid protocol, which came into force in 1998, achieves that balance through three key obligations.

First, it commits parties to the comprehensive protection of the Antarctic environment and designates Antarctica as a natural reserve devoted to peace and science.

Second, it sets out the principles for environmental protection, requiring an environmental impact assessment of all activities before they are allowed to proceed.

Third, the Madrid protocol bans activities harmful to the Antarctic environment, such as commercial mineral resource activity, damage to historic Antarctic sites and the harmful disturbance of wildlife.

What Bill C-42 does is it provides the legislative basis needed to implement the requirements of the Madrid protocol in Canada. Canadian tour companies and scientists are already voluntarily complying with the protocol using the approval mechanisms established by other nations . . .

[P]assage of the bill . . . will enable Canada to do its fair share to protect this last common wilderness as a legacy for people in the future.

(House of Commons Debates, June 13, 2003, pp. 7275-76)
(Débats de la Chambre des Communes, le 13 juin 2003, pp. 7275-76)

B   STATEMENTS IN RESPONSE TO QUESTIONS / DÉCLARATIONS EN RÉPONSE AUX QUESTIONS

1   Environment / Environnement

(a)   Cartagena Protocol / Protocole de Carthagène

M. Bernard Bigras (Rosemont — Petite-Patrie):

[L]ors des négociations du Protocole de Carthagène, le Canada faisait partie du groupe de pays, dont les États-Unis, qui souhaitaient que le protocole soit sous l'autorité de l'Organisation mondiale du commerce, ce que ne prévoient pas les dispositions actuelles du Protocole sur la biosécurité.

Est-ce que le gouvernement fédéral entend respecter sa signature et dire non à la demande d'appui des États-Unis de contester devant l'OMC l'interdiction de l'Europe sur les importations d'OGM, et ratifier immédiatement le Protocole de Carthagène sur la biosécurité?

Hon. David Anderson (Minister of the Environment):

We are trying hard to ensure that the environmental considerations are indeed a major component of any decision on the trade side. Therefore, we look with favour to the WTO taking environmental concerns into account as a fundamental part of its discussions.... [W]e will be pursuing that avenue to ensure both with the Cartagena protocol and with many others that we achieve the best environmental protection we can through this method.

(House of Commons Debates, January 31, 2003, p. 3014)
(Débats de la Chambre des Communes, le 31 janvier 2003, p. 3014)

(b)   Great Lakes / Grands Lacs

Ms. Paddy Torsney (Burlington):

Mr. Speaker, the Great Lakes hold about 20% of the surface fresh water in the world and the entire drainage basin measures some 750,000 square kilometres on both sides of the Canada-U.S. border.... [W]hat [is] the government... doing to reduce pollution and restore areas harmed by pollution in this precious Great Lakes basin?

Hon. David Anderson (Minister of the Environment):

[A]s part of the Government of Canada's ongoing commitment to restore the Great Lakes basin ecosystem ... 14 projects will be funded under the Great Lakes sustainability funding, which totals some $600,000. They include the Burlington, Hamilton and Scarborough areas... The projects focus on restoring habitat for fish and wildlife, developing new ways of managing waste water and preventing agricultural runoff.

(House of Commons Debates, November 28, 2002, p. 2014)
(Débats de la Chambre des Communes, le 28 novembre 2002, p. 2014)

(c)   Kyoto Protocol / Protocole de Kyoto

M. Gilles Duceppe (Laurier — Sainte-Marie):

[L]e gouvernement affirme, au sujet du Protocole de Kyoto ... que "le Canada s'est engagé à respecter d'ici 2012, certaines obligations en matière de réduction des émissions de gaz à effet de serre.

Si le Premier ministre est ... déterminé à ratifier sans détour le Protocole de Kyoto, pourquoi ... parle-t-il de respecter "certaines obligations" et non pas toutes les obligations du Canada?

Le très hon. Jean Chrétien (Premier ministre):

[C]'est l'intention du gouvernement canadien de respecter les critères qui veulent que d'ici 2012, nous aurons réduit de 6 p. 100 les émissions de CO_2 au Canada, par rapport à la situation qui existait en 1990.

(House of Commons Debates, October 1, 2002, p. 49)
(Débats de la Chambre des Communes, le 1er octobre 2002, p. 49)

Mr. James Moore (Port Moody — Coquitlam — Port Coquitlam):

[T]he United States and Australia have chosen to develop their own emissions reduction targets rather than committing themselves to the unachievable goals of Kyoto. Other nations such as Argentina, Chile and Mexico have not committed to a firm Kyoto target. All of our major free trade partners, the U.S., Mexico and Chile, are working on their own solutions.

Why can we not have a made-in-Canada solution to Kyoto that balances our economic and environmental needs for the future?

Hon. David Anderson (Minister of the Environment):

Canada did choose its own target just as other countries have done. Furthermore, Canada has developed a made-in-Canada plan with the cooperation of the provinces and territories. All 14 governments have been working on this for the last five years ... [T]he principal issue ... about climate change is that it is a global problem and it has to be dealt with on a global basis.

(House of Commons Debates, November 4, 2002, p. 1230)
(Débats de la Chambre des Communes, le 4 novembre 2002, p. 1230)

Mr. Stephen Harper (Leader of the Opposition):

[W]hen the government ratifies Kyoto does it intend to ratify the whole accord including sections dealing with international emissions trading?

Hon. David Anderson (Minister of the Environment):

[W]hen we ratify the Kyoto accord we will be ratifying the Kyoto accord. However ... what we have for implementation is a made in Canada plan. That made in Canada plan ... will not include the incorporation of the so-called Russian hot air; in other words, a reduction which has no impact on the environment by reducing emissions.

(House of Commons Debates, December 3, 2002, pp. 2203-4)
(Débats de la Chambre des Communes, le 3 décembre 2002, pp. 2203-4)

(d)   Madrid Protocol / Protocole de Madrid

Mr. Peter Adams (Peterborough):

Canadians are increasingly active in Antarctica ... [W]hen will Canada ratify the protocol for environmental protection under the Antarctic treaty, commonly known as the Madrid protocol?

Hon. David Anderson (Minister of the Environment):

[I]t is high time that Canada ratified the Antarctic treaty. The protocol is essential to protect one of the world's most sensitive and interesting ecological regions ... [R]atification [the Protocol] is expected by the end of the year.

(House of Commons Debates, April 7, 2003, p. 5173)
(Débats de la Chambre des Communes, le 7 avril 2003, p. 5173)

(e)   Space Exploration / Exploration de l'espace

Mme Yolande Thibeault (Saint-Lambert):

[N]ous avons tous été consternés par le désastre de la navette *Columbia* en fin de semaine dernière ... Dans un tel contexte, est-ce que le ministre peut nous informer de ses intentions quant à l'avenir du programme spatial canadien?

L'hon. Allan Rock (ministre de l'Industrie):

Depuis 40 ans, le Canada travaille étroitement avec la NASA dans un vrai partenariat ... Canada and its Space Agency are determined to continue the international effort in space exploration ... [W]e will work closely with NASA, assisting it to determine the cause of the tragedy, and we will fly again with the Americans.

(House of Commons Debates, February 3, 2003, p. 3065)
(Débats de la Chambre des Communes, le 3 février 2003, p. 3065)

2   *Foreign Affairs / Affaires étrangères*

(a)   Afghanistan / Afghanistan

Mr. Larry Bagnell (Yukon):

[A] year after the September 11 attacks a Canadian presence is needed in Afghanistan to visibly work with agencies to restore and protect school programs for young Afghan children and women ... [W]hat is the Government of Canada doing ... to help with Afghanistan's reconstruction efforts?

Mrs. Marlene Jennings (Parliamentary Secretary to the Minister for International Cooperation):

[T]hrough CIDA, Canada has been and continues to be present in Afghanistan's reconstruction efforts. Since 9/11, Canada has committed over $160 million to Afghanistan. Of that amount, $22 million has been provided for reconstruction and development initiatives, including vocational training for women and primary education. CIDA does work on the ground with reputable organizations like UNICEF, CARE Canada and the Red Cross.

(House of Commons Debates, November 8, 2002, p. 1502)
(Débats de la Chambre des Communes, le 8 novembre 2002, p. 1502)

Ms. Anita Neville (Winnipeg South Centre):

[W]e have recently read reports that Canada could be considering a return to Afghanistan. [Is] this ... true?

Hon. John McCallum (Minister of National Defence):

Canada has been approached by the international community for assistance in maintaining peace and security in Afghanistan for the UN mandated mission in Kabul. Canada is willing to serve with a battle group and a brigade headquarters for a period of one year, starting late this summer. We are currently in discussion with a number of potential partners.

(House of Commons Debates, February 12, 2003, p. 3467)
(Débats de la Chambre des Communes, le 12 février 2003, p. 3467)

(b)   Algeria / Algérie

M. Michel Guimond (Beauport — Montmorency — Côte-de-Beaupré — Île d'Orléans):

[A]u dernier Sommet de la Francophonie, qui s'est tenu à Beyrouth et auquel participait le premier ministre canadien, les participants, en présence de l'Algérie, ont réaffirmé leur volonté de travailler au maintien de la paix dans le monde, et plus particulièrement dans l'espace francophone.

Le site Web du ministère des Affaires étrangères identifie l'Algérie comme un endroit à éviter pour les touristes canadiens. Est-ce que le ministre des Affaires étrangères peut nous dire s'il partage la mise en garde de son ministère?

L'hon. Bill Graham (ministre des Affaires étrangères):

[L]e Canada est très fier de sa participation à la Francophonie et nous sommes fiers de la participation du premier ministre à Beyrouth.

Évidemment, nous travaillons avec tous les pays de la Francophonie. L'Algérie reste, dans certaines régions, un pays non sécuritaire. C'est naturellement notre devoir d'informer les citoyens canadiens de ce fait, mais nous continuons de travailler avec l'Algérie, avec la Francophonie et avec le monde afin d'essayer d'établir la paix dans toutes les régions du monde.

(House of Commons Debates, October 21, 2002, p. 679)

(Débats de la Chambre des Communes, le 21 octobre 2002, p. 679)

Mr. Mac Harb (Ottawa Centre):

[I]n October of 2002 the Minister of Citizenship and Immigration ... announced special measures to deal with the Algerian file ... Since the minister just returned from a trip to Algeria three weeks ago, could he report on that visit?

Mr. Sarkis Assadourian (Parliamentary Secretary to the Minister of Citizenship and Immigration):

During his active visit to Algeria, the minister met with the minister responsible for overseas community, ministers of foreign affairs, justice and interior, as well as the prime minister of Algeria and the president. The minister also expressed a desire to establish a working group with these ministers to address issues related to the movement of people. Further, the minister also met with editors of major newspapers to discuss the situation in Algeria. He also met with Algerian human rights NGOs to discuss the situation of human rights in Algeria.

(House of Commons Debates, February 7, 2003, pp. 3304-5)

(Débats de la Chambre des Communes, le 7 février 2003, pp. 3304-5)

(c) Armenia / Arménie

Mr. Svend Robinson (Burnaby — Douglas):

On June 13 this year the Senate passed a motion calling upon the Government of Canada to recognize the 1915 genocide of the Armenians and to designate April 24 of every year hereafter throughout Canada as a day of remembrance for the 1.5 million Armenians who fell victim to the first genocide of the 20th century[3] ... Will the government ... join with the

---

[3] See Recognition and Commemoration of Armenian Genocide, *Debates of the Senate* (Hansard), June 13, 2002, pp. 3044-45.

French government and many other elected bodies around the world and support this ... recognition of the Armenian genocide?

Hon. Bill Graham (Minister of Foreign Affairs):

[T]he government shares with the people of Armenia the sorrow as a result of the terrible tragedy and loss of life in those awful circumstances during the course of the breakup of the Ottoman Empire.

I met recently with the Speaker of the Armenian legislature, who was here, and with various Armenian members of their legislature. We continue to examine this question. The Armenian people know that the government sympathizes with their cause and sympathizes with the suffering they had, and we will continue in that line.

(House of Commons Debates, October 3, 2002, p. 247)

(Débats de la Chambre des Communes, le 3 octobre 2002, p. 247)

(d)   Caucasus Region / Région du Caucase

Mr. Sarkis Assadourian (Brampton Centre):

Recently the secretary of state [for Central and Eastern Europe and the Middle East] visited Azerbaijan, Georgia and Armenia to meet with government officials and business dealers to broaden Canada's contacts in the rapidly developing Caucasus region. Will the secretary of state share with us his views on this very important visit and the outcome he achieved?

Hon. Gar Knutson (Secretary of State (Central and Eastern Europe and Middle East)):

My visit to Azerbaijan, Armenia and Georgia was clearly a success. I was well received and met with all three presidents. This is a critical time for the region as all three countries face challenges ranging from systematic corruption, conflicts and poverty. Notwithstanding these challenges, there are many positive signs in these countries as they move through transition from being former soviet republics to democratic countries enjoying the benefits of a free market economy. I believe that Canada and our business community have a large role to play in providing assistance to these countries.

(House of Commons Debates, November 25, 2002, p. 1839)

(Débats de la Chambre des Communes, le 25 novembre 2002, p. 1839)

(e)   China / Chine

Mr. Svend Robinson (Burnaby — Douglas):

Amanda Zhao, a young Chinese student living in Burnaby, was murdered last week. This followed brutal attacks on a number of Korean women in the months immediately preceding. It took over a week for the RCMP to publicize Amanda's disappearance and the Chinese consulate was not informed as international protocol requires.

What steps is the minister taking to ensure that there will be a full, vigorous, public review of the circumstances ...?

Hon. Wayne Easter (Solicitor General of Canada):

I would like to extend my deepest sympathy to Ms. Zhao family and friends for their loss under such tragic circumstances.

[T]he RCMP is conducting an internal review of the matter and it has already indicated that it will make the results of that review public.

(House of Commons Debates, October 25, 2002, p. 912)
(Débats de la Chambre des Communes, le 25 octobre 2002, p. 912)

(f)   Congo

M. Gérard Binet (Frontenac — Mégantic):

[N]ous avons appris récemment le terrible massacre de Congolais dans l'est de ce pays ... [Q]uelle est la contribution du Canada au processus de paix dans la République démocratique du Congo?

L'hon. Denis Paradis (secrétaire d'État (Amérique latine et Afrique) (Francophonie)):

[L]'action du gouvernement canadien se traduit par un appui politique et financier au processus de paix, notamment par le biais l'accord du Dialogue inter-congolais. Notre envoyé spécial auprès de ce pays, Marc Brault, travaille étroitement avec les Nations Unies, avec nos partenaires internationaux ainsi qu'avec les parties congolaises concernées. À la demande des Nations Unies, le Canada participe au Comité international de garantie sur l'Accord de Pretoria, dont la première réunion se tient aujourd'hui à Kinshasa. Nous nous concentrons, avec notre ambassade à Kinshasa, sur la sécurité des Canadiens qui sont dans la région.

(House of Commons Debates, April 10, 2003, pp. 5361-62)
(Débats de la Chambre des Communes, le 10 avril 2003, pp. 5361-62)

(g)   Cuba

M. David Price (Compton — Stanstead):

[Le] secrétaire d'État pour l'Amérique latine, l'Afrique et la Francophonie ... revient de Cuba après la première visite ministérielle canadienne depuis mars 1999. Après cette mission, comment le Canada estime-t-il avoir atteint ses objectifs?

L'hon. Denis Paradis (secrétaire d'État (Amérique latine et Afrique) (Francophonie)):

[N]ous avons soulevé la question du tourisme. Il y a 400 000 Canadiens qui vont à Cuba chaque année. Nous avons soulevé aussi avec les Cubains l'importance de l'investissement canadien. Nous sommes les deuxièmes investisseurs à Cuba. Nous allons également mettre sur pied des ententes pour faire en sorte que nos PME, nos petites et moyennes entreprises puissent être davantage présentes. Nous avons aussi soulevé la question des droits de la personne et de la démocratie. Dans la poursuite du dialogue, nous avons convenu que nous devrions avoir des échanges de parlementaires.

(House of Commons Debates, November 7, 2002, p. 1459)
(Débats de la Chambre des Communes, le 7 novembre 2002, p. 1459)

(h)　French in International Institutions / Utilisation du français dans les institutions internationales

M. Bernard Patry (Pierrefonds — Dollard):

On note que l'utilisation de la langue française au sein des institutions internationales accuse un recul. Le ministre pourrait-il nous dire ce qu'il entend faire pour promouvoir l'utilisation du français dans ces mêmes institutions internationales?

L'hon. Denis Paradis (secrétaire d'État (Amérique latine et Afrique) (Francophonie)):

[L]e Canada s'occupe activement de la promotion du français dans les organismes internationaux. Lors du Sommet de la Francophonie de Beyrouth et lors de la dernière conférence ministérielle à Lausanne, j'ai annoncé que le gouvernement du Canada allait allouer 500 000 dollars pour favoriser l'utilisation du français dans les organismes internationaux à New York et Washington, plus précisément à l'ONU et à l'Organisation des États américains.

(House of Commons Debates, January 29, 2003, p. 2844)
(Débats de la Chambre des Communes, le 29 janvier 2003, p. 2844)

(i)　Haiti / Haïti

M. Bernard Patry (Pierrefonds — Dollard):

Compte tenu du fait que l'actualité politique nous rappelle de façon quotidienne la dure réalité de la situation en Haïti, est-ce que le secrétaire d'État peut nous faire part des préoccupations du Canada à cet égard?

L'hon. Denis Paradis (secrétaire d'État (Amérique latine et Afrique) (Francophonie)):

[L]e Canada est très préoccupé de la situation en Haïti. Ce sont 8,5 millions de personnes qui vivent dans un état de pauvreté et de misère extrêmes. Relativement à la Francophonie, nous avons la déclaration de Bamako. À l'intérieur de l'Organisation des États américains, nous avons la charte. Ces deux instruments véhiculent des valeurs qui sont propres aux Canadiens, des valeurs de démocratie, de droits de la personne et de bonne gouvernance, valeurs qui semblent ne pas être contenues dans le dictionnaire haïtien. Le Canada demande l'aide de la communauté internationale pour apporter son appui à l'Organisation des États américains, afin que tous nous puissions venir en aide au peuple haïtien.

(House of Commons Debates, February 18, 2003, p. 3716)

(Débats de la Chambre des Communes, le 18 février 2003, p. 3716)

(j)   International Civil Aviation Organization / Organisation de l'aviation civile internationale

M. Mario Laframboise (Argenteuil — Papineau — Mirabel):

[L]'édition du 10 décembre dernier du quotidien *Le Devoir* titrait: "Ottawa a fait languir l'OACI pour lui donner une leçon," et ajoutait: "L'organisme international pourra enfin prendre possession des locaux mis à sa disposition par Québec." Est-ce que le ministre ... peut nous confirmer que l'Organisation de l'aviation civile internationale peut, dès à présent, occuper ses nouveaux locaux sans que soit remise en question l'intégralité des avantages dont elle et les 33 États membres siégeant au Conseil jouissent en vertu des accords qui lient le Canada à l'organisation?

L'hon. Bill Graham (ministre des Affaires étrangères):

[C]ette affaire très complexe est une question immobilière. Il y a eu des négociations entre ... le gouvernement provincial du Québec, le gouvernement fédéral et cette institution internationale. Nous allons essayer de compléter cela aussitôt que possible dans le but de garder cette importante institution internationale à Montréal, non seulement pour servir les Canadiens mais tout le monde.

(House of Commons Debates, February 12, 2003, p. 3469)

(Débats de la Chambre des Communes, le 12 février 2003, p. 3469)

(k)   Iraq / Irak

Mme Francine Lalonde (Mercier):

Peut-on obtenir l'engagement du gouvernement qu'il est hors de question que le Canada participe à des frappes contre l'Irak sans que les Nations Unies ne l'aient décidé?

L'hon. Bill Graham (ministre des Affaires étrangères):

[L]a politique de ce gouvernement a toujours été d'agir par le biais des Nations Unies. Nous appuyons les Nations Unies; nous avons appuyé

le président Bush lorsqu'il est venu aux Nations Unies; et nous continuons d'appuyer une solution à cette grave crise par le biais d'un moyen
multilatéral.

(House of Commons Debates, October 1, 2002, p. 54)

(Débats de la Chambre des Communes, le 1ᵉʳ octobre 2002, p. 54)

Mme Francine Lalonde (Mercier):

[L]e projet de résolution que les États-Unis ont rendu public retire beaucoup de pouvoir à l'ONU dans le règlement du conflit irakien. Premièrement, les inspecteurs seront accompagnés par des soldats américains;
deuxièmement, il appartiendrait aux États membres, pas à l'ONU, de
juger si l'Irak fait preuve de bonne volonté ou s'il faut utiliser la force.
   Maintenant qu'il connaît la position américaine, est-ce que le gouvernement appuie toujours la résolution des États-Unis?

L'hon. Bill Graham (ministre des Affaires étrangères):

Cette résolution sera débattue au sein du Conseil de sécurité. Dès que le
Conseil de sécurité aura décidé, parce que c'est au Conseil de sécurité de
décider, nous avons dit que le gouvernement canadien soutiendra le Conseil de sécurité sur les conditions de l'entrée des inspecteurs en Irak.

(House of Commons Debates, October 3, 2002, p. 248)

(Débats de la Chambre des Communes, le 3 octobre 2002, p. 248)

M. Stéphane Bergeron (Verchères — Les Patriotes):

[U]ne compagnie montréalaise ... se voit privée d'un contrat de 40 millions de dollars pour l'exportation d'ambulances à l'Irak, en raison de la
position du gouvernement américain à l'égard de ce pays. Le ministre m'a
répondu, et je le cite:

   nous continuons notre collaboration avec les autorités américaines
   pour réduire les tensions dans la région et ne pas donner du matériel
   aux Irakiens dans ces circonstances.[4]

Comment le ministre des Affaires étrangères peut-il faire une telle affirmation, alors qu'il sait très bien que la vente de matériel humanitaire,
comme des ambulances, s'inscrit parfaitement dans l'esprit du programme de l'ONU régissant le commerce avec l'Irak?

L'hon. Bill Graham (ministre des Affaires étrangères):

Les exportations vers l'Irak ont besoin de l'approbation de l'ONU parce
que c'est l'ONU qui octroie les permis d'exportation. Dans le cas d'un

---

[4] Hon. Bill Graham (Minister of Foreign Affairs) in response to the question of Mr.
Stéphane Bergeron (Verchères — Les Patriotes), *House of Commons Debates*, October 28, 2002, p. 963.

permis octroyé par les Nations Unies, le Canada l'approuve et l'exportation a lieu. C'est un malentendu de prétendre que ce sont les autorités américaines qui empêchent cette exportation. C'est une décision prise par tous les pays par l'entremise de l'ONU.

(House of Commons Debates, October 31, 2002, p. 1146)
(Débats de la Chambre des Communes, le 31 octobre 2002, p. 1146)

Mr. Stephen Harper (Leader of the Opposition):

[T]oday a group of European nations, including Italy, Poland, Hungary, Spain, Portugal, Denmark and the Czech Republic, has issued a declaration declaring support for the multilateral coalition of nations led by Australia, Britain and the United States pursuing the unconditional disarmament of Saddam Hussein ... Is the government now prepared to unequivocally join and support this coalition of nations?

Hon. David Collenette (Minister of Transport):

[T]he government is unified on one position and that is that the United Nations is the final determinant as to whether or not action should be taken in Iraq.

(House of Commons Debates, January 30, 2003, p. 2958)
(Débats de la Chambre des Communes, le 30 janvier 2003, p. 2958)

(1)   Ivory Coast / Côte d'Ivoire

M. Yves Rocheleau (Trois-Rivières):

Le 18 septembre dernier, le gouvernement de la Côte d'Ivoire a subi une tentative de coup d'État, fragilisant ainsi les assises d'un gouvernement démocratiquement élu.
    Avant que la situation ne dégénère et ne devienne incontrôlable, comme cela s'est produit il n'y a pas si longtemps dans d'autres pays africains, est-ce que le gouvernement canadien a l'intention de réaffirmer son appui au gouvernement ivoirien, qui a été élu démocratiquement en octobre 2000?

Le très hon. Jean Chrétien (premier ministre):

[L]ors de notre rencontre de la semaine dernière à Beyrouth, tous les chefs de gouvernement ont discuté, au cours de la séance plénière, de la situation en Côte d'Ivoire.
    Nous travaillons tous collectivement pour nous assurer que le gouvernement démocratique demeure en place. Un comité de chefs de gouvernement, présidé par le président Wade, du Sénégal, travaille à ce sujet. Nous espérons que la situation va bientôt redevenir normale dans ce pays.

(House of Commons Debates, October 23, 2002, p. 798)
(Débats de la Chambre des Communes, le 23 octobre 2002, p. 798)

M. Mac Harb (Ottawa-Centre):

[C]onsidérant les réactions suivant la signature de l'accord en Côte-d'Ivoire, est-ce que le ministre responsable de l'Afrique peut nous informer sur la situation en Côte d'Ivoire, particulièrement quant à la sécurité des Canadiens qui demeurent dans ce pays?

L'hon. Denis Paradis (secrétaire d'État (Amérique latine et Afrique) (Francophonie)):

[J]'étais en communication tout à l'heure avec notre ambassadeur en Côte-d'Ivoire, M. Émile Gauvreau. Nos Canadiens, au nombre de 500, sont en sécurité. L'ambassade a préparé un plan d'évacuation pour parer à toute éventualité. Toutefois, ce matin, la situation était revenue au calme. Notre ambassade est à nouveau ouverte et notre ambassadeur nous dit que les Ivoiriens attendent un discours rassurant du président dans les prochains jours.

(House of Commons Debates, January 30, 2003, p. 2963)
(Débats de la Chambre des Communes, le 30 janvier 2003, p. 2963)

(m)   Latin America / Amérique latine

Mme Yolande Thibeault (Saint-Lambert):

[Q]uelle est la réaction du gouvernement canadien eu égard à la lutte antiguérilla et aux tensions entre la Colombie et le Venezuela?

L'hon. Denis Paradis (secrétaire d'État (Amérique latine et Afrique) (Francophonie)):

[L]e président de Colombie ... déploie des efforts pour ramener à la raison les forces révolutionnaires en Colombie, lesquelles détiennent à l'heure actuelle 3 000 otages ... We support the efforts of the Organization of American States regarding peace in the region. We ask the international community, and more particularly the neighbouring countries, to give support and to provide solidarity so that violence will be alleviated in Colombia and in the whole region.

(House of Commons Debates, February 26, 2003, p. 4042)
(Débats de la Chambre des Communes, le 26 février 2003, p. 4042)

(n)   Mexico / Mexique

Ms. Paddy Torsney (Burlington):

Last week the President of the Queen's Privy Council for Canada and Minister of Intergovernmental Affairs signed a memorandum of understanding with Mexico's Secretary of the Interior, Santiago Creel, to cooperate on federalism ... [W]hat this MOU will mean for Canadians and for Mexicans?

Mr. Joe Peschisolido (Parliamentary Secretary to the President of the Queen's Privy Council for Canada and Minister of Intergovernmental Affairs):

This is the first time that Canada has signed a memorandum of understanding on federalism with another country. Mexico is working very diligently on this active reform program and it is important for Canada to enhance and work with Mexico in this process. The areas of cooperation in this field include transparency and accountability, intergovernmental affairs and intergovernmental relations.

(House of Commons Debates, February 5, 2003, pp. 3182-83)
(Débats de la Chambre des Communes, le 5 février 2003, pp. 3182-83)

(o)   Middle East / Moyen-Orient

Mr. Walt Lastewka (St. Catharines):

The secretary of state [for Central and Eastern Europe and the Middle East] will be visiting the gulf region next week. In light of the increased tension in the area due to Iraq, would the secretary of state please tell us what he hopes to accomplish during this visit?

Hon. Gar Knutson (Secretary of State (Central and Eastern Europe and Middle East)):

[M]y trade mission to the gulf next week, accompanied by 30 Canadian companies, including SNC-Lavalin and EnCana, ... will stress that Canada's relationship with the Arab world is not simply one-dimensional. We can help achieve regional stabilities through strengthening our economic ties while at the same time conveying messages of Canadian values.

However, I will have the opportunity to sit down with leaders of these countries and convey Canada's desire to see a resolution of the current impasse regarding Iraq and the absolute necessity of getting the weapons inspectors back to work.

(House of Commons Debates, October 2, 2002, p. 137)
(Débats de la Chambre des Communes, le 2 octobre 2002, p. 137)

Mr. Stockwell Day (Okanagan — Coquihalla):

Prime Minister [of Canada] spent his weekend at the francophonie summit rubbing elbows with a world renowned self-proclaimed terrorist whose stated goal is to disrupt any prospects for peace in the Middle East.

Why did the Prime Minister at some point during this conference ... not publicly condemn this terrorist and demand an apology from the

Lebanese president who was already himself making one-sided comments about the Middle East situation?

Hon. Bill Graham (Minister of Foreign Affairs):

[T]he Prime Minister was one among many world leaders, presidents of many countries invited to an event to address the opening of the francophonie summit. Lebanon, the host country, has control of the invitations. Those invitations are not vetted by the Prime Minister or any other attendee.

The francophonie summit permits us an opportunity for dialogue on cultures, on civilizations, on human rights and on other issues.

Our policy on Hezbollah is clear. We condemn its military wing as terrorists and we engage in dialogue with those with whom we wish to gain peace.

(House of Commons Debates, October 21, 2002, p. 680)
(Débats de la Chambre des Communes, le 21 octobre 2002, p. 680)

(p)   Nuclear Disarmament / Désarmement nucléaire

Mr. David Price (Compton — Stanstead):

[F]our days ago Pakistan tested surface to air ballistic missiles. That same day India chose to respond by testing a conventional surface to air missile. Today Pakistan has again conducted missile tests. [What is] the [government] response to these very disturbing developments?

Hon. David Kilgour (Secretary of State (Asia-Pacific)):

[A]fter Pakistan's test last Friday, Canada expressed deep regret and urged a halt to nuclear development. Today we reiterate that as tensions in the region remain high, these tests are particularly counterproductive and serve only to undermine efforts by the international community to bring a lasting peace.

In the interests of regional and international security, Canada urges both Pakistan and India to de-escalate and resume dialogue immediately.

(House of Commons Debates, October 8, 2002, p. 475)
(Débats de la Chambre des Communes, le 8 octobre 2002, p. 475)

Mr. Sarkis Assadourian (Brampton Centre):

The world has recently discovered that North Korea has secretly developed a weapon of mass destruction and has admitted to the capability to manufacture nuclear weapons. Reports state that the North Koreans presently have at least two long range nuclear weapons ... [W]hat effect this will have on Canada's foreign policy in the region and what action has been taken to face this challenge?

Hon. Bill Graham (Minister of Foreign Affairs):

[W]e are obviously very concerned by the recent developments arising out of North Korea. We have communicated to the republic of North Korea the fact that the normalization of relations with North Korea will entirely depend upon its abandoning these weapons of mass destruction and its present program.

We continue to provide humanitarian aid for people in that country who are suffering. We have made it clear to that administration and those people that for them to enter into the family of nations and have regular contacts we must be assured that they are not a threat to the peace and security in the region.

(House of Commons Debates, October 22, 2002, pp. 750-51)
(Débats de la Chambre des Communes, le 22 octobre 2002, pp. 750-51)

Ms. Libby Davies (Vancouver East):

U.S. war planners have refused to rule out the possible use of nuclear weapons on Iraq. Will the Prime Minister make it clear that the government is opposed to the use of these weapons by any nation, including the U.S., and that these weapons must be abolished?

Hon. Bill Graham (Minister of Foreign Affairs):

[W]e are opposed to the use of nuclear weapons or any weapons of mass destruction. We have constructively worked through the international community at the disarmament commission in Geneva which I attended last year. We have consistently been working with all the powers, both to reduce the number of and to eliminate nuclear weapons, consistent with the non-proliferation treaty, and ultimately all weapons of mass destruction.... It is an important part of our foreign policy.

(House of Commons Debates, February 21, 2003, pp. 3866-67)
(Débats de la Chambre des Communes, le 21 février 2003, pp. 3866-67)

(q)　Sri Lanka / Sri Lanka

Mr. Derek Lee (Scarborough — Rouge River):

[B]etween March 18 and 21 the sixth session of peace talks between the government of Sri Lanka and the Liberation Tigers of Tamil Eelam were held in Hakone, Japan ... [What are] the results of those ... discussions ... and ... how is Canada helping to bring peace to that region?

Hon. David Kilgour (Secretary of State (Asia-Pacific)):

[R]egarding the ceasefire, the two parties have reaffirmed their commitment to peace by strengthening the mandate and capacity of the Sri Lankan monitoring authority ... Canada continues to support the process through ongoing humanitarian aid, supporting the form of the federations being made available to both sides in order to find models of federalism that work practically around the world.

(House of Commons Debates, March 31, 2003, p. 4920)
(Débats de la Chambre des Communes, le 31 mars 2003, p. 4920)

(r)   Turkey / Turquie

Miss Deborah Grey (Edmonton North):

One of Canada's NATO allies, Turkey, has asked for help to protect its borders in light of a possible war in Iraq. It is requesting emergency consultations under NATO's mutual defence treaty.... [I]s Canada prepared to pre-deploy troops to Turkey?

Right Hon. Jean Chrétien (Prime Minister):

Canada has always been ready for any situation. Because Turkey is Iraq's neighbour it is normal that it wants to be ready in case there is a conflict there. We all hope that this preparation will not be needed.

(House of Commons Debates, February 10, 2003, p. 3353)
(Débats de la Chambre des Communes, le 10 février 2003, p. 3353)

(s)   Ukraine

Mr. Walt Lastewka (St. Catharines):

[T]he country of Ukraine requires assistance to strengthen the country's agricultural infrastructure ... [What is] CIDA's agricultural technical assistance with the Ukraine?

Hon. Susan Whelan (Minister for International Cooperation):

[T]he Canadian International Development Agency will be contributing $6 million over five years to a Saskatchewan-Manitoba-Alberta government partnership to help provide technical assistance in agriculture for the Ukraine. One of the common themes that came out of our new policy on agriculture ... is that we need to harness Canadian expertise.

(House of Commons Debates, April 9, 2003, p. 5295)
(Débats de la Chambre des Communes, le 9 avril 2003, p. 5295)

(t)   Zimbabwe

Mr. Keith Martin (Esquimalt-Juan de Fuca):

[T]he expulsion of Zimbabwe from the Commonwealth expires next month unless the suspension is renewed. Given the fact that people are still being tortured and murdered by Mugabe's thugs ... will the [government] ... support the continued expulsion of Zimbabwe from the Commonwealth ...?

Hon. Bill Graham (Minister of Foreign Affairs):

We have been following this extremely closely. We continue to urge on President Mugabe to change the conditions in his country. [W]e remain in contact with our colleagues ... to see if we can work something through with the troika before we make any precipitous steps ... [W]e want to work ... in a way that recognizes the best interests of the people of Zimbabwe.

(House of Commons Debates, February 18, 2003, pp. 3717-18)
(Débats de la Chambre des Communes, le 18 février 2003, pp. 3717-18)

3   Health / La Santé

Ms. Bonnie Brown (Oakville):

[I]t is estimated that tuberculosis kills more than two million people worldwide every year. The overwhelming majority of these deaths happen in developing countries ... [W]hat is the Canadian government doing to address this deadly and entirely preventable disease?

Hon. Susan Whelan (Minister for International Cooperation):

[T]wo years ago Canada led the world by investing in the global drug facility and helped reduce the cost for tuberculosis drugs from $15 per person to $10 per person, U.S. Yesterday at the World Conference on Lung Health in Montreal, I was pleased to accept the International Union Against Tuberculosis and Lung Disease award in recognition of Canada's leadership in the fight against tuberculosis. Further, I committed Canada to continue the fight yesterday by announcing $80 million over four years to the stop tuberculosis partnership.

(House of Commons Debates, October 7, 2002, p. 364)
(Débats de la Chambre des Communes, le 7 octobre 2002, p. 364)

Mr. Svend Robinson (Burnaby — Douglas):

Recently studies for the Romanow Commission have noted that trade deals like NAFTA and the GATS may block the expansion of medicare to include a national plan for home care, pharmacare and dental care.

Will the government take immediate steps to prevent any further privatization in the health care field to prevent private health care companies from claiming massive compensation under NAFTA and GATS?

M. Jeannot Castonguay (secrétaire parlementaire du ministre de la Santé):

[I] 1 est évident qu'à l'heure actuelle, la loi canadienne assure à tous les Canadiens que les soins de santé qui seront médicalement nécessaires seront fournis. Il est évident également que ce gouvernement-ci est très conscient de l'importance de réviser notre structure de système de santé pour les années à venir. C'est pourquoi nous attendons avec beaucoup d'enthousiasme à la fois le rapport Romanow et le rapport Kirby, qui nous permettront de voir comment on va aborder la situation pour les années à venir. Je peux assurer tous les Canadiens ... que notre système de santé sera protégé.

(House of Commons Debates, October 24, 2002, p. 869)
(Débats de la Chambre des Communes, le 24 octobre 2002, p. 869)

Ms. Colleen Beaumier (Brampton West — Mississauga):

The recently released UN AIDS report confirms that the AIDS pandemic is worsening. There are currently 42 million people living with HIV world-wide. This will increase to 50 million by 2005. More than 95% of new infections are in developing countries ... [W]hat is Canada doing about this?

Hon. Susan Whelan (Minister for International Cooperation):

[I]n addition to the $50 million announced by our Prime Minister for the international AIDS vaccine initiative, and in addition to the $150 million committed by the government for the global health fund to fight HIV-AIDS, tuberculosis and malaria, today I was able to announce an additional $19 million toward six initiatives in developing countries around the world, which includes a $2 million increase to the core fund for UN AIDS ... We are committed to putting more resources toward HIV and AIDS.

(House of Commons Debates, November 28, 2002, pp. 2011-12)
(Débats de la Chambre des Communes, le 28 novembre 2002, pp. 2011-12)

4 *World Health Organization / Organisation mondiale de la santé*

Mr. Svend Robinson (Burnaby — Douglas):

In the fight against atypical pneumonia or SARS the World Health Organization plays an absolutely critical role. Yet, when Taiwan asked the World Health Organization for help to assist its 23 million people, the WHO said no since Taiwan is not a member ... Will the [government] ... support Taiwan at the World Health Organization?

Hon. Bill Graham (Minister of Foreign Affairs):

Taiwan is not eligible for membership in the World Health Organization as it is not a member of the United Nations. Its observer status would require consensus from all members ... The government has been active in working with Taiwan and all governments to ensure that the Taiwanese government receives help through all the possible channels. We will continue that constructive policy.

(House of Commons Debates, March 27, 2003, p. 4821)
(Débats de la Chambre des Communes, le 27 mars 2003, p. 4821)

Mr. Grant Hill (Macleod):

SARS is a health issue that is significantly important to Canadians. The Ontario government has taken preventive steps. However, when the federal government was asked by the World Health Organization to screen all outgoing passengers, the minister said no. I would like her to explain that.

Hon. Anne McLellan (Minister of Health):

[I]n response to the WHO recommendation, we do have screening procedures in place ... [W]e have been in constant contact with the WHO ... [T]he WHO believes the procedures we have in place at Pearson International Airport in relation to outgoing passengers meet its recommendations. [Moreover,] ... the WHO ... has asked us to post those procedures so that other countries can learn from what we are doing and perhaps put in place similar procedures.

(House of Commons Debates, April 1, 2003, pp. 4987-88)
(Débats de la Chambre des Communes, le 1 avril 2003, pp. 4987-88)

4   Human Rights / Droits de la personne

(a)   China / Chine

Mr. Deepak Obhrai (Calgary East):

Canadians continue to be concerned with human rights violations in China. [T]his week the Chinese minister in charge of religious affairs visited Canada ... [Did] the government [take] ... this opportunity to tell the Chinese that Canada views these human rights violations with serious concern and that they must be stopped [?]

Hon. Bill Graham (Minister of Foreign Affairs):

[W]e speak out regularly about the human rights situation, both in Tibet and in China ... We have two positions with the Chinese government. We remonstrate with them, we point out where we believe they are strongly in the wrong, and we also try to work with them to upgrade their human rights record by bringing them Canadian expertise in the courts and the human rights record in China.

(House of Commons Debates, February 21, 2003, p. 3866)
(Débats de la Chambre des Communes, le 21 février 2003, p. 3866)

(b) Immigration

Mme Madeleine Dalphond-Guiral (Laval-Centre):

[P]endant que le ministre des Affaires étrangères recommande aux citoyens du Canada d'éviter de se rendre en Algérie, "étant donné les activités terroristes qui se poursuivent dans certaines régions de ce pays", son collègue de l'Immigration maintient la fin du moratoire sur les renvois des ressortissants algériens, alléguant que "les citoyens algériens ne courent aucun risque en étant renvoyés dans leur pays."

Comment le ministre peut-il défendre la levée du moratoire et expliquer que, malgré une guerre civile sanguinaire qui a fait plus de 150 000 morts, on permette le renvoi de gens installés ici depuis des années, alors que leurs enfants, nés au Canada, pourraient en principe rester ici?

L'hon. Denis Coderre (ministre de la Citoyenneté et de l'Immigration):

Dans un premier temps, le but de la levée du moratoire est de régulariser le système. Le Canada n'a aucune intention de faire une expulsion massive et aucune intention non plus d'accorder une amnistie générale. Chaque cas est spécifique et est examiné avec compassion et pour des raisons humanitaires. Nous pourrons prendre des décisions de façon à acheminer les dossiers correctement.

Toutefois, nous avons aussi le devoir de mettre en place un système intègre, où nous trouvons l'équilibre entre la vigilance et l'ouverture.

(House of Commons Debates, October 8, 2002, p. 476)
(Débats de la Chambre des Communes, le 8 octobre 2002, p. 476)

(c) Iran

Mrs. Betty Hinton (Kamloops, Thompson and Highland Valleys):

[I]n Iran 400 people have recently been stoned or hung and 270 of those people have been women. With 60 million Iranians at risk ... [a]re there specific resolutions before the United Nations on human rights violations in Iran and [what] ... has the government done ... to protect those human rights?

Hon. Bill Graham (Minister of Foreign Affairs):

[A]s to the specific resolutions that will come up before the Human Rights Commission ... I raised ... [this issue] with the Iranian foreign minister when I met with him at the United Nations General Assembly. We have always taken these concerns to the Iranian authorities and we insist absolutely that Iran's place in the world depends on its willingness to conform to international human rights standards. We will work with the government and the people of Iran to give them the chance to do that.

(House of Commons Debates, November 7, 2002, p. 1458)
(Débats de la Chambre des Communes, le 7 novembre 2002, p. 1458)

(d)　Multiculturalism / Multiculturalisme

M. Gérard Binet (Frontenac — Mégantic):

[L]e Réseau international sur la politique culturelle a été créé à Ottawa en 1998 à l'initiative ... du gouvernement du Canada.

Ce réseau compte actuellement 53 pays membres de toutes les grandes régions du monde. Son objectif est d'instaurer un dialogue sur les questions touchant la diversité culturelle dans le contexte de la mondialisation ... [Qu'est-ce que] le gouvernement du Canada ... fait ... pour la promotion de la diversité culturelle sur la scène internationale?

Mme Carole-Marie Allard (secrétaire parlementaire de la ministre du Patrimoine canadien):

[L]a ministre du Patrimoine canadien se trouve présentement à Paris afin de rallier le plus grand nombre possible de pays autour d'un instrument juridique qui, une fois adopté et ratifié, aura pour effet de protéger la culture lors de la conclusion de traités commerciaux. La ministre prendra la parole devant plusieurs tribunes, dont la Chambre de commerce Canada-France et l'UNESCO.

(House of Commons Debates, February 4, 2003, p. 3141)
(Débats de la Chambre des Communes, le 4 février 2003, p. 3141)

(e)　Racial Profiling / Profilage racial

Mr. Brian Masse (Windsor West):

Citizens from ... Windsor West have been stopped at the border, detained for as long as two hours, fingerprinted and photographed both when entering the U.S. and again when returning to Canada. All this was based solely on racial origin and country of birth, and they are Canadian citizens now. Will the Prime Minister ... intervene with ... George W. Bush to defend the rights of Canadian citizens ... ?

Hon. Elinor Caplan (Minister of National Revenue):

[S]ince the tragic events of September 11 of last year, both Canada and the United States have not only been on the highest state of alert but we have also enacted joint smart border initiatives ... [T]he goal is to have a safe, secure and efficient border.

(House of Commons Debates, October 8, 2002, pp. 476-77)
(Débats de la Chambre des Communes, le 8 octobre 2002, pp. 476-77)

(f) Right to Consular/Diplomatic Access / Droit à l'accès consulaire/diplomatique

Mr. Svend Robinson (Burnaby-Douglas):

Last July, Omar Khadr, a 15-year-old Canadian citizen, was arrested by the U.S. army in Afghanistan. To date, the U.S. has allowed the Red Cross access but has refused all Canadian consular access, in blatant violation of international law.... What action is the government taking ... to defend the rights of this young Canadian citizen from this abuse of U.S. power?

Hon. Bill Graham (Minister of Foreign Affairs):

This young man in an unfortunate situation was arrested in the course of having been accused of killing an American serviceman in the course of a conflict. There is no consular access in the course of conflicts or we would have had consular access to all of our prisoners during the second world war ... We have requested to the United States to have access and it has assured us that we will have access. The Red Cross has assured us that the young man's health is in good condition. We continue to press the United States to ensure that his rights will be protected.

(House of Commons Debates, October 2, 2002, p. 135)
(Débats de la Chambre des Communes, le 2 octobre 2002, p. 135)

Mme Francine Lalonde (Mercier):

[U]n travailleur forestier de Pohénégamook, dans le Témiscouata, se retrouve en prison pour avoir omis de déclarer un achat d'essence fait à la frontière des États-Unis. Il risque d'y rester jusqu'à Noël et les gens de la région sont inquiets.

Est-ce que le ministre des Affaires étrangères compte accentuer ses pressions auprès des autorités américaines pour s'assurer que M. Michel Jalbert soit traité équitablement dans cette affaire?

L'hon. Bill Graham (ministre des Affaires étrangères):

[N]ous avons naturellement demandé l'accès diplomatique pour cette personne. C'est un incident bien malheureux. Évidemment, les autorités américaines sont libres de faire ce qu'elles estiment nécessaires pour assurer la sécurité sur leur territoire. Naturellement, nous défendons toujours les intérêts des Canadiens et nous le ferons aussi dans ce cas, comme nous le faisons dans tous les cas qui concernent des Canadiens aux États-Unis.

(House of Commons Debates, October 29, 2002, p. 1034)
(Débats de la Chambre des Communes, le 29 octobre 2002, p. 1034)

Ms. Alexa McDonough (Halifax):

Seventy-six days ago, 32-year-old Canadian citizen Maher Arar ... was returning to Canada through the U.S. from a family vacation. He was apprehended, interrogated and deported without legal counsel first to Jordan and then to Syria, a country he left at the age of 17.

These actions violate international law and they violate his rights as a Canadian citizen ... When can the wife and kids of Maher Arar expect him home in Canada?

Hon. Bill Graham (Minister of Foreign Affairs):

[W]e are remaining in constant contact with the Syrian authorities to ensure that we have consular access to Mr. Arar. Our ambassador has met with him. We will continue to make sure that he receives consular access. We are making all representations possible to try to get the return of Mr. Arar to his family and to Canada as soon as possible.

(House of Commons Debates, December 12, 2002, p. 2629)
(Débats de la Chambre des Communes, le 12 décembre 2002, p. 2629)

5   *International Criminal Law / Droit pénal international*

(a)   International Criminal Court / Cour pénale internationale

Mme Francine Lalonde (Mercier):

[L]ors d'une allocution à la population américaine hier, le président George Bush a soutenu que les généraux irakiens pourraient être jugés pour crimes de guerre s'ils obéissaient à des ordres de Saddam Hussein en posant des gestes cruels et désespérés.

Est-ce que le Premier ministre est d'accord avec le président Bush qui veut se faire juge et partie et déterminer lui-même qui est un criminel de guerre?

Ms. Aileen Carroll (Parliamentary Secretary to the Minister of Foreign Affairs):

[T]he president has continued to focus on the United Nations Security Council as the proper forum for discussion and debate. He also said and acknowledges as we do that is where the important decision regarding a new resolution will be taken, and it is from that body's actions that decisions will comply.

Our emphasis has always been that it is the Security Council that should be dealing with the Iraqi situation, multilaterally through the United Nations. The obligations of Iraq are to the Security Council. It is that body that should be taking the lead in ensuring the resolution is respected.

Mme Francine Lalonde (Mercier):

[L]a réponse aurait dû être la suivante: Il n'appartient pas au président des États-Unis de déterminer qui est un criminel de guerre et qui ne l'est pas. Cette tâche revient à un tiers neutre, en l'occurrence la Cour pénale internationale.

Est-ce que le Premier ministre va profiter de la circonstance pour intervenir auprès du président Bush afin que celui-ci reconnaisse l'autorité de la Cour pénale internationale, y compris sur ses propres généraux?

Le très hon. Jean Chrétien (Premier ministre):

[L]es Canadiens ont été parmi les principaux initiateurs pour établir cette Cour internationale. Nous espérons qu'elle pourra jouer le rôle qu'elle doit jouer dans les années à venir pour tous les pays.

À ce moment-ci, les Américains ne veulent pas se soumettre, mais je pense qu'ils devraient reconsidérer, faire comme les autres pays et nous donner la possibilité d'avoir une cour internationale pour régler ce genre de conflit. Je pense qu'il y a dans le traité suffisamment de protection vis-à-vis des citoyens d'un pays pour que tout le monde puisse signer cet accord en toute sécurité.

(House of Commons Debates, October 8, 2002, p. 474)
(Débats de la Chambre des Communes, le 8 octobre 2002, p. 474)

(b) Terrorism / Terrorisme

Mr. Stockwell Day (Okanagan — Coquihalla):

[A]t the APEC conference this weekend in Mexico, 11 Asian countries, along with Australia and the United States, have signed on to a coalition to shut down the terrorist group Jemaah Islamiah, the group believed responsible for the 200 bombing murders in Bali. Why was Canada not included on that coalition list?

Hon. John Manley (Deputy Prime Minister and Minister of Finance):

[T]he government of Australia sought Canada's support for listing Jemaah Islamiah as a terrorist entity by the UN. We reviewed the request. We, along with 20 other countries, including the United States, European countries and Asian countries, submitted a letter of support for this listing to the United Nations.

We expect that the group will be added to the UN list by the end of today, at which time it will automatically be designated by Canada under our own UN suppression of terrorism regulations.

(House of Commons Debates, October 25, 2002, p. 914)
(Débats de la Chambre des Communes, le 25 octobre 2002, p. 914)

Mr. Mauril Bélanger (Ottawa — Vanier):

[S]hortly after the September 2001 terrorist attacks on the United States, cement barriers went up around the American embassy here in Ottawa. We were told that they were erected in order to provide greater distance from the street in the event of a car or truck bomb attack thereby providing greater security for the people in the embassy ... In providing greater protection for the people in the embassy, are we not, by the same token, putting the Canadians neighbouring the embassy at greater risk? If not, what assurances can he give us to that effect?

Hon. Wayne Easter (Solicitor General of Canada):

[W]e are very much aware of the inconvenience as a results of the extra security measures around the U.S. embassy.

I am advised by the RCMP that in consultation with the community partners, it is working with stakeholders to reach satisfactory solutions for residents and businesses in the area and at the same time ensuring the safety and security of our international community and residents in the national capital region.

(House of Commons Debates, October 28, 2002, p. 960)
(Débats de la Chambre des Communes, le 28 octobre 2002, p. 960)

Right Hon. Joe Clark (Calgary Centre):

In April CSIS confirmed that it had been monitoring Hezbollah terrorist activity in Canada since at least 1999. That same year in Montreal CSIS questioned Mohamedou Ould Slahi, who recruited two of the terrorist pilots. The week following the September 11 attacks ... the Prime Minister said in the House: "There is no link to any group in Canada with what happened in New York and Washington last week."[5] Is that still the government's position?

Hon. Wayne Easter (Solicitor General of Canada):

[W]e have now listed seven entities and are taking the necessary steps to ensure that our efforts are justified and effective. CSIS is doing its job in

---

[5] Right Hon. Jean Chrétien (Prime Minister) in response to the question of the Right Hon. Joe Clark (Calgary Centre), *House of Commons Debates*, September 18, 2001, p. 5250.

protecting international security and safety of Canadians, and doing the necessary investigations to see if other listings should come forward.

(House of Commons Debates, October 31, 2002, p. 1141)
(Débats de la Chambre des Communes, le 31 octobre 2002, p. 1141)

6 *International Humanitarian Law / Droit international humanitaire*

Ms. Beth Phinney (Hamilton Mountain):

Southern Africa is currently facing a major humanitarian crisis. The governments of several southern African countries have declared national disasters due to actual and anticipated food shortages.

This year, people in a number of countries in Africa, including refugees and internally displaced people, still have great unmet needs, with several million children going hungry ... [W]hat is the government doing to address these very urgent needs?

Hon. Susan Whelan (Minister for International Cooperation):

Canada is deeply concerned about the crisis facing several of the south African countries. On Monday I had the opportunity to meet with Jim Morris, who is the executive director of the World Food Program, inform him of our continued commitment to address this crisis and announce that Canada would be contributing an additional $7.9 million immediately, raising our total from $34.2 million to $42.1 million, to deal with the famine in southern Africa.

(House of Commons Debates, November 6, 2002, p. 1351)
(Débats de la Chambre des Communes, le 6 novembre 2002, p. 1351)

Mr. Svend Robinson (Burnaby — Douglas):

When the Prime Minister announced a special $500 million fund for Africa at the G-8, he told Canadians it would lift Africa out of poverty ... Given the performance of some Canadian businesses in Africa, including Talisman Energy, Acres International and the five mining companies in Congo recently found in violation of international UN regulations, will the minister agree to independent monitoring of their performance and an assessment of the development impact of this money?

L'hon. Denis Paradis (secrétaire d'État (Amérique latine et Afrique) (Francophonie)):

[L]e plan NEPAD, le Nouveau partenariat pour le développement de l'Afrique, qui est proposé par les Africains, pour l'Afrique, mentionne tout d'abord que, pour avoir de l'investissement en Afrique — et c'est la seule façon qu'ont les Africains de s'en sortir, disent-ils — il faut avoir des progrès en démocratie, en droits de la personne et en bonne gouvernance.

C'est le plan d'attaque pour l'Afrique. À cela, l'an passé, au Canada, nous avons voté en cette Chambre ... un fonds spécial de 500 millions de dollars pour faire en sorte d'aider l'Afrique à s'en sortir.[6]

(House of Commons Debates, November 18, 2002, p. 1547)
(Débats de la Chambre des Communes, le 18 novembre 2002, p. 1547)

Ms. Beth Phinney (Hamilton Mountain):

[T]he Prime Minister pledged at the G-8 summit in Kananaskis to increase Canada's investment in basic education in Africa. The international community also pledged to achieve by 2015 the six objectives of Education for All agreed to in Dakar in 2000. The Minister for International Cooperation is currently participating in the high level group meeting on Education for All in Abuja, Nigeria. What concrete measures is Canada taking to support education in developing countries?

Mrs. Marlene Jennings (Parliamentary Secretary to the Minister for International Cooperation):

[T]oday the Minister for International Cooperation announced that Canada, through CIDA, will provide $10 million per year over the next five years to both Mozambique and Tanzania. This is over and above our regular support for education to both these countries.

The minister also announced the funding of $5 million over the next five years to the UNESCO Institute for Statistics to help monitor the international community's work in meeting the objectives of Education for All.

(House of Commons Debates, November 19, 2002, p. 1621)
(Débats de la Chambre des Communes, le 19 novembre 2002, p. 1621)

Mr. John Harvard (Charleswood — St. James — Assiniboia):

There are more than 11 million Ethiopians in need of humanitarian assistance today and another 3 million need to be closely monitored. No one

---

[6] The 2001 budget (December 10, 2001) established the $500 million Canada Fund for Africa, a government program to provide funding for activities that will "help reduce poverty, provide primary education for all and set Africa on a sustainable path to a brighter future." (See Hon. Paul Martin (Minister of Finance), Fiscal Statement [The Budget], *House of Commons Debates,* December 10, 2001, pp. 8075, 8081). As for the introduction of Bill C-49 (Budget Implementation Act, 2001), see *House of Commons Debates,* February 5, 2002, p. 8679 (First Reading); March 18, 2002, p. 9787 (as passed by the House of Commons).

wants a repeat of the 1984 tragedy when mass starvation caused widespread suffering and death in Ethiopia ... [H]ow is the Government of Canada through CIDA responding to this emergency?

Hon. Susan Whelan (Minister for International Cooperation):

On January 16 the Government of Canada announced an additional $40 million in emergency assistance. Assistance will be delivered in partnership with the World Food Program, the Canada Food Grains Bank and other NGOs which will bring our total contribution to $47 million since September. Canadians are providing a leadership role in dealing with the drought and the famine in Ethiopia. We will continue to monitor the situation very closely.

(House of Commons Debates, January 29, 2003, p. 2842)
(Débats de la Chambre des Communes, le 29 janvier 2003, p. 2842)

7   *Trade and Economy / Commerce et économie*

(a)   Africa / Afrique

Mr. Tony Tirabassi (Niagara Centre):

[T]he Prime Minister and the government have continuously supported trade initiatives with impoverished nations, so that all involved may better participate and benefit in this new era of globalization ... [T]he Minister for International Trade will be leading a trade mission to Africa in November.

Given the challenges that Africa faces related to trade and development, what can Canadian companies gain by participating in the upcoming trade mission?

Hon. Pierre Pettigrew (Minister for International Trade):

[Y]es indeed, I will be leading a trade mission to South Africa, Nigeria and Senegal from November 15 to 26.

It is becoming quite clear that as Africa modernizes its private and public sectors, many African economies are looking outward to meet the demands and challenges of modernization.

Canadian companies have a lot to offer, particularly when it comes to education, technology and infrastructure. This mission will enable Canadian companies to develop new trading partnerships and a market that is ripe for Canadian products and services.

(House of Commons Debates, October 21, 2002, p. 682)
(Débats de la Chambre des Communes, le 21 octobre 2002, p. 682)

(b)   Canadian International Trade Tribunal / Tribunal canadien du commerce

M. Stéphane Bergeron (Verchères — Les Patriotes):

[L]'été dernier, le Tribunal canadien du commerce extérieur publiait les résultats de son enquête sur le dommage causé à l'industrie canadienne de l'acier. Reconnaissant qu'il y avait eu dommage pour cinq catégories de produits en cause, il recommandait l'imposition de contingents tarifaires pour quatre d'entre elles ... [L]e ministre des Finances reconnaîtra-t-il que l'imposition de contingents tarifaires ne réglera pas le problème?

L'hon. John Manley (vice-premier ministre et ministre des Finances):

[D]epuis le rapport, nous avons travaillé étroitement avec les entreprises et avec l'industrie de l'acier ... [L]'industrie s'oppose à l'imposition d'un tarif sur les importations des États-Unis. Cela pourrait créer un problème avec l'OMC, comme nous l'avons vu cette semaine avec les tarifs imposés par les États-Unis. Alors, il faut certainement trouver une méthode pour régler la situation, mais il faut considérer la décision du tribunal et les options qui nous sont disponibles.

M. Stéphane Bergeron:

[C]omme le signalait le ministre, l'an dernier, les États-Unis ont décidé d'exempter le Canada des mesures de sauvegardes ... Le gouvernement entend-il, de la même façon, exclure les États-Unis de l'application de toute mesure?

L'hon. John Manley:

Malheureusement, le tribunal a déterminé que le problème vient non seulement d'ailleurs, mais aussi des importations des États-Unis. Alors, pour faire exactement ce qu'il a demandé et ce que l'industrie a demandé, il faut exclure les États-Unis. C'est fondé sur une détermination tout à fait différente au Canada qu'aux États-Unis et cela pourrait nous causer des problèmes avec l'OMC.

(House of Commons Debates, April 10, 2003, pp. 5357-58)
(Débats de la Chambre des Communes, le 10 avril 2003, pp. 5357-58)

(c)   Canadian Wheat Board / Commission canadienne du blé

Hon. Lorne Nystrom (Regina — Qu'Appelle):

As the minister [for International Trade] knows, the American government has once again attacked the Canadian Wheat Board by slapping a

duty of some 12% and 10% on Canadian durum and spring wheat ...
[W]hat specific action is the minister taking to stand up for ... the ...
Board?

Hon. Pierre Pettigrew (Minister for International Trade):

[T]he American administration has been harassing Canadian wheat producers. We will continue to defend them in this Doha development round.
Even though it was not part of the negotiating mandate, the Americans are
pursuing the Canadian Wheat Board, and we will continue to stand up for
it because we believe it is doing a great job on behalf of Canadian farmers.

(House of Commons Debates, May 5, 2003, pp. 5809-10)
(Débats de la Chambre des Communes, le 5 mai 2003, pp.
5809-10)

(d)   Economic sanctions / Sanctions économiques

Mr. Rahim Jaffer (Edmonton — Strathcona):

[T]he United States and the United Kingdom have placed an important
resolution before the United Nations Security Council. That resolution
would lift the economic sanctions on Iraq and allow for the reconstruction
to continue ... [Will] the Government of Canada ... support ... the U.S.
and U.K. resolution?

Hon. Bill Graham (Minister of Foreign Affairs):

We wish to see the sanctions lifted as quickly as possible. We are actively
participating and looking not only at humanitarian relief, but also at how
we can help reconstruct and rebuild Iraq. In so doing, we want to work
with the international community in the fullest way possible ... through
agencies of the United Nations. We will be looking at ways in which we can
play the most positive role for the benefit of the Iraqi people.

(House of Commons Debates, May 15, 2003, p. 6317)
(Débats de la Chambre des Communes, le 15 mai 2003, p. 6317)

(e)   Free Trade Area of the Americas (FTAA) / Zone de libre-
échange des Amériques (ZLÉA)

Mr. Mac Harb (Ottawa Centre):

[L]ast year the Government of Canada, in conjunction with its partners,
was able to release the text of the negotiating agreement of the free trade
area of the Americas.... [W]ill ... the Government of Canada ... continue
to play a leadership role [in these negotiations]?

Mr. Pat O'Brien (Parliamentary Secretary to the Minister for International Trade):

[I]n April 2001, in Argentina, the hemispheric trade ministers made history when they endorsed Canada's proposal to release the draft text of the FTAA. Later this week the minister will be in Quito, Ecuador, and he will again be seeking consensus from his colleagues to have the release of the updated text.

The release of the negotiating text has been an important improvement in trade negotiations, including at the WTO. Canada's leadership in pushing for greater transparency will ensure greater buy-in by our citizens.

(House of Commons Debates, October 30, 2002, p. 1077)

(Débats de la Chambre des Communes, le 30 octobre 2002, p. 1077)

Mme Francine Lalonde (Mercier):

Est-ce que le ministre reconnaîtra que l'absence d'un ... fonds de développement social [pour amoindrir le choc que pourrait causer à certains pays l'implantation de la ZLÉA] explique en grande partie la résistance de certains pays d'Amérique latine à l'endroit de la ZLÉA?

L'hon. Bill Graham (ministre des Affaires étrangères):

[I]l est évident que notre but, le but de tous les pays, est d'avoir un système de commerce qui contribue à la prospérité et donc à la justice sociale dans tous les pays. L'établissement d'un fonds de développement est une chose dont on devrait discuter, mais nous avons déjà pour cela plusieurs banques importantes, comme la Banque pour les Amériques et la Banque mondiale. Le gouvernement canadien croit que nous avons actuellement les outils en place pour aider les pays en voie de développement ... [N]ous allons continuer de travailler avec ces pays pour leur prospérité et pour la justice sociale à travers les Amériques.

(House of Commons Debates, May 6, 2003, p. 5869)

(Débats de la Chambre des Communes, le 6 mai 2003, p. 5869)

(f)   NAFTA's Chapter 11 / Chapitre 11 de l'ALÉNA

Mme Francine Lalonde (Mercier):

[N]otre capacité d'intervenir en matière de santé et d'environnement est encore une fois questionnée en raison du chapitre 11 de l'ALÉNA. Alors qu'une étude démontre que le gouvernement pourrait être poursuivi à la suite d'une éventuelle réforme du système de santé, un tribunal vient de condamner le Canada à payer plus de huit millions de dollars à S.D. Myers pour avoir émis une ordonnance sur l'exportation de BPC.

Le ministre du Commerce international peut-il nous assurer que des dispositions semblables à celles du chapitre 11 de l'ALÉNA ne se retrouveront pas dans d'autres accords comme la ZLÉA?

L'hon. Pierre Pettigrew (ministre du Commerce international):

Dans le cas de S.D. Myers, notre gouvernement a déjà déterminé d'aller devant la Cour fédérale. Nous avons déjà pris la décision d'aller devant la Cour fédérale et nous attendons le résultat de cela. Alors avant de sauter aux conclusions, on doit aller là.

Pour ce qui est de la santé, je l'ai dit à chaque fois: ce n'est pas parce qu'on l'évoque dans un rapport, le système de santé canadien et la Loi canadienne sur la santé ne sont pas menacés par nos accords internationaux, ni par la Zone de libre-échange ni par le GATT ou l'Organisation mondiale du commerce, sous sa forme actuelle, présente ou future.

(House of Commons Debates, October 22, 2002, p. 752)
(Débats de la Chambre des Communes, le 22 octobre 2002, p. 752)

M. Réal Ménard (Hochelaga — Maisonneuve):

[H]ier, un des négociateurs de la ZLÉA a déclaré que le Canada voulait reproduire le chapitre 11 de l'ALÉNA dans l'entente avec les trois Amériques. Ce chapitre permet à des entreprises de poursuivre les gouvernements pour des pertes de profits potentiels et a donné lieu, jusqu'à présent, à des excès ou des interprétations abusives.

Comment le vice-premier ministre peut-il concilier cette déclaration du négociateur avec celle du ministre du Commerce international, qui a affirmé à plusieurs reprises vouloir remplacer ce chapitre par un autre qui ne permettrait pas aux investisseurs de poursuivre les États?

Mr. Pat O'Brien (Parliamentary Secretary to the Minister for International Trade):

[I]t is quite clear that Canada does not advocate the replication of the chapter 11 clause that exists in NAFTA, in the FTAA or in other international agreements.

Having said that, obviously our investors need protection for their investments overseas. There has been a remarkable increase in Canadian investment overseas and that investment must and will be protected.

(House of Commons Debates, October 25, 2002, p. 913)
(Débats de la Chambre des Communes, le 25 octobre 2002, p. 913)

(g)   Organization for Economic Cooperation and Development (OECD) / Organisation de coopération et de develloppement l'économiques (OCDE)

Ms. Bonnie Brown (Oakville):

[T]he OECD recently completed a comprehensive review of Canada's regulatory system. The title of the report, "Regulatory Reform in Canada: Maintaining Leadership through Innovation," suggests that the OECD's assessment was very positive.

Could the government House leader tell us how Canada's regulatory system measures up, according to the OECD?

Hon. Don Boudria (Minister of State and Leader of the Government in the House of Commons):

[E]ach year the OECD releases reports reviewing member countries and their ability to provide high quality regulation. This year Canada was acknowledged as not just a regulatory reform pioneer, and we all know that, but more important, "a consistent leader and vigorous innovator in regulatory reform." With the Prime Minister's smart regulation agenda, it will get even better.

(House of Commons Debates, October 29, 2002, p. 1034)
(Débats de la Chambre des Communes, le 29 octobre 2002, p. 1034)

(h)   Softwood Lumber / Bois d'œuvre

Mr. John Duncan (Vancouver Island North):

[T]he U.S. Department of Commerce is ... proceeding with its divide and conquer tactics. This time it is targeting the provinces rather than industry. When is the trade minister going to ... use his federal mandate to stop these U.S ... tactics?

Hon. Pierre Pettigrew (Minister for International Trade):

[T]he strategy of our government has been very clear from day one on this. It is to find a long-term, policy-based strategy.
    Now ... we resume discussions with the Americans to identify such a long-term, policy-based solution. We are going to the courts to get support from the WTO and NAFTA that the Canadian case is right. We are discussing with the Americans to identify an earlier resolution to this conflict. This is what the government is doing now.

(House of Commons Debates, October 1, 2002, pp. 54-55)
(Débats de la Chambre des Communes, le 1ᵉʳ octobre 2002, pp. 54-55)

M. Paul Crête (Kamouraska — Rivière-du-Loup — Témiscouata — Les Basques):

[D]ès le début de la crise du bois d'œuvre, nous savions que, juridiquement, le Canada avait toutes les chances de remporter cette guerre commerciale qui l'oppose aux États-Unis. Toutefois, la crainte exprimée dès le départ était à l'effet que les Américains souhaitaient gagner du temps et ainsi éliminer des concurrents, une fois le litige réglé, en ne prévoyant pas d'aide pour les entreprises du secteur du bois d'œuvre.
    Le gouvernement fédéral n'abdique-t-il pas ses responsabilités en laissant à elles-même les entreprises forestières?

L'hon. Pierre Pettigrew (ministre du Commerce international):

Nous savons très bien que la cause canadienne est forte et solide. Nous avons réussi à franchir un premier pas au mois de juillet avec le panel de l'Organisation mondiale du commerce, qui a donné raison au Canada. Je crois que cela a été entendu à Washington.

C'est la raison pour laquelle du côté du ministère du Commerce international, on essaie à l'heure actuelle de reprendre une partie de l'initiative. On va justement essayer de voir en fonction des circonstances actuelles ce que la loi américaine permettrait. S'il y a des changements de circonstances, on pourrait avoir un changement de régime.

Notre approche fonctionne. On les poursuit devant les tribunaux et, en même temps, on a des discussions pour améliorer la situation et accélérer le dossier.

(House of Commons Debates, October 8, 2002, p. 472)
(Débats de la Chambre des Communes, le 8 octobre 2002, p. 472)

(i) Technology / Technologie

Mr. Walt Lastewka (St. Catharines):

[I]n an increasingly digitalized world ... what action the government is taking to ensure that our students, many of them employed in small businesses, have access to the technology and information they need to succeed?

Hon. Allan Rock (Minister of Industry):

[I]n the world as we now know it Internet access and awareness of how to use the Internet are fundamental to both economic growth and social justice.

One of the achievements of which the government is very proud is that we have made Canada the most connected nation in the world. Last week an OECD report confirmed that and pointed out that we have the best ratio of students to computers of any country measured.

We will continue to do that to make sure our children have the tools to succeed in the future.

(House of Commons Debates, November 5, 2002, p. 1305)
(Débats de la Chambre des Communes, le 5 novembre 2002, p. 1305)

(j) World Trade Organization (WTO) / Organisation mondiale du commerce (OMC)

Mr. Tony Valeri (Stoney Creek):

Recently, senior U.S. officials, including trade representative Zoellick and commerce secretary Evans, made the bold proposal that all WTO countries eliminate tariffs on manufactured goods no later than 2015 ... What is the Canadian response to this proposal?

Hon. Pierre Pettigrew (Minister for International Trade):

[T]he United States proposal is bold, it is innovative and it does indeed merit careful consideration. Our tariffs are generally very low and many goods already enter Canada duty free. We are committed to the further reduction or even elimination of barriers that remain in markets of interest to Canadian exporters. We must also call for the full consideration of the needs of developing countries.

(House of Commons Debates, December 10, 2002, p. 2521)
(Débats de la Chambre des Communes, le 10 décembre 2002, p. 2521)

Mr. Mac Harb (Ottawa Centre):

The WTO from time to time reviews the trading policies of its members ... [W]hat has the WTO found in its latest review of Canada's trading policies[?]

Hon. Pierre Pettigrew (Minister for International Trade):

Canada has been recognized by the WTO as one of the world's most transparent and liberal traders. The WTO recognizes that sound economic policies and an outward looking trade regime have allowed Canada to maintain economic growth in the face of a global economic slowdown.

(House of Commons Debates, March 17, 2003, p. 4252)
(Débats de la Chambre des Communes, le 17 mars 2003, p. 4252)

Mr. Mark Eyking (Sydney — Victoria):

[T]here is concern among Canadians about what we are giving up at the WTO negotiations with respect to services. There is concern that there is no transparency ... [H]ow can [the government] ... ensure that Canadian values will not be negotiated?

Hon. Pierre Pettigrew (Minister for International Trade):

[T]oday ... we tabled our initial offer in Geneva ... [S]ome of Canada's closest trading partners, including the United States, Australia and the European Union, have now agreed to follow our lead and release their own initial offers. We are committed to an open and transparent approach to these negotiations.

(House of Commons Debates, March 31, 2003, pp. 4917-18)
(Débats de la Chambre des Communes, le 31 mars 2003, pp. 4917-18)

Mr. Rick Casson (Lethbridge):

The director general of the WTO issued a statement saying that it was a great disappointment that negotiators missed the deadline on agriculture. Canada contributed to the breakdown of talks due to its rejection of the Harbinson Report. In short, Canada sided with the developed countries such as the EU against the developing countries in Africa and South America. Will the minister explain [this]?

Hon. Pierre Pettigrew (Minister for International Trade):

We did not reject the Harbinson modalities ... We continued to promote Canada's interest. We want major, serious reform in the international trade routes for agriculture. We want the elimination of export subsidies. We want a substantial reduction in the production subsidies and the domestic subsidies. That is our agenda and we will pursue it at the WTO.

(House of Commons Debates, April 3, 2003, pp. 5108-9)
(Débats de la Chambre des Communes, le 3 avril 2003, pp. 5108-9)

8 Law of the Sea / Droit de la mer

(a) 200 mile limit / Zone de 200 milles

Mr. Loyola Hearn (St. John's West):

[T]he Minister of Fisheries and Oceans has ... said that we cannot extend jurisdiction beyond the 200 mile limit, nor can we impose custodial management. Russia, however, has requested the United Nations to extend its boundaries to take in almost half of the Atlantic, and 30 other countries are lined up ready to move. Why is Canada not taking such action?

Hon. Robert Thibault (Minister of Fisheries and Oceans):

[W]e held a forum in Newfoundland last week where experts in international law came together to discuss this matter, to see what the ramifications would be and what the possibilities would be. We have already extended the 200 mile limit.

(House of Commons Debates, February 24, 2003, p. 3914)
(Débats de la Chambre des Communes, le 24 février 2003, p. 3914)

(b) Fisheries / Pêches

Mr. Rodger Cuzner (Bras d'Or — Cape Breton):

[T]he cod stocks in the north sea have been in decline for a number of years and are now at their lowest recorded levels. Other stocks around Scotland and Ireland are also very low. Given this evidence, the International

Council for the Exploration of the Sea has recommended a closure of cod fisheries in several European areas and the implementation of recovery plans.

Could the Minister of Fisheries and Oceans comment on the similarities between the current European context and Canada's recent experience with groundfish declines?

Hon. Robert Thibault (Minister of Fisheries and Oceans):

In 1992, Canada went through much similar circumstances. We have had to invest over $3.5 billion in economic development packages and bought back 3,600 licences.

(House of Commons Debates, November 27, 2002, p. 1945)
(Débats de la Chambre des Communes, le 27 novembre 2002, p. 1945)

Mr. Peter Stoffer (Sackville — Musquodoboit Valley — Eastern Shore):

[L]ast year the Russian ship *Olga* had 49 tonnes of cod, which is under a moratorium, in its hold ... I have a Russian manifest of another ship that had the equivalent of 650,000 pounds of groundfish in its hold on April 8, 2002 in Bay Roberts, Newfoundland. Why does the government ... do nothing to the foreigners?

Hon. Robert Thibault (Minister of Fisheries and Oceans):

On occasion some of those vessels which are out fishing for over a year at a time visit many fishing waters, transship from one vessel to the other and can have their results of fishing not only in the waters of Canada's jurisdiction but in other parts of the world. We verify and if we do not like it, we take action when there are illegal activities.

(House of Commons Debates, April 30, 2003, p. 5640)
(Débats de la Chambre des Communes, le 30 avril 2003, p. 5640)

Treaty Action Taken by Canada in 2002 / Mesures prises par le Canada en matière de traités en 2002

compiled by / préparé par
ANDRÉ BERGERON

I BILATERAL

Australia

Protocol amending the Convention between Canada and Australia for the Avoidance of Double Taxation and the Prevention of Fiscal Evasion with Respect to Taxes on Income. Canberra, 23 January 2002. *Entered into force:* 18 December 2002.

China (People's Republic of)

Agreement between the Government of Canada and the Government of the Hong Kong Special Administrative Region of the People's Republic of China on Mutual Legal Assistance in Criminal Matters. Hong Kong, 16 February 2001. *Entered into force:* 1 March 2002.

Costa Rica

Free Trade Agreement between the Government of Canada and the Government of the Republic of Costa Rica. Ottawa, 23 April 2001. *Entered into force:* 1 November 2002.

Agreement to Amend Annex IV.1 (Specific Rules of Origin) of the Free Trade Agreement between the Government of Canada and the Government of the Republic of Costa Rica. Quito, 1

November 2002. *Entered into force:* 1 November 2002.

Agreement on Environmental Cooperation between the Government of Canada and the Government of the Republic of Costa Rica. Ottawa, 23 April 2001. *Entered into force:* 1 November 2002.

Agreement on Labour Cooperation between the Government of Canada and the Government of the Republic of Costa Rica. Ottawa, 23 April 2001. *Entered into force:* 1 November 2002.

Czech Republic

Convention between Canada and the Czech Republic for the Avoidance of Double Taxation and the Prevention of Fiscal Evasion with Respect to Taxes on Income. Prague, 25 May 2001. *Entered into force:* 28 May 2002. CTS 2002/11

Germany (Federal Republic of)

Agreement between Canada and the Federal Republic of Germany for the Avoidance of Double Taxation with Respect to Taxes on Income and Certain Other Taxes, the Prevention of Fiscal Evasion and the Assistance in Tax Matters; Protocol to the Agreement

André Bergeron is Treaty Registrar in the Legal Advisory Division at the Department of Foreign Affairs / Greffier des Traités, Direction des consultations juridiques, Ministère des Affaires étrangères.

between Canada and the Federal Republic of Germany for the Avoidance of Double Taxation with Respect to Taxes on Income and Certain Other Taxes, the Prevention of Fiscal Evasion and the Assistance in Tax Matters. Berlin, 19 April 2001. *Entered into force:* 28 March 2002. CTS 2002/6

Israel
Exchange of Notes (April 4 and 22, 2002) Constituting an Agreement between the Government of Canada and the Government of the State of Israel amending Chapters Three and Five of the Free Trade Agreement between the Government of Canada and the Government of the State of Israel. Jerusalem, Ottawa, 22 April 2002. *Entered into force:* 5 July 2002. CTS 2002/10

Korea (Republic of)
Exchange of Notes between the Government of Canada and the Government of the Republic of Korea amending Articles V.4 and VII of the Agreement between the Government of Canada and the Government of the Republic of Korea for Co-operation in the Development and Application of Atomic Energy for Peaceful Purposes. Seoul, 10 July 2002. *Entered into force:* 10 July 2002. CTS 2002/14

Lebanon
Agreement between the Government of Canada and the Government of the Lebanese Republic on Air Transport. Beirut, 18 May 2000. *In Force Provisionally:* 18 May 2000. *Entered into force:* 26 August 2002.

Agreement between the Government of Canada and the Government of the Lebanese Republic Regarding Cooperation on Consular Matters of a Humanitarian Nature. Beirut, 13 April 2000. *Entered into force:* 1 October 2002. CTS 2002/16

Mexico
Exchange of Letters between the Government of Canada and the Government of the United Mexican States

Constituting an Agreement Amending the Tariff Schedules to Annex 302.2 of the North American Free Trade Agreement Mexico, Ottawa, 12 December 2001. *Entered into force:* 1 January 2002. CTS 2002/15

Moldova
Convention between the Government of Canada and the Government of the Republic of Moldova for the Avoidance of Double Taxation and the Prevention of Fiscal Evasion with Respect to Taxes on Income. *Protocol signed* Chisinau, 4 July 2002. *Entered into force:* 13 December 2002.

Mongolia
Convention between the Government of Canada and the Government of Mongolia for the Avoidance of Double Taxation and the Prevention of Fiscal Evasion with Respect to Taxes on Income and on Capital. Ottawa, 27 May 2002. *Entered into force:* 20 December 2002.

Norway
Convention between the Government of Canada and the Government of the Kingdom of Norway for the Avoidance of Double Taxation and the Prevention of Fiscal Evasion with Respect to Taxes on Income and on Capital. Ottawa, 12 July 2002. *Entered into force:* 19 December 2002.

Slovenia
Convention between the Government of Canada and the Government of the Republic of Slovenia for the Avoidance of Double Taxation and the Prevention of Fiscal Evasion with Respect to Taxes on Income and on Capital. Ljubljana, 15 September 2000. *Entered into force:* 13 August 2002. CTS 2002/12

United States of America
Exchange of Notes between the Government of Canada and the Government of the United States of America Constituting an Agreement to Improve Bilateral Security through Enhanced Military Cooperation with Respect to

Maritime, Land and Civil Support Functions. Ottawa, Washington, 5 December 2002. *Entered into force:* 5 December 2002.

Exchange of Notes between the Government of Canada and the Government of the United States of America Constituting an Agreement under the Treaty between the Government of Canada and the Government of the United States of America Concerning Pacific Salmon, done at Ottawa on January 28, 1985. Washington, 4 December 2002. *Entered into force:* 4 December 2002.

Uruguay
Treaty between Canada and the Oriental Republic of Uruguay on Mutual Legal Assistance in Criminal Matters. Ottawa, 10 July 1996. *Entered into force:* 1 March 2002. CTS 2002/4

Agreement on Social Security between the Government of Canada and the Government of the Eastern Republic of Uruguay. Ottawa, 2 June 1999. *Entered into force:* 1 January 2002. CTS 2002/2

II MULTILATERAL

Aviation
Protocol Relating to an Amendment to Article 50(a) of the Convention on International Civil Aviation. *Signed:* Montréal, 26 October 1990. *Ratification:* 19 April 1991. *Entry into force* for Canada: 28 November 2002.

Defence
Treaty on Open Skies. *Signed:* Helsinki, 24 March 1992. *Signed* by Canada: 24 March 1992. *Ratification:* 21 July 1992. *Entry into force* for Canada: 1 January 2002. CTS 2002/3

Disarmament
Inter-American Convention on Transparency in Conventional Weapons Acquisitions. *Signed:* Guatemala, 7 June 1999. *Signed* by Canada: 7 June 1999. *Ratification:* 18 October 1999. *Entry into force* for Canada: 21 November 2002.

Environment
Amendment to the Montreal Protocol on Substances That Deplete the Ozone Layer. *Signed:* Beijing, 3 December 1999. *Acceptance:* 9 February 2001. *Entry into force* for Canada: 25 February 2002.

Human Rights
Amendment to Article 43(2) of the Convention on the Rights of the Child. *Signed:* New York, 12 December 1995. *Ratification:* 17 September 1997. *Entry into force* for Canada: 18 November 2002.

Optional Protocol to the Convention on the Rights of the Child on the Involvement of Children in Armed Conflict. *Signed:* New York, 25 May 2000. *Signed* by Canada: 5 June 2000. *Ratification:* 7 July 2000. *Entry into force* for Canada: 12 February 2002. CTS 2002/5

International Courts
Rome Statute of the International Criminal Court. *Signed:* Rome, 17 July 1998. *Signed* by Canada: 18 December 1998. *Ratification:* 7 July 2000. *Entry into force* for Canada: 1 July 2002. CTS 2002/13

Internationally Protected Persons
Convention on the Safety of United Nations and Associated Personnel. *Signed:* New York, 9 December 1994. *Signed* by Canada: 15 December 1994. *Ratification:* 3 April 2002. *Entry into force* for Canada: 3 May 2002. CTS 2002/7

Navigation
Amendments to the Convention on the International Maritime Organization. *Signed:* London, 4 November 1993. *Entry into force* for Canada: 7 November 2002. *Acceptance:* 23 June 1995.

Nuclear
Convention on Assistance in the Case of a Nuclear Accident or Radiological Emergency. *Signed:* Vienna, 26 September 1986. *Signed* by Canada: 26 September 1986. *Ratification:* 12 August 2002. *Entry into force* for Canada: 12 September 2002.

Terrorism

International Convention for the Suppression of Terrorist Bombings. *Signed:* New York, 15 December 1997. *Signed by Canada:* 12 January 1998. *Ratification:* 3 April 2002. *Entry into force* for Canada: 3 May 2002. CTS 2002/8

International Convention for the Suppression of the Financing of Terrorism. *Signed:* New York, 9 December 1999. *Signed by Canada:* 10 February 2000. *Ratification:* 19 February 2002. *Entry into* force for Canada: 10 April 2002. CTS 2002/9

Trade

Exchange of Letters (21 November and 12 December 2002) Constituting an Agreement between Canada, the United Mexican States and the United States of America Rectifying Annex 300-B, Annex 401, Annex 403.1, the Uniform Regulations for Chapters Three and Five and the Uniform Regulations for Chapter Four of the North American Free Trade Agreement. *Signed:* Mexico, Ottawa, Washington, 12 December 2001. *Signed by Canada:* 12 December 2001. *Entry into force* for Canada: 1 January 2002. CTS 2002/17

Agreement on Mutual Acceptance of Oenological Practices. *Signed:* Toronto, 18 December 2001. *Signed by Canada:* 18 December 2001. *Ratification:* 27 November 2002. *Entry into force* for Canada: 1 December 2002.

I BILATÉRAUX

Allemagne (République fédérale de)
Accord entre le Canada et la République fédérale d'Allemagne en vue d'éviter les doubles impositions en matière d'impôts sur le revenu et de certains autres impôts, de prévenir l'évasion fiscale et de fournir assistance en matière d'impôts; Protocole à l'Accord entre le Canada et la République fédérale d'Allemagne en vue d'éviter les doubles impositions en matière d'impôts sur le revenu et de certains autres impôts, de prévenir l'évasion fiscale et

de fournir assistance en matière d'impôts. Berlin, 19 avril 2001. *En vigueur* le 28 March 2002. RTC 2002/6

Australie
Protocole modifiant la Convention entre le Canada et l'Australie en vue d'éviter les doubles impositions et de prévenir l'évasion fiscale en matière d'impôts sur le revenu. Canberra, 23 janvier 2002. *En vigueur* le 18 Décembre 2002.

Chine (République populaire de)
Accord d'entraide juridique en matière pénale entre le gouvernement du Canada et le gouvernement de la Région administrative spéciale de Hong Kong de la République populaire de Chine. Hong Kong, 16 février 2001. *En vigueur* le 1er Mars 2002.

Corée (République de)
Échange de notes entre le gouvernement du Canada et le gouvernement de la République de Corée modifiant les articles V.4 et VII de l'Accord de coopération entre le gouvernement du Canada et le gouvernement de la République de Corée concernant le développement et l'utilisation de l'énergie nucléaire à des fins pacifiques. Séoul, 10 juillet 2002. *En vigueur* le 10 juillet 2002. RTC 2002/14

Costa Rica
Accord de libre-échange entre le gouvernement du Canada et le gouvernement de la République du Costa Rica. Ottawa, 23 avril 2001. *En vigueur* le 1er novembre 2002.

Accord relatif à la modification de l'Annexe IV.1 (Règles d'origine spécifiques) de l'Accord de libre-échange entre le gouvernement du Canada et le gouvernement de la République du Costa Rica. Quito, 1er novembre 2002. *En vigueur* le 1er novembre 2002.

Accord de coopération environnementale entre le gouvernement du Canada et le gouvernement de la République du Costa Rica. Ottawa, 23 avril 2001. *En vigueur* le 1er novembre 2002.

Accord de coopération dans le domaine du travail entre le gouvernement du Canada et le gouvernement de la République du Costa Rica. Ottawa, 23 avril 2001. *En vigueur* le 1ᵉʳ novembre 2002.

États-Unis d'Amérique
Échange de notes entre le gouvernement du Canada et le gouvernement des États-Unis d'Amérique constituant un accord concernant l'amélioration de la sécurité bilatérale par une collaboration militaire accrue en ce qui a trait aux fonctions d'appui maritime, terrestre et civil. Ottawa, Washington, 5 décembre 2002. *En vigueur* le 5 décembre 2002.

Échange de notes entre le gouvernement du Canada et le gouvernement des États-Unis d'Amérique constituant un Accord dans le cadre du Traité entre le gouvernement du Canada et le gouvernement des États-Unis d'Amérique sur le saumon du Pacifique, fait à Ottawa le 28 janvier 1985. Washington, 4 décembre 2002. *En vigueur* le 4 décembre 2002.

Israël
Échange de notes (4 et 22 avril 2002) constituant un accord entre le gouvernement du Canada et le gouvernement de l'État d'Israël modifiant les chapitres trois et cinq de l'Accord de libre-échange entre le gouvernement du Canada et le gouvernement de l'État d'Israël. Jérusalem, Ottawa, 22 avril 2002. *En vigueur* le 5 juillet 2002. RTC 2002/10.

Liban
Accord entre le gouvernement du Canada et le gouvernement de la République libanaise concernant la coopération en certaines matières consulaires à caractère humanitaire. Beyrouth, 13 avril 2000. *En vigueur* le 1ᵉʳ octobre 2002. RTC 2002/16

Accord entre le gouvernement du Canada et le gouvernement de la République du Liban concernant le transport aérien. Beyrouth, 18 mai 2000. *En*

vigueur provisoire le 18 mai 2000. *En vigueur* le 26 août 2002.

Mexique
Échange de lettres entre le gouvernement du Canada et le gouvernement des États-Unis du Mexique constituant un Accord modifiant les listes tarifaires de l'Annexe 302.2 de l'Accord de libre-échange nord-américain. Mexico, Ottawa, 12 décembre 2001. *En vigueur* le 1ᵉʳ janvier 2002. RTC 2002/15

Moldova
Convention entre le gouvernement du Canada et le gouvernement de la République de Moldova en vue d'éviter les doubles impositions et de prévenir l'évasion fiscale en matière d'impôt sur le revenu; Protocole *signé:* Chisinau, 4 juillet 2002. *En vigueur* le 13 décembre 2002.

Mongolie
Convention entre le gouvernement du Canada et le gouvernement de la Mongolie en vue d'éviter les doubles impositions et de prévenir l'évasion fiscale en matière d'impôts sur le revenu et sur la fortune. Ottawa, 27 mai 2002. *En vigueur* le 20 décembre 2002.

Norvège
Convention entre le gouvernement du Canada et le gouvernement du Royaume de Norvège en vue d'éviter les doubles impositions et de prévenir l'évasion fiscale en matière d'impôts sur le revenu et sur la fortune. Ottawa, 12 juillet 2002. *En vigueur* le 19 décembre 2002.

République tchèque
Convention entre le Canada et la République tchèque en vue d'éviter les doubles impositions et de prévenir l'évasion fiscale en matière d'impôts sur le revenu. Prague, 25 mai 2001. *En vigueur* le 28 mai 2002. RTC 2002/11

Slovénie
Convention entre le gouvernement du Canada et le gouvernement de la République de Slovénie en vue d'éviter les doubles impositions et de prévenir

l'évasion fiscale en matière d'impôts sur le revenu et sur la fortune. Ljubljana, 15 septembre 2000. *En vigueur* le 13 août 2002. RTC 2002/12

Uruguay
Traité d'entraide judiciaire entre le Canada et la République orientale d'Uruguay. Ottawa, 10 juillet 1996. *En vigueur* le 1er mars 2002. RTC 2002/4

Accord sur la sécurité sociale entre le gouvernement du Canada et le gouvernement de la République orientale de l'Uruguay. Ottawa, 2 juin 1999. *En vigueur* le 1er janvier 2002. RTC 2002/2

II MULTILATÉRAUX

Aviation
Protocole portant amendement de l'article 50 a) de la Convention relative à l'Aviation civile internationale. Montréal, le 26 octobre 1990. *Ratification:* 19 avril 1991. *En vigueur* pour le Canada: 28 novembre 2002.

Commerce
Échange de lettres (21 novembre et 12 décembre 2002) constituant un accord entre le Canada, les États-Unis d'Amérique et les États-Unis du Mexique rectifiant l'annexe 300-B, l'annexe 401, l'annexe 403.1, le Règlement uniforme des chapitres trois et cinq et le Règlement uniforme du chapitre quatre de l'Accord de libre-échange nord-américain. Mexico, Ottawa, Washington, le 12 décembre 2001. *Signée* par le Canada: 12 décembre 2001. *En vigueur* pour le Canada: 1er janvier 2002. RTC 2002/17

Accord d'acceptation mutuelle des pratiques oenologiques. Toronto, le 18 décembre 2001. *Signé* par le Canada: 18 décembre 2001. *Ratification:* 27 novembre 2002. *En vigueur* pour le Canada: 1er décembre 2002.

Cours internationales
Statut de Rome de la cour pénale internationale. Rome, le 17 juillet 1998. *Signé* par le Canada: 18 décembre

1998. *Ratification:* 7 juillet 2000. *En vigueur* pour le Canada: 1er juillet 2002. RTC 2002/13

Défense
Traité sur le régime "Ciel ouvert." Helsinki, le 24 mars 1992. *Signé* par le Canada: 24 mars 1992. *Ratification:* 21 juillet 1992. *En vigueur* pour le Canada: 1er janvier 2002. RTC 2002/3.

Désarmement
Convention interaméricaine sur la transparence de l'acquisition des armes classiques. Guatemala, le 7 juin 1999. *Signée* par le Canada: 7 juin 1999. *Ratification:* 18 octobre 1999. *En vigueur* pour le Canada: 21 novembre 2002.

Droits de la personne
Amendement au paragraphe 2 de l'article 43 de la Convention sur les droits de l'enfant. New York, le 12 décembre 1995. *Ratification:* 17 septembre 1997. *En vigueur* pour le Canada: 18 novembre 2002.

Protocole facultatif à la convention relative aux droits de l'enfant, concernant l'implication d'enfants dans les conflits armés. New York, le 25 mai 2000. *Signé* par le Canada: 5 juin 2000. *Ratification:* 7 juillet 2000. *En vigueur* pour le Canada: 12 février 2002. RTC 2002/5

Énergie nucléaire
Convention concernant l'assistance en cas d'accident nucléaire ou de situation d'urgence radiologique. Vienne, le 26 septembre 1986. *Signée* par le Canada: 26 septembre 1986. *Ratification:* 12 août 2002. *En vigueur* pour le Canada: 12 septembre 2002.

Environnement
Amendement au protocole de Montréal relatif aux substances qui appauvrissent la couche d'ozone. Beijing, le 3 décembre 1999. *En vigueur* pour le Canada: 25 février 2002. *Acceptation:* 9 février 2001.

Navigation
Amendements à la Convention portant création de l'Organisation maritime internationale. Londres, le 4 novembre 1993. *En vigueur* pour le Canada: 7 novembre 2002. *Acceptation:* 23 juin 1995.

Personnes jouissant d'une protection internationale
Convention sur la sécurité du personnel des Nations Unies et du personnel associé. New York, le 9 décembre 1994. *Signée* par le Canada: 15 décembre 1994. *Ratification:* 3 avril 2002. *En vigueur* pour le Canada: 3 mai 2002. RTC 2002/7

Terrorisme
Convention internationale pour la répression des attentats terroristes à l'explosif. New York, le 15 décembre 1997. *Signée* par le Canada: 12 janvier 1998. *Ratification:* 3 avril 2002. *En vigueur* pour le Canada: 3 mai 2002. RTC 2002/8

Convention internationale pour la répression du financement du terrorisme. New York, le 9 décembre 1999. *Signée* par le Canada: 10 février 2000. *Ratification:* 19 février 2002. *En vigueur* pour le Canada: 10 avril 2002. RTC 2002/9

Cases / Jurisprudence

Canadian Cases in Public International Law in 2002-3 / Jurisprudence canadienne en matière de droit international public en 2002-3

compiled by / préparé par
KARIN MICKELSON

Diplomats — status in Canada

Note. See *Copello* v. *Canada (Minister of Foreign Affairs and International Trade)*, 2003 FCA 295 (Federal Court of Appeal). This was an appeal from a decision of the Federal Court, Trial Division, noted at (2002) 40 Canadian Yearbook of International Law 557, in which the court dismissed the appellant's application for judicial review seeking to quash a decision of the Minister of Foreign Affairs and International Trade that requested that the appellant, an Italian diplomat, leave Canada. In dismissing the appeal, Linden J.A. expresses agreement with the reasoning of Heneghan J. at trial that a declaration of *persona non grata* is not a legal issue and therefore the minister's decision is not justiciable. He notes that although it may seem unfair that Canada can expel a diplomat from within its borders without ever having to justify its decision in court, this traditional power exists in order to foster friendly diplomatic relations between nations. It is also in accordance with principles of international law. Diplomats are guests in the foreign countries in which they live and work. Diplomatic status carries with it certain privileges and immunities, but the purpose of these privileges and immunities is not for the benefit of individual diplomats. Rather, as

Karin Mickelson is in the Faculty of Law at the University of British Columbia.

reflected in the preamble to the Vienna Convention on Diplomatic Relations, these privileges and immunities attach to diplomatic agents in order "to ensure the efficient performance of the functions of diplomatic missions as representing States." Consequently, the usual rules of administrative law — those concerned with procedural fairness and the rule of law — do not apply.

Sovereign immunity

Schreiber v. *Canada (Attorney General)*, [2002] 3 S.C.R. 269, 2002 SCC 62. Supreme Court of Canada.

The Federal Republic of Germany had sought the extradition of the plaintiff. The plaintiff then commenced an action claiming, *inter alia*, damages for personal injuries suffered as a result of his arrest and detention prior to being released on bail. This was an appeal from a decision of the Ontario Court of Appeal, noted at (2000) 38 Canadian Yearbook of International Law 423, upholding a decision by which the action against the Federal Republic of Germany was dismissed on the ground that the Federal Republic of Germany enjoys sovereign immunity, as codified by the State Immunity Act, R.S.C. 1985, c. S-18. At issue was whether certain exceptions to immunity found in the act applied. Section 4 of the act provides an exception to immunity in circumstances in which the foreign state has submitted to the jurisdiction of the court. Section 6(a) of the act provides an exception to immunity in any proceedings relating to personal injury.

The appellant's argument under the section 4 exception to immunity was two-fold. First, section 4(2)(b) provides that a foreign state is not immune if it submits to the jurisdiction of a court by initiating proceedings in the court. Here, according to the appellant, Germany initiated the proceedings by requesting that Canadian authorities go before the Ontario Superior Court of Justice on behalf of Germany to arrest and imprison him. Second, section 4(5) provides that where a foreign state submits to the jurisdiction of the court, that submission is deemed to be a submission by the state to the jurisdiction of one or more courts by which those proceedings may, in whole or in part, subsequently be considered on appeal or in the exercise of supervisory jurisdiction. The appellant argued that section 4(5) applies because the Superior Court of Justice is only exercising a "supervisory jurisdiction" over the arrest warrant proceedings initiated by Germany, the legality of which is now challenged by the appellant.

With regard to section 4(2)(b), LeBel J. notes that Germany did not initiate the judicial proceedings as its request to arrest and imprison the appellant was made to the executive branch of government pursuant to the extradition treaty. It was the Minister of Justice who authorized the Attorney General to apply for an arrest warrant. The appellant's tort liability action against the government of Germany is an action that is separate and distinct from the extradition process initiated by Germany. There is nothing in the wording of the legislation or in the extradition treaty to suggest that Germany would impliedly waive its sovereign immunity from law suits in the Canadian courts every time it exercised its treaty-based right to request extradition.

With respect to section 4(5), LeBel J. agrees with the Attorney General's submission that section 4(5) simply extends the waiver of immunity arising from proceedings that fall within section 4(2) or section 4(4) to include appeals from, or judicial review of, those proceedings. As the appellant's lawsuit does not fall within either section 4(2) or section 4(4), it is outside the scope of section 4(5).

LeBel J. goes on to note that it would be contrary to the concepts of comity and mutual respect between nations to hold that a country that calls upon Canada to assist in extradition only does so at the price of losing its sovereign immunity and of submitting to the domestic jurisdiction of Canadian courts in matters connected to the extradition request, and not only in respect of the extradition proceeding itself.

The argument in relation to the section 6(a) exception was that the mental distress, denial of liberty, and damage to reputation that the appellant suffered due to his wrongful arrest and imprisonment was a "personal injury" and that immunity does not apply. LeBel J. begins by addressing an argument raised by the intervener, the United States of America, which would severely restrict the scope of application of the exception. The United States asserts that a distinction must be made between *acta jure imperii* and *acta jure gestionis* in determining whether any of the exceptions to immunity under the State Immunity Act are applicable. Each of the exceptions to immunity depends, it is submitted, on the nature of commercial or other private law conduct underlying the claim. The intervener relied on the reference before this court in *Re Canada Labour Code*, [1992] 2 S.C.R. 50, where La Forest J. writing for the majority, stated that the common law developed a new theory of restrictive immunity under which courts extended immunity "only to acts *jure imperii* and not to acts *jure gestionis*," and went on to observe that the

State Immunity Act was a "codification that is intended to clarify and continue the theory of restrictive immunity, rather than to alter its substance." According to the intervener, this comment implies that the *jure imperii/jure gestionis* distinction that underlies the theory of restrictive immunity applies to the entire act.

In reply to this submission, the appellant argued that when Parliament enacted the State Immunity Act in 1982, it codified that distinction in section 5 of the act. It also created a new exception, the death or personal injury exception at section 6(a), which did not exist at common law. Had Parliament intended to limit the exception in section 6 by the *jure imperii* and *jure gestionis* distinction, it would have incorporated the distinction into the statutory exception.

LeBel J. accepts the appellant's argument on the irrelevance of the *jure imperii/jure gestionis* distinction for a number of reasons. First, the wording of section 6(a) clearly states that this exception applies to all torts committed by a foreign state that cause death or personal injury. Second, *Re Canada Labour Code* is inconclusive on this issue. In that reference, the court considered only section 5 of the act (the commercial activity section), which does indeed codify the restrictive theory of immunity but does not deal directly with any other of the exceptions under the act. Furthermore, most of the international law authorities cited by the parties appear to accept that the personal injury exception does not distinguish between *jure imperii* and *jure gestionis* acts; LeBel J. mentions the European Convention on State Immunity and the International Law Commission's "Draft Articles on Jurisdictional Immunities of States and Their Property." He also notes that the interpretation advanced by the United States would deprive the victims of the worst breaches of basic rights of any possibility of redress in national courts. Given the recent trends in the development of international humanitarian law enlarging this possibility in cases of international crime, such a result would jeopardize at least in Canada a potentially important progress in the protection of the rights of the person.

The main issue is whether the Court of Appeal erred in holding that the term "personal injury" in section 6(a) of the State Immunity Act applies only to claims of physical injury and does not apply to wrongful arrest and imprisonment. The Court of Appeal followed its earlier decision in *United States of America* v. *Friedland* (1999), 182 D.L.R. (4th) 614, noted at (2000) 38 Canadian Yearbook of International Law 419, which was under appeal in the Supreme Court of Canada at the time *Schreiber* was being heard in the Court of Appeal. The appeal in *Friedland* was subsequently discontinued. Doherty J.A. found that the *Friedland* case was dispositive of the appellant's submission that his claim fell within the section 6(a) exemption to state immunity and found no basis for departing from the earlier decision.

LeBel J. agrees that *Friedland* established that the scope of the exception in section 6(a) is limited to instances where mental distress and emotional upset were linked to a physical injury. For example, psychological distress may fall within the exception where such distress is manifested physically, such as in the case of nervous shock. LeBel J. also refers to a statement made by McKinlay J.A. in an earlier Ontario Court of Appeal decision in *Walker* v. *Bank of New York Inc.* (1994), 16 O.R. (3d) 504, noted at (1994) 32 Canadian Yearbook of International Law 361, which had indicated that the scope of personal injury covered by section 6 is not merely physical, but could include mental distress, emotional upset, and restriction of liberty. It seems clear that statement in *Walker* was made in *obiter* and that such finding had no bearing on the case before that court. Doherty J.A. was correct when he chose to rely on *Friedland* in reaching his decision to dismiss the appellant's appeal, as it seems consistent with the position taken in academic writings and international law sources. The applicable case law and academic writings seem to indicate that the term "personal injury" generally denotes "physical" injury. A few secondary sources of international law have also limited the term "personal injury" to "physical injury" in the context of the personal injury exception to immunity. LeBel J. cites the International Law Commission's commentaries on its "Draft Articles on Jurisdictional Immunities of States and their Property" and the *Explanatory Reports on the European Convention on State Immunity and the Additional Protocol*.

LeBel J. then addresses the views expressed by the intervener Amnesty International, which advanced the proposition that the right to the protection of mental integrity and to compensation for its violation has risen to the level of a peremptory norm of international law that prevails over the doctrine of sovereign immunity. Some forms of incarceration may conceivably constitute international human rights violations, such as an inordinately long sentence or abusive conditions. However, incarceration is a lawful part of the Canadian justice system. Without evidence of physical harm, to find that lawful incarceration amounts to compensable mental injury would be to find that every prisoner who is incarcerated by the Canadian penal system is entitled to receive damages from the state. Mental injury may be compensable in some form at international law, but neither the intervener nor any other party has established that a peremptory norm of international law has now come into existence that would completely oust the doctrine of state immunity and allow domestic courts to entertain claims in the circumstances of this case.

In the case at bar, there is no conflict between the principles of international law, at the present stage of their development, and those of the domestic legal order. International law sets out some general principles with respect to the origins and uses of sovereign immunity, but the domestic law sets out very specific exceptions to the general rule of sovereign immunity. The questions at stake fall within the purview of the domestic legislation. Indeed, it can be argued that the domestic legislation is more specific than the rules set out by the international legal principles and, as such, there would be little utility in examining international legal principles in detail. In other cases, international law principles might have a more direct impact and the disposition of the matter might turn on their interpretation and application. In this appeal, the case turns on the interpretation of the bilingual versions of section 6(a) of the State Immunity Act rather than the interpretation of international law principles.

The State Immunity Act creates exceptions to the classical and broad-ranging principles of state immunity. Section 6(a) lifts the immunity in respect of proceedings for "death or personal or bodily injury" or, in the French version of the Act, "*les actions découlant ... des décès ou dommages corporels survenus au Canada.*" Under the principles governing the interpretation of bilingual and bijural legislation, where there is a difference between the English and French versions, the court must search for the common legislative intent that seeks to reconcile them. The gist of this intellectual operation is the discovery of the essential concepts that appear to underlie the provision being interpreted and that will best reflect its purpose, when viewed in its proper context.

In this case, the French version is the clearer and more restrictive of the two versions. A failure to consider the key ideas underpinning the French version might lead to a serious misapprehension as to the scope of section 6(a). It would broaden its scope of application to such an extent that the doctrine of state immunity could be said to have been largely abrogated whenever a claim for personal injury is made. Therefore, the guiding principle in the interpretation of the section 6(a) exception, more consonant with the principles of international law and with the still important principle of state immunity in international relations, is found in the French version of the provision. It signals the presence of a legislative intent to create an exception to state immunity that would be restricted to a class of claims arising out of a physical breach of personal integrity, consistent with the Québec civil law term "*préjudice corporel.*" This type of breach could conceivably cover an overlapping area between physical harm and mental injury, such as nervous stress; however, the mere deprivation of freedom and the normal consequences of lawful imprisonment, as framed by the claim, do not allow the appellant to claim an exception to the State Immunity Act. This claim seems to be more in line with a Canadian Charter of Rights and Freedoms claim of deprivation of rights and is properly dismissed against the respondent, Germany.

Treaties and principles of international law — Domestic application

Commissioner of Competition v. *Falconbridge Ltd.* (2003), 225 D.L.R. (4th) 1. Ontario Court of Appeal.

This was an application for leave to appeal under section 35 of the Mutual Legal Assistance in Criminal Matters Act, R.S.C. 1985, c. 30 (4th Supp.) from a judgment that dealt with an application by the respondent, the Commissioner of Competition, for a sending order under section 15 of the act, applications by the appellants to have search warrants and evidence gathering orders set aside and seized records returned to them, applications by the appellants for certain declarations concerning the application of the act and the Treaty between the Government of Canada and the Government of the United States of America on Mutual Legal Assistance in Criminal Matters, and an application for the continuation of a sealing order. The leave application and the appeal were heard together. While leave to appeal was granted, the appeal was dismissed.

The case arose out of a grand jury investigation in the United States concerning possible violations by the appellants and others of the Sherman Act. In 1999, the United States made a request of the government of Canada for assistance under the treaty in connection with possible anti-trust offences under the Sherman Act. The Minister of Justice approved the request and sent it to the Commissioner of Competition as the "competent authority" within the meaning of the treaty and the act. On the basis of *ex parte* applications by the Commissioner, the application judge issued search warrants under section 12 of the act. After the searches were completed, on the basis of *ex parte* applications, the application judge made evidence-gathering orders under section 18 of the act. The appellants then brought applications to set aside the warrants and the evidence gathering order. The respondent brought an application for a sending order in relation to the warrants only.

Among the issues on appeal were two issues involving the interpretation of certain provisions of the act and the treaty: whether the Sherman Act offences constitute "offences" within the meaning of the act, and whether the act contains a reciprocal offence requirement. The arguments in relation to the first issue hinged on the meaning of the word "offence" defined in section 2(1) of the act as "an offence within the meaning of the relevant agreement." The word "agreement" is defined in section 2(1) of the act to mean "a treaty, convention or other international agreement that is in force, to which Canada is a party and that contains a provision respecting mutual legal assistance in criminal matters." Article 1 of the Treaty between the Government of Canada and the Government of the United States of America on Mutual Legal Assistance in Criminal Matters contains the following definition of the word "offence":

(a) for Canada, an offence created by a law of Parliament that may be prosecuted upon indictment, or an offence created by the Legislature of a Province specified in the Annex;
(b) for the United States, an offence for which the statutory penalty is a term of imprisonment of one year or more, or an offence specified in the Annex.

The appellants' argument was that to come within that provision, the offence for which the United States seeks assistance must, upon conviction, carry with it a mandatory minimum prison term of one or more years. They maintain that the Sherman Act offences in the present case do not meet that test because although they contemplate a maximum prison term of three years, they do not require a mandatory minimum term of imprisonment of at least one year.

Rosenberg and Moldaver JJ.A. express agreement with the analysis and conclusion of the application judge, who found that the appellants effective insert the words "mandatory" and "minimum" in the definition of offence when they are not necessary to the plain meaning. They note that there is no reason why the words "mandatory" and "minimum" should be read into the definition of "Offence for the United States" under the treaty. To do so would be to twist the plain language of the provision and add requirements that are contextually out of place and inconsistent with the fair, large, and liberal interpretation to which acts and treaties of this nature are entitled. Writing the words "mandatory" and "minimum" into the "offence" provision for the United States would also lead to the illogical conclusion that the parties to the treaty intended a gross imbalance in the range of cases for which the United States would be required to assist Canada. For Canada, under Article 1 of the treaty, an offence includes "an offence created by a law of Parliament that may be prosecuted upon indictment." That definition would of course include hybrid offences, many of which are punishable by a maximum term of six months imprisonment if the Crown elects to proceed summarily. In other words, acceptance of the appellant's argument would mean that Canada could seek assistance for offences that have a maximum punishment of six months, with no minimum term prescribed, whereas the United States could only seek assistance for offences with a mandatory minimum prison term of one or more years. Such an interpretation is rejected as unrealistic and contrary to the intention of the parties. They conclude that the Sherman Act offences in the present case are "offences" within the meaning of the act.

The second issue, regarding the requirement of reciprocity, hinges on the interpretation of section 8(1) of the act, which provides: "If a request for mutual legal assistance is made under an agreement, the Minister may not give effect to the request by means of the provisions of this Part *unless the agreement provides for mutual legal assistance with respect to the subject-matter of the request*" [emphasis added]. The appellants focus on the words "with respect to the subject-matter of the request." They submit that those words refer to (or at least include) the offence for which the requesting state is seeking assistance and that to determine their true meaning, regard must be paid to the organizing principle of reciprocity that informs both the treaty and the act. Following this approach, they submit that in enacting section 8(1) of the act, Parliament intended that assistance should be denied when the offence for which the requesting state seeks assistance is not, in substance, an offence in Canada. In support of their position, the appellants rely upon the reasons of Owen-Flood J. in *United States of America* v. *Stuckey*, (1999) 181 D.L.R. (4th) 144 (B.C.S.C.), noted at (2000) 38 Canadian Yearbook of International Law 425, which held that when Canada receives a request under the treaty from the United States, Canada must have, under the terms of the treaty, a reciprocal right to make a request to the United States on the same subject matter. In other words, the subject matter on which the request is founded must come within the definitions given in the treaty as to the meaning of the term "offence" both in Canada and in the United States. There must be a particular reciprocity in that any offence in the request must also be, in substance, an offence within the requested state.

Rosenberg and Moldaver JJ.A., holding that the application judge reached the correct conclusion, express disagreement with the analysis of Owen-Flood J. There are several reasons for holding that section 8(1) does not incorporate "a reciprocal offence requirement." The appellants are not advocating a "dual criminality" requirement, which is addressed and expressly rejected in the treaty. Rather, they maintain that it contains a "reciprocity of offence" requirement that they define as "a reciprocal right to make a request with respect to the same subject matter." In other words, according to the appellants, the focus of section 8(1) is not on conduct but on the content of the offence for which assistance is being sought and specifically, whether an offence exists in Canada that can be said to be the substantial counterpart of the foreign offence

Section 8(1) does not contain a "reciprocity of offence" requirement. The distinction proposed by the appellants, namely that section 8(1) does not require dual criminality but does require offence-based reciprocity is formalistic, not in keeping with the spirit and intent of the treaty, and capable of leading to illogical results. If correct, it would mean that Canada could not provide assistance in cases where an American offence is without substantive Canadian counterpart, even though the conduct underlying the American offence would, if committed in Canada, constitute a criminal offence. In consequence, Canada could well find itself in the illogical situation of being unable to render assistance in the investigation of a particular offence but quite able, in respect of the same offence, to extradite someone for trial, notwithstanding the far graver consequences attached to extradition than legal assistance. This result would make no sense.

That is not to say that we as a nation should be unconcerned about the prospect of rendering assistance in circumstances where, for example, the foreign law is one that we do not adhere to and find socially or politically unacceptable. On the contrary, the concern is a legitimate one. The authority to deal with such matters has been entrusted to the Minister of Justice under Article V of the treaty headed "Limitations on Compliance." Specifically, section 1(b) of that article provides that the requested state may deny assistance to the extent that "execution of the request is contrary to its public interest as determined by its Central Authority." Under Article 1, "Central Authority" is defined for Canada as "the Minister of Justice and officials designated by him." "Public Interest" is defined as "any substantial interest related to national security or other essential public policy." The words "other essential public policy" are very broad, and they provide the minister with the authority needed to refuse a request for assistance in circumstances where, for example, the lending of assistance in respect of a particular offence unknown to our law would shock Canada's collective social conscience.

Second, the plain wording of section 8(1) of the act does not support the reciprocal offence requirement advocated by the appellants. On the contrary, to the extent that the words "with respect to the subject-matter of the request" refer, among other things, to the offence under investigation in a foreign state, there is no reason why the word "offence" should take on a different meaning from the meaning ascribed to it in the treaty. The act itself defines the word "offence" to mean "an offence within the meaning of the relevant agreement." In the present case, given that the word "offence" in the treaty has a different meaning for Canada than for the United States, it seems apparent that insofar as section 8(1) is concerned, so long as the minister is satisfied that the offence under investigation by the United States is one that is covered by the treaty, using the definition of offence for the United States, nothing more is required. Under section 8(1), the minister would then go on to determine whether the type of assistance sought was covered by the treaty. If so, the requirements of section 8(1) would have been met.

Rosenberg and Moldaver JJ.A. recognize that such an interpretation places Canada in the position of providing assistance in situations for which it would never have occasion to make a demand. Yet that is precisely what the treaty envisages. Grafting a reciprocal offence requirement onto section 8(1) of the act would not only be out of step with the treaty, it would fly directly in its face. Interpreting section 8(1) in the manner suggested here takes into account the fact that under section 8(1), the minister may only implement a request for assistance if "*the relevant treaty*" provides for mutual legal assistance with respect to the subject matter of the request. In other words, under the act, the minister's authority to give effect to a request for assistance is limited by the four corners of the relevant treaty. The significance of that limitation becomes apparent when a comparison is made of the various treaties that Canada has entered into with different nations. Without going into detail, it is apparent that the various treaties differ in terms of the types of assistance that may be rendered and the types of offences for and circumstances under which investigative assistance may be given, including in some instances, a requirement of dual criminality.

Rosenberg and Moldaver JJ.A. note that even if they had interpreted section 8(1) to contain a reciprocal offence requirement, that requirement would have been met in this case. The Sherman Act offences for which the United States seeks assistance are in essence, restrictive trade practice offences and their Canadian counterparts are found in section 45 of the Competition Act. The restrictive trade offences in the two jurisdictions are not identical. They do, however, relate to the same subject matter, they have the same object, and they address fundamentally the same conduct. This is not a situation in which the subject matter of the American law is unknown to our law or contrary to our basic values. On the contrary, the offences in the two jurisdictions are closely connected.

Fuentes v. *Canada (Minister of Citizenship and Immigration)*, [2003] 4 F.C. 249, 2003 FCT 37. Federal Court Trial Division.

This was an application of judicial review of an adjudicator's decision finding the applicant to be an inadmissible person for permanent residence in Canada under clause 19(1)(f)(iii)(B) of the Immigration Act, which deals with membership in an organization that there are reasonable grounds to believe is or was engaged in terrorism. The adjudicator interpreted "terrorism" as not being restricted to actions against civilians.

Lemieux J. found that the adjudicator's decision could not stand, *inter alia*, because it departs from the delineation by the Supreme Court of Canada in *Suresh* v. *Canada (Minister of Citizenship and Immigration)*, [2002] 1 S.C.R. 3, noted at (2002) 40 Canadian Yearbook of International Law 570, of what terrorism constitutes. In *Suresh*, the Supreme Court of Canada adopted a definition of terrorism focused on the protection of civilians — a central element in international humanitarian law whose foundation rests on the four Geneva Conventions adopted on June 12, 1949, and its two additional Protocols, all of which have been incorporated into and made part of Canadian law. Article 50 of Protocol I [Protocol Additional to the Geneva Conventions of 12 August 1949, and relating to the Protection of Victims of International Armed Conflicts] defines a civilian as basically anyone not taking up arms in an armed conflict that excludes members of armed forces, militia, and volunteer groups taking up arms, members of a resistance group and inhabitants of a non-occupied territory who, on the approach of an enemy, spontaneously take up arms to resist the invading forces. Protocol II [Protocol Additional to the Geneva Conventions of 12 August 1949, and relating to the Protection of Victims of Non-international Armed Conflicts] to the 1949 Geneva Conventions applies to non-international armed conflicts — that is, conflicts between the armed forces of a state and dissident armed forces or other organized armed groups, under responsible command and in control over a part of the state's territory. Protocol II proscribes either side committing acts of terrorism (see subparagraph 2(d) of Article 4). Also prohibited are "[a]cts or threats of violence the primary purpose of which is to spread terror among the civilian population" (see paragraph 2 of Article 13).

There are other key elements in the definition of terrorism adopted by the Supreme Court of Canada, namely: (1) civilians or other persons must not be taking an active part in hostilities in situations of armed conflict that again brings into play concepts known in international public law; and (2) the purpose of the act intending to cause death or serious bodily harm (which are crimes known in domestic law and in international law (war crimes or crimes against humanity)), which gives that act its quality of terror, must be, by its nature or context, to intimidate a population or to compel a government or international organization to do or to abstain from doing any act. The Supreme Court of Canada was quite conscious that the concept of terrorism can and is the subject of political manipulation and this is why it wished to circumscribe its scope by identifying precise elements of what terrorism is while at the same time, at the margins or on the fringe, not closing the class to terrorist activity. This allows for some flexibility and some means of adaptation. In addition, by choosing the definition of terrorism it did, the Supreme Court harmonized and gave space to each of the key concepts found in section 19 of the act: subversion, terrorism, crimes against humanity, war crimes, and ordinary crimes. Each of those concepts are distinct and have separate roles to play in law.

Mack v. Canada (Attorney General) (2002), 217 D.L.R. (4th) 583. Ontario Court of Appeal.

This was an appeal from an order to strike a claim brought by the appellants seeking a public apology, damages and other remedies arising out of the moneys paid to the government of Canada in respect of the so-called "Head Tax" and other effects of the Chinese Immigration Acts, enacted between 1885 and 1923. In a decision noted at (2001) 39 Canadian Yearbook of International Law 577, Cumming J. of the Ontario Superior Court of Justice had struck the claim pursuant to the Rules of Civil Procedure, R.R.O. 1990, Reg. 194, on the basis that it was plain and obvious that the claim could not succeed.

Among the arguments raised by the appellants was that their claim supports a cause of action based on customary international law. In particular, they argued that it is not plain and obvious that customary international law did not condemn racial discrimination during the period of the impugned legislation and, to the extent that it did, Canada was legally bound to abide by it and can be held accountable for failing to do so. They maintained that Cumming J. had failed to consider their customary international law argument and its impact on the viability of their claim.

The appellants rely on a number of sources to establish the pre-1947 existence of a customary international law prohibiting racial discrimination. These include national and international judicial decisions; individual opinions expressed by some members of Parliament; Canada's membership in the League of Nations and its participation as a signatory to the Treaty of Versailles; Canada's participation as a signatory to various treaties regarding the abolition of slavery; the constitution of the International Labour Organization and various declarations emanating from it; and writings of various international law scholars. In addition, the appellants point to the Canadian Bill of Rights and the Charter, characterizing each as a codification of pre-existing rights, including the right to be free from racial discrimination. The Attorney General of Canada submits that the source materials referred to by the appellants fall short of establishing a pre-1947 international custom prohibiting racial discrimination. According to the Attorney General, these materials, properly construed, represent pockets of enlightenment in an era when the protection of human rights did not figure prominently on the international scene.

Moldaver and MacPherson J.A. cite the writings of scholars that support the view that the development of international human rights was of a "revolutionary" nature and can largely be traced to the adoption of the United Nations Charter in 1945 and the Universal Declaration of Human Rights in 1948. Furthermore, they note that to the extent that national judicial decisions from the pre-1947 era are relevant, the cases relied upon by the appellants are of limited assistance since they do not address the issue at hand but relate instead to the separation of powers under sections 91 and 92 of the Constitution Act, 1867. In any event, they must be read in light of *Cunningham* v. *Tomey Homma*, [1903] A.C. 151 (P.C.), a more recent decision and one of higher authority in which the Privy Council held that a statute that restricted entitlement to vote on the basis of race was both *intra vires* and a valid exercise of provincial power. *Cunningham*, a decision of the final appellate court of the day, stands in stark contradiction to the appellants' assertion that a customary international law prohibiting racial discrimination existed in that era.

As for the foreign decisions cited by the appellants in support of their customary international law argument, these are examples of foreign domestic law, not customary international law and thus not binding on Canada. In any event, the appellants do not suggest that Canada adopted those decisions or the principles enunciated in them during the relevant time frame. In sum, based on the evidence presented, it is plain and obvious that the appellants cannot succeed in establishing the existence of a pre-1947 customary international law prohibiting racial discrimination that would render the impugned legislation invalid. For that reason alone, the customary international law pleading must fail. However, even if the evidence presented by the appellants was capable of passing the threshold test, the action would nonetheless have been halted because of the well-established principle that customary international law may be ousted for domestic purposes by contrary domestic legislation. Applying that principle to this case, to the extent any customary international law prohibiting racial discrimination may have existed during the relevant time frame, it was clearly ousted by the impugned legislation. Accordingly, for that reason as well, the customary international law aspect of the claim must fail.

Moldaver and MacPherson J.A. also express agreement with Cumming J.'s conclusion on the issue of unjust enrichment. The appellants had argued that the impugned legislation could not constitute a juristic reason for any enrichment and corresponding deprivation because of its inconsistency with Canadian constitutional and customary international law. The appellants' submissions relating to juristic reason cover precisely the same ground as their submissions on the Charter and customary international law issues. Rejection of the latter necessarily entails rejection of the former.

Pfizer Canada Inc. v. *Canada (Attorney General)*, [2003] 4 F.C. 95, 2003 FCA 138. Federal Court of Appeal.

These were three appeals, heard at the same time, from the same order of Blanchard J. [[2003] 1 F.C. 423 (T.D.)] dismissing applications for judicial review of the decision of the Minister of Health refusing to list certain Canadian patents on the patent lists pursuant to section 4 of the Patented Medicines (Notice of Compliance) Regulations, SOR/93-133 (as amended by SOR/98-166, s. 3). In each case, the minister refused to list the Canadian patents because the filing date of the applications for those Canadian patents did not precede the filing date for submissions for notices of compliance (NOCs). The minister took the position that, pursuant to subsection 4(4), he could only list a Canadian patent where an application was made for such a patent prior to the filing of a submission for an NOC. In all of these cases, there had been an application for a US equivalent patent prior to the filing of a submission, but, in each case, the application for the Canadian patent was not made until after the filing of NOC submissions.

The appellants argued that the term "filing date" in subsection 4(4) of the regulations is not confined to the date an application is filed for a Canadian patent but instead means the "priority date" of a Canadian patent based on as, in these cases, the date of filing applications in the United States for patents that, in each case, preceded the date of filing submissions under the regulations for notices of compliance.

The Applications Judge, having held that the standard of review of the minister's decision was correctness, the issue being a question of law, concluded that the words "a filing date," read in their entire context and in their grammatical and ordinary sense, harmoniously with the scheme of the act and the intention of Parliament, should be interpreted to be exhaustive and refer solely to the filing date for an application for patent in Canada.

Strayer J.A. characterizes the essential issues on appeal as, first, whether the reference to "a filing date" in subsection 4(4) of the regulations includes a priority date based on an earlier foreign filing or whether the provision is at least ambiguous; and, second, whether international conventions should be resorted to in order to determine the meaning of "a filing date," and, if so, whether they are determinative. Having concluded that the meaning of "filing date" in subsection 4(4) is clear and unambiguous and is confined to the filing of an application in Canada, Strayer J.A. turns to the argument made by the appellants that this interpretation of sub-section 4(4) is prohibited by three international instruments: the Paris Convention for the Protection of Intellectual Property, the North American Free Trade Agreement, and the TRIPS Agreement.

Strayer J.A. concludes that there is no need to resort to these instruments in this case, based on the long-established jurisprudence that while Parliament is presumed not to intend to legislate contrary to international treaties or general principles of international law, this is only a presumption: where the legislation is clear, one need not and should not look to international law. If a statute is intended to implement an international convention, then the latter becomes a proper aid to interpretation. That is not the situation in the present case. It has not been demonstrated that the Patented Medicines (Notice of Compliance) Regulations were adopted for the purpose of implementing any of the international instruments on which the appellants rely.

Furthermore, none of the instruments relied on, even if applied directly to override the clear language of the regulations, would dictate the result insisted upon by the appellants. Some of these instruments require "national treatment" — that is treatment as favourable for nationals of other parties to the conventions, as is accorded to a member's nationals by that member. This is the essence of paragraph 1 of Article 2 of the Paris Convention and paragraph 1 of Article 3 of the Agreement on Trade-Related Aspects of Intellectual Property Rights (TRIPS). Subsection 4(4) of the regulations as the Applications Judge has interpreted that it in no way conflicts with this obligation. The requirement that it imposes on an originator, to file a patent application in Canada before making a submission for an NOC, is in no way tied to nationality. It applies equally to Canadian originators as to originators from any of the countries who are members of the Paris Convention or TRIPS. Indeed the appellants who complain herein are all Canadian companies. Similarly the most-favoured-nation treatment required by Canada under Article 4 of TRIPS is in no way denied by subsection 4(4) of the regulations, for the same reason. Its provisions apply to all "first persons" who want to make submissions for an NOC in Canada, regardless of nationality.

The other important international obligation invoked by the appellants is found in Article 4B of the Paris Convention. This is based on the right of priority established by Article 4A. A person filing an application for a patent in any member country enjoys a right of priority for its patent, based on the date of original filing, in respect of any subsequent filing (within prescribed time limits) in another member state. Article 4B goes on to provide in part that "any subsequent filing in any of the other countries of the Union . . . shall not be invalidated by reason of any acts accomplished in the interval, in particular, another filing, the publication or exploitation of the invention, the putting on sale of copies of the design, or the use of the mark, and such acts cannot give rise to any third-party right." By Article 1701(2) of NAFTA, Canada is obliged to give effect to this convention and is bound to comply with these articles by paragraph 1 of Article 2 of TRIPS.

Subsection 4(4) of the regulations as interpreted by the Applications Judge in no way "invalidates" a patent first filed in another member of the Union where that patent is invoked for purposes of priority in a filing for a Canadian patent. That priority is specifically protected by section 28.1 of the Patent Act. Nor do the regulations give rise to any third-party patent rights that could detract from the priority based on a foreign filing. The owner of a foreign patent can prosecute his Canadian patent application with his priority recognized, as long as he does it within one year. He has access to our courts to withstand challenges to his application, to object to other conflicting applications, and to seek redress for infringement of his patent once it is issued in Canada.

Instead, the regulations provide an extra administrative process tied to the protection of public health, designed, on the one hand, to assist the development and preparation for marketing of generic drugs at a time prior to the issue of an NOC when their sale would still be an infringement of a current patent. At the same time, it gives patentees extra protection: by merely applying for prohibition they can normally prevent the issue of an NOC to a generic for twenty-four months. This system is, not surprisingly, confined to the protection of patents that have, or will have, force in Canada. The universe of special remedies is confined to existing or potential Canadian patents. Yet this in no way detracts from the priority to which convention member patents are entitled in Canada with respect to the prosecution of Canadian patent applications. All that is required to achieve recognition in the Canadian regulatory system under consideration is to file a Canadian patent application prior to filing a submission for a notice of compliance. The appellants were at liberty to file such patent applications in Canada prior to filing their submissions but they did not do so.

In spite of what the appellants seem to imply, the Paris Convention does not confer immediate enforceability in Canada of a patent applied for, or obtained in, another member country. While it gives certain priorities to its holder in prosecuting a Canadian patent application, that holder or its affiliate must still apply in Canada for a patent before being able to enforce it. The regulations are in no way inconsistent with this principle. Article 1702 of NAFTA provides that a party may provide more extensive protection of patents than already required (for example, by the Paris Convention), and such protection "must not be inconsistent with this Agreement" (*inter alia,* inconsistent with the Paris Convention incorporated by subparagraph (c) of Article 1701(2)). While arguably the regulations represent "more extensive protection," there is nothing inconsistent with the Paris Convention in requiring the holder of a convention patent to apply for the same patent in Canada before being able to enjoy the extra enforcement rights under the regulations just as he has to do to exercise enforcement rights under the Patent Act generally.

Therefore, even if resort should be had to the international conventions to interpret subsection 4(4), this provision is correctly understood to require the filing of a Canadian patent application prior to delivery by a first person of a submission for a notice of compliance.

Québec (Minister of Justice) v. *Canada (Minister of Justice)* (2003), 228 D.L.R. (4th) 63. Québec Court of Appeal.

On February 19, 2002, Bill C-7, entitled Act in Respect of Criminal Justice for Young Persons and to Amend and Repeal Other Acts, was given Royal Assent. The corresponding act, the Youth Criminal Justice Act, S.C. 2002, c. 1 (YCJA), was slated to come into force in April 2003. On September 5, 2001, the Québec government referred a number of questions relating to Bill C-7 to the Court of Appeal. One question asked whether the proposed provisions of Bill C-7, particularly those in Part 4 (sections 38 to 82) and Part 6 (sections 110 to 129), are incompatible with international law, especially the Convention on the Rights of the Child and the International Covenant on Civil and Political Rights, which were ratified by Canada with the support of all the provinces and territories, and to which the Québec government had declared it was bound.

The court begins by addressing a number of preliminary matters raised by the fact that this question calls for conclusions constituting simple declarations of incompatibility, as opposed to conclusions that the provisions in dispute are invalid or inoperative. First, what are the legal effects in domestic law of the simple ratification of the two international treaties involved? Second, what are the legal effects of a simple declaration of incompatibility? Third, is it useful and timely for the court to make any such declaration?

Addressing the first preliminary question, the court notes that the parties agree that simple ratification of an international treaty by the executive branch, as in this case, does not give the treaty force of law or any coercive effect in domestic law, unless it is subsequently incorporated into domestic law through the legislation of Parliament. A reference in a statute is not sufficient, and, thus, a simple "whereas" in the preamble of the YCJA that refers to the Convention on the Rights of the Child is therefore insufficient. However, even though the international treaties were not incorporated into domestic law, it does not necessarily mean that they are of no utility in that area. The fact that the YCJA mentions the convention in its preamble creates a relative interdependence between the YCJA and the convention. Although that interrelation is of limited impact, it can nevertheless guide the courts in interpreting domestic legislation. In the event of doubt, or ambiguity between the YCJA and international law, it can be presumed that Parliament legislates in a manner that respects Canada's international commitments, even if it may legislate in a manner inconsistent with them. Hence, in the case at bar, the convention and the covenant can merely serve as tools for interpreting the provisions of the YCJA whose scope would otherwise be ambiguous.

The situation may be different from an international standpoint. Violation of international treaties can incur the state's international liability, which may, in fact, have only moral importance and political influence. The court notes that states are bound only by that to which they have explicitly agreed. Neither the work preliminary to the drafting, signing, and ratifying of an international treaty, nor the subsequent analyses of the application of the treaty by the signatory states, therefore has any coercive effect, even from an international standpoint. The preliminary work, particularly if explicitly referred to in the convention, can at best be used as a tool for interpreting the convention.

On the question of the legal effects of a simple declaration of incompatibility, the court notes that its remarks regarding the first preliminary question explain why both the Attorney General of

Québec and the intervening party sought a simple declaration of incompatibility, not a declaration of invalidity of the provisions of the YCJA that allegedly cannot be reconciled with the treaties. It is evident that, from strictly judicial and legal standpoints, such a declaration is unlikely to have any direct effect, given the power of Parliament to legislate, even against the terms of an agreement that the executive branch has ratified. From an international standpoint, neither the convention nor the covenant provides for sanctions in the event of the violation by a state of its obligation or even a mechanism for filing a complaint. The two treaties provide for the preparation and transmission of periodic reports on the progress made by the signatory states or on their violations. The recommendations made by international authorities responsible for monitoring the implementation of the treaties have merely a political impact, at least directly. Internationally, a declaration of incompatibility would therefore have the sole effect of subjecting the Canadian state to the criticism of those authorities. In other words, the consequence would be chiefly non-juridical. From a domestic standpoint, it also would have no coercive effect. At best, it could serve as a means of applying pressure on, and prompting, Parliament to amend the contentious provisions. But even then, the effects of the judgment would be essentially political.

In relation to the third preliminary question, regarding the usefulness and timeliness of such a judgment, the court notes that the scope of section 1 of the Court of Appeal Reference Act is very broad, and no provision limits in any way the government's power to rule thereon. References, whether by the federal government to the Supreme Court or by provincial governments to courts of appeal, customarily ask the court to express an opinion on the validity of one or more aspects of a bill. Given this, it is frequent and normal for a government to also seek the opinion of the court as to the compatibility of the provisions of its bill with other statutes or, as in this case, with international treaties. It is only occasionally, if not exceptionally, that a level of government contests, by a declaratory reference, the validity of the statute of another level of government.

In the case at bar, from an international standpoint, the answers to the government's questions have no legal effect, and their consequences would be purely political. The same would be true from the standpoint of domestic law, and the court may appear to be used as a political instrument. Inasmuch as the convention may serve as an instrument for interpreting what constitutes, in criminal matters, the fundamental right of children under section 7 of the

Charter, a declaration of incompatibility may then have an impact in terms of the applicability of section 1 of the Charter. Within those confines, it may be said that the question asked is justiciable and legal in nature. For that reason, it should be considered.

Having dealt with the three preliminary questions, the court proceeds to survey relevant provisions in the Convention on the Rights of the Child and the International Covenant on Civil and Political Rights. Both the Attorney General of Québec and the intervening party had argued that the specific provisions of the two international treaties at issue must be, if not supplemented, then at least interpreted, in light of instruments drawn up prior to their drafting and ratification. These are, in particular, instruments that have been the subject of resolutions by the General Assembly of the United Nations, such as the 1985 United Nations Standard Minimum Rules for the Administration of Juvenile Justice (Beijing Rules), the 1990 United Nations Guidelines for the Prevention of Juvenile Delinquency (Riyadh Guidelines), and the 1990 United Nations Rules for the Protection of Juveniles Deprived of Their Liberty. The treaty provisions must also be considered in light of the observations and recommendations of the convention implementation committees.

After pointing out that international public law is founded on the principle of recognition of the sovereignty of states and that its corollary is that states are bound only by that to which they explicitly consent, the Attorney General of Canada stressed that the international treaties must be interpreted by means of the rules of interpretation codified in Articles 31 and 32 of the Vienna Convention on the Law of Treaties. Article 31 of the Vienna Convention stipulates, among other interpretive means relevant to this case, that "any subsequent agreement between the parties regarding the interpretation of the treaty or the application of its provisions" must be taken into consideration, while Article 32 states that "[r]ecourse may be had to ... preparatory work" when necessary to confirm the interpretation resulting from the application of Article 31. That is, what the authors in international public law call "soft law," an expression used to designate non-coercive written instruments of an instructive nature, to which Canadian courts can refer, not as a coercive source of law, but to confirm that a principle whose existence in Canadian law has been noted by the court, is also recognized internationally. In this case, the Beijing Rules, the Riyadh Guidelines, and the United Nations Rules for the Protection of Juveniles Deprived of Their Liberty are such instruments.

Following a survey of relevant provisions in these instruments, the court reiterates that the only coercive provisions in international law for the signatory states are those in the convention and the covenant. The others are merely instruments for interpreting the philosophy and wording where necessary. The distinction is important in this case, since, to the extent that the wording and interpretation of a provision of the convention do not reflect the philosophy or the wording of the instruments that preceded or followed the convention's ratification, those instruments are irrelevant to the question that we have been asked. It must immediately be pointed out that, for example, Article 3 of the convention, does not necessarily reflect all the rules adopted prior to it.

Before conducting a comparative analysis of the contentious provisions of the YCJA in terms of the convention and the covenant, the court notes that several preliminary remarks must be made. The specific conclusions of the Attorney General of Québec do not deal with the underlying philosophy of the impugned provisions of the YCJA in terms of the convention and the covenant. They deal exclusively with the compatibility of certain specific provisions with the commitments explicitly made by Canada in international law through the ratification and signing of all of the explicit provisions in the convention and the covenant. In other words, the court is not asked to express an opinion about the philosophy and spirit underpinning the impugned provisions, as opposed to the philosophy and spirit of the international instruments, but solely to determine whether the specific provisions of the YCJA contradict or are compatible and reconcilable with the corresponding provisions of the international treaties.

The provisions of the YCJA cannot be considered in a vacuum. They must be read in the context of the YCJA as a whole, including its preamble and all its other provisions. Furthermore, their compatible or incompatible nature cannot be dissociated from their potential concrete application to specific cases that will possibly be submitted to the decision-maker designated by the YCJA. A pragmatic approach is required in order to determine whether certain seemingly contrary provisions can be reconciled in the framework of their functional application to specific cases.

From the outset, it is important, from that standpoint, to immediately point out that Article 3 of the Convention on the Rights of the Child, which sets forth the guiding principle and philosophy, is also aimed at the decisions of courts, not only those of legislative bodies. The judges eventually responsible for applying the YCJA and, to do so, for interpreting it, will be at the front line of its application. It must be borne in mind that Article 3 does not make the child's best interests the only consideration; it does not rule out consideration of other paramount factors, such as the protection of the public, in decisions, whether legislative or judicial. In this regard, Article 3 does not go as far as the Beijing Rules, which may appear to bring into conflict the minor's well-being, as the most important objective, and the other considerations. In such a case, the wording of the convention takes precedence, not that of the preliminary written instruments. Moreover, the specific reference to the convention in the YCJA preamble and to the rights that young persons may accordingly enjoy necessarily forces the decision-makers designated in the YCJA to consider the best interests of the young person at the administrative or judicial stage in every decision they must make in the young person's regard. Article 3 of the convention provides a clue to the way in which the powers conferred on decision-makers under the authority of the YCJA should be interpreted. Pursuant to the preamble and the resulting rules of interpretation, all references to interests other than the child's well-being in the YCJA, and more specifically in the provisions in dispute, must be read, interpreted, and applied in light of Article 3 of the convention. First of all, that article recognizes the best interests of the child as a paramount consideration in the decisions to be made, without excluding other factors that are also essential and paramount. Although, at first glance, the wording of certain articles implies that the protection of the public is the paramount objective, one very quickly realizes that the YCJA recognizes that society can be truly protected only by a system that takes into consideration the needs of young persons so as to facilitate their rehabilitation.

Finally, it must be pointed out that "incompatibility" is a strong term. Two statements that contradict each other are incompatible. Once the statements can be reconciled, either through interpretation or application, they cannot be considered incompatible. The court then proceeds to undertake an analysis of the provisions involved.

Sections 3, 38, 39 and 83 of the YCJA

According to the Attorney General of Québec and the intervening party, the use in these provisions of the terms "long-term protection of the public" and "the protection of society" (section

3(1)(a)), and "fair and proportionate accountability" (section 3(1)(b)(ii) and section 3(1)(c)) reflect a philosophy that is incompatible with that of Article 3 of the convention, since it places on an equal footing the protection of the public and the criminal accountability of the young person, on the one hand, and the young person's best interests, on the other. The same is said to be true of sections 38, 39, and 83, in regard to both the objective based on the protection of the public and the sentencing of the young person.

Article 3 of the convention in no way bars decision-makers from considering factors other than the best interests of the young person. Nothing in section 3(1) of the act justifies the conclusion that, through simple enumeration, the impugned terms establish a priority in favour of the protection of the public and in favour of measures to sanction the offence solely in proportion to its seriousness. Subsection 3(1) must be read in light of not only Article 3 of the convention but also section 3(2), which obviously refers to the young person's rehabilitation and reintegration into the community. Furthermore, the measures listed in section 3(1)(c) and (d) are precisely what is contemplated in Article 5 of the Beijing Rules, which specifically refers to the proportionality principle.

Sections 38, 39, and 83 deal with the sentence and the custody and supervision of the young person once the sentence is handed down. Here, a dual reproach is made: section 38, by referring in section 38(2) to section 3, is said to be incompatible with Article 3 of the convention, and those provisions allegedly give priority once again to the seriousness of the offence and favour custody or even imprisonment. The preceding remarks about section 3 of the act are also valid in regard to the first argument. As for the second, it must be recognized at the outset that the wording of section 38 is not very clear, with the result that there is a major divergence of opinion between the two parties. Subsection 38(1) of the YCJA first stipulates that the imposition of a sentence on a young person must target his or her rehabilitation and reintegration into the community. The second paragraph of that section stipulates that the court determines the youth sentence in accordance with the principles set forth in section 3, which indicates that the criminal justice system for young persons must focus on their rehabilitation, among other things. However, section 38(2)(c) and (e) seem to scale back this general objective of reintegration into the community by apparently subordinating it to the more specific objective of "the seriousness of the offence and the degree of responsibility of the young person for that offence" (section 38(2)(c)).

The Attorney General of Québec sees in this provision the legislator's intention to make proportionality the primary objective of the sentencing regime. He believes that, by thus subjecting one of the main purposes now pursued by the YOA to the achievement of the other, the legislator fundamentally upsets the delicate balance previously sought between the protection of the public and the needs of young persons.

The court does not share this point of view. Section 38 must not be considered in isolation from the other provisions of the act — a proper reading of the act suggests that neither guiding principle must take precedence over the other. A court to which the case of a young person is referred must necessarily seek a balance between the two in imposing a youth sentence. The argument of the Attorney General of Québec seems to disregard section 38(2)(e) and section 39(2), (3), and (5), which provide that custody or imprisonment be subject to the obligation to impose the least restrictive sentence possible that offers the best chance of rehabilitation and reintegration into the community, since custody cannot be substituted "for other [more appropriate] social measures."

In addition, all these reservations and qualifications must themselves be interpreted in light of the preamble of the act and, therefore, in light of Article 3 of the convention. Finally, custody and imprisonment are in no way excluded by the international treaties. On the contrary, the covenant refers to them explicitly in Articles 10.2(b) and 10.3, as well as in subparagraphs (b) and (c) of Article 17.1 of the Beijing Rules. As for the convention, it explicitly recognizes the possibility of detention or imprisonment of a child, but it specifies that this must be a measure of last resort, in effect for the shortest appropriate period of time.

In light of the preceding, the court is of the opinion that the YCJA gives decision-makers, in accordance with Article 6.1 of the Beijing Rules, the discretion and power required to apply the four provisions in dispute in a manner that is compatible and reconcilable with the covenant and the convention and also in accordance with the philosophy underpinning the international treaties. The court therefore believes that sections 3, 38, 39, and 83 of the YCJA are not incompatible with either the Convention on the Rights of the Child or the International Covenant on Civil and Political Rights.

Sections 13 and 67 of the YCJA

The Attorney General of Québec and the intervening party argued that sections 13 and 67 would make the youth justice court similar to adult courts and, accordingly, subject young persons to adult courts. The Attorney General of Québec contended that those provisions create confusion between the specialized court for young persons and adult courts and subject young persons to adult courts, contrary to the provisions of the Beijing Rules and the international treaties.

The court does not agree. Section 13 of the YCJA enshrines the priority given to the specialized court for young persons and subjects justices of the Superior Court of criminal jurisdiction to all the provisions of the YCJA by imposing on them the same obligations in regard to the young person as those of judges of the specialized court. Moreover, except in the case of murder or the other highly exceptional offences contemplated in section 469 of the Criminal Code, the option referred to in section 67 depends on the free choice of the young person alone. The aim of those provisions is to give a young person the same right as that which an adult has. That protection supplements all the others specifically provided for young persons under the YCJA. Those two provisions must also be considered in light of Article 14 of the covenant, which explicitly provides for the right of the child, like any other accused, to be assisted and represented by the legal counsel of his or her choice. Finally, in regard to the offences referred to in section 469 of the Criminal Code, the exclusive jurisdiction conferred by that section on the justice of the Superior Court is nonetheless subject to the protections established in Article 13. The court is therefore of the opinion that there is no incompatibility between sections 13 and 67 of the YCJA and the provisions of the international treaties.

Sections 61, 62, 64, 70, and 72 of the YCJA

Sections 61, 62, 64, 70, and 72 concern the imposition of adult sentences on young persons for certain offences. According to the Attorney General of Québec and the intervening party, those provisions create a presumption contrary to the best interests of children that the imposition of adult sentences under the Criminal Code must be the norm for young persons in cases of "presumptive offences," defined in section 2(1) — that is, all serious violent offences. They believe that that would mean that imprisonment must be the norm in such cases.

At first glance, that appears to be incompatible with Articles 3.1, 37(a) and (b), and 40.1 of the convention as well as with Articles 5.1 and 17.1(a), (b), and (c) of the Beijing Rules. Whereas the Convention on the Rights of the Child, as interpreted in light of the

Beijing Rules, emphasizes the best interests of the child and the child's specific circumstances, as well as measures of rehabilitation and reintegration into the community instead of imprisonment, the provisions of the act cited earlier seem to focus, in sentencing, on the seriousness of certain "presumptive" offences. At first glance, the child's best interests do not even seem to have been a paramount consideration in the drafting of those few legislative provisions. Is this really so?

Section 61 can be disregarded since it simply provides that the provincial executive branch can exempt young persons of fourteen to sixteen years of age from the application of the contentious provisions. This provision is absolutely neutral and cannot be said to be, in and of itself, incompatible with the international treaties. The impugned presumption is stated in section 62. Pursuant to sections 62, 72, and 73, an adult sentence is, in principle, imposed on a young person who has committed a presumptive offence when fourteen to eighteen years of age. Moreover, section 64 allows the Attorney General to apply for an order that a young person be liable to an adult sentence in the framework of a court decision that the offence for which the adolescent has just been found guilty constitutes a serious violent offence (section 42(9)), if the young person has already been found guilty of an offence other than a presumptive offence, but one for which an adult would be liable to imprisonment for more than two years.

The strictness of this principle is, however, relieved by certain mechanisms open to the parties. For example, section 63 gives a young person who may be liable to an adult sentence the right to make an application for an order that he or she not be liable to such a sentence. That application must be granted automatically by the court if the Attorney General does not oppose it. Furthermore, the Attorney General can waive, under section 65, the imposition of an adult sentence on the young person, in the case of a presumptive offence contemplated in paragraph (a) of the definition of that term in section 2(1) (murder, attempt to commit murder, manslaughter, and aggravated sexual assault). Conversely, if the Attorney General opposes the application of a young person not to be liable to an adult sentence, the onus will be on the young person to demonstrate to the court the elements provided for in section 72(1) of the act. The onus is on the party that applies for the non-imposition (section 63(1)) or the imposition (section 64(1)) of an adult sentence, as the case may be (section 72(2)). Among the criteria that must be proven to exist by the claimant according to section 72(1) and (2) are the seriousness of the offence, the circumstances of its perpetration, the background and previous record of the young person, the age, maturity, and character of the young person, and any other relevant factor in favour of the application.

Once the claimant has proven the existence of the facts or circumstances related to the application, it is up to the court, in light of all of those factors, to decide whether the young person is liable to an adult sentence or a youth sentence. In that regard, it is important to stress that section 72(1)(a) obliges the court to order the non-imposition of an adult sentence in all cases where it believes that a youth sentence consistent with the principles and objectives set forth in section 3(1)(b)(ii) and section 38 (proportionality and the least restrictive sentence possible) is sufficient. Hence, even within the parameters established by section 72(1), the court has complete discretion. It has sufficient discretionary power within the meaning of Articles 6.1 and 6.2 of the Beijing Rules, to which the preamble of the convention refers, to apply in its decision Article 3 of the convention, to which the preamble of the YCJA refers.

In other words, and notwithstanding the establishment of the presumption under sections 62 and 72, nothing in those provisions prevents the decision-making court from stressing the rehabilitation and reintegration into the community of the young person and imposing on him or her the least restrictive sentence possible, in compliance with sections 3 and 38, interpreted in light of Article 3 of the convention. Thus, the application of the impugned provisions can be reconciled with the objectives of the international treaties, and the court is therefore of the opinion that they are not incompatible with those objectives.

Section 75 and Section 110(2)(b) of the YCJA

Section 75 and section 110(2)(b) establish, as a presumptive rule, the publication of the identity of a young person found guilty of such "presumptive offences." These two provisions undeniably constitute a marked exception to the rule of confidentiality, which has been recognized as one of the paramount elements in facilitating a young person's reintegration into the community, by protecting him or her from the shame of a criminal conviction.

A young person's right to protection of his or her privacy, the standard of confidentiality of which is a crucial factor, is explicitly contemplated in Articles 8.1 and 8.2 of the Beijing Rules and implicitly contemplated in Articles 40.1 and 40.2(b)(vii) of the convention. Those international instruments clearly stipulate that, "in principle," nothing must be divulged that could lead to the identification of a juvenile delinquent. However, the wording does not make that rule absolute, given that what is affirmed, in principle, is subject to exceptions. In this regard, as in regard to sentencing, the objective of reintegration into the community is a paramount consideration.

Section 110(1) of the YCJA in fact confirms the publication ban and the standard of confidentiality recommended in the convention. It is the rule. Subsection 110(2) constitutes the exception limited to "presumptive offences" of which a young person is found guilty and for which he or she receives an adult sentence, or to a young person concerning whom the Attorney General has given notice of an application to seek an adult sentence under section 64 of the YCJA. Furthermore, that exception is also limited by the court's discretion and by the measures provided for in that regard in section 75(1) and (3).

Given the court's discretion and the fact that the rule established by the international treaties does not formally exclude the exceptions, the court is of the opinion that the grounds invoked in support of its conclusion regarding the preceding sections concerning adult sentences are also valid in regard to the exception to the rule of confidentiality. In applying the test in section 75(3), the court must, in fact, consider the rule of confidentiality to be fundamental to the objective of rehabilitation and reintegration into the community, and to be the basic standard. Given this, the court is of the opinion that there is no formal contradiction and therefore no incompatibility between section 110(2)(b) and the international treaties.

Sections 76 and 92 of the YCJA

Ultimately, whereas all of the provisions of the YCJA cited earlier are said to be incompatible with the convention, sections 76 and 92 are said to directly contradict the explicit provisions of the covenant. They provide for the possible imprisonment of young persons with adults. According to the Attorney General of Québec, the two provisions contradict Article 10(3) of the covenant, which lays down the rule that juvenile delinquents must be separated from adults in all respects.

The same rule is, in fact, laid down in Article 37(c) of the convention, which provides, as an exception, for a case where the best interests of the child require the opposite. The Attorney General of Québec acknowledges, in his factum, that this article of the convention is, however, unopposable in Canada, which, at the time of ratification of the convention, recorded an explicit reservation in regard to the provision, in the following terms: "The Government of Canada accepts the general principles of article 37(c) of the Convention, but reserves the right not to detain children separately from adults where this is not appropriate or feasible." A similar reservation was also recorded by several other states that signed the convention. This article of the convention is therefore unopposable in Canada under Article 19(c) of the Vienna Convention on the Law of Treaties.

This is why the Attorney General of Québec sought only a declaration of incompatibility of those two provisions and the corresponding provision of the covenant. For his part, the Attorney General of Canada pointed out that Article 31(3) of the Vienna Convention requires that a treaty be interpreted taking into consideration "any subsequent agreement between the parties regarding the interpretation of the treaty or the application of its provisions" (the convention is an agreement subsequent to the covenant). Under that rule, the exception in Article 37(c) of the convention — that is, regarding the child's best interests — must therefore be added to Article 10(3) of the Covenant.

Although it is correct that section 76(1) stipulates that a young person liable to an adult sentence and sentenced to imprisonment can be ordered to serve his or her sentence in either a youth custody facility separated from any adult or a provincial correctional facility for adults, or, in the case of a sentence of more than two years, a penitentiary, that provision of a general nature must be read in light of section 76(2), which compels the same court to order placement in a youth custody facility, that is, separate from any adult who is detained or held in custody, unless the best interests of the young person require the opposite which is in keeping with the covenant, read in light of Article 37(c) of the convention. As for the exception resulting from the words "if the safety of the other inmates requires it," it is difficult to consider it incompatible with the spirit and philosophy of the international treaties. Moreover, section 84 of the YCJA reiterates the rule, subject to section 76 and sections 89 to 93, that the young person must be held separate from any adult who is detained or held in custody. In short, there is no doubt that the basic rule established by the YCJA is that a young person must be held separate from adults, which is not only compatible but in compliance with the covenant.

As for section 92, it applies exclusively to those who may be considered former young persons who have become adults after beginning to serve their sentence. In such a case, the court may order, upon an application by the provincial director, either the transfer of the young person who has become an adult to a provincial correctional facility for adults, or the young person's transfer from such a facility to a penitentiary if the remainder of the sentence is two years or more. The court must hear a young person who has become an adult and balance its decision on the basis of, on the one hand, that person's interests and, on the other, the interests of the public, even though the former young person has reached full age. The court is of the opinion that there is no incompatibility between that provision and the covenant.

In response to Question 2 of the reference of the Attorney General of Québec regarding the incompatibility of Bill C-7 with the Convention on the Rights of the Child and the International Covenant on Civil and Political Rights, the court concludes that the provisions involved are not incompatible with the international treaties ratified by Canada.

Zrig v. *Canada (Minister of Citizenship and Immigration)*, [2003] 3 F.C. 761, 2003 F.C.A. 178. Federal Court of Appeal.

This was an appeal pursuant to subsection 83(1) [as am. by S.C. 1992, c. 49, section 73] of the Immigration Act, R.S.C. 1985, c. I-2 from a judgment of Tremblay-Lamer J., noted at (2002) 40 Canadian Yearbook of International Law 582, which dismissed the appellant's application for judicial review of a decision by the Immigration and Refugee Board. The Refugee Division had concluded that the appellant was not a refugee within the meaning of the United Nations Convention Relating to the Status of Refugees, on the ground that he should be excluded because of the provisions of Article 1F(b) and (c), which provide that the convention shall not apply to any person with respect to whom there are serious reasons for considering that he has committed a serious non-political crime outside the country of refuge prior to his admission to that country as a refugee (1F(b)); or he has been guilty of acts contrary to the purposes and principles of the United Nations (1F(c)).

The main issue raised by the appeal was according to the interpretation of Article 1F(b) of the convention. It took the form of two questions certified by the judge. First, are the rules laid down by the Federal Court of Appeal in *Sivakumar* v. *Canada* ([1994] 1 F.C.

433), on complicity by association for purposes of implementing Article 1F(a) of the United Nations Convention Relating to the Status of Refugees, applicable for purposes of an exclusion under Article 1F(b) of the said convention? Second, if so, can a refugee status claimant's association with an organization responsible for perpetrating "serious non-political crimes" within the meaning of that expression in Article 1F(b) of the United Nations Convention Relating to the Status of Refugees, entail the complicity of the claimant for purposes of applying the said provision simply because he knowingly tolerated such crimes, whether committed during or before his association with the organization in question?

The appellant, a Tunisian citizen, had been involved as a member and a leader of an organization in Tunisia, the "Mouvement de la tendance islamique" (MTI), which had later changed its name to Ennahda. The Refugee Division had reviewed a considerable amount of evidence regarding the MTI/Ennahda, and had noted that it is a movement that supports the use of violence: it is composed of an armed branch that uses terrorist methods and is financed by several countries and movements. This branch of the movement is involved in assassinations and bombings. The ultimate aim of the movement is the creation of an Islamic state in Tunisia. MTI/Ennahda committed twelve crimes that may be described as serious non-political crimes. It is plain from the evidence that not only was and is the claimant a member of MTI/Ennahda, but he has held important offices within that movement. Given the claimant's important role within MTI/Ennahda, the tribunal concluded that he was aware of the crimes committed by the organization and, accordingly, that he shared the aims and goals of his movement in the perpetration of those crimes. The Refugee Division concluded that the appellant's fear of being persecuted for his political opinions was valid, since there could be no doubt that if he returned to Tunisia he would be imprisoned, tortured, or killed. However, in view of his involvement and his position as a leader in MTI/Ennahda, there were serious reasons for considering that the appellant was an accomplice in the commission of serious non-political crimes, as well as serious reasons for considering that the appellant was guilty as an accomplice "of acts contrary to the purposes and principles of the United Nations." He must therefore be excluded from the definition of a refugee, despite the existence of a reasonable fear of persecution.

Nadon J.A. (Létourneau J.A concurring) notes that in *Sivakumar,* the Federal Court of Appeal concluded in connection with the application of Article 1F(a) of the convention that an individual could be held responsible for acts committed by others on account of his close association with those others. The appellant argued that the rules relating to complicity by association for the purposes of Article 1F(a) are not applicable so as to exclude him under Article 1F(b). In the appellant's submission, the Refugee Division and the judge gave Article 1F(b) an excessive meaning, which is contrary to the restrictive and limited interpretation that such an exceptional provision should be given. In so doing, the purpose of Article 1F(b) was not observed.

In the appellant's submission, the intention of the signatories of the convention was to ensure that persons committing non-political crimes could not avoid extradition proceedings, criminal prosecution or the execution of a sentence of imprisonment in their countries by seeking refugee status in a third country. Since there is no direct or indirect evidence to link him to the crimes ascribed to him by the Refugee Division, the appellant argued that he could not be excluded under Article 1F(b). He further submitted that he could not be the subject of any type of criminal prosecution since there is no physical proof to connect him in any way whatever with the commission of the crimes ascribed to him. The appellant concluded by submitting that the deduction of complicity by association for establishment of a serious non-political crime is contrary to Article 1F(b) of the convention.

In support of his arguments, the appellant referred to a number of judgments of the Supreme Court of Canada, including *Canada (Attorney General)* v. *Ward,* [1993] 2 S.C.R. 689, and *Pushpanathan* v. *Canada (Minister of Citizenship and Immigration),* [1998] 1 S.C.R. 982. Nadon J.A. notes that the references to Article 1F(b) in these judgments are *obiter.* Nadon J.A. goes into more detail on *Pushpanathan,* in which Bastarache J. had stated that "Article 1F(b) is generally meant to prevent ordinary criminals extraditable by treaty from seeking refugee status, but that this exclusion is limited to serious crimes committed before entry in the state of asylum"(at paragraph 73). Nadon J.A. cannot find any intention in the remarks of Bastarache J. to limit the non-political crimes covered by Article 1F(b) to those which are extraditable under a treaty. Such a limitation would be surprising to say the least, since first it is in no way contained in the wording of Article 1F(b), and, second, the limitation would lead to an absurd situation in which extraditable criminals would be excluded from refugee protection whereas offenders whose crimes were not extraditable crimes would not be excluded because Canada had not concluded an extradition treaty with the country in which the serious non-political crimes were committed. Rather, the comments by Bastarache J. are simply an indication of the nature and seriousness of crimes that may fall under the Article 1F(b) exclusion — that is, serious crimes to which the extradition treaties might be fully applicable. It is important to bear in mind that the issue in *Pushpanathan* concerned the interpretation of Article 1F(c) of the convention and, in particular, whether an individual who had pleaded guilty to the crime of drug trafficking in Canada could be excluded from the definition of a refugee because of the application of Article 1F(c). The Supreme Court's judgment in *Pushpanathan* did not have the effect of making the rules on complicity by association stated by this court in *Sivakumar* and other cases inapplicable.

There is no basis for making any distinction between Article 1F(a) and Article 1F(b), so far as the rules laid down by this court in *Sivakumar* are concerned. First, it should be noted that the two paragraphs deal with the commission of serious crimes. Article 1F(a) refers to a crime against peace, a war crime, or a crime against humanity. Needless to say, these crimes are all crimes that can only be described as serious. Under Article 1F(b), the exclusion results from the commission of a serious non-political crime by the refugee status claimant. Both paragraphs describe the nature of the crimes that will result in the exclusion of someone who has committed them. In order to exclude persons covered by Article 1F(a) and (b), it will be necessary to show that there are "serious reasons for considering" that the serious crimes identified were committed, but it will not be necessary to attribute any one specifically to the claimant. This test applies to both Article 1F(a) and Article 1F(b). Accordingly, in considering an exclusion based on Article 1F(b), the Refugee Division will be justified in excluding a claimant from refugee protection if it has serious reasons for considering that a serious non-political crime was committed for which the claimant may be held responsible.

The interpretation of Article 1F(b) which the plaintiff is asking the court to adopt conflicts with the very wording of the article. Additionally, this interpretation has been categorically rejected by other courts in other jurisdictions. While acknowledging that the court is not bound by those judgments, Nadon J.A. shares the viewpoint of those courts on the interpretation of Article 1F(b) and notes that it is preferable, where possible, for the courts of the signatory countries to an international convention to adopt the same interpretation of the provisions of that convention. Consequently, the answer to the first question certified by the judge will be yes.

The question of whether the crimes committed by MTI/Ennahda can be attributed to the appellant as an accomplice by association takes in the second question certified by the trial judge. The answer to such a question necessarily depends on the facts of the case. In the case at bar, in view of the evidence, the Refugee Division concluded that the appellant had to be held responsible for the crimes attributed to MTI/Ennahda, as an accomplice by association. In the Refugee Division's opinion, the appellant was not just a member of the movement but someone who performed important duties. In view of his function in the movement, the fact that he never left the movement, although he was able to do so, and the fact that at the time of the hearing before the Refugee Division he was still a member of the movement, the Refugee Division concluded that he should be held responsible by association for the crimes attributed to MTI/Ennahda. Additionally, the Refugee Division considered that in the case at bar the appellant's mere membership in the movement sufficed to make him responsible, since MTI/Ennahda existed primarily for limited and brutal purposes. Given that the Refugee Division's findings of fact were not unreasonable, the crimes attributed to MTI/Ennahda may be ascribed to the appellant as an accomplice by association in accordance with the rules set forth in *Sivakumar.*

Décary J.A., concurring in the result, reaches the same conclusion as to the outcome of the appeal for different reasons, which leads to a different answer to the first question certified. Décary J.A. notes that there is no unanimity on the general meaning to be given to Article 1F(b), and where there is any consensus, it is not always easy to determine what it is. What is certain is that this is an area that is constantly changing. It should also be borne in mind that the disparity results from the system itself, which requires the courts of the countries of refuge to interpret the convention, rather than an international body, and inevitably they do so in terms of their own legal cultures. It is true that in theory unanimity should be sought when interpreting an international document: it would be achieved in the case at bar if the courts of the signatory countries recognized that the authors of the convention intended to interpret the word "crime" in Article 1F(b) in accordance with domestic law. Of course, the meaning of the word "crime" would then vary with the state. This is the result intended by the system, which is readily understandable given that what is being done is to determine the types of criminal against which a country of refuge feels it must protect itself. When an international convention refers to domestic law, the rule that such a convention should not be interpreted in accordance with a single legal system obviously does not apply.

This is the first time that this court has had to consider the concept of "complicity by association," which is recognized in international criminal law in relation to Article 1F(b) of the convention. None of the decisions to which the court was referred dealt directly with the point at issue, namely whether the rules on complicity in traditional criminal law or the rules on complicity in international criminal law should be applied in determining whether there has been a "crime" within the meaning of Article 1F(b).

A reading of precedent, academic commentary, and the actual wording of Article 1F of the convention, leads to the conclusion that the purpose of this section is to reconcile various objectives that can be summarized as follows: ensuring that the perpetrators of international crimes or acts contrary to certain international standards will be unable to claim the right of asylum; ensuring that the perpetrators of ordinary crimes committed for fundamentally political purposes can find refuge in a foreign country; ensuring that the right of asylum is not used by the perpetrators of serious ordinary crimes in order to escape the ordinary course of local justice; and ensuring that the country of refuge can protect its own people by closing its borders to criminals whom it regards as undesirable because of the seriousness of the ordinary crimes that it suspects such criminals of having committed. It is this fourth purpose that is really at issue in this case.

These purposes are complementary. The first indicates that the international community does not wish persons responsible for persecution to profit from a convention designed to protect the victims of their crimes. The second indicates that the signatories of the Convention have accepted the fundamental rule of international law that the perpetrator of a political crime, even one of extreme seriousness, is entitled to elude the authorities of the state in which he committed his crime — the premise being that such a person would not be tried fairly in that state and would be persecuted. The third indicates that the signatories do not wish the right of asylum to be transformed into a guarantee of impunity for ordinary criminals whose real fear was not being persecuted, but being tried, by the countries they were seeking to escape. The fourth indicates that while the signatories were prepared to sacrifice their sovereignty, even their security, in the case of the perpetrators of political crimes, they wished on the contrary to preserve them for reasons of security and social peace in the case of the perpetrators of serious ordinary crimes. This fourth purpose also indicates that the signatories wanted to ensure that the convention would be accepted by the people of the country of refuge, who might be in danger of having to live with especially dangerous individuals under the cover of a right of asylum.

Décary J.A. agrees with Nadon J.A.'s treatment of *Ward* and *Pushpanathan*. With respect to the latter, he notes that in his view Bastarache J. did not intend to limit the application of Article 1F(b) to extraditable persons. It is clear that the question of extradition was central to the discussion and Bastarache J. was not wrong to attach great importance to it. However, the fact remains that the framers of the convention had other concerns to reconcile, and they did so by using language that goes beyond the concern with extradition. Moreover, it would have been surprising if the signatories, who expressly discussed extradition in the *travaux préparatoires*, had disregarded that term in adopting the final wording, if their intention was to limit the application of the article to cases of extradition or to crimes defined in extradition treaties. An interpretation that is closer to the intention of the signatories would be that the word "crime" was used to apply to any crime recognized by ordinary criminal law and that the word "serious" was used to ensure that exclusion would only be justified by ordinary crimes the seriousness of which corresponded to the crimes generally associated with extradition. The signatories placed their emphasis on the "seriousness" of the crime, not the fact that the crime could formally be, or had been, the subject of extradition proceedings.

It is thus easy to understand why, in dealing with "non-political crimes," the courts of the signatory countries have tended to refer to extradition treaties in defining the seriousness of such crimes and why those courts have tended to limit these "political crimes" to crimes in which the political aspect transcended everything else. It is a sort of compromise, which allows states to leave their borders open to genuine political criminals and close them to persons who have committed non-political crimes the seriousness of which, for example, approximates to crimes generally covered by extradition treaties. It follows that under Article 1F(b) it is possible to exclude both the perpetrators of serious non-political crimes seeking to use the convention to elude local justice and the perpetrators of serious non-political crimes that a state feels should not be allowed to enter its territory, whether or not they are fleeing local justice, whether or not they have been prosecuted for their crimes, whether or not they have been convicted of those crimes and whether or not they have served the sentences imposed on them in respect of those crimes.

Décary J.A. notes that while in agreement with the reasoning of Nadon J.A. up to this point, he parts company when Nadon J.A. applies the concept of complicity by association indiscriminately whether Article 1F(a) and (c) or Article 1F(b) is in question. Article 1F(a) and (c) deals with extraordinary activities, that is, international crimes in the case of Article 1F(a), or acts contrary to international standards in the case of Article 1F(c) These are activities that can be characterized as extraordinary because they have been criminalized by the international community collectively for exceptional reasons, and their nature is described in international instruments (Article 1F(a)) or in terms of such instruments (Article 1F(c)). One feature of some of these activities is that they affect communities and are conducted through persons who do not necessarily participate directly in them. In order for the persons who really are responsible to be held to account, the international community wished responsibility to attach to the persons, for example, on whose orders the activities were carried out or who, aware of their existence, deliberately closed their eyes to the fact that they were taking place. It is in these circumstances that the concept of complicity by association developed, making it possible to reach the persons responsible who would probably not have been responsible under traditional criminal law. Fundamentally, this concept is one of international criminal law.

Article 1F(b) is of a completely different order and is designed for different purposes. The phrase "serious non-political crime" requires that three conditions be met: there must be a crime, the crime must be a non-political one, and the crime must be serious. The courts and commentators have so far considered the second and third conditions, probably because it was generally assumed that the first condition simply required there to be a "crime" within the meaning of the ordinary criminal law of the country of refuge. The English wording of Article 1F(b) justifies this approach. It speaks of a "serious non-political crime," and it is the word "non-political" that is rendered in French by "*de droit commun.*" "Crime" in English is of course "crime" in French, and "serious" in English is "*grave*" in French. The word "*crime*" can only be understood in its ordinary meaning in criminal law, as opposed to those crimes said to be international that are covered by Article 1F(a), namely crimes against peace, war crimes, or crimes against humanity, and as opposed to the *"délit"* (crime) referred to by the French version of Article 33 of the convention. In short, on the question that arises here the wording of Article 1F(b) seems clear.

Article 1F(b) deals with ordinary crimes, non-political crimes, which are committed in the ordinary course of life in a society. The international community acting collectively has not defined such crimes. Such crimes are not defined by the convention: on the contrary, Article 1F(b) incorporates concepts of domestic law. Strictly speaking, it can be said that crimes recognized in extradition treaties have been the subject of international consensus and constitute serious non-political crimes in the eyes of the international community; but such crimes are not international crimes in themselves and are defined in terms of the applicable domestic law. Although in practice it is assumed that such ordinary crimes, which are usually the subject of extradition treaties, generally constitute serious crimes, the other crimes will be the subject of debate and each time the question will arise as to whether an act is an ordinary crime, and, if so, whether it is a serious crime within the meaning of the convention. In the absence of an international consensus on the seriousness of a crime, a court that has to interpret the convention will naturally look to its domestic law, while striving to reconcile this with the law of other states so far as possible. In Canada, the court will more readily rely on Anglo-American precedents. If in this context, the court comes to the conclusion that there are serious reasons for considering that a crime recognized as such in Canadian law has been committed, and that this crime is a serious one, it will apply the exclusion mentioned in Article 1F(b).

In short, complicity by association is a method of perpetrating a crime that is recognized in respect of certain international crimes and applied in the case of international crimes covered by Article 1F(a), and by analogy in the case of acts contrary to the international purposes and principles sought by Article 1F(c). This method of perpetration is not recognized as such in traditional criminal law.

Article 1F(b) refers to the "ordinary criminal law." Once the crimes covered by Article 1F(b) differ from those covered by Article 1F(a) and (c), it follows that a method of perpetration accepted with respect to one is not necessarily applicable to the others. A state may undoubtedly argue, as in the case at bar, that a given crime falls both under Article 1F(b) and under Article 1F(c), but this must still be established in the legal framework appropriate to each one.

It goes without saying that in emphasizing extraditable crimes the assumption is that the crimes in question are crimes recognized in ordinary criminal law. These crimes are only crimes in terms of the criteria laid down in domestic law, and in Anglo-Canadian law among these criteria is the concept of a "party to the offence." It is hard to see, for example, how the concept of complicity by association, developed in relation to international crimes, to the extent that it differs from the concept of a "party to the offence," could transform into an extraditable crime one that was not a crime in domestic law.

In addition to these textual arguments, there is one argument of judicial policy that seems to be of the highest importance: it would not be advisable to import into Article 1F(b) of the convention concepts borrowed from international instruments such as the Charter of the International Military Tribunal and the Rome Statute of the International Criminal Court. International criminal law has developed in a particular, initially military, context, which has nothing to do with the context in which domestic law developed. The Rome Statute cannot really be transposed to domestic law. It applies in Article 5 to "the most serious crimes of concern to the international community as a whole." The crimes in question are the crime of genocide, crimes against humanity, war crimes, and the crime of aggression. The first three of these crimes are defined in great detail in Articles 6, 7, and 8. Article 9 states that the "Elements of Crimes" that will assist the court in interpreting Articles 6, 7, and 8 will be those adopted by a two-thirds majority of the members of the Assembly of states parties. Article 21 indicates that the applicable law is "[i]n the first place, this Statute, Elements of Crimes and its Rules of Procedure and Evidence," "[i]n the second place . . . applicable treaties and the principles and rules of international law, including the established principles of the international law of armed conflict" and "[*f*]*ailing that, general principles of law derived by the Court from national laws of legal systems of the world*" (emphasis added). Articles 22 to 23 define "the general principles of criminal law," including in Article 25 that relating to "individual criminal responsibility," and this article sets out a series of rules covering various types of complicity. Only this last article can be transposed into domestic law with impunity, subject to certain qualifications.

In short, the Rome Statute is a complete criminal code. It governs the crimes against humanity and the war crimes covered in Article 1F(a) of the convention. It only refers to the traditional criminal law by default ("failing that"). Article 1F(a) must now be interpreted in light of the statute, *inter alia*. Saying that the rules laid down by the statute also apply to crimes covered by Article 1F(b) would be to distort the meaning of the said article and give it a scope that the signatories of the convention never foresaw or intended.

In sum, it is not possible to apply to Article 1F(b) the rules developed by the courts with regard to Article 1F(a) and (c). Decary J.A. notes that unlike Nadon J.A., he feels that the court's previous judgments in *Sivakumar* and other cases are of little value when Article 1F(b) is to be interpreted. While there is an analogy between Article 1F(a) and Article 1F(c), such that there is no danger of distorting the concept of "complicity" by applying it to either one, there is no such analogy between Article 1F(a) and (c) on the one hand and Article 1F(b) on the other. What is more, those previous judgments were rendered in a very fluid international context and should probably be updated to take account, for example, of the Rome Statute.

This leads to the question of whether in Canadian criminal law the crimes committed by the organization of which the appellant is a member can be attributed to him. The appellant did not argue, or is no longer arguing, that the crimes committed by the organization were not serious crimes or that they were of a political nature. However, once it is established that the appellant did not commit those crimes himself, the question that arises is the following: in Canadian law, can the appellant, as a result of the fact that he was a member of the organization that committed them, be regarded as a person in respect of whom it is possible to have serious reasons for considering that he committed them?

Counsel for the minister did not argue in this court, nor apparently in the lower courts, that there were serious reasons for considering that the appellant was a party to the offences committed by the Ennahda movement, within the meaning of sections 21 and 22 of our Criminal Code. Accordingly, counsel for the appellant did not have to examine this possibility either. As these are separate questions of law and fact from those that have been considered from the outset by the minister himself, by the Refugee Division, and by the Federal Court Trial Division, and since the solution is not self-evident, it would not be proper for this court to make a ruling in this regard at this stage. In the circumstances, it would be proper to refer the matter back to the minister for him to reassess the appellant's case in light of these reasons. However, in view of the conclusion arrived at with regard to Article 1F(c), it will be unnecessary to do this.

The Refugee Division also based the appellant's exclusion on Article 1F(c), indicating that in its opinion there were serious reasons for considering that he had committed acts contrary to the purposes and principles of the United Nations. The motions judge did not feel it necessary to deal with Article 1F(c): she was entitled to limit her consideration to Article 1F(b), since in her view that article by itself justified his exclusion.

The Refugee Division had concluded that in its view terrorism had become an act contrary to the purposes and principles of the United Nations at least from 16 January 1997 onwards, the date of adoption of a resolution by the General Assembly of the United Nations on "Measures to Eliminate International Terrorism." Décary J.A. notes that the Refugee Division may have erred on the side of caution in taking this view. It is not impossible that there was an international consensus on certain forms of terrorism, including the one at issue in the case at bar, before January 1997. However, it is not necessary to decide the point since it was established in the case at bar, during the hearing before the Refugee Division, which ended in May 1999, that the Ennahda movement was at that time a terrorist group within the meaning of the resolution. It was further established before the Refugee Division that on November 28, 1998, the appellant said he was still a member of the movement. Accordingly, it was open to the Refugee Division to conclude, based on the evidence presented of the appellant's position in the movement, that there were serious reasons for considering that the appellant had been guilty by association of terrorist acts contrary to the purposes and principles of the United Nations within the meaning of Article 1F(c) of the convention.

Canadian Cases in
Private International Law in 2002-3 /
Jurisprudence canadienne en matière de
droit international privé en 2002-3

compiled by / préparé par
JOOST BLOM

A   *Jurisdiction / Compétence des tribunaux*

1   Common Law and Federal

(a)   Jurisdiction *in personam*

Jurisdiction by consent — attornment

Note. In *Imagis Technologies Inc.* v. *Red Herring Communications Inc.* (2003), 15 C.C.L.T. (3d) 140 (B.C.S.C.), defendants from the United States, who had filed a statement of defence and a demand for the production of documents, were held to have attorned to the jurisdiction and deprived themselves of the right to argue *forum non conveniens*. *Cincurak* v. *Lamoureux* (2002), [2003] 2 W.W.R. 743, 8 Alta. L.R. (4th) 354 (Q.B.), decided that defendants who had filed a statement of defence were not entitled to seek a stay on the basis of a choice of forum clause in favour of the courts of British Columbia. To give effect to the clause at this stage, after the limitation period in British Columbia had run, would be unfairly prejudicial to the plaintiffs.

Constitutionally based territorial limits on jurisdiction

Wood v. *Gabriel Resources Ltd.* (2003), 10 B.C.L.R. (4th) 252 (British Columbia Court of Appeal)

The plaintiff, then resident in Colorado, was hired in 1996 by Gabriel to be its president. Negotiations for the contract were concluded in British Columbia and the plaintiff signed it in Colorado. Gabriel was a company that operated internationally. At one time,

---

Joost Blom is in the Faculty of Law at the University of British Columbia.

it had business in Australia and it had some involvement with a property in Romania. At the time that the plaintiff was its president, its shares were traded on the Vancouver Stock Exchange, but its head office was in Colorado because that was where the plaintiff lived. The plaintiff left Gabriel in 1998. Later in that year, Gabriel's head office moved to British Columbia, where its new president was based. In 2000, the head office moved to Ontario, after which Gabriel had no assets or operations in British Columbia. In 2001, the plaintiff, now resident in Ontario, brought an action in British Columbia against Gabriel and an associated company, seeking damages for constructive dismissal. The defendants applied for a declaration that the British Columbia court had no jurisdiction *simpliciter* (that is, no constitutionally sufficient basis for exercising jurisdiction) because the litigation had no real and substantial connection with the province. Alternatively, they sought to have the court decline jurisdiction on the ground of *forum non conveniens*.

The Court of Appeal affirmed the chambers judge's decision that the court lacked jurisdiction *simpliciter*. Neither Gabriel's past connections to British Columbia, nor its registration in British Columbia as an extra-provincial company, were a sufficient basis for the British Columbia court to take jurisdiction.

Marren v. Echo Bay Mines Ltd. (2003), 226 D.L.R. (4th) 422, 13 B.C.L.R. (4th) 177 (British Columbia Court of Appeal)

Brown and Marren brought a wrongful dismissal action in British Columbia against their former employer, a federally incorporated mining concern that carried on business in Nunavut, Ontario, and Alberta and had its executive office in Alberta. They had entered into the employment contract in Alberta, where both were then resident, to work in a mine in Nunavut. The mine closed in 1998. Brown, who still lived in Alberta, and Marren, who had moved from Alberta to British Columbia in 1997, intended to seek certification of their action as a class action by all the former employees of the mine who resided in and outside British Columbia. The plaintiffs had obtained leave to serve the defendant *ex juris* pursuant to Rule 13(3) of the British Columbia Rules of Court. The defendant applied to set aside the service *ex juris* or to decline jurisdiction. In response, the plaintiffs purported to amend their statement of claim to assert that service *ex juris* was authorized without out leave under Rule 13(1)(m), as the claim was based on contract and the defendant had assets in the jurisdiction. The chambers judge held that the court had jurisdiction *simpliciter* because the litigation had a real and substantial connection with the province. He also held that the court should not decline jurisdiction in favour of Alberta or Nunavut, and gave the plaintiffs leave to amend their statement of claim to invoke Rule 13(1)(m).

On appeal, the court held that the British Columbia Supreme Court had no jurisdiction *simpliciter.* The chambers judge had erred by viewing authority to serve *ex juris* as presumptively establishing a real and substantial connection. The *Spar Aerospace* case (noted later under 2. Québec, Action personnelle — compétence internationale — Article 3148 C.c.Q.) did not equate the Québec rules of court dealing with the competence of the courts with a real and substantial connection. Rather, it limited the reach of the real and substantial connection imperative to interprovincial disputes, and suggested that each of the grounds listed in Article 3148(3) C.C.Q. seemed to be an example of a real and substantial connection between the province of Québec and the action. The assumption of jurisdiction is governed by principles of comity, order, and fairness. The facts that the plaintiffs' claim was founded on a contract and that the defendant had assets in the province were only the starting point of the inquiry. The residence in British Columbia of one of the plaintiffs, and the defendant's owning passive assets in the province, were too tenuous to be a real and substantial connection. The defendant's only contact with British Columbia with regard to the claims the plaintiffs advanced was the deposit of Marren's salary into a British Columbia bank account, a consequence of his having moved to British Columbia after he became an employee. The plaintiffs argued that they would enjoy advantages in a British Columbia court, including a six-year limitation period and class proceedings. Such considerations were relevant to a *forum non conveniens* issue but not to establishing jurisdiction *simpliciter.*

Note. Plaintiffs also failed to jurisdiction *simpliciter* (an expression that now has the imprimatur of the Supreme Court of Canada: see the *Unifund* case, noted below under D. Choice of law, 1. Common law and federal, (a) Contracts — statutory regulation of contracts — constitutional limitations) in the following cases. *Deureneft Deutsche-Russische Mineralöl Handelsgesellschaft mbH* v. *Bullen* (2003), [2004] 1 W.W.R. 535, 37 C.P.C. (5th) 22 (Alta. Q.B.), held that there was no real and substantial connection between Alberta and counterclaims brought by an Alberta resident and his company against a German corporation and its Gibraltar and Canadian subsidiaries, arising out of a contract with the Gibraltar subsidiary for the opening of oil wells in Russia. *Saleh* v. *United Arab Emirates* (2003), 15 C.C.L.T. (3d) 231 (Ont. S.C.J.), found no real and substantial connection between Ontario and claims for alleged torture that took place in the United Arab Emirates. *Greco* v. *Flemming* (2003), 33 C.P.C. (5th) 238 (Ont. S.C.J.), found that the Ontario court had no jurisdiction in an action by an Ontario resident against residents of New York State arising out of a motor vehicle accident in New York. The court applied the eight factors in *Muscutt* v. *Courcelles* (2002), 213 D.L.R. (4th) 577 (Ont. C.A.) (noted in "Canadian Cases in Private International Law 2001-02" (2002) 40 Can. Y.B. Int'l L. 583). (For the eight factors, see the note of *Incorporated Broadcasters Ltd.* v. *Canwest Global Communications Group*, below under (d) Shareholder claims — Relief against oppression.) An important consideration (relevant to factor eight) was that, on the evidence submitted as to New York law, a New York court would not recognize an Ontario judgment where the only basis for the Ontario court's jurisdiction was that the victim lived there and so suffered loss there.

A real and substantial connection was found in the following cases. *Na* v. *Renfrew Security Bank & Trust (Offshore) Ltd.* (2003), 16 B.C.L.R. (4th) 345, 35 C.P.C. (5th) 381 (S.C.), was a claim by a refugee claimant resident in British Columbia against a Cyprus trust company, whose managing director lived in British Columbia, for the return of a US $1 million deposit. In *Armstrong* v. *Servier Canada Inc.* (2002), 24 C.P.C. (5th) 103 (B.C.S.C.), British Columbia residents brought claims against French pharmaceutical firms for injury allegedly caused by taking a diet drug, the firms having been involved either in testing the drug in Canada or importing it into Canada. *ABN Amro Bank N.V.* v. *BCE Inc.* (2003), 44 C.B.R. (4th) 1 (Ont. S.C.J.), had Ontario-based banks suing a Québec-based telecommunications company, which was present in Ontario, on the basis that it was independently liable for loans the banks had made in Québec to a subsidiary. (See the note of this case below, under Declining jurisdiction — *forum non conveniens* — defendant present in the jurisdiction.) *C.B. Distribution Inc.* v. *BCB International Inc.* (2003), 33 C.P.C. (5th) 203 (Ont. S.C.J.), was an action by a Canadian exporter against its United States customs broker for negligent advice relating to the American duties applicable to Brazilian cane sugar refined in Canada. In *Subramaniam* v. *Shelter* (2002), 61 O.R. (3d) 136, 23 C.P.C. (5th) 180 (S.C.J.), an Ontario resident, who was riding as passenger in a truck owned by an Ontario company and being driven by an Ontario resident, was injured in a collision in Nebraska with a vehicle owned by a resident of the state of Washington and driven by a resident of New Jersey. He sued the owner and driver of the truck and the owner and driver of the other vehicle. The real and substantial connection with Ontario of the claims against the foreign defendants was found in the close relationship of those claims with the ones against the Ontario-resident defendants, over whom the court undeniably had jurisdiction.

Service ex juris — grounds

Note. Two Alberta-resident employees of the Department of National Defence sued an Ottawa-based company and the federal Crown for various torts in connection with conduct that had deprived the plaintiffs of royalties on inventions that the plaintiffs said had been used on military hardware in many countries. The claim was held not to be for torts committed in Alberta: *Murray* v. *Canada (Attorney General)* (2003), 14 Alta. L.R. (4th) 330 (Q.B.).

Declining jurisdiction — exclusive choice of forum clause

Z.I. Pompey Industrie v. *Ecu-Line N.V.*, [2003] 1 S.C.R. 450, 224 D.L.R. (4th) 577 (Supreme Court of Canada)

The defendant agreed to ship certain photo-processing equipment from Antwerp to Seattle, in the state of Washington. It carried the goods to Montreal, Québec, and there transferred them to a railway for onward shipment to Seattle, despite having been instructed that rail transport was not to be used. The bill of lading, however, permitted the defendant to use any mode of transport whatsoever and to transship the goods from one method of transport to another without notice to the shipper or the consignee. The equipment was damaged in the course of the railway transit, and the shipper and consignee brought an action against the defendant in the Federal Court of Canada. The defendant applied for a stay of the proceedings on the basis of a clause in the bill of lading by which the parties agreed that Belgian law would be the proper law of the contract and the courts in Antwerp would be the proper courts to determine any claim or dispute arising out of the bill of lading.

The prothonotary of the Federal Court held that the plaintiff had a persuasive argument that the clause ceased to have effect after the deviation from the agreed transport in Montreal. To the objection that this was an issue to be decided at trial, he answered that denying a stay, on the ground that there was a strong case that the clause ceased to operate, was effectively the same as granting an interlocutory injunction. It left the trial judge free to decide the merits, and any prejudice to the defendant in having to litigate in Canada could be compensated by costs. The prothonotary's decision was upheld by a judge of the Trial Division. The Federal Court of Appeal affirmed the refusal of a stay. It held that the approach in *The "Eleftheria,"* [1969] 2 All E.R. 641, [1969] 1 Lloyd's L.R. 237 (P.D.), which was to require the plaintiff to show "strong cause" why the agreed choice of forum should not be enforced, had been superseded by later cases in England. These cases, thought the court, had replaced the "strong cause" test with the "tripartite test" for the granting of an interlocutory injunction. On this new test, the party seeking the stay had to show that there was a serious issue to be tried, a risk of irreparable harm to its interests if the clause was not upheld, and a balance of convenience in favour of a stay. This was in essence the approach that the prothonotary had taken.

The Supreme Court of Canada unanimously reversed the decision of the Federal Court of Appeal and held that the action should have been stayed. Forum selection clauses are common components of international commercial transactions. They are generally to be encouraged by the courts because they create certainty and security in transaction, derivatives of order and fairness, which are critical components of private international law. The "strong cause" test remains relevant and effective and no social, moral, or economic changes justified the departure advanced by the Court of Appeal. It is essential that courts give full weight to the desirability of holding parties to their agreements. There is no reason to consider forum selection clauses to be non-responsibility clauses in disguise. In any event, the "strong cause" test allows judges to take improper motives into consideration in relevant cases and prevent defendants from relying on forum selection clauses to gain an unfair procedural advantage.

Moreover, the tripartite test used in the Court of Appeal was inappropriate to the issue. The authorities cited by the Court of Appeal did not deal with private international law. The tripartite test was a significant and unjustified departure from the jurisprudence of the Federal Court and of provincial courts as well as those of other jurisdictions. Public policy also offered compelling reasons for upholding the "strong cause" test. Applying the tripartite test would render most forum selection clauses unenforceable, creating commercial uncertainty by unduly minimizing the importance of contractual undertakings. Instead of requiring a plaintiff to demonstrate a "strong cause" not to enforce a forum selection clause, it would place the burden on the applicant for a stay to establish the elements of the tripartite test. The components of that test were also ill-suited to the task at hand. Determining the likelihood of success on the merits of the case, the first part of the test, is designed to allow the motions judge to deal with the legal issues in preliminary proceedings without prejudice to the final adjudication on the merits. By contrast, deciding whether to uphold a forum selection clause normally involves no adjudication of the merits at all because it decides where the case is to be heard. As for showing irreparable harm, the second part of the test, no instance could be imagined in which a defendant could demonstrate that it would suffer irreparable harm from having to defend in a Canadian court.

The court also rejected as without merit the argument that forum selection clauses should be given little weight because the bills of lading in which they were contained are contracts of adhesion. Bills of lading are typically entered into by sophisticated parties familiar with the negotiation of maritime shipping transactions who should, in normal circumstances, be held to their bargains. The forum selection clause in this particular contract might well have been negotiated because of the freight forwarder's insistence that the cargo be transported solely by sea. There was no evidence that the bill of lading was the product of grossly unequal bargaining power that would invalidate the clause.

It was also wrong for the lower courts to have got into the question whether there had been a deviation from the agreed voyage and whether that had deprived the clause of its effect. Issues respecting an alleged fundamental breach of contract or deviation therefrom should generally be determined under the law and by the court chosen by the parties in the bill of lading. The "strong cause" test, once it is determined that the bill of lading otherwise binds the parties (thus not affected by, for example, public policy, fraud, or grossly uneven bargaining positions), constitutes an inquiry into questions such as the convenience of the parties, fairness between the parties, and the interests of justice, not of the substantive legal issues underlying the dispute. The Court of Appeal's approach would allow parties to remove their claims from the reach of a widely framed forum selection clause merely by alleging various types of wrongful conduct. The clause clearly embraced disputes about fundamental breaches or deviations. Applying forum

selection clauses according to their terms, without seeking to evaluate the merits of the dispute, was also sound from a policy point of
view. Stay applications should be brought quickly after commencement of the suit and, consequently, the parties will have limited
knowledge and information about the strength or weakness of their
opponent's case.

Note. The reasons in the lower courts were more or less summary
in nature. The resulting confusion is illustrated by the vagueness on
the question of onus. The prothonotary seemed to say that *denying*
a stay was analogous to giving the plaintiff an interlocutory injunction against enforcement of the clause, whereas the Court of
Appeal apparently thought that *granting* a stay was to be equated to
an interlocutory injunction in favour of the defendant. Orthodoxy,
in the form of the "strong cause" principle, rightly triumphed in
the end, but it should have prevailed much earlier in the process.

It is worth noting that as of August 8, 2001, the Federal Court has
had no discretion to stay proceedings arising from the carriage of
goods by water on the ground of a forum selection clause in certain
circumstances, including where the actual port of loading or discharge, or the intended port of loading or discharge under the contract, is in Canada (Marine Liability Act, S.C. 2001, c. 6, s. 46(1)).
The section did not apply to this case, which was commenced
before it came into force. The court admitted (at para. 38) that Parliament had apparently deemed it appropriate to limit the scope of
forum selection clauses by facilitating the litigation in Canada of
claims related to the carriage of goods by water having a minimum
level of connection to Canada. The court observed, however, that
the provision did not undermine the general law about the "strong
cause" test. Rather, it indicated Parliament's intent to broaden the
jurisdiction of the Federal Court only in very particular instances
that can easily be ascertained by a prothonotary called upon to
grant a stay of proceedings pursuant to the forum selection clause
in a bill of lading. It in no way mandated a prothonotary to consider
the merits of the case.

Green v. *Jernigan* (2003), 18 B.C.L.R. (4th) 366 (S.C.), found no
"strong cause" for departing from a clause in a trust deed that stipulated that Nevis was the exclusive forum for disputes relating to
the trust. By contrast, in *Friesen* v. *Norwegian Cruise Lines Inc.* (2003),
12 B.C.L.R. (4th) 394 (S.C.), an exclusive choice of Florida as
forum in a cruise ship ticket was not enforced against a British
Columbia-resident passenger who sued for injuries from a fall when

the Bahamian-registered ship was in Alaskan waters. The plaintiff lacked the resources to litigate in Florida, and for the defendant, a Bermuda corporation whose management was based in Florida, defending this action in British Columbia would not be significantly more burdensome than it would be in Florida.

A forum selection clause was defeated in *Cincurak* v. *Lamoureux*, [2003] 2 W.W.R. 743, 8 Alta. L.R. (4th) 354 (Q.B.), because the defendant had attorned to the jurisdiction some time before invoking the clause, and in *Na* v. *Renfrew Security Bank & Trust (Offshore) Ltd.* (2003), 16 B.C.L.R. (4th) 345, 35 C.P.C. (5th) 381 (S.C.), because the choice of forum, construed *contra proferentem*, was not exclusive. An attempt to avoid an agreed choice of forum in favour of Alberta, on the basis that the clause did not apply to claims for negligence and breach of fiduciary duty, was unsuccessful in *Scalas Fashions Ltd.* v. *Yorkton Securities Inc.* (2003), 17 B.C.L.R. (4th) 6, 35 B.L.R. (3d) 286 (C.A.). The tort and fiduciary duty claims arose out of the contractual relationship and so were subject to the clause, which referred to "any dispute."

Declining jurisdiction — arbitration agreement — international commercial arbitration

Dalimpex Ltd. v. *Janicki* (2003), 228 D.L.R. (4th) 179, 64 O.R. (3d) 737 (Ontario Court of Appeal)

Dalimpex was the Canadian importer of products made by Agros, a Polish company, until Agros terminated the arrangement and replaced Dalimpex with a new company, one of whose senior officers was Dalimpex's former employee. Dalimpex sued the former employee, his company, and Agros in breach of contract (the employee), conspiracy (all defendants), and intentional interference with contractual relations (Agros). Agros commenced arbitration proceedings before the Polish Court of Arbitration against Dalimpex, based on a clause in their contract, claiming that Dalimpex owed Agros for goods delivered and for payments that Agros had made on a guarantee of Dalimpex's line of credit. The Court of Arbitration held that it had jurisdiction and made an award in Agros's favour. Dalimpex's appeal from this conclusion was currently pending. Agros now moved for a stay of Dalimpex's action in Ontario and a referral of the underlying issues to the Court of Arbitration in Poland, pursuant to the International Commercial Arbitration Act, R.S.O. 1990, c. I.9. Agros also applied for recognition and enforcement of the arbitration award under the same act.

The chambers judge refused the stay because the tort claims being made in the action were outside the scope of the arbitration agreement. The Divisional Court reversed and ordered a stay until final disposition of the arbitration in Poland. The judge on Agros's application for enforcement held that the award should be enforced but made a "provisional" order to that effect, which would be vacated if the Polish courts set aside the award. Dalimpex appealed from both decisions, and Agros cross-appealed against making the order for enforcement "provisional."

The Court of Appeal held that a stay was mandatory unless it was clear that the dispute was outside the scope of the arbitration agreement, that a party was not bound by the agreement, that the application was out of time, or (under Article 8 of the UNCITRAL Model Law implemented by the act) that the arbitration agreement was null and void, inoperative or incapable of being performed. If any of these issues was arguable, it should be referred to the arbitral tribunal. This dispute could reasonably be interpreted as one falling within the interpretation or execution of the agency agreement between Dalimpex and Agros and therefore within the arbitrators' jurisdiction.

On the enforcement question, the judge had had no power to make a provisional award. The proper course was to adjourn the application under Article 36(2) of the Model Law pending the outcome of the appeal in Poland. If the appeal succeeded the award would be gone. If the appeal failed, the enforcing court in Ontario could still be asked to decide whether the dispute was in fact within the arbitrators' jurisdiction. The arbitrators' decision on that point was not binding on an enforcing court (Article 36(1)(a)(iii) of the Model Law).

Declining jurisdiction — *forum non conveniens* — defendant resident in the jurisdiction

ABN Amro Bank N.V. v. *BCE Inc.* (2003), 44 C.B.R. (4th) 1 (Ontario Superior Court of Justice) (application for leave to appeal dismissed (2003), 44 C.B.R. (4th) 25 (Ont. Div'l Ct.))

Several banks, the plaintiffs, had made unsecured loans to Teleglobe, a subsidiary of BCE. Their credit agreements with Teleglobe, which were negotiated primarily in Québec, where Teleglobe and BCE had their main offices, stipulated that they were governed either by Québec or New York law and were subject to the exclusive jurisdiction of the courts of Québec or New York. The plaintiffs brought the present action in Ontario against BCE, claiming that it either was the alter ego of Teleglobe, or had guaranteed Teleglobe's debts to them. BCE applied for a dismissal or a stay of the action on the ground that the court lacked jurisdiction or, alternatively, should decline jurisdiction on account of the forum selection clause in the credit agreements.

The Ontario court held that it had jurisdiction and refused a stay. Jurisdiction existed because there was personal jurisdiction over BCE, which had an ongoing presence in Ontario, and because the case had a real and substantial connection with Ontario, applying the factors enumerated in *Muscutt* v. *Courcelles* (2002), 213 D.L.R. (4th) 577 (Ont. C.A.) (noted in "Canadian Cases in Private International Law 2001-2" (2002) 40 Can. Y.B. Int'l L. 583). (For a fuller treatment of these factors, see the note of *Incorporated Broadcasters Ltd.* v. *Canwest Global Communications Group,* below under (d) Shareholder claims — relief against oppression.)

As for *forum non conveniens,* the court canvassed the ten factors listed in *Spar Aerospace* (see below under 2. Québec, Action personnelle — competence internationale — Article 3148 C.c.Q.): (1) the residence of the parties, witnesses, and experts; (2) the location of the evidence; (3) the place where the contract was negotiated and executed; (4) the existence of proceedings between the parties in another jurisdiction; (5) the location of the defendant's assets; (6) the law to be applied to the claims; (7) the advantages, if any, that were conferred upon the plaintiffs by their choice of forum; (8) the interests of justice; (9) the interests of the parties; and (10) the need to have the judgment recognized in another jurisdiction. When all these were weighed together, BCE had not demonstrated that Québec was the more appropriate forum. LeBel J., in *Spar Aerospace* at paragraph 81, had emphasized the exceptional quality of the *forum non conveniens* doctrine and the desirability of minimizing the uncertainty and inefficiency that would be created by its too frequent use.

Note 1. The judge's reference to the "exceptional" nature of the *forum non conveniens* doctrine, as stressed in the *Spar Aerospace* case, is regrettable. The Supreme Court of Canada focused on that expression because it appears in the *forum non conveniens* provision of the Quebec Civil Code and goes hand in hand with the comparatively narrow jurisdictional grounds for which the code provides. In the Canadian common law jurisdictions, which traditionally employ broader jurisdictional grounds, the doctrine of *forum non conveniens,* far from being exceptional, is a necessary and often-used corrective to the expansiveness of the rules for jurisdiction. To seek to discourage its use is likely to increase, rather than reduce, the uncertainty and inefficiency of this area of law in the common law jurisdictions.

Note 2. Forum non conveniens was at issue in the following cases, in which the defendant was resident in the province. *Brown* v. *Kerr-McDonald,* [2003] 3 W.W.R. 146, 9 Alta. L.R. (4th) 179 (Q.B.), was an Alberta action where all the parties were from Alberta but the motor vehicle accident out of which the action arose had happened just over the border in Saskatchewan; a stay was refused. In *1279022 Ontario Ltd.* v. *Posen* (2003), 172 Man. R. (2d) 169, 34 C.P.C. (5th) 94 (Q.B. Master), affd. (2003), 179 Man. R. (2d) 108, 38 C.P.C. (5th) 85 (Q.B.), thirty-three individuals sued an Alberta company, several Manitoba companies, and a Manitoba-resident individual in connection with certain franchise agreements. The court rejected the defendants' argument that the Alberta franchise legislation, which applied to the relevant agreements, gave exclusive jurisdiction to the courts of that province. The court found that the defendants' connections with Manitoba, together with the plaintiffs' preference for litigating there, made the court *forum conveniens.* In *Lloydminster (City)* v. *Carlyle* (2003), 232 Sask. R. 76 (C.A.), a stay was granted on the ground that Alberta was the more appropriate forum for a Saskatchewan city's action against the Alberta-resident creators of a public monument; the city is on the border between the two provinces. The court affirmed, on the jurisdictional point, the decision noted in "Canadian Cases in Private International Law 2001-2" (2002) 40 Can. Y.B. Int'l L. 596.

Declining jurisdiction — *forum non conveniens* — defendant resident outside the jurisdiction

A large number of cases reported this year dealt with *forum non conveniens* in actions brought against defendants who were outside the province. The non-residents' applications for a stay were unsuccessful in the great bulk of them. These were *Waldron* v. *Kist,* [2003] 5 W.W.R. 145, 171 Man. R. (2d) 204 (Q.B.) (Manitoba residents suing New York resident for misrepresentations made to them about a Canadian investment); *Caspian Const. Inc.* v. *Drake Surveys Ltd.* (2003), 174 Man. R. (2d) 263, 26 C.L.R. (3d) 297 (Q.B. Master), affd. 2003 MBQB 281 (Manitoba company, as prime contractor on a project in Alberta, suing its Alberta subcontractor); *Zimberg* v. *Housatchenko* (2003), 172 Man. R. (2d) 157 (Q.B. Master) (Manitoba resident suing in respect of an investment in a Manitoba business, though part of the contractual arrangements were governed by Ontario law); *Load Runner Logistics Ltd.* v. *Transport Seblac Inc.*, [2003] 7 W.W.R. 158, 171 Man. R. 92d) 214 (Q.B.) (Manitoba transport company suing Québec customer on a contract to carry goods from the United States to Alberta); *Burgess Transfer & Storage Ltd.* v. *Helipro International, a Division of Aero Aerospace* (2003), 215 N.S.R. (2d) 231 (S.C.) (Nova Scotia carrier suing out-of-province customer on a contract to move goods from British Columbia to Prince Edward Island); *Pearl* v. *Sovereign Management Group Inc.* (2003), 37 C.P.C. (5th) 143 (Ont. S.C.J.) (Ontario customer suing British Columbia vendor on contract for purchase of vending machines); *C.B. Distribution Inc.* v. *BCB International Inc.* (2003), 33 C.P.C. (5th) 203 (Ont. S.C.J.) (Ontario exporter suing its United States customs broker for giving negligent advice); *Polar Foods International Inc.* v. *Jensen Tuna Inc.* (2002), 218 Nfld. & P.E.I. R. 6, 27 C.P.C. (5th) 376 (P.E.I. S.C.) (Prince Edward Island seller suing Louisiana purchaser on contract for ongoing sale of fish); *Saskatchewan Wildlife Federation* v. *Vantage Financial Services Inc.* (2003), 239 Sask. R. 1 (Q.B.) (Saskatchewan non-profit organization, as customer, suing a Massachusetts firm on a contract to provide mailing services for solicitation of donations); *Branco* v. *American Home Assurance Co.* (2002), 226 Sask. R. 114, 45 C.C.L.I. (3d) 170 (Q.B.) (former Saskatchewan resident, now living in Portugal, suing several parties in connection with injuries suffered while working at a mine in Kyrgyzstan, the claim against the only non-consenting defendant being most conveniently heard with the other claims arising out of the accident); and *Stephan* v. *591346 B.C. Ltd.*, [2003] 2 W.W.R. 159, 224 Sask. R. 112 (Saskatchewan resident suing British Columbia and Saskatchewan residents in respect of the purchase of a ski chalet in British Columbia).

A stay was granted in *Bray* v. *Standard Commercial Corp.* (2002), 29 C.P.C. (5th) 256 (Ont. S.C.J.), in which an Ontario resident sued an American client for failure to pay him commissions on sales of tobacco to American purchasers whom the plaintiff had introduced to the defendant. The contract was most closely connected with the United States because it was made there, governed by United States law, and the breaches of it involved acts done in the United States. The argument that the plaintiff enjoyed a legitimate advantage in the Ontario court because the Ontario limitation period had not yet run, whereas the American one had, was without merit. Since limitation periods are a matter of substantive law, the American limitation period would apply in the Ontario court to claims based on an American contract.

Declining jurisdiction — *lis alibi pendens*

Note. The common law has not developed a principle of *lis alibi pendens,* but views the existence of parallel proceedings in another jurisdiction merely as one factor relevant to the question of *forum conveniens.* In *Design Recovery Inc.* v. *Schneider* (2003), 230 Sask. R. 231 (Q.B.), the plaintiff commenced a breach of contract action in Ontario, where all the parties resided, and then commenced a second action in Saskatchewan that was identical except for making claims of an equitable interest in a house that the defendant owned in that province. The Saskatchewan action was stayed on the ground that Ontario was clearly the appropriate forum. Securing, by registration of a certificate of pending action, real property in Saskatchewan for the satisfaction of an eventual Ontario judgment was not a reason to permit duplication of actions or avoid the application of *forum conveniens* principles. See also *Chaplin* v. *Chaplin,* noted below under (e) Matrimonial actions — matrimonial property.

(b) Class proceedings

Class including non-residents

Boulanger v. *Johnson & Johnson Corp.* (2003), 226 D.L.R. (4th) 747, 64 O.R. (3d) 248 (Ontario Divisional Court) (motion for leave to appeal filed in the Ontario Court of Appeal (court file M29822))

A resident of Ontario, as representative plaintiff, brought a class action against the manufacturers and distributors in Canada of a brand-name drug, Prepulsid, used for the treatment of intestinal disorders. The drug was claimed to have injured patients and the defendants were sued for fraud, negligence, breach of fiduciary duty, breach of contract, and failure to warn. The federal food and drug regulatory authorities were also sued for negligence. The intended class included patients who had taken the drug while resident outside Ontario, which is permitted by the Class Proceedings Act, 1992, S.O. 1992, c. 6, as it has been interpreted by the courts.

The statement of claim included claims that non-resident victims might have under the legislation of other provinces, including subrogated claims on behalf of provincial health insurers, claims by family members for loss of care or companionship, and rights analogous to those provided by Ontario's trustee legislation. The defendant argued that the representative plaintiff could not assert claims that were inapplicable to herself and applied to have them struck out.

The motions judge refused to strike out the claims. The Divisional Court upheld that decision. The scheme of the act demonstrated the legislature's intention to permit a representative plaintiff, prior to the certification motion, to plead causes of action that are not the representative plaintiff's personal causes of action but are the causes of action of members of the class, asserted by the plaintiff in a representative capacity. Class proceedings are such from their commencement, and, therefore, when a proceeding is commenced in accordance with the act, members of the class who are not named as a plaintiff but whose claims are asserted in accordance with the act are like parties to the action. It was not plain and obvious that the claims based on the legislation in other provinces had no chance of meeting the "common issues" criterion for certification. They had in common the issues of the defendants' acts or omissions before Prepulsid was ingested by any member of the public. Moreover, the claims on behalf of provincial health insurers were essentially the same claims. In any event, the defendants had not put any of the relevant statutes before the court to support their contention that the claims had no common issues. The plaintiff, however, would need to amend the statement of claim to plead the relevant statutes of other provinces, because for the purpose of the Rules of Civil Procedure the laws of other provinces were to be treated as material facts.

Note. The opposite conclusion was reached in *McNaughton Automotive Ltd.* v. *Co-operators Gen. Ins. Co.* (2003), 66 O.R. (3d) 112, 2 C.C.L.I. (4th) 236 (S.C.J.), in which the plaintiff alleged that automobile insurers across Canada had violated the legislatively mandated statutory conditions of their policies in the way that they had compensated for total losses of the automobile. Residents of other provinces, whose claims were based on policies issued there, were excluded from the class because the statutes differed too much from province to province, and the claims from other provinces had insufficient connections with Ontario.

(c) Corporations and shareholders

Shareholder actions — relief against oppression

Incorporated Broadcasters Ltd. v. Canwest Global Communications Group
(2003), 223 D.L.R. (4th) 627, 63 O.R. (3d) 431 (Ontario Court of
Appeal) (application for leave to appeal dismissed, 11 Dec. 2003
(S.C.C.))

The individual plaintiffs, Epstein and Morton, resident in Ontario,
had been associated in the 1970s with Asper in the creation of Can-
West Broadcasting (Broadcasting), a Manitoba corporation that at
first operated only a Winnipeg television station. The three individuals also invested in Global Television, a network that had run
into financial difficulties. The parties' relationship deteriorated in
the 1980s, and in 1989 Epstein and Morton sold their interest in
Global Television to Asper's company, CanWest Global. They continued, however, to own about a 29 per cent stake in Broadcasting
through a holding company. They were directors of Broadcasting
and a subsidiary that held its (by now four) television licences.
Through the 1990s, Epstein and Morton were at odds with Asper
about his use of his majority ownership of Broadcasting, through
CanWest Global, to lessen their role in Broadcasting's affairs and
the management fees they earned from their involvement with it.

In March 2001, they and two corporations they owned commenced the present action in Ontario against Asper, CanWest
Global, and subsidiaries of CanWest Global that held shares in
Broadcasting or held assets for it. All the defendant corporations
were federally incorporated with management based in Manitoba.
In May 2001, Asper caused Broadcasting to be amalgamated with
another company to form CanWest (2001), a Manitoba corporation all of whose shares were owned by a subsidiary of CanWest
Global. Morton and Epstein received special shares in CanWest
Global in lieu of their former shares in Broadcasting. The plaintiffs
amended their statement of claim to take account of the new situation. The plaintiffs sought a declaration that CanWest Global and
its affiliates had exercised its control over Broadcasting in a manner that was oppressive or unfairly prejudicial to the interests
of Morton and Epstein (via their holding company) as minority
shareholders, contrary to the Canada Business Corporations Act
(CBCA), R.S.C. 1985, c. C-44. The plaintiffs sought further declarations that CanWest Global had contravened the CBCA by improperly favouring the interests of Asper and his companies, had

broken fiduciary duties to Morton and Epstein and their companies, had diverted corporate opportunities from Broadcasting, and
pushed through an amalgamation that was oppressive and unfairly
prejudicial to and unfairly disregarded the interests of Morton and
Epstein. The plaintiffs sought an order that CanWest Global purchase Epstein and Morton's special shares, and pay an accounting
of profits and damages for breach of several contracts that Morton
and Epstein had with CanWest Global.

Upon the defendants' application to stay the proceedings on the
ground of lack of jurisdiction or *forum non conveniens*, the motions
judge held that there was no real and substantial connection
between the litigation and Ontario so that the court lacked jurisdiction. The action was in essence an oppression action relating to
the affairs of a Manitoba corporation, and the bulk of the decisions
being challenged had been made by directors of that corporation
in Manitoba. He held in the alternative that Ontario was *forum
non conveniens* for the action. The Ontario Court of Appeal held
that jurisdiction existed, but upheld the motions judge's decision
on *forum non conveniens*.

The motions judge had erred in applying the real and substantial
connection test. That is a test for asserting jurisdiction over defendants that are not present in the jurisdiction. There is no constitutional impediment to asserting jurisdiction over a person having a
presence in the province. All the corporate defendants were present
in Ontario because they were federally incorporated companies that
carried on business and had offices in Ontario. Since Asper was a
non-resident of Ontario, the real and substantial connection test did
apply to jurisdiction over him personally, but it was clearly satisfied
on the basis of the criteria set out in *Muscutt* v. *Courcelles* (2002), 213
D.L.R. (4th) 577 (Ont. C.A.) (noted in "Canadian Cases in Private
International Law 2001-2" (2002) 40 Can. Y.B. Int'l L. 583). First,
there was a connection between Ontario and the plaintiffs' claim,
since the plaintiffs were all residents of Ontario, and they relied on
the statutory cause of action in section 241 of the CBCA, which
gives a complainant access to the courts for a remedy against oppressive conduct by a CBCA corporation or its affiliates. Second, Asper
did business in Ontario through his corporations and came regularly to Ontario in that connection. Third, it was not apparent that
there would be any unfairness to Asper in taking jurisdiction.
Fourth, and conversely, there was no apparent unfairness to the
plaintiffs in not taking jurisdiction. Fifth, the fact that all the other
defendants were present in Ontario militated in favour of finding a

real and substantial connection. Sixth, Ontario courts would recognize a judgment from another province based on jurisdiction such as was being proposed. Seventh, as *Muscutt* held, jurisdiction is more easily established in interprovincial than in international cases. The eighth factor, comity and the standards of jurisdiction, recognition and enforcement prevailing elsewhere, was not relevant in an interprovincial case. Cumulatively, therefore, the factors pointed in favour of taking jurisdiction over the claims against Asper.

As for the question of *forum non conveniens,* the judge was right to characterize the action as concerning the internal management of Broadcasting. The plaintiffs alleged that in their conduct with respect to Broadcasting, the defendants had contravened the CBCA and that many of the breaches took place in Ontario. It was an arguable point whether section 241 of the CBCA extended the right to bring an oppression action to shareholders of a non-CBCA company, even if it was an affiliate of a CBCA company, as Broadcasting was. However, even assuming the plaintiffs' position was right, Manitoba had been shown to be a more appropriate forum for the litigation than Ontario. The Court of Appeal applied the eight factors enumerated in *Eastern Power Ltd.* v. *Azienda Comunale Energia & Ambiente* (1999), 178 D.L.R. (4th) 409 (Ont. C.A.). First, the dispute was localized in Manitoba more than in Ontario, although the Ontario factors were stronger than the motions judge had allowed. Second, the applicable law was largely federal, making this a relatively neutral factor. Third, the location of most of the witnesses was in Manitoba rather than Ontario. Fourth, the key witnesses were evenly divided between the two provinces. Fifth, the location of the evidence was a neutral factor because the evidence also was evenly divided between the two provinces. Sixth, the jurisdiction where the factual matters arose was a factor that weighed in favour of Manitoba. Broadcasting's board meetings were mostly there, and many of the acts complained of arose from decisions made there. Seventh, the residence or place of business of the parties was Ontario more than Manitoba, given that all the plaintiffs resided there, the corporate defendants carried on business there, one corporate defendant had its registered office in Ontario, and another had its registered office in Québec. The eighth factor, juridical advantage, was not an issue.

Although the eight factors, taken together, favoured Manitoba only slightly, the appropriate jurisdiction was not just a matter of contact-counting. Viewed from the perspective of order and fairness, Manitoba was clearly the more appropriate forum. The location of the dispute and the jurisdiction where the factual matters arose, which both favoured Manitoba, were considerably more important in the context of this case than factors such as the location of the parties. The case was about the dissatisfaction of minority shareholders with the way they were and continued to be treated by two companies based in Manitoba. One, Broadcasting, was a Manitoba corporation and the other, CanWest Global, was a federal corporation resident in Manitoba. Reasons of justice, necessity, and convenience called for the matter to be sorted out by the Manitoba Court of Queen's Bench.

Note. By constructing their action around the CBCA, the plaintiffs had sought to avoid the usual territorial limitations on statutory remedies with respect to provincially incorporated companies. It is usually assumed that only a court in the province of incorporation has jurisdiction to entertain causes of action founded on the provincial corporations statute. *Nord Resources Corp.* v. *Nord Pacific Ltd.* (2003), 263 N.B.R. (2d) 205, 35 B.L.R. (3d) 260 (N.B.Q.B.), held that only a New Brunswick court has jurisdiction in an oppression action by shareholders of a New Brunswick corporation, and *forum non conveniens* is therefore not in question. Likewise, *Noble* v. *Noble* (2002), 33 C.P.C. (5th) 175, affd. (7 April 2003), Doc. no. C39231 (Ont. C.A.), held that only an Ontario court had jurisdiction to hear a former wife's oppression action in respect of the Ontario corporation that she owned with her ex-husband, notwithstanding that the rest of their matrimonial property and support claims were, by a consent order in their divorce proceedings, to be heard in California. See also *West* v. *Wilbur* (2002), 255 N.B.R. (2d) 218 (N.B.Q.B.), application for leave to appeal dismissed (2003), 257 N.B.R. (2d) 85 (N.B.C.A.), in which the court held it had no jurisdiction to grant injunctions in respect of the corporate affairs of foreign companies.

Oppression actions invoke the power of the court actually to intervene in the conduct of corporate affairs, and so it is hard to see any court other than one in the jurisdiction of incorporation being able to exercise this power. An analogy can be drawn with actions involving title to foreign immovables. Under the so-called rule in *British South Africa Co.* v. *Companhia de Moçambique*, [1893] A.C. 602 (H.L.), these can only be heard in the jurisdiction where the immovable is situated. (See also the note above under (c) Actions Relating to Property — title to foreign immovables.) The rationale for the rule is that only the court of the *situs* has the power to affect directly the title to the property. Territoriality is not axiomatic when it comes to jurisdiction in actions for breaches of other forms of legislation, like securities laws, that create rights to compensation for certain wrongs related to corporations. See *Pearson* v. *Boliden Ltd.*, noted below under D. Choice of Law, 1. Common Law and Federal, (b) Corporations and shareholders — civil actions for breach of securities legislation.

(d)   Actions relating to property

Title to foreign immovables

   Note. In *Mountain West Resources Ltd.* v. *Fitzgerald* (2002), 6 B.C.L.R. (4th) 97 (C.A.), a British Columbia company sued its Arizona-resident president, alleging that he had broken his fiduciary duty to the company by taking in his own name certain mineral, oil, and gas claims in Nevada. The chambers judge held that the British Columbia court had no jurisdiction because the claim involved title to foreign immovables. The Court of Appeal set aside the judge's order and remitted the matter to the lower court on the ground, *inter alia*, that the judge had not considered the plaintiff's position that its claim was based, not on title, but on personal obligations of loyalty that the defendant owed to it, and so was not subject to the rule about foreign immovables.

(e)   Matrimonial actions

Support obligations

   Note. In *Muzechka* v. *Muzechka* (2002), 324 A.R. 327 (Q.B.), an Alberta court took jurisdiction to vary a 1983 award for support made corollary to a divorce in Saskatchewan. The respondent had submitted to the Alberta court's jurisdiction. This was an agreement that the court should have jurisdiction, one of the grounds on which jurisdiction may be taken in a variation proceeding (Divorce Act, R.S.C. 1985, c. 3 (2nd Supp.), s. 5(1)(b)).

Matrimonial property

   Note. In *Chaplin* v. *Chaplin* (2003), 237 Sask. R. 115, 41 R.F.L. (5th) 35 (Q.B.), notwithstanding that the wife had commenced proceedings in British Columbia for a division of family assets, the Saskatchewan court allowed the husband's action for division, which was started later, to continue despite the wife's argument that

Saskatchewan was *forum non conveniens*. There were roughly equal family assets in the two jurisdictions, and the decisive factor was that the husband was ninety years old and ill and could not travel outside Saskatchewan. See also *Walker* v. *Walker* (2003), 211 N.S.R. (2d) 197, 35 R.F.L. (5th) 222 (S.C.), holding that, under Nova Scotia legislation, the court's jurisdiction over divorce proceedings supported jurisdiction to vary an Ontario order for division of property, and *McLean* v. *McLean* (2003), 36 R.F.L. (5th) 107 (Ont. S.C.J.), which held that Ontario, where most of the family property was, should take jurisdiction in the wife's action to divide the property although the husband lived in Peru and the parties' matrimonial property rights were governed by Peruvian law as the law of their last common habitual residence (Family Law Act, R.S.O. 1990, c. F.3, s. 15).

(f) Infants and children

Custody — declining jurisdiction

Note. Where the mother had moved with the daughter from Saskatchewan to Alberta, in violation of a Saskatchewan court order giving her interim custody on condition that she not change the daughter's residence without thirty days' notice to the father, the Saskatchewan court refused the mother's application to decline jurisdiction in favour of Alberta. She should not benefit from her wrongful actions and, anyway, Saskatchewan was the *forum conveniens* because the evidence as to the child's welfare was mainly to be found there: *Giles* v. *Beisel* (2003), 229 Sask. R. 177 (U.F.C.). See also *Brouillard* v. *Racine* (2002), 33 R.F.L. (5th) 48 (Ont. S.C.J.), in which the court declined jurisdiction in favour of Québec, where the child had mostly lived.

Child abduction — Hague Convention on the Civil Aspects of International Child Abduction

Aulwes v. *Mai* (2002), 220 D.L.R. (4th) 577, 209 N.S.R. 92d) 248 (*sub nom. A.(J.E.)* v. *M.(C.L.)*) (Nova Scotia Court of Appeal)

The mother and father were divorced in Iowa in 1993 and were awarded joint custody of their daughter, than aged one. In 1995, the mother applied to the Iowa court to terminate the father's visiting rights on the ground that he had sexually abused the daughter; the court dismissed the application. Fearing that the court would order the father's visitation rights reinstated, the mother obtained passports with false information, secretly left Iowa with the daughter, and moved to British Columbia. Shortly afterwards, she remarried. In 1997, she, her new husband, and their newborn daughter moved with the elder daughter to Nova Scotia. The second marriage ended in 2001 and the younger daughter left the mother to live with her father. After that, the elder daughter rarely saw her stepfather or half-sister. As a result of the Nova Scotia divorce proceedings, the father in Iowa learned for the first time of his daughter's whereabouts and telephoned her. The daughter was afraid he would take her away from her mother. The father applied for the return of the daughter under the Child Abduction Act, R.S.N.S. 1989, c. 67, which implements the Hague Convention. The mother conceded that her removal of the child from Iowa had been in violation of the father's custody rights, and on appeal did not contest the trial judge's finding that a return to Iowa would not expose the daughter to a grave risk of physical or psychological harm or otherwise place her in an intolerable situation (Article 13(b) of the convention). The trial judge ordered the daughter's immediate return to Iowa, but the mother argued on appeal that the judge had failed to give effect to her daughter's own wishes (Article 13), and to the fact that the daughter was now settled into her new environment in Nova Scotia (Article 12).

The Court of Appeal affirmed the trial judge's decision, subject to certain transitional provisions. The trial judge had not been wrong to discount the child's own views. She was dependent on, and probably influenced by, her mother. Once it was found that a return would not pose a grave risk of physical or psychological harm to her, that really determined that her own wishes should not be given great weight. One of the policies underlying the convention is to deter child abduction, and that policy is promoted by certainty that return will be ordered. For that reason, courts should not be too ready to give effect to the "settled into the environment" exception. The exception should be applied only where circumstances had weakened the case for entrusting the courts of the habitual residence with the issues relating to the child's best interests. Here, the child's links to Iowa could not be ignored, and neither could the justice or logic of entrusting the child's interests to the courts of that state. In addition, the child's circumstances in Nova Scotia were not all that settled, given the breakup of the mother's second marriage and the uncertainty as to whether mother and daughter could stay in Canada, now that immigration officials were investigating whether they should be deported as having entered the country illegally.

Since the mother was willing to accompany the girl to Iowa, the mother was ordered to return with her daughter to Iowa within a month. Subject to any order that might be made in Iowa, they should proceed to the mother's sister's home in Des Moines.

Note. Jabbaz v. *Mouammar* (2003), 226 D.L.R. (4th) 494 (Ont. C.A.), a mother and child had lived with the father in California, but now that the father had moved to Ontario the immigration status was uncertain and there was a risk that they would be deported from the United States. This was held not to amount to an "intolerable situation" under Article 13(b) so as to prevent the child from being ordered returned to her mother's custody in California. An argument that to force a violation of United States immigration laws would be against public policy was also rejected. The motions judge was in no position to determine what the immigration status of the mother and the child was or what United States immigration officials might do. Also, the courts should be slow to graft a public policy exception onto a law whose purpose was to promote the certainty of return of children. In *Proia* v. *Proia* (2003), 41 R.F.L. (5th) 371 (Alta. Q.B.), a return of children to France was refused on the ground that the children had become ordinarily resident in Alberta when they (the mother and father moved there from France) intended to stay. The mother's keeping them in Alberta after the father returned to France was therefore not wrongful retention under the convention. An earlier determination to the contrary by the French courts did not affect the matter.

(g)   Anti-suit injunctions

Note. When they were sued in New Jersey for selling a defective cosmetics product to a buyer resident there, Ontario-resident defendants brought proceedings in Ontario for an injunction that would prevent the plaintiff in the New Jersey action from continuing the proceedings there. The applicants argued that Ontario was the more appropriate forum. The Ontario court held that, although it appeared Ontario was indeed the *forum conveniens*, no injunction should be granted against foreign legal proceedings until the *forum non conveniens* argument had been put to the foreign court, which the applicants had not done: *Elga Laboratories Ltd.* v. *Soroko Inc.* (2002), 61 O.R. (3d) 324, 27 C.P.C. 95th) 293 (Ont. S.C.J.). Only special circumstances, which were not present, would justify pre-empting the foreign court's right to consider the issue first. In *R.P.C. Inc.* v. *Fournell* (2003), 33 C.P.C. (5th) 174 (B.C.S.C.), an injunction was also refused. The court of the state of Georgia had rejected an argument that it was *forum non conveniens* and the British Columbia court held that, given the facts, that decision should be respected. *Western Union Ins. Co.* v. *Re-Con Building Products Inc.* (2002), 7 B.C.L.R. (4th) 343, 41 C.C.L.I. (3d) 78 (B.C.S.C.), refused an injunction to the Canadian insurer of a Canadian manufacturer against the latter's suing the insurer in California, where the manufacturer itself was being sued in a class action for defects in its building products that were sold there. The British Columbia and the California court had each rejected arguments that they were *forum non conveniens,* so parallel proceedings would continue. The British Columbia Court of Appeal gave the insurers leave to appeal ((2002), 7 B.C.L.R. (4th) 354, 44 C.C.L.I. (3d) 22), but the appeal seems to have been discontinued.

2   Québec

(a)   Action personnelle

Compétence internationale — Article 3148 C.c.Q. — principe constitutionnel du "lien réel et substantiel" — applicabilité

Spar Aerospace Ltd. c. *American Mobile Satellite Corp.,* [2002] 4 R.C.S. 205, 220 D.L.R. (4th) 54 (English version only) (Cour suprême du Canada)

Motient, une société américaine, a conclu un contrat avec Hughes Aircraft, aussi une société américaine, en vue de la construction d'un satellite. Hughes a sous-traité à Spar la fabrication du matériel de communication formant la charge utile au satellite à son établissement au Québec. Le satellite a été lancé en orbite. L'essai en orbite qui a suivi a été une réussite et Motient a accepté l'engin spatial. Motient a alors engagé trois sociétés américaines pour faire les essais de station au sol et pour surveiller et contrôler le rendement du satellite. Le satellite a subi de graves dommages pendant l'évaluation et Hughes a refusé de payer Spar les primes de rendement prévues dans le contrat. Spar a intenté une action au Québec contre Motient et les trois autres sociétés américaines, alléguant que les signaux de communication envoyés de la station au satellite avaient provoqué une surcharge, ce qui avait causé de graves dommages. Elle a réclamé des dommages-intérêts pour la perte de primes de rendement, les pertes que l'atteinte portée à sa réputation occasionera et les dépenses engagées pour faire l'évaluation des dommages causés au satellite. Le siège social de Spar est situé en Ontario et toutes les défenderesses sont domiciliées aux États-Unis, où a eu lieu la négligence alléguée. Les défenderesses ont présenté des requêtes pour exception déclinatoire, contestant la compétence des tribunaux du Québec, selon l'article 163 C.p.c. et l'article 3148 C.c.Q. En outre, deux d'entre elles ont sollicité le rejet de l'action en invoquant la doctrine du *forum non conveniens* conformément à l'article 3135 C.c.Q. La Cour supérieure du Québec a rejeté les deux requêtes en confirmant la compétence des tribunaux du Québec. La Cour d'appel a confirmé cette décision.

La Cour suprême du Canada a rejeté le pourvoi des défenderesses. Les trois principes de courtoisie, d'ordre et d'équité servent de guide pour trancher les principales questions de droit international privé: la simple reconnaissance de compétence, le *forum non conveniens*, le choix de la loi applicable et la reconnaissance des jugements étrangers. Les règles qui gouvernent l'ordre du droit international privé au Québec sont codifiées et elles couvrent un vaste éventail de sujets étroitement liés, dont la compétence du tribunal et les pouvoirs discrétionnaires qu'il possède pour l'élimination des tribunaux inappropriés. Les règles en question permettent également aux tribunaux québécois de reconnaître et d'exécuter les décisions étrangères. Les tribunaux doivent interpéter ces règles en examinant d'abord le libellé particulier des dispositions du C.c.Q. et ensuite en cherchant à savoir si leur interprétation est compatible avec les principes qui sous-tendent les règles. Comme les dispositions du C.c.Q. et du C.p.c. ne renvoient pas directement aux principes de courtoisie, d'ordre et d'équité, et qu'au mieux ces principes y sont vaguement définis, il est important de souligner que ces derniers ne constituent pas des règles contraignantes en soi. Ils servent plutôt de guide à l'interprétation des différentes règles de droit international privé et renforcent le lien étroit entre les questions en litige.

Conformément au paragraphe 3148(3) C.c.Q., les tribunaux du Québec peuvent exercer leur compétence quand: (1) une faute a été commise au Québec; (2) un préjudice y a été subi; (3) un fait dommageable s'y est produit; ou (4) l'une des obligations découlant d'un contrat devrait y être exécutée. En l'espèce, l'intimée a établi *prima facie* qu'elle avait subi un préjudice au Québec. La preuve a démontré que l'entreprise exploitée au Québec avait établi sa propre réputation indépendamment de la réputation nationale de Spar. La preuve a aussi démontré que l'installation située au Québec a subi un préjudice en raison du refus de verser les primes, même si ces versements devaient être effectués à son siège social à Toronto, en Ontario. En outre, dans le contrat de sous-traitance conclu entre Spar et Hughes pour la fabrication de la charge utile, on décrit Spar comme étant située à Ste-Anne-de-Bellevue. Ce fait tend à renforcer son argument selon lequel sa réputation était réellement associée à son entreprise exploitée au Québec. Si les faits tels qu'allégués sont avérés, il semble que toute atteinte à la réputation de Spar a été subie à son établissement situé dans la province de Québec, et non à son siège social en Ontario. De plus, rien dans le libellé du paragraphe 3148(3) ne donne à penser que seul le préjudice direct peut être utilisé pour rattacher l'action au ressort. En dernier lieu, le montant symbolique des dommages-intérêts que réclame Spar pour l'atteinte portée à sa réputation n'a pas à être discuté pour régler la question de la compétence, mais ce montant peut constituer l'un des nombreux facteurs à considérer dans une demande fondée sur le *forum non conveniens.*

La Cour supérieure a conclu à bon droit en l'espèce que l'atteinte à la réputation de Spar satisfait de manière suffisante à l'exigence relative au "préjudice" du paragraphe 3148(3). Mais la Cour d'appel a commis une erreur en concluant que l'atteinte à la réputation dont Spar allègue avoir été victime à son entreprise située au Québec constituait un "fait dommageable." Si l'on veut interpréter le "fait dommageable" d'une manière conforme à l'évolution de la règle et de façon à éviter la redondance des trois autres motifs énoncés au paragraphe 3148(3), celui-ci doit se rapporter à un événement qui, donnant naissance à un préjudice, attire une responsabilité sans faute. Rien de tel n'est invoqué en l'espèce.

L'exigence d'un "lien réel et substantiel" énoncée dans les arrêts *Morguard Investments Ltd.* c. *De Savoye,* [1990] 3 R.C.S. 1077, et *Hunt* c. *T & N Plc.,* [1993] 4 R.C.S. 289, n'est pas un critère additionel auquel il faut satisfaire pour déterminer la compétence des tribunaux québécois en l'espèce. Premièrement, ces arrêts ont été jugés dans le contexte de conflits de compétence interprovinciaux, et leurs conclusions précises ne peuvent facilement déborder de ce contexte. Deuxièmement, il ressort des termes explicites de l'article 3148 et des autres dispositions du Livre dixième du C.c.Q. que ce système de droit international privé vise à assurer la présence d'un "lien réel et substantiel" entre l'action et la province de Québec, et à empêcher l'exercice inapproprié de la compétence du for québécois. Il est douteux que le demandeur qui réussit à faire la preuve de l'un des quatre motifs d'attribution de compétence énumérés au paragraphe 3148(3) ne soit pas considéré come ayant satisfait au critère du "lien réel et substantiel," du moins aux fins de la simple reconnaissance de compétence, étant donné que tous les motifs énumérés (la faute, le fait dommageable, le préjudice, le contrat) semblent être des exemples de situations qui constituent un lien réel et substantiel entre la province de Québec et l'action.

La doctrine du *forum non conveniens,* telle que codifiée à l'article 3135 C.c.Q., constitue un contrepoids important à la large assise juridictionnelle prévue à l'article 1348. En vertu de l'article 3135, un tribunal québécois compétent à juger un différend peut exceptionnellement refuser d'exercer sa compétence s'il estime que les tribunaux d'un autre pays sont mieux à même de juger l'affaire. En l'espèce, la juge des requêtes a étudié les facteurs pertinents et a conclu qu'aucune autre juridiction n'était manifestement plus appropriée que le Québec et que l'exercice exceptionnel de ce pouvoir n'était pas justifié. Il n'y a aucune raison d'intervenir dans cette décision. Vu la nature exceptionnelle de la doctrine qui ressort du libellé de l'article 3135, et compte tenu que les décisions discrétionnaires ne sont pas facilement modifiées, les défenderesses n'ont pas établi les conditions qui auraient pu forcer la Cour supérieure à décliner sa compétence en raison du *forum non conveniens.*

Note. This case is as important for the common law jurisdictions of Canada as it is for Québec, but its implications on the common law side must be examined with care. The first important point is the exclusion from international cases of the "real and substantial connection" criterion laid down by *Morguard* and *Hunt,* because the basis of the test is found in federal constitutional principle. It is hard to know whether the court, by so holding, meant that provinces can go as far as they like in giving their courts jurisdiction in international cases. The tendency has been to regard the appropriate minimum level of connection needed to support jurisdiction as being more, not less, substantial in international than in interprovincial cases. Even though *Spar* was an international case, the court went to considerable pains to show that the jurisdictional rules in the Quebec Civil Code were, in fact, compatible with the "real and substantial connection" criterion. This is the second major point in the case. The rules of court in common law provinces generally include broader jurisdictional grounds than those in the Civil Code, and lower courts are holding with some frequency that an action lacks a real and substantial connection with the province even though it satisfies one of the rules for service *ex juris.* (See the cases noted above, under 1. Common Law and

Federal, (a) Jurisdiction *in personam* — constitutionally based territorial limits on jurisdiction.) The deference paid to the Québec jurisdictional rules in the *Spar* case may encourage a relaxation of the "real and substantial connection" test for jurisdiction *simpliciter* in other provinces, which in itself would not be altogether a bad thing. The current approach arguably involves too much overlap between jurisdiction *simpliciter* and *forum non conveniens.*

However, the third point in the *Spar* case is the restrictive view taken of *forum non conveniens*, in the sense of emphasizing its "exceptional" nature (while stressing, somewhat contradictorily, that even in Québec it is "an important counterweight to the broad basis for jurisdiction set out in art. 3148" (at para. 57). This can probably be traced to the fact that *forum non conveniens* was not part of Québec private international law until it was introduced by the new Civil Code in 1994. By design, Article 3135 uses the term "exceptionally" to limit the doctrine's application. The jurisdictional principles in the common law provinces need tempering by *forum non conveniens* more than the Québec rules do. It will be a pity if the *Spar* case is used in common law provinces to restrict the use of *forum non conveniens*, because it will mean a reversion to the bad old days when courts virtually invited the selection of an inappropriate forum for tactical reasons, by hardly ever depriving a plaintiff of his or her chosen forum. There are already signs that courts will be tempted to avail themselves of *Spar* in this way. (See *ABN Amro Bank N.V.* v. *BCE Inc.,* noted above under 1. Common Law and Federal, (a) Jurisdiction *in personam* — declining jurisdiction — *forum non conveniens* — defendant resident in the jurisdiction). So if *Spar* is applied too enthusiastically outside Québec, the result may be lenient jurisdictional rules that are harder to challenge on constitutional grounds and, at the same time, harder to control with *forum non conveniens.*

Compétence internationale — recours collectif — exception déclinatoire

Option Consommateurs c. *Servier Canada Inc.,* [2003] R.J.Q. 470 (Cour supérieure du Québec)

Dans le cadre d'une requête pour autorisation d'exercer un recours collectif présentée par Option consommateurs à son encontre, Biofarma a soulevé une exception déclinatoire en alléguant que seuls les tribunaux français sont compétents pour connaître le litige. Biofarma se fonde sur le fait qu'elle est une société française, ayant son siège social en France et constituée en vertu des lois françaises. Elle ajoute en plus n'avoir aucun lien ou rattachement avec le Québec. Biofarma est convaincue que tout jugement rendu contre elle par la Cour supérieure du Québec ne serait pas exécutoire en France et que cette absence de compétence des tribunaux québécois doit être décidée avant l'instruction de la requête au stade de l'autorisation. Option consommateurs présente une requête visant à faire déclarer irrecevable et prématurée la requête de Biofarma en exception déclinatoire. La Cour a accueilli la requête de Option consommateurs. Après avoir procédé à une revue de la jurisprudence pertinente, la Cour conclut que le juge saisi de la requête en autorisation constitue le meilleur forum pour débattre de la question de la compétence en regard de Biofarma. Le juge pourra alors choisir d'entendre la requête de Biofarma dès le début de l'audition, ou de l'intégrer comme moyen de contestation de la requête pour autorisation d'exercice d'un recours collectif ou encore, d'entendre la requête après avoir décidé si le recours satisfait les critères de la requête pour autorisation d'un recours collectif. Par ailleurs, le Tribunal défère la détermination de la compétence de la Cour supérieure à l'égard de Biofarma au juge saisi de l'instruction de la requête en autorisation de recours collectif.

B   Procedure / Procédure

1   Common Law and Federal

(a)   Commencement of proceedings

Service of process abroad

Note. In *Grant* v. *Grant* (2003), 34 C.P.C. (5th) 374, 38 R.F.L. (5th) 89 (B.C.S.C.), personal service of a statement of claim, translated into French, on the defendant in France was held to be in good service for the purposes of the British Columbia Rules of Court, notwithstanding that it was not a mode provided for by the Hague Convention on the Service Abroad of Judicial and Extra-Judicial Documents in Civil or Commercial Matters (see R. 13(12)). The defendant's assertion that a French lawyer had advised her that the service was invalid under French law, by way of explanation of why she had not responded to the service, was not evidence.

(b)   Interlocutory orders

Note. The court in *Green* v. *Jernigan* (2003), 18 B.C.L.R. (4th) 366 (S.C.), set aside a *Mareva* injunction (an interlocutory injunction restraining a party from removing assets from the jurisdiction) on the grounds that the court should decline jurisdiction in the action on the basis of a choice of forum clause in the trust deed that was the basis of the claim, and because the plaintiff had not made full and frank disclosure in its *ex parte* application for the injunction.

(c)   Obtaining evidence abroad for local proceedings

Judicial request for examination

Note. See *Manitoba (Attorney General)* v. *Murray* (2003), [2004] 1 W.W.R. 158, 172 Man. R. (2d) 191 (Q.B.), giving effect to the request of an Italian court to examine a Manitoba lawyer on the basis that he was thought to hold certain property as trustee for a man who owed maintenance to his Italian-resident wife. A treaty between Canada and Italy providing for evidence to be taken in Canada had not been properly proved. However, the request appeared to be authentically issued by a foreign court of competent jurisdiction for purposes of a judicial proceeding beyond the dis-covery stage. The examination of the lawyer was ordered under the Manitoba Evidence Act, C.C.S.M., c. E150, s. 82(1).

(d)   Remedies

Damages — foreign currency — conversion

Amertek Inc. v. *Canadian Commercial Corp.* (2003), 229 D.L.R. (4th) 419, 39 B.L.R. (3d) 163 (Ontario Superior Court of Justice) (notice of appeal to Ontario Court of Appeal filed 8 Sept. 2003)

The main defendant was a federal Crown corporation that pro-vided government guarantees for certain export contracts. Its primary customer was the United States government, which since 1956 had agreed to permit the defendant, and no other Canadian company, to bid on United States defence contracts free of the restrictions that otherwise applied to foreign contractors. Officials of the defendant had persuaded the plaintiff, an Ontario manufac-turer of truck bodies, to take on the performance of a contract for the manufacture of fire trucks for the United States military. The defendant had originally made the contract with the United States on behalf of a Québec company that had proved unable to carry out its obligations. The plaintiff lost a great deal of money on the contract and was forced to the verge of bankruptcy. It sued the defendant corporation for having misled it by concealing the fact that the procurement contract had been very substantially under-bid by the Québec company and by assuring the plaintiff that the subcontract would be a viable one for it. O'Driscoll J. held the defendant liable for breach of fiduciary duty towards the plaintiff, breach of warranty, unjust enrichment, and abuse of process (for trying to push the plaintiff into bankruptcy to get rid of it).

The defendant's motive was found to have been the avoidance of its own liability to the United States government if the latter had to re-procure the contract because the defendant could not fulfil the contract for the supply of the trucks. Along with other items awarded in Canadian dollars, the plaintiff's damages included an award of US $26,507,000 as the probable amount of the liability the defendant had avoided, which the judge viewed as a profit the defendant had made from its wrong. For conversion of this sum to Canadian currency, the judge applied section 121(3) of the Courts of Justice Act, R.S.O. 1990, c. C.43, which makes the presumptive date for conversion the date when the judgment is paid, which counsel had agreed could be taken as the date that judgment was released. Under section 121(3), the court has a discretion to con-vert as of another date if using the presumptive date would be inequitable. The judge considered the date when the cause of action arose (when the plaintiff committed itself to the losing subcon-tract), which was in October 1985 — the date when the defendant would have been liable for the cost of re-procurement, which was found to be in October 1990; and the date the action was begun, in October 1996. The exchange rate had fluctuated considerably during the period. The judge saw no reason to depart from the pre-sumptive date.

Note. The interest of the *Amertek* case, aside from its excoria-tion of malfeasance by public servants, lies in the example it offers of damages awarded in foreign currency to a Canadian plaintiff for wrongs done in Canada. Also significant is the substitution, by consent, of the judgment date for the payment date, which is the presumptive rule in the legislation. It seems that the certainty of a judgment for a fixed amount in Canadian dollars was more attrac-tive to the parties than the theoretical precision of a judgment denominated in foreign currency, to be converted at the time of payment.

C   *Foreign Judgments / Jugements étrangers*

1   Common Law and Federal

(a)   Conditions for recognition or enforcement

Judgment given on the merits

Note. The victim of an automobile accident in British Columbia sued her own insurer in actions in both the state of Washington, where she lived, and British Columbia. The insurer obtained a summary judgment in Washington. The British Columbia court refused to recognize it as making the victim's claim *res judicata,* because the basis for the Washington decision was unknown and so could not be taken as a decision on the merits: *Mulcahy* v. *Farmers Ins. Co. of Washington* (2002), 3 B.C.L.R. (4th) 113, 40 C.C.L.I. (3d) 158 (S.C.).

Jurisdiction of the original court — consent — submission by the defendant

Note. Unsuccessfully seeking leave to appeal from a default judgment of a foreign court was held a submission to the jurisdiction of the court, in *Roy* v. *Connors Bros. Ltd.* (2003), 227 D.L.R. (4th) 735, 263 N.B.R. (2d) 166 (Q.B.).

Jurisdiction of the original court — consent — contractual agreement to submit

Note. In *Zaidenberg* v. *Hamouth* (2002), 9 B.C.L.R. (4th) 303 (S.C.), the debtor under a New York default judgment being sued upon in British Columbia argued by way of counterclaim that he had been induced to enter into the contract on which the action had been brought by the judgment creditor's fraud. He said this invalidated the clause in the contract by which he, the debtor, agreed to submit to the jurisdiction of the New York courts. The British Columbia court held that the alleged fraud was "intrinsic" fraud in that the debtor could have raised it before the foreign court. Such fraud was not a ground for impeaching the merits of the judgment. In any event, the fraud did not affect the validity of the agreement on choice of forum.

Jurisdiction of the original court — no consent — real and substantial connection with the foreign jurisdiction — arbitration clause

United Laboratories Inc. v. *Abraham* (2002), 62 O.R. (3d) 26, 26 C.P.C. (5th) 156 (Ontario Superior Court of Justice)

United Labs, an Illinois-based manufacturer and distributor of industrial cleaning products, hired Abraham in 1993 to be its vice-president of international sales Canada. In 1996, the relationship was changed so that Abraham was an independent contractor instead of an employee. The contract provided that any disputes between the parties that could not be settled by negotiation would be subject to arbitration, with the governing law to be the law of Ontario. When United Labs notified Abraham that the contract was terminated, he served United Labs with a notice of arbitration, which United Labs rejected as premature because there had not been any attempt to negotiate a settlement. United Labs subsequently brought an action for damages in Illinois against Abraham and several corporations, alleging that after his termination, Abraham and the other defendants had illegally accessed United Labs' voicemail system. Neither Abraham nor the other defendants took steps to defend the Illinois action, apparently because Abraham assumed all his differences with United Labs would be settled by arbitration. Abraham received notice from the Illinois court that he should show cause why default judgment should not be entered against him. He did not respond.

United Labs sued Abraham and M Ltd., one of the other Illinois defendants, in Ontario for malicious falsehood. Abraham, M Ltd., and P Inc., another Illinois defendant, sued United Labs and others in Ontario claiming injunctive relief and damages. No one sought a stay of these actions. Eventually, United Labs applied in Ontario for the appointment of an arbitrator. The arbitration led to a mediated settlement in which Abraham and the corporations agreed to pay United Labs $50,000 in settlement of all claims except those in the Illinois action.

Default judgment was entered in the Illinois action, and the judge awarded over US $500,000 in damages, including $200,000 punitive damages. United Labs sued on this judgment in Ontario. Abraham and the other Illinois defendants argued that the Ontario settlement made the claims in the Illinois action *res judicata,* or made the pursuit of them an abuse of process. They also argued that the Illinois court lacked jurisdiction because of the arbitration clause, and that the judgment was unenforceable because it was for a penalty.

The trial judge rejected these arguments. A foreign money judgment creates a new, distinct cause of action. Any argument based on *res judicata* or abuse of process should have been put to the Illinois court. Moreover, the Ontario settlement expressly did not extend to the matters being litigated in Illinois. Nor could Abraham now argue that the arbitration clause in his contract applied to the claims in the Illinois proceeding and therefore rendered the Illinois judgment unenforceable for lack of jurisdiction. An arbitration clause does not oust the jurisdiction of a court. It was incumbent on the defendants to bring proceedings to persuade the Illinois court that it had no jurisdiction in the face of the arbitration agreement. As for the argument that the Illinois judgment was penal in nature, the Ontario judge held that the award was not in favour of the state or at the suit of the state, and in any event it was compensatory in nature. The litigation had a real and substantial connection with Illinois, as the defendants had conceded, and the default judgment was therefore enforceable.

(b)   Registration under uniform reciprocal enforcement of maintenance orders legislation

Confirmation of provisional order — original court's application of its own law

S.(C.J.) v. *S.(R.R.S.)* (2003), 227 D.L.R. (4th) 540, 39 R.F.L. (5th) 410 (British Columbia Supreme Court)

Since 1993, the husband had been subject to an order of the British Columbia court to pay the wife child support and spousal support. In 1997, he lost his job with a Canadian national company and moved to England. He paid no support after that time. In 2001, the British Columbia authorities, acting under the Family Maintenance Enforcement Program, took steps to enforce the support order. In the ensuing proceedings in the English Magistrates' Court, the husband obtained a provisional order reducing slightly the amount of child and spousal support payable, and canceling more than £10,000 of arrears. The transcript of the proceeding indicated that the magistrates had considered themselves bound by case law to remit any arrears more than twelve months old, save in exceptional circumstances. The British Columbia court, upon being asked by the husband to confirm the provisional order, refused to confirm the order in so far as it cancelled arrears. Section 31(1) of the Interjurisdictional Support Orders Act, S.B.C. 2002, c. 9, provides that when an applicant outside British Columbia applies to vary support obligations, the entitlement to receive support for a child must be determined according to the law of the jurisdiction in which the child ordinarily resides or, if there is no entitlement under that law, the law of British Columbia. In this case, the children were ordinarily resident in British Columbia. British Columbia law did not remit arrears except where the enforcement of them would be grossly unfair, which was not the case.

Note. See also *Finn* v. *Finn* (2003), 37 R.F.L. (5th) 103 (Ont. S.C.J.), where the court refused to confirm a Newfoundland provisional order for the forgiveness of arrears because the applicant had not made full and frank disclosure to the Newfoundland court, including the fact that another judge had previously refused to forgive the arrears, and he had shown the Ontario court no change in circumstances that would justify the forgiveness of the arrears.

2   Québec

(a)   Compétence internationale du tribunal étranger

Article 3168(4) C.c.Q. — obligations découlant d'un contrat devaient être exécutées à l'étranger

Labs of Virginia Inc. c. *Clintrials Bioresearch Ltd.,* [2003] JQ N° 3395, JEL/2003-255 (Cour supérieure du Québec)

Labs of Virginia demande à la Cour supérieure du Québec de reconnaître et déclarer exécutoire un jugement rendu par défaut le 4 avril 2000 en Caroline du Sud et condamnant Clintrials Bioresearch Ltd. et Bio-Research Laboratoires de Montréal à lui payer 163 259,62 $ US représentant 252 072,84 $ Can. Ce jugement fait suite au non-paiement par les défenderesses du coût de 70 singes rhésus ainsi que 60 singes femelles de type cynomolgus commandés à Virginia et livrés par elle. Les défenderesses soutiennent que Virginia aurait livré des singes infectés par la tuberculose dont plusieurs ont dû être euthanasiés. En juillet 1997, Clintrials a intenté, à Montréal, une action en dommages-intérêts contre Animal Breeders, propriété de Virginia, pour les animaux perdus. Cette poursuite est toujours pendante aujourd'hui. Virginia soutient que le jugement américain rencontre toutes les conditions énoncées aux articles 3155 à 3168 C.c.Q., particulièrement aux paragraphes (3) et (4) de l'article 3168, alors que Clintrials et Bio-Research invoquent que l'article 3168(4) exige que toutes les obligations découlant du contrat aient été exécutées à l'étranger afin que le tribunal étranger soit compétent, ce qui ne serait pas le cas en l'espèce.

La Cour supérieure a rejeté la requête de Virginia. En vertu de l'article 3168(3) C.c.Q., une autorité étrangère n'aura compétence que si une faute et un préjudice se sont produits dans cet État étranger. De même, selon l'article 3168(4), un tribunal étranger ne sera compétent en matière d'inexécution contractuelle que si toutes les obligations découlant du contrat devaient être exécutées dans l'État étranger. L'intention du législateur est donc de restreindre les champs de compétence des autorités étrangères par rapport aux champs de compétence interne. En l'espèce, au moins deux des obligations contractuelles devaient être exécutées à Montréal: la délivrance des singes et le paiement des animaux. D'autre part, contrairement à ce qu'invoque Virginia, toute la cause d'action n'est pas survenu en Caroline du Sud et jamais les défenderesses n'ont reconnu la compétence du tribunal de la Caroline du Sud puisqu'elles n'y ont jamais comparu.

Article 3155 alinéa 1 C.c.Q. — absence de compétence du tribunal étranger quand les tribunaux québécois ont compétence exclusive — article 3129 C.c.Q. — exposition à une matière première provenant du Québec

Worthington Corp. c. *Atlas Turner Inc.,* [2003] R.J.Q. 1197 (Cour supérieure du Québec)

Une cour de l'État de New York a condamné Worthington et Atlas, dont le siège social est situé au Québec, à dédommager Elaine Ronsini pour le préjudice subi par son mari, aujourd'hui décédé, à la suite d'une amiantose qui aurait été causée par une exposition à de la fibre d'amiante produite par Atlas. Atlas s'est toujours défendue en alléguant que l'amiante ne provenait pas de ses mines. Pour satisfaire la condamnation solidaire prononcée contre elle et Atlas, Worthington a dédommagé Ronsini et se considère maintenant subrogée dans les droits de cette dernière jusqu'à concurrence de la somme payée pour Atlas. Worthington demande donc la reconnaissance et l'exécution du jugement rendu dans l'État de New York ordonnant à Atlas de lui payer 979 802,20 $ Can. Atlas soulève les exceptions prévues aux alinéas 1, 3 et 5 de l'article 3155 C.c.Q. pour appuyer sa thèse du refus de reconnaître le jugement new-yorkais. Elle plaide qu'en vertu des articles 3129 et 3151 C.c.Q., le tribunal de New York n'avait pas compétence pour rendre tel jugement. Quant à Worthington, elle réplique en soulevant l'inconstitutionnalité de ces dispositions. Les dispositions se lisent comme suit:

3129   Les règles du présent code s'appliquent de façon impérative à la responsabilité civile pour tout préjudice subi au Québec ou hors du Québec et résultant soit de l'exposition à une matière première provenant du Québec, soit de son utilisation, que cette matière première ait été traitée ou non.

3151 Les autorités québécoises ont compétence exclusive pour connaître en première instance de toute action fondée sur la responsabilité prévue à l'article 3129.

La Cour supérieure a rejeté la requête de Worthington. La demande de Worthington de condamner Atlas à lui payer une somme d'argent est irrecevable. En effet, Worthington doit exercer au Québec un recours récursoire contre Atlas alors que Ronsini, à titre de liquidatrice, pouvait demander l'exécution directe du jugement au Québec; la subrogation n'a pas eu pour effet de transférer à Worthington le bénéfice de la solidarité dont jouit Ronsini. Par ailleurs, la reconnaissance du jugement étranger est la règle. L'allégation d'Atlas fondée sur l'article 3155 alinéa 5 C.c.Q. à l'effet que le montant très important de la condamnation rendrait le résultat contraire à l'ordre public dans les relations internationales ne peut être retenue. De même, le moyen soutenu par Atlas et basé sur l'article 3155 alinéa 3 C.c.Q. à l'effet que la reconnaissance du jugement violerait les règles essentielles de la procédure parce qu'elle a été privée du droit d'offrir une défense pleine et entière doit être rejeté. Atlas ne peut demander de réviser des faits et le droit de la cause entendue par les tribunaux new-yorkais et ayant aujourd'hui force de chose jugée. Cependant, le moyen fondé sur l'article 3155 alinéa 1 C.c.Q., qui traite de l'absence de compétence du tribunal new-yorkais pour rendre le jugement doit être accueilli puisque seuls les tribunaux québécois avaient compétence en l'espèce. Enfin, la question de la constitutionnalité des articles 3129 et 3151 C.c.Q. n'a pas à être tranchée car seuls les articles 3155 et 3165 C.c.Q. sont applicables en l'espèce et qu'ils n'ont pas de portée extraterritoriale susceptible d'entacher leur validité constitutionnelle. Vu la preuve non contredite faite par Atlas quant à l'origine de l'amiante qu'elle utilisait dans ses produits, la reconnaissance, au Québec, du jugement rendu à New York est refusée pour le motif énoncé à l'alinéa 1 de l'article 3155 C.c.Q.

D *Choice of Law (including Status of Persons) / Conflits de lois (y compris statut personnel)*

1 Common Law and Federal

(a) Contracts

Proper law — insurance contract

Note. Provincial insurance legislation generally includes a provision deeming an insurance policy that is issued in the province, covering property in the province or an insurable interest of a person resident in the province, to be governed by the province's law. For an application of such a provision, see *Re Laidlaw Inc.* (2003), 46 C.C.L.I. 93d) 263 (Ont. S.C.J.). As noted there, the drafting, and perhaps the effect, of the provisions differ significantly from one province's act to another.

Statutory regulation of contracts — constitutional limitations

Unifund Assurance Co. v. *Insurance Corp. of British Columbia,* [2003] 2 S.C.R. 63, 227 D.L.R. (4th) 402 (Supreme Court of Canada)

Two residents of Ontario were injured in a collision with a tractor-trailer in British Columbia. The victims brought an action against the driver, owner, and repairer of the truck, all residents of British Columbia, in that province and were awarded damages. The Insurance Corporation of British Columbia (ICBC) was the third party liability insurer for all the defendants. The victims also received no-fault benefits from Unifund, their own insurer, as provided by law in Ontario. In an action brought in Ontario, Unifund sought to recoup the victims' no-fault benefits from ICBC (which had an address for service in Ontario) on the basis of section 275 of the Insurance Act, R.S.O. 1990, c. I.8. That provision created a statutory right on the part of an insurer that had paid no-fault benefits to a victim of an automobile accident to be indemnified by the wrongdoer's insurer if the wrongdoer's vehicle was a heavy commercial vehicle. British Columbia law had no comparable provision for shifting the cost of no-fault benefits to a liability insurer. On the contrary, it expressly prevented such loss-shifting by section 25(5) of the Insurance (Motor Vehicle) Act, R.S.B.C. 1996, c. 231. This said that a liability insurer was not liable to pay the victim damages to the extent that they represented a claim by a victim's insurer to be reimbursed for the payment of no-fault accident insurance benefits to the victim. The explanation for this rule was probably that ICBC is the sole provider of mandatory automobile insurance in British Columbia and so would usually be insuring both sides. Nevertheless, the provision expressly extended to the reimbursement of no-fault benefits paid under an automobile insurance policy issued outside British Columbia. The sum at stake between the two insurers was about $750,000.

The Ontario legislation required the parties to go to arbitration if there was a dispute about a claim for reimbursement of no-fault benefits paid. When Unifund applied to the Ontario court for an order that ICBC go to arbitration on Unifund's claim, ICBC applied for a stay or dismissal of the application on the ground that British Columbia law, not Ontario law, governed the matter. ICBC contended that, as a matter of constitutional law, Ontario law could not apply to subject-matter that was extraterritorial in relation to Ontario. Alternatively, ICBC sought a stay on the ground of *forum non conveniens*. The motions judge granted the stay on the latter ground. The Ontario Court of Appeal allowed Unifund's appeal and ordered ICBC to go to arbitration, holding that any dispute as to jurisdiction or the applicable law was a matter for the arbitrator.

On further appeal, the Supreme Court of Canada held, by a majority of four to three, that there was no basis for ordering the arbitration. The Ontario reimbursement provision was constitutionally inapplicable to ICBC, because its application would not respect the territorial limits on provincial legislative jurisdiction. Those limits are a matter of a sufficient connection among the province, the subject matter of the legislation, and the individual or entity sought to be regulated by the legislation. A "real and substantial connection" sufficient to permit the court of a province to take jurisdiction may not be sufficient for the law of that province to regulate the outcome. The applicability of otherwise competent provincial legislation to out-of-province defendants is conditioned by the principles of order and fairness that underlie Canadian federal arrangements. These principles, being purposive, are to be applied flexibly. Different degrees of connection may be required, according to the subject matter. Here, ICBC was not authorized to sell insurance in Ontario, its insured vehicles in this case did not enter Ontario, the accident took place outside Ontario, and ICBC benefited from the deduction of statutory accident benefits, not by virtue of Ontario law, but by the law of British Columbia. The fact that the Ontario legislature had chosen to attach legal consequences to an event (the accident) taking place elsewhere did not extend its legislative reach to a resident of "elsewhere." The decision of the British Columbia legislature to attach legal consequences (the deduction) in that province to an event that occurred in Ontario (the no-fault benefit payments) did not bring ICBC into the orbit of the Ontario legislature for the purpose of taking away the British Columbia benefit in favour of an Ontario insurance company.

Like all other out-of-province insurers, ICBC had filed with the Ontario authorities a power of attorney to accept service on its behalf, an undertaking to submit to the jurisdiction of the Ontario courts, and an undertaking not to raise any defence under one of its policies that might not be set up if the policy had been issued in Ontario in conformity with Ontario law. These arrangements were aimed at litigation arising directly out of a motor vehicle accident itself. They were not a consent to having the law of Ontario apply to an accident that took place in British Columbia.

The dissenting judges thought that Ontario had jurisdiction *simpliciter* in the case, because ICBC, by participating in the reciprocal interjurisdictional insurance scheme, had subjected itself to the jurisdiction. It was not unfair that insurers involved in the interprovincial scheme, having accepted the risk of harm to extraprovincial parties under the agreement, should be considered to have attorned to the jurisdiction of Ontario's courts. ICBC had not presented any evidence so far that Ontario was *forum non conveniens*, but could raise that argument before the arbitrator. As for the constitutional issue, the dissenting judges said that, as valid provincial legislation, section 275 of Ontario's Insurance Act could affect matters that, although they had extraprovincial elements, were sufficiently connected with the province. Interinsurer indemnification was a "matter" that was sufficiently connected to Ontario so as to render the statute applicable to ICBC.

Note 1. In this case, what should have been a choice of law issue was transformed into a constitutional one. The underlying question was whether the Ontario indemnification rule applied as between Unifund and ICBC. One surmises that it took a constitutional, rather than private international law, form because the immediate question was the jurisdiction of the Ontario court to require ICBC to go to arbitration with Unifund. If ICBC had presented the nonapplicability of the Ontario rule as a choice of law argument, it might have given Unifund more of an opening to respond that the question went to the substance of the claim and so should be left to the arbitrator. Because ICBC couched the question in terms of the constitutional applicability of the rule to itself, it was easier for ICBC to persuade the courts (at least the highest court) that it went to the foundation of the arbitrator's jurisdiction.

It is worth speculating on what would have happened if the choice of law issue in *Unifund* had been addressed directly. The first question would have been to characterize Unifund's claim. One possibility would be to characterize the Ontario rule as equivalent to a statutory right of subrogation. On that basis, it is fairly clear that Unifund would have had a valid claim because its right would have been seen as part of the rights that Ontario law attached to the insurance contract between Unifund and the victims, a contract of which Ontario law was the proper law (*Régie de l'assurance automobile du Québec* v. *Brown* (1990), 71 D.L.R. (4th) 457 (N.B. C.A.) (application for leave to appeal dismissed, [1991] 1 S.C.R. vi)). The characterization of the claim as a subrogated one is doubtful, because the claim was not by way of enforcing, for Unifund's benefit, the insureds' existing claim against the person who had negligently injured them. The claim was a new one, distinct from the insureds,' created wholly by the statute. The better view is to regard it as a *sui generis* right, not falling into any of the usual choice of law categories.

A *sui generis* right requires a *sui generis* choice of law rule to be formulated. The statutory right of indemnity given to the payer of Ontario no-fault benefits is part of an integrated regulatory scheme for the compensation of road accident victims. Each province has its own version of such a scheme. Because the different parts of each scheme are so highly integrated, it is desirable that only one province's scheme should apply to any particular accident. Therefore, it makes sense to make the choice of law decision using the connecting factor or factors that provides the most workable delineation of the schemes' respective spheres of operation. The most obvious one, and the one on which the interprovincial (indeed, North American) automobile insurance arrangements have been based, is the place of the accident.

Whether this analysis is correct or not, in resolving these problems the choice of law method is demonstrably superior to the constitutional method. It may, and in this case probably does, lead to the same outcome, but it has the merit of looking at the whole picture as a systemic problem, by asking what choice of law rule will best decide whose law should apply in this type of case. This is better than just looking at a particular instance of it from the side of one jurisdiction only, by asking whether the application of the particular statutory rule is prevented by the limits on Ontario's constitutional power. Moreover, to go first to the constitutional question is putting the cart before the horse. Conflict of laws principles determine the application of legislation. If under conflict of laws principles, a statute does not operate extraterritorially, there is no constitutional issue. The issue only arises if the legislature expressly purports to override the otherwise applicable conflicts principles and, by doing so, claims to regulate matters that are outside its constitutional competence.

Note 2. Another case arising out of provincial rules relating to the liability of automobile insurers to reimburse other insurers was *Matt (Litigation Guardian of)* v. *Barber* (2002), 216 D.L.R. (4th) 574, 45 C.C.L.I. (3d) 13 (Ont. C.A.). The Alberta Health Plan had paid medical expenses for the (now) Alberta-resident victim of an accident in Ontario, and made a subrogated claim for the amount in an Ontario action against the parties who were liable for the accident. The court held that the right of subrogation created by Alberta law, although otherwise valid in Ontario, was overridden by s. 267(1)(b) of the Insurance Act, R.S.O. 1990, c. I.8, which bars subrogated claims for benefits that the victim received from any medical or hospitalization plan.

Statutory regulation of contracts — mandatory provision imposed by the proper law

Dinney v. *Great-West Life Assurance Co.* (2002), 169 Man. R. (2d) 317, 33 C.C.P.B. 208 (Manitoba Queen's Bench)

Great-West brought a motion to determine whether certain provisions of the Pension Benefits Act, C.C.S.M., c. P32, applied to beneficiaries of its pension plan who were employed outside Manitoba. The court had already decided in class proceedings that certain of Great-West's pensioners had not received the full amount of the increments to which they were entitled. There were 129 pensioners who were employed outside the province. Nothing in the text of the plan indicated an intention that more than one law should govern it. The court held that the extra-provincial employees were included in the class. The parties intended the plan and the vesting provisions to be interpreted according to the law of Manitoba. The proper law of the plan was therefore Manitoba law, and there was no reason why the entitlement of the non-resident pensioners should depend on the laws of other provinces. An Ontario case that reached a contrary conclusion (*Régie des rentes du Québec* v. *Pension Commissioners of Ontario* (2000), 189 D.L.R. (4th) 304 (Ont. Div'l Ct.)) was distinguishable because the pension plan in that case expressly made the beneficiaries' rights subject to the pension benefits laws of the province in which they were employed. The court acknowledged that another province's legislation might mandatorily give certain rights to beneficiaries employed in that province, and that Manitoba law might have to defer to such legislation, but that was not the situation here.

Note. Pension benefits standards legislation, such as consumer protection or securities legislation, alters contractual rights by way of imposing rights and obligations on the parties to certain types of transactions. If, as in *Dinney*, the legislation is part of the proper law of the contract, it will usually apply, irrespective of whether the court that is asked to apply it is a court in the enacting jurisdiction or elsewhere. If the legislation is not part of the proper law, the issue is more difficult. As far as a court in the enacting jurisdiction is concerned, the legislation must be applied if its terms demand that it apply. Usually, the application of rules of this type hinges, either expressly or impliedly, not on the proper law of the contract but on where the activity being regulated takes place. Prospectus and disclosure requirements in securities laws, for example, usually apply to any distribution of securities that takes place in the jurisdiction: see *Pearson* v. *Boliden Ltd.*, noted immediately below under (b) Corporations and shareholders. If the issue arises before a court that is not in the enacting jurisdiction, the question is whether the mandatory rule of jurisdiction A can impose itself on a contract whose proper law is the law of jurisdiction B, where the court faced with the issue is not a court of jurisdiction A but a court of jurisdiction B or C. Generally speaking, the common law answer is no: see *Avenue Properties Ltd.* v. *First City Development Corp.* (1986), 32 D.L.R. (4th) 40 (B.C.C.A.) (prospectus requirement for the solicitation of investments in subdivided real estate).

(b)   Corporations and shareholders

Civil actions for breach of securities legislation

Pearson v. *Boliden Ltd.* (2002), 222 D.L.R. (4th) 453, 7 B.C.L.R. (4th) 245 (British Columbia Court of Appeal) (application for leave to appeal dismissed, 18 Sept. 2003 (S.C.C.))

A class action was commenced in British Columbia on behalf of all those who had bought shares in Boliden in an initial public offering and who had lost all or part of their investment because a tailings dam at Boliden's mine had failed, causing major environmental damage. The action was against Boliden's directors and officers, and was based on the statutory cause of action in section 131 of the Securities Act, R.S.B.C. 1996, c. 418, for material misrepresentations in a prospectus for an offering of securities. Boliden had filed a prospectus with the securities authorities of all ten Canadian provinces, and shares had been bought throughout Canada and in Europe and the United States. Boliden applied to exclude from the class all those whose investment had been solicited in other provinces whose law did not have a statutory cause of action of this type (New Brunswick and the Northwest Territories), under whose law the action was statute-barred (Alberta), or where a different form of prospectus had been used (the United States and Europe). The chambers judge refused to exclude such claimants from the class without first having a summary trial as to the questions raised.

On appeal, the British Columbia Court of Appeal held that claimants must be excluded if they were solicited in a jurisdiction that gave them no cause of action of this type. The British Columbia Securities Act did not give a cause of action to those who had been solicited in, and had purchased shares in, another province. The provincial statutes were aimed at protecting the public from certain acts or conduct taking place within the respective provinces. The *lex loci delicti* choice of law rule for torts does not apply directly to the question which provincial Act might found a cause of action for misrepresentations in a prospectus. Although each of the provincial acts on its face was of universal application, the court should follow the constitutional principle that the province in whose territory the securities were distributed has the jurisdiction to regulate the distribution and to attach civil consequences to non-compliance. Such an approach to the choice of law question provided a principled way through the thicket of the many extra-provincial aspects that will be involved in any national securities distribution. As well, it comports with what a reasonable investor would expect — that when he or she purchases shares offered under a distribution taking place in a province, the securities legislation of that province will govern the filing of the prospectus, its contents, and the rights and obligations of the parties thereunder. It also comported with the assumptions that underlie current regulatory practice in Canada.

Where it was clear on the evidence before the chambers judge that there was no statutory cause of action under the law of the relevant jurisdiction (the court found this to be so in Alberta, New Brunswick, and the Northwest Territories), claimants whose investments had been solicited and made in those jurisdictions were excluded. As for claimants from the remaining jurisdictions in Canada and from abroad, the matter was remitted to the chambers judge to examine disclosure and filing requirements and the consequences of non-compliance, in order to determine whether a cause of action existed under the laws of those jurisdictions.

(c)   Torts

Applicable law

   Note. In *Britton* v. *O'Callaghan* (2002), 219 D.L.R. (4th) 300, 62
O.R. (3d) 95 (Ont. C.A.), Ohio law was held to govern the right
of an Ontario resident to sue both an Ontario-resident owner and
driver and an Ohio-resident owner and driver for injuries he suffered when, as passenger, he was injured in a road accident in Ohio.
The bar on civil actions that, at the relevant time, existed under the
Insurance Act, R.S.O. 1990, c. I.8, s. 267.1(1), only came into play
if the plaintiff's claims were governed by Ontario law, which in this
case they were not. See also *Bezan* v. *Vander Hooft* (2003), 333 A.R.
215 (Q.B.), applying the *lex loci delicti* rule to hold that an Alberta
resident who was in an accident in Saksatchewan was bound by the
Saskatchewan bar on civil actions and had recourse only to the no-
fault benefits payable under the Saskatchewan insurance scheme.

(d)   Property

Transfer inter vivos — *tangible movables* — *personal property security*

Toronto-Dominion Bank v. *RNG Group Inc.* (2002), 61 O.R. (3d) 567,
38 C.B.R. (4th) 110 (Ontario Superior Court of Justice)

   RNG, an insolvent company based in Ontario, had leased from
GE certain motor vehicles that were located in other provinces. GE
registered its security interest in the vehicles in the provinces where
the vehicles were located but not in Ontario. The receiver denied
GE's claim of priority with respect to the vehicles on the ground
that GE ought to have registered its security interest in Ontario,
according to the Personal Property Security Act [PPSA], R.S.O.
1990, c. P.10. Section 7(1) says that "the validity of a security interest in goods that are of a type that are normally used in more than
one jurisdiction, if the goods are equipment or inventory leased or
held for lease by a debtor ... shall be governed by the law of the
jurisdiction where the debtor is located at the time the security
interest attaches." GE applied for an order that it had priority, arguing that section 7(1) did not apply because the motor vehicles were
not equipment that RNG leased or held for lease to others. The
receiver maintained that the words about leasing to others modified "inventory" but not "equipment," and relied upon a decision of
the Alberta Court of Appeal that had so held on the corresponding,
but not quite identical, provision of the Alberta PPSA.

The court held for the receiver. The Alberta decision was persuasive because the definition of "equipment" in section 1 of the PPSA excludes goods held for lease, and so it would not make sense to read section 7(1) as referring to equipment leased or held for lease to others. The difference in wording between the comparable provisions in Alberta and Ontario was immaterial (Alberta inserted a second "are" before "inventory"). No public policy or disclosure reason would justify the distinction suggested by GE. An important feature of PPSA legislation across Canada is uniformity among the PPSA statutes and the personal property security provisions of the American Uniform Commercial Code. As noted by the Alberta Court of Appeal, inconsistent interpretations would defeat one of the major purposes of these acts by defeating settled expectations and transactions based on them. Moreover, interpreting similar provisions differently from province to province would produce conflicting registration procedures and potentially create a *renvoi* under conflicts principles.

Note. See also *GMAC Commercial Credit Corp. Canada* v. *TCT Logistics Inc.* (2002), 36 C.B.R. (4th) 37, 4 P.P.S.A.C. (3d) 107 (Ont. S.C.J.), which also concerned the operation of the PPSA provisions relating to equipment.

Transfer inter vivos — *maritime lien*

Note. A maritime lien was held created by the supply of necessaries to a vessel in Malta, by virtue of a provision in the supply contract that it was to be governed by the law of the United States, which, unlike Maltese law, created a lien in favour of the supplier. The lien gave the holder an *in rem* claim in a court in Canada, where the vessel had been arrested: *Kirgan Holding S.A.* v. *The Panamax Leader* (2002), 225 F.T.R. 273 (F.C.T.D.).

(e)   Husband and wife

Recognition of foreign divorce

Jahangiri-Mavaneh v. *Taheri-Zengekani* (2003), 66 O.R. (3d) 272, 39 R.F.L. (5th) 103 (Ontario Superior Court of Justice)

The wife, then resident in Iran, married the husband, then resident in Canada, in February 1997, and immigrated to Canada a year later. In April or May 1998, at the husband's instruction, she returned to Iran to live with her parents-in-law. In November 2001, the husband divorced her according to Iranian law. She left his parents' home, re-immigrated to Canada, and now sought spousal support. The husband objected that they were no longer married and that the court lacked the jurisdiction to order support. The court held that the Iranian divorce had to be recognized on the ground that the wife had been ordinarily resident in Iran for a year preceding the commencement of divorce proceedings (Divorce Act, R.S.C. 1985, c. 3 (2nd Supp.), section 22(1)). She may not have wanted to live in Iran, but intention was not determinative of ordinary residence. In any event, she had a real and substantial connection with Iran and the divorce could be recognized on that ground as common law (section 22(3) of the act). The fact that she was divorced against her will was not a ground for refusing recognition. Courts should be slow to deny recognition to a foreign divorce. To the extent that she felt she lacked free choice in the matter, it was due to cultural factors rather than some form of duress or oppression. It was not for a Canadian court to superimpose Canadian cultural values on those of Iran. Because the divorce took place outside Canada, the support provisions of the federal Divorce Act did not apply. Nor could spousal support be ordered under the relevant Ontario legislation, as the parties were no longer spouses.

2 Québec

(a) Statut personnel

Mariage — divorce étranger — reconnaissance

M.(G.) c. F.(M.A.), [2003] R.J.Q. 2516 (Cour d'appel du Québec)

G.M. porte en appel le rejet de la Cour supérieure de sa requête déclinatoire des procédures en divorce entreprises à la fois au Québec et en Louisiane. Les parties sont les parents de J. Après avoir vécu à la Baie James et à Montréal, la famille s'installe aux États-Unis, soit en Louisiane. Elles se séparent en 2002. M.A.F. intente une action en séparation de corps à Montréal. En septembre 2002, une action en divorce est déposée au nom de G.M. devant la Cour civile de New Orleans en Louisiane. L'avocat montréalais de G.M. dépose une requête au Québec affirmant que M.A.F. s'est soumise à la juridiction du tribunal de New Orleans qui est désormais le seul compétent quant au divorce et demandant à la Cour supérieure de décliner compétence. Cette requête est rejetée aux motifs que le déclinatoire est de nature exceptionnelle et que l'action en divorce a été intentée au Québec avant celle en Louisiane, ce qui

rendrait impossible la reconnaissance et l'exécution au Québec de
la décision rendue en Louisiane. G.M. conteste ce dernier jugement.
La Cour d'appel a rejeté l'appel. La Cour supérieure du Québec
a été le premier tribunal saisi d'une action en divorce. M.A.F. a
décidé de participer aux procédures de divorce intentées par G.M.
en Louisiane et n'a jamais contesté la compétence du tribunal
de New Orleans de prononcer la fin du lien matrimonial et de statuer sur certains aspects financiers. La Cour conclut que la Cour
supérieure était compétente au moment de l'audition de la requête
et le juge de première instance a eu raison de rejeter la requête
en déclinatoire quant à l'action en divorce. Il aurait cependant dû
accueillir la requête en suspension de l'action en séparation de
corps jusqu'à ce qu'il soit établi qu'elle devenait sans objet en raison du divorce à être prononcé en Louisiane ou à Montréal. Cette
erreur est cependant sans conséquence puisqu'un jugement de
divorce a été prononcé en Louisiane et a rendu sans objet l'action
en séparation.

(b)   Obligations

Régime matrimonial

P.(L.) c. *B.(F.)*, [2003] R.J.Q. 564 (Cour supérieure du Québec)

La femme, canadienne, et le mari, marocain et citoyen canadien,
s'épousent au Maroc, y résident et y mènent un train de vie luxueux.
Pendant les vacances, ils occupent une résidence au Québec. Lors
de la séparation, la femme s'établit au Québec avec l'enfant née
de cette union. Plusieurs procédures furent intentées devant les
tribunaux québécois et marocains. Du consentement des parties,
le Tribunal a d'abord tranché la question de la reconnaissance
du jugement de divorce rendu par la Cour marocaine, décidant que
la Cour supérieure du Québec a compétence pour statuer sur la
présente. La femme réclame la garde de l'enfant, le partage de la
société d'acquêts, une prestation compensatoire et une pension
alimentaire ou une somme globale de 1 000 000 $. Pour sa part, le
mari soumet que les demandes de la femme quant au partage de la
société d'acquêts sont injustifiées; la loi marocaine s'appliquant en
l'espèce. De plus, il ne voit aucune justification à l'octroi d'une
pension alimentaire ou d'une somme globale.
La Cour a accueilli les requêtes en partie. Selon l'article 3123
C.c.Q., le régime matrimonial et le mode de partage des biens
prévus par le système judiciaire marocain doit régir les parties. La

dernière résidence commune des parties étant celle de Rabat, la loi marocaine doit s'appliquer quant au partage du patrimoine familial, à l'exclusion du Code civil. Quant à la pension alimentaire payable par le mari, le Tribunal souligne son intention de cacher sa situation financière. Des présomptions de fait seront donc utilisées à partir des dépenses effectuées. En tenant compte du fait que seuls les biens de ce dernier situés au Québec pourront faire l'objet d'exécution, le Tribunal fixe une somme globale composée de tous les actifs au Québec ainsi que 250 000 $. La garde de l'enfant est confiée à la femme. Le mari devra payer 900 $ mensuellement pour les besoins de leur fille. Les droits d'accès du mari sont suspendus considérant la possibilité d'enlèvement.

Book Reviews / Recensions de livres

Theory of International Law. By G.I. Tunkin, foreword by L.N. Shestakov, translated, introduced, and edited by W.E. Butler, 2nd edition. London: Wildy, Simmonds and Hill Publishers. 2003.

The first edition of this work, published by G.I. Tunkin in 1970,[1] was a landmark event in Russian international legal scholarship. No previous Soviet treatment of international law covered a comparable range of issues, matched its analytical and rigorous examination, and displayed equally wide-ranging familiarity with pertinent writings, Soviet and non-Soviet alike. Tunkin continued revising the first edition until his death. On the one hand, he condensed it significantly — he excised entirely its chapters explaining how international law affected relations between socialist countries, and he expunged various quotes from the Communist party. On the other hand, he preserved its focus on the international legal issues that preoccupied Soviet jurists in the Khrushchev and the Brezhnev eras. His ongoing labours found their consummation in the edition reviewed here.[2]

Tunkin's standing among Soviet international jurists of his vintage alone suffices to impart more than passing interest to this edition. From the mid-1950s until he died in 1993, he bestrode Russian

---

The views expressed in the foregoing review are solely the author's views and should not be taken as expressing any views of the Department of Justice Canada.

[1] G.I. Tunkin, *Teoriya mezhdunarodnogo prava* (Moscow: Mezhdunarodnye otnosheniya, 1970). English-language readers know the first edition as G.I. Tunkin, *Theory of International Law,* translated and introduced by W.E. Butler (Cambridge, Massachusetts: Harvard University Press, 1974).

[2] This edition represents a translation of G.I. Tunkin, *Teoriya mezhdunarodnogo prava,* edited by L.N. Shestakov (Moscow: Izdatel'stvo "Zertsalo," 2000).

international legal scholarship as no jurist since F.F. Martens (1845-1909) had done.[3] He outstripped contemporary Soviet jurists by combining distinguished academic appointments at home and abroad with a prominent role in formulating Soviet foreign policy in the post-Stalin era. His scholarly works underwent translation into various languages, including English, French, Spanish, German, Arabic, Chinese, Japanese, and Vietnamese. More than any other contemporary Soviet international jurist, he could expound authoritatively a theory of international law mirroring Marxist-Leninist ideology and Soviet geopolitical relations from the early 1950s onwards. Most likely, his exposition in the present edition will remain that era's foremost exposition of Soviet thinking on international law — if not the foremost exposition of Soviet international legal thought generally.

A central pillar of Tunkin's theory of international law was his conviction that capitalist and socialist countries could coexist under norms of general international law. From 1956, he advanced a theory of "peaceful coexistence," in which general international legal norms arose through agreement between states.[4] As Butler has correctly remarked, this theory underpinned cooperation between capitalist and socialist countries at least until the Soviet Union collapsed in 1991.[5]

More immediately, Tunkin's theory of "peaceful coexistence" informed his exposition of the international legal issues treated in the present edition. He addressed six issues: how the 1917 Russian Revolution affected international law; how norms of contemporary general international law arise; what the central role of agreements between states in creating international legal norms implies about

---

[3] Martens's career and contributions to international legal scholarship are analyzed in V.V. Pustogarov, *Fedor Fedorovich Martens-yurist, diplomat*, 2d ed. (Moscow: Mezhdunarodnye otnosheniya, 1999).

[4] Tunkin's early writings on "peaceful coexistence" include: G.I. Tunkin, "Mirnoe sosuchestvovanie i mezhdunarodnoe pravo" (1956) 7 Sovetskoe gosudarstovo i pravo 3; G.I. Tunkin, *Osnovy sovremennogo mezhdunarodnogo prava: uchebnoe posobie* (Moscow: Vysshaya partiynaya shkola pri TsK KPSS, 1956); and G.I. Tunkin, "Coexistence and International Law" (1958) XCV Recueil des cours 1. He was not the only Soviet international jurist who advanced theories of "peaceful coexistence" from the mid-1950s: B. Meissner, "Die Entwicklung der sowjetischen Völkerrechtslehre," in B. Meissner, *Sowjetunion und Völkerrecht 1917 bis 1962* (Cologne: Verlag Wissenschaft und Politik, 1963) 52 at 57 ff.

[5] G.I. Tunkin, *Theory of International Law* (London: Wildy, Simmonds and Hill Publishers, 2003) at xix-xx.

international law more broadly; how international law interacts with foreign policy and diplomacy; the international legal character of contemporary inter-state organizations; and the implications of international law for state responsibility. He also addressed these issues in the first edition, and the views he advanced there largely anticipate the corresponding views put forward here.

A scholarly apparatus accompanies Tunkin's theory of international law. The apparatus contains a glossary of Russian international legal terms and their English counterparts, a table of treaties and United Nations General Assembly resolutions to which he refers, and an index. It also contains an up-to-date bibliography of Tunkin's scholarly works. The bibliography not only depicts him as remarkably industrious and erudite, but it also illustrates how wide-ranging his interests in international law were and implicitly marks him as unusually well-equipped to expound a comprehensive theory.

Tunkin's reflections on the draft Charter of the International Tribunal for the Consideration of Cases Concerning Crimes Committed in the Territory of Former Yugoslavia merit especial comment. They are dated March 31, 1993 — that is, slightly less than five months before he died — and they comprise his last known statement on international law. Although the present edition includes no attempt to explain how they relate to his theory of international law, arguably a critical response to them would have been helpful. Happily, this gap does not detract greatly from the high standard of scholarship that the present edition — in Butler's eminently readable translation — achieves.

However admirable its scholarship might be, though, the present edition's long-term significance to Russian international legal scholarship remains a subject for scholarly enquiry. One might conjecture that Tunkin's theory of international law still informs to some degree the ideas held by his former students and colleagues. While his theory of "peaceful coexistence" was a product of its age, other elements of his theory can better withstand the passage of time. Yet this reviewer has argued elsewhere that Russia's international jurists have attempted assiduously since 1991 to acquaint themselves with late imperial Russian international legal scholarship.[6] Which theories of international law have, in fact, won the greatest support among post-Soviet Russia's international jurists?

---

[6] E. Myles, "'Humanity,' 'Civilization' and the 'International Community' in the Late Imperial Russian Mirror: Three Ideas 'Topical for Our Days'" (2002) 4(2) J. Hist. Intl. L. 310 *passim*.

A painstaking examination of the post-Soviet works on international law is necessary to answer convincingly this query. Until this examination takes place, a definitive answer as to whether Tunkin's theory will hold primarily historical interests or will exert an abiding influence on Russian international jurists will remain infeasible.

Eric Myles
Department of Justice Canada, Toronto

Determining Boundaries in a Conflicted World: The Role of Uti Possidetis. Par Suzanne Lalonde. Montreal et Kingston: McGill-Queen's University Press, 2002, 347 pp.

Si le Québec accède un jour à l'indépendance, quelles seront les frontières internationales de ce nouvel État? Depuis plus d'une dizaine d'années cette question retient l'attention non seulement des politiciens et des commentateurs politiques, mais également de plusieurs spécialistes du droit international. Au début des années 1990, à la suite de l'échec de l'accord du Lac Meech, le gouvernement québécois de l'époque avait mis sur pied la "Commission sur le processus de détermination de l'avenir politique et constitutionnel du Québec" pour étudier les possibilités qui s'offraient au Québec, en particulier le scénario d'un Québec indépendant. Lors des audiences de cette commission, l'éminent professeur de droit international public et ancien ministre sous le gouvernement du Parti québécois, Jacques-Yvan Morin, déclarait "qu'on ne peut pas modifier les frontières d'une province, sans son consentement. C'est une règle de droit constitutionnel canadien, et, de surcroît, en droit international ... c'est la règle de l'*uti possidetis* ... qui font qu'on entre dans l'indépendance avec le territoire qu'on avait avant." Cinq spécialistes internationaux consultés par la commission tenaient des propos très semblables.[1] Plus de dix ans après la conclusion des travaux de cette commission, Suzanne Lalonde remet ce constat en question dans un ouvrage qu'elle consacre à l'*uti possidetis*. Le dernier chapitre de son livre traite, entre autres, de l'application de ce concept à un éventuel Québec souverain. Auparavant, l'auteure retrace l'évolution du concept, démontrant savamment ses nombreuses permutations au fil des années.

Le premier chapitre explore les origines lointaines de l'expression, d'abord en droit romain puis dans les débuts du droit

---

[1] Les experts en question étaient les suivants: Thomas M. Franck, Rosalyn Higgins, Alain Pellet, Malcolm N. Shaw, et Christian Tomuschat.

international. Initialement l'*utis possidetis* était invoqué dans les litiges entre particuliers concernant des terrains ou des immeubles. Son objet, sauf exceptions, était d'accorder la possession à titre provisoire à la personne qui occupait les lieux disputés en attendant que l'autorité judiciaire saisie de la question se prononce de manière définitive sur le litige. Omise dans le Code de Justinien, l'expression, sans qu'on sache véritablement pourquoi sinon qu'elle a trait à la possession, est récupérée par les premiers auteurs de droit international qui l'assimilent au "*status quo post bellum.*" En vertu de ce principe, un État conserve la possession des territoires qu'il occupe effectivement au terme d'un conflit à moins qu'un traité de paix ne prévoit autrement. Cette nouvelle notion de l'*uti possidetis* diffère nettement du droit romain parce que, non seulement elle ne concerne plus les individus mais les États, mais elle vient aussi consacrer de manière permanente une possession acquise par la force.

La notion évolue une fois encore au début du 19ᵉ siècle, avec la création de nombreux États en Amérique latine. Comme le rappelle Lalonde, ces États adoptent comme frontières internationales les divisions administratives coloniales existant au moment de leur indépendance,[2] laissant à plus tard la détermination précise de leurs frontières respectives. Depuis la notion d'*uti possidetis* est toujours associée à l'accession à l'indépendance d'un État. Par conséquent, Lalonde entreprend une étude de la notion moderne de ce concept dans le chapitre consacré à la pratique des États latino-américains. Elle commence à développer la thèse que, contrairement à ce qu'avancent un grand nombre de publicistes du droit international, l'*uti possidetis* n'est pas une règle d'application générale.

L'auteure examine la pratique des États de l'Amérique latine, en prêtant une attention particulière à leurs constitutions, aux traités conclus et à la résolution de divers conflits territoriaux. Elle tire plusieurs constats importants:

(a) Au moment de l'indépendance les nouveaux États n'ont pas remis en question le fait que les frontières de leur territoire correspondaient aux anciennes frontières coloniales. Par contre, la détermination précise des frontières a donné lieu à d'importants différends.

---

[2] Comme le note Suzanne Lalonde, puisque les deux puissances coloniales, l'Espagne et le Portugal, avaient précédemment convenu de diviser entre elles l'ensemble du continent sud-américain, le choix des anciennes frontières coloniales comme frontières internationales signifiait que les nouveaux États renonçaient implicitement à recourir à la force pour l'acquisition de territoires.

(b) Même si au moment de l'indépendance les nouveaux États ont accepté les frontières héritées de l'époque coloniale, ces frontières ne correspondaient pas uniformément à une division coloniale précise. Les frontières de certains États, par exemple, épousent des unités coloniales très larges; d'autres, des unités incluses dans ces unités plus importantes.

(c) Certains États, étant donné les circonstances entourant leur accès à l'indépendance, ont préféré d'autres frontières que les frontières coloniales peu de temps après leur indépendance.

(d) L'intention originale des États était de résoudre les questions de délimitation frontalière sur la base du concept de l'*uti possidetis*. Ce concept, cependant, n'a pas servi énormément dans les opérations de délimitation en Amérique latine. Suzanne Lalonde note qu'une comparaison de la carte de l'Amérique latine sous le règne espagnol et au début du vingtième siècle démontre que les frontières coloniales ne constituaient pas plus de 10 p. 100 des nouvelles frontières internationales un siècle après l'indépendance.

(e) Il n'y a pas de consensus sur le sens de l'expression *uti possidetis*. S'agit-il de l'*uti possidetis de facto,* c'est-à-dire du territoire effectivement géré par une entité administrative coloniale au moment de l'indépendance ou de l'*uti possidetis de jure,* c'est-à-dire non pas le territoire effectivement occupé au moment de l'indépendance mais plutôt le territoire colonial juridiquement identifié par l'État comme division administrative? Cette différence d'opinion concerne surtout, comme le note l'auteure, la délimitation des territoires d'anciennes colonies portugaises et espagnoles et moins des territoires autrefois sous le contrôle de la même puissance coloniale. Notons toutefois que Lalonde, contrairement à l'étude qu'elle fait plus tard de l'Afrique, ne distingue pas nettement, à ce stade de son étude, entre les frontières convenues entre puissances coloniales et les frontières strictement internes, tracées par un seul État dans sa colonie. Pourtant cette distinction justifierait peut-être en partie la coexistence de ces deux conceptions de l'*uti possidetis.*

(f) L'expression *uti possidetis* n'apparaît presque jamais dans les constitutions et les traités des États latino-américains au 19ᵉ siècle. L'auteure n'a trouvé le terme que dans dix des 210 instruments examinés. Elle note, par ailleurs, que plusieurs de ces constitutions et traités indiquaient que les États héritaient de frontières coloniales.

(g) Le tracé des frontières de plusieurs États au 19ᵉ siècle et dans la première moitié du 20ᵉ siècle a été déterminé davantage par l'issue de conflits armés que par l'*uti possidetis*.

(h) Le concept de l'*uti possidetis* est inséré dans quelques traités d'arbitrage visant à régler des litiges frontaliers. Dans certains cas, toutefois, l'arbitre est autorisé à recourir à d'autres principes que celui de l'*uti possidetis*. En effet, les frontières tracées par l'État colonial sont souvent ambiguës. Étant donné que de larges portions de territoires sont inexplorées, il n'est pas surprenant que le tracé d'une carte ne reflète pas toujours fidèlement la réalité sur le terrain et qu'il est nécessaire de recourir à d'autres critères que l'*uti possidetis*. De même, deux documents coloniaux pertinents peuvent être contradictoires.

Indéniablement, ces conclusions de l'auteure ébranlent quelque peu les certitudes quant à l'importance de l'*uti possidetis juris* dans la détermination des frontières en Amérique latine. Elles soulèvent bien des questions sur le statut véritable de l'*uti possidetis juris* en Amérique latine, mais il serait prématuré, sans d'abord répondre à ces questions, de déduire que ce principe ne constitue pas une règle coutumière, à tout le moins régionale.

Que Lalonde réussisse à discréditer une règle pourtant si souvent associée avec la pratique en Amérique latine peut paraître surprenant. Pour exécuter ce tour de force, l'auteure redéfinit le concept de l'*uti possidetis,* lui prêtant une portée plus limitée que celle généralement acceptée. L'auteure reconnaît que la plupart des publicistes assimilent la politique du 'statut quo colonial' avec celle de l'*uti possidetis.* Elle concède que si l'on retient cette définition "every constitution and every treaty that defines a state's territory by reference to a former colonial unit . . . is considered an example of the application of the *uti possidetis* principle in Latin America." Selon cette définition, il est difficile de nier le statut de l'*uti possidetis* comme règle de droit international.

Lalonde préconise une définition plus étroite de l'*uti possidetis:* "The second interpretation of the principle identifies the colonial status quo policy as the core value and *uti possidetis juris* as one of several principles relied upon to delimit the boundaries of the colonial entities that succeeded in achieving independent statehood." Sur la base de cette définition, l'auteure déclare qu'on ne peut conclure que la règle de l'*uti possidetis* possède les attributs d'une règle de droit coutumier, car la pratique des États manque d'uniformité et l'*opinio juris* semble manqué.

Pourquoi mettre de l'avant une définition non traditionnelle de l'*uti possidetis*? Afin d'expliquer cette préférence, Suzanne Lalonde souligne, notamment, que la règle du statut quo est conforme aux règles de succession et qu'il n'y a pas lieu de trouver une autre justification. Ces règles servent à conférer un titre à un État alors que l'*uti possidetis* aide à préciser la portée de ce titre par la détermination de ses frontières. Peut-on vraiment penser que les règles de succession des États expliquent l'adoption des frontières coloniales existantes par la myriade de nouveaux États succédant à un État colonial? Si oui, en vertu de quelle règle de succession des États existante à l'époque? L'auteure élabore très peu sur cette question pourtant au cœur de son argumentation. Par conséquent, si la définition suggérée par Suzanne Lalonde mérite un examen plus approfondi, il faudrait, avant de l'adopter, explorer attentivement les règles de succession acceptées à l'époque et, plus généralement, se demander si on peut vraiment dissocier la 'politique du statut quo colonial' de la règle de l'*uti possidetis*.

Même en acceptant la définition retenue par Suzanne Lalonde, son examen de la pratique soulève quelques interrogations. Est-ce vraiment pertinent que l'expression *uti possidetis* se trouve dans très peu des documents examinés. La réponse à cette question dépend de la nature des dispositions? Étaient-elles de nature à faire appel à ce concept? Par ailleurs, le fait que plusieurs différends frontaliers aient été résolus en appliquant d'autres critères que l'*uti possidetis* suffit-il pour nier son statut de règle? Il semble que dans bien des cas les États ont fait référence à ce principe initialement, pour ensuite l'abandonner au profit d'autres critères lorsque ce dernier s'avérait insuffisant pour diverses raisons identifiées par l'auteure. Selon elle, cela signifie que la règle de l'*uti possidetis* repose sur le consentement des Parties et par conséquent ne constitue pas une règle d'application générale.[3] Elle fonde son propos, toutefois, sur ces cas où les États ont convenu d'écarter la règle de l'*uti possidetis*. Le fait que les États peuvent s'entendre pour ne pas appliquer une règle semble suggérer que la règle s'applique en l'absence d'un accord au contraire. Qu'on accepte ou non la conclusion de Suzanne Lalonde que l'*uti possidetis*, selon sa définition, ne constitue pas une règle de droit coutumier et ce même pour l'Amérique latine, son étude a néanmoins le mérite de démontrer que, quel que soit le statut de ce concept, son application a eu des

---

[3] L'auteure fait un argument semblable, aux pp. 124 et 125, lorsqu'elle discute de l'arbitrage frontalier entre Dubai et Sharjah.

effets limités. En effet, dans bien des cas, soit la preuve n'était pas de nature à permettre le seul recours à ce concept pour déterminer les lignes précises d'une frontière contestée, soit les événements survenus depuis l'indépendance imposaient de nouvelles frontières.

Suzanne Lalonde réserve les dernières pages de ce chapitre au principe de l'occupation effective, principe qu'en conclusion de l'ouvrage elle propose comme une alternative à celui de l'*uti possidetis*. Elle note que ce critère a joué un rôle déterminant dans la délimitation des frontières entre d'anciennes colonies espagnoles et des puissances étrangères et même, dans certains cas, entre les États issus de la colonisation espagnole. Elle renforce sa critique de l'*uti possidetis* en citant divers publicistes de la première moitié du 20e siècle qui contestent l'importance donnée à ce concept. Il est dommage, toutefois, qu'elle n'ait pas accordé la même importance à la doctrine contraire.

Poursuivant un plan chronologique, dans le chapitre 3, Lalonde examine le rôle de l'*uti possidetis* dans la détermination des frontières après la Première Grande Guerre. Elle se penche en particulier sur trois dossiers: les îles Âland, la zone de Taba et la frontière entre la Palestine et la Transjordanie dans le triangle de Semakh. Dans le premier cas, la solution adoptée semble être une application de l'*uti possidetis*. En concluant à la souveraineté de la Finlande sur les îles Âland, la Commission nommée par la Société des Nations ne faisait que confirmer le territoire finlandais existant avant l'indépendance de ce pays. Toutefois, l'auteure note que non seulement plusieurs autres facteurs ont été pris en considération, mais qu'en plus il n'est pas fait expressément mention du principe de l'*uti possidetis*. Comment, affirme-t-elle, peut-on penser qu'il s'agit d'une règle contraignante alors qu'on n'y fait même pas référence dans une affaire où elle semble pourtant pertinente? Elle en conclut, et c'est là nous semble-t-il une conclusion défendable, que cette affaire "lends little support to the proposition that by the turn of the century *uti possidetis* had become a general principle of international law for the determination of boundaries." Le cas de la zone de Taba présente des similarités avec celui des îles Âland, car un tribunal d'arbitrage a conclu dans cette affaire qu'une ligne frontalière interne était subséquemment devenue une frontière internationale. L'auteure refuse toutefois de voir là une application de l'*uti possidetis* car, à son avis, la frontière en question aurait été internationalisée dès sa création. Elle souligne, d'une part, qu'il s'agissait d'une frontière avec l'Égypte, un État quasi indépendant à l'époque et, d'autre part, que la frontière avait été imposée à la Turquie à la suite des pressions britanniques. Il est toutefois difficile d'accepter la thèse de la création d'une frontière internationale dans une zone qui, en droit, relevait à l'époque de la souveraineté d'un seul État. L'argument que le concept de l'*uti possidetis* ne semble pas avoir influencé le résultat car les Parties semblent l'avoir ignoré est plus convaincant. Dans le cas de la frontière entre la Palestine sous mandat et la Transjordanie, l'auteure démontre que les Britanniques ont modifié la frontière administrative établie par l'Empire ottoman. Dans la mesure, toutefois, où cette modification concernait des territoires sous contrôle britannique et non des territoires accédant à l'indépendance, on s'écarte un peu du statut de l'*uti possidetis*. En fin de chapitre, Lalonde conclut qu'il est douteux qu'après la Première Guerre mondiale on puisse considérer l'*uti possidetis* comme un principe général de droit international. Malgré les réserves précitées, cette conclusion nous apparaît fondée. Comme le souligne l'auteure, le concept semble avoir été ignoré dans les réorganisations territoriales de l'époque.

Si ce chapitre sur l'après-Grande Guerre n'apporte pas énormément au débat sur le statut de l'*uti possidetis*, en revanche, le chapitre suivant sur la pratique africaine est aussi capital pour la thèse de l'auteure que celui sur l'Amérique latine, ces deux continents étant communément perçus comme les pierres d'assises du concept. Comme elle l'a fait pour l'Amérique latine, Lalonde se dissocie de la majorité des publicistes qui voient dans l'acceptation des frontières coloniales en Afrique une manifestation de la règle de l'*uti possidetis*. S'appuyant sur de nombreux documents de l'époque, elle affirme que la grande majorité des États africains nouvellement indépendants ont choisi de conserver leurs frontières coloniales, par crainte que la remise en question de ces frontières ne plonge l'ensemble du continent dans une grave crise et non parce que la règle de l'*uti possidetis* dicterait ce résultat.

Par un examen fouillé des documents entourant la création de l'Organisation de l'unité africaine, l'auteur convainc le lecteur que, contrairement à l'affirmation d'éminents publicistes du droit international, le principe de l'*uti possidetis* en Afrique n'a pas son origine, expressément ou implicitement, dans les documents fondateurs de cette organisation ou dans la rencontre du Caire. Il n'y a là rien de bien étonnant. Il est normal que des États indépendants insistent sur l'intégrité de leur territoire plutôt que sur le critère légitimant les frontières existantes. La période critique pour déterminer si le principe de l'*uti possidetis* a été appliqué en Afrique semble être le moment même de l'indépendance de ces États. À ce sujet, Lalonde observe que, contrairement à l'Amérique latine où l'indépendance a été le fruit d'une révolution, en Afrique l'indépendance a été accordée à un nombre d'entités coloniales précises. Autrement dit, ce ne sont pas les nouveaux États qui ont convenu, au moment de leur accession à la souveraineté, d'accepter les frontières coloniales existantes. Les colonies sont plutôt devenues des États indépendants avec leurs frontières coloniales existantes. Il serait utile d'étudier les motifs juridiques de la dévolution de territoires par les puissances coloniales. Selon les recherches de Lalonde, en ce qui concerne les États africains, il semble que l'*uti possidetis* n'ait pas constitué, du moins expressément, un motif d'acceptation du statut quo.

Lalonde souligne une autre distinction entre la situation américaine et africaine. En Amérique latine, les frontières coloniales étaient déterminées, du moins du point de vue de la majorité des États anciennement sous l'Empire espagnol, par référence aux titres juridiques — *uti possidetis juris.* Dans les États africains, par contre, les frontières coloniales existantes ont été officialisées au moment de l'indépendance, par le concept de l'occupation effective. On peut aussi qualifier cette pratique, comme l'explique l'auteure dans son étude de l'Amérique latine, de *uti possidetis de facto.* D'ailleurs, dans son commentaire sur l'affaire du *Différend frontalier entre le Burkina Faso et le Mali,* sur laquelle nous reviendrons ci-dessous, Lalonde ne rejette pas d'emblée que ce type d'*uti possidetis* puisse constituer une règle de droit international en Afrique: "Therefore, if African practice is to be equated with the *uti possidetis* principle, it should at least be assimilated to the much less influential *uti possidetis de facto* formula." Les frontières au moment de l'indépendance sont alors toujours héritées de la situation coloniale, mais elles peuvent différer de manière significative selon qu'on adopte l'*uti possidetis juris* ou *de facto.*

Dans son étude de la pratique africaine, l'auteure passe en revue trois affaires récentes où des instances internationales ont eu à trancher des différends frontaliers en Afrique et se sont prononcées directement sur le statut de l'*uti possidetis* sur ce continent. Deux de ces affaires, *Guinée* c. *Guinée-Bissau* et *Guinée-Bissau* c. *Sénégal,* traitent de frontières délimitées par une convention internationale conclue entre deux États coloniaux avant l'indépendance des États africains concernés. Lalonde observe, à bon escient il nous semble, qu'il n'y a pas lieu dans ces affaires d'étendre la notion de l'*uti possidetis* à des frontières fixées par un accord international. Les tribunaux auraient pu tirer les mêmes conclusions en appliquant les règles de succession des États. L'auteure donne aussi une série de raisons persuasives pour conclure que l'*uti possidetis* ne devrait pas servir à délimiter les zones maritimes. Il aurait été utile d'indiquer, par contre, si l'une ou l'autre ou les deux Parties avait soulevé le principe de l'*uti possidetis* dans leur plaidoirie dans chacun de ces litiges.

L'affaire qui retient le plus l'attention de l'auteure est le *Différend frontalier entre le Burkina Faso et le Mali*. Elle précise, avec raison, que c'est l'affaire la plus souvent invoquée pour appuyer la proposition que l'*uti possidetis* est un principe général de droit international. La Chambre de la Cour internationale de justice saisie de l'affaire devait rendre une décision conforme au "principe de l'intangibilité des frontières héritées de la colonisation." Il ne s'agit donc pas de l'intangibilité de n'importe quelles frontières, mais bien de frontières découlant de la décolonisation. La Chambre aurait pu, sur cette base, reconnaître la pertinence de l'*uti possidetis* dans ce litige. Elle va beaucoup plus loin, affirmant que le concept est rattaché à l'indépendance de tout État, qu'il soit américain, africain ou autre. La Chambre n'explique vraiment pas ce passage de l'*uti possidetis* d'une règle régionale, américaine ou africaine, à une règle universelle. L'auteure cherche à combler ce vide, non pas pour démontrer qu'une règle d'application générale existe, mais plutôt pour expliquer que la pratique de l'Amérique latine sur laquelle la Chambre aurait pu se fonder réfute en fait l'existence d'une telle règle, pour les raisons mentionnées dans le chapitre précédent. Au terme de ce chapitre, l'auteure insiste sur la nature consensuelle de l'*uti possidetis*. Elle rejette la suggestion de certains auteurs selon laquelle on peut présumer que la règle s'applique à moins que les Parties ne conviennent autrement. Pourtant, comme nous l'avons mentionné plus tôt, le fait que des Parties s'entendent pour ne pas appliquer l'*uti possidetis* peut aussi suggérer l'inverse.[4]

Le cinquième chapitre constitue une exception au plan jusque-là chronologique. Il est consacré non pas à une période précise de l'histoire, mais à l'étude d'une série de concepts pertinents en

---

[4] D'ailleurs, au chapitre suivant, à la p. 170, Lalonde semble accepter cette proposition: "While pronouncements of the ICJ had undoubtedly endowed the *uti possidetis* principle with some normative status in international law, cases and state practice supported the conclusion that at its strongest, *uti possidetis* constituted a presumption in favour of the continuity of pre-independence borders."

matière de frontières. Ce chapitre semble néanmoins un prolonge-
ment du précédent, car l'objectif principal est de démontrer, par
l'étude de ces concepts que, contrairement à ce qui est affirmé
dans l'affaire *Guinée* c. *Guinée-Bissau*, il n'y a pas lieu d'étendre le
concept d'*uti possidetis* aux frontières internationales fixées par un
accord entre deux États coloniaux avant l'indépendance. L'intangibilité de ces frontières serait ainsi protégée par d'autres règles
du droit international. En d'autres mots, l'auteure veut démontrer
que le recours au principe de l'*uti possidetis* n'est pas nécessaire
pour préserver le statut quo en Afrique. Son argument sur le principe de l'intégrité du territoire est particulièrement intéressant.
L'auteure soutient que ce principe empêche les États coloniaux
de modifier des frontières internes avant l'indépendance. Parmi
les autres sujets examinés, mentionnons les règles de succession
d'États, la règle du *rebus sic stantibus*, le principe *nemo dat* et le droit
à l'autodétermination.

Dans son dernier chapitre, avant de conclure, Lalonde aborde les
événements récents en ex-Yougoslavie ainsi que les conséquences
territoriales de l'accession du Québec à l'indépendance. Elle
examine d'abord les trois premières Opinions de la Commission
Badinter dans le dossier de l'ex-Yougoslavie et leurs répercussions
en droit international. De l'Opinion 1, elle questionne la conclusion de la Commission que l'État yougoslave était en train de se dis-
soudre puisque l'entité fédérale ne remplissait plus les critères de
représentativité et de participation des entités fédérées. En effet, la
Commission n'aurait pas dû fonder sa décision sur la seule structure constitutionnelle interne de l'État. Elle aurait dû se demander
plutôt si l'État conservait un contrôle effectif sur la population et le
territoire. Le fait que l'État n'était plus en mesure de fonctionner
comme État fédéral aurait alors été un facteur à prendre en compte
pour évaluer l'effectivité réelle de l'État. Évidemment, la Commission aurait pu, même en adoptant cette approche, arriver au constat
que l'État yougoslave se dirigeait vers la dissolution. Pour Lalonde,
l'analyse de la crise yougoslave comme un processus de dissolution
et non une série de sécessions entraîne des conséquences importantes, puisque la Commission n'a pas alors à se prononcer sur
la difficile question de la relation entre l'autodétermination et
l'intégrité territoriale de l'État existant. De l'Opinion 2, l'auteure
critique l'interprétation de l'*uti possidetis* voulant que, même avant
l'indépendance, les frontières internes des républiques yougoslaves
ne pouvaient être modifiées. Pour Lalonde, cela signifie que la
Commission décidait à l'avance quels acteurs pouvaient accéder à

l'indépendance par l'exercice du droit à l'autodétermination. L'*uti possidetis* concerne en effet la transformation des frontières internes en des frontières internationales comme conséquence de l'indépendance. Le concept n'opère pas pour imposer certains résultats avant l'indépendance, ni pour déterminer qui a droit à l'autodétermination. Elle reprend les mêmes commentaires dans son analyse critique de l'Opinion 3. L'essentiel de son propos sur cette opinion, par contre, a trait à la conclusion de la Commission que l'*uti possidetis* s'applique dans un contexte non colonial. Lalonde observe que la Commission appuie son raisonnement sur une lecture parcellaire de la décision de la Cour internationale de justice dans l'affaire du *Différend frontalier entre le Burkina Faso et le Mali* et qu'une lecture de l'ensemble de la décision démontre que la Cour discutait de *l'uti possidetis* uniquement dans un contexte colonial.

Après son étude des opinions de la Commission, Lalonde examine l'argument voulant que cette nouvelle conception de l'*uti possidetis,* indépendamment des failles dans l'analyse de la Commission, est dorénavant largement acceptée. Elle relate comment les autorités des nouveaux États issus de l'ancien État yougoslave ont progressivement accepté que les frontières internes soient transformées en des frontières internationales, pour des considérations politiques et non juridiques. La même remarque s'applique en ce qui concerne la position de l'Union européenne. Une solution s'est imposée pour toutes sortes de considérations non juridiques. Lalonde insiste sur l'absence d'une articulation juridique clairement fondée sur l'*uti possidetis*. Dans bien des cas, toutefois, il n'est pas facile de déterminer si la pratique des États ou, en l'espèce, de l'Union européenne et du Conseil de sécurité, est complètement dénuée de motivations juridiques. Lalonde fait d'ailleurs allusion à l'opinion contraire d'autres spécialistes. De plus, les partisans de l'existence d'une règle d'*uti possidetis* s'appuient sur les événements survenus en Union soviétique et en Tchécoslovaquie. On peut en effet se demander pour combien de temps on pourra nier l'existence d'une règle si les frontières de chaque nouvel État indépendant reflètent systématiquement des frontières internes antérieures? En d'autres mots, peut-on déjà ou viendra-t-on à déduire d'une pratique uniforme l'*opinio juris* requise?

Lalonde étudie enfin la pertinence de l'*uti possidetis* dans le débat sur l'avenir du Québec. Elle examine en détail les conclusions présentées par les cinq spécialistes du droit international à la Commission sur le processus de détermination de l'avenir politique et constitutionnel du Québec. Selon ces spécialistes, les frontières de cette province deviendraient automatiquement des frontières internationales en cas de sécession. Lalonde rappelle que les spécialistes n'ont pas reconnu au Québec un droit de sécession, mais plutôt le droit d'un gouvernement sécessionniste de réussir l'indépendance en établissant un contrôle effectif sur un territoire défini. Naturellement, la question clé est de savoir quel serait ce territoire? De l'avis de Lalonde, et contrairement aux conclusions des spécialistes, l'absence de droit à la sécession emporte logiquement l'absence de droit à un territoire précis. Seul le degré d'effectivité exercé par un nouvel État sur un territoire déterminera les frontières de celui-ci. Comme l'observe avec raison Lalonde, il pourrait être plus difficile de réaliser le degré d'effectivité souhaité dans une situation de sécession par opposition à une dissolution. Elle rejette aussi la conclusion des spécialistes que l'*uti possidetis* s'applique maintenant dans une situation non coloniale. Elle observe que leur analyse est fondée sur une interprétation, à son avis erronée, de la décision de la Cour internationale de justice dans l'affaire du *Différend frontalier entre le Burkina Faso et le Mali* et sur l'opinion de la Commission Badinter qui, elle-même, comme nous l'avons mentionné précédemment, s'appuie aussi sur l'affaire *Burkina Faso*. De plus, l'auteure rejette l'appréciation des spécialistes selon laquelle la pratique récente en Yougoslavie et en URSS consacre l'élargissement de la portée de l'*uti possidetis* à des situations non coloniales. Lalonde est d'avis que cette pratique n'est pas expliquée par une obligation qu'auraient les États d'accepter d'anciennes frontières internes. Les déclarations des républiques soviétiques, au moment de leur indépendance, n'incluraient pas de demandes que les frontières internes deviennent des frontières internationales. Toutefois, dans le contexte de l'époque, il n'est pas facile d'exclure que les répliques, "en s'engageant à reconnaître leur intégrité territoriale respective et l'inviolabilité des frontières existantes," faisaient ainsi implicitement référence aux frontières jusque-là internes. De plus, que les frontières issues de la disparition de l'Union soviétique ou encore de la Tchécoslovaquie aient finalement été fixées par des ententes entre les Parties concernées n'écarte pas la possibilité que ces ententes aient été fondées sur des considérations relatives à l'*uti possidetis*. En revanche, si la signification juridique de la pratique des États n'est pas toujours claire et permet souvent diverses interprétations, l'absence de référence expresse à l'*uti possidetis* par les acteurs directement impliqués dans les cas d'indépendance récents, exception faite de la Commission Badinter, vient fortement appuyer l'analyse de Lalonde.

En conclusion, Lalonde explique pourquoi, indépendamment du statut de l'*uti possidetis* aujourd'hui, il ne serait pas sage de faire de ce concept le critère principal pour la détermination des frontières dans l'avenir. Contrairement aux cas de décolonisation où s'opposaient à distance un État colonial et une colonie, la sécession ou la dissolution d'un État moderne signifie une brisure d'un même territoire. Dans ces conditions, il n'est guère certain que l'*uti possidetis* représente toujours la solution la plus susceptible de favoriser le règlement pacifique d'un conflit. Les groupes mécontents des résultats de l'application de la règle de l'*uti possidetis* pourraient résister à une telle solution, comme le démontre le conflit yougoslave. Les débats sur la question au Canada démontrent bien que cette solution ne fait pas l'unanimité. Toutefois, la même objection pourrait être soulevée contre tout autre critère suggéré. Donner la priorité au critère de l'effectivité, comme le propose Lalonde, invite les Parties concernées à se disputer cette effectivité. Le choix de l'une ou l'autre de ces solutions suscitera inévitablement la grogne des perdants. Dans ces conditions, déterminer quelle solution est moins dommageable à la paix et sécurité n'est pas chose facile. Pour cette raison, en conclusion, Lalonde retourne à la conception romaine de l'*uti possidetis,* suggérant que ce principe peut garantir provisoirement le statut quo en attendant la détermination de frontières définitives par une instance internationale. Le fait que dans les conflits récents les frontières internes aient été retenues comme frontières internationales suggère, toutefois, qu'il ne faut pas écarter à la légère le résultat auquel conduit l'*uti possidetis*. Une autre option serait peut-être de geler provisoirement la situation, comme le suggère Lalonde, tout en créant une présomption en faveur de l'*uti possidetis*. La Partie préconisant une autre approche aurait alors le fardeau de démontrer pourquoi, exceptionnellement, les frontières internes ne devraient pas devenir des frontières internationales. La présence de minorités importantes et de peuples autochtones au sein d'une entité, leur appui ou leur opposition à la dissolution ou à la sécession, de même que la structure constitutionnelle projetée par le nouvel État constitueraient alors vraisemblablement des facteurs à considérer dans la détermination finale des frontières. Soulignons que dans sa conclusion Lalonde attache, avec raison, beaucoup d'importance aux droits des minorités et des peuples autochtones touchés par la dissolution ou la sécession d'un État.

En somme, Suzanne Lalonde cerne admirablement bien les arguments centraux du débat sur le statut de l'*uti possidetis*. D'un côté, ceux et celles qui, comme elle, rejettent l'existence d'une règle en la matière, insistent notamment sur l'absence de référence à ce concept dans de nombreuses situations où il aurait été pertinent de l'invoquer, sur le nombre de différends frontaliers réglés par consentement plutôt que l'application d'une règle précise et sur l'existence de règles de droit international autres que l'*uti possidetis* pour expliquer le choix de frontières internes comme frontières internationales. De l'autre côté, un nombre de spécialistes appuient l'existence d'une règle en se fondant sur une pratique récente quasi uniforme, de même que sur l'acceptation de ce principe par des instances internationales importantes. Le grand mérite de l'ouvrage de Suzanne Lalonde est d'explorer la question sous de multiples facettes et d'avoir jeté un bon éclairage sur ce premier point de vue, tout en exposant l'argument inverse. Si cet ouvrage ne vient pas régler le débat sur l'*uti possidetis*, il l'enrichit sans contredit. Gageons qu'il deviendra un ouvrage incontournable dans ce débat juridique et qu'il sera aussi chaudement discuté dans d'éventuels nouveaux débats référendaires au Québec.

YVES LEBOUTHILLIER
Faculté de droit, Section de common law, Université d'Ottawa

Analytical Index / Index analytique

THE CANADIAN YEARBOOK OF
INTERNATIONAL LAW

2 0 0 3

ANNUAIRE CANADIEN
DE DROIT INTERNATIONAL

(A) Article; (NC) Notes and Comments; (Ch) Chronique;
(P) Practice; (C) Cases; (BR) Book Review
(A) Article; (NC) Notes et commentaires; (Ch) Chronique;
(P) Pratique; (C) Jurisprudence; (BR) Recension de livre

Index of Cases /
Index de la jurisprudence

———

85: Art 23 DSU –

98,   "   " – cannot prevent other Tribs from operating .